An Alphabet Of Tales

An Alphabet of Tales.

EARLY ENGLISH TEXT SOCIETY.
ORIGINAL SERIES. No. 126.
1904.

"These Tales are brief as the books of our childhood."

OXFORD
HORACE HART: PRINTER TO THE UNIVERSITY

Early English Text Society.
ORIGINAL SERIES. 126.

An Alphabet of Tales.

AN ENGLISH 15TH CENTURY TRANSLATION OF THE

ALPHABETUM NARRATIONUM

OF

ETIENNE DE BESANÇON.

FROM ADDITIONAL MS. 25,719 OF THE BRITISH MUSEUM.

EDITED BY

MRS. MARY MACLEOD BANKS.

PART I. A—H.

LONDON:
PUBLISHED FOR THE EARLY ENGLISH TEXT SOCIETY,
BY KEGAN PAUL, TRENCH, TRÜBNER & CO., LTD.
DRYDEN HOUSE, 43 GERRARD STREET, SOHO, W.
MDCCCCIV

NOTE.

For facility of reference this text quotes the Harleian MS. 268, and the Arundel MS. 378, of the British Museum, at all points where these Latin copies of Etienne de Besançon's collection of exempla throw any light on difficult or confused readings. A further clearing-up will be undertaken in the notes, which with an introduction and a glossary are to follow Part II.

Words and letters which have been obliterated or worn away from the MS. are restored conjecturally in brackets; words and letters inadvertently omitted by the writer of the MS. are also conjecturally supplied in brackets, but in italic, to distinguish them from those for which the MS. leaves a space. Capitals have been given to names of persons and places, and have been left in some common nouns as they stand in the MS.; modern punctuation has been adopted throughout. Scribal errors are corrected by footnotes. Signs standing in earlier MSS. for final -e are represented by a small stroke curved to the right or left, only the diminutive curl after short r has been left out.

A list of *errata* will be printed with Part II, also an Index to the Tales.

AN ALPHABET OF TALES.

I.

Abbas non debet esse nimis rigidus. Vnde Anselmus.

Som tyme *þer* was ane abbott þat asked cowncell of Saynt Anselme, & sayd vnto hym[1], "what sall w[e] do with childer þat er nuryshid & broght vpp in our clostre? ffor," he sayde, "we sese nott day & nygh[t to] bete þaim, & yitt þai er ay þe langer þe wers." And þan Saynt Anselme answerd hym agayn [&] sayd, "ye spend full wele your nuryshyng & your almos, þat of[2] men makis b[estis], ffor, & þou sett in my garthyn a yong plante of a tre, & closyd it rownde aboute, strayte on [evur]-ilk side, þat it mot nott sprede furth no bewis, whatkyn a tre wolde spryng þeroff? ffor sut[h, an] vnprofitable tre. On þe same maner of wise," he said, "do ye; ye kepe strayte in your clostre chi[lder] & yong men, with ferdnes & thretyngis, so at þai may hafe no libertie; whar-oppon it happe[ns], for als mekill as þai fele in you anence þaim selfe no maner of luff nor swettnes, nor hafe no fai[th][3] of no gudenes afterwerd in you, þerfor it happyns of þaim be a mervolos maner, & a wrichid. ffo[r] evur as þai grow & waxis in bodis, Right so in þaim growis haterid & suspecion of all[4] [yit]; and þerfor, for als mekull as þai of no man war nurisshid in trew nor in perfite charite, þerfo[r þai] may not luke of no man, bod with a sowr cowntenance and a froward luke." *et c*9.

II.

Abbas debet esse compaciens peccatoribus.

We rede in a buke þat is callid 'Vitas Patrum,' how som tyme þer was a monke þat happen[yd] on a tyme to syn flesshlie with

[1] MS. hyr.

[2] *After* of, bestis makis men, *erased*.

[3] Latin MSS. fidem boni. (This reference and others following, are to the Latin MSS. Harl. 268, and Arundel, 375, in the British Museum).

[4] Latin MSS. omnis mali.

a woman; & he went & schrafe hym þerof vnto ane of his brethyr, ane alde monke. And þis monke tuke not his confession tendirlie, bod chiddid hy[m], & flate *with* hym, & said he was vnworthi to be a monke & for to bere þe name of þer ordur, becauce he fell so lightlie vnto flesshlie temptacion; To so mekull att, when þai war partid, þis y[ong]er monke began to fall in a despare, So þat on a nyght he gat hym se[cular] wede, & stale away oute of his cell, and liffid as a seculer man in þe werld. So on a ty[me] as he went be þe way, it happend be þe dispensacion of almiȝti God, hym happend to mete *with* ane abbott þat hight Appollinius, whilk þat knew þe cauce of his gate oute of his ordur, whilk abbott comfurthid hym *with* fayr wurdis, and said vnto hym þus: "turn agayn, brother, vnto þi sell, & hafe no mervell at þou, at is a yong man, be tempid *with* syn, ffor I my selfe, now in myne olde age, is hugelie tempid *with* þe same syn." So, þurgh his comfurthable wurdis, þis monke turnyd agayn vnto his cell. And þan þis Abbott Abbollinius on a tyme come vnto þis olde monke cell dure, þat had made þis yong man to despayre, & þer he prayed[1] at þis olde monke myght somwhatt fele of þe temptacion of his oder bruder, & at his oder bruder myght be delyverd. And when he had done his prayer, he was war of a little blak felow like a man of Ynde, shotand byrnand aro[ws] at þis olde man, vnto so mekull at þis olde monke was so stirrid *with* syn & temptacion of his bodye, þat he stale oute of his ordur in-to þe werld. So on a tyme þis abbot come vnto hym þer he was, & said vnto hym: "Turn agayn in-to þi cell, & hafe compassion on þi neghburs." And þan þis abbott went vnto his prayers, & prayed for hym; [& he co]me home vnto his cell, & onone he was delyverd of his temptacion.

III.

Abbas discretus peccatores a peccato retrahit.

We rede in 'Vitis *Patrum*' þat in þe tyme of Valencian þer was a passand [fayr maydyn] þat hight Thaysis, whilk maydyn

[1] MS. prayer.

hur modir in all hur yong age lete [do accordand to] hur will[1]. So when hur moder deyed, sho become þe moste common strompyd in all þe land, vnto so [m]ykill þat men come vnto hur infenytelie. So þer was ane Abbott þat hight Pasuncius[2], whilk [þ]at, when he harde tell on hur, he tuke oppon secular wede, & tuke in his purs a shelyng, [and] went vnto hur and gaff hur þis shelyng to lat hym hafe his will of hur. And sho [grawn]tit, & led hym up into a chambre, and when sho was in þe chambre, hur bed was [ga]ylie dyght & clenlie, & sho did of hur clothis & went þerto, & bad hym com vnto hur. And þan he spirryd hur iff þer wer no mor privalie place þat he & sho mott lie samen in, and sho said, "yis." And þan he said, "Go we þerto." And sho led hym þerto, & sayd: "Sir, & þou drede any man, Be nott aferde, for here commys no man, nor no man may nowder se the nor me. And if þou be ferde for Godd, or drede Hym, dowte nott þatt whar-euer we [b]e, Almyghtie God seis vs." And þan þis olde Ablott askid hir þuff sho knew almighti [G]od, And sho answerd agayn & said þat sho knew almyghti God & att his kyngdom was for to com; & also sho said þat turmettrie & payn sulde be for syn. And þan he answerd hur agayn & said: "Thow þatt knowis almyghty [*God*], why hase þou loste and myschevid so many sawlis as þou hase done? for þou mon nott alonelie be dampnyd in þine awne sawle, bod also þou[3] mon giff acompte for þer sawlys at þou hase dampned." And when sho hard þis, sho ffell down on hur kneys att his fette, & wepid sore, and made mekull sorow; & evyn furth-with all þat evur sho had getty[n] *with* hur syn and hur wrichidnes, aforn all þe peple sho put it in a greate fy[re &] burnyd[4] itt; and so, be cowncell of þis abbott, not alonelie for hur syn-doyng, bod s[o] sho tuke itt vppon hur to name all-myghti God, sho was sparred in a cloce cell iij yere, and grete penance was enioynyd hur for hur syn; and emang all hur oþer penance, þis was hur[5] prayer: "Qui plasmasti me, miserere mei! Thow Lord at made me, hafe mercie on me!" And when sho had bene þer iij yere,

[1] Latin MSS. quam mater eius a pueritia statuit in prostibulo.

[2] Harl. MS. prasencius, Arun. MS. pasuncius.

[3] MS. *repeats*, bod also þou.

[4] *After* burnyd, id, *erased*.

[5] MS. his.

þis Abbott had in a reuelacion̄ a knowlege þ*at* alƚ hur synys was forgiffyn̄ hur[1]. þan this abbott tuke hur furth of þis celƚ, and sho tolde hym̄ þat sho had made a grete pakk̄ of alƚ hur synys, and þat sho layd' eu*er*-ilk̄ day in hur eye-syght, and eu*er* þis pakk wex les & les, vnto þ*er* was noght lefte in it; & þ*er*by sho wiste þ*at* hur synys was forgiffyn̄ hur wit*h*in þat iij yere penance doyng. *et c*⁹.

IV.

Abbas debet esse elemosinarius.

Frendis, we rede how þat þ*er* was ane Abbott þ*at* hight Petrus Damanus[2], and [on a tym]e he made a grete feste; and vnto þis feste he garte by a grete fyssh̄ þat [coste] xx d'; and onone it was soden̄ & sett befoɼ hym̄. And as he sett att [mea]te, þ*er* come vnto his yate a pure man̄; and wit*h* a greate noyse & a cry [he besogh]t þ*at* þe Abbott wold' giff hym̄ þe beste mete[3] þ*at* stude befoɼ hym̄; [& þe] Abbott harde hym̄, and wit*h* a gude harte sent hym̄ itt, þe fyssch þat had' coste hym̄ xx d', evyn̄ hale as it was; and a monke bare hym̄ it. And onone as he had it delyverd', þis monk̄ lukid aft*er* þis pure man̄, & he saw hym̄ stegh̄ vnto hevyn̄ wit*h* þe dubler & þe ffissh̄ in his hand'. And he went in, and' tolde þe abbott. And þis abbott þankid almyghti God', & trustid þ*at* it was God Hym̄ selfe þat come to feche his almos at his yate. *et c*⁹.

V.

Abbas debet esse conformis subditis in vestib*us* *et* victualib*us*.

We rede how som tyme þ*er* was ane Abbott, þat eu*er*-ilk day fure gaylie att his meate, & w[ent] eu*er* gaylie arayed', & lett for no coste, bod boght of þe beste mete & drynk & clothis þat he cuthe gett for any sylver, aft*er* his astate. So it happend on̄ a day when̄ he had gaylie farn̄ att his meate, and his brether in þe covent had farn̄ bod badlie, & had little mete to ete, it happend

[1] MS. *repeats*, all hur synys. [2] *For* Petrus Damianus. [3] MS. mece.

af*ter* meate þat he mett ane of his brethir, a monk, & *with* a grete haste & a prowde cowntenance he bad hym̄ faste his erand'. And þis monke tarid, & went nott furth*with* as þe Abbott bad hym̄. And þe Abbott saw þis, & sayd vnto hym̄ *with* a grete indignacion̄: "ffra*ter*! fra*ter*! no*n* audisti que iussi? Brother, brother," said' he, "þou harde nott whatt I com*m*awndid þe?" Than̄ þis monke ansswerd' hym̄ agayn̄ & said', "ffor suthe I know wele I am̄ your bruther, bod trewlie nowd*er* your kirtyll nor your cowle, nor your welefare at your meate is my sister; for fra ye far̄ wele at your meate, ye rakk nevur & we þ*at* sulde be your brethir fare neu*er* so ill; & if ye may gett gay clothyng & gude, ye rakk neu*er* how we fare." *et* c^9.

VI.

Abbas int*er*du*m* debet gaudere cu*m* subditis suis.

We rede in þe life of Saynt Anton̄ how on̄ a tyme ane archer, þat was a gude sh[oter], fand Saynt [*Anton*] syttand emang his brethir makand merie *with* þai*m*. And þis archer was displesid' þer*with* & þoght þai sulde hafe bene in þ*er* clostre, & tente þ*er* buk*is* & þ*er* serues, & nott hafe bene att no sporte nor no welefare. And onone Saynt Anton̄ purseyvyd' his menyng, and callid hym̄ to hym̄, & bad hym̄ putt ane of his arows in his bow, & shote als fer as he myght, & he did' so; and þan̄ bad hym̄ take a noder, and do on̄ þe same wyse, and he did as he bad hym̄; & þan̄ he bad hym̄ take a thrid', & dràw hys bow als fer as he myght, at it mott fle far fro hym̄. And þan̄ þis archer[1] [*answerd*] hym̄ agayn̄ and said', "Sir, I dar nott, for I may happen̄ draw so fer þat I may breke my bow, & þat wold' I nott, for þan̄ I monde make mekull sorow." Than̄ Saynt Anton̄ sayd' vnto hym̄ agayn̄, "loo! son̄, þus it is in þe werke of allmyghtie God'; ffor and we draw it oute of mesur, we may sone breke itt; þat[2] is to say, and we halde our̄ brethir so strayte in aw þatt þai com̄ to no myrth nor no sporte, we may lightlie[3] cauce þai*m* to breke þ*er* ordur. And herefor̄ vs muste som̄ tyme lowse our̄ pithe, & suffre þai*m* hafe som̄

[1] MS. archerd'. [2] MS. þan. [3] MS. lighlie.

recreacioṅ & disporte emang aƚƚ þ*er* other chargis, as Catoṅ says, Int*er*pone·tuis int*er*du*m* gaudia curis." *et c*⁹.

Abbas malus et*er*nalit*er* punit*ur*. Infra de Ebrietate.

Abbas no*n* mansuetem[1] debet corrig*er*e. Inf*r*a de correcc*ione*.

VII.

Abbas quantu*m* potest debet p*ecca*tores reuocare.

We rede how soṁ tyme þ*er* was a thefe þat had many other thevis at his reule a[nd] gou*er*nance, & he was prince & maist*er* of þai*m* aƚƚ, vnto so mekuƚƚ þat w*it*h his robro[rie &] his thifte he di*s*troyed nerehand' aƚƚ þe regioṅ þat he dwelte in, in spolyng now of ane & now of a noder. So þ*er* was ane Abbott þat harde teƚƚ of hyṁ, & he tuke a gude hors, & þe beste clothis þat he had, & rade into þe wud þ*er* þis thieff lay; and onone he was takeṅ w*it*h þis thieff & his felows; and þis abbott askyd þai*m* what þai wolde w*it*h hyṁ; And þai [an]sswerd' hyṁ agayṅ & said', þai wold' hafe his hors & his clothis. And þis abbott [a]nsswerd' þai*m* agayṅ & said', "ye saƚƚ hafe þai*m* aƚƚ redie; for þe gudis of God, þai er̄ com*m*oṅ, and I hafe worṅ & occupied' þies gudis þis many yeris, and þ*er*for̄ it is right at ye hafe þai*m* now & vse þai*m* als long as I hafe done." And þaṅ þis maist*er* thefe said' vnto þis abbott, "Sur, þis day we wiƚƚ seƚƚ aƚƚ þis gere, and bye vs such thyng as vs nedis vnto our̄ fyndyng." & þaṅ þis Abbott said' vnto þis maist*er* thieff, "Whi laburs þou þus, & puttis þi selfe in so grete pereƚƚ as þou dose, for þi lifelod'? Coṁ w*it*h me vnto our̄ abbay, & I saƚƚ so ordand' at þou saƚƚ nott myster to be a thief no mor̄." Thaṅ þis thief said', "Sur abbott, I may not eate your benys nor your cale, nor I may not drynk your thyṅ ale." Thaṅ þis abbott ansswerd' hyṁ & said', "I saƚƚ giff the gude fissch & flessh to ete, & gude wyne to drynk." So vnnethis yit he wold' graunt þ*er*to, bod yit att þe laste he went home w*it*h þis abbot, & þoght he wold' prufe whethir he wold' holde his p*ro*mys or noght. So þis Abbott garte ordayṅ for hyṁ a fayr chawm*er* & a fayre bed', and assigned hyṁ a monk to seryff hyṁ, & for to gar hyṁ hafe aƚƚ þing þat he

[1] MS. mansuentem.

desirid. And euer-ilk day when þis thief had etyn & dronken of þe beste meate þat cuthe be getten, þis monke, be commandment of his abbott, befor þis thieff ete no thyng bod brede & watir. And when þis monk had done þus a long while, on a day þis thief said vnto hym, "bruthir! whatt grete syn hase þou done, þat þou pynys þi selfe so evur-ilk day with brede & watir? hase þou slayn any men?" And þis [*monk*] sayd, "Nay, sur, God forbede þat euer I kyll any man." Than þis thief askid hym if he had done any fornycacion or avowtrie, or done any sacrelege; and þan þis monke saynyd for merveil & said, "sur, whi say ye so? I hafe bene broght vp in þis abbay of barn litill, & I tuchid nevur no womman with syn." Than this thief was compuncte, & said vnto hym selfe, "A! how wrichid & vnhappie am I, þat hase done so mekull ill as I hafe done, as thifte, & mansslaghter, fornycacion, & avowtrie & sacrelege; & I neuer fastid nor did no penance." And þan þis thief garte call þis abbott vnto hym, & fell on kneis befor hym, & besoght hym þat he myght[1] be receyvid into þe abbay to be a bruther; & he grawntid hym, and so he was made a monke in þat abbay. And afterward he become so gude a man & so halie, þat he passid all his other brethir in gude lyfe & abstinence, & in gude reule of religion & holynes.

VIII.

Abbas non debet eligi per preces carnales.

Hubertus, in a buke þat he makis 'De Dono Timoris,' tellis how som tyme þer was ane abbott, and when he sulde dye, he besoght his brethir þat when he was deade [þai] wolde chese his suster son, þat[2] was a monke of þe same place, to be Abbott; and so þai did. So on a tyme as þis new Abbott walkid in his garthyn beside a well, [he] harde a huge voyse makand a grete mornyng & a sorow, & þat mervaluslie, and onone þis abb[ott] coniurid it. And when he had so done, It told hym þat it was þe saule of the Abbott a[t] was his eame, whilk it said was in grete payn, & byrnyd, and all becauce þat he, er he dyed, desirid his brethir to make hym þat was his sybman Abbott. And þan þe new abbott, his suster son,

[1] MS. *repeats*, þat he myght. [2] MS. þas.

said; "How may þou byrn in so grete payn, & be in so calde a well [as] þou ert in?" þan þis spiritt bad þis abbott go into þe kurk & take þer a copir candilstik, [&] bryng it with hym & caste it into þe well, & So he did. And onone, as it was casten into þe well, it was meltid as it had bene wax þat had bene putt in-to þe fire. And when þis new abbott saw þis, onone he renowncid his abboship, & garte chese a noder. And fro thens furth he neuer hard þis voice agayn.

IX.

Abbas bona monasterij non debet amicis dare.

We rede how som tyme þer was ane abbott of Saynt Pantaleus[1] in Colan, þat hight Cesari[us], & he had a bruther þat was a merchand; & euer when þis merchand come vnto hym, he wolde giff hym a grete substance of money of his monasterie. And many yeris þis money at [his] bruther gaff hym, he mengid it with his awn in his merchandice, & euer his gudis fa[ylid] hym, & he loste all þat evur he did. Not-with-stondyng, afor his bruther was abbott, he [w]a[s] a wurthie merchand, & was a riche man & he did gretelie vnto his bying and his sellyng. So on a tyme þis abbott his bruther sent after hym, when he harde of his rewle, and said vnto hym; "Bruther, whi wastis þou þus vilauslie þi substance & þi gudis bothe vn[to þi] confusion & myne?" Than þis merchand ansswerd hym agayn & said, "I liff als skantlie as I can, & diligentlie I kepe all my merchandice, and I wote neuer how it behappens vn[to me], ffor my felows profettis & waxis riche men, & I defayle & waxis pure." So he tuke his lefe att his bruther & wente home. And so, as he went hamwerd, he fell into a grete compunccion, & trustid he had done som grete syn, þat causid his gudis to fall away from hym be grevans of all-mighti God. So he avisid hym, and went to a preste and shrafe hym, & tolde hym all his life. And þis preste ansswerd hym & said; "The money at þou hase taken of þi bruther, it is stoltherye, & it wastis þi money and þi gudis, and þerfor fro hens furth take no mor money of hym, & þou sall do wele enogh. And with þat litle þat is lefte

[1] Harl. MS. Pentaleonis, Arun. MS. Panthaleonis.

the make þi m*er*chandice, & halfe of þi winnyng alway restore agayn vnto þe abbay, ewhils þou hafe payde agayn all att þi bruther lente the, & liff of þe toder halfe of þi wynnyng"; and so he did. And wit*h*-in a while he waxid so riche, at he restorid all agayn þat his bruther had giffen hym; and þan he was a passand riche man. So on a tyme þis abbot had grete m*er*vayle of hym & saide vn[to] hym; "how erte þou waxen riche so sodanlie, & wit*h*in a while was bod a pure man?" And heansswerd hym agayn & said; "Bruther abbott, als long as I reseyvid þ[e] substance & þe gudis of þi brethers of the, I was eu*er* pure & bakstad; and þou did grete syn att gaff me itt, for þou did bod stale it fro þi brether & gaf me it. And eu*er* sen I forsuke to take swilk stolethery, I hafe abundid & waxin ryche of gudi[s]; and þ*er*for I will no mor of þi money, for þuf all þou hase it in gou*er*nance, yitt itt is þi brethers als wele as thyne." *et c*9.

X.

Abbas in vestib*us* *et* in calciamentis humilem se debet ostendere.

We rede of ane Abbott off Ceustus ordur, how he on a tyme come vnto Philipp, þat was kyng of Romayns, for dyvers nedis of his howse, for to speke wit*h* hym. So þe kyng beheld his hose & his shone, & þai war passand strayte & clenlie done vppon; and when he had con[s]ydurd þis, he askid þis abbott of whyne he was; and þis abbott ansswerd hym agayn & sayd, "Sur, I am abbott of a full pure howse." And þan þe kyng said agayn vnto hym, "Sur, þat semys wele be your hose & your shone þat your howse is made passand pure, for þai er costios & dere." And wit*h* þis wurd þis abbott was confusid, & neu*er* aft*er* ware so costios hose nor shone, nor so strayte as he did befor.

XI.

Abb*a*tis simplicitas plus p*ro*dest aliqu*ando* Conuentui q*u*am ipsius calliditas. de bona vxore.

We rede how þ*er* was a monk of Clariuall þat was Abbott þ*er*, & his name was Petur, & he was a passand innocent man. So hym̄ happynd̄ cn̄ a day he[1] was [a]ssignyd̄ for to go, & a monke *with* hym̄, to speke *with* a knyght þat had tane mykull of þis abbott gudis fro hym̄, and said̄ þai war his awn̄; and þis knyght mett þis abbott at a place apoyntid̄, *with* a grete menyay of his kyns-men̄ *with* hym̄. And when̄ þai wer mett, The abbott said vnto þis knyght, "Thow ert a cristen̄ man̄; and þ*er*for & þ*ou* will say[2] of suthfastnes & be þi treuth at þies gudis er þine, I wull trew the, & fro hens furthe speke no more þ*er*off." And when̄ þe knyght hard̄ þis he was passand fayn̄, & forsid̄ litle of suthefastnes, and said̄ þat on̄ suthfastenes & be his treuthe, þase gudis war his & not þe abbays. Than̄ þe abbott sayd̄, "thyne be thay"; and þus þai p*ar*tid̄, & þe abbott lefte hym̄ þis gude. Than̄ þis knyght went home & tolde his wife, and sho as a gude woman̄ was ferd̄ þ*er*of, & said̄ vnto hur husband̄; "fforsuthe, Sur, þ*ou* hase done dissaytefullie agayn̄ yone holie abbott. Be war, for bod if þ*ou* restor agayn̄ vnto yone abbott þe gudis at þ*ou* hase takyn̄ þ*er*fra, þ*ou* sall want my felowshup̄"; and þurgh hur cowncell & hur saying he was agaste. And cn̄ þe morn̄ he went vnto Clarevall abbay, & come vnto þe abbott, & renowcid all þies gudis & forsuke þai*m*, & restorid̄ þe abbay agayn̄, and prayed̄ þe abbott for to forgyff hym̄ þat wrong at he had done vnto hym̄.

Abbas durus ad simplicitatem et hospitalitatem divisioni subiacet. Infra de histrionibus.

XII.

Abbas infirmis mult*um* debet condescendere.

Som tyme þ*er* was ane abbott of Cistus, þ*a*t hight Cesarius, comandid̄ vnto a monk of his þat was seke, þat he sulde eate flessh; and þis monke obeyid̄ his com*m*andment, þuff all it was agayn̄ his will, and said̄ vnto his abbott; "and I pray you for charitie þat ye wull vuchesafe to eate flessch *with* me." And̄ onone þis abbott g*r*auntid̄ & sett hym̄ down̄ be þe monke, & tuke a morsell of [flessc]h oute of þe seke man̄ platir & eate it. So it happend̄ þat

[1] MS. þai. [2] MS. said.

with-in ij dayes after, þis abbott went vnto a kurk whar þer was a man þat had a fend in hym, and onone as þis abbott saw hym, he spak vnto þe fend & said. "O! þou ill spirit! I coniure þe & chargis the þurgh þat charite be þe whilk laste day I ete flessh for my monke sake, at þou tarie here no langer, bod pas furth of þis man." And onone þis fende fled & went furth of þis man, becauce þe fire of charite was so hate þat he myght not suffer it.

XIII.

Abbatissa semp*er* subiectas sibi in dissiplina d*e*bet regere, *et* ad be*a*tam mariam vi*r*ginem deuocionem habere.

Som tyme þ*er* was a non þat was ane abbatiss of a grete place, and sho was called gude of gou*er*nans bothe in wurde & dede; & *with* a spi*r*ituall luf sho did þe cure þat sho had taken of hir sisters. & *with* grete aw & straytnes, þe co*n*gregacion att sho had gou*er*nan[s] of, sho co*m*pellid to kepe þ*er* ordur. Not*with*stondyng, þurgh entysing of þe devull, sho lete hur carvur, þat was hur awn syb-man, hafe at do *with* hur, so þat sho conseyvid and was *with* childe. And for all þat, yit sho lett nott, bod kepyd diligentlie emang hur susters þe rigur of disciplyne. Than it happend þat sho wex grete & drew nere hur tyme, & hur susters þe non*n*ys purseyvid, & was passand fayn þ*er*of, becauce sho wa[s] so strayte vnto þai*m*, at þai myght have a cauce to accuse hur in. And hur accusers gaite write vnto þe bisshop & lete hym wete þ*er*of, and desirid hym to com vnto þ*er* place and see hur. So he grawntid, and þe day of hym com*m*yng drew nere. And þis abbatis, þat was grete *with* childe, made mekull sorow & wiste neu*er* what sho might do. And sho had a p*r*ivay chapell *with*-in hur chawm*er*, þ*er* sho was wunt daylie als devoutlie as sho cuthe to say our ladie matyns. And sho went in þ*er* & sparrid þe dure vnto hur, and fell devoutelie on kneis befor þe ymage of our ladi, & made hur prayer vnto hur, & wepid sore for hur syn and besoght vr ladie for to helpe hur & safe hur, þat sho war not shamyd when þis bisshopp come. So in hur p*r*ayers sho happend to fall on slepe, and our ladie, as hur thoght, apperid vnto hur *with* ij angels, & comfurthid hur & said vnto hur in þis man*er* of wise; "I hafe hard þi prayer, and I hafe getten of my son forgifnes of þi syn, & delyverans of þi co*n*fusion." And onone sho was delyvur of hur childe, & our ladie chargid þies ij angels to hafe it vnto ane h*er*mett, & chargid hym to bryng it vp vnto it was vij yere olde; and þai did as sho com*m*aundid þai*m*; & onone our ladie vanysshid away. And þan þis abbatiss wakynd & grapid hur selfe, & feld hur selfe delyvurd of hur childe, & hole & sownde; & sho thankid almighti God & our blissid ladie þat þus h[ad] delyvurd hur. In þe mene while on a day, þis bisshop come & went into þe chapitr howse, & callid all þe nonnys aforn hym; & þis abbatis wold hafe gone vp & sett hur in hur stede be þe bisshop as sho was wunte to do; and þis bisshop reprovid hur & chargid hur to go furth of þe chapitr, & said sho was not wur[thi] to be þ*er*-in. & when sho was gone he sent ij clerkis aft*er* hur to examyn h[ur], & to serche whethur sho wer *with* childe or noght; & þai cuthe fynde no takyn on hur þat sho sulde be *with* childe. And þai come vnto þe bisshop & tolde hym þat sho was innocent of þat at sho was accusid of. Neu*er*-þe-les þis bisshop mystristid þai*m*, & trowid þai had takyn som money of hur, & he said he wolde serge hur hym selfe; & so he did, & he cuthe not fynde in hur no synge þat sho sulde be *with* childe. And þan þis bisshop fell downe befor hur on his kneis, & askid hur forgifnes of þe wrong at he had done vnto hur; and all þai*m* þat had accusid hur, he chargid at þai sulde be putt oute of þe place. And þis abbatis besoght hym nay, and forgaff þai*m* at þai had saide vppon hur. And þan sho tuke þis bisshop in confession & tolde hym all how it had happend hur, & how owr ladie had delyverd hur; and þis bisshop had grete m*er*vayle þ*er*of, & sent þies ij clerkis vnto þis hermett to luke if it wer so or noght. & þai broght þe bisshopp wurd fro the h*er*mett, þat ij yong men had broght hym þis childe, & said þat our ladie com*m*aundid hym to kepe it vij yere. And when it was vij yere olde, þis bisshop tuke it & garte putt it vnto þe skule, & it encrecid gretelie in vertue & con*n*yng, vnto so mekull þatt when þis bisshop decesid, he was made bisshop after hym nexte succedyng.

XIV.

Abbatissa pura *et* munda debet esse corpore *et* temptacionib*us* omnino resistere.

We rede be tellyng of olde fadurs, how þat þ*er* was a holie abbatis, and sho was gretelie vexid xiij yere wit*h* þe syn of fornycacion, & eu*er* when sho was tempid sho prayed all-myghti God to send hur strenth to wit*h*stond þis temptacion, & not for to mofe it away. So on a tyme þe spiritt of fornycacion apperid vnto hur bodelie & said; "þou hase ou*er*-com*m*en me." & sho answerd agayn & said, "I hafe not ou*er*com*m*en þe, bod my Lord Ie*su* Criste hase ou*er*com*m*en þe." *et* c*etera*.

XV.

Abbatissa non debet esse in vestib*us* *et* lectis nimis delicata.

We rede in a fable how at þe lopp & þe gutt on a tyme spak to-gedre, & emang þ*er* oþ*er* talkyng, athir of þai*m* askid other of þ*er* lugyng, & how þai war herberd & whare, þe night next befor. And þe lopp made a grete playnte & said, "I was herberd in þe bed of ane abbatice, betwix ij white shetis, opon a softe matres, & þ*er* I trowed to hafe had gude h*er*berie, for hur flessh was fatt & tendre, & þ*er*of I trowid to hafe had my fyll. & furste, when I began[1] for to bite hur, sho began to cry & call on hur maydyns, and when þai come, onone þai lightid candels & soght me, bod I hid me to þai war gone. & þan I bate hur agayn, & sho come agayn & soght me wit*h* a light, So þat I was fayn to lepe oute of þe bed. And so all þis nyght I had no reste, bod was chasid & charrid & vnnethis gatt away wit*h* my life." Than answerd þe gowte & said, "I was herberd in a pure wom*m*ans howse, & onone as I prikkid hur in hur thomble ta, sho rase & uettid a grete boll full of clothis, & went wit*h* þai*m* vnto þe watir, & stude þ*er*-in wit*h* me vp to hur kneis; so þat, what for calde & for holdyng in þe watir, I was nere-hand slayn." And þan þe lopp said,

[1] MS. *repeats*, furste.

"This night will we [cha]nge our h*er*bery"; & so þai did. & on þe morn þai mett agayn; & þan þe lopp said vnto þe gowte, "þis night hafe I had gude herberie, for þe wom*m*an þat was þine oste yisternyght was so werie and so yrke, þat I was sekurlie h*er*berd *with* hur, & eate of hur blude als mekull as I wold." And þan answerd þe gutt & said vnto þe lopp, "þou gaff me gude cowncell yistreven, for þe abbatiss vnder-nethe a gay cou*er*lade, & a softe shete and a delicate, cou*er*de me & nurisshid me all nyght. & als sone as I prikkid in hur thomble ta, sho wappid me in furris, & if I hurte hir neu*er* so ill, so lete me alone, & laide me in the softests place of þe bed, & tribulde me nothyng. And þ*er*for als lang as sho liffis I wil[l] be h*er*berd *with* hur, for sho makis mekill of me." And þan said þe lopp, "I wull be h*er*berd *with* pure folke als lang as I liff, for þ*er* may I be in gude reste & ete my fyll, & no bod[ie] lett me." And þus þe gowte abade *with* riche folk & þe lopp *with* pure folk. *et c*^9.

XVI.

Abscondere. Abscondere debet mulier pulc*r*itudinem sua*m* ne aliquis in ea*m* offendat.

Eaclides[1] tellis how att þ*er* was a mayden whase name was Alexandria, þat garte cloce hur selfe in a grete grafe, & tuke hur meat att a little hole, to so mekull þat x yere to-gedyr sho saw neu*er* nowder man nor wom*m*an, nor shewid nevur hur visage to no creatur. So on a tyme, þ*er* come a man vnto hur hole, & spirrid whi sho was closid þ*er* & wolde not com oute. And sho answerd agayn & said, "Som tyme þ*er* was a yong man þat lukid on my fayrehede, & þurgh þat luke his saule was hurte *with* syn; & þ*er*for or I sulde be sene for to hevie any man, me had leu*er* be closid in þis grafe als lang as I liff, þan for to noy þe saule þat is made vnto þe liknes of almighti God." And þan þis man askid hur how sho might liff so; Sho answerd agayn & said, "fro þe begynyng of þe day I fall in hand *with* my prayers, & forther-mor of þe day I wurk lyne werk, and þan I þink of holie martyrs, confessurs, & virgynnys,

[1] Latin MSS. Heraclides.

and þan I take me meate & drynk; and þan again evyn I go to ryste, & þ*er* I wurschup allmyghti God. And þus I abide þe ende of my life wit*h* a gude hope, & a belefe þat I sall be savid on þe day of dome." *et c*9.

XVII.

Absolucio. Absolucio eciam valet post mortem.

We rede of a monke þat hight Hub*er*tus, whilk þat when he sulde dy, he askid straytlie þat þe abbott myght com vnto hym & assoyle hym, as he did other of his brether þat dyed. And þis abbott was fro home, & in þe mene while [þis] monke deyed. And when þe abbott come home þai tellid hym, and þis abbo[tt] went vnto þe altar þ*er* þis monk was berid, & sett hym down on his kneis & prayed for hym. And as he satt in his prayers, hym þoght þis monke rase oute of his grafe & come vnto hym, & said, "Benedicite!" right as he had bene o life, and askid a due absolucion. So þis abbott, gretlie astonyd þ*er*-wit*h*, Said, "miseriatur tüi *et c*9, *et* absolu-*cio*nem." And þan þis monk askid hym penans. And þis abbott wiste neu*er* whatkyn penance sulde be giffen vnto þai*m* at wer deade; and he com*m*andid hym þat he sulde be in purgatorie vnto he had said a mes for hym. And when þe monk hard þis, he cryed so horrible, þat all þe abbay hard, on þis man*er* of wise; "O! þou man wit*h*-oute m*er*cie! þat hase com*m*andid me to be so long in þe grete payn of purga[*to*]rie[1]." And wit*h* þat he vanysshid away.

XVIII.

Absolucio ad-huc valet post mortem.

We rede in þe life of Saynt Gregur how at þ*er* was ane abbott of a monast*er*ie off Saynt Gregories, and he come vnto Saynt Gregur & tolde hym how þat he had a monk in his place þat vsid for to cone mony vnder-nethe þe erth, & wolde not lefe it for no com*m*andmente. And Saynt Gregur sent for hym, & chargid o payn of cursyng to lefe it. So wit*h*-in a while after, þis monke dyed, & Saynt Gregur wuste nott. And when he was enformed þ*er*of,

[1] MS. purgarie.

he was wrothe þ*at* þis monke died vnasoylid. And he wrote his absolucion in a scrow of papir to assoyle hym of þe said sentans of cursyng, and gaff it vnto ane of his dekyns, & com*m*andid him to go vnto þis monke grafe þ*er* he was berid, & rede it ou*er* hym. And he did so, and vppon þe nyght aft*er*, þis monk þat was deade apperid in a vision vnto his abbott, & tolde hym þ*at* fro he was dede vnto he was asoylid he was in grete payn, bod fro þe howr þat he was asoylid he went vnto blis, & was delyverd of all his payn. *et c*.

XIX.

Abstinencia. Abstinencia debet esse discreta.

We rede in '*Collacionib*us* *Patrum*,' how þat a gude halie abbott, þat hight Moyses, on a tyme said of hym selfe in þis man*er* of wise; "I remembre so for to hafe dispysid þe appetite of mete & drynke, so at ij dayes or iij, mete nor drynke was neu*er* in my mynde. And I hafe so abstenyd me fro slepe, not-wit*h*-stonding I was attemptid gretlie þ*er*to be þe devull, þat many nyghtis & many [*dayis*][1] I slepid neu*er* a dele, bod bad my prayers vnto almyghti God. And yitt I felid my selfe, þat I had dyvers tymys mor hurte wit*h* outrage takyng of meate & drynk & slepe þan wit*h* abstinens þ*er*off." Bod monk*is* er not so now o dayis, for or a monk wantid now ane howr slepe, or a negg of his s*er*ves in his dissh, hym had levur þat his howse was in xx li dett. And so war nott monk*is* in olde tyme[2].

XX.

Abstinencia singularis in com*m*itate est repr*e*hensibilis.

We rede in a buke þat is callid '*Vitæ*[3] *Pat*r*um*,' how on a tyme, all þe monkis þat was in ane abbay opon a solempne fastyng-day ete sam*en* in þ*er* fratur. And emang þ*aim* þ*er* was one þat bad bryng hym salte, for he ete no bulid meate. And he þat he bad bryng hym salte was occupied wit*h* oþ*er* laburs, and forgatt to

[1] Latin MSS. ut p*er* pl*ures* dies ac noctes.
[2] This tale is very different from the Latin version.
[3] MS. Vitas.

bryng hym itt; & þan þis monk callid þer-for agayn. And þis servand cried vp opon hyght and bad som man bryng salte vnto þis monke, for he ete no bulid mete. And þan rase vp one alde monk & said vnto þis monk þat callid for salte; "Bruther, it had bene mor expedient vnto þe þis day for to hafe etyn flessh in þi cell, þan for to hafe made þis voyce of þine abstinence emange so many of þi brethir."

XXI.

Abstinencia mod*er*ata p*ro* loco et t*em*pore displicet diabolo.

Jacobus de Vet*ria*co[1] tellis how þat þ*er* was a holie Saynt þat hight Maria de Oginiez, whilk þat oft sithes punysshid hur selfe w*ith* grete abstinence. So on a tyme sho refresshid hur w*ith* mete, & as sho satt etand sho was war[2] of þe devull; & w*ith* a grete [con]tenans & ane angrie he said vnto hur; "Beholde þis gluton! how ferventlie sho etis!" And sho satt still & vmbethoght hur, & knew his falssett well enogh, & ete on. & eu*er* þe devull wolde hafe lett hur for to hafe etyn, becauce he wulde sho had dyed for defawte; and ay þe mor he lett hur to ete, þe mor sho ete. And he saw at sho wolde not lett to ete for hym, bod at ay þe langer he laburd hur, þe more sho ete. [&] w*ith* a grete crying & a noyse he vanyshid away fro hur, & neu*er* aft*er* trubled hur nor did hur harm.

XXII.

Admirabilis abstinencia.

We rede in 'Vitis[3] P*atrum*' how þat þ*er* was a gude holie alde man, & xl yere he drank nevur; & evur he wulde take a vessell & fulfill it w*ith* wyne & hyng it in his chawm[re] þat he mott daylie se it. So on a tyme his brethir askyd hym whi he did so, and he answerd agayn & said, "I do it to þis entent, þat when I se þat þing at I desire, þat w*ith* abstinens þ*er*of I may suffre mor payn; and so of almyghti God I sall have more mede."

[1] MS. Vet*r*iano. [2] *After* war, vi, *erased*. [3] MS. Vitas.

XXIII.

Abstinencia refrenat concupiscenciam in re habita que fuerat concupita vel desiderata.

We rede ex 'Dictis Patrum' how þat þer was som tyme a man of religion, þat be temptacion of þe devull covett gretle to ete spyce. So on a tyme he boght hym spice, & wulde not ete þerof, bod hang it befor hym þat he mott se itt. & becauce he wolde not be ouercommen with covatice þerof, he wolde neuer eate þeron nor tuche itt, Bod euer when he saw itt, punysshid his body þerwith becauce þat it desirid it.

XXIV.

Abstinencia interdum vincit diabolum inpugnantem.

We rede in 'Vitis[1] Patrum' how at þer was a freer þat was so gretelie tempid with þe devull, þat euer-ilk day, at iij of þe bell, he fell into so grete a honger, þat he myght not suffer it. So on a tyme he said vnto hym selfe, "Benedicite! how is it with me, þat I am so turment with suche a honger at iij of þe bell in þe mornyng, so þat I may nott forbere meate no day vnto vj of þe clokk, or ix, or none?" And euer-ilk day befor none, not-withstondyng all þis honger, he wuld say his matyns, his mes, & his oþer prayers[2] ilk day or he ete any meate, as þe rewle of his religion askid, and þan he wulde sett hym down & take hym meate; and þus he did many day. So on a day when he had bene at his prayers, he walkid vp & down in a garthyn, & hym thoght þer come so swete a savur oute of his parcell bed & his erbis, þat he was so replete þerwith þat ij or iij dayes hym liste nevur at e[ate]. And yit hym thoght þat he was als strong of hym selfe as he had etyn sufficient at evur-ilk mele tyme. *et c^9.*

XXV.

Abstinencia a nimis potu reddit hominem cautum in consilijs et facundum in verbis.

Helinandus, a grete clerk, writand of þe life & maners of one þat hight Romulus, þat was one of þe foundors of Rome, wrate

[1] MS. Vitas. [2] MS. prayes.

oñ hym̃ in þis maner of wise & said, þat agayns þis Romulus suld go vnto þe cowncell howse, he wold not drynke, & in-esspeciall wyne, bod in esy quantitie iij dayes befor. So oñ a tyme a gude mañ of Rome, þat purseyvid his condicioñ, said vnto hym̃, "Thow Romull*us*! and all meñ did as þou duse, wyne sulde not be in Rome in so grete dayntie as it is. For & no mañ wolde drynk no mor þerof þan þou Duse, it sulde not be so dere as it is." *et c*[9].

XXVI.

Abstinencia indiscreta est nimis periculosa.

Cesarius tellis how a devull in liknes of ane aungell apperid evur-ilk day vnto a monke wheñ he was at his meate, & shewid hym̃ alway halfe a lafe, & bad hym̃ no mor bod þat. And þe monke did evur as he bad hym̃, & *with*-in a shorte while he wex passand wayke. And þer fell a swyngyllyng in his hede þat he wex fonde *with*, & mad as a guse; & so he contynued vnto he deyid. *et c*[9].

Abstinencia a carnib*us* est necessaria. Infra de gula.

XXVII.

Abstinencia. Abstinentib*us* deus p*ro*videt de necessarijs.

Saynt Gregorie tellis how þat ane abbott, þat hight Honoratus, & his fadur & his moder, oñ a tyme made a feste vnto his frendis. And þer was at þis feste a childe þat was ane of his kynsmeñ þat satt att þe burd, and wheñ þai bad hym̃ eate flessh, he wolde eate none, for grete abstinens þat he vsyd. And þai þat satt abowte lowgh at hym̃, & askid hym̃ in skorñ, señ he wolde nott ete flessh, if he wold eate any fyssch. & he answerd agayñ & said, "Ya." & he had it. And in þe mene while at þai talkid þus *with* hym̃, happend þai*m* want watir; & þañ þer mawnciple went vnto þe well & drew watir. And as he was drawand, þer happend of Sodentie a fyssh to com̃ in-to þe bukett, & þat a grete; & he was fayñ þerof, & broght it in & lete þe abbott se itt. & þe abbott garte sethe it, & it was so foysonable þat it fande þe childe and all at was att meate fyssh enogh at a mele. *et c*[9].

Accepcio p*er*sonar*um*. Accepcione p*er*sonar*um* multi decipiuntur. Infra de iudicio humano.

XXVIII.

Accidia. Accidia multos retrahit a bono op*er*e.

Cesarius tellis how þat a monk on a tyme was so tempyd *with* sleuthe & slugisnes, þat evur when he sulde rise vnto matyns, he was eu*er* stryken into a grete ferdnes & a fayntnes, to so mekull þat he supposid hym selfe þat it was a sekenes. & ilk nyght, when his brethir went to matyns, he happed his hede *with* clothis & lay still. So it happend on a gude night, all his brether, when þai hard þe bell, rase & went to matyns. And when þai wer gone, he thoght he wold ryse & go *with* þai*m*, & bukkled vpward. And onone þis slugisnes come on hym, & causid hym lay hym down agayn & happ hys heade. And sodanle he hard a voyce þat was vnknowen to hym, as hym þoght, speke vnder his hede, & said, "Noli surg*er*e; noli sudore*m* tuu*m* int*er*rumpere. Rise nott, bod ly still, & lett not þi selfe to swete; for & þou do, it will hurte the." & þan he was halfe agaste, & liftid up his hand & saynyd hym. And onone it smate in his mynd þat it was bod ane illusion of þe devull & a fantasie, & onone he rase vp & went to matyns *with* hys brether. And fro thens furth, he was neu*er* slugissh to rise & go vnto Goddis serves, nor þat fayntnes nor þat swete come neu*er* on hym aftre.

Accidia in or*atione* est vitanda. Infra de dormire in or*atione*.

XXIX.

Accidia causatur frequent*er* ex eo q*uo*d homo ociosus no*n* cogitat circa vtilia aliqua.

We rede In 'Vitis[1] P*atrum*' vnto þ*er* was ane man of religion þat sayd vnto his bruther þat was ane olde man, "what sall I do? for

[1] MS. Vitas.

I sit in my cell & duse noght, bod is made slugis *with* slewth." Than þis olde man answerd hym & sayde, "hase þou not sene turment þat is for to com? for & þou pryntid þaim in þi harte, and þi Cell war full of wormys evyn vnto þi nekk, þou sulde suffer it pacientlie & be nothyng slugyssh þer*with*, bod take it mekelie."

XXX.

Accusacio. Accusat demon pecc*ato*res et scribit pecc*ata* eor*um*.

Saynt Bede tellis in 'Gestis Anglor*um*,' how at þ*er* was a knyght in Englond þ*at* was a dughti man in armys, bod he was corrupte in maners. And on a tyme hym happend to fall passand seke. And þe kyng come vnto hym, & comforthed hym, & bad hym be of gude chere. And [he] ansswerd agayn & said þat he myght nott, ffor he was passand ferd þat hys seknes suld cover on hym. And þe kyng come to hym a nod*er* tyme & co*m*furthed hym, & bad hym take gude harte vnto hym & be of gude chere. And he ansswerd agayn & said þ*at* he myght not, for it was to late, for he said; "I am demyd & dampnyd; ffor a litle while or ye come in, [þer] was here ij fayr yong men, and one sett hym at my bed hede, & a noder at my fete. And þai said, 'This man mon dye. And þ*er*for lat us se if we hafe any right in hym.' And þe tone of þai*m* tuke oute of his bosom a buke writtyn all *with* gold letters. And he soght all þe buke þurgh, & he cuthe fynd nothyng of me bod a few gude dedis þat I did in my yowthed, or I cuthe syn deadlie; & þ*at* he shewid me, & I was passyng glad þ*er*off. And þan þ*er* come in ij fowle fendis, & þe tane of þai*m* broght *with* hym a grete blak buke, and þ*er*-in was wretten all þe evull dedis þat evur I did. And þai said vnto þies ij angels; 'wharto stond ye here al day *with* hym þis? ye hafe no right in hym, for þis many yeris was þ*er* nothyng of hym wrettyn in your buke.' Than þe angels ansswerd & sayd, 'Thai say suthe, & þ*er*for go we hyne.' And þis done, þies fendis cuttys me in sonder *with* ij sharpe swerdis; and þe tone begynys at my fute, and þ*at* other at my heade, & þai smyte me now on myne eyn, & I hafe loste my sight, and now fro my fute þai com̄ vnto my harte." And when̄ he had þus said he swelte, *et c*⁹. This tale is gude to tell agayns þai*m* þat er slaw in penance doyng, or at will not lefe syn̄ or it lefe þai*m*. *et c*⁹.

¶. Accusat Angel*us*. Infra ffideiussor.
¶. Accusat demon. Infra demon.
¶. Accusant Sa*n*cti. Infra Epi*scopus*. ij.

XXXI.

¶. Accusare fr*atr*em no*n* expedit semp*er*.

As holie fadurs tels, we rede how þ*er* was a holie religious man̄, þat askid his abbott, þat hyght Joseph, & said; "And I se my bruther do a tryspas, it is gude vnto me to layn̄ itt?" And þan̄ þis old Abbott answerd hym̄ agayn̄ & said, "When̄ som̄ evur we hide þe syn̄ of owr brutber, almighti God hydis owr syn̄, & when̄ som̄ evur we vtter þe synys of owr brether, þan̄ almightti God vtters our syn̄." This tale is gude to tell vnto þai*m* þat luffis to sklander þ*er* evyn̄ cristen̄. *et c*⁹.

XXXII.

Accusacio frequent*er* est falsa.

We rede de Sa*ncta* Marina, how at þ*er* was a seculer man̄ þat had a doght*er* alone, & no ma childer. So on̄ a tyme he betuke þis barn̄ vnto his fadur to kepe, and went hym̄ [se]lfe vnto ane abbay & made hym̄ a monke. And when̄ he had bene þ*er* a while, eu*er* when̄ he thoght of his yong doghter he was passand hevie. And when̄ þe abbott pursayvid þis, he askid hym̄ whi he was so hevie & so sad. And he fell down̄ vnto hym̄ on̄ his kneys wepand, & said, "ffadur abbott! I hafe a son̄ þat I hafe lefte in þe cytie, & evur when̄ I thynk opon̄ hym̄, my harte is sore & passand hevie." And yitt he wold not tell hym̄ þat it was a doght*er*, bod at hit was a son̄. And þe Abbott bad hym̄ go þ*er* for, & bryng it into þe place, & kepe it wi*th* hym̄, & giff it meate & drynk, & lern̄ itt. And so he did, and cled it in mans clothyng & callid it Marinus. And he warnyd þat on̄ no wyse no man̄ sulde know þat it wer a wom*m*an̄, for drede þat it fell in-to temptacion of þe devull. And when sho was xvii yere olde, þis monk hur fadur dyed, and sho was lefte alone. & no man knew bod at sho was a man, & eu*er*-ilk bodie luffid hur. So on a tyme sho was made ane offisur in þe abbay, for to folow þ*er* car & lede wud & fewell vnto þ*er* brewhowse, & so sho did; and ilka nyght sho lay in þe brewhowse. So on a tyme þe brewster doghter happend to be w*ith* childe w*ith* a knyght at *ser*vid þe abbott, and in þe mene while þis Marinus was made a bruther of þe place, & sho said þat he was þe fadur þ*er*of, & had getten it. And þe abbott garte call þis Marin*us* furth, & examynd hym whethur þat he had done þis dede or noght. And þan þis Marin*us* answerd w*ith* a grete sighyng & said, "ffadur abbott! I hafe synnyd, & I ask penance for my syn, & I pray you & all my brether to pray for me." And þan þe Abbott wex wrothe w*ith* hym & putt hym furth of þe abbay, and feste hym be þe fute w*ith* a chyne w*ith*-oute þe abbay yate, and all men mott wonder on hym, & wolde lat no man giff hym meate bod att he beggid for Godd*is* sake of þai*m* þat come in & oute. And when þe childe was att spanyng, þis brewster doght*er* broght it vnto hym & lefte it w*ith* hym. And þis holie virgyn Marin*us* tuke it w*ith* gude will, & w*ith* meate & drynk at þai at come in & oute gaff hur, sho broght it vpp, þuf all it war a noder mans & not hurs. So at þe laste hur brethir had co*m*passion of hur, & besoght þ*er* abbott, att he wold forgiff hur hur trespas, trustyng alway at sho was man & no wom*m*an, ffor sho had þan bene feste at þe yate v yere. And þis Abbot forgaff hur at requeste of his brethir, & tuke hur in & garte putt hur vnto al man*er* of vile occupasions w*ith*-in þe abbay, & to be *ser*vand vnto evur eman; & sho was so, & tuke it plesandlie. So w*ith*-in[1] a while sho dyed; and when þis abbott saw at sho was deade, he said vnto hys brethir, "Loo! now may ye se whatkyn a syn sho did, & yitt sho shrafe hur neu*er* þ*er*of, nor askid forgifnes." And þan he com*m*andid wassh hur bodie, & berie hur far fro þe abbay. And when þai wasshid hur & fand þat sho was a wom*m*an, þai weppid & made grete sorow becauce þai turment hur, þat was a wom*m*an of so gude co*n*v*er*sacion &

[1] *After* w*ith*, *some letter erased.*

penance, so vnrightwuslie. And when þe abbot saw at sho was a wom*m*an, he fell opon his kneis & bett opon his breste, and besoght hur of forgifnes, and com*m*andid þat hur bodie sulde be berid in þe kurk, in ane oritorie. And opon þe same day þis damysell at bare þis childe was vexid *with* a fend, & come vnto þe abbay & askid m*er*cy at hur grafe; & þ*er* sho was delyverd, and grawntid who aght þe child. & þ*er* sho abade in þe oratorie vij dayes, & þan sho was delyverd. And in þ*at* same oratorie vnto þis day, be merett*is* of þis holie vi*r*gyn, is many wurthi meracle done, þurgh v*er*tue of God & þis holie maydyn.

Adu*er*sitas. Adu*er*sitas p*r*esens est aliqu*ando* signu*m* boni. Infra de p*ro*sp*er*itate.

Adoracio. Adorari debet corpus Chr*ist*i in om*ni* loco. Infra de milite. v.

XXXIII.

Adulator. Adulator freque*n*t*er* honoratur, *et* verax homo contempnitur.

Esopus tellis in his fables, how þ*er* was ij men, ane a trew man & a nod*er* a lyer. And þai come to-gedur in-to þe region of apis. And emang þai*m* was a chefe ape, þat satt in a hye sete þat was ordand for hym emang all þe tod*er* apis. And he askid þai*m* many questions; emangi*s* all oþ*er* he said vnto þai*m*; "Quis sum ego? who am I?" And þis lyeransswerd agayn & sayd, "Sur, þou erte ane Emp*er*our, & þies abowte þe er þi duk*is* & þine erlis & þi barons." And onone as he had þus said, þis ape com*m*andid hym to hafe a grete reward. And þan þis trew man saw how þis lyer was rewardid, and said p*r*ivalie vnto hym selfe, "Now, sen he þis at did bod make[1] a lye hase had suche a grete reward, I mon[2] hafe a grete reward for my suth saying." And þan þis ape askid þis trew man & said, "who am I?" And he ansswerd agayn & said, "Thow ert bod ane ape, and all þies oþ*er* apis er like þe." And onone as he had þus said, he com*m*andid all þe tod*er* apis for

[1] MS. made. [2] MS. *repeats*, mon.

to bite hym & skratt hym *with* þ*er* tethe & þ*er* naylis; & so þai did, to he vnnethis gatt away *with* his life. This tale is gude to tell agayn flat*er*ers, & agayns þai*m* þ*at* wull here no thyng bod at is to þ*er* plesur.

XXXIV.

Adulator no*n* est audiendus.

We rede how som tyme a man þat hyght Seutonius, þat was a grete lord, on a tyme was at a game*n* in þe Emp*er*our p*re*sens, and þe Emp*er*our com*m*ond & talkyd *with* his meneyay; & emang all his oþ*er* saying, he sayd þat þis Seutonius was a gude lorde, and ane evyn & a iuste. And his meneya was glad þ*er*of þ*at*[1] þe Emp*er*our com*m*andid þ*er* maist*er*, & callid hym lord. And on þe morn when he was comme*n* home vnto his place, þo þat callid hym lord, he was passand wrothe *with* þai*m*, & made a decre & bad þai*m* neu*er* call hym lord, for, he said, þ*er* was no lord bod one.

Adulator ho*min*em sup*ra* se[2] frequent*er* p*er* mendacium extollit. Infra de Augurrio. iijo.

XXXV.

Adult*er*iu*m*. Adult*er*a vxor no*n* est tenenda.

We rede how þat one þat hight Genulphus[3] in Frawnce, boght a well, & he was a wed man & he was a holie man[4]; & when he come home in-to Burgundie þ*er* he dwelte, he fand þe same well sprongen in his garthen. So on a day, þis Genulphus[3] & his wife walkid same*n* in þ*er* garthyn & sett þai*m* down be þe well; & he reprovid hur for avowtrie, & said it was tellid hym at a noder man held hur beside hym; & sho denyed it & said nay. Than he said vnto hur; "Bare þine arm & take vp a little stone in þe bothom of þis well, & if þine arm com vp vnhurte I sall trow at þou ert innocent of þis at is put on[5] the." And sho trowed at sho had bene sekur enogh, & showid in hur arm in-to þe well. And when sho drew it oute, it was as it had bene scaldid *with* þe fyre. And

[1] *After* þat, his mene, *erased*.
[2] MS. *repeats*, supra se.
[3] Lat. MSS., Gangulphus, Gengolphus.
[4] MS. *repeats*, & a wed man.
[5] MS. *repeats*, on.

þan þis holie man said vnto hur; "Lo! now aperis þe treuth of þi falsett, and þerfor fro hens furth þou sall neu*er* be my felow." & he devidid his gude in two & gaff hur þe to halfe, & lete hur dwell be hur one. And *with*-in a litill whill a cleık þat held þis Genulphus [1] come to hym on a nyght when he lay slepand in his bed, & slew hym. And when he was berid he did m*er*acles. And when his wife hard tell at he did m*er*acles, scho skornyd hym & said on þis man*er* of wise; "It is als trew at Genulphus duse m*er*acles, as it is at myne ars syngis." And onone hur ars made ane vglie noyse, and wolde not lefe for noght sho cuth do. And evur after, opon þe fryday at hur husband suffred m*ar*tyrdom on, wekelie when sho spakk any wurd, hur ars began to syng & make ane vglie noyse, & wold neu*er* lefe it on þe fryday whils at sho liffid. *et c*⁹.

XXXVI.

Adult*er*iu*m* punit deus in hac vita.

Petrus Damanus [2]. On a tyme when he was at þe cetie of *P*arissh [3], opon þe day befor þe ffest of Gervasij & *P*rothasij, a man of þe cetie rase tymelie in þe mornyng & drafe his oxen vnto a fer pastur; & þis man had þe axis ill. And one of his neghburs p*ur*seyvid þat he was gone vnto þe feld, & he fenyd hym as he had shakyn in þe axis, & come in-to þis mans howse shakand, & went into þe bed to þe wife. And þe wyfe trowed þat it had bene hur husband þat had com*m*en fro þe felde shakand in þe axis, & sho hawsid hym, and onone he defowlid & went his wais. And *with*-in a while after, hur husbond come home passand seke, & bad hur make hym a cuche þat he myght lig on. And þe wife reprevid hym, & sayd sho mott thole hym "go vnto þe kurk of þase holie martyrs *with* othe[*r*] chr*ist*en men, & here dyvyne *ser*ves." And hur husband was gretlie astonyd *with* hur language, & askid hur what sho mente; and sho tellid hym all þe matyr. And onone as sho had told hym, he consayvid þat bothe he & sho was desayvid; and when þai come vnto þ*er* selfe, þai besoght God to venge þ*er* harmys, and at it myght be opynlie knowen

[1] Lat. MSS., a cl*er*ico adult*er*o occisus est. [2] *For* Damianus.
[3] Latin MSS. apud permensem vrbem.

who did þis avowtrie. And onone þ*er* neghbur þat did þis avowtre was vexid *with* a fend, & skratt & bete hym̄ selfe, & went in-to þe kurk, & þ*er* he was so mad þat now he wold clymbe vp als hye as he myght, & sodanlie fałł down̄ agayn̄ vnto þe erthe; & now he wold ryn̄ agayn̄ þe wałł *with* his hede, & now he wolde sodanly fałł down̄ vnto þe erth. & þus he did ewhils he swelte aforn̄ ałł þe pepułł.

XXXVII.

Adult*er*ium eciam aues abhorrent.

Cesarius tellis how som̄ tyme þ*er* was in a knyghtis garth a [storkis][1] neste; and þ*er* was bathe þe male and þe femałł. And on̄ a tyme when̄ þe male was away, sho lede a nod*er* fewle do avowtrie *with* hur; and eu*er* when̄ he had done, sho wolde go vnto a dike at was beside þe place, & þ*er* sho wold wassh hur. And þis knyght had grete m*er*vełł here-of, & garte make a hedgyng ou*er* þis dyke, at sho mot nott wyn̄ þ*er*to. So on̄ a tyme when̄ sho had truspasid, sho come & soght þe watir to wassh hur in, & sho myght noght wyn̄ þ*er*to. And in þe mene wile come hur male, and onone he purseyvid þat sho had fawtid, and *with* his byłł he strake a grete strake at sho lay stiłł *with*. And becauce he was nott of myght and power to sla hur be his one, þ*er*for he gaderd samen a grete co*m*pany of [storks], & *with*-in ane how*er* þai come on̄ hur *with* a grete wudnes, & in sight of þe knyght and ałł men̄ in þe cowrte, þai flow opon̄ hur & slew hur as a wriche. Loo! surs, how burdis hatis avowtre; þ*er*for me thynk þat men̄ & wom*men*̄ sulde hate it mekułł more.

XXXVIII.

Aduocatus. Aduocator*um* cautele aliqua*n*do su*n*t p*er*iculose.

We rede how som̄ tyme þ*er* was a yong [*man*] þat feste hym̄ at þe scule *with* Pictagoras, for to be a sophister & lern̄ eloquens, & for to know þe crafte of disputyng in ałł man*er* of cawsis, and he agreid *with* hym̄ to giff hym̄ a grete dele of money. So on̄

[1] MS. has here a gap; the scribe could not read the Latin, "nidus erat ciconiar*um* maris," so left the space empty.

a day he come in-to þe cowrte, & pleyd *with* þe men of courte & þe iudgies, & ou*er*-come þai*m*. And so þurgh techyng of þis Pictagoras he habu*n*did eu*er* mor & mor in eloquens & in sutis in þe law, to so mekull, he was more desyrid to pley in þe law þan was his maist*er* Pictagoras. So on a day as þai wer bothe in þe courte befor þe iudgies, þis Pictagoras said vnto hym; "Redde mi*h*i quod peto; Gyff me at I ask the; Siue *pro* te, Siue cont*ra* te; Owd*er* for þe or agayn; and here-in I wull dispute. And yf I dispute for the, I wull say þou aw me my hyre be cou*n*an[d]. And if I dispute agayns þe, my hyre is awyng me be þe law; & so þou ert ou*er*com*m*en, & I ou*er*com the." And þan he ansswerd agayn & said, "Maist*er*, þou sall vnderstond þat [þou] sal be ou*er*com*m*en bothe ways; for if þe law *pro*cede for me, be þe sentance of þe law I sall aw þe no thyng, for I ou*er*com þe. And if þe *pro*cede be agayns me, I sall aw nothyng be cou*n*and, for I am not ou*er*com*m*en." And þe iudgis fell in hand *with* þis matir, and in a lang day þai cuth not make ane end þ*er*off.

XXXIX.

Aduocati eciam silenciu*m* vendu*n*t.

Helenandus. Demostenes[1] on a tyme askid Aristodem*us*[2], þat was a maker of talis, what he tuke eu*er* in þe cowrte when he spakk. And he ansswerd agayn, & said he tuke a besand of golde. And he ansswerd agayn & sayd, "I take more to hold my tong agayns þai*m* þat pleyis in þe law. For my tong is bou*n*, & may not speke bod if it be lowsid *with* bandis of sylu*er*."

Aduocator*um* cautele aliquando su*n*t necessarie. Infra v*b*i agit*ur* de cautela.

XL.

Aduocati q*ui*a in vita vendu*n*t linguas suas, ipsis in morte priuant*ur*[3].

Aduocatis, becauce in þ*er* lifis þai sell þ*er* tonges, when þai er dead þ*er* tongis er takyn fro þai*m*; as we rede of one þat hight

[1] MS. Helenandus de Mostene. [2] MS. Aristodimus.
[3] Heading supplied from Lat. MSS.

Cesarius, þ*at* was ane aduocatt in Saxonia. So on a tyme Sekenes come on hym & dy suld he. And agayn he suld dy, he began at yiske; & evyn sodanlie his tong was takyn away, so þ*at* no man cuthe fynde in his mouthe þat he had no tong when he was dead. And rightwuslie he loste his ton[g] when he was dead, becauce he solde it when he was on lyfe.

XLI.

Aduocat*us* sicut consueu*i*t viuens, ita moriens vult [þer] iudicia p*ro*cedere cont*ra* deum.

Jacobus de Vet*ri*aco tellis how Som tyme þ*er* was a reprovable aduocatt; & on a tyme when he was seke & lay in his bed, bown to dey, þe preste broght hym þe holie Sa[cra]ment, & desyrid hym to resayve itt. And he answerd agayn as he was wu[nt to] do in cawsis of þe law, & sayd; "I will nott resayve þe sac*r*ament bod if it be de[m]yd at I resayfe itt, and whethir I sall take it or noght." And all at stude about said it was right at he tuke itt, & þai said þai gaff dome þ*er*in. And he answerd agayn & said: "ye hafe no power for to deme me, for ye [þ*at*] er no bett*er* þan myselfe, is bod evynlyng*is* wit*h* me." And þ*er*for he said he wold appele fro þ*er* wykkyd sentan[s]. And emang þis vnthrifti language he gaff vp his gaste. *et* c9.

XLII.

Aduocatus petens inducias mortis non optinet, qui eciam in causis inducias non concessit.

Jacobus de Vet*ri*aco tellis how som tyme þ*er* was ane Aduocatt, when he lay seke & was in passyng, he saw many fendis. And he was passand ferde, & askid a respett of almi3tti God, þ*at* he mot liff a litle while langer. And becawse he wolde neu*er* giff a respett in no cawsis in þe law, bod if it war to p*ro*longe þe cauce & hurte his adu*er*sarie, þ*er*for he myght not opteyne of almighti God þat at he askid, bod dyed furth-wit*h* in myserie & in wrichidnes.

XLIII.

Aduocati puniuntur in inferno.

We rede how þ*er* was a holie man þat on a night was ravisshid in a vision, & hym thoght he saw hell; & þ*er* he saw Nero boyland hym in hate byrnand golde. And onone he se aduocatt*is* command vnto hym, and he said vnto þai*m*: "O! ye aduocattis, my frendis, þat whils ye liffid sellid mens trew cawsis, com hedur vnto me! for þis place is kepid to you & me." *et c⁹.*

XLIV.

Affectus carnalis no*n* debet esse in religiosis.

We rede how at þ*er* was a man of religion þ*a*t was a holie man, and a sustir of his, þat he luffid passandlie wele, happend to fall seke. And he wolde not als mekull as com furth of his abbay to vysitt hur & se hur. Than sho, becauce sho wolde giff hym none occasion to syn, sho sent a man vnto hur bruther, & bad hym pray þat he wold go in-to his sell & pray for hur, þat, *with* þe grace of God, sho mott se hym in hevyn. And sho did so aft*er*ward.

XLV.

Affectus carnalis debet rep*r*imi.

We rede, ex '*Dictis Patrum*,' how abbott John had a suster, whilk þat fro hur yowthed forward conu*er*sid all-way in a gude purpos, to so mekull scho taght hur bruther, & made hym for to lefe þe vanyties of þis werld, & go vnto ane abbay & make hym monk. And þ*er* he abade xxiiij yere, & neu*er* come oute. So on a tyme his suster desyrid gretelie to speke *with* hym, and sent oft sithes vnto hym l*ett*res, and desirid hym þat he wold com vnto hur as in way of charitie, at sho mot se hym, & at þai myght be glad to-gedur of þ*er* yowthid and or þai deyid. And he excusid hym eu*er*, & wrote vnto hur agayn & said he wolde nott. þan sho wrote agayn vnto hym, & said sen he wolde not com unto hur, itt was nedefull att sho sulde com vnto hym. And þis abbot þan tuke ij of his brethir *with* hym; & when he come vnto his suster yate, he cried & said, "Com̄ furthe & se pylgrames!" And sho come furth̄ & knew hym̄, & so did he hur; & yitt nowder of þaim spak ma wurdis to oþer, þat nowþer of þaim sulde ken̄ oþer be voyce. And when̄ þai had dronken̄ watir togeder, þis abbott & his monkis went home agayn̄ vnto þer abbay. And with-in a litle while after, his suster wrote vnto hym̄ agayn̄, & desirid hym̄ agayn̄ to com̄ vnto hur; and he answerd agayn̄ & said, "I come vnto þe and þou gaff me watir, & I tuke it of þi hand & dranke itt; and þerfor it suffisis vnto the at þou saw me. And þerfor pray for me, & I sall pray for the; for I wull com̄ no ner the." *et* c^9.

Affectus viri naturaliter inclinatur ad mulierem. Infra de Concupiscencia.

Affectum eternalem[1] non debent sequi Religiosi. Infra de Sanguineis[2].

XLVI.

Ager. Agrorum [terminos[3]] transponentes et inuasores puniuntur in hac vita.

Cesarius tellis how þat in Colayn̄ þer was a husband-man̄ þat hyght Henrie; and sekenes tuke hym̄, & he drew vnto his dedeward. And evur hym̄ thoght þat þer was enence his mouthe a grete burnand stone hyngand, euer in like to hitt hym̄. And as hym̄ thoght, þe hete þeroff burnyd hym̄ hugelie. And he cried horrible & said; "Behold þis stane þat hyngis befor my face, how þat it burnys me!" And þan̄ þai garte call a preste, & he was shrevyn̄. Neuer-þe-les, it profettid hym̄ noght, and þe preste said vnto hym̄; "Son̄, vmthynk þe if þou hafe dissayvid any man̄ be þis stane." And at þis wurde he vmthoght hym̄ & said; "A! Sur, I hafe now gude mynde how I remevid þis stone in þe feld, to þe entent þat I wolde enlarge myne awn̄ grownd & mynys oþer mens grownd." And þan̄ þe preste tolde hym̄ at þat was þe cauce; and he shrafe hym̄ þeroff, & promyssid to make amendis þerfor. And þus hitt wanysshid away, & he was delyverd

[1] Latin MSS. *have* carnalem. [2] Latin MSS. *have* consanguineis.
[3] From the Latin MSS.

of þat horrible vision, & liffid af*ter* many day, & made a restitucion & become a gude ma[n].

XLVII.

Agror*um*[1]. Adhuc de agris.

Cesarius tellis how þatt in þat same contreth þ*er* was a husbond, & when he sulde dye, þe devull come aforn hym *with* a byrnand stake, and thretid hym þat he sulde þruste itt in at his mouthe. And he wiste neu*er* whi, bod whatt way as eu*er* he turnyd hym, þe devull was eu*er* at þe mouthe on hym *with* þis stake. So he vmthoght hym what it sulde mene; and at þe laste, he remembrid hym how, on a tyme, he had remoud a stake of þe same mesur & lenthe oute of his awn feldis into a knyghtis felde þat was nerehand hym, to enlarge his awn grond *with*. And þan when nede cachid hym, he garte his meneya ga take it vp, & sett agayn whare it stude, & sent vnto þe knyght & prayed hym to forgiff hym. And þis ansswerd & said; "I wote not *þ*eroff, bod sen he was fals to me, latt hym alone to he be wele punysshid." And eu*er* þe devull abade still *with* [*þe*] stake, & wold eu*er* hafe putt it in his mouthe. Than He sent agayn vnto þe knyght, & prayed hym forgiff hym for Godd*is* sake, & he wold nott. And þan he send vnto hym his wyfe & his childre wepand, þat besoght hym for charitie to forgiff hym þe trispas at he had done vnto hym; "for he liffis *with* mekull sorow, and he may not dye or ye forgiff hym." And þan þe knyght said; "Now I will forgiff, for now I am well vengid." And fro þat hour, all þe ferdnes of þe devull sesid away fro hym. *et c9*.

Allexij co*n*fess*oris. Infra de Paciencia. iiiii.

Alexandri magni[2]. Infra de sup*er*bia. v. et de morte. ixo. et xvo. Et de Vindicta. ijo.

XLVIII.

Agnetis Virginis et martiris.

We rede in hur m*er*acles how þat þ*er* was a preste þat s*er*vid in a kurk of Saynt Agn[es], whilk þat on a tyme was hugelie vexid

[1] *After* Agrorum, and, *erased*.

[2] MS. magno.

with temptacion̄ of his flessħ; bod becauce þ*at* he wold̄ nott offend̄ allmyghti God̄, he besoght þe pope þat he wold̄ giff hym̄ lefe to be weddid̄. And þe pope, considuryng his gudenes & his symplenes, gaff hym̄ a ryng, & bad hym̄ go home vnto a fayr̄ ymage of Saynt Agnes, þat was paynttid̄ in his kurk, & on̄ his behalfe charge hur þat sho sulde suffre hym̄ wed hur. And þe preste come home & chargid̄ þe ymage as þe pope bad [hym]. And onone sho putt furtħ hur ryng-fynger & p*ro*fird̄ it to hym̄, & he putt on̄ þe ryng. And [*sho*] drew in hur fynger agayn̄, And onone alƚ man*er* of temptacion[1] passid̄ away fro þis preste. And in Rome in hur[2] kurk, at þis day, þe same ryng shewis yitt on̄ hur fynger, & is closid̄ into þe burde agayn̄. *et c*ᵒ.

Amandi co*n*fessoris. Infra de infante, i.
Ambicio. Ambicioso totus mu*n*dus no*n* sufficit.

XLIX.

Ambiciosi rep*r*imendi su*n*t a sapientib*us*.

We rede how þat on̄ a tyme, ane of þe p*ro*phettis sayd vnto Alexander; "And so wer þat our goddis wolde þ*at* þe statur of þi bodie war like vnto þi covatusnes, All þis werld̄ mott nott resayfe þe; for þan̄ þou might putt þine one hand̄ in-to þe far side of þe este, & þe toder vnto þe fer side of þe weste. Knowis þou nott att grete treis, þai er lang in growyng? & yitt þai may be cutt down̄ in ane howr̄. And he is a fule þat pullis not down̄ frute when̄ þai er moste ripe. Therfor̄ vuise the, þatten̄ when̄ þou erte att hyeste of þi brawnchis, at þai be nott cutt in sonder & þou falƚ down̄, ffor, as þou may see, a lion̄ is som̄ tyme meate to smale burdis. And þ*er* is nothyng so stabylƚ[3], bod vmwhile þ*er* is p*ar*celƚ þ*er*in. And if þou be a god̄, þou aght to giff ben*e*fice vnto mortalƚ folk, & nothyng take fro þai*m*. And if þou be a man̄, vmthynk þe alway what þou erte, for it is grete folie vnto the to thynk so lang of oþ*er* folk at þou forgett þi selfe." *et c*ᵒ.

[1] MS. temptacid.
[2] *After* hur, hu, *erased.*
[3] Latin MS. cui p*er*iculu*m* no*n* sit ab inualido deniq*ue*.

Ambicio qu*ando*q*ue* inducit ho*min*em ad p*er*petrand*um* homicidiu*m*. Infra vbi agitur de Archidiacono.

Ambiciosi freque*nter* cu*m* confusione frustrantur. Infra vbi agitur de Simonia.

L.

Ambicio inducit ho*min*em ad faciend*um* co*n*uenciones cu*m* diabolo.

We rede in þe 'Cronicles of Saynt Siluester' of a pope þat hyght Secundus[1], how furste he was a monke, and þan̄ afterwerd' he made homage vnto þe devuƚƚ, p*ro*mysyng hym̄ to do what þing so he com*m*anddid hym̄. And þe devuƚƚ hight hym̄ at he sulde hafe evur what þing so he desyrid; and he spak oft sithis w*ith* þe devuƚƚ. And evur he encresid' so in sciens & in con*n*yng, at Ottonus, at was Emp*er*our, and Rob*er*t, þat was kyng of Frawnce, wer his scolers. So be p*ro*curyng of þe devuƚƚ, he was made archbisshopp*e* of Bononience[2]. Syne he was made a cardinaƚƚ, and at þe laste he was made pope. So on̄ a tyme as he was spekand w*ith* þe devuƚƚ, he askid' hym̄ how long he sulde liff, and he ansswerd' hym̄ agayn̄ & said', vnto he sang mes in Jer*usalem*; and w*ith* þis wurde he was passand glad', & þoght it sulde be long or he sang any mes þ*er*, or yit go thedur in pylg*ra*mage. So it happend' afterward' in þe lentren̄, þat he said' mes in Rome in a kurk þat hight Jer*usalem*; and when̄ he was at mes he hard' a grete noyse of devuls, and he feƚƚ so seke þat he felid' hym̄ selfe þat hym̄ burd dye; and þan̄, þuf aƚƚ he war nevur so wykkid' in[3] liffyng, ye[*t*] he had com*p*un*c*cion̄, & made mekuƚƚ sorow for his syn̄. And he besoght God of m*er*cye, & wold' not dy in dispayr. And þ*er* he made ane oppyn̄ confession̄ of aƚƚ his syn̄ befor*e* þe peple, and he com*m*andid' þ*at* all þase membris þat he had s*er*vid' þe devuƚƚ w*ith* suld be cutt off, & at þe carcas of his bodie sulde be

[1] For Sylvester II.

[2] For Bononia, = Bologna. MS. Arund. Factus e*st* Arc*h*iep*iscop*us Remensis.

[3] *After* in, liffid', *erased.*

þut in a carte, & whethir-som̄-evur at þe catell led it, at þer it sulde be berid; and so þe pepull did. And þai led it in-to þe kurk of [Sai]nt Johñ Lateranencis; & þer it was berid. And in tokyñ þat almyghti God had mercie of hym̄, hys grafe spryngis als wele smale crusyll bonys as oyle yit vnto þis day[1]. *et c^o*.

Ambicio inducit hominem ad negandum deum et scripto suo firmare. Infra de Theophilo, vbi agitur de Maria, dei genitrice.

LI.

Ambrosij Confessoris.

We rede in 'Historia Tripartita' how oñ a tyme, at þe cetie of Cessalonye, þer fell a stryfe betwix þe iudgies & þe comons, to so mekull att þe comoñ peple stanyd þe comons to dede. And wheñ Theodosius, þat was Emperour, hard tell[2] hereof, he garte kyll þaim þat did no truspas, with þaim at did þe trispas. So oñ a tyme afterward, wheñ þis Emperour wolde hafe commeñ in-to þe kurk, þis holie mañ, Ambros, mete hym̄ att þe dure & forbad hym̄ þat he suld com̄ in, sayand oñ þis maner of wise; "O, þou Emperour! whi knawis þou nott þi presumpcioñ after so grete a hastenes? O, þou Emperour! att erte a prynce, & hase imperiall power, It semys þe at resoñ sulde ouer-com̄ þi power, & nott þi power resoñ: how dar þou þat with þine eeñ hase beholdeñ þi servand dye, trede with þi fete opoñ þis holie paymente? And how dar þou holde vp þi handis vnto God, þat yitt droppis with blude þat is innocent? And how dar þou resayfe þe holie sacrament in bread or wyne, wheñ, þurgh þe hastines of þi wurde, innocent blude is wronguslie spylte? And þerfor, Go þi ways, þou þat ert boun with syñ, and amende þi fawte, & do away þe band att þou ert bun with, and þou may hafe a medcyñ to amend þe with, & þou will." And with þies wurdis þis Emperour obeyid hym̄, & made sorow and went home agayñ to his place; & þer

[1] MS. Arund. Et in signum misericordie, sepulcrum ipsius, tam ex tumultu ossium quam ex sudore, presagium est Pape morituri, sicut in eodem sepulcro litteris est exaratum.

[2] MS. *repeats*, tell.

he wepud, & made mekull sorow, & sayd vnto hym selfe on þis man*er* of wyse; "The kurk is oppyn to þai*m* þat er my s*er*vandis, & it is sparrid vnto me þat am ane Emp*er*our." And þan ane þ*a*t was maist*er* of all his knyghtis, þat hight Ruffin*us*, come vnto Saynt Ambroce and besoght hym to assoyle þe Emp*er*our. And when Saynt Ambros saw hym, he sayde; "O, þ*o*u Ruffin*us*! at was doar & cowncelur of such a dede, þink*is* now no shame to speke agayns þe magestie of almighti God? I lat þe witt, & þe Emp*er*our com here, I sall forbid hym to entyr into þis holie place vnto he take his penans for his tyrandrie, and þat done I will resayve hym gladlie." And þis Ruffin*us* went & tolde þis vnto þe Emp*er*our. And þan þis Emp*er*our said; "I will go vnto hym at I may take rightwus penans for myne vnrigh[*t*]wusnes dedis." So on a tyme he wente agayn vnto þe kurk, and Saynt Amb[ros] come agayn & forbad hym, & said; "whatt penans hase þ*o*u done for all þi wykkednes?" & þe Emp*er*our answerd agayn & sayde; "It longes vnto þe to giff me penans, & it is my parte to obey the, & do at þ*o*u com*m*andis me." And þan he shrafe hym vnto þis [Am]brosius, & enionyd hym penance. And þis Emp*er*our tuke it so thankfullie, þat for his opyn syn he did oppyn penans. *et c*ᵒ.

LII.

Ambrosij Confessoris.

We rede in '*Historia* Trip*ar*tita' how on a tyme, when þis Theodosius þe Emp*er*our come in-to þe wher, þis Ambros com*m*yn vnto hym & askid hym what he beheld þ*er*; and he answerd agayn & said, "I come in to behold how cristen men reseyvis þ*er* sacrament." The[n] Saynt Ambros sayd vnto hym, "O þ*o*u Emp*er*our! þies inward placis er ordand for prestis; And þ*er*for go furth, and þ*er* abyde *with* other vnto þ*o*u be howseld." And onone þe Emp*er*our did as he bad hym." So on a tyme eft*er*ward þis Emp*er*our went vnto Costantynople, & stude þ*er* in þe kurk *with*-owten þe where. And þe bisshopp þ*er* went vnto hym & com*m*aundid hym to go into þe quere. And þan þe Emp*er*our sayde; "vnnethis yit I may knaw whatt differens is betwix ane Emp*er*our & a preste, ffor yitt vnnethis hafe I fon̄ þe treuth̄. Notw*ith*stondying I can̄ v*er*elie fynde at my maist*er* Ambros is wurthi to be made a bisshopp̄." *et c⁹.*

LIII.

Amicicia. Amicus verus ecia*m* morti se exponit p*ro* amico.

We rede how þ*at* Pictagoras had ij disciples, & þai was passand gude frendis, & ather luffid' wele other. And þ*at* one hight Damon̄ & þe toder Phicias. So on̄ a tyme Dionisius, þ*at* was a tirand, wolde hafe slayn̄ þe tone of þai*m*, & he þ*at* sulde be deade askid lefe þat he myght go home & ordand' for his wife & his howshold', & he sulde com̄ agayn̄. And þe toder become his borgh̄, & bade behynd' hym̄ in his stede. And when̄ þe day come, þis disciple come nott agayn̄, & þan̄ eu*er*e man̄ demyd' þe toder, þat was his suertie, to dye for hym̄. And þis man̄ at was suertie sayde he dowtid' nothyng þe constance of his frend', and p*re*sent hym̄ befor̄ þis tyrand, & bad hym̄ do w*ith* hym̄ what he wolde & asoyle hys frend'. And þan̄ þis tyrand' had grete m*er*vayle of his witt, & for his trew frenship̄ he forgaff þai*m* bothe. *et c⁹.*

LIV.

Amici necessitatib*us* ecia*m* est subueniend*um*.

Senec tellis how a philosophur þat hight Archisilus[1] had a frend' þat was bothe seke & pure. And for shame he wold' latt no man̄ witt at he was so, And when̄ þis philisophur vnd*er*stude þis, he callid' þis frend' vnto hym̄, & lete hym̄ witt in p*ri*vatie betwix þai*m* two þat he wolde helpe hym̄, & sulde make hym̄ hale of his sekenes; & he tuke a grete sachell & fyllid it full of money p*ri*valie, & bande it vnto his side agayns his long in stede of a playstre. And þe tod*er* man trowid' it had bene so. And þis he did to the entent at a[2] man̄ þat is shamefull vnprofitable sulde titter fynde þat he desyrid', þan̄ þat þing att he askid'.

[1] MS. Harl. Archelisas philosophus. MS. Arund. Achesilas.

[2] Latin MSS. vt h*omo* inutiliter verecundus.

LV.

Amicicia vera multum est laudabilis.

We rede how þ*at* in þe tyme of Pipinius þ*at* was kyng of France, þ*er* was two childer, and þai war passand like. And þe tone was ane Erle son þ*at* hight Auernus, and þe toder was a knyght son þ*at* hight Bericanus, whilk þ*at* was born vnto Rome for to be baptisid when þai war big childre. Not-wit*h*stondyng afor þ*at*, in a cetie at was callid Luca þ*er* þai war broght vp togedur, þai wer grete felows, & ather luffid other passand wele; and att Rome þai wer bothe to-gedur baptisid of þe pope. And he namyd þe erle son Amelius, and þe knyght son Amicus. And he gaff ather of þai*m* a copp of wud þ*at* was passand like. And þai thankid hym & went þ*er* wayes. And þ*er* was betwix þai*m* so grete felaschup & so grete evynhed of will, at þai wolde neu*er* ete nor slepe bod to-gedur. So on a tyme þis Amicus hard tell þ*at* his fadur was dead, & att malicious men wold take his heritage fro hym. And als hastelie als he cuthe, he went vnto[1] his oþ*er* frend at tell hym, & he cuthe not fynd hym. So als sone as þis Amelius ha[rd] tell at his frend Amicus fadur was dead, and he went vnto hym att comfurth hym, and he cuthe neu*er* fynde hym. So þis Amicus happend to be lugid at a wurthi mans place, & happend to tarie þ*er*, & weddid þe gude mans doght*er*. And þis Amelius soght hym to ij yere was passid, & þan a pilgrem tolde hym þ*er* he was, & how he was expulsid oute of his awn contre. And þis Amelius doffid his cote & gaff þis pylgram, & bad hym pray vnto God "þ*at* I mot sone fynde hym." And þe same day att evyn, Amicus mett þis pylgram and haskid hym if he saw oght þis Amelius. And þis pylgram answerd hym agayn & said, "wharto spirris þou me? Ert þou nott Amelius att askid me if I saw oght to day[2] Amicus? fforsuth I can nott wytt, ffor þou hase changid bothe [þi] hors & þi harnes & also þi felashup." And he answerd agayn & say[*d*]; "Nay, I am not Meli*us*, bod I am Amicus þ*at* sesis not for to seke hym." And þe pylgram

[1] *After* vnto, hym, *erased.*

[2] *After* day, Amelius, *erased.*

tolde hym̄ þat he sulde fynde hym̄ at Parissħ. And he went vnto *Parissħ* & fande hym̄ *þer*. And þai kissid', and wer athir fayn̄ of other. And þai went in-to cowrte to king Charlis, and onone þis Amicus was made þe kyngis tresurer, and Amelius was made karvur. And þai war fayr yong men̄ & wise and discrete, and þai war wurshuppid & had in grete dayntie *with* evur eman̄. So on̄ a tyme þis Amicus went & vissytt his wiffe, and tarid *with* hur, & Amelius bade still in þe courte. So it happend hym̄ priualie to lie by þe kyngis dogh*ter*, And when̄ he had done he tolde it in privatie vnto ane erle þat hight Ardericus, þatt was sworn̄ to hym̄ to be hym̄ trew frend' many day befor. And he went & accusid' hym̄ vnto þe kyng. And he said' nay to it, & oblissid' hym̄ to feght *with* hym̄ in þe quarell. And þe day was appoynttid' þai*m* be þe kyng at þai suld' feght vppon̄. And in þe mene while Amicus come home, & Amelius teld' hym̄ all; and he blamyd hym̄ greteli þ*er*for. And on̄ þe day att þai sulde feght, þis Amicus did on̄ Amelius armur & went into þe place for to feght for hym̄, and our-come þis Ardericus & smate of his head'; and þan̄ þe kyng gaff hym̄ his dogh*ter*. And þis done, þis Amelius went vnto Amicus howse, and þe wife trowid þat it had bene Amicus, and when̄ she wold' owder kis hym̄ or hals hym̄, he putt hur away from̄ hym̄. And herefor sho was passand' hevie, and tolde hur neghburs þe cauce of hur hevynes, & how he wold' eu*er*-ilk nyght, when̄ þai lay to-gedur, lay a nakid swerd' betwix þai*m* and said', & sho lay nere hym̄, he sulde kill hur. And þis done, þis Amicus & Amelius changid' þ*er* clothyng agayn̄, and Amicus went home vnto his awn̄ howse, and sent Amelius agayn̄; & he wed þe kynges dogh*ter*. And belife after þis, Amicus happend to wax lepre. And he wex so pure vnto so mekull he was so fowle, þat his wife and his childre put hym̄ fro þai*m*. So on̄ a tyme he was so compulsid' *with* honger and *with* wrich[id]nes, þat he went vnto þis Erle Amellius[1] place, and þ*er* he layed hym̄ down̄ befor þe ya[tt], & knokkid *with* his tables as lepre men̄ duse. And þe Erle hard', & sent hym̄ brede and flessħ & a drynk in þe copp þat þe pope gaff hym̄ at Rome. And þe man̄ at broght itt putt it

[1] *Under* Amellius, Avellius, *erased.*

oute of þe erle copp into þe lepre mans copp; & hym thoght þat þase coppis wer passand like, and went in & tolde þe Erle how at þis lepre man had a copp þat was passand like his copp. And he garte feche hym in to hym; & Amicus tolde hym all þe [1] proces how þat it had happend *with* hym. And þis Erle & his wife wepud & made mekyll sorow for hym, & hight hym þat he sulde hafe gude enogh whils þat he lyffyd. So on þe night after, as þis Amicus lay in his bed, þe aungell Gabriell apperid vnto hym, & bad hym byd Armelius sla his two sonnys at he had, & sprenkle hym *with* þe blude of þai*m*, & he sulde be hale of all his lepre: and he did so. And when he had tolde hym he was passand hevye. Neu*er*-þe-les he remembrid of þe faith & gude treuth at he had done vnto hym, and he come vnto þe bed þ*er* his childre lay, & *with* grete wepyng & mornyng he drew his swerd & tuke his childre and hedid þai*m*. And he put þ*er* bodies & þ*er* hedis to-gedur in myddest þe bed, & coverd þai*m* and gaderd þ*er* blude in a vessell, & come to Amicus þ*er* he lay & al by-sprenkled hym þ*er*with, and said in þis man*er* of wise; "*Diuine* Iesu Ch*riste*, qui fidem ho*min*ib*us* s*er*vare p*re*cepisti, et leprosu*m* v*er*bo sanasti, þis my trew felow vuchesafe to hele of his lepre, for whose luff I was not ferd to shed my childre blude." And onone he was clensid, & þis Ameli*us* cled hym in his beste clothyng. And all þe bellis in þe place rang be þ*er* one. And þis cowntes askid whi þai rang & þ*er* cuthe no bodie tell hur. So þis Erle *with* grete murnyng & sarow went into þe chawm*re* agayn, þ*er* he had slayn his childer, & he fande þai*m* ligand in þe bed, laykand sam*en* in als gude quarte as evur þai wer. And þ*er* was abowte bathe þ*er* nekkis ij cerkles as þai had bene ij rede thredis. And þan he was fayn, & went vnto his wyfe & tolde hur all þe p*ro*ces, how at it had happend hym. And fro thens furth bothe he & sho liffid in chastitie. And a fend vexid so Amicus wife, þat onone [2] he made ane ende of hur. And be strenth of þis Erle, þis Amicus went in-to þe contre þ*er* he dwelte, & ou*er*-com it & made it to be subgett vnto hym; & þ*er* he liffid many day in a holie life, & þan aft*er*ward be p*ro*ces of tyme, Ameli*us* & Amicus dyed bothe, and wer berid

[1] MS. *repeats*, þe. [2] MS. ononone.

in placis far in sondre. So not-*with*stondyng, afterward be grete miracle, þai wer bothe fun̄ in[1] a grafe ligand for þer trew luff. *et c*.

LVI.

Amici semper [mutuam] debent seruare honestatem.

Valerius tellis how þat þer was ij frendis, and þe tone desyrid þe toder to do for hym̄ ane vnrightwus thyng. And he wold not do itt for hym̄. And þan̄ he said vnto hym̄; "what is þi frenship wurth vnto me when̄ þou will not do for me at I pray þe?" And he answerd agayn & said, "what profettis þi frenship vnto me, when̄[2] þu desyris me for to[3] do for þe þat þing þat is vnhoneste, and agayn my treuthe?" *et c*.

Amicum mala de amico dixisse non est de facili credendum. Infra vbi agitur de credere.

LVII.

Amicus Debet probari ante necessitatem.

We rede how som tyme þer was ij merchandis in Egipte, þe tone of Egipte and þe toder of Baldac[4], þat know wele athir other be þer name, & luffid passandlie wele to-gedur. & þis Marchand of Baldac come into Egipte, & þe merchand þer reseyvud hym̄ thankfullie, and a grete while he festid hym̄ & all his meneya. So when̄ a sennett was passid, þis merchand of Baldac happend to fall passand seke, And þai went & gatt hym̄ lechis; and a leche felid his powce[5] & lukid his watir, bod he cuthe fynde no sekenes in hym̄. So at þe laste he oppynd his harte privalie vnto þe gude man̄ of þe howse, & tolde hym̄ how þat all his sekenes was for luff of a maydyn̄ þat þis merchand of Egipte had in his howse, becauce he wold wed hur vnto his wife. And when̄ þis merchand wuste at it was herefor, he gaff hym̄ þis mayden̄ vnto wife, and gaff hym̄ a grete dele of gude with hur. And when̄ he had wed hur, he tuke hur & all his meneya & wente into his awn̄ contre. So be

[1] MS. &.
[2] MS. *repeats*, when.
[3] MS. *repeats*, forto do.
[4] MS. Waldac; Harl. MS. Daldac; Arund. MS. Baldac.
[5] MS. pownce.

proces of tyme after, it happend þis *mer*chand' of Egipte to lose his gudis & to wax passand pure, to so mekull þat he come vnto þe contrey of Baldac bothe nakid & hongrie on ane evyneng, and þ*er* wold' no man luge [*hym*]; & he went & layde hym down in a kurk porche. So þ*er* happend' þ*at* evynyng in þe town a man to be slayn, & no man wiste who did itt. And þe men of þe town rase up & soght þis mans queller, & þai*m* happend' to fynd' þis man likkand' in þe kurk porche. And when þai had fon hym, þai said all þ*at* it was he þat did þe dede; and he grauntid at he did itt, þuff all he did it nott, beyng in will to end his pou*er*tie *with* dead. And þai tuke hym & putt hym in *pri*son þat nyght, & on þe morn þai had hym vnto þe galos att hang hym. And þis oþ*er* *mer*chand' þat was his frend' come *with* many oþ*er* to se hym dede. And when he saw hym, onone he knew what he was, and þan he said'; "Leve, ye dampe ane Innocent, ffor I slew þe man my selfe & not he." And þai[1] take hym & lete þe toder go. And a lurdan, at did þe dede, stude emang oþ*er* men & saw, & he remordid' in his conciens & said'; "Nowder of þies two did itt, I did it my selfe." And þan þai lete þe toder go & tuke hym. And þe iudgies had grete *mer*vell here-off, And tuke þai*m* all iij, & had þai*m* vnto þe kyng. And onone þai tolde hym all þe *proces*; and becauce of þ*er* treuth he *par*dond' þai*m* ilkone. And þan þis *mer*chand' of Baldac *par*tid' his gudis evyn in two, and gaff it vnto þis pure *mer*chand', & he tuke it & went agayn into his awn contrey, and afterward' was als riche as eu*er* he was.

LVIII.

Amicus in necessitate *pro*batur.

We rede how þ*er* was a man in a contrey þat was takyn & had to þe kyngis cowrte, & sulde die. And he come vnto a man þat he luffid' passand'[2] wele, & prayed hym to helpe hym in þat grete nede; [*and he said vnto hym*][3], "I hafe oþ*er* frendis at I luff als wele as I do the, & þ*er*for will nott go *with* the, bod I sall giff þe a garment to happ þe *with*." And þan he mett [with] a secund' frend' þat he luffid' bettir, & he prayed' hym to go *with* hym & helpe

[1] MS. þan. [2] MS. passid. [3] Latin MSS. qui dixit.

hym; & he said he wold go *with* hym a little way, bod he myght not tarie, he wold co[m] sone agayn. And þan he mett *with* his thrid frend, þat he luffid bod litill, and *with* grete shame he prayed hym to helpe hym. And he answerd agayn & sayd; "I hafe y[it] in my mynde a little gude turn at þou did me *with* vsurie, and yitt I sall reward t[he], ffor I sall putt my sawle for þi sawle." Frendis! ye sall vnderstond þat þis ffurst frend is we[*r*]ldly possessions, whilk þat when we dye giffis vs bod a wyndyng clothe to lap vs in. And þe second frend is owr kynsmen and our frendis, þat[1] gase *with* vs vnto we com att owr grafe. And þe iij frend is almighti God, whilk þatt putt bothe His life & His sawle for His frendis when He suffred His passion.

LIX.

Amicus ecia*m* prop*ter* necessitatem debet p*ro*bari.

We rede how þe fadir taght his son for to prufe his frende, & saide; "Take & sla a calfe & lay it in salte. And when þi frende com*m*ys vnto the, tell hym þ*at* þ*o*u haste slayn a man, & pray hym for to go berie hym p*ri*valie 'þat þou be not suspecte, nor I nowder; And so þou may safe my life.'" And his furste frend at he come to & tolde þis matier answerd hym & said; "Nay, bere hame þe deade man *with* þe, for he sall not com in my howse; ffor as þu hase done sall þou answer, for me." And so he went fro frend to frend, & ilkone answerd hym in þis wise. And þan he come vnto a frend of his fadurs, telland hym; And he bad hym go bere hym in-to his howse, and said he sulde do it & kepe it p*ri*vay enogh. And he sent oute his wife & all his howse meneya, and wente & grufe it hym selfe. And when þat he had done, he told hym all how he had done, & þankid hym for his kyndnes.

LX.

Amicis ecia*m* delinquentib*us* est parcend*um*.

Valerius tellis how att þ*er* was a tyrand in Athens, & he had a fayr dought*er*. And þ*er* was a yong felow þat luffid hur wele and wold hafe had hur to his wife. So on a tyme hym happend

[1] MS. *repeats*, þat.

to mete hur in ane oppyn place, and befor hur modir he kissid hur. And þe wyfe went & tolde þis tyrant hur husband, & walde hafe garte smyte of his hede. And þis tyrand answerd agayn & said; "If we sla þ*aim* þat luffis vs, what sulde we do *with* þ*aim* att hatis vs?" And þus he answerd manlie, & þoght for luf þat þis yong man had vnto þis doght*er* of his, þat[1] he luffid hym agayn & wolde not suffre hym hafe none ill.

LXI.

Amicis ecia*m* Conuicia et obprobria int*er*du*m* su*n*t condonanda.

Valerius tellis how that þ*er* was a tyrand þat on a nyght satt att supper *with* a man þ*at* hyght Crasippus. And as þai fell at supper þai fell att varyans. And þis Crasippus was so angrie and flate so, þ*at* þe frothe sprang at þe mowthe of hym, becauce he mot not venge hym. Neu*er*-þe-les þis tyrand suffred hym becauce he was in his howse. And on þe morn when he was comme*n* vnto hym selfe, he com vnto þis Crasippus & tolde hym soberlie of his anger, and forgaff hym itt.

Amici mors debet pacient*er* tolerari[2]. Infra de morte, xiiij.

LXII.

Amici falsi multa p*ro*mittu*n*t que no*n* implent.

We rede in 'Libro de dono Timoris' how þ*at* þ*er* was a nygromansier, and he had a dissiple; And he fenyd hym þat he luffid his maist*er* passyng wele. And he beheste his mast*er* mekle þing and he wolde helpe att he war riche. And his maist*er* thoght to prufe hym, whethir he said treuth or noght. And be his enchawntment*is* he garte hym thynk at he was ane Emp*er*our. And when it was lattyn hym witt þ*at* þ*er* was mekull lande voyd, hym þoght his maist*er* come vnto hym and p*r*ayed hym to be myndefull of his

[1] MS. yit. [2] So in the Latin MSS. The English MS. has, tollari.

*pro*mys, and at he wolde giff hym̄ som̄ lande. And he answerd' agayn̄ & askid' hym̄ what he was, & said' he knew hym̄ noght. And his maist*er* said'; "I am̄ he þat gaff vnto you aƚƚ þies gud[is]; and becauce now ye ken̄ me noght, Now I saƚƚ take aƚƚ away fro you." And *with* þat he v[a]nysshid' his enchawntement, & þ*er* was oght nott lefte of aƚƚ þat hym̄ þoght he saw. In like wise wiƚƚ God do vnto riche men̄ þat whils þai er pure *pro*myssis enogħ vnto Almighti God', and when̄ þai er riche, þan̄ þai wiƚƚ not ken̄ nor giff Hym̄ noght, þat is to say, giff noght for His sake. *et* c⁹ ad libitu*m*.

Amici su*n*t m*u*lti ficti[1]. Infra vbi agitur de fidelitate.

LXIII.

Amor Castus in om*n*ib*us* est laudandus.

We rede in 'Vita Beati Lupi' how he had in his howse a holie virgyn̄ þat was his p*re*decessur doghter, & he luffid' hur passandli wele, and his howsold' bakbate hym̄ þ*er*for̛. So on̄ a tyme, befor̛ þai*m* aƚƚ, he tuke hur abowte þe nekk̄ & kyssid' hur, & said' vnto þai*m* on̄ þis mane*r* of wise; "Other mens wurdis saƚƚ neue*r* noy a man̄, how þ*a*t evur þai say, whome þat his consciens fylis noght." For he luffid God aboue al thyng, and so wiste he wele þat sho did'; and þ*er*for̛ he luffid' hur *with* a meke mynde.

LXIV.

Amor carnalis p*e*ru*er*tit in ho*m*i*n*e fidem.

We rede in 'Vita S*anct*i Basilij,' how þ*er* was a wurthi man̄ þat had a fayr doghter; and he had a yong boy vnto his *ser*vand'. And he luffid' þis damyseƚƚ so hartlie wele þat he was in poynt to dye for hur. So he went vnto a nygromansier and agreid' *with* hym̄ þat he sulde gett hym̄ þe luff hur. And he, evyn̄ befor̛ þis yong felow, raysid' a grete meneya of fendis, and þe grete fende said' vnto hym̄; "And þ*o*u wiƚƚ at I fulfiƚƚ þi wiƚƚ, make me

[1] MS. facti, but Latin MSS. ficti.

a wrytyng *with* þi hand[1] þat þou forsakis God & þi cristendom, & at þou sal be my *ser*vand, and for to dwell *with* me for evur." And he grawntid þerto, and wrote it & delyverd it vnto hym. And þis done, þir fendis made þe harte of þis maydyn so for to kyndell in þe luff of þis [boy][2], to so mekull sho fell on hur kneis befor hur fadur & cried on hym & said; "Hafe m*er*cie on me, fadur! for I am hugelie trubled for þe luff of suche a yong man, and þ*er*for I p*r*ay you latt me hafe hym to husband, or els I mon dye." And when hur fadur hard þis, he said: "Alas! what is happend vnto my doght*er*? I purposid to hafe marid þe *with* a wurshupfull man, and þou erte streken in þe luste of a yong lad." Neu*er*-þe-les be cowncell of his frendis, he lete hym hafe hur, & gaff hym a porcion of his gudis *with* hur. And when þai had bene wed a while, sho pursayvid þat he wold nowder sayn hym nor com into þe kurk to here no dyvyne *ser*ves. And þe neghburs trowid at he was not cristend; and sho went & tolde hym. And he said þai lyed, and sho said þat sho wold not trow hym bod if he wolde go *with* hur vnto þe kurk on þe morn. And þan he saw þat he myght no langer kepe it cowncell, and told hur all how þat it had happend hym. And sho made mekull sorow, and went vnto Saynt Basyll & tolde hym. And he askid hur husbond if he wold reverte agayn to Criste; and he sayde þat he wold full fayn, bot he myght nott; "for I am sworn vnto þe devull and hafe denyed Criste, & hafe writtem my dede þeroff & delyverd it vnto þe devull." And þan þis Basilius told hym þat God was m*er*cifull, & if he wold shrife hym of his syn & do his penans þ*er*for, þat God wold forgiff hym. And he tuke hym and blissid hym *with* þe cros, & put hym in a howse be his one in grete penance xlti dayes. And in þe mene while þ*er* was harde grete crying of fendis þat apperid vnto hym, bod ilk day þis Basilius come vnto hym and comfurthed hym. And eft*er* þis he tuke hym befor all his clergie & þe pepull, & had hym vnto þe kurk. And þe devull come þat all men might se, & wold hafe taken hym fro hym, and þis yong man cried & said; "holie fadur! helpe me!" And þan þe devull said at all myght here; "Basyll, þou duse me wrong; for I come

[1] MS. *repeats*, writing, *here*. [2] MS. maydyn.

not to hym̄, bod he come to me, & forsuke Criste, & was sworn̄ vnto me. And þ*er*-of I hafe his writyng in my hand'[1]. And Saynt Basill & his[2] clergie sett þ*aim* down̄ & made þ*er* prayer for hym̄, & sodanlie þis chartyr fell down̄, & þis holie man̄ tuke it vp̄ in his hand & opynd' it & shewid' it vnto þis yong man̄, & askid hym̄ if he kend itt. And he said; "ya, sur, for I wrote it my selfe." And he burnyd' it & had hym̄ vnto þe kurk, & delyvurd' hym̄ vnto his wife, & bad hym̄ be a gude man̄; & so he was evur after.

Ama*n*te*m* carnalit*er* expedit elongare. Inf*ra*, Clementis in p*r*incipio.

Amor carnalis ecia*m* magnoru*m* adiutoriu*m* requirit. Infra vbi Agitur de arte magica, ij.

Amor carnalis ecia*m* p*r*opinquis no*n* p*ar*cit. Infra de co*n*tricione, iij *et* vj.

Amor carnal*is* Cr*ist*ianos Iudeis coniu*n*gi facit. Inf*ra* de cont*r*icione, iiij.

Amor carnalis ho*min*em qu*and*oq*ue* p*er*iculo exponit. Sup*ra* de Amicicia, viij.

LXV.

Andree Apo*st*oli.

We rede in[3] 'Libris Lombardoru*m*,' how som tyme þ*er* was ane olde man̄ of lxxx[4] yere olde. Ande on̄ a tyme he sayde vnto Saynt Andrew þe apostill, þ*at* all þe tyme of his life he had vsid' evur lichorie. And Saynt Andrew prayed' vnto God for hym̄ þ*at* he myght be delyverd' þeroff; & so he was a while[5], bod onone he turnyd agayn̄ vnto þe syn̄ as he was wunte to do. Not-wi*th*-stondyng he bare opon̄ hym̄ a euange[ll] wretten̄. So on̄ a tyme he come vnto þe bordelhouse to fulfill his luste, and onone a commo*n* wom*m*an̄ mett wi*th* hym̄, & said' vnto hym̄ in þis man*er* of wise; "O! þou olde man! go þi ways! go þi ways! for þou

[1] MS. *repeats*, þerof.
[2] *After* his, maydyn, *erased*.
[3] Harl. MS. ex lege Lombardicis. *For* 'Legenda Lombardica.'
[4] *After* of, xl, *erased*.
[5] MS. has also, onone he fell þerto, at the foot of the page.

arte þe Angell of God. And þ*er*for tuche me noght, ffor I se vppon þe many m*er*vaylis." And þan þis olde man, beyng astonyd gretelie *with* þis comon womm*an* language, remembred how þat he had vppon hym þe evangell. & þan he went agayn vnto Saynt And[*r*]ew & tolde hym all, & prayed hym to pray for hym. And þan Saynt Andrew wepid for hym & sayd; "I sall [no] meate eate vnto tyme I know if our Lord will hafe m*er*cie of þe or noght." And so he lay in [h]i[s] prayers & fastid v dayes. & þan þ*er* come vnto Saynt And[r]ew a voyce þat sayd; O! þou Andr[ew]! our Lord hase grauntid þe att þis alde man sal be savid. Bod as þou *with* fastyng hase made þe lene, Right so muste hym chastes his flessh *with* fastyng if he sal be savid." And so he did, & fastid sex dayes brede & watir, & eft*er*ward sex monethis; & afterward he was a gude man, & decesid in gude life. And þan þ*er* come a voyse vnto Saynt Andrew & said; "Be þi holie pray*er* [1], Nicholas þat I had loste hafe I getten agayn."

LXVI.

Andree Ap*osto*li.

We rede on [*a*] tyme how a yong man said vnto Saynt Andrew in p*r*ivatie; "My mod*er* on a tyme þoght me passand fayr, & desyrid me to hafe att do *with* hur. And when sho saw þat on no wise I wolde consent vnto hur, sho went vnto þe iudgies of þe law & accusid me to þai*m* þat I had done it *with* hur. And þ*er*for I [2] pray þe" he said, "to pray for me, at I be nott wrongoslie putt to dead [3]. Not-*with*stondyng me had levur suffer to take my deade wronguslie, þan [4] for to hafe corrupte my [5] moder." So on a day þis yong man was broght vnto þe bar befor a iudge, and Saynt Andrew felowid hym thedir; and þe moder stude furthe & accusid hur son fellie, saying þat he wold hafe lyen by hur. And þis yong [*man*] stude still & spak no wurde. Than Saynt Andrew spak vnto þe moder & sayde; "O! þou crowelleste of womm*e*n! be þi fals [6] luste, þow wolde distroy þine awn son." And þan þis moder sayd vnto

[1] MS. pray.
[2] MS. he.
[3] MS. *repeats*, wrongoslie.
[4] MS. þat.
[5] *After* my, br, *erased.*
[6] *After* fals, þ, *erased.*

þe iudge; "Sur, when my son wold hafe done þis dede *with* me, & I had avoydid hym, þan he went vnto þis man." And þan þe iudge wex wrothe, & com*m*andid þis yong man to be put in a lyn sekk, enoyntyd *with* pykk & tar, & so to be casten in a depe watir; and he com*m*awndid att Saynt Andrew sulde be put in *pri*son. And þis done, Saynt Andrew knelid down & made his prayers, & sodanlie þ*er* fell a grete thondre & ane erd-quake, & smate down eu*er*ilk a man vnto þe erth. And þis wom*m*an was burnyd to dede *with* a thondre-bolte, & fell down to assh. And þan Saynt Andrew made his *pra*yer agayn, & all sesid; and þus þe iudge & all þ*at* wer aboute wer tornyd vnto þe f[aith].

LXVII.

Andree Ap*ost*oli.

We rede how on a tyme þe devull apperid vnto a c*er*tayn bisshopp[1] þat had grete devocion vnto Saynt Andrew, in form & lyknes of a fayr mayden, & said vnto hym on þis man*er* of wise; "Sur, I wulde be shreven at you & at no noder." & þis bisshop graunntid, not-*with*stondyng it was agayns his will. And þan sho sett hur down & said; "Sur, I am yong & passand fayr, as ye may se; and I am a kyngis doght*er*, and my fad*er* wolde hafe marid me vnto a wurthi *pri*nce, and I am fled away & wold not hafe hym, becauce I had avowed my virginitie vnto almighti God. And becauce I harde tell of your halines, þ*er*for I am com*m*en vnto you for refute." Than þis bisshopp had grete m*er*vayle of hur fayrnes & hur gudelie language, & sayd vnto hur; "Dogh*ter*, I latt þe witt for þi gude entent, þ*at* what at evur I hafe sall be þine; and I *pra*y þe þis day for to dyne *with* me." And þan sho answerd hym agayn & said; "Nay, holie fadur, desire it nott, nor pray me not þ*er*to, þ*at* no suspecte rise betwix vs þ*at* myght hurte þi gude name and þi fame." And þis bisshopp answerd hur agayn & sayd; "We sall not be be our one, & þ*er*for þ*er* sall no suspecion ryse of vs." So þis bisshopp went to meate, and þis wom*m*an was sett enence hym in a chayre. And all þe meat-while þis bisshopp beheld hur, & had grete m*er*vayll of

[1] MS. *repeats*, vnto a bisshopp.

hur fayrnes; & sho p*ur*ceyvid þis, & encresid hur fayrenes ay more & more, vnto so mekle at þis bisshopp was wowndid gretlie in his harte *with* flesshlie luste, vnto so mekle þat he thoght to aske hur if sho wulde latt hym ly by hur. And þan sodanlie þ*er* come vnto þe yate a pylgram, & knokkid & askid meate for Godd*is* sake. Than þis wom*ma*n desyred þe bysshopp þat he sulde hafe no meate vnto at he had essoynyd iij questions þ*at* sho suld ask hym. And þe furste question was þis, What was þe grettest m*er*vayle & fayrest þing þ*at* evur God made in leste rowme? And a messang*er* come vnto þe pylgram & askid hym it; and þe pylgram ansswerd agayn & sayd, þat it was þe dyu*er*sitye & fayrnes of a mans vysage; "ffor & all men," he said, "war sam*en*, þat was fro þe byggynyng of þe werld vnto þe endyng, yit ij sulde nott be fon to-gedur þat war lyke in visage in all man*er* of thyng; & all þe wittes of a man is sett in þat litle rowm." So þis messang*er* come in & told þe bisshop, & he & all men sayd þe pylgram had ansswerd well. And þan sho sent hym a noder question, and þat was þis; [1] Whether was hyer heven or erthe? And he ansswerd agayn & sayde[2] þat erth was hyer þan hevyn, "quia in celo emp*i*rio ibi est corpus Chr*ist*i, q*uo*d est sup*er* om*n*es celos." And when þe messanger come *with* þis, sho said þatt sho sulde sende hym a war question þan owther off þe tother was, and þat was þis; How far space it was betwix hevyn & erth? And þan he ansswerd agayn & said; "He þat sent þe vnto me knowis þ*at* bettyr þ*an* I doo, ffor I fell neu*er* fro hevyn to erthe, & he fell fro hevyn vnto hell þ*at* is vnd*er* þe erth, & þ*er*for he mett itt; ffor þ*at* wom*ma*n at bad þe spyr me þies questions is þe devull, þat putt hym in lyknes of a wom*ma*n." And when þe messanger harde þis, he had grete wunder, and went in & befor all men, & told all as he bad hym. And all att was aboute had grete m*er*vayle, and sodanlie þe devull vanysshid away *with* a grete thonder & a levenyng; and þe bisshop & all þe felowschip saynyd þai*m*, & onone it cesid. Than he garte send furth[3] to seke þis pylgram, & þ*er* cuthe no man fynd hym.

[1] Lat. MSS. v*bi* terra est altior celo? Ille autem respondit; "In celo empireo, v*bi* corp*us* *Christi*."

[2] *After* sayde, & he said, *erased.*

[3] *After* furth, þis, *erased.*

Than þis bisshopp come vnto hym selfe, & had grete sorow for þe temptacion þat he was fallen in, & shrafe hym þeroff & tuke his penans þerfor. And afterward he had knowlege be revelacion, þat þis pylgram was Saynt Andrew. And fro thyne furth, evur after whils he liffid, he had more devocion vnto Saynt Andrew þan he had befor.

LXVIII.

Angelus. Angelis fetent peccata ho*minum*.

We rede in '*Vitis Patrum*' how, on a tyme, ane angell in a mans lyknes come & went *with* ane h*er*mett a grete way. So þai*m* happend com be a caryon þat had liggen dead many day, & it stynkid ill; and þis h*er*mett helde his nece, at he sulde nott fele savur þ*er*of. And þis aungell askid hym whi he helde his nece, and he answerd hym agayn & said; "Becauce I may not fele þis savur." And þai went on furth, & onone þai mett a fayr yong man cled in gay clothyng, þat had a fayr garland on his head, þat rade opon a gay hors in a sadle all of gold & sylver. And when þai wer a gude way fro hym, þis angell in a mans liknes stoppyd his nease-thrillis. And when þis h*er*mett saw, he had grete m*er*vall þ*er*of, & said vnto hym; "whi stoppis þ*ou* þi nece so, & stoppid þai*m* nogt right now?" And he answerd agayn & said; "yone yong man þ*at* is so prowde & full of syn, stynkis mor vglie in þe sight of God & all his aungell, þan done all þe carion of þis werld in syght or felyng of crysten men." *et c*.

Angelus accusat pecc*at*ores. Infra de fideiussor[*e*]. ij.

LXVIII *a*.

Angelus actus n*ost*ros dinum*er*at.

As we rede of ane h*er*mett þat had a cell far fro þe watir. *et c*. Vt infra de laborare, ij.

LXIX.

Angelus a morte corp*or*ali lib*er*at.

Cesarius tellis how þ*er* was a damysell in a chylde liknes þat went in felowshup w[ith] a thefe be þe way, & wiste nogt what he was. & þis thefe gaff hur to bere a paghald of gere þat he had stoln. So it happend at þe men att aght þis gude folowid after þis thefe, & onone as he hard noyse of rynyng of þaim, & he gatt away, & lete þis damysell alone *with* þis stoln gude. And þis childe was takyn *with* þis thifte & demyd to be hanged; & when sho cuthe gett no skosacion to helpe hur *with*, bod at sho trewid vereli[e] to dye, sho shrafe hur vnto þe preste & tolde hym all þe proces. So þai went & soght þis thefe in þe wud & fande hym, & tuke hym; and when he was taken he[1] alegid for hym selfe, & said þat þis paghald was not of his, & þerfor he said þat þai at þe stoln gude was fun *with* sulde suffre þe penance. And þus he alegid þat þe childe sulde be dede & not he. So be cowncell of þe preste, þer was broght furth a hote yrn to prufe þe treuth *with*; and þis damysell tuchid þis hote yrn & hur hand was nothyng byrnyd. And when þe thefe tuchid itt, his hand was grevuslie burnyd, and so þe thiefe was hanged & þe mayden delyverd. So þe kynsmen of þis thieff wex wrothe *with* þis, and tuke down þis thieff, & hanged vp þis damysell. And onone þer come ane aungell & helde hur vp, so at sho felid no grevans bod a grete swettnes, & hard a passand swete melodie, in þe whilk it was tolde hur þat a sister saule of hurs, þat hight Agnes, was had vnto hevyn, and at sho suld at ij [*yere*] ende after folow hur. And þer sho hang ij dayes; & þan hirdmen trowid at sho had bene dead, & cut down þe rape & went sho sulde hafe fallen down; bod scho was sustenyd *with* ane angell & lattyn down be little & litle, vnto sho stude evyn opon þe erth. And þan þe aungell sayd vnto hur; "Now erte þou fre; Go whethur þou will." And sho said sho purposid go vnto þe cetie of Veron[2]; & onone *with*-in a stownde sho was sett nere þe cetie of Veron[2], & þan þe aungell told hur þat sho was *with*-in iij myle of þis cetie. And þis happend att þe cetie of Auguste, & þat is vij day iorney fro Veron[2].

Anima purgatur in loco quo peccauit. Infra de pena. Anima punitur cum persona cum qua peccauit. Infra de penitentia et Purgatorio.

[1] MS. le. [2] *For* Verona.

A*nim*e aliqu*ando* ab amicis iuvantur. Infra de apostata, iij.

A*nim*a punitur *secundum* qualitatem p*eccat*i. Inf*r*a de purgatorio.

Animosus debet esse miles in bello. Inf*r*a de milite, vj.

LXX.

Annu*n*ciacio Dom*in*ica.

The feste of þe annu*n*ciacion of our ladie aght to be had in grete reu*er*ens, & to be wurshuppid *with* grete devocion; and opon þat day aght þe Ave Maria ofte to be said, as we rede of a knyght þat was a passand ryche man, notw*ith*stondyng he went & made hym a monke in þe Ceustos ordur. And þuf all he cuthe no l*ett*re on þe buke, yit for his hy burthe[1] he was taken in & putt emang monk*is*. And a maist*er* was delyverd vnto hym to lern hym on þe buke; and he cuthe lern hym no thyng bod þies ij wordys, Ave Maria. And þat he was evur h*ar*pand on, to so mekill þ*at* whid*er* as eu*er* he went, or what thyng som evur he did, he was evur sayand Ave Maria. So at þe laste hym happynd to dye, & was berid w*ith* other monk*is*; and þ*er* sprang oute of his grafe a fayr lelie, and on evur-ilk a lefe þ*er*off was wreten, Ave Maria, w*ith* golde l*ett*res. And þe monk*is* ran þ*er*to & grufe down in his grafe to þai[2] fande þe rute of þe lelie, & þai fand how it sprang furth of his mouthe. And be þat þai vnderstude þat he said þase ij wurdis, Ave Maria, w*ith* grete deuocion. And þ*er*for our ladie wold lat þai*m* hafe knowlege.

LXXI.

Ave Maria dict*um* deuote lib*er*at hom*in*em de potestate diaboli.

We rede how som tyme þ*er* was a knyght þat was a thieff, and vsid forto rob men be þe way. So on a tyme þ*er* come be þe way a man of religion, and onone he was taken w*ith* þis knyghtis men,

[1] MS. *here repeats*, yit. [2] MS. þe.

þat was thevis. And when þai had taken hym he prayed þaim speciallie to hafe hym to þer maister; and when he come afor þe knyght he prayed þe knyght þat he wold latt hym se all his men; and he grauntid, & garte feche all his men. And when þat all was befor hym, þis holie man of religion askid þis knyght if þer was all, and þai said, "ya"; and he sayd it was not sa. So þai lukid aboute þaim, & one of þaim sayd þat þe chamberlayn was wantand. And þe knyght sent for hym & he come, bod yit it was *with* ill will. And when he saw þis holie man of religion, he starte bakk & glorid *with* his een as he had bene wude, & wulde com no ner for noght at no man cuthe do. Than þis holie man said vnto hym; "I adiure þe in þe name of God at þou tell me what þou erte, and wharefor þou come hedur." And þan he ansswerd agayn & sayd; "Allas! now moste me ned*is* tell what I am! I am," he said, "a fend, & I made me like a man, & I hafe wunte *with* þis knyght þis xiiij yere, & alway ligen in wayte if I cuthe wache what day he sayd not, 'Aue Maria'; ffor what day he had faylid þeroff, I sulde hafe strangled hym; and what day as he said þat Ave, I had nevur power on hym, nor not mot hafe. And all þe tyme þat I hafe bene *with* hym he faylid nevur a day, bod he said it a tyme of þe day." And when þe knyght hard þis, he was hugelie astonyd & had grete mervayle, & fell down on his kneis befor þis holie man, & askid hym forgifnes, & was shrevyn, & tuke penance and amendid his life. And þis holie man commandid þis fend at he sulde go his ways, and nevur aftur presume to dissese any creatur þat had deuocion vnto our ladie, Saynt Marie. *et c9*.

Antiphonam Regina celi Angeli cantauerunt.
Infra de Maria. x.

LXXII.

Antonij Abbatis.

We rede in 'Vitis Patrum,' how on a tyme as Saynt Anton lay in a den in wildernes, a grete multitude of fendis come vnto hym and rafe hym, & toylid hym, to so mekle he was nerehand dead.

And his brether went & soght hym, & fand hym nere dede; & þai wepud & made grete sorow, and fechid hym home. So on a nyght when he was amendid, & all his brethir was oslepe, he garte bere hym agayn vnto þe sayd den: and as he lay þer, & many wowndis vppon hym, he lukid evur when þir fendis suld com agayn. Than þai come in liknes of wilde bestis, & *with* þer hornys & þer tethe þai rafe his flessh, & wowndid hym hugelie. Than sodanlie þer apperid a mervaylus light, & þies fendis fled; & sodanlie Saynt Anton was hele of all his wowndis. So att þe laste he vnderstude þat þer was almighti God Hym selfe; & þan he said; "A! gude Jesu! whar was þou? whar was þou? whi was þou not *with* me in þe begynyng, at þou mot hafe helpid me, and helid my wowndis?" And our Lord answwerrid hym agayn & said; "Anton, I was here, bod I abade to se þi batell; and becauce now at þou hase manlelie ouercommen þine enmys, I sall make þi name to be knowen þurgh all þis werld, and þe for to be wurshuppid."

Antonius recreatur cum fratribus. Supra de Abbate.

Apparicio. Apparet quandoque deus. Infra de leproso.

Apparet quandoque beata virgo. Infra de beata Maria. et alibi[1] in pluribus locis.

Apparent quandoque angeli. Supra de angelo.

Apparent demones. Infra de Maria. viij.

Apparent mortui. Infra de morte, fere totum, et de suffragijs.

Appetitus est reprimendus. Supra de abstinencia, X et V.

LXXIII.

Apostasia. Apostate religionis quandoque corporaliter puniuntur.

We rede how þer was offerd vnto Damyanus, in an abbay þat Saynt Gregur byggid *with*-in þe wallis of þe cetie of Rome, a childe be his fader & his moder; and when he come vnto mans age, he

[1] MS. et in alij pluribus locis.

forsuth forsuke þis Abbay, & went into þe werlde, & tuke hym a wyfe. So afterward hym happend for to fall seke, and he garte bere hym vnto þis abbay, & þ*er* he lay; & on a tyme, sodanlie, befor his wyfe & all þat was aboute, he began to cry faste, & said þat Saynt Andrew & Saynt Gregur had bett hym grevuslie; and when he had ligyn a while, he said at þai had dongen hym becauce he went oute of þe abbay & tuke hym a wyfe. And a while after he sayd þai bett hym agayn becauce he skornyd pure men, & wulde giff þai*m* noght; "& now," he said, "þai bete me becauce I tuke wronguslie vi d of a man & wulde not giff hym þai*m* agayn; & now I hafe for ilk peny a lassh" and wit*h*in ane howr or ij after, he rase oute of his bed, & did on hym a hayr & a scapularie þat lay by hym, and ran vnto þe kurk, and said þat, be þe grace of God, he was delyverd of all þis betyng. & he garte make his bed in þe same kurk, & garte a monke go vnto mes; and evyn onone, as þe gospell was red, he endid his life. And þe monk*is* had his bodie to wassh it, & þai fand vppon his bodie wowndis & yedders of þe betyng þat he said he was bett wit*h* þase halie Synttis for þe trispas at he had done. *et c9*.

LXXIV.

Apostata red[*i*]ens ad religione*m* pacient*er* debet ferre qua*m*cu*m*q*ue* penitenciam.

We rede in 'Vitis P*atrum*,' how þat þ*er* was ij fadurs þat war tempid wit*h* þe spiritt of fornicacion, & þai went into þe werld & tuke þai*m* wyfis. So on a tyme þe tone of þai*m* said vnto þe toder; "whatt hafe we won in þis our vnclennes, sen we consayfe þat eu*er*lastand payn mon folow itt, & we hafe forsaken þe life of angels? And þ*er*for latt us turn agayn, & be as we wer in wilde[*r*]ness." And þai went agayn vnto þ*er* cellis, and was reclusis a full yere, and had nothyng bod a porcion of bread & watir evurilk day. And when þe yere was done, þe tone of þai*m* had a pale face, & þe toder a fayr face; & his brethir askid hym whi his face was so pale, & he answerd agayn and said; "I hafe a pale face for I had mynd of þe paynys of hell, whilk þat

I mond hafe bod if I did penance for my syn." And þe tod*er* said his face was so fayr for he thoght of þe gudenes of allmightti God, & had a grete comfurth & a ioy þat he was delyverd oute of þe paynys of hell; & þerfor he said, he had grete comfurth when he purseyvid þat he was delyverd of so grete a p*er*ell, & þan put agayn in so grete wurthines. And when þ*er* brethir hard þis, þai vnderstude att þai wer of evyn penance. *et c*9.

Apostate reue*r*tentes freque*nter* deuocius se habent. Inf*ra* de p*eniten*cia, ijº.

LXXV.

Apostate aliqu*ando* ecia*m* mali peiores efficiuntur.

Cesarius tellis how þ*er* was som tyme a yong man þat made [*hym*] of a monk of Ceustos ordur, and þuff[1] all he was gretelie movid be a bisshop at was his Cussyn to com oute of þe place, yit neu*er*-þeles he wolde nott, bod abade still & was professid, & eft*er*ward made a preste. So afterward be temptacion of þe devull, he gatt oute of his place & went vnto a grete co*m*pany of thevis; & he, þat was gude emang his brethir, was þ*er* þe warste of all. So on a tyme, at þe sege of a Castell, hym happend to be hurte *with* ane arow, & was bown to dye. And men abowte cownceld hym to shryfe hym, and he answerd & sayd; "What may shrifte p*ro*fett me, þat hase done so many grete trispasis?" And þe p*re*ste told hym þat þe m*er*cie of God was more þan was all hys syn. And þan he began to shryfe hym, & sett hym down on his kneis befor þe preste; and God sent hym swilk cont*ri*cion þat eu*er* when he began to shryfe hym, he sighed & wepid so sore þat he mott not speke a wurd. So at þe laste he tuke his spiritt vnto hym & sayd; "Sur, I hafe synnyd ofter þan þ*er* is gravell in þe see, and I hafe gane oute of myne ordur and felashippid me *with* thevis & lurdans, & slayn many a man. And if þai be savid I mon nott, ffor I hafe violatt & fylid many mens wyvis, & þ*er* chuldre, & burnyd þ*er* howsis, & done many other infenyte illis." And þe p*re*ste was bod a fule & said; "Maior est iniquitas tua qua*m* veniam m*er*caris:

[1] MS. if.

þi syn & þi wikkednes is more þan evur þou may gett forgiffnes off." And he answerd agayn & said; "Sur, I am a clark, & I hafe sene þis written, 'Quacum*que* hora ingemisc*er*it pecc*at*or, *et cetera* : Whatt how*r* som eu*er* þat a synn*er* forthynk*is* his syn, & shryvis hym clene þ*er*of, almighti God will forgiff hym.' And þ*er*for I beseke you for Godd*is* sake to enioyn me som penance for my syn." And þan þe preste said; "I wate nevur what penance I sulde enioyne þe, for þou arte bod a loste man." Than he answerd agayn & said; "Sur, sen þou will not enioyn me penance, I sall enioyn my selfe penance; And þ*er*for I bynd my selfe to be ij M Ł.[1] yere in purgatorie; & after þat at I may hafe forgifnes of my syn of allmyghti God." And þan he askid þat he myght be howseld, and þis fond p*re*ste wolde not howsell hym. Than at þe laste, he prayed hym write his confession in a scrow, and at he wold giff it vnto þe bisshopp þat was his cussyn; and þe preste hight hym þat he suld do so. And þan he dyed & his sawle went vnto purgatorie, as he had bon it to do. And þe p*re*ste offerd þis cedull vnto þis bisshopp; and when þe bisshopp redd itt he was passand hevie & wepud, & said þus vnto þe preste; "þ*er* was neu*er* man þat I luffid so wele whikk, & þ*er*for I sall luff hym deade." And in þat yere he sente þurgh all his bisshoppryke, & garte do message & oders prayers & suffrage of halie kurk for hym. And at þe yere end he aperid vnto hym w*ith* a pale & a lene face, & tolde hym þat be his suffrage þat he garte do þat yere for hym, & did hym selfe, he was remytt of a M Ł yere þat he sulde hafe suffred in þe payn of purgatorie; & if he wold do als mekull for hym þe nexte yere, he said he sulde be clene delyverd þ*er*off for evur. And þis bisshop garte do for hym þe secund yere as he did þe furste. And when þis was done, as þe bisshop was syngand a mes for hym, he apperid vnto hym in a white cowle, & w*ith* a passand fayr face, & sayd; "Almiȝtti God reward þe at þou hase done for me; for be þi besynes I am delyverd in þies ij yere of þe paynys of ij M Ł yere in purgatorie. And þ*er*for I thanke the, for now I go vnto paridice vnto evurlastand blis." *et c*[9].

[1] M Ł. *omitted, and added above the line.*

Apostate habentes firmum propositum redeundi si sic moriantur saluat eos, *et* reddit eis habitum monachalem. Infra de voluntate que pro facto reputatur.

Apostata a fide aliqu*ando* a deo e*ciam* corporaliter punitur. Infra de benedicta.

LXXVI.

Apostolus. Ap*osto*lor*um* memoria *et* deuocio est utilis.

Cesarius tellis how som tyme in þe cetie of Colayn þ*er* was so grete a fyre, þ*at* a grete parte of þe cetie was brente. So þ*er* was a c*er*tayn wom*m*an in þe cetie, þat wasshid & amendid for hur hyre all þe clothis þat belonged vnto þe kurk of þe apostels. And sho had a howse all of wud, harde be þe kurk, and when þe wykkid fyre was in howsis nere-hand hur, hur doght*er* began to bere oute hir howsshold; & hur mod*er* bad hur lefe, & wolde nott latt hur, bod garte hur bere in all agayn. And sho lokkid þe dure faste, & wente in-to þe kurk, & had grete faythe in þe apostels, & sett hur downe afor þai*m* & prayed in þis man*er* of wise; "O! ye holie apostels! & eu*er* I did you any trew or gude s*er*ves, kepe my howse & my gudis þat is þ*er*in." Lo! þis was a m*er*valos fayth of a wom*m*an! And þan þe fyre þat burnyd, still owr-hippid þis lawnderer howse, so þat nowder it nor hur gudis þat was þ*er*-in was byrnyd, þuf all þai wer in myddeste þe fyre; & þus hur howse was savid þurgh fayth, & belefe þat sho had vnto þe apostels. *et c*[9].

LXXVII.

Aqua quasi solida stetit non fluens.

Saynt Gregorie tellis, how at þe Cetie of Terenence[1], þe flude þat is callid Artose bolnyd up so, þat it come vnto þe kurk of Saynt Zenon þe martyr; and yit, þuf all þe duris wer oppyn, it come not

[1] Latin MSS., apud Verenensem urbem, = Verona.

in; and it sparrid vp þe kurk-duris & þe wyndows, as it had bene turnyd into a thyng þat had bene faste as þe stone wall, vnto so mekull þat mekle peple þat was in þe kurk war sparrid in *with* þe watir, & myghte not wyn oute. And yitt when þai come vnto þe kurk-dure, þai might take þai*m* wat*er* & drynk þ*er*off. And þus, þurgh þe gude prayers of þis holie m*ar*tir, þe watir was many day as a wall vnto þai*m*, & myght nott entir in-to þat holie place. *et c*⁹.

LXXVIII.

Archidiaconus ad episcopatu*m* aspirans p*er*pet*r*auit homicidiu*m*.

We rede in 'Libro de Dono Timoris,' how som tyme þ*er* was in Ducheland ane archdekyn þat desirid gretelie to be a bisshopp, & co*n*tyrfetid her-for þe bisshoppis deade; & he garte lay a grete stane abown þe yate at þe bisshopp vsid to go in att þe kurk att; and þ*er* was owr þe yate ane ymage of our ladie. And on a tyme, as þe bisshop went befor all his felaship, & sett hym down to wurshup þis ymage on his kneis, þis stane was put down, & smate oute his h*er*nys. And onone aftre, þis archedekyn was made bisshopp, & made a grete feste at his stallyng. So at þis ffeste þ*er* was a grete p*r*ince þat s*er*vid hym, & sodanlie he was ravisschid into a vision, & þ*er* he saw our ladie *with* a grete multitude of aungels & Sayntis, berand þe bisshopp head at þe harnys was strekyn oute off, and p*re*sent it vnto Almiȝtti God, sayand on þis man*er* of wise; "dere Son! yit þis my s*er*vand hede bledis; & yit his succidur þe homycide, at garte sla hym, ioyes of his dignytie at he hase after hym." And þan our Lord askid hur whome he sulde send vnto hym. And sho said; "Lo! yonder is his s*er*ver." And þan our Lorde com*m*anddid hym in payn of dethe, þat he sulde *with*-oute co*n*tynnance tell þe bisshopp all þat evur he had bothe hard & sene. And þan he come vnto hym selfe & wepud, & went in & told opynlie vnto þe bissho[p], befor all at þ*er* was, all þat he had bothe hard & sene. And when þis bisshopp had hard hym oppynlie befor all men, he wex wude & swelte. *et c*⁹.

Archiep*iscopus* a demonibus[1] portatur. Infra de demone.

Arma religioso*rum* su*n*t vestes eo*rum*. In*fra* de Religione.

Arma mon*achi* possu*n*t temp*or*e et loco ex causa[2] . . . Inf*ra* de bello.

Arnulphi Metens*is*. Infra de Remissione.

Arsenij senatoris *et* heremite. Infra de odore *et* de pecc*ato*, de solitudine *et* vigilia. *et c*.

LXXIX.

Aspectus debet esse compositus.

Tullius tellis how þat Pericles[3] & Sophocles war made dukis at Athenys. And oñ a tyme, wheñ þai went to speke to-gedur in a cowncelhows of suche thyngis as was necessarie vnto þe cetie, þ*er* happend a fayr yong mañ to go be a wyndow at þai sett enence. And þis Sophocles spak vnto Pericl*es*[4] & sayd; "Se! yond*er* gois a fayr yong mañ!" And he answerd hym agayñ & said; "Sur, it semys a mañ of cowncelƚ, not alonelie to kepe stiƚƚ his handis & his tong, bod also for to kepe his eeñ c*on*tynent froñ aƚƚ man*er* of ydiƚƚ sightis in tyme þat he is at conceƚƚ."

LXXX.

Assenecħ historia.

As we rede in þe furste yere of þe vij plentyfuƚƚ yeris þat was in Egipte, Kyng Pharao sent Josepħ to gadr samen cornys þat he cuthe gett in þe bowndis of Cleopilas, of whilk regioñ Pytaphar[5] þe preste was prince. & he was a wise mañ & grete of cowncelƚ *with* Pharao; and he had a doght*er* þat hight Assenecħ, and sho

[1] MS. demonijs. Latin MSS. have, de demonib*us* deportatur.

[2] MS. leaves a space here. Harl. MS. Arma mon*achi* possunt tempore *et* loco. In*fra* de bello. Arund. MS. Arma mon*achi* possunt tempore *et* loco ex cau*sa*. In*fra* de bello.

[3] MS. paricles.

[4] MS. perich.

[5] MS. Pyckaphar.

was a passand fayr maydcn emang all o*þer*; & *with* þ*at* sho was passand statelie & prowde, & thoght skorn be evur-ilk comm*on* man. And sho was kepid so at no man saw hur. And þ*er* was ioynyd uppon þis Putyphar howse a towr, at was grete & hy, & in þe top þ*er*of was a cenacle, þat had in it x chawmers; of þe whilk þe furst was grete & fayr, & dight *with*-in *with* p*re*cious stonys; and in þat was þe goddis of Egipte, of golde & of sylu*er*, at þis Assenech did sacryfice vnto. & evur-ilk day sho offerd vnto þai*m*. And þe secund chawm*er* lay hur clothyng in, & hur gold & hur sylver & hur p*re*cious stonys; and in þe iij chawm*er* war all þe gudis of þe lande, & þ*er* was hur buttrie; and in þe toder war vij maydyns þat s*er*vid þis Assenech, *with* whame spak nowder childe nor man; and in Assenech chawm*er* was þ*er* iij wyndows, ane at þe suthe, a noder at þe este, & þe iij at þe weste: & at þe northe was hur bed, onowrnyd *with* gold & sylu*er*, p*re*cious stonys, & gay clothis of purpur & sylk at sho slepid in, & þ*er* sat neu*er* man on þat bed. And aboute þis towre was þ*er* ane entre *with* a hy wall, *with*-in þe whilk þ*er* was fayre treis & frutefull of dyvers kyndis; & þ*er* was a fayr spryng & a well. And þis Assenech was a mekull large wom*m*an as Sarra was, & als wise as Rebecca, & als fayr as Rachell. So þis Joseph sent vnto þis Putiphar & lete hym witt at he wald com vnto hys place & se itt; & he was fayn þ*er*of, & lete his dogh*ter* hafe knowlege, & said he wolde marie hur vnto hym. And sho was wrothe þ*er*-*with*, & said scho wold be giffen vnto no man at was in thraldom as Joseph was, bod rather vnto a kyngis son. So as þai war spekand sam*en*, one come & tolde þai*m* at Joseph come. And þis Assenech fled in-to hur cenacle, vp into þe topp of þe towre. And Joseph come rydand in Pharao carte, þat was all of gold, & iiij white hors drew it, & þai had brydyls all of gold; & Joseph was cled in a white cote & in pall & purpur wovyn *with* golde, & a crown of p*re*cious gold opon his head, & aboute it was xij p*re*cious stonys, & he had in his hand a golden wand of þe kynges, & a branch of oliff full off fatt frute. And þis Putiphar & his wife come & mett hym, and wurschippid hym, and Joseph went in-to þis entrie, & þai sparrid þe duris af*ter* hym. & at þe laste he was war of Assenech oute at a wyndow, and sho saw hym. And þan sho was gretelie trubled *with* wurd at sho had hard on hym, and þan sho said; "Beholde! þe son is comm*e*n fro hevyn to shyne vppon vs in his cowrs; and I wiste not," sho said, "at Joseph was þe son off Godd. What man myght hafe so grete fayrnes, & what wom*m*ans wambe myght bere so grete a light?" And þan Joseph went vnto Putiphar hows, & þai wasshid his fete. And þan Joseph asked what wom*m*an þat was þat he saw in þe cenacle oute at þe wyndow, & þai tolde hym. & he was aferd þat sho was hevye vnto hym, as sho was vnto other þat sent vnto hur messangers *with* grete giftys; & eu*er* sho keste þai*m* agayn att þai*m* *with* grete[1] skorn & dedyne. And þan said Putiphar; "Sur, my doght*er* is a mayden, & hatis evur-ilk man, for sho saw neu*er* man bod me & the at sho saw þis day. And if þou will, sho sall com & speke *with* the." And þan Joseph thoght þat & sho hatid eu*er*-ilk a man, sho sulde not be vnbehuvable vnto hym. And þan he said vnto hur fadur; "and your doght*er* be a mayden, I luff hur as my sustre." And hur moder went & fechid hur down & broght hur befor hym, and hur fadur bad hur hals hur bruther, þ*at* hatid all women as sho did all men. And sho halsid hym & sayde; "Ave b*e*n*e*dic*te* a deo excelso! hayle þou blissid, comm*e*n fro Almyghti God!" and þan he said agayn; "Ben*e*dicat te deus q*u*i viuificat om*n*es; God blis þe þat whikkens all creaturs." And Putiphar bad his doghter kys Joseph; and sho wolde hafe done so, & he lett hur *with* his hand & said; "It semys nott a man þat wurschuppis Almyghti God to kys a wom*m*an þat wurshuppis mawmett*is* þat er defe & dom." And when sho hard hym say so, sho was passand hevye & wepid. And Joseph was sorowfull for hur, & laid his hand on hur heade & blissid hur. And þan sho was merie & p*ar*tid *with* hym & went vnto hur bed. And what for ioy & what for drede, sho fell seke, & did penans for þase fals godd*is* at sho had wurshuppid, and forsuke þai*m*. And when Joseph had etyn, he tuke his lefe & went his way, & said he sulde com agayn þat day viij dayes. And when he was gone, þis Assenech did on blak clothyng in token of hevynes & sparrid hur dure, & keste down all hur ydolsis, & keste hur supper vnto

[1] *After* grete, giftis, *erased*.

hundis, & putt assh opon hur head, & laid hur down on þe payment & wepid bitterlie vij dayes. And on þe viij day come Joseph & tuke hur vnto wyfe & wed hur. *et c⁹.*

Asinus portat usurarium ad patibulum. Infra de sepultura.

Asinus custoditur a leone. Infra de Leone.

Asinus legatus tribus perit. Infra de legato.

LXXXI.

Avaricia. Auarus quanto plus congregat, tanto deus aliquando ei occasionaliter subtrahit.

We rede in 'Vitis Patrum' how þat som tyme þer was a garthener, & all þat evur he gatt off his labur, he gaff it in almos, so þat vnnethis he kepid vnto hym selfe to fynd hym mete & clothe. So afterward be intysyng of þe devull, he lefte his almos-giffyng, & gaderd samen a grete some of money þat he myght liff with in his age. So afterward þer happend a surans for to fall in hys lymbe, þat his fute rotid off. And he spendid all his money in lechecrafte, & was neuer þe better; and att þe laste, be cowncell of a gude leche, he garte cutt it off. And opon þe same nyght at it was cutt off, as he lay in his bed sorowand & mornand, þer apperid vnto hym ane angell & said; "Whar is now þe money att þou gaderd samen to liff with in þine elde? What may þat now helpe the att þou had hope in?" And he ansswerd agayn & said, "I hafe synnyd, & I will now no mor do soo." And þis aungell tuchyd his fute, & it was restorid agayn. And þe leche come to hym agayn on þe morn, & fand his fute hale, & hym gravand as he was wunt to do in þe felde. Lo! Surs, þus he was restorid for his gude dede, þuff all he lefte it, and þerfor ye may see at God will hafe no gude dede vnrewardid.

LXXXII.

Avaricia a temporali promocione impedit.

Saynt Gregor tellis how one þat hight Constancius, at was cussyn vnto Bonyface, on a tyme sellid his hors for xij d of gold, & he putt þaim in his kiste; & in þe mene while he[1] went his way. So on a tyme pure men come vnto þis pope Bonyface, & askid hym almos passand faste; & he was in þe kurk & had nothyng to giff þaim. So he trustid gretelie in his cussyn, at he had gude, & went vnto his kiste & brak it, & tuke oute þies xij golde penys & gaff þaim vnto pure folke. So þis Constancius come agayn & fand his kyste breken, & *with* a grete rumor & a cry he come vnto the pope, & bad hym giff hym his xij d. agayn. & *with* his crying þis pope wente into the kurk & was gretlie sterid, & evyn standand he liftid upp his handis vnto allmyghti God, & made his prayer. & sedandlie he grapid in his bosom & fand xij d. of gold, & he keste þaim in þis wude preste skyrte, & said; "Behold! now þou hase þe xij d. of gold at þou askid me; Bod þou sall vnderstand, þat af*ter* my decese þou sall neu*er* be pope nor bysshop of þis kurk, as þou trowis to be; and all becauce off þi covatusnes, at þou will giff God no þing of þat at he sendis the."

LXXXIII.

Avaricia est qua*n*doq*ue* causa amissionis temp*or*aliu*m*, *et* vniu*s* avaricia toti vni congregacioni nocet.

Cesarius tellis how þat a monk som tyme of Ceustus ordur, þat was Celerer, was tempid *with* covatice. So on a tyme in barganyng he begylid a pure wedow. So it happend þat same yere our Lord sent such weddur þat stroyed all þe vynys þat langed vnto þe abbay, so at þ*er* wyne had nowder colour nor savor. And þe abbott, seyng þis, trowed þat it come for somwhatt at God was displesid *with* þaim fore. And he went vnto a holie mayden þat hight Acelina, & besoght hur mekely at sho wold aske in hur prayers of almyghti God, at sho mot know be reuelacion what was þe cauce here-off; and so sho did. & it was answerd hur be allmyghti God, þat it was for þe fraude & þe gyle þat þis celerer did vnto þis pure wedow. And yit it was said mor vnto þaim be almyghti God in þis wise; "Yit I sall tuche hym *with* a plage." & so it happen[d] þat a knyght þat wonnyd beside þaim

[1] *After* he, dyed, *erased.*

in þatt yere, sodanlie of ill will, opon a night sett fyre in þ*er* lathis, & burnyd up all þ*er* warn-store at þai had of corn. And þan þe plage cesid, & þe monke shrafe hym clenelie of all hys synnys, & come vnto amendment.

LXXXIV.

Auaricia retrahit ab elemosinis faciendis.

Jacobus tellis how at þ*er* was a wom*m*an, & hur husband gaff hur keys & kepyng of all at evur þai had. And sho was so sparand, at sho wolde giff nothyng for Goddis sake vnto pure folke, nor vnto þai*m* at mysterd. So at þe laste hur happend to dye, & hur neghburs owncellid hur husband to dele som almos to pure folke for hur saule. And he answerd agayn & sayde; "Whils scho liffid hur selfe, sho wolde nothyng dele nowder for hur selfe, nor for me; & þerfor I will now nothyng dele for hur."

Auaricia *eciam* a debita oblacione in missa retrahit. Inf*ra* de obl*acio*ne in offertorio.

Auaricia hospitalitatem impedit. infra de hospitalitate.

Auarus moriens a pecunia no*n* potest sep*ar*ari. Infra[1] de Vsurario.

Aue Maria no*n* potest demon audire, sed fugit. Infra, demon.

Ave Maria liberat a potestate Demonis. Sup*ra* de annu*n*ciacione.

LXXXV.

Auditus. Audire se*r*monem impedit demon.

Jacobus de Vet*ri*aco tellis, how som tyme þ*er* was a religious man, and as he was sayand a se*r*mon in a kurk on a tyme, he saw þe devull in þe kurk. & þ*er* he adiurid hym, & chargid hym on Godd*is* behalfe, þat he sulde tell hym his name, & what he was. And þis Deuyll answerd & said; "I am a fend, & I am callid

[1] MS. Supra.

Claudens Aurem, Ere sparrer. And I hafe other iij felows, and ane is callid Claudens Cor, a nodér, Claudens Os, & þe thrid, Claudens Bursam. The furst sparis a mans harte, þat he may not hafe contricion for his syn. The second sparis his mouthe, þat he sall not shryfe hym, & þe thrid sparis his purs, þat he sall make no satisfaccion nor dele none almos-dede, at his syn may be forgyffyn hym. And I my selfe sparis a mans eris, þat he sall nott here noo gude prechyng, þat sulde cauce hym to forsake his syn."

LXXXVI.

Audientes *verbum* dei deus audiet, Et nolentes audire non audiet.

Jacobus de Vet*riaco* tellis, how som tyme þer was a husband-man þat wald nott here of almyghti God. So on a tyme hym happend to dye, and when he was born vnto þe kurk, & þe prestis & þe clerkis was besy aboute hys dirige-doyng, in syngyng & redyng aboute his bodie, þe crucifix, at stude vp in þe rude-lofte, lowsyd his handis fra þe rude, & stoppid his eris þat he sulde nott here þai*m*. And all þat was in þe kurk, when þai saw þis, had grete me*r*vayle þeroff. And þan þe preste said vnto þe pepull; "Know ye whatkyn a tokyn þis is? ye know ve*r*elie, þat he this at lies here had neue*r* will in all his life to here þe wurd of Godd, nor at no man sulde speke off Hym. And þe*r*for he is now in þe power of þe devull; and þe*r*for þe crucifix now stoppis his eris, þat he here nott þe prayers þat we syng & say for hym." And so þai all lefte þe*r* prayers & wolde pray no more for hym; & þan the crucifix putt vp his armys as þai war befor. *et c*.

Audire missam est multu*m* vtile. Inf*r*a de Incepcione.

LXXXVII.

Auguriu*m* aliquando est verum.

We rede in 'Historia Eccle*s*iastica' how on a tyme Herodes Agrippa come vnto Rome, & þe*r* he was passand famyliari *with* one þat hight Gayus, þat was þe Emp*er*our cussyn. So on a day, as Herod was in a chariott *with* þis Gayus, Herod lifte vp his handis vnto hevyn & said; "Wold God at I mott se yone alde man deade, þat is Emp*er*our, & at þou war lorde of all þis werld." And when he had hard þis Herod say so, he went vnto Tyberius, þat was Emp*er*our, & tolde hym. And he wex passand wrothe þ*er*with, & garte putt Herod in *pri*son þ*er*for. So on a day as þai satt in *pri*son, he & his felous, þai war war of ane owle sytt in þe bewis of a tre. & þan one of þai*m*, þat was wiseste of þai*m* all, said vnto Herod; "dowte þe noȝt, for þou mon sone be delyverd, & be so gretelie enhawnsid & þai þat er þi frendis sal be þine enmys; & in þis *pro*sp*er*itie þou sall dye." So *with*-in a little while aft*er*, þis Tyberius dyed, and þis Gayus was chosyn Emp*er*our. And he tuke vp þis Herod oute of *pri*son & gretelie enhawnecid hym, & made hym þe chefe kyng in all Iurie.

LXXXVIII.

Augurriu*m*. Sicut supra.

Josephus tellis þat when Herod come vnto Cesarie & all þe men of þe contre come vnto hym, he had on clothyng of clothe of golde & sylu*er*. So on a day he satt in þ*er* mote-hall, & þe son bemys shane opon his clothyng. & þai þat saw hym thought at þ*er* was ij sonnys, one at schane on hym, & a noder at shane oute of hym; & so þai tuke a grete ferdnes for hym, to so mekull at þai said on þis man*er* of wise; "hedertoward we dred yone man bod as a man, bod fro hyne-furth we sall wurshupp hym abown þe natur of man"; vnto so mekull þat, þurgh þe adulacion of þe pepyll, he supposid hym selfe more for to be a god þan a man. So on a day as he satt vnder-nethe a tre, he was war of ane owle syttand in þe tre abown his head; and þ*er*by he wiste þat he sulde sone dy, & said; "Lo! surs, I, þat am your lord, mon now dy." For he knew be þe sight of þis owle, þat he sulde dy *with*-in v dayes after. And onone he was smytyn *with* seknes, and v dayes wormes knew hym so in his bowels þat at þe laste he [1] expired & dyed.

[1] MS. de.

LXXXIX.

Augustinus.

We rede how oñ a tyme þ*er* was a mañ þat had a grete deuocioñ vnto Saynt Austiñ. & oñ a tyme he come vnto a monk þat kepid Saynt Austyñ shryñ, & gaff hym̃ a grete dele of money, & besoght hym̃ to giff hym̃ a fyngre of Saynt Augustyñ. And þis monke [*tuke*] a noder dead mans fynger & wappid it in a sylkeñ clothe, & gaff hym̃ it & tolde hym̃ þat it was Saynt Austyñ fynger. And he tuke it *with* grete reu*er*ens, & alway wurschippid it als deuotelie as he cuthe, & wolde putt it to his mouthe, his eyñ & vnto his breste. So almighti God, seyng þe faith of þis mañ, als wele m*er*cifullie as m*er*valuslie, gaff vnto þis mañ a fynger of Saynt Austyñ. And he went home þ*er*with in-to his contreth; & þ*er* it did grete m*er*acles, vnto so mekull at þe fame þ*er*of come vnto þe monast*er*ie þ*er* Saynt Austyñ was shrynyd. And þe Abbott examynd þis monke þ*er*of, & he said at it was bod a dede mans fynger at he gaff hym̃, & not Saynt Austyns. And þe Abbott & his brethir oppynd his fertir & lukid, & fand þat a fynger of his was away. & wheñ þe abbott knew þe treuth, he putt þis monke oute of his offes, & punysshid hym̃ grevuslie for þat at he had done.

XC.

Augustinus.

Wheñ Saynt Austyñ liffid, vpponñ a tyme as he satt redand oñ a buke, he was war of a fend berand a grete buke in hys armys. And Saynt Austyñ [1] adiurid hym̃, & chargid hym̃ oñ Goddis behalfe at he sulde tell hym̃ whatt was wrettyñ in þat buke. & he said þ*er* was wrettyñ mens syns. & Saynt Austyñ chargid þat [*fend*], & þ*er* war wretteñ any of his syns, þat he sulde latt hym̃ se þai*m*, at he myght rede þai*m*. & he shewid hym̃ þe buke, & he cuthe fynd nothyng þ*er* wretteñ of hym̃ selfe, bod at a tyme he had forgetteñ to say his evynsong. & he com*m*aundid þis fend þat he suld abide þ*er* still vnto he come agayñ. & he went into þe kurk, & devoutelie sayd his complyñ & divers other gude orysons &

[1] Austyñ, *omitted and added above the line.*

prayers, & þan he come agayn & chargid þis fende to latt hym se þat place agayn in þe buke. And þis fend turnyd þis buke ouer & ouer & soght it, bod he cuth not fynde nothyng bod a voyde place. And þan he was wrothe, & said vnto Saynt Austyn; "þou hase fowlie deseyvid me. Me forthynkis now at evur I shewid the my buke, for be þe vertue of þi prayer þou hase done away þi syn." And with þis he wanysschid away & was confusid.

XCI.

Ad-huc de Sancto Augustino.

We rede how on a tyme þer was a womman þat mysterd cowncell, & sho come vnto Saynt Austyn & fande hym at his studie. And sho come vnto hym & salusid hym, & he wold nowder luke on hir nor answer hur. And sho stude still & vmthoght hur, & trowid þat for his halynes he wold not behold a wommans face. And sho come ner hym and told hym hur erand, and he wolde not answer hur nor als mekle as ans move hym. And when sho saw þis, sho went away fro hym with grete sorow & hevynes. And on þe morn after, when he had said his mes & þe same womman was þer-att, after þe sacryng-tyme sho was ravisshid in hur spyritt, and sho thoght þat sho was afor þe iugement of almighti God; and þer, as sho thoght, sho saw Saynt Austyn, faste disputand of þe ioy of þe holie Trinytie. & as hur thoght, þer was a voyse at said vnto hur; "when at þou come vnto Saynt Austyn, on þis maner of wyse he was disputand of þe ioy of þe holie Trynytie; and þat he thynkys on wele enogh. Bod go now vnto hym boldlie, & þou shall fynd hym meke enogh, and he sall giff þe gude cowncell." & sho did so; & he harde hur with gude will & gaff hur his beste cowncell.

XCII.

Ad-huc de Sancto Augustino.

Som tyme þer was a man þat was ravisshid in his spiritt, & he saw many Saynttis in grete ioy; & emangis all oþer hym thoght þat he cuthe not se Saynt Austyn. And he spyrrid one of þe

Saynttis whar Saynt Austyn was, and he answerd agayn & sayd; "Saynt Austyn is in a hy place; þer he is disputand of þe ioy of þe holie Trinytie. Thus men may Se þat he is a holie Saynt."

XCIII.

Avis. Avium Vanitas siue ludus grauiter punitur.

Petrus Clunacensis[1] tellis how som tyme þer was a knyght þat was in purgatorie, whilk þat was a gude man & luffid wele for to herber pure folk; bod whils he liffid he had a grete delectacion to layke *with* fewlis; and when he was purgid in purgatorie of all his oþer synnys, þat for þis syn þer come evur vnto hym a thyng like a burde, & gretelie turment hym. *et c^9*.

XCIV.

Avis oratio est exaudita aliquando.

Cesarius tellis how som tyme þer was a burd þat was lernyd to speke. So on a tyme sho flow away in þe feldis, & þe Goshalk sewid after hur & wold hafe kyllid hur. And when sho saw hym com, as sho was lernyd at home, sho began to cry, & sayd; "*Sancte* Thoma! adiuua me! A! Saynt Thomas, helpe me!" And onone þis goshalk fell down dead, and þis burd esskapid & had none harm. Lo! surs, what vertue it is to call on Saynt Thomas, martir of Cantyrbery, in any tribulacion!

XCV.

Baptismus in forma debita debet celebrari.

The Cronycles tellis how som tyme þer was a bisshopp of Arryans[2], and on a tyme he baptisid a man þat hight Barba. And he said in þis maner of wise; "Baptizo te, Barba, in *nomine patris per* filium, in *spiritu sancto per* filium *et spiritum sanctum*," to þe purpos þat he wold shew whilk of þaim was leste. And sodanlie þe watir was away, and he þat sulde hafe bene crystend ran vnto þe kirk, & was cristend þer.

[1] MS. Climacensis.

[2] Harl. MS. *episcopus* arrianus.

XCVI.

Balliuus no*n* debet poni in officio paup*er* vel auarus.

Valerius[1]. We rede how þat when þ*er* was a varyans emang þe senaturs of Rome, whethir of ij men at was ordand þ*er*to sulde be sent for a speciall erand vnto þ*er* captan, So þai vmthoght þai*m* at þai wold aske cownceli att Sup*er*cipius[2] Affricanus, at was a lernyd man & dwelte emang þai*m*. And so þai dyd, & þai all abade of his answer. And when he saw þies ij men, of whilk þe tone sulde be sent furth þis message, he consydurd at þe tone of þai*m* was pure & covatus, & þe toder ryche & sparand & bod a chynche, [&] he sayd vnto þe senaturs in þis man*er* of wyse; "Me plesis not at nowder of þies sulde be sent þis message; ffor þe tane of þai*m* hase noght, and no man*er* of þing is enogh vnto þe toder; & þ*er*for such men sulde be no baillays, nor go no messagies."

XCVII.

Balliuor*um* freque*n*s mutacio non est vtilis.

We rede how on a tyme Tyberius Cesar askid Josephus whi he wold not change ofte his Baillays & his s*er*vandis, [&] he answerd agayn & sayd þat he wold spare þe peple; ffor baillays & s*er*vand*is* þat er long in offes hase ans enogh, & will not all-way be gad*er*hand vnto þ*er* selfe; & eu*er* þai þat er putt in of new er gredye, & gaders sam*en* vnto þ*er*selfe all þat evur þai may. "And þis," he said, "I can shew you be exsample of a man þat was wowndid & lay in þe way. And a grete multitude of fleis come vnto his wownd & satt þ*er*-on & bate hym; & he was so sore þat he myght nott remew þai*m* away. So þ*er* come a man & fand hym & had compassion on hym, and onone he drafe away þies fleis & killid þai*m* at satt vppon his wownd. And þan þe wowndid man said vnto hym on þis maner of wise; 'Thow hase done me ane ill turn, ffor þe fleis at þou hase slayn & dongen away war now fillid wit*h* my blude, & þ*er*for evur þe langer þai wold hafe bytten me þe les. Bod þe fleis þat will com vnto my wownd of new, will bite me war

[1] MS. We rede how þat Valerius, when, &c. [2] *For* Scipio.

& þai wold hafe done; & þerfor me had levur at þai had byddin styll, [*þan*] þatt other þat er hongry suld com & pryk me war þan þai did.'" et cetera.

XCVIII.

Balliuus hic iniuste iudicans alibi iudicabitur.

We rede in 'Libro de Dono Timoris,' how þat[1] on a tyme a philosophur, when he saw a thief led to be hanged with a baillay, this philosophur said; "Lo! þe gretter thieff ledis þe les thieff to hangyng." And so it happens oft sithes now-of-dayes; ffor commonlie þe lytle þieff is hanged, Bod his resettyr & his mayntynnuer is savid. et cetera.

XCIX.

Balliui frequenter munera recipiunt sed non faciunt quod promittunt.

Som tyme þer was a ballay of a grete lordshup, þat made a feste grete and costios vnto þe weddyng of a son of his. So þer was a tenand in þe lordshup, þat had a grete cauce þer in þe cowrte to be determynd befor þe Stewerd. And agayn þis baillay son sulde be wed, he come vnto þe baillay & said; "Sur, I pray you stand for me befor þe stewerd in þe courte, at I may hafe ryght, & I sall giff you a fatt cow to your son weddyng." & he tuke þe cow & sayd þat he suld. So þis mans aduersarie harde tell here-off, and he come vnto þis baillay wyfe & gaff hur a fatt ox, & besoght hur at sho wold labur vnto hur husband þat he wold answer for hym agayns his aduersarie in þe courte. And sho tuke þe cow & laburd vnto hur husband, & he promysid hur at he suld fulfill hur entent. So bothe þe parties come into þe courte afor þe Stewerd, & put furth þer cawsis, & þe baillay stude still & spak not a wurd for nowdur of þaim, vnto so mekyll at he þat gaff þe ox was like to be castyn. And þe man þat gaff hym þe ox said vnto þe baillay; "Sur, whi spekis nott þe ox?" and þe baillay

[1] MS. þan.

answerd' hym̄ agayn̄ & sayd'; "ffor suthe! þe ox may nott speke, ffor þe cow is so fayr & so gude þat sho wilł nott latt hym̄ speke."

Hec fabula valet ad quoscumque iudices, *et quod* munera peruertunt iudicium, *et quod* mulieres sepius optinent magis quam viri.

C.

Basilius.

We rede how som tyme þer was a holie hermett, þat saw þis Basilius on̄ a tyme walk in his pontificalł abbett; & he þoght dedeyn̄, & had a dispyte þeratt, & demyd in hym̄ þat he had a delectacion̄ & a pride in þis clothyng. So sodanly þer come a voyce vnto þis hermett, & sayd on̄ þis wise; "Thow hase more delectacion̄ in grapyng of þi catt tayle, þan̄ Basilius hase in his gay pontificalł clothyng." *et c⁹.*

Basilius Iuuenem a diabolo eripuit. Supra de amore. Basilius mortem Iuliani apostate procurauit. Infra de vindicta.

CI.

Basilius oracione sua mortem suam prolongari fecit.

.We rede þat when̄ Saynt Basylł was seke & drew nere vnto his deadward', he commandid' to gar feche vnto hym̄ on̄ þat hight Joseph, þat was a Iew, whome þat he had sene be reuelacion̄ at sulde be a crysten man̄. And þis Joseph was passand' connyng in grapyng of þer vaynys at war seke, and he come vnto hym̄ & felid' his[1] vaynys. And Saynt Basilł askid' hym̄ how hym̄ thoght of hym̄[2], & he answerd' agayn̄ & sayd'[2]; "Sur, þou salł dye or þe son̄ sett." And þan̄ Saynt Baslł sayd'; "what & I dye nott or to-morn̄?" And þis Jew said'; "Sur, þat may not be; for þou erte bod a dede man̄; for vnnethis wilł þi life & þi saule byde samen ane howr." Than̄ Saynt Basilł sayd vnto hym̄; "what wilł þou

[1] *After* his, fel, *erased.* [2] MS. *repeats, from* &, *to* sayd.

say & I liff vnto to-morn at vj of þe clok?" And þan þis Jew answerd agayn & said; "and þou liff, I wote wele þat I mon dye." And þan þe Saynt answerd hym agayn & said; "fforsuth þou sais suthe, for þou sall dye fro syn and liff vnto Cryste." And þe Jew answerd hym agayn & sayd; "I wote what þou says, and if þou liff so sall I do." Than þis holie man made his prayer vnto almyghtti God at his life mott be ekyd, at þat man mott be savid. So þis Jew went his wayes & come agayn on þe morn, and fand þis holie man liffand. And he fell down on his kneis and wurshuppid crystemmens Godd. And þan þis holie man, yitt als ill as he myght, rase up & went vnto þe kurk, & baptisid hym his awn handis. And when he had done, he went home agayn & layed hym down; and abowte none of þe same day he passyd vnto almighti God.

CII.

Basilius veniam *pro* pecc*at*is mulieri impet*r*auit.

We rede how þ*er* was a wom*m*an þat wrate all hur synnys in a byll; and emangi*s* all oþ*er* sho wrate a grete syn at sho had done, & þis byll sho delyverd vnto Saynt Basyll & prayed hym to pray for hur þat hur synnys myght be forgiffen hur. And he sett hym down on his kneis & made his prayers for hur. And þan he oppynd þis byll, & þis wom*m*an *with* hym, and all hur synys war away, out-take þis grete syn. And þan sho prayed hym, þat as he *with* his prayers had getten hur forgifnes of all hur od*er* synys, at he wold so pray for hur att sho mott be forgiffen of þat syn. And he bad hur go away from hym, & sayde he was a syn*n*er & mysterd forgyfnes of his syn als wele as sho did. And sho wolde nott away, bod abade still *c*riand on hym to *pray* for hyr[1]. And he bad hur go vnto Saynt Effrem, & he myght grawnt hur at sho askid. And when sho come att Saynt Effrem & told hym, he sent hur agayn vnto Saynt Basyll & bad hur go fast, at he wer nott dead or sho come. And when sho come, men was berand hym vnto his grafe. And þan sho began to cry & said; "all-myghti God deme betwix þe & me; for when þou might hafe prayed for me, þou sent me

[1] MS. hym.

vnto a noder." And sho keste þis bill vpp[on] his bere, & *with*-in a while sho tuke it agayn & opynd it, and fande all hir syn clene done away oute þeroff.

Bede *pre*sbit*er*i. Infra de *pre*dicacione. I.

CIII.

Bellu*m*. Bellare no*n* expedit sine magna causa.

We rede how þat Cesar Augustus, þat was moste noble in batayle, eu*er* denyed to take batell on hand bod if it war mor for hope of avayntage þan[1] drede of harm. For he saide þat in were a little *pro*fett myght nott make amendi*s* vnto þe grete harm þat com*m*ys of feghtyng; "ffor," as he said, "& a man fysshid *with* a huke all of gold & gatt a little fyssh, & at þe laste his huke war broken away, þe takyng of þat fyssch myght not make amendis vnto þe los þat he had of his golden huke."

CIV.

Bellantes debent e*ss*e cauti *et* exp*er*ti.

Justinus tellis how þat kyng Alexander chose not to go *with* hym in his weris yong men, nor þai*m* þat was in þe[2] flowr of þ*er* youthe[d][3], bode alde knyght[*is*] þat war wise, & had vsyd batels & cuthe gyff gude cowncell, at had bene in weris *with* his fadur. And suche men he trustid for gude knyght*is* & made þai*m* maisters of his chyvalrie. And he sayde þat in batayll a man sulde nott þink of cowardnes nor of fleyng away, bod rather of havyng victorye, and at a man suld giff no truste vnto his fete, bod vnto his wapyn þat was in his hand.

CV.

Bella procurat Diabolus frequent*er*.

We rede how on a tyme when þe grete Emp*er*our Henrie at a grete cetie held his whisson-tyde, a little befor mes, when þai sett burdis in þe hall, þ*er* began a grete fray, so þat grete blude was shed betwix þe chamberlayns of þe archbysshopp & þe Abbott-

[1] MS. þat. [2] MS. þ*er*. [3] MS. youther.

of Sulden; and all for ather of þ*aim* wold hafe sett þ*er* lord*is* sete next þe Emper*our* sete. For þe Abbott of Suldan fyndyn vnto þe emp*erour* when hym mysters, LX Ml of harnessid men. And herfor he had a privalege of old tyme grawntid, þ*at* he sulde att grete festys sytt nexte þe Emp*erour* on his right hand. So þe p*ar*tis onone war stillid & þe mes begon. And when þai war att þe laste end of þe sequens, & had songen þis vers; "hunc diem glor*iosum* fecisti"; onone all þat was in þe kurk hard a voyce say þus; "hunc diem bellicosu*m* Ego ffeci." And in confusion of þe fend, þe Emp*erour* garte begyn þe sequens agayn *with* grete deuocion; & all þe meate at was ordand for hym & his meneya, he garte dele it furth-*with* vnto pure men for Godd*is* sake. *et c*[9].

Bellare possu*n*t religiosi cum armis[1] in spe diuini auxilij, defendendo ius su*mmum*. Infra de Religioso.

Bellare nesciunt ho*min*es concordes. Infra de Concordia.

Bellant ecia*m* aliqua*n*do post mortem inimici. [[2] Infra de Odio.]

CVI.

Beneficia impensa ecia*m* bruta a*ni*m*a*lia recognoscunt.

Damianus tellis how som tyme merchandis of Venys wer opon þe se, & gretlie vexid *with* stormys, so at þai wyste neu*er* whar þai war. So att þe laste þai fand ane Ile in þe see, & þ*er* þai landid & tuke þ*aim* ffressch wat*er* & wud, & such as þ*aim* nedid. And þai cuthe fynd no creatur þ*er* bod wilde bestis. So at þe laste, as a meneya of þ*aim* went vp in a cragg to gett þ*aim* wud, þai fande how þat a dragon had taken a lyon & wold hafe devowrid hym & drawen hym into his den; and þai fell on þis dragon *with* þ*er* wapens & kyld hym, & delyverd þe lyon & lete hym go. And evur-ilk day als lang as þai lay þ*er*, þis lyon was nott vnkynd, & he broght þ*aim* owder a swyne or a schepe new slayn, a little

[1] Latin MSS., sine armis. [2] Reference from Lat. MSS.

befor none of þe day, evyn in þe skyn as he had taken itt. Lo! how frendlie ane vnresonable beste rewardid þaim þat did hym gude & savyd his lyfe. *et c*.

CVII.

Beneficia conferenda sunt Dignis.

Seneca tellis þat he þat hase benefice in giffyng sulde do as þai do at playes at þe ball; for & a man caste a ball fro hym to a noder, & he to hym agayn, No doute, of patten from þe tone of þaim it will fall vnto þe erth. Bod a gude player will vmwhile caste þe ball ferrer & vmwhile nerrer, at he at is a gude player may play *with* hym. Right so sulde it be betwix hym þat giffis þe benefis & hym þat takis it, for he þat giffis it suld se þat he þatt he gaff it to war able for to take it, & kepe it fro þe erthe; þat is to mene, þat he cuthe reule it to þe plesur of God.

Beneficia acquisita male malu*m* exitu*m* habent. Infra De Blasfemia.

Beneficia multa ecia*m* prestat deus[1] inuitis. Infra Inuitus.

CVIII.

Benedictio. Benedicendus est cibus *et* potus antequam sumatur.

We rede how þat þer was som tyme a holie mayden in a monasterie of virgyns. And on a day as sho went into hur garthyn, sho saw ane herbe þat is callid letes, and sho desyrid to eate þeron gretelie; & sho tuke þerof & blissid it nott & ete þer-on, for sho forgatt at bliss it. And onone sho was taken *with* a fend & fell down; and þer come vnto hur a holie man þat hyght Equirius, & purseyvid þat a fend was in hur, & commandid hym to go oute of hur. And þan þis fend cryed & said; "Allas! whatt hafe I done? I satt opon þe letes, & sho come & tuke me vp & bate me." & vnnethis for all þis holie mans comm*a*ndment, wald he go oute of hur. *et c*.

[1] MS. *here repeats*, eciam.

CIX.

Benedicti Abbatis.

Saynt Gregur tellis how on a tyme opon passh day *þer* was a gude holie preste, & ordand hym bettyr meate in wurshup of þe day. And our Lorde apperid vnto hym & sayd; "Thow ordans delicious meattis for þi selfe, & my *ser*vand Benett, in such a place, suffres grete honger." And onone þis *pre*ste rase & tuke meatt *with* hym & soght hym. And at þe laste *with* grete labur & sekyng he fand hym, & sayd vnto hym; "Ryse, & lat vs take vs meate & drynke to-gedur, ffor þis day hafe I broght þe meatt, and it is passch day." And he ansswerd agayn & sayd, "I knaw wele þat þis day is passch day, ffor cauce att þou erte com*men*." And he had bene so lang oute of mans felaschup þat he had clene forgetten what day att passh day was. Than þis *pre*ste said vnto hym; "ffor suthe þis day is þe solempnitie of þe resurreccion of our Lord, and *þer*for as þis day it acordis nott for þe to lyff in abstinens; ffor I was sent vnto the and bedyn bryng þe meatt." And þan þai bothe thankid almyghti God & sayd *þer* prayers, & tuke þai*m* meat to-gedur in wurshup of þe resurrecion of our Lord. *et c*[9].

CX.

Bene*d*ictus Diabolu*m* expulit a iuuene.

We rede how som tyme *þer* was a monk þat hight Gregorie, and in no wise he myght nott lang abyde att dyvyne *ser*ves, nor at his *pra*yers, bod evur when his other brether sayd *þer* prayers or *þer* serves, onone he went furth and made hym to do som other labur. So on a tyme his Abbott, Saynt Benett, was war of a lytle blak boy led hym oute be þe shurte of his clothis. So on a day when he went furth, & þis lurdan led hym oute, þan Saynt Benett strake þis yong monk *with* a wand & bad hym go in agayn, & abide in his *pra*yers as his other brethir did. & so for ferd of þis strake of Saynt Benett, þis fende at was in a blak boy lyknes durst nevur after com & feche hym furthe. *et c*[9].

CXI.

Benedictus sp*iritu*m elacionis a iuuene expulit.

Saynt Gregur tellis þat on ane evynyng when þis holie man was at his supper, þ*er* stude befor hym a yong gentylman þat come of a hy kynrid, & helde þe candyll. So þis yong man was prowde, & þoght scorn þ*a*t he sulde hold þe candyll, & sayd *with*-in hym selfe on þis man*er* of wyse; "what is he þis at syttis att supper & I holde candell vnto and duse such s*er*ves? what am I þat I sulde seryff hym þis?" and þan þis holie man sayd vnto hym; "Bruther, Cros & mark þi harte! what is þat att þou spekis vnto þi selfe?" and he callid one of his brethir & com*m*anddid hym to take þe candill fro hym & halde it, & com*m*awndid hym to go vnto hys chambre & take his reste. & þis yong man was so asshamyd þat he knew his thoght, þat neu*er* after he was prowde nor thoght disdeingne to done hym s*er*ves. *et c*[9].

CXII.

Barnardus.

We rede how on a tyme as Saynt Barnard was p*re*chand, and all þat was aboute hym lythed hym *with* gude deuocion, þ*er* entred into his harte suche a temptacion þat, as hym thoght, rownyd vnto hym & sayde; "Behalde, & se now how wele þou p*re*chis, & how gladlie þatt þe pepull heris þe, & how wyse and wyttie þou erte callid in þi p*re*chyng!" And þis holie man, felyng hym selfe styrrid *with* þis temptacion, tarid a while in his s*er*mon, and or he passyd any forther or made ane ende, he began to wax hevy & pensie for þis thoght. And onone he was comfurthid þurgh þe helpe of allmyghti God. And p*r*ivalie he answerd vnto þis temptacion in þis man*er* of wise; "þou fals temptacion! be the I began nott, nor be the I sall nott end." And þan he procedid in his s*er*mon & made a gude ende. And onone þis temptacion recedid away, and he had it nevur after.

CXIII.

Ad-huc de S*ancto* Barnardo.

We rede on a tyme þat as Saynt Barnard rade in þe contrey, hym happend to be harbard at a gude husband howse. And when þai had suppid, þis husband sayd vnto hym; "Sur, what aylis you at ye forsake þe labur þat is in þis werld & gase vnto religion? for in your p*ra*yers ye may hafe als gude a thoght here as þ*er*." So Saynt Ba*r*nard tellid hym many cawsis, & at þe laste he thoght he wold ou*er*com hym, & sayd; "Go a little from vs, & say þi pat*er* nost*er* w*ith* all þe entente & gude deuocion at þou can, & if þow end it & þinke of no noder þing or þou hase done, I sall giff þe my hors; & beheste me be þe faythe of þi bodie, þat & þou thynk of any other þing, at þou sall tell me." And þis husband was glad & grawntid here-to, trowyng to wyn þis hors, & went a litle asyde, & baldlie went in hand w*ith* his pat*er* nost*er* & sayde it. & when he wa[*s*] skantlie at þe myddest þ*er*of, a besy thoght smate in his harte, & þat was þis; þat & he wan þe hors, whethur he sulde hafe þe sadle & þe brydill w*ith* hym or noght. And þis done, w*ith* grete contricion he went vnto Saynt Barnard agayn, and told hym what þoght come in his mynde in þis p*ra*yer-saying: and þus he had not þe hors. & fro thens furthe, he had nevur p*re*su*m*pcion in his mynde of his p*ra*yers-saying w*ith*-oute temptacion neu*er* after.

CXIV.

Ad-huc de S*ancto* Barnardo.

On a tyme as Saynt Barnard come into Normundie, a wom*man* come vnto hym & tolde hym þ*a*t þe space of vj yere sho was gretlie tempid w*ith* a fend to fall vnto lichorie, eu*er* when sho was in hur bed. And ay it bad hur at sho sulde nott tell Saynt Barnard þ*er*off. And Saynt Barnard gaff hur his staff, & bad hur þ*at*, when sho went to bed, sho sulde lay itt in hur bedd by hur; and sho did so. & onone he come, bod he myght not com nere þe bedd. And þan he thred hur, & said þat when Saynt Barnard was gone he sulde venge hym opon hur. & on þe morn sho went vnto Saynt Barnard & told hym; & he garte call samen all þe peple vnto þe kurk, and commawndid þat ilk man sulde hafe a candyll byrnand in his hand. And with all þase candels he cursid þis fend & entirditid hym, & [1] commawndid þat he sulde neuer fro thens furth com att þis womman agayn. And þus sho was delyverd fro all þis illusion of þe fende.

CXV.

Blasfemia in deum grauiter punitur.

Som tyme þer was a man þat had a son of xv yere age, whilk þat he luffyd passandlie wele, & broght hym vp tenderlie. And þis childe had in condicion þat when any thyng displesid hym, onone he wolde blasfeme þe name of God. So þe pestelence come & tuke it, so þat it burd dye. & when he had þe spottys þe fadur held hym vp in his armys; and þis childe saw wykkid spirittis com vnto hym-ward & said; "helpe fadur!" And when his fadur saw hym quake for drede, he askid hym what at he saw; & he ansswerd agayn & said, þat ill men come vnto hym & wolde take hym; & he began to blasfeme almyghti God, & with þatt he swelte.

Blasfemus per oracionem eciam post mortem ad penitenciam reuocatur. Infra de Oracione. ij.

CXVI.

Blasfemus visibiliter a deo punitur.

Damianus tellis how þat in Burgundie þer was a proude clerk & a covatus. So hym happend, be power at was gyffen vnto hym, to take wranguslie vnto hym selfe þe kurk of Saynt Maurys. So on a tyme as he hard mes, in þe end of þe gospell he hard þis clauce red; "Qui se humiliat exaltabitur, et qui se exaltat humiliabitur," [&] þis wrichid clerk made a skorn þerat & sayd þat it was fals. For he said, & he had mekid hym unto hys enmys, he had not

[1] MS. gaff a commawndid.

had þe riches & þe prophett of þat kurk. And furth-*with* a levynnyng like a swerd went in at þe mouthe of hym þat spak, as he was spekand, & onone it killyd hym. *et c9.*

CXVII.

Aliqu*ando* blasfemus corporalit*er* punitur.

Damianus tellis þat at Bolayn ij frendis at wer gossops satt to-gedur sam*en* at meate at a feste; and þai war servid of a boylid cokk. & þe tone tuke his knyfe & kutt it in sonder in pecis; & he putt þ*er*on peper & musterd. And when he had done, þe toder sayd vnto hym; "Gossop, þou hase broken þis cokk so þat, & Saynt Petur wolde nevur so, it myght nevur com sam*en* agayn." And the tod*er* ansswerd hym agayn & sayd; "Not now, & Saynt Petir, bod also & *Cr*iste hym selfe wold comm*a*wnd, þis Cokk sulde nevur ryse." And onone as he had sayd, þis cokk starte vpp *with* his fedurs on, & clappid sam*en* hys wengis & krew; & þai mot se clefe in his fedurs all þe liquor at was putt on hym. & *with* þe sprenclyng of his wengis, þe pep*er* & þe sauce light vppon bathe thies gosseps, & *with* þat þai wer streken *with* a lepre whilk held þai*m* vnto þ*er* lyvis end, & made ane end of þai*m*.

CXVIII.

Blasfemus aliqua*n*do statim vita p*r*ivatur.

Cesarius tellis how on a tyme ij men played at þe dyce, and when þe tane of þai*m* began to lose, he began to wax wrathe *with* þe toder & speke grete wurdis, & rauie & flite *with* God for þat he wan nott. And þe tod*er*, when he hard hym flite *with* God & speke grete wurdis, flate *with* hym agayn & bad hym hold his tong; & he wold not, bod evur when he loste, blasfemyd owder God or our Ladie. So as þai satt threpand þus, þai*m* þoght þai hard a voyce aboue þai*m* þat sayd; "I hafe suffred hedur-toward iniurie & wrong to be done vnto my selfe, bod I will nor may not suffre no langer þe iniurie & wrong done vnto my moder." And onone he þis att laste, as he lenyd opon þe tabels, was sodanlie

strekyn *with* a wown þat all men myght se, & bafid att his mouthe & swelte.

Bos totus vno die ab uno com*m*estus est. Infra de com*m*estione.

Bubo aliqu*ando* est signu*m* eventuu*m* futuror*um*. Sup*ra* de augurrio.

CXIX.

Bupho. Mirabilis fabula de Buphone.

Cesarius tellis how som tyme in þe Dioces of Colayn, a man þat hyght Theodoricus hurte a tade, & when he had hurte hur sho stude vp ayeyns hym on hur hynderfete; & he waxed wrate þ*er*wi*th*, & tuke ane yrn & slew hur. Bod, att is m*er*valus to tell, sho gatt life agayn, & in a purpos to venge hur, sho persewid aft*er* hym; & ans or twyce eu*er* wi*th* a spade he smate hur in sonder. At þe laste he burnyd hur, & it p*ro*fettid hym no thyng; to so mekull þat, for ferde of hur, he durste not slepe in no place apon þe erthe, vnto so mekull þ*at* on nyghtis he garte hyng his bed att a hy balke. So on a day hym happend ryde on huntyng & a felow wi*th* hym, & he sett spell on ende & tolde hym all þe cace. Sodanlie he lukid behynd hym, & þis tade was clymmand in his hors tayle & walde fayn hafe bene att hym, and he began to cry. And his felow sayde; "Be war! for þe devull is in þi hors tayle, & wold be up att þe." & he lightyd & slew itt. A noder tyme as he satt at ale emang felowshup, he was war of þis tade syttand on a poste in þe syde of a wall, and onone as he saw hur he cryed & sayde; "lo! surs! yonder is a fend þat I mon nevur be delyvurd of or he venge hym on me." And onone be cowncell, he nakend þe tane of his legis & lete þe tade com vnto it, & sho gatt hym be þe leg & bate hym; & when sho had done, he putt hur of wi*th* hys hand. And he tuke a rasur, & all þe bitt at sho had byttyn, he cutt it oute & keste it from hym; & onone þis pece bolnyd m*er*valoslie als grete as a fute-ball & breste; & þus he was delyverd. *et c*[9].

Canonicus. Canonici debent deuote dicere officiu*m* diuinu*m*. Infra de Cl*er*ico.

Canonicus ad altare pure *et* mu*n*de debet ministrare. Inf*ra* de co*n*t*r*icione.

Canonicus amore mulieris qua*n*doq*ue* decipit*ur*. Inf*ra* de cont*r*icione.

Canonico possu*n*t adaptari multa[1] que dicuntur inf*ra* de cl*er*ico.

Canis. Canes aliqui su*n*t fortissimi. Inf*ra* de fortitudi*ne*.

Canis. Canes dilig*unt* d*omi*nos suos. Infra de dileccione.

CXX.

Cantus p*ro*p*r*ius multos decipit q*ui* credunt ben*e* cantare *et* pessime ac vilissime cantant.

Jacobus de Vet*r*iaco tellis how þat þ*er* was a preste þ*at* trowid' he was a passand' gude synger, not-wi*th*-stondyng he was not so. So on̄ a day þ*er* was a gentyl-wom*m*an̄ þ*at* satt behynd' hym̄ & hard' hym̄ syng, & sho began̄ to wepe; and he, trowyng þ*at* sho wepid' for swettnes of his voyse, began̄ to syng lowder þan̄ he did' tofor̄; & ay þe hyer sho hard hym̄ syng, þe faster wepud sho. Than̄ þis p*re*ste askid' hur whi sho wepud' so as sho did', and sho answerd' hym̄ agayn̄ & sayd'; "Sur, I am̄ a pure gentill-wom*m*an̄, & þe laste day I had no calfe bod one; & þe wulfe come & had it away fro me; and evur when̄ þat I here you syng, onone I remembre me how þ*at* my calfe & ye c*r*ied like." And when̄ þe preste hard' þis, onone he thoght shame, & remembred hym̄ þ*at* þat þing at he thoght was grete lovyng vnto God', was vnto Hym̄ grete shame and velany; & fro thens furth̄ he sang nevur so lowde. *et c*⁹

[1] MS. adaptari multi multa.

CXXI.

Cantando multi vana*m* gl*or*iam appetu*n*t et ideo aliquando a deo puniuntur.

Cesarius tellis how som̄ tyme þ*er* was a monk at þe Mownte of Cassian̄, þat had a passand swete voyce. So on̄ þe pascħ evyn̄, when̄ he suld' blis þe candyƚƚ of þe pascaƚƚ, he sang it in̄ a moste swete voyce, to so mekuƚƚ þat ilk bodie þat hard' hym̄ þoght his voyce was a dulcett melodye. & onone as þe pascaƚƚ was blissid', sodanlie it was away, and' his prior and his brethir trowid' þat it was so taken̄ away sodanlie becauce of his pride & his elacion̄ *et c⁹*.

CXXII.

Cantus clamosos[1] Deus parum̄ reputat et demon approbat[2].

Cesarius tellis how on̄ a tyme, when̄ clerkis wer syngand' & makand a grete noyse, a religious man̄ was war of a fend' syttand' in a hy place in þe kurk, holdand' opyn̄ a grete sekk in his left hand'. And with his right hand' he putt þe voyces of þai*m* at sang into his sekk. So when̄ þai had done þ*er* sang, þai made a grete lawde þ*er*of & a grete com*m*endacion̄. & he þ*at* saw þe vysion̄ answerd' & sayd'; "fforsuthe ye sang wele, bod ye fillid' a tome sekk evyn̄ fuƚƚ *with* your sang." And þai had grete m*er*veƚƚ þ*er*-off, and spyrrid' hym̄ what he ment, & he told' þai*m* aƚƚ what at he saw, & how. *et c⁹*.

CXXIII.

Cantoris spec*ie*m[3] diabolus aliquando sum*i*t.

Cesarius tellis of a clark þat som tyme had a swete voyce, to so mekuƚƚ þat men̄ at hard' hym̄ syng þoght þat it was a grete delite to here hym̄. So on̄ a day a religious man̄ happend' to here hym̄ harpe, and onone as he harde hym̄ he sayd' in þis man*er* of wyse; "This voyce & þis melodie is not of a man̄ bod, rather of þe devuƚƚ."

[1] MS. clamosus. [2] MS. approbatt. [3] *After* speciem, dui, *erased.*

And all men m*er*vayld of þis at he said, & evyn furthw*ith* he co[*n*]iuryd hym; & þe fend onone went his way, & lefte þe bodie as a dead, dry caryon; & so þai mott wit at it was a dry caryon.

CXXIV.

Cantare vel ecia*m* scrib*ere*, vel eciam referre aliqua crimina scurilia, uel inhonesta carmina, non expedit. *et c*.

Valerius tellis of one þat was a passand famos poett, þ*at* hight Aurilegus[1]; and for cauce of his oppynyons, þe contre at he dwelte in da*m*nyd his bukys & exilde hym selfe, and all be-cauce at his bukys spakk of vnclennes of liffyng & of gest*is* & enchawntement*is*. þ*er*for þai wold nott suffer hym abide emang*is* þai*m*, at his bukis suld not be ensample to ill vnto þ*er* contre afterward when he was dead.

Cantare aliqu*ando* expedit nouas historias s*anctorum*. Inf*ra* de deuoc*ione*. vj.

CXXV.

Cantanda est letania contra tribulaciones.

Joh*annes* Damacenus tellis how on a tyme, att þe cetie of Constantynople, þ*er* was t*r*ibulacion, & peple went aboute þe kurk in þ*er* prayers to pray God to sese itt; [&] a childe sodanlie emang þe peple was taken vp vnto hevyn, & þ*er* he was taght þe sang of þe latenye. And sodanlie he was sett agayn emang þe peple & began þe letany hym selfe, & told þe clerk*is* how þai sulde syng after hym. & So þai did; and þis done onone þe t*r*ibulacion cesyd.

CXXVI.

Cantus humilis cu*m* cordis deuocione plus placet deo q*ua*m voces in celu*m* arrogant*er* eleuare.

Cesarius tellis how on a tyme in þe Ceustus ordur, when þe psalm was begon in a medull voyce, & all þe monkis felowd aft*er*

[1] Lat. MSS. Archilegus.

in þe same voyce, a prowde yong monke began at sett it vp abown þaim iij notis; and þuf all þe old monkis resistid hym, yit som þat was on his syde fell in tone vnto hym and helpyd hym, and so he requorid. & þe old monkis, for disclander of Goddis serves, lete hym alone; and onone þer was sene com oute att his mouthe a fend in lykkenes of a byrnyng yrn, & went evur fro man to man þat helpyd hym, & burnyd þaim.

Captiuitas. Captiui aliquando miraculose liberantur. Infra de Maria. ij.

Carcer. Carceratos soluit beata virgo. Infra de odio. j.

Caritatiue *et* non arroganter debet frater accusari. Infra de inuidia. ij.

Caritate deficiente eciam *et* alia deficiunt. Infra de hospitalitate. iij.

Caritate vrgente interdum soluitur ieiunium. Infra de hospitalitate.

CXXVII.

Caro. Carnis eciam temptacione Sancti quandoque vexantur.

Heraclides tellis, in 'Libro Paradisi,' how on a tyme a holie monk þat hight Helyas, þat was a virtuos man & had grete petie & mercye of wommen, had vndernethe his gouernance in a monasterie CCC wommen. And when he had contynued in þis occupacion ij yere, and was bod of xxx[ti] or xl[ti] yere age, sodanlie he was attempyd with his flessh, and onone as he felid þis, he went oute of his monasterie ij dayes in-to wyldernes, & made hys prayer in þis maner of wyse; "Diuine deus meus, *et* c[9]. Lord, I beseke þe owder to remefe þis temptacion from me, or els sla me!" So at evyn sodanlie he fell opon a slepe, & hym thoght þer come vnto hym iij angels þat sayd; "Why went þou furth oute of þe monasterie of þies wommen?" And he answerd & said, for he was ferd þat owder he sulde noy þaim, or þai hym. And þai sayd þai suld delyver hym of þis drede, and bad hym go home & take charge of þaim agayn. And he grawntyd þerto & made þaim ane athe at he sulde do so. And þai layd hym down, & one of þaim held his handis & a-noder his fete, & þe thrid with a rasur cutt away bothe his balok-stonys, not at it was done, bod as hym thoght it was done; and þan þai askyd hym if he was any better, & if he was any bettyr þan he was befor. And he answerd agayn & sayd; "I vnderstand þat a hevie burdyn is taken fro me, and þerfor I trow þat I am delyverd of þat at I was full ferd for." And with-in v dayes he went agayn in-to his monasterie, & liffid þerin afterward xl[ti] yere. And as holie fadurs says, fro thens forward such a thoght come nevur after in his mynde.

Carnales cogitaciones a sanctis beneficia dei auferunt. infra de predicacione. iij.

Carnalis cogitacio accepta a sanctis demones letificat. Infra de cruce. ij.

Carnalem temptacionem demon frequenter procurat. Supra de Sancto Andrea et eciam vbi agitur de Sancta cruce. ij.

Caro mouetur ad modicum tactum mulieris quemque. Infra de Sancto leone.

CXXVIII.

Carnale peccatum committere sanctos procurat demon[1].

We rede of olde Thebens[2] þat was a preste son of þe old law, & on a day as he saw his fadur sacrefie vnto þe ydolsis & fals goddis, he was war of þe devull & all his chyvalrie standand by; and hym þoght at þe devull was sett in chayre, and all þis felaschup

[1] Lat. MSS. Carnale peccatum committere sanctos prius curat demon. Eng. MS. committere plus sanctos, etc.
[2] Latin MSS. Senex Thebensis.

come afor hym & made þ*er* acom*m*pti*s* of þ*er* wykked temptacions. And one come & sayd, þat wit*h*-in þat xxx^{ti} dayes he had made many men ilk one to sla oþ*er*; and a noder sayd þ*at* wit*h*-in xx^{ti} dayes he had drownyd many men in þe see; and þe thrid said þat he had bene at a weddyng, & þ*er* he had made ilk one to sla other. And when þai had said, he com*m*anddid ilk one of þai*m* to be betyn, fore becauce þai had occupyd so lang tyme & done so litle labur. So at þe laste þ*er* come one & sayd þat he had bene besye xl^{ty} [*yere*] [1] to stir a monke þat was in wyldernes vnto syn, & vnnethis þat same nyght he had stird hym to do fornycacion. And þan þe grete devull rase oute of þe chayre & kissyd hym & sett his crown on his heade, & sayde þat he was wurthi lovyng, & to be sett in þe chayr, for he had done a grete cure.

Carnali temptacione mediante diabolus viru*m* vel mulierem i*n*duc*it* ad negandu*m* deu*m*. Sup*ra* de amicicia. ij.

CXXIX.

Carne*m* com*m*ouens diabolus *eciam* in sa*nct*is pe*r* formam mulieris, inducit eos in desp*er*acionem.

We rede how som tyme þ*er* was a monke þat was of a grete abstinence & lay in a den, & full of v*er*tues & gude liffyng. So on a tyme, be temptacion, he tuke a p*re*sum*p*cion & þoght his [2] holines come more of hym selfe þan of God; [*and*] þe devull on ane evynyng fenyd hym selfe in lyknes of a wom*m*an goand wyll in þe wyldernes, and come vnto his den dure, & callid & said sho was a wery wom*m*an & had gane will, & sett hur down on hur kneis & besoght hym to hafe m*er*cie on hur. And, "Sur," scho said, "it is now nere nyght, & I beseke þe lat me lig to to-morn in a hyrn of þi den, att wylde bestis sla me not and eate me." And he had com*p*assion on hur & graw[*n*]tid hur. And þan sho went in & tolde hym þe cauce of hur gate will. And wit*h* hur fayr speche

[1] Latin MSS. *per* xl annos.

[2] MS. *repeats* his.

& hur swete wurdis, sho smate his harte in-to a luste & a lykyng, & sho made hym̄ such cownttenans & flaghter, þat it luste lenyd vnto hur ay mar & mare. So þis monke was so attempyd *with* hur, þat he rase & tuke hur in his armys & hawsid hur, & þoght to hafe done his luste & his lykyng *with* hur; & sho began to giff a huge cry & ane vglie, & slippid oute of his handis. And þan he hard a grete multitude of fendis in þe ayr, þat sayde; "O! þou monk, at was so extollid in hevyn, how depe now þou erte drownyd in hell! Vmthynke þe how he þatt heightens hym̄ selfe mon be lawuyd." And þan þis monk fell into a despayr, & was nere-hand evyn wude, & gaff hym̄ selfe vnto all vnclennes & syn, & eft*er*ward dyed in wykkid lyffyng. *et c⁹*.

CXXX.

Carnales motus su*n*t p*er* affliccione*m* corporis rep*ri*mendi.

We rede in 'Vitis P*atrum*' how þ*er* was a c*er*tayn wom*ma*n þat made beheste vnto yong men þat sho was felowshuppid *with*, þat sho sulde gett oute ane old holie man oute of his cell. And sho come vnto his cell & fenyd hur ane erand, & he lete hur in; & onone he was strekyn *with* a co*n*cupiscens to syn *with* hur; and onone as he felid þis, he made a fyre & burnyd þe fyngers of bothe his handys, at þai smertid so at it putt away all his temptacion. And þis wom*ma*n layde hur down in a noke of his cell & slepyd, & in hur slepyng sho dyed. And on þe morn þies yong men come vnto hym̄, and þis olde man sayd vnto þaim̄; "will ye se how þis childe & doghter of þe devull hase burnyd my fyngers? and lo! whar sho lyes slepand!" And þai went vnto hur & wold hafe wakend hur, & þai fande hur dead. And þan þis old man made his prayers vnto almiȝttie God, & raysyd hur fro deade vnto life, & bad hur be a[1] gude wom*ma*n, & temp no mor no men.

Carnales motus dom*ina*ndi su*n*t disciplinis et ieiunijs.
Inf*ra* de temptacione.

[1] MS. as.

Carnalis temptacio aliqu*ando* extinguitur or*ati*onib*us* sa*n*c*torum*. Sup*ra* de Agnete.

CXXXI.

Carnis temptacio rep*ri*menda est eciam in senib*us*.

Heraclides tellis of hym̄ selfe & sais þus; "when̄ on̄ a tyme I was gretelie tempyd' *with* temptacion̄ of my flessħ, I went vnto a man̄ þat hight Pachonius, þ*at* dwelte in wyldernes a solitarie, and tolde hym̄ my dissese, whilk at I durste not for shame tell att hame vnto Euag*er*us, þat was my maist*er*. And he answerd' me in þis man*er* of wyse, & sayd'; 'Be it not vnto þe a new thyng at þ*ou* suffers, ffor I hafe bene þis xl^ti yere in my p*r*ayers, & liffid' in my cell ane old' man̄ as þou may see, & evur restreynyd' me from̄ þat temptacion̄; and now þis laste xij yere, þat temptacion̄ fell opon̄ me & wolde neu*er* away fro mee; and þan̄ I thoght att I was destitute of þe helpe of allmyghti Godd', & þoght þat me had levur dy þan̄ for to concent vnto syn̄. And I nakynd' me & went furtħ of my cell & layid' me befor a wylde beste, & wold' hafe bene devowrid' & slayn̄; & sho come & lykkid me from my hede vnto my fete, & went hur way. þan̄ I vmthoght mee þat God wold' spare mee, & I turnyd agayn̄ vnto my cell; and þan̄ *with*-in a while aft*er*, þe devull *tra*nsfygurd' into liknes of a fayre damysell þat I had' sene befor, & com̄ vnto me & sat down̄ on̄ hur kneis afor me, & stirrid' and' movid me so, at I had nere-hand' desyrid' to hafe had at do *with* hur. So at þe laste I vmthoght me & I wex wrathe *with* hur, & gaff hur a grete strake *with* my right hande; & onone sho vanysshid' away. And þan̄ I went vnto wyldernes, & þ*er* I fande a s*er*pent, & I tuke it vp̄ in my hand' & fretid itt, & put it vnto my membres, to th'entente þat I mot be p*er*ysched' *with* þe bytyng þ*er*off. And sho wolde nothyng bite me. And þan̄ I hard' a voyce at sayd' vnto me; 'Go hame & *with*stand' þi temptacion̄, ffor almiȝti God hase sufferd' þe to be tempid' becauce at þou sulde know þine infirmyte & þi frelenes, and at þou sulde beseke God for to helpe þe.' And þan̄ I went home vnto my cell, & contynowid' in[1]

[1] MS. *repeats*, in.

my prayers, & bade in a faste belefe þat þurgh þe helpe of allmyghtie God I mott *with*-stond temptacion; & so I thank God I hafe done hedur-toward.'"

CXXXII.

Carnis temptacion*em*[1] reprimu*n*t fetor *et* horror mulieris mortue.

We rede in 'Vitis P*atrum*' how þ*er* was a bruther þat gretelie was turment *with* mynd of a wom*m*an þat he saw som tyme. So on a tyme a nod*er* bruther of his come & tolde hym at sho was dead; and on þe nyght aft*er* he come þ*er*, he hard tell sho was berid, & he grufe down vnto hur & beheld þe fayr clothe at sho was wappid in, and he tuke hur vp & had hur vnto his cell. And a litle while aft*er* sho began to stynke, and he tuke hur oute & sayd, when he lukid on hur; "Lo, flessh! now þou hase desyre, ffyll now þi luste on hur!" And on þis man*er* of wise he chastid hym selfe many day, vnto hym ill temptacion went away from hym.

Carnales motus p*er* lesione*m* corp*or*is qu*andoque* su*n*t rep*ri*mendi. Inf*ra* de castitate. v.

CXXXIII.

Carnales motus in se corp*oraliter* extinxisse nemo debet gloriari.

We rede of a man þat hight Paphencius, how on a tyme he liffid so straytlie many yeris, so þat he trowid he was delyverd fro flesshlie concupiscens, & vnto so mekull þat he was so strang in his selfe, þat he mott *with*stond any temptacion of þe devull. So on a tyme he had burnyd his hand ill, & his brethir come & made a medcyn & layd þ*er*-vnto; and he made grete sorow & was passand hevie þat be instigacion of þe devull his hand was burnyd; and aft*er* þis hevynes he fell on slepe, and ane angell aperid vnto hym

[1] MS. tempacioni.

& sayd; "Whi erte þou hevie, sen þou may not suffer a little burnyng of erdlie fyre, & kepis in þi selfe a movyng of a flesslie luste? Go & take a naked fayr mayden & se hur ons, & if þou fele þi harte for to be in tranquillite & reste, Than þou may wele wete þat þou may, *with*-oute grete hurte, suffre a little burnyng of fyre." *et* ꝯ.

CXXXIV.

Castitas. Castitate*m* mittit deus illam indigentib*us* [1].

Gregorius Nazarenus tellis, when he duelie kepid hym in chastitie & was bod a yong man, & lernyd philosophi att Athenys, he saw in a dreme, as hym thoght he saw syttand by hym redand ij fayr wom*men*, one on his right side & a noder on his lefte syde. And hym[2] þoght he[3] durst not for brekyng of his chastite behold þa*im*, nor he durst not aske þa*im* whyne þai come nor what þai wold. And þai beheld hym & sayd; "yong man! be not hevie, for þou knowis vs wele enogh; ffor þe tone of vs is wisdom & þe toder is chastite, and we erte sent hedur to dwell *with* þe; ffor þou hase ordand for vs in þi hard harte a ioyfull habitacle & a merie."

CXXXV.

Castitas in vxore est multu*m* laudabilis.

Jeronimus tellis how þ*er* was som tyme[4] a noble man þat hight Duellus, & he was ane alde man & a wayke of bodie, & he wed a maydyn þat hight Yliana. So on a tyme his neghburs & he fell at debate, & ane of þa*im* vpbrayed hym & sayd his ande stynkyd, & his mouthe, & said his yong wife was ill warid on hym. And he was displesid þ*er*-*with* & went hame. And onone as his wife saw his cowtenans, sho askid hym whi he was so hevie; and he blamyd hur & said he was wrothe *with* hur becauce sho wold neu*er* sen þai wer wed tell hym at his ande stynkid; for, he said, & sho had tellid hym he suld hafe done som medcyn þ*er*for

[1] Latin MSS. *have* diligentib*us*. [2] MS. me. [3] *Under* he, I, *erased*.
[4] MS. *inserts*, man, *here*.

to distroy itt. And sho said; "Sur, I sulde hafe done so, bod all oder mens and duse so as yours duse." *et c*9.

Castitatis violatores ecia*m* aves puniunt. Sup*ra* de adult*er*io.

Castitatis amore vita corp*or*alis contempnitur. Inf*ra* de virginitate. I.

Castitatis amore p*r*op*r*ia pat*r*ia relinquenda est. Inf*ra* de Clemente. iij.

CXXXVI.

Castitatis amore eciam membra corporis contempnu*n*tur.

Jacobus de Vet*r*iaco tellis[1] how som tyme þ*er* was a myghti prince þat was fowndur of a nonrie þat stude nere-hand hym; & he covett gretelie a fayr non of þe place, to hafe hur vnto his lemman. & notw*ith*stondyng, nowder be prayer nor be gyfte he cuthe ou*er*com hur; & at þe laste he tuke hur away be strang hand. And when men come to take hur away, sho was passand ferd, & askid þai*m* whi þai tuke hur oute of hur abbay more þan hur other sisters. And þai answerd hur agayn & sayd, becauce sho had so fayr een. And onone as sho hard þis sho was fayn, & sho garte putt oute hur een onone, & layd þai*m* in a dissh, & broght þai*m* vnto þai*m* & sayd; "Lo! here is þe ene at your maist*er* desiris, & bid hym lat me alone, & lose nowd*er* his sawle nor myne." And þai went vnto hym þ*er*w*ith* & told hym, & he lete hur alone; & be þis mene sho kepid hur chastite. & w*ith*-in iij yere aft*er* sho had hur een agayn als wele as evur had scho, þurgh grace of God.

CXXXVII.

Castitatis exemplo *et* amore totu*m* corpus aliqu*ando* exponitur in p*er*ic*u*lo.

We rede how on a tyme, when þe cetie of Leodone*ns*[2] was wastid be þe Brabans, many wom*m*en & maydens & od*er*, for luff of

[1] Tellis, *repeated and erased.*

[2] Latin MSS. Leodiens*is* ciuitas.

chastite put þ*aim* in grete perell of þ*er* bodis. So as one of þ*aim*, to safe hur chastite, putt hur in grete perell of þe watir, ij of hur enmys come vnto hur in a bote, & drew hur into þ*er* shipp, to þe entent at þai wold devowre hur maydenhede. And sho had levur hafe gane agayn into þe watir & hafe bene drownyd, þan at þai had defowlid hur. And sho lepe oute of þe shipp into þe watir, and *with* strenthe of hur lowpyng þe bote drownyd, & þase ij men war bathe drownyd; and sho be þe grace of allmyghti God was savid, & come hole & sownde vnto þe land. *et c*°.

Castitatis amore p*ul*c*r*itudo debet abscondi. S*upra* de abscond*ere et* inf*ra* de pulc*r*itu*dine*.

Castu*m* pueru*m* Maria virgo sibi desponsat. Inf*ra* Marie genit*r*icis dei.

Casta*m* reginam Maria virgo delib*era*t. Infra Marie genet*r*icis dei.

Castus homo ecia*m* int*er* m*e*ret*r*ices castitate*m* s*er*uare debet. Inf*r*a de m*e*ret*r*ice *et* iuv*ene*. ij.

Castitate*m* sua*m* s*er*uare volens mulier int*er*du*m* includi debet, *et* viris non apparere. Sup*r*a de Assenech.

CXXXVIII.

Castitatem viri p*er*icli*ta*ri faciunt tempus, locus, *et* mulier alliciens.

Saynt Jerom tellis in þe 'Legent of Saynt [*Paul*[1]] þe H*er*mett,' how Decius, at som tyme was Emp*erour*, tuke a yong chr*isten*-man & garte lay hym in a softe bed, whar þ*er* was temp*er*ans of þe ayr & sownd of watir rynyng, & syngyng of burdis, and gude smell of flowris, & he garte bynd hym þ*er* so *with* rapis, þat he myght nowder stur hand nor fute, nor helpe hym selfe. So as he lay, þ*er* come vnto hym a yong wenche & a fayre, bod scho was not clene of hur bodie, & laid hur done be þis yong man & made hym dalyans. And when he felid at sho had movid his flessh vnto

[1] So in the Latin MSS.

syn & he mot not helpe hym selfe, nor no mau*er* of wapyn had to fend hym *with* fro hur, he bate in sonder his tong & spitt it in hur face. And *with* þe wark þ*er*of his temptacion recedid away. *et c*.

CXXXIX.

Cautela. Cautela bona frequent*er* est necessaria.

Valerius tellis how ij men þat was sam*en* at hoste *with* a wom*m*an þat held hostre, lefte on a tyme *with* hur a grete sowme of money, vnd*er*nethe þis condicion, at sho suld not delyver it bod if þai bothe come vnto hur sam*en* þ*er*for. So *with*-in a little while aft*er*, þe tane come þ*er*for, & sayid his felow was dead, & begylid hur & made hur to delyvur hym þe mony; and he went þ*er**with* our se into a noder contre. And onone fro he was gone, þe toder come vnto hur & askid hur þis money, and sho ansswerd agayn & sayd sho was redie to giff þis money, bod sho wold not delyver it or he & his felow bothe sam*en* come þ*er*for, as þai had bothe bedyn hur do; & þus sho excusid hur.

Cautela fraudulenta rep*re*hensibilis est. Sup*ra* de aduocatis.

CXL.

Cecus aliqu*ando* audacius p*er*transit[1] malu*m* passu*m* q*u*am videns.

We rede in 'Libro de Dono Timoris,' how þ*er* was a blynd man þat had a boy þat led hym be þe way; & þai come on a tyme vnto a strayte place whar þ*er* was not bod a little bryg & a strayte, & þis boy durste not lede hym ou*er* itt, & stude still & told hym. And þe blinde man bad hym go ou*er* it baldlie, and þe boy sayd he durste not; & he gatt þe boy in his nekk & bad hym poynt

[1] MS. *repeats here,* aliqu*ando*.

þe way with his staff, & he suld felow it; & he did so. & þis blynd man went ou*er* þe bryg baldlie be tellyng of þe lityll boy.

Cecu*m* esse corporalit*er* aliqu*an*do p*r*odest a*n*i*m*e.
Infra de paciencia.
Cecus ecia*m* inuitus illuminatur a deo. Inf*r*a Invitus.

CXLI.

Celandu*m* est secretu*m*.

Macrobius[1] tellis how þ*er* was a nobyll captayn in Rome þat hight Papirius; & when he was a childe *with* his fadur, on a day he went *with* hym vnto the cowrte, and when he come home his moder askid hym what at þe senaturs & þe wyse men of Rome said at þ*er* cowrte & þ*er* p*ar*lement. And he answerd hur & sayd þat it was not lawfull to tell, for he þat tellid it mond be dead þ*er*for. And sho tuke a wand & bett hym, and he saw þat hym burd nedes tell hur somwhat, & he fenyd in þis man*er* of wyse & sayd, þ*er* all þe cowncell att þe senaturs had at do at þ*er* p*ar*lement was for to witt whedur it was more necessarie þat a man sulde hafe ij wyvis, or a wom*m*an ij husbandis. And sho went & told it vnto hur com*m*edurs, & tellid þai*m* all þe town our, so þat on þe morn aft*er*, wurd come þ*er*-of vnto þe senaturs þat þe cowncell of þ*er* p*ar*lement shulde be dis-curid be þis little childe; & þai garte feche hym aforn þai*m*, & spyrrid hym what þat was at he had tellid his moder, & he tolde þai*m*[2] all þe p*ro*ces. And þan þe senaturs ordand þat fro thens furth no childe, bod alonelie he, sulde com into þ*er* p*ar*lement *with* his fadur, for perell of tellyng of þ*er* cowncell; & afterward hym happend be þe wyseste man in all Rome.

CXLII.

Celari debent defectus amicoru*m*.

Ruffinus tellis þat on a tyme when þe Emp*er*our Constantyne went into a place whar þ*er* was gaderd many brethyr same*n* at

[1] MS. Mocrobius. [2] MS. *repeats*, þaim.

a cowncell, he fand at þai had emang þai*m* many debatis & stryvis; and he tuke of þai*m* a byll of all þ*er* debatis & þ*er* stryvis, & putt it in his bosom, & when he come home he burnyd it, at neu*er* man suld se it after, as *pre*stis sulde do *with* confession. And afterwerd he sayd, when þai askid hym whi he had done so, in þis maner of wise; "Si vidissem sac*er*dotem vel aliqu*em* eor*um* q*ui* monachali hab*i*tu su*n*t amicti, et c[9]. And I saw a *pre*ste or a monke doyng syn, rather I suld hide hym *with* my mantyll, þan disclander hym." *et* c[9].

CXLIII.

Cibus. Cibarior*um* sup*er*fluitas semp*er* est ab om*n*ib*us* vitanda.

Saynt Jerom tellis of a philosophur þat hight Epicurus, þat, if all he was a sewer of voluptuosite, at he mott sett his felicite þ*er*in, neu*er*-þe-les he fillid his bukis & said, þat appyls & oþ*er* vile meatis sulde be vsid; þat[1] other metis sulde not hafe mor payn in inquiryng þan luste in abusyng. For he sayd we mott nott all-way giff hede vnto wisdom, if we thoght all-way of habundans of our meate.

CXLIV.

Cibus mod*er*atus *et* vniformis causat sanitat*em* *et* pulc*r*itudi*n*em corp*or*alem.

Helynandus tellis how on a tyme a bisshopp askid a yong man of Religion, how it happend þat he was haler & fayrer in his closter þan he was when he was in þe werld. And he answerd agayn & sayd; "For here I liff well & clenlie; ffor as for þe furste, here I hafe my heall, and as for þe secund, I am here fayr, & so I mott not do in þe werld; for þ*er* I liffid in fylthe, & so I did not here." þan þe besshopp askid hym whatt at he had etyn þat day, and he ansswerd agayn & said, "enogh." And þe bisshopp sayd he askid

[1] Latin MSS. eo q*uod* exquisite ep*u*le maiore*m* pena*m* h*abe*ant inquirendo, q*ua*m voluptate*m* in abutendo.

hym̄ not of quantite, bod of qualitie; "bod what ete þou yisterday, & what to[1]-day?" And he answerd agayn̄ & said; "yisterday I ete cale and pes, & to-day I eete pes & cale, & to-morn̄ I mon̄ eate pess *with* cale, & *after* to-morn̄ I mon̄ eate cale *with* pease." & þus be a fayr circumstans he broght aboute his sentans, so þat he mot shew at acordyng diett makis a man̄ both fayr & hale of his bodie. *et c⁹.*

Cibo eodem vtentes non semper equaliter meliorantur in corpore. *Supra* de apostatis. ij.

Cibum sumere sine benediccione non est bonum. *Supra* de benediccione.

CXLV.

Cibo spirituali sustentatur corpus aliquando sine corporali.

Jacobus de Vetriaco tellis, þat þe appetite of meate was so wastid in Saynt Marie of Oginiez[2], þat a grete while scho mott vnnethis take any meatte; so þat som tyme be viij dayes, & som tyme be x dayes, sho ete neuer meate. & yit it was a grete mervayle, for, for all þis, nowder warkid hur hevud, nor sho lefte not þe labur of hur handis, & sho was als strang to labur on̄ þe laste day as sho was on̄ þe furste; and if sho wold hafe etyn̄ þase dayes, sho myght nott, vnto[3] þe sensualitie þat come of hur spiritt come vnto þe selfe agayn̄. And som tyme when̄ sho was be hur selfe, som̄ tyme be xxx^{ti} dayes, sho wolde neuer ete meate. And many dayes sho wold neuer speke wurd bod þis alone; "I wull resayfe my sacrament." & daylie sho reseyvid it in privatie. And when̄ v wowkis was done, þan̄ scho oppynd hur muthe & spakk & reseyvid bodelie meatt. *et c⁹.*

Ciconia adulterium abhominatur *et* punit illud. *Supra* de adulterio. iij.

[1] MS. do. [2] MS. Ogimiem.

[3] Harl. MS. donec sensualitas que a *spiritu* quasi absorta fuerat ad se ipsam rediret.

CXLVI.

Cineres. Cine*r*es sacri deuote su*n*t recipiendi.

Cesarius tellis how þ*er* was in a cetie ij meñ, & þai satt at myrth & at ale oñ fastyngang[9] evyñ vnto mydnyght in a taverñ; & in þe mornyng þai war so [1] thristie at þai went thedur agayñ, & sett þai*m* at þe ale vnto þai rang to mes. And wheñ þai saw gude meñ wend vnto þe kurk, one of þai*m* sayd vnto þe toder; "Now hafe we abydyñ our lang. Go we vnto þe kurk & take our ass." And þe toder answerd hym agayñ in skorñ, & sayde; "Sitt still, & I sall giff þe ass." And he tuke vp ass & kest opoñ his hede, & he oñ his. And furth-wit*h* þai war punyshid for þ*er* scorñ, ffor þai felid so mekull duste, bathe aboute þ*er* hedis & þ*er* facis, as it had bene blawñ opoñ þai*m* wit*h* a payr of belows. And wheñ þai felid þis, þai begañ to cry; and wheñ þai oppynd þ*er* mouthe, so mekill ass went in-to þ*er* throtis, at þai war nerehand werid. And þai wer ledd into dyvers placis whar þ*er* was no duste, as into medows & in garthyns & in selers, bod it p*ro*fettid nothyng at þai myght defend þai*m* fro þis duste of ass at was abowte þ*er* hedis, to, att þe laste, þai war bothe whirkenid þ*er*-wit*h* & deyid: & þat had þai for þ*er* skornyng.

CXLVII.

Clementis.

We rede how þat Matidiana, þat was moder of Saynt Clemett, was a [2] passand fayr womma*n*, & hur husband broþ*er* fell amoros of hur, & laburd hur hugelie; & sho wulde neu*er* consent vnto hym for to cauce hym & his bruther, hur husbond, to be at debate. And sho vmthoght hur þat sho wolde go oute of þe contre a while, and sho fenyd a dreme & told hur husband at þ*er* was a voyce at come vnto hur in hur slepe, & bad hur go furth of þe cetie wit*h* hur ij sonnys, Faustus & Faustinus, vnto tyme itt callid hur agayñ, and els sho & bothe hur sonnys mond be perysshid & distroyed. And wheñ hur husband hard þis, he had grete me*r*vayle þeroff,

[1] MS. *repeats*, so. [2] MS. *repeats*, n.

& he sent his wyfe & hir ij sons, & a parte of his meneya *with* þaim, vnto Athenys, and held Clemett at home *with* hym, þat was bod v yere olde. And as þai war sayland be þe se, þ*er* shup brakk, and þis moder loste hur sonnys & went þai had bene drown; & yit sho gatt to land & clam vp on a cragg. And þ*er* scho dwelt a grete while *with* a wom*man* þat had þe p*ar*lesie. So þis Matidiana handis fell benombe for sorow of hur husband & hur chuldre, so þat sho mot nothyng welde hur handis; so þat þai wer evyn as deade & at sho had no felyng of þaim. And afterward hur husband sent vnto Athenas, & hard no tithandis nor wurd of his wyfe nor of his childer. & he putt Clemett in a gude mans gou*er*nans, & gatt hym a ship & went to seke his wyfe and his childre, & so he contenyd xx yere. And in þe mene while, þis Clemett drew vnto Saynt Petur, and told hym what was happend vnto his fadur & his moder. So on a tyme Petur & Clemett vnto-come þ*er* þis Matidiana begid hur meatt. And Saynt Petur askid hur whi sho beggid & wolde nat wyrk for hur meate, & sho ansswerd agayn & sayd, þat hur handis was[1] benombe & scho mott not welde þa*im*, & teld hym all þe p*ro*ces how it had happend *with* hur husband & hur & hur childre. And þan Petur said vnto hur; "as for Clemett þi son, I can shew þe hym." And when sho hard þat sho swonyd & fell down vnto þe grownd; & Petur tuke hur vp be þe hand & led hur vnto Clemett. And when Clemett saw his maist*er* Petir ledand a wom*man* be þe hand, he began to smyle; and onone as þis wom*man* come vnto Clemett, sho hawsid hym in hur armys, & kissid hym & fell down in swone; & he putt hur from hym & trowed sho had bene wude, and made hym passand wrathe *with* Petur. And þan Saynt Petur said; "what duse þou, son Clemett? Putt not þi moder away fro the." And when Clemett hard þis, he wepud, & tuke vp his moder, & fell evyn down vnto þe erth hym selfe for fayn; & att þe laste he tuke knowlege vnto his moder. And in þe mene whlie Aquila & Niceta, þat war becom*men* þe discipuls of Petur, wer not þ*er* p*re*sent, and when þai saw hur þai spurrid faste what sho was, and Clemett told þa*im* how at sho was his moder; and Saynt

[1] *After* was, v, *erased.*

Petur tellid þaim all þe proces. & þan þai tuke a knowlege vnto hur & sayd, "fforsuth we ij [1] er Faustus & Fa tinianus, & þis is our muder, & Clemet is our brother." & þai kyssid sam*en* *with* grete wepyng & Ioy. And *with*-in a while aft*er* þ*aim* happend þe grace of God to fynd þ*er* fadur; and þus all þ*er* sorow turn in-to myrthe & Ioy.

CXLVIII.

Clericus *ratione* status sui h*ab*uit plura p*r*ivilegia [2].

We rede how þat a poett, þat hight Valerius, wulde neu*er* ryse vnto Iulius Cesar when he come in-to þe company of poett*is*, as it had bene a man þ*at* had nott kend his magestie; and he did it all becauce he trustid hym selfe was moste hye in *compary*-ton of studie & lernyng. And he askid hym whi he wuld not ryse vnto hym, & he said he wold nott for þ*er* was no place of temp*or*altie nor of feghtyng in armur, bod all of turnyng of bukys & volums.

CXLIX.

Clerici non debent te*r*rena appetere, sed virtute*m* *et* honestate*m*.

We rede of Pyocinus [3] þe filosophur, when he was ordand to make enornement*is* of vertues, (so þat at he taght, he suld not shew þe [4] exsample of oþ*er* men bod rather be exsample of hym selfe), becauce he mot sitt still in ryst & pease, he chose hym vnto a quiete place, wher he sulde here no noyse of no creatur; & þ*er* he hedid all man*er* of þing how God ordand þ*aim*. And *with*-in a while fro he had bene þ*er*, he had in contempte all man*er* of wurshup & said þ*er* was no trew wurshup bod conn*y*ng; ffor þat, he said, was most delicious, þe whilk att mans witt cuthe ymagyn off trewthe in a mans saule. *et* c.

Clericis necessaria est facundia. Infra de facundia.
Clerici aliqu*ando* false infamantur. Inf*r*a de infamia. i° *et* ij°.

[1] *After* ij, fa, *erased*.
[2] MS. privaleg'a.
[3] MS. Arundel, Protin*us*.
[4] MS. þe.

Clerici incontinentes vix in fine continent. Infra de con*tr*icione.

Clerici filiab*us* iudeor*um* se com*m*iscent. Inf*ra* de cont*r*icione. iiij.

Clerici qui de sacra scriptura legunt, opere debent adimplere. Inf*ra* de Sciencia, primo.

Clerici debent in scripturis diligent*er* studere. Inf*ra* de studio.

Clerici ecia*m* int*er* meretrices castitatem seruare debent, *et* ad hoc faciend*um* alios induc*ere*. Inf*ra* de muliere meret*r*ice.

CL.

Clerici in eccl*es*ia deuote debent dicere officiu*m* diuinu*m*.

Jacobus de Vet*ri*aco tellis how on a tyme a holie man, as he was in the quere, he was war of þe devull & a hevie sakk [1] evyn full on his bakk. & þis holie man chargid hym to charge hym att tell hym whatt he bare in þat sekk at was so hevy. & he answerd agayn & sayd; "here in þis sakk er silappis & wurdis þat er ou*er*hippid, & also versis of þe salter & wurdis er mombled þat þir prestis & þies clerkis hase stolne in þis matyn-while." & þan þis holie man askid hym what he hight, and he said þat he hight Titiuillus. And hereof þis holie man made ij vers & sayd; "Fragmina v*er*bor*um* Titiuillus colligit hor*um*, Et fert [2] ad for*um* quo p*re*mia reddat [3] eor*um*." *et* c*9*.

CLI.

Clerici no*n* debent studere in uanis.

Jacobus de Vet*ri*aco tellis how on a tyme at Parissh, it happend þat a scoler, when he was dead, apperid vnto his maister cled all in p*ar*chemyn writyn, wit*h* smale letters wretten þeron. And

[1] MS sall. [2] MS. ferte. [3] MS. reddit.

emang all oþer questions his maister askid hym what bement þat garment att was so light, & þe letters att was wretyn þervppon. And he answerd agayn & sayd; "ilkone of þies letters er hevyer vnto me þan war þe weght of þis grete kurk & I bare it on my nek"; and shewid hym þe kurk of Saynt German at was þer, & sayd; "þies er sophyms & subtelties, whare-in I wastis all my dayes, & I may not tell what hete at I am turment *with* all my dayes vnder-nethe þis cape. Bod & þou will hold furth þi hand, I sall shew þe be a dropp." And he putt furth his hand, and þer fell þer-opon as it had bene bod a dropp of swete. And it was so hate at it thirlid his hand þu[*r*]gh as it had bene þe sharpe schote of ane arow. And onone þis maister as he saw þis, he lefte þe logykk skule, & made hym a monk of Ceustus ordur. And he made þies ij versis & sayd; "linquo coax ranis, cra corvis, vanaque vanis; Ad logicam pergo que mortis non timet ergo." And he become a gude man; & als long as he liffid þer was a hole þurgh his hand. *et c*.

Clerici aliqu*ando* carnali amore mulier*um* decipiuntur. Inf*ra* de cont*r*icione.

Clerici in sacris ordinib*us* positi mu*n*do corde *et* corpore debent ministrare. Inf*ra* de Contricione. iiij.

Cogitaciones varie occurru*n*t orantib*us*. Sup*ra* Barnardi. ij.

Cogitacionib*us* frequent*er* immiscet se sup*er*bia vt bona op*er*a p*er*dat, sed p*ro*pt*er* hoc non sunt dim*i*ttenda. Sup*ra* Barnardi. i.

CLII.

Cogitacionibus malis impeditur aliquis ne *orati*ones facte p*ro* se ab aliquo exaudiantur.

We rede in '*Vitis Patrum*,' how þer was a man þat was gretlie tempid *with* temptacion of his flessh: and he luked vnto a gude ald man & lete hym wete þ*er*of, & p*r*ayed hym to pray for hym; and so he did. & when he had long prayed for hym he mendid no þing, & þis olde man m*er*veld gretlie at his prayer was not hard. So on a nyght as he lay in his prayers, he saw in a vision þis yong man sittant, & evull spyrittis in lyknes of wom*m*en playand befor hym, & makand hym grete myrth; and he saw þis yong mans gude angell[1] grete wroth becauce he wold nott ryse & make his prayer vnto almighti God. And þan þis olde man sayd vnto þis yong man; "Bruther! þe fawte is þine þ*at* þe prayers þat er prayed for þe er nott harde. For þou hase a delectacion in evull thoghtis, and it is impossible to remofe ill thoghts fro the w*ith* other mens prayers, bod if þou doo som labur þ*er*in þi selfe. For it is w*ith* the as it is w*ith* a man þat is seke; ffor & a man þat is seke will nott abstene hym fro guttus meatis, what p*ro*fettis it to do vnto hym any cure of lechecrafte?"

CLIII.

Cogitaciones ex toto nemo fugere possit.

We rede how on a tyme a c*er*tayn man of religion made playnt vnto a holie abbott þatt hight Pastor, þat he had so many thoghtis of syn in his mynde þat he was like to be perisshid þ*er*w*ith*. And he had þis monke in-to a playn felde vppon a fayr day, whar þe wynde blew, & he bad hym hald obrade his skyrte & take þe wynde & bere it hame. And he answerd agayn & said he myght nott. And þan þe abbott said; "No more may þou lett þoghtis to com in þi harte & þi mynde, bod itt is þy parte to with-stond þai*m*." *et c*[9].

Cogitacio de diu*er*sis contristat vel letificat ho*mi*nem, vnu*m* reddit pallidu*m*, aliu*m* rubicundu*m*. S*upr*a de apostata. ij.

[1] MS. ans, *with* g *written over the* s, *to make* angell.

CLIV.

Cogitacio de morte multum est vtilis.

We rede ex '*Dictis Patrum*,' how a yong man sayd on a tyme vnto ane old man; "what sall I do? for I am like to be slayn with fowle þoghtis." And þis ald man answerd hym agayn & said; "Son, a womman when sho will spane hur child, sho will enoynt hur pappis with bitter þing, att hur childe, when he wolde sowke, sulde lett when he felid bytternes. And þerfor putt in þi thoght þe bitternes of dede, & of þe paynys þat er ordand in hell & in purgatorie for syn in tyme to com, and onone þies evill þoghtis sall recede away fro the." *et c^9*.

Cogitacio faciens comparacionem de delicijs presentibus ad supplicia eterna multum est vtilis. infra de delicijs. ij.

Cogitacio miserie proprie *et* nature defectibilis retrahit hominem a malo. Infra de contemptu sui.

Cogitacio purgatorij vel inferni inducit hominem ad penitenciam. Infra de penitencia. iiij.

CLV.

Cogitacio perpetuitatis penarum inferni aliquando conuertit hominem.

Jacobus de Vetriaco tellis how þer was som tyme a seculer man þat was passand delicate. So on a tyme he vmthoght hym in his mynde, ffurst, if a thowsand of dampnyd sawlis myght be delyverd fro payn, and his thoght answerd hym & sayd, "nay." þan if a hondreth Mᵗ mott be delyuerd, & his thoght said, "nay." þan if a thowsand thowsand myght be delyverd, & his thoght said, "nay"; and þan if als many thowsand mot be delyverd as þer was droppis of watir in þe see, & euer it said, "nay." And as he was in þies thoghtis he was gretlie trubled & waxid ferd. So sodanlie he vmthoght hym & said vnto hym self þat þai þat giffes þer luff vnto þis werld war passand blynd & fonde, þat for a little tyme att þai mon liff þ*er*in, for þe transitorie delites and vanyties þ*er*off, fallis in-to eu*er*lastand dampnacion & payn of hell.

CLVI.

Cogitacio finis in om*n*ib*us* ope*r*ib*us* est multu*m* necessaria.

We rede in 'Libro de Dono Timoris,' how on a tyme þ*er* was a yong man þatt went vnto a fayre; and when he had walkid abowte, & sene many shappis & mekull chafir to sell, at þe laste he come vnto a shop þ*er* ane old man [st]ude; & he had as who say no thyng to sell. And þis yong man askid hym what at he had [1] to sell. And þis alde man answerd & sayd he had to sell wisdom; and þis yong man sayd þat he wolde by itt, and askid hym whatt he sulde pay þ*er*for. And he said, "a hondreth mark." And þe toder þoght itt mekull, nott-withstondyng he payed hym itt. And when it was payed, þis olde man taght hym þis wysdom & said; "In om*n*i ope*r*e cogita *pr*imo ad qu*em* finem venire potes, vn*de* *versus*; 'Quicquid agas ope*r*is finem *pr*imo mediteris.' þat is to say, in all þi werkis, evur at þe begynyng vmthynk þe whatt will com of þe endyng." And when þis yong man hard þis, hym forthoght hys bargan & traystid þat he had bene deseyvid. Than þis olde man said; "Go þi wais home! and forgett nott þis at I tolde þe, bod write itt in þi howse ou*er* þi hallyng, & in þi wyndows, & on þi duris, & on þi vessell, & in oþ*er* dyvers places in þi howse; & þou shall fynd att it sall be þe best chafir at evur þou boght." And he wente home & did so. And emang all oþ*er* he garte browde þis reson opon a clothe þat he was vsid to be shavyn wi*th*. So on a tyme þis yong man had enmys þat come vnto a barbur att vsid to shafe hym, & hyrid hym for a grete som of money to sla hym when he shufe hym; & he tuke þ*er* money & grawntid þat he sulde do so. And when þis barbur come to shafe þis gude man, as he was in wetyng of hym he lukid vpon þe raster clathe; & he was somwhatt letterd & red þis reson. And onone as he had red it, he vmbythoght hym what ende wald com of þis

[1] MS. *repeats*, hym what he had.

treson & he did itt. & he said vnto hym selfe þus; "and I sla þis man I mon be slayn þerfor." And he began to wax faynt & hevie & swownyd. And onone as þis gude man saw hym fare so, he steppid vnto hym & lifted hym vp on his fete, and comfurthed hym & askid hym whatt hym aylid. And he prayed hym to hold hym excusid & be not wrothe & he sulde tell hym, & he essurid vnto hym þat he suld not be wrothe. And þan þis barbur sett þe spell on end & tolde hym all þe dede. & he forgaff hym & bad a noder man shafe hym. And þan he thankid God & þe wisdom þat he boght, for þus he fand þat it savid þ*er* lifes bothe. *et c*[9].

CLVII.

Colu*m*ba. Colu*m*bar*um* nutricio non placet Deo.

Cesarius tellis how som tyme þ*er* was a knight þat luffid wele to bryng vp & brede dowvis in his place in his chaw[*m*]ber-endis, & in dyvers oþ*er* places. And his curatt tolde hym þat it was grete syn vnto hym for to kepe so many of þai*m* to-gedur, for als mekull as þai hurte & wastid his neghburs cornys. So on a day he tuke a skuttylfull of corn & callid þai*m* to-gedur & gaff þai*m* meate. And when þai wer all to-gedur befor hym, he spak vnto þai*m* wi*th* a clere voyce þat all men myght here, and sayde on þis man*er* of wyse; "Ye dowvis! If it be Goddis will att ye bide wi*th* me, dwell still, or els I com*m*awnd you in Goddis name at ye rise vp, & flee away faste." And att þis wurde, onone all þies dowvis rase vpp, & flow clene away in a grete flokk. And neu*er* after fro thens furth þai come agayn vnto his place. *et c*[9].

Columba sac*er*doti indigno sacr*amentum* aufert. Inf*r*a de sac*er*dote indigno.

Comes a de*m*one iniquo viuus portatur in infernu*m*. Inf*r*a de demone. vj.

Comiti *possunt* adaptari multa que dicu*n*tur inf*r*a de p*r*incipe *et* Iudice.

Comitissa p*r*opt*er* ornatu*m* vestiu*m* dampnatur. Inf*r*a de ornatu. I.

CLVIII.

Com*m*endacio vel com*m*essio. Com*m*endare vel com*mitt*ere se diabulo nimis periculosum est.

Helinandus[1] tellis how on̄ a tyme þe archedekyn̄ of Aurilianens suld go vnto Rome. And he *pra*yed a chanon̄ of his to graunt hym̄ a clerk of his to go *with* hym̄, þat hight Nathanael, þat was a trew *ser*vand vnto hym̄; for hym̄ þoght at he was necessarie vnto hym̄ in his iorney. And þis clerk, þuf all it was agayns his will, went *with* hym̄, & he made hym̄ his purs-maister. Soo when̄ þai come nere Rome, þis Archdekyn̄ was bod a chynche, & he askid þis clerk a rekkenyn̄ & a compte of þ*er* expensis straytlie vnto þe leste halpeny. And þ*er* þai fell vnto rekenyng & varid; & þis clerk betuke hym̄[2] selfe vnto þe devull, als witterlie as evur he was in fonte-stone, bod it was as he sayde. So þai went on̄ flytand. And as þai went owr at a brygg our a grete watir, þis clerk happend to fall by þe brygg & was drownyd. And he had made a cou*n*and befor *with* þis Chanon̄ þ*at* was his maist*er*, þat whethur of þai*m* dyed furste, *with*-in xxx[ti] dayes, & he myght, suld com̄ vnto his felow, & hide no thyng bod tell hym̄ clerelie how it stude *with* hym̄. So on̄ þe nyght afterward, as þis chanon̄ lay in his bed wakand, & a byrnand lampe befor hym̄, þis Nathanaell clerk stude befor hym̄, cled as hym̄ thoght all in a fayre cape made of feddurs. And þis chanon̄ was nothyng aferd of hym̄, bod was well apayed of his com*m*yng, and said vnto hym̄; "Nathanael! welcom̄ home! Is nott þe archedekyn̄ com*m*en̄?" and he ansswerd agayn̄ & sayd; "Nay, sur, bod I am̄ com*m*en̄ as I made cou*n*and *with* you þ*at* I suld do; and I am̄ now dead & I *pra*y you to helpe me, for I am̄ in grete turmentt*is*." And he askid hym̄ whi, sen̄ he liffid so honestlie & so trewlie as he did. And he sayd agayn̄; "Sur, forsuthe it sulde hafe bene wele *with* me, bod þis day I was sodanlie grevid, & betaght my selfe vnto þe devull: and I *pra*y you warn̄ als many as ye may, at þai do neu*er* so as I did, ffor þai þat will com*m*end þ*er* selfe vnto þe devull, þai giff hym̄ power of þai*m*; & so did I

[1] MS. Belmandus. [2] MS. *repeats*, hym̄.

þis day, & þ*er*for I was drownyd, & for no noþ*er* þing am I in payn." And þan þis chanon askyd hym, sen þat he was in payn, how it was þat he had on so fayr a cape. And he answerd agayn & sayd; "Sur, þis cape is hevyer vnto me þan war þe gretteste towr in all þis werld & it wer on my bakk. And þe fayrnes þ*er*of is a belefe of forgifnes þat I hafe, if at I be trewlie p*r*ayed for." And þan þis chanon hyght hym þat at hys power he sulde pray for hym. And w*ith* þat he vanysshid away; & he hard neu*er* more on hym.

CLIX.

Com*m*estio. Comedit aliqu*ando* vnus plus q*u*am plures.

Solinus tellis how som tyme þ*er* was a strang knyght, a man like a grete giand, and he was a grete weryor & alway had þe victorie whar-evur he faght. So on a tyme as he was in batall, he was passand hongrie, & he gatt in hys armys ane ox, and bare it a-way ane acre lenthe; & w*ith* his neve he slew it & made meatt þ*er*of, and ete it vp att ons all be his one. And it grevid hym at þat tyme no þing; bod w*ith*-in a little while aftre, he þat had victory of all oþ*er* men in batell, þurght his awn folie deyed away.

Comedens cibos no*n* licitos punitur. Inf*r*a de gula. ij.

Comedere pluries in die p*r*opt*er* hospites caritas est. Inf*r*a de hospit*alitat*e. ij.

CLX.

Com*m*unio. Communicare[1] freque*nter* volentes no*n* su*nt* p*ro*hibendi.

Cesarius tellis how þat in þe dioces of Leodonens[2], in a town þat hight Chorenbar[3], was þ*er* a wom*m*en þat desirid greatlie oft sithis

[1] MS. comminicare.
[2] Latin MSS. Leodiensis.
[3] Harl. MS. Corebam. Arund. MS. Chor*en*bar.

to be howseld. So on a night, as sho lay on a cowche sayand hur prayers, almiȝti God come in-to hur chawmer, & bare in his handis þe box at þe sac*r*ament was in in þe kirk, and þ*er* come aungels *with* hym, syngand þis sang; "speciosus forma *pro* filijs ho*minum et c*9." And he stude befor hur & said; "Becauce þe p*re*ste denyed to giff þe my bodie, I sall howsell þe myne awn handis." & he did so, & tuke ane hoste oute of þe box & gaff hur, & went his wayis. And þ*er* was in þe same chawmber a noder religious wom*m*an þat saw all þis, and on þe morn sho went vnto þe preste, and askid of hym how many hostis war in þe sacrament-box in þe kurk; and he saide þat wiste he wele enogh. & he oppynd þe[1] box & luked & fand þat one was away; & yit all was lokkid as þai war wunte to be; & þan he had grete m*er*vayle, & wepud & made mekill sorow, and had grete m*er*[*v*]ell how þis mott happen. And þan þis wom*m*an comfurthid hym & told hym all þat evur sho saw, & whar þe hoste was becom*m*en, & cownceld hym þat fro thens furth he sulde nevur gruche to giff þai*m* þe howsyll þat askyd itt, & it war nevur so ofte. *et c*9.

Com*m*unione nemo debet p*r*ivari qui *secund*um consciencia*m* sua*m* est sufficient*er* confessus, *et* ad satisfaciend*um* paratus. Infra de Iusticia.

CLXI.

Communica*n*ti[2] no*n* est administranda hostia no*n* consecrata.

Cesarius tellis how þat Maister Maurice, þat was bisshopp of P*a*rissh, on a tyme was vexid *with* so grete a seknes in his head, þat it strake in-to his brayn, & tuke away his witt & his mynde from hym. So at þe laste he come vnto hym selfe, & axkyd to be howseld; & þai þat wer abowte was ferd at he had bene fallen in-to a wudenes; & þai cownceld þe preste to feche ane hoste þat was vnsacred & giff hym; and so he did. And onone as he come wit*h*-in þe thresshwold of þe dure, þis bisshopp cryed

[1] *After* þe, buke, *erased.* [2] MS. Comminicanti.

with a clere voyce & sayde; "hafe it away! hafe it away! for þat is not[1] my Lorde." And all þat was abowte hym had grete wonder here-off; and þan þe *preste* wente agayn & broght *with* hym þe *verray* sacrament. And þis bisshopp *with* grete devocion reseyvid it, þurgh vertue of þe whilk he come agayn vnto his right mynde. And so he in full faythe & charitie passid vnto Godd.

CLXII.

Com*m*unio[2] famem corporalem repellit.

Som tyme þ*er* was a wom*m*an þ*at* þe lefe of hur curatt was euerilk Sonday[3] howseld, and þat day aft*er* sho tuke no bodelie meatt; and yitt sho was nothyng hongrie. And onone as hur curatt purseyvid þis, he went vnto þe bisshop & told hym; & he bad hym take ane hoste þat was vnsacred & gyff hur; and so he dyd. & þis wom*m*an purseyvid it noght, bod tuke it *with* gude deuocion & went home; & onone as sho come home, sho was so hungred, þat, as sho thoght, had sho nott titter getten hur meatt sho sulde hafe dyed furth-with. Yit not*with*stondyng sho ran agayn vnto þe *preste*, & trowed þis honger had bene com*m*en on hur for hur syn*n*ys, and *with* grete wepyng how þat was taken fro hur þat God had giffen sho told hym. And when he hard þis he was greatlie reioysyd þ*er*off, & þankyd God, & went *with* hur vnto þe kurk & gaff hyr þe *verray* sacrament. And þurgh þe vertue hereoff all hur hungre was swagid, & þis grace þat was *with*drawen from hur was giffen hur agayn: and onone as þe bisshopp hard þis he þankid almighti God þ*er*off.

CLXIII.

Com*m*unio ecia*m* fortitudi*n*em corporalem confert.

Som tyme þ*er* was a wurthi knyght whilk þat did many eniuries vnto Lowis þat was Erle of Losens, & to his men. So on a tyme þis erle *com*plen*y*d hym of þis knyght vnto his frendis. So on of þai*m* was a wurthi man & sayd; "I dar vnd*er*take þat I sall take hym, & I may be sekur þat none of you sall do hym no bodely

[1] Not, *omitted and added above the line.*

[2] MS. Comminio.

[3] *Under* Sonday, day, *erased.*

harm̄." And þe erle & all̄ made hym̄ surans; and þis worthi man̄ gatt þis knyght and delyverd̄ hym̄ vnto þe erle. And þe erle, in savyng of his athe, garte make a depe graffe; & he tuke þis knyght & wappid̄ hym̄ in softe clothis & layd̄ hym̄ þ*er*in, & garte caste erthe on̄ hym̄, & so smorid̄ hym̄ to dead̄. And þe frendis of þis knyght co*m*plenyd̄ of þis wurthi man̄ vnto þe Emp*er*our̄ Frederike, & said̄ þat he for a grete som̄ of money had taken̄ þis knyght & solde hym̄ vnto þe Erle. And þe Emp*er*our garte call̄ hym̄ before hym̄, & wolde hafe garte putt hym̄ to deade herefor̄, and he cuthe not be excusyd̄ for nothyng att he cuthe say. And þan̄ at þe laste he knew þ*at* hym̄ selfe was nott giltie as þai sayd̄, and oblissid̄ hym̄ to profe þatt as right & law wolde; & þ*er* he was demyd̄ to feght þ*er*for̄. And so a day was sett, & his enmys gatt a strang knyght to feght wit*h* hym̄. And on̄ þe day att þai sulde feght vppon̄, þis wurshupfull̄ man̄ shrafe hym̄, & wit*h* gude deuocio*n* reseyvid̄ hys sacrament & went boldlie into þe place þ*er* þai sulde feght; & his enmy come in manlelie agayns hym̄. And onone as þai mett, þis man̄ att was hyrid̄, þat all̄ men hard̄, asked̄ hym̄ if he had etyn̄ oght þat day. And þis wurthi man̄ answerd̄ agayn̄ & sayd̄; "ya, I hafe reseyvid̄ & ete þis day þe bodie of almighti God̄." And þis other lurdan̄ answerd̄ hym̄ agayn̄ & sayd̄; "fforsuthe, & þou had̄ eatyn̄ þe devull̄ þis day, I sall̄ feght wit*h* þe & ou*er*thraw þe." And evyn̄ furthwit*h* after þis wurde of blasfemyng, almiȝti God tuke his strenth̄ from̄ hym̄ & strenthid̄ þis other wurthi man̄ so, þat his enmy þat was hyrid̄ agayns hym̄ had no more strenth̄, nor myght no more stand̄ to feght wit*h* hym̄ þan̄ he had bene a childe, vnto so mekull̄ he gaff our̄ þe batell̄ & held̄ hym̄ selfe as owrecom*m*en̄. And þus þis trew knyght, be etyng of þe bodie of almighti God̄, had a glorious victorie.

Com*m*unio ecia*m* vitam corporalem prolongat[1]. Inf*r*a de p*r*edone.

Com*m*unio qu*a*n*d*oq*ue* a p*r*op*r*ietarijs religiosis non p*er*mittit se recipi[2]. Infra de p*r*oprietate.

[1] MS. prolongatt. [2] MS. non permittit sed recipit.

Com*m*unicant[1] frequent*er* tam̄ boni q*u*am mali indifferent*er*. Inf*ra* de eukaristia.

Com*m*unio ecia*m* a mortali pec*cato*[2] ret*r*ahit. Inf*r*a de obstinacione. ij.

CLXIV.

Com*m*unione*m* aliqu*ando* impedit pollucio nocturna, *et* aliqu*ando* non.

Cassianus tellis how he knew som tyme a man of religion, þat gaff hym gretelie vnto chastitie bothe of his harte & of his body, with grete mekenes; noghtwithstondyng he was tempid with grete ludificacions on þe nyght. And evur when he ordand hym to ressayfe his sacrament, on þe nyght befor evur he was pollutt in his slepe. And when he for ferdnes had lang time abstenyd hym fro his mess-saying, for ferdnes hereoff he went vnto ane olde bruther of his & told hym þe mater & askid hym cowncell þ*er*in. And he vmthoght hym þat þ*er* was nowder in þis man sup*er*fluitie, nor at his mynd was giffen vnto suche illusions, & þ*er*bie hym thoght at it was nowder syn of his bodye nor of his mynde, he cownceld hym baldlie to go vnto his mes & reseyfe þe holie sac*r*ament, þat not be þis disseyte þe medcyn of þe helefull medcyn & remedy sulde be lefte. And be þis cowncell he went vnto mes & boldelie resayvid þe sacrament: and be þe vertu þ*er*off þe custom at he was wunte to hafe of þis illusion fro thens-furt sesyd.

Com*m*unioni p*ossunt* adaptari multa que dicuntur inf*r*a de eukaristia.

CLXV.

Comp*ar*aciones odiose sunt.

Agellius tellis how þat when Aresto[*ti*]le þe philosophyr wexid olde, all his scolers & þai þat vsid his facultie come vnto hym

[1] MS. comminicant.

[2] MS. pp-ccō.

& prayed hym to tell þaim þat, when he was dead, who sulde succede & be þ*er* maister in his steade. And þ*er* was in his scole ij p*r*incipallis, Thofrastus and Memedemus. And þan Arestotile garte bryng hym bere & mead þatt he myght drynk of þaim bothe befor all his scolars. And when he had tastid of bathe, he com*m*endid ather of þaim. Neu*er*-þe-les he sayd þat bere was þe bettyr, becauce it was þe elder. And þus p*r*iualie *with*-outen lakkyng or com*m*endacion of owder p*ar*tie (*þai purseyvid*) þat Thofrastus sulde be þ*er* maister after hym when he was dead.

CLXVI.

Compassio natu*r*alit*er* inest mulierib*us*. *et* c^9^.

Valerius tellis how on a tyme þ*er* was a womman þat had done a grete trespas agayns þe law, & sho was broght þ*er*for befor þe justice, & þ*er* sho was demyd þat on a c*er*tan day after hur head sulde be smyten of. And sho was com*m*andid to p*r*ison, & he þat had hur in kepyng had petie on hur and gaff a dought*er* of hurs, at was a womman, lefe ilk day to com vnto hur; & ay when sho come in he serchid hur þat sho broght nothyng *with* hur, & it was com*m*andid hym þat sho suld neu*er* hafe meate afor scho sulde dy. So when he fand sho abade on life many dayes *with*-owten meate, on a tyme when hur doghter come, he serchid hur & he fand þat sho had sustenyd hur moder life *with* hur mylk of hur pap; & he thoght þis a grete m*er*vayle & went & told þe iustice. And þe iustis he[*r*]for had compassion on hur & forgaff hur hur tryspas for hur doghter sake.

Compati debent viri *sancti* eciam malis. Inf*r*a de obediencia. vij.

Compaciendu*m* est *eciam* animalib*us* brutis. Infra de obediencia. vij.

Compati d*e*bent co*n*fessores co*n*fitentib*us* cont*r*itis. Inf*r*a de cont*r*icione.

Compati d*e*bent confessores confitentib*us*. Sup*r*a de abbate. ij[a].

CLXVII.

Compaciendu*m* est leprosis.

Jacobus de Vet*ri*aco tellis how som̄ tyme þ*er* was a worthi ladie, & sho had grete petie of seke folk, & speciallie of lepre men̄. And hur husband was a myghti man̄, & he had lepre folk in so grete vgsomnes þat he myght not suffer to se þai*m*, nor lat þai*m* com̄ *with*-in his howse. So on̄ a day as a lepre man̄ was cryand at his yate, þe ladie come to hym̄ & askid hym̄ if he wold owder eate or drynk, and he answerd agayn̄ & sayd; "I am̄ here hugelie turment *with* hete of þe son̄, & I wiłł nowder eate nor drynk bod if þou take me into þi place." And sho answerd agayn̄ & sayd; "knowis þou not how my husband vgis to see lepros men? & he wiłł onone com̄ home fro huntyng, & if he fynde þe *with*-in his place, happelie he wiłł sla bothe þe and me." And he wepid & made sorow. So at þe laste þis ladie might no langer se hym̄ wepe, & sho tuke hym̄ vp̄ in hur armys & bare hym̄ into hur place, and þan̄ sho p*ra*yed hym̄ to eate. He said agayn̄ he wald nowder eat nor drynk bod if sho bare hym̄ vnto hur chamber & layde hym̄ in hur awn̄ bed, & þ*er* he wolde riste hym̄ awhile & þan̄ he wold eate. And he made so mekułł sorow þat sho mot not suffre itt, þat sho had hym̄ vnto hur chawm*er* & laid hym̄ in hur bed, & sho laid a softe cod vnd*er*nethe his head & happed hym̄ *with* a gay coue*r*lad. And þis done, onone hur husband come home fro huntyng & bad hur oppyn̄ hym̄ þe chamber dure, & he wold lay hym̄ down̄ & slepe a while; & sho was ferd at he suld sla bothe þe lepre man̄ & hur, & made hur to tarie a while, & wolde not com̄ & oppyn̄ þe dure redelie. & he seyng at sho tarid & wold nott com̄, brest oppyn̄ þe dure in a grete anger and went in-to þe chambr̄. And onone he come bakk agayn̄ & mett his wyfe & sayde vnto hur; "Now þou hase done wele; for þou hase arayed our bed on̄ þe beste wise, bod I m*er*vayłł whare þou gat so gude spicis þurgħ whilk ałł our chawm*er* is fyllid so fułł of gude savir *with*, for onone as I come into þe chaw[*m*]ber, þ*er* was þ*er*in so swete a savur at me thoght I was in paradice." And when̄ sho þ*at* befor̄ was ferd for hur dead hard þis, sho went in-to þe chamber *with* hym & fand it as he sayde; & þan sho told hym all how scho had done; & þai lukid in þe bed and þis lepre man was away. And þan hur husbond þat befor was als wude as a lyon, wex als meke as a lambe, & evur afterward luffid God & leplere men better.

Compati debet p*re*latus subditis temptatis. Sup*ra* de abb*at*e. ij.

CLXVIII.

Compaciend*um* e*st* amplius peccatis hominu*m* q*uam* reb*us* temporalib*us* p*ro*prijs.

Saynt Gregor tellis; "we rede of a gude holie man þat had no þing to lif on all yere bod a little corn þat he had gravyn þe erd of, & sawen hym selfe. So on a tyme when he had shorn it & broght it home, ane ill man þat luffid hym nott sett fyre in his lathe, & burnyd vp þe corn and all. So a man hard tell þ*er*off & come vnto hym & said; 'allas! fadur, what is happend vnto þe? wo is me for þe.' And he ansswerd agayn *with* a chere as he had bene nothyng grevid & said; 'wo is me for þat at sall happyn vnto hym þatt did þis dede!' as he had not sett be hys awn herm, bod rather be þe toder mans syn." *et c^9^*.

Compositus debet esse homo in sensib*us* exte*r*iorib*us*, vt habetur sup*ra* de Aspectu.

CLXIX.

Concordia multu*m* est necessaria habitantib*us* ad inuicem.

We rede in 'Vitis P*atrum*' how som tyme þ*er* was ij brether þat dwelte sam*en* many yeris, & þai varid neu*er* nor neu*er* was wrothe. So on a tyme þe tone said vnto þe toder; "latt vs make debate betwix vs as other men of þis werld dois." And þe toder ansswerd

& sayd þat he wuste neu*er* what debate was; & þan þe toder sayd vnto hym; "lay down þi hude betwixt vs two and I sall say it is myne, & þou sall say, 'nay! it is myne.' And here-of sall a debate brede betwix vs." And þai laid down þis hude betwyx þai*m*, and þe tone said; "it is myne"; & þe toþ*er* said; "nay! it is myne." þan þe tother sayd; "it is þyne; & þ*er*for take it vp & don it on þi hede & go þi ways." And þus þai p*ar*tid & nowder of þai*m* mott nor cuthe discorde wit*h* oþ*er*.

Concubina sac*er*dotis punitur. Infra de luxuria.

CLXX.

Co*n*cupicencia carnalis naturalit*er* ad mulierem inclinatur.

We rede in þe storie of Barlaam how þ*er* was a kyng þat had a son; and when he was new born, wyse lechis þ*at* saw it told hym þ*at* hym burde gar kepe it to it war x yere olde, þat it saw no þing bod meate & drynk & clothis & a wom*ma*n to kepe it, & els it suld dye. And so he dyd; & at x yere end he garte bryng befor it all man*er* of þing*is*, þat it mott se þai*m* & know what att þai war; & þ*er* was b[r]oght befor hym gold & sylu*er*, & hors & catell, & evur as he askid what þai war men tolde hym. And when yong wom*men* & maydyns come befor hym & he saw þai*m*, he askid beselie what at þai hight, & what þing*is* þai wer. And þai þat wer aboute answerd hym & said; "yone er devils þat begylis men." And when he had sene all man*er* of þingis, þai broght hym vnto þe kyng his fadur; and he askid hym of all thyngis þat he had sene, whilk he luffid beste. And he answerd agayn & sayd: "Fadur, forsuthe nothyng els bod devuls þat disseyvis men, ffor of þai*m* alonelie befor all oþ*er* is my harte sett."

Concupiscencia gule est rep*ri*menda. *Sup*ra de abstinencia.

Confessio facta in scriptis valet. *Sup*ra de Basilio. iij°.

CLXXI.

Confessio delet peccata de Sciencia Diaboli.

We rede in þe '*Meracles* of Saynt Constantyn[1],' how on a tyme when Saynt Lamfranke at was bisshop of Ca[*n*]turberie sayde mes þer, sodonlie a yong monke, þat suld hafe red þe gospell at þe same mes, was afore þe gospell taken *with* a fend; vnto so mekull at þai þat come before, what at evur þai had done & had not bene shrevyn þerof, he wold hafe teld þaim it. And som þat shamyd *with* þer syn, went & shrafe þaim clene þerof for ferd of hym. And when þai come agayn before hym he spirrid whatt þai war & whar-for þai come; & had no knowlege þat þai had bene at hym befor. *et c*[9].

CLXXI .

Confessio nocet Demoni.

Cesarius tellis how þer was a doctur of Dyvinitie þat was a gay *pre*chur, & he hight Thomas. And when he was seke & bown to dye, he was war of þe devull standdand in a noke of þe chawmbre þer he lay, and he coniurid hym & spirrid hym many thyngis. And emang all oþer thyngis he askid hym what noyed hym & his felos moste. And he said att no þing noyed nor hurte þaim so ill as did confession; ffor when a man is in deadlie syn, all his membres is bon, & he may not mofe hym; and onone as he is shrevyn, þan is he lowse, and redie vnto all gudenes. And when þis holie doctur had hard hym say þus, he thankid God & gaff vpp his sawle in-to hevyn.

Confessio mundat peccatorem *et* peccatum occultat. Supra de adulterio[2]. iij.

Confessio a visibili *et* horribili[3] pena liberat. Supra de agro. j.

[1] Arundel MS. Ex mira*culis sancti* Con*stantini* Can*tuaris*; celebra*nte sancto* Lanfranco Cantuaris archiepiscopo missam. The Harleian MS. has; Ex miraculis sancti Dunstani Cantuaris; celebrante sancto Lanfranco Cantuaris Archiepiscopo missam.

[2] MS. alulterio.

[3] MS. corrigibili. Latin MSS. horribili.

Confessio tarda aliqu*ando* valet. Sup*r*a de ambicione. iij.

CLXXIII.

Confessio pura celat pecc*atu*m *et* recidiuu*m* manifestat.

Cesarius tellis how som̄ tyme in þe Dioces of Traiecte, þ*er* was a fysscher þat was a fornicatur. & on̄ a tyme he was ferd' to be putt vp at þe sene [1]; & he went vnto a preste & shrafe hym̄ of alƚ his syn̄, and when̄ he had done þ*at*, if he war accusid' he mot sekurlie deny it, & suffer þe burnyng of a hate yrn̄ as þ*er* was vse to þai*m* at denyed it. And so he did', and þis hate yrn̄ þat he bare noyed' hym̄ no þing. So aft*er*ward he fell þ*er*to agayn̄. And on̄ a tyme he ferid' ou*er* a watir *with* a man̄ þatt had knawlege of his mysgou*er*nans; & þis man̄ spak vnto hym̄ & said'; "I m*er*velƚ, & so duse many mo, þat þe hate yrn̄ byrnyd þe noght; for we knew wele enoghe at þou was giltie, & hase occupyed it syne." & he answerd' agayn̄, & sayd' þe hate yrn̄ noyed hym̄ no more þan̄ did puttyng of his hand' in-to þe watir; & *with* þat he putt his hand' into þe watir. And onone [2], be þe rightwusnes of alƚ-myghti God', þat hym̄ hy schameles when̄ he was a penytent, becauce of turnyng agayn̄ vnto his syn̄, þ*er* he was punysshid'; & onone as he tuchid' þe watir it was vnto hym̄ as byrnand' fyre. For als sone as his hand' was in þe watir he gaff a grete cry & tuke vp his hand'; and alƚ þe skyn̄ lefte behynd' in þe watir. And þan̄ he told' þai*m* alƚ how it happend hym̄.

CLXXIV.

Confessio pura delet pecc*at*a a memoria confessoris qu*andoque*.

Cesarius tellis how þat [3] on̄ a tyme, as a grete meneyay of pylgrams saylid' to-gedur ou*er* þe se, þ*er* felƚ suche a tempeste in þe

[1] Latin MSS. timens in synodo accusari.

[2] Latin MSS. mira dei iustitia, qui mis*er*icorditer penitente*m* custodiuit iuste, *et* iuste recidiuante*m* punivit.

[3] MS. þan.

se, at þe shipmen war ferd at þai sulde all dye. And þan spak one att was emang þai*m* att was a grete synn*er* & sayde; "þis tempest is fallyn on vs becauce I am a grete synner; and I pray you all att ye will here my confession." And þai all held þ*er* tong; & he told so mekull horrible venom of syn at þai*m* irkid to here hym. And onone as he had done, þurh þe m*er*cie of almighti God þ*er* fell a grete calme in þe see, & þe storm sesyd so sone at eu*er*e man had m*er*vall þ*er*off. And when þai come vnto þe havyn, almyghti God tuke oute of þ*er* aller myndis all þase synys þat he had shrevyn hym off als verelie as þai had neu*er* harde tell of one of þai*m*.

Confessio pura a confusione temporali lib*er*at. Inf*r*a de famulo. v.

CLXXV.

Confessio eciam a morte corporali lib*er*at.

We rede how som tyme in þe cetie of Arthebatenc*is*[1], a yong pure clerk sayd vnto a goldsmyth þ*at* þ*er* sulde com vnto his howse a m*er*chand, þat wald by of hym sylu*er* vessell of dyvers form. And when he had told hym þis, þis goldsmyth wold fayn hafe solde his chaffer, & com*ma*wndid one of his men to go home & feche suche vessell & bryng þai*m* vnto suche a clerke howse. And a sister of þis goldsmyth broght þai*m* þedur þis clerk lay in wayte of hym & his suster as þai come in at þe dure, & slew þai*m* bothe, & cut þai*m* in pecis & keste þai*m* in a sege. And when þis goldsmyth meneya saw he tarid long & come not home, þai went vnto þis clerkis howse & spirrid after þ*er* maist*er* & his suster. And þis clerk denyed hym & sayd he come nott þ*er*; & þai areste hym & a brud*er* & a sist*er* þat he had, & broght þai*m* befor þe[2] iustice of þ*er* law, & þ*er* þai cuthe not agaynsay þ*er* gilde, for þe man was fon *with* þai*m*, & þe sylu*er* vessell bothe; and þai war demyd all to be brent. þan þis suster said vnto hur[3] brother þe clerke;

[1] MS. Harl. In ciuitate Att*r*abanensc. MS. Arund. In ciritate Atrabacesi.

[2] MS. *repeats*, þe.

[3] *After*, hur, h, *erased*.

"Bruther, I suffer þis fo[*r*] þe. And sen we may nott esshew þe payn of dead at we er demyd vnto, lat vs shryfe vs of owr syn, at we may so esshew þe eu*er*lastand payn of hell." And bothe þe brethir wuld nott. Noght-*with*-stondyng sho sh afe hur of hur syn vnto a preste *with* grete wepyng & h*er*tlie cont*r*icion; and þan þai wer all takyn & boun vnto a stokk, and a grete fyre made abowte þai*m*. And þe clerk & his bruther fell in a dispayr & war burnyd vp; & þis damysell þurgh hur trew confession was kepyd harmeles. & yit þe bandis at sho was bou*n* *with* wer burnyd, & sho felid no more of þe hete of þe fyre, þan it hadd bene þe blaste of a dew wynd.

CLXXVI.

Confessio simulata vel tamen furtiua[1] no*n* delet pecc*at*a de sciencia diaboli, sed tantum vera confessio illa delet.

Cesarius tellis þ*at* on a tyme in Braban þ*er* was a man bou*n* in a howse þ*at* had a fend in hym, whilk fend cawsid þis man to vpbrayd ilkone at come in *with* syns at þai had done & war nott shrevyn off. So þ*er* was a man in þe town þat gretelie desyrid to se hym & here hym speke, bod he was ferd þat he suld vpbrayde hym *with* his syn. And for ferd here-of he went & shrafe hym of all his synys vnto a preste, bod he kepid *with*-in hym a will to fall vnto syn agayn; and he trowid þat he was sekur enogh & wente boldelie into þe howse vnto þis man. And onone as he come in, þis man at was bun cryed & said; "A! welcom, frend! com ner! for þou hase wele whittend þe." & onone, þuf all he war shrevyn, yit he told all his synnys oppynlie vnto all þat stude abowte; & þe man þoght he was gretlie confusid becauce his syns wer so fowle, and he was passand hevye & turnyd agayn vnto þe preste, & tolde hym all how it happend. And he shrafe hym agayn *with* a full wyll neu*er* to syn agayn. And þan þe preste bad hym go baldlie agayn and he sulde no more shame hym; and

[1] MS. fulcina. Latin MSS. *as above.*

he did so. And when he come into þe howse, one at was þ*er* said vnto þis man at was bun; "lo! þi frend is commen agayn." And he askid whilk was he. And þai said; "he þis att þou vpbraydid right now *with* so fowle synys at þou sayd at he had done." And he answerd hym agayn & said; "I vpbraydid hym noght, nor I knaw none ill of hym." And fro thens furthe eu*er*ilk man trowed att he was bod a lyer, & wolde truste no thyng at he sayd. *et c*9.

CLXXVII.

Confessio ex corde facta celat pecc*ata*.

We rede how on a tyme þ*er* dwelte in a town a knyght, & he had a fayr wyfe; & þe preste of þe town held hur. And it was tolde þe knyght, & he wolde nott onone giff faythe þ*er*to; not-*with*stondyng he had þai*m* evur in suspecion, & he wold nowd*er* latt þe pr*este* nor his wyfe witt at he had þai*m* so. So on a tyme he prayed þe preste at he wolde go *with* hym to speke *with* a man a myle or ij thens. And he said yis, and went *with* hym vnto a noder town, whar þ*er* was a devull in a man at wolde tell eu*er*ilk man of all þe synys at evur þai had down þat þai wer not welc shrevyn of. And þis preste was aferd þat þe knight broght hym þedur for to aske þis devull of his dedis, & he went & soght a preste and þ*er* was nane in þe town. And þan he went privalie into þe stabyll þ*er* þe knight*is* man had sett vp þ*er* hors, & he fell on his kneis befor þe knyghtis man, & prayed hym þat he wold here his confession, for he was so seke he was bown to dye. And þ*er*, *with* grete contricion he made a full confession vnto þis man, & besoght hym to enione hym penance: and þan þis servand sayd; "Sur, I am no preste; I know nott whatt penance I sulde enione you, bod þat penance at ye wolde enione a noder prest and he war shrevyn at you of a like syn, þat sall be your penance." And þis done he went on boldlie *with* þe knight vnto þis man at had þis devull in hym. And þan þis knight askid hym if he kend oght *with* hym selfe; and he sayd, Nay, he knew no þing *with* hym. þan he askid hym what he cuthe say of þe preste, &

he sayd þat he cuthe say nothyng of hym. And when he had sayd so, he turnyd his tong oute of þe language at þe knyght vnderstude, & spak Latyn & said; "In stabulo mundatus est; he was clensid in þe stabyll." & þe preste vnderstude what he sayd, & so did none oþer att was þer. & he was fayn & thankid God & went home with þe knight agayn, & lefte þis werld & went & made hym a monke in Ceustus ordur & become evur after a gude man.

CLXXVIII.

Confessio *facta* diabolo in loco sac*er*dotis aliquid p*ro*dest.

Jacobus de Vet*ri*aco tellis how at þ*er* was a man þat had done many grete synys at he was neu*er* shrevyn of, & so hym happend fall seke & was like to dye. And þe devull was ferd at he suld shryfe hym vnto som preste, & come vnto hym hym selfe in liknes of a preste, & cownceld hym to shrife hym. And þis man trowed at he had bene a preste, & shrafe hym to hym *with* gude will of all his synys *with* grete cont*ri*cion. And þis done, þe devull sayd vnto hym; "Bruther, þies syn*n*es er grevus, and þ*er*for I enione þe to penance at þou schryfe þe noght of þai*m* vnto no noder man, for þai may gretlie sklander þe"; and þan þe devull went his wayes. And onone þis man dyed; and þ*er* come aungels & fendys vnto his sawle, & þe fendis sayde; "he is owres, for he was neu*er* schrevyn vnto no preste." And þe aungels sayd þat he had made a confession, for he was contrite; and þuf all it was þe devull at he was shrevyn, yitt he trowed þat he had bene a preste. And þis sawle was broght befor þe hie iugement of almyghtti God; & he demyd it for to be putt agayn in þe body, at þe bodi eft mot be shrevyn vnto a preste, and so it was. *et c*9.

Confessio pura reddit sac*er*dotem dignu*m* sacrame*n*to misse. Inf*r*a de sac*er*dote. vj.

Confessio cum[1] p*r*oposito recidiuandi no*n* valet. Infra de contricione. j.

[1] MS. sine.

Confessionem impedit demon quantu*m* potest. Inf*r*a de demone. xj.

Confessio penam corporalem inflicta*m* delet. Inf*r*a de h*er*etic*is*. i. *et* de Maria.

Confessio amissa a viuo, fit qu*andoque* a mortuo resussitato *pre*cib*us* *sanctorum*. Inf*r*a de Francisco *et* oracione.

CLXXIX.

Confessor in aliquo casu no*n* tenetur confessione*m* celare.

Cesarius tellis how þ*er* was a monke of Ceustus ordur, & he confessid hym vnto his Abbott, how þat þuff all he war no preste, yit he said mes; and he wold not lefe nowdur be prayer, nor charge, nor com*mand* of his abbott. And þis abbott told þis case vnto a *cer*tan *per*son and sent it vnto pope; and he answerd agayn & said it was no co*n*fession, it was bod a blasfemyng, and "a confessur," he sayd, "aw not be þe law to layn such a blasfeme, whar-þurgh grete *per*ell myght fall vnto all holie kurk." And þus he was dischargid of mes-saying. *et c*[9].

Confessor no*n* celans co*n*fess*io*nem est causa multor*um* malorum. Infra vbi agitur de Maria Dei genitrice.

CLXXX.

Confessor incontinens m*u*ltociens potest esse occasio dampnacionis.

Cesarius tellis how þ*er* was a riche huswyfe þat had done many horrible syn*n*ys; & sho had grete sorow for þai*m* in hur harte, and yit sho wold nevur shryfe hur of þai*m*. So þ*er* was a yong *pre*ste þat sho had broght vp of barn little hur self; & sho tuke suertie of hym & shrafe hur unto hym of all hur syn*n*ys. And when he had hard hur confession he was lathe to displease hur, & cowncelд hur to fulfyll þe luste & þe likyng of hur bodie; & scho wold nott, bod abade in *par*fite cont*r*icion. And when he saw þat, he discurid hur synys to ilk man & diffamyd hur. And sho was so gude a wom*ma*n at no man trowid hym, bod held hur a gude wom*ma*n & cowntid hym bod for a fule.

CLXXXI.

Confessor ec*iam* in cautela *et* in inte*r*rogando[1] multis est occasio pecc*ati*.

We rede how on a tyme a maydyn come & shrafe hur vnto a preste; and he as ane vnwyse confessur began to tempe[2] hur vnto syn, & gaf hur comfurthe þ*er*in þ*at* sho sulde contynue. And so sho contynued it so lang at sho cuthe neu*er* lefe it[3].

CLXXXII.

Confessor discretus ecia*m* nolentes pe*r* discrecione*m* sua*m* ad penitenciam inducit.

Cesarius [*tellis*] how þ*er* was a man þat had done many horrible syn*n*ys, and when he had shrevyn hym þ*er*of vnto a preste, he wolde resayfe no penance, bod said he myght do none; to so mekull, & þe pr*e*ste enionyd hym neu*er* so lityll penance, yit he wolde nott g*r*aunte þ*er*to. So his confessur askid hym if he myght say eu*er*-ilk day his pater no*ster*. & he tuke hym þ*er*to & did itt. And almighti God sent hym suche grace, þat he come agayn oft-sithes & asked evur more penans, vnto þe preste had enionyd hym sufficient penance for his syn.

Confessor discretus debet esse co*m*paciens *et* condescendens peccatorib*us*. Sup*r*a de Abb*ate*.

[1] Harl. MS. incautus in inte*rr*ogando. Arun. MS. as above.
[2] *After* tempe, hym, *erased*.
[3] Latin MSS. Virgo queda*m* cuida*m* sacerdoti confitebat*ur*. Ille sicut impruden*s* cepit de pecc*atis* sibi ignotis inte*rr*ogare. Que mox de eis in *tantum* cepit temptari quod, sicut postea retulit alt*eri* sac*er*doti, vix de illis pecc*atis* continuit.

CLXXXIII.

Confessor dure loquens confitentib*us* aliquando contra se ips*um* p*ro*uocat eos.

We rede in 'Libro de Dono Timoris' how þat a man þat was in syn happend on a tyme to be in p*er*ell of his dead; and he made a vow þat, & he mot esskape, he sulde shrife hym. And so hym happend be delyverd; & þe maist*er* of his felowship went & shrafe hym vnto a preste h*er*mett, & he shrafe hym vnto þe same. And þis p*re*ste gretlie blamyd hym for his syn, & sent hym vnto þe pope; & þis man wexid hym gretlie and slew hym, and did þe same *with* ane oþ*er* confessur. And þe thrid confessur hard hym mekelie & spak frendlie vnto hym, & tretid hym, and enionyd hym to penance one thyng alonelie, & þat was; þat when somevur he saw any man dead, he suld helpe to berie hym & he myght, & putt hym in þe erth, and at he sulde þinke of deade. And so he did oft-sythis; & att þe laste he began devowtelie to þinke on his estate, & went in-to wyldernes, & þ*er* he liffid & dyed in grete penance. *et c*[9].

CLXXXIV.

Confidencia. Confidendu*m* no*n* est in senectute vt p*ro*pt*er* hoc magis homo p*er*iculis se exponat.

We rede in 'Vitis P*atru*m' how þat ane olde man of religion was seke in Egipte, and he wold algatt*is* go home vnto his frendis at he mot be *with* þai*m* to he wer seke, & not emang his [1] brether to noy þai*m*. And þe abbot Moyses bad hym go noght, þat he fell not into fornicacion. And he was hevy þ*er*with & sayd his bodie was dead fro all man*er* of swilk luste. And he went on his ways to his frendis; & a damysell of hur devocion kepid hym. And when he was coverd of his sekenes, he lay by hur & gatt hur *with* child. And when þis child was born, þis olde man tuke it in his

[1] *After* his, breke, *erased.*

armys opon a grete festiuall day, & come into þe kurk þer*with* befor all his brether & all oþ*er* þat þ*er* was; and his brethir wepid & made sorow for hym. And þan he said vnto þai*m*; "See ye þis childe? Lo! þis is þe son of inobediens; be war!" he said, "þ*er*for, ye brether, & take ensample be me, for þis I dyd in myne elde. And þ*er*for I pray you h*er*telie pray for me." And he went into his cell; & þ*er* he abade all his life-days in grete penau*n*ce & prayer.

Confidencia est h*ab*enda in s*an*c*t*is[1] de rebus temporalib*us*. Inf*ra* de S*anct*o Nicholao.

Confidend*um* no*n* est in quolibet. Inf*ra* de gula. iiij.

CLXXXV.

Confusio orta de peccato p*er*petrato aliqu*ando* est occasio boni.

Cesarius tellis how on a tyme a yong man gatt a non *with* child; and he was so confusid þ*er*-*with*, & so ferd at he sulde be descried þat he had done suche a truspas, & no man had hym in suspecion, þat he went vnto ane abbay of a strayte ordur & made hym a man of religion, & þ*er* abade in grete devocion & prayer all his life. *et cetera*.

CLXXXVI.

Confusio aliquando est causa mortis.

Helinandus tellis how þat shipmen on a tyme come vnto a philosophur þat hight Omerus, & spirrid hym a question & he cuthe not in no wise essoyne it. And becauce he cuthe not, þai said he was bod a fule, & cuthe no wisdom. And he was so confusid & esshamyd þat *with*-in a little while after he dyed for sorow.

[1] So the Latin MSS. The English version *has*, in *sanctis temporalibus*.

CLXXXVII.

Congregacio aliquando dirigitur *per* aliquem bon*um*.

Isidorus tellis how [*when*] þat Philip̄ þat was king of Macedonie was at Athenys, he askid of þe cetie at þai sulde delyvir hym̄ x wyse men [1], and he sulde breke vp his sege. And when̄ a man̄ þat hight Demonstrues [2] harde tell þis, he fenyd þis fable & told it emang þe cetisyns of Athenys; how þat, on̄ a tyme, wulfis desyrid of shep*er*dis at þai & þai myght be made frendis. And þe shep*er*dis þoght none ill & grawntid & was made frendis *with* þai*m*. And þan̄ þe wulfis askid of þies shep*er*dis at þai mott hafe þ*er* doggis at kepid þ*er* shepefald delyverd; ffor as þai sayd, þai wold be occasion̄ and cauce to gar þai*m* fall att debate agayn̄. And þe shep*er*dis agreid þ*er*to, & delyverd þai*m* þ*er* doggis þat war wunte for to kepe þ*er* faldis. And þan̄ þe wulvis killid þies howndi*s*; & when̄ þai had so done, þai come & werid vp all þe shepe att was in þe flokk. "And þus," he sayd, "will Philipp̄ þe kyng do *with* vs, þat is to say, take away our wise men̄ & owr oraturs; and when̄ he hase so done, þan̄ he wyll mys-chefe vs & sla vs, & all þat er in þe cetie of Athenys."

CLXXXVIII.

Consanguinitas. Consanguinei no*n* sunt a viris s*anct*is sustentandi nisi in iure suo p*ro*prio.

We rede in þe life of Abbott Pastur, how þ*er* was a Iustice of þe contre, & he desyrid to se þis Abbott, and he mot nevur com to at se hym̄. And þis iustis saw þat, & he garte take þe sist*er* son̄ of þis abbott, & said he was a thiefe & putt hym̄ in p*ri*son̄, & sayd & þis abbott Pastor wold com̄ vnto hym̄ & pray hym̄ for hym̄, he suld delyver hym̄ hym̄. And þan̄ þe moder of þis childe come vnto þis abbott cell dure, and callid þ*er*-att & besoght hym̄ to speke *with* hur, & he wolde no wurd answer. And when̄ sho saw þatt, sho wepid & made mekull sorow, & sayd; "And þou had

[1] *After* men, at, *erased*. [2] Latin MSS. Demostrues.

a harte & bowels of yrn̄ & mott not be movid *with* no compassion̄, yit at þe leste marke, þou suld hafe compassion̄ of þine awn̄ blude, þi sist*er* son̄." And þan̄ þis abbott sent wurd vnto þis iustis & sayd; "Pastor filios non gen*er*au*it*; Abbott Pastor gatt nevur child." And when̄ þis iustis saw at þe abbott wold not com̄ hym̄ selfe & p*ra*y for hym̄, he said & he wold send wurd for hym̄ be mowthe he suld send hym̄ hym̄. And þan̄ þis Abbott sent hym̄ wurd & sayd; "Examyn̄ þe cauce as þe law wyll, & if he be wurthi to dye lat hym̄ dy; or els do *with* hym̄ as þou plesis." *et c*9.

CLXXXIX.

Consciencia bona frequent*er* timet [1].

We rede in 'Historia Trip*ar*tita,' þat on̄ a tyme when̄ Iulianus Apostata at a grete ffeste tyme, in man*er* as emp*er*ours dose, garte encens be sett befor hym̄, he made crysten̄ men̄ to com̄ knelyng aforn̄ hym̄ & *ser*ve hym̄ þ*er*-of. & he gart hide fals mawmett*is* vnd*er*-nethe a clothe befor hym̄, at þe cristen̄ men suld not se þ*aim*; & þe *cr*istenmen̄ wiste nothyng þ*er*of. And when̄ þis was done, he garte bare þies & told þe *cr*isten̄ men̄, & threpid of þ*aim* at þai had done sac*r*ifice vnto his godd*is*, & offred þ*aim* encence. And when̄ þai harde þis, þai cryed & made mekull sorow, and desyrid at þ*er* right hand*is* at þai broght it vp̄ *with* sulde be cutt off for penance *et c*9; þuff all þai þoght not of no sacrifice vnto fals godd*is*.

CXC.

Consciencia pecc*ati* [2] no*n* potest quiescere.

We rede in 'Libro de Dono Timoris,' how on̄ a tyme þ*er* was a riche man̄, & he luffid wele to go to sportis & to grete festis. So on̄ a tyme, as he was be hys ane, hym̄ happend to vmthynk hym̄ of his synnys, & so he contynued; and his consciens was so gretlie

[1] The Latin MSS. *conclude, vbi non est timendum.*

[2] So Latin MSS. The English version *has*, peccato.

turment þ*er*-*with* at he mott hafe no reste. And þ*er*for evur when̄ suche a thoght come in his mynd, he wald evur caƚƚ vnto hym̄ one of his neghburs to hald a talk *with* hym̄, & for to putt suche thoghtis oute of hys mynde.

Consecracio eccl*es*ie. Infra de dedicacione.

CXCI.

Consilio bono est acquiescend*um*.

We rede how on̄ a tyme ane archer gatt a little burd þat is callid a nightgale, & he gatt oute his knyfe & wold hafe slane hur. & þan̄ sho spakk vnto hym̄ & sayd; "þou man̄! whatt may my dede *pro*fett þe? For þou may not fyƚƚ þi body *with* me, bod & þou wiƚƚ latt me go, I saƚƚ gif þe for my rawnson̄ iij wisdoms, whilk & þou kepe, saƚƚ be grete *pro*fett vnto þe." And when̄ he hard hur speke he was gretelie astonyd, & sayd þat & sho cuthe teƚƚ hym̄ any new þing*is* at mot *pro*fett hym̄, he suld latt hur go aƚƚ redie; & sho essurid hym̄ at sho suld. And as for þe furste, sho bad hym̄ neu*er* to desyre to gett þat þing at he myght not gett; and make not sorow for þat þing þat is v*er*ely loste & can̄ neu*er* be requoverd; and as for þe thrid, "Gyff not truste vnto eu*er*ilk wurd at þou heris." And þis done he lete hur fle þ*er* sho wold; and sho gatt hur vp into a tre & þoght sho wald witt wheþ*er* þies wisdoms sulde turn̄ hym̄ vnto any profett or nay. And sho said vnto hym̄; "A! wo be vnto þe! for þou hase had þis day ane iƚƚ cownceƚƚ; for þ*er* is *with*-in my body a p*re*cious stone callid a Margarite, þat is of grete v*er*tue, and it is more þan̄ ane egg." And when̄ he hard þis, he made mekuƚƚ sorow at he had lattyn̄ hur go, & desyrid hur to com̄ agayn̄, & made aƚƚ þe crafte att he cuthe to gett hur. And þan̄ sho sayd vnto hym̄; "Now I know þat þou erte bod a fule. I bod þou suld not make sorow for þat þing þat was loste and irrecou*er*able, & I bad þou suld not be besy to labur for þat þing at þou may nott gett, & þou mak*is* mekil[1] sorow at þou hase loste me, & laburs to gett me agayn̄, & I wiƚƚ not com̄ att þe. And I bad þou sulde not trow eu*er*-ilk wurd att

[1] MS. mekis.

þou hard, & þou trowis at þ*er* be in my bodye a p*re*cious stone mor þan ane egg; & all my bodie is nott so mekull as halfe ane egg. And þ*er*for as I fand þe a fule, so will I lefe þe." & *with* þat sho flow away syngand þies ij versys; "Non nimis amissis doleas, nec om*n*e quod audis credas, nec cupias id quod habere nequis."

CXCII.

Consilio inhonesto *eciam* si sit vtile, no*n* est adquiescend*um*.

Tullius tellis how som tyme þ*er* was a man þat hight Themistenes, & on a tyme he told vnto þe men at dwelte in Athens þat he cuthe tell þai*m* a cowncell þat war for þ*er* commo*n* p*ro*fett. Bod he said þat it was noght necessarie þat all men suld witt it, & þ*er*for he desyrid þai*m* at he myght hafe ane to tell it to. And þai assigned hym a man þat hight Aristes, and he told hym & sayd: "A grete shyp of Lacedonye is com*m*en vnto þe haven; and it wer ane ethe þing & a p*ro*fitable to men of þe cetie to go & take oute all þe riches þ*er*-of." And when þis Aristes hard þis, he went to þe cowncell in-to þe cetie & told þai*m* þat he had hard a p*ro*fitable cowncell, bod it was nowder treuth nor honestie; and þ*er*for he sayd he wold not concent þ*er*to.

Consilio bono frequen*ter* pecc*at*or ad penitenci*am* *et* satisfaccionem attrahit*ur*. Infra de vsurario *et* multis aliјs locis.

Consilio malo p*er*dit homo corpus *et* a*n*i*m*am. Inf*ra* de h*er*etico.

Consilio bono fit iustu*m* iudiciu*m*. Infra de *pro*misso.

Consilio bono pecc*atu*m dimittitur *et* te*m*p*er*ancia augetur. S*upr*a de abb*at*e.

Consiliu*m* gratis debet dari paup*er*ib*us*. Sup*ra* Augustini. iij.

CXCIII.

Consolacio diuina cor ad se tot*um* attrahit et replet dulcedine.

Jacobus de Vet*ri*aco tellis of[1] our ladie Saynt Marie, þat when sho norisshid hym in his youthed and sho had ligen *with* hym iij dayes in bed laykand, hur wold hafe þoght it bod ane hour; & sho wold layke so long *with* hym at he wold be bathe hon[*g*]rie and threstie. And ay þe hongreer & þe thristier at he was, þe more sho desyrid to hald hym in hur armys; and if he wold hafe bene furth, sho wold cry & hold hym still betwix hur armys. And som tyme sho wold bere hym in hur armys iij dayes, & kis hym & play *with* hym in dyvers placis, becauce sho had so mekull comforth of hym in hur harte; for als mekull as sho knew þat he was bothe verray God & man.

CXCIV.

Consolacio diuina debet p*recibus* impetrari.

We rede in 'Libro de Dono Timoris' of a wom*man* þat was devowte; & on a tyme when sho wantyd comfurth at sho was wunte vnto, & was ferd at it suld tary lang or it come, & when at it war commen at it suld sone pas away, and sho spakk vnto hur awn v*er*tues at was *with*-in hur & sayd; "My faythe! go þou vnto my Lord God, & charge Hym be all þe articles þat er trowed in Hym þat He com vnto me & comfurth me. & my mynde! Be þou His hoste, & ordan for his h*er*berie. And my luff! Luke þou make Hym gude chere. And my charitie! It acordis to þe to hold Hym still, at He pas not away." And when sho had þus chargid all hur vertues, onone sho was putt in a m*er*valos grete comfurth, at *con*tynued *with* hur lang & recedid noght away from hur.

Consolatur Deus[2] aliquos in sacr*amento* altaris. Inf*ra* de sacramento. j.

[1] Harl. MS. de *sancta* Maria de Ogniez. Arund. MS. de *sancta* Maria de Origine. This English version is entirely corrupt.

[2] So the Latin MSS. The English MS. *has*, Consolatur Deus in aliquo in aliquo sacramento, &c.

Consolacione*m* recipiunt aliqu*ando* s*anct*i creaturis vel f*act*is. Sup*ra* abb*at*is vi[1] *et* inf*ra* de Ioh*anne* Euua*n*gelista.

Consolatur Deus t*r*ibulatos. Sup*ra* de Antonio.

Consolacio Diuina subt*ra*hitur ab hijs qui consolacione*m* h*ab*ent in amicis carnalib*us*. Infra de P*er*egrino. ij°.

CXCV.

Consolacio diuina allicit ho*min*em ad manend*um* in eccl*es*ia.

Cesarius tellis of a monk̄ of Ceustus ordur, þat had a grace and a lefe, for feblenes att his body was in, for to ly in his bed' & not com̄ att matyns at mydnyght; & yitt for al̄l̄ þat he myght not reste in his bed in matyn̄ tyme, bod þat reste at he had, hym̄ burd' hafe it in þe kurk̄. So on̄ a day his brether chalangid' hym̄ þ*er*for̄, & said' sen̄ he was so wayke of hym̄ selfe, at hym̄ wer bettir for to reste hym̄ in his bed' þan̄ for to com̄ vnto þe kurk̄, & specialli becauce he had lefe. He ansswerd' agayn̄ & said'; "When̄ I here my brethir syng, & I be not *with* þai*m*, þan̄ I am̄ m*er*voloslie trubled' and turment in my harte; & þan̄ I wax hevy when̄ I vmthynk me þat þe comfurth̄ at God duse vnto þai*m* þ*er* did it som̄ tyme þ*er* vnto me. & þuf al̄l̄ I may nott helpe þai*m*, yit it comfurthis me gretelie to here þai*m*."

CXCVI.

Consolacio diuina non conceditur adm*i*ttentib*us* alienam.

Cesarius tellis how som tyme þ*er* was a monke in Ceustus ordur, and he was[2] a leche & ran̄ þurgh̄ þe cuntre ilk day, þat vnnethis he wolde be att hame at his abbay on̄ hy dayes. So it happend' opon̄ a night, in þe solempnyte of our̄ Ladie, as he stude at matyns

[1] MS. ij.

[2] MS. *repeats*, was.

syngand emangis his felos, he saw our Ladie Saynt [*Marie*] com̄ in-to þe where, & broght a boyste full of lectuarie; & sho putt þerof in-to evur-ilk monk mouthe *with* a spone. And when̄ sho come att hym̄ sho said; "þou mysters not of my lectuarie, for þou erte a leche & takis þine awn̄ comfurth at þe full": & so he had none. And fro þine furth, bod if he had bene compellid, he wold neu*er* oute of his abbay, nor he had neu*er* af*ter* dayntie of bodelie medcyn̄. So þe next ffeste of our Ladie sho come agayn̄, & did vnto þe monkis as sho did before; and when̄ sho come att þis monk, sho said vnto hym̄; "Becauce þou hase had mor comfurth of me þan̄ þou had of þi lechecrafte or [1] of þi medcyns, þ*er*for I sall giff þe of my medcyns." And when̄ he had tastid þ*er*off, onone he feld suche a swetnes, þat eu*er* fro thens furth he was so stable in his ordur þat he refusid all man*er* of oþ*er* þing.

CXCVII.

Constans debet e*ss*e religiosus in om*n*ib*us*, tam p*ro*sp*er*is q*u*am adu*er*sis.

Cesarius tellis of a monk of þe same ordur, þat did many grete m*er*acles. So his abbott askid hym̄ on̄ a tyme, how he had þat grace befor all his brethir to do so many m*er*acles. And he answerd agayn̄ & said; "I wote nevur, for I pray no more, nor fastis no more, nor wakis no more, þan̄ duse myne other brether, nor laburs no more; bod I know [2] a thyng. Ther may no p*ro*sp*er*ite make me prowd, nor none adu*er*sitie make me displesid nowder of my selfe nor of oþ*er*." And þe abbod askid hym̄ & said; "Was þou not trubbled when̄ suche a knyght byrnyd our grange?" And he answerd agayn̄ & sayd; "Nay! for I betaght þe reward þerof vnto almighti God; and wheþ*er* I hafe mekull or little, eu*er* I thank allmighti God þ*er*of, & takis it *with* gude will, ffor I hafe dispysed & forsaken̄ all þe riches of þis werld." *et c*ᵒ.

Constans debet e*ss*e p*re*latus in hijs que p*er*tinent ad officiu*m* suu*m*. S*upr*a Ambrosij. vj.

[1] MS. of of.

[2] *After* know, n and some other letter, *blotted*.

Constans debet esse bonus subditus [in bono][1] *contra* prelatum ullum. Infra Hillarij.

Constans debet esse miles in bello. Infra[2] de Milite. vj.

Constans debet esse quilibet in bono opere incepto. Infra[2] de nouicio.

Constantes Deus adiuvat in necessitate. Infra de virginitate. iij.

Constans omnia suffert propter Deum. Supra de compassione.

Constantinus imperator. Supra de eodem.

CXCVIII.

Consuetudo peccandi minuit timorem.

Saynt Gregur tellis how *þer* was on a tyme a man þat opon þe Pasch-evyn corrupte a maydyn. So opon þe morn he was ferd for to go into þe kurk, att þe devull suld hafe no power of hym. Not-*with*stondyng, at þe laste he went in for shame *with* a grete ferdnes. And so he did on þe secund day, & was les ferd; & on þe iij day he was leste ferd of all. And þus he did vnto vij dayes was passid, and þan he was nothyng ferd, & wold not shryfe hym þerof. & onone after he dyed a sodan dead. And when he was laid in his grafe, *þer* come sodanlie a grete low into his grafe & burnyd ewhils *þer* was lefte a morcell of hys bodie to burn opon, & to it was clene wastid.

Consuetudo eciam naturam aliquando alterat. Infra de lupo *et supra* de Andrea.

Consuetudo[3] mala difficile tollitur. *Supra* de aduocato. iiij.

Consuetudo bona semper est seruanda. Infra de milite, v, *et* de Aue. ij.

[1] So Arund. MS. [2] MS. Supra. [3] MS. *inserts* eciam here.

CXCIX.

Contemplacioni modus apponendus est.

Heraclius[1] tellis how þat Alexandrus[2] Macharius told hym on a tyme & sayd, þat som tyme a vayne covatice of thoghtis of vanytie occupyed his mynde, at he wald certayn dayes contynuallie bere hys mynd vnseu*er*able, to so mekull þat he wald spar his duris at no man sulde speke *with* hym, nor hafe ane ansswer of hym. And he wold flite *with* his awn mynd & say vnto hit; "vmbe-se þe att þou fall not fro hevyn vnto erth; ffor þ*er* þou hase þi creatur & all angels & saynttis. Think of all þies." And þus he contynued ij dayes & ij nyghtis; and þan he felid þe devull prikkid hym so, att hym þoght att all his cell fell opon hym.

CC.

Contemplacioni sic est insistend*um*, vt accio no*n* necligatur.

We rede in 'Vitis P*atrum*' how a bruther on a tyme come in pylg*ra*mege vnto a place of monkis þat was at þe mownt*e* of Synay, & þ*er* he say þe monkis labur & grafe þat þai suld saw corn. And he said vnto þai*m* in þis mane*r* of wise; "Whie wurke ye for meatt þat will do bod waste & p*er*issh away? Remembre yo*u* of Marie Magdalyn, how sho did no bodelie labur, & yitt our Lord sayde þat sho had chosyn þe bettir parte." And when þ*er* abbott harde tell of þis, he bad a disciple of his giff þis man a buke, & putt hym in a cell þat nothyng was in. And at howr of none þis man lukid furth if any man callid hym to mete; & þ*er* was none att callid hym. And after none þe abbott come vnto hym & sayde; "how duse þou?" And he ansswerd agayn & sayd; "Sir Abbott! Ete none of your brethir no meate to-day?" and þe abbott sayd; "yis." And þan he askid whi þai callid not hym to dener; & þan þis abbott ansswerd hym & sayde: "Thow

[1] Latin MSS. Heraclides. [2] Latin MSS. Alexandrin*us* Machari*us*.

erte a *spiritual* man & mysters no meatt; and we er flesshlie men & bus nedelyngis eatt; & *þerfor* we wurk *with* oure handis." And when þis[1] bruther hard þis, he began to forthynk at he had said, & sayd vnto hym selfe; "Now I know wele att it is necessarie to ioyn þe life of Martha *with* þe life of Magdalen: þat is to say, vmwhile to vse *spiritual* life & vmwhile to vse contemplatyfe life," & þan he fell to werk and did as þai did.

Con*tem*placio rapit ho*min*em extra se vt aliqu*ando* sensu*m* no*n* habeat. Sup*ra* Augustini. iij.
Co*n*templacionem[2] inte*r*mittere inte*r*du*m* expedit. Inf*ra* de Ioh*ann*e Euua*n*gelista.

CCI.

Co*n*temptus mu*n*di. Co*n*tempni debent *omn*ia exemplo ph*ilosoph*or*um*.

Saynt Jerom tellis of a man þat hight Socraticus, and on a tyme his gudis wer all tane fro hym safeyng a mantill. And he had a disciple þat hight Diogenes, & he had no gude lefte bod a skrip and a taberd & his vvermest clothe to hyll hym with; & in his scrip he bare his meatt. And he had no howse bod a tome ton, & hym þoght þatt was a noble howse; & in wynt*er* when it was cald, he wald evur turn þis ton mouthe vnto þe sowthe, & in sommer he wald turn it into þe northe, & evur as þe son turnyd wold he turn his ton. And he had kepid hym no gude bod alonelie a copp of tre to drynk opon. So on a tyme he saw a childe take vpp watir in þe luff of his hand & drynk þ*er*of; and when he saw þat he caste away his copp & sayd þat he wiste neu*er* þat natur had giffen a man a vessell to drynk off. *et c*[9].

Contempni [et] elongari debet turba ho*minum*. Infra de solitud*in*e[3]. i. ij. *et* iij.

[1] MS. his. [2] MS. contemplacioni. [3] MS. solicitudine.

CCII.

Contempni debent dignitates.

Heraclides tellis how þat a gude holie man þat hight Animonus[1] opon a tyme was gretlie desirid to be a bisshopp with þe common peple, to so mekull þe cetisens tuke hym & sayd he suld be þer bisshopp magre his tethe. And he saw þat he myght not esskape þaim, and he tuke ane yrn & pullid of his lefte ere of his heade hard be þe rutis, at all men mot se. And þan he said; "Now may ye see at I may nott be a bisshopp, for þe law will not at a man be made a bisshopp & owder of his eris be off." And þan þer was a bisshopp þat hight Dorotheus, & he said vnto [*þe*] peple þat þe Iewis kepid þat law; "Bod emang vs Cristen men I doute not þat & a man bothe eris war cutt off, & his maners wer gude & honest, bod he wer wurthie to be a bisshopp & myght be made ane." And when þe peple hard þis þai said he sulde be þer bisshopp magre his tethe. And when he saw þat, he was wrothe, & said; "fforsuth! and ye make me bisshopp, I sall cutt oute my tong at ye sall nott witt what I say." And when þai hard þis, þai lete hym go.

Contempni potest mundus eciam inter amicos carnales. Infra de pecunia. iiij.

Contemptum mundi inducit aliquando memoria mortis. Infra de memoria mortis in pluribus narracionibus, *et* supra de cogitacione. iiij.

Contemptum mundi inducunt transitoria que sunt in mundo. Supra de Ambicione. ij.

Contemptum mundi inducit aliquando falsitas amici. Supra de Amico. vj. vij. *et* x.

Contempnentes sacramenta ecclesie aliquando moriuntur sine ipsis. Infra de Sortilegio. j.

[1] Latin MSS. *Animosus.*

CCIII.

Continens debet [motus][1] sensualitatis *et* co*m*plexionis nat*ur*al*is* reprimere.

Cassianus tellis þat when Socrates þe philosophur be co*m*plexion off his bodye was disposid vnto many synys, so on a tyme þ*er* was a man þat beheld hym ons, & sayd he had þe een of child body. And Soc*r*ates disciples þoght þai wold bete hym for þe skorn he gaff þ*er* maist*er*; and þ*er* maist*er* wulde not latt þai*m*, bod garte þai*m* lefe & do hym no skath; "for it is wit*h* me as he said, bod I wit*h*-draw me fro þat at I am desposid to."

Continens ecia*m* habita op[*p*]ortunitate p*e*ccandi se custodit. Infra de temptacione carnis.

Continens ecia*m* mortem sustinet anteq*u*am p*e*cc*a*to consensiat. Infra de temptacione carnis. j.

CCIV.

Contricio p*er*fecta nulla*m* pena*m* corporale*m* formidat.

Cesarius tellis how on a tyme when a p*r*este was p*r*echand & telland of synnys & þe paynys of hell, a wom*m*an cried vnto hym & sayd; "Sur, whatt sall wurth of p*r*estes lemmans?" And he knew sho was bod a symple thyng & answerd halfe in sporte & said; "Thai sall nevur be savid bod if þai crepe into a hate oven." And sho was a p*r*estis lemman, & sho tuke not þis wurde in bowrte, bod on a day sho hate a grete oven, and no-bodie wit*h* hur; & when it was rede hate sho sparrid þe duris to hur & crape into it. And onone sho was burnyd to dead. And þ*er* was a grete felashupp of men & wom*m*en standand sam*en* wit*h*-oute, nerehand hur place, and þai*m* þoght þai saw a white dowfe fle fro hur howse vnto heven. And þai had grete wonder þ*er*off, and brak upp hur duris; & þai fande hur burnyd of dead in þe oven, & þai drew hur oute & berid hur in þe felde as men duse wit*h* þai*m* att kyllis þ*er*

[1] Latin and English MSS. *have* homo *instead of* motus.

selfe. So afterward allmighti God wold latt it be knawen þat sho slew not hur selfe of malece nor of ill will, bod for penans & obediens; opon nightis þ*er* was sene a huge light abowte hur grafe. & þan þai tuke hur vpp & layd hur in Crystens mans beriall.

CCV.

Contricio p*er*fecta ecia*m* sine confessione delet pecc*a*t*a*.

Cesarius tellis how on a tyme þ*er* was a scoler at P*ar*issh, þat had done many vglie syn, & he wold not shrife hym of þai*m* for shame; notw*it*h*s*tondyng h*er*telie cont*r*icion ouer-come his shame, & on a tyme he come vnto þe p*r*iour of Sayntꝰ Victors, & wold hafe bene shrevyn. & þ*er* was so mekull cont*r*icion in his harte, & so many sobbis in his breste, & so many syghyng*is* in his throte, & so many teris in his een, þat he mot not speke nor say a wurd. And when þe p*r*iour saw þis, he bad hym go & write his syn; and so he did, and come agayn, & yitt for sorow he myght not speke a wurd, bod gaff þis byll vnto þe p*r*iour. And he red it, & hym thoght þe synnys wer so grete at he desyrid þe scolar þat he mott latt his abbott se itt, at he myght aske hym cowncell þ*er*in. And he lete þe abbott se it; and when þe abbott lukid þ*er*-vppon, he cuthe se nothyng wretten þ*er*in; & þan he said vnto þe p*r*iour; "What may I rede here, whar right noght is wretten?" And when þe p*r*iour saw þatt, he had grete wondre þ*er*of & said; "Sur, forsuthe a yong man wrate his confession here-vppon, and I redd it my selfe; bot now I se þat God is m*er*cifull, þat gracioulie hase behalden his contricion and forgiffen hym his syn." And þus bothe þe abbott & þe p*r*iour told þis scolar & assoylid hym; and þus w*it*h grete ioy & myrth he went fro þai*m* home vnto his lugyng.

CCVI.

Contricio p*er*fect*a* pecc*a*t*a* remittit.

Cesarius tellis how som tyme þ*er* was a wom*m*an þat lete hur awn son gett hur a barn; and when þis barn was born, sho bare it in hur armys vnto Rome, & þ*er* wit*h* grete wepyng & sorow, sho shrafe hur vnto Pope Innocent afor all his cardinallis. And þe pope enioynyd hur vnto penance at sho suld com befor hym on þe morn in þe same clothyng at sho had on when sho went to syn wit*h* hur son. And on þe morn sho did of all hur clothyng, and in hur sarke alone sho come afor þe pope, and said sho was redi to fulfill whatt penance som-eu*er* he wold enioyn hur. And when þe pope saw þatt, he said vnto hur; "þi syn is forgyffen the." And one of þe cardynals when he hard þis, began to gruche agayn þe pope, & said he demyd vnsufficientlie. And þan þe pope said vnto hym; "and I hafe demyd ill, þe devull entre into me; and if I hafe wele demyd, þe same happen þe, becauce at þou gruchid here-in." And onone att all saw at wer aboute, þe devull began to vex þis cardinall, becauce att he gruchid þat þe pope declarid vnto þis wom*m*an þat hur syn was forgyffyn hur.

Contric*io* p*er*fect*a* p*er* op*er*a manifestatur. Inf*r*a de peni*tenci*a. ij.

Contricio aliqu*ando* excitatur a p*resen*t*i*a bonor*um*. Inf*r*a de visitacione. j.

CCVII.

Contricio p*er*fecta liberat a confusione temporali.

Cesarius tellis how som tyme þ*er* was in England a clark þat was a chanon in Lincoln Mynster, and he was nere sybb cussyn vnto þe bisshopp. & þ*er* was a Iew wonnyd in þe town, & he had a fayr dought*er*: and þis clerk laburd hur so att sho p*ro*mysid hym att he suld lyg by hyr, bod sho said hur fadur luffid hur so wele & kepid hur so þat þai myght nott com sam*en* bod on Gude Fryday nyght; ffor þan þe Iewis hase a bludie flux, & þai vse little to be occupyed or com forward. And when þat night come, þis chanon hafeyng no mynd of þe Passion of Criste þ*at* he suffred as þat day, come vnto hur & lay wit*h* hur vnto on þe morn. And hur fadur rase & come in-to þe chambr þ*er* sho lay, & saw a man in bedd wit*h* his dought*er*, & he thoght for to hafe slayn hym. And when he lukid on hym, he knew wele enogh at he was þe bisschoppis cussyn, and þerfor he was aferd to sla hym; & he cryed *with* a hedus voyce & sayd; "O! þou fals Christen man! what duse þou here in syn þis day? What is þi faith? Be þe dome of God rightwuslie þou ert giffen in-to owr handis; and warn it wer for drede of þe bisshop at þou ert cussyn vnto, onone I sulde sla the." And þus *with* grete confusion he showed hym oute att þe dure; and he went home, & happend þat day, þat is to say Pasch-even, to be assigned be þe bisshopp to be his dekyn in serves tyme & rede þe pistle; & he was ferd as on such a day to commytt his offes vnto ane other man, for drede of suspecte; & he was also ferd to com nere þe altar & þe halie sacrament *with* so grete syn as he was in. And yitt for shame he myght nott fynd in his harte to shryfe hym, so he was þus ouercommen *with* shame, & did on his mes clothis, & stude att þe altar befor þe bisshopp. And sodanlie þis Iew and a grete meneya of oþer Iewis *with* hym come in att þe mynster dure *with* a huge durdom & a noyse, ffor to make complaynt vnto þe byssbopp of his cussyn. And als tyte as þis yong chanon saw þaim, he wex pale & was passand ferd, and made his prayer vnto God in his harte, & sayd þus; "Lorde Iesu! delyuer me & safe me shameles of þis Iewis at þis tyme, and I beheste þe hertelie þat I sall shryfe me of þis syn & make a sethe þerfor; & fro hens furth I sall no more offend þe." So þis bisshopp saw þies Iewis & had grete mervayle whatt þai did in þe kurk, & speciallie suche a day; and he commaundid þaim to stand, & askid þaim what þai mente. And onone as þai wold hafe accusid þis clerk, be þe vertue of God, þai wer all dombe, & myght nott speke. & when þe bisshopp saw þaim gaspe *with* þer mowthis agayns hym & mott speke no wurde, he trowid att þai come for illusion of þe sacrament, & *with* indignacion[1] he commanddid þaim to be put oute of þe mynster. And þis clerk felid att God had had mercie on hym; & when serves was done, he went vnto þe bysshopp & shrafe hym, and afterwerd made hym a monk in Ceustus ordur. And þai garte cristen þis damysell, & made hur a non of þe same ordur; and afterward þai bothe wer gude halie liffers.

[1] MS. *with* indignacion &.

CCVIII.

Cont*r*icione sola deficiente, co*n*fessio nec aliqua bona sufficiunt ad pecc*at*i dimissio*n*em.

Som tyme þ*er* was a yong man þat was a chanon in Parissh, þat liffid incontinent and delicatelie, & did many grevos syn. So on a tyme he was passand seke, & shrafe hym & made sorow for his syn & hight to amend hym, and reseyvid his sacrament, & was enoyntid; and so he dyed & was wurthelie berid. So wit*h*-in a few dayes after he was deade, he apperid vnto ane þat he was familiarie wit*h*, & told hym þat he was dampnyd, & said þuff all he war shreven & howseld & enoyntid, & beheste to do penance, yit he said he forgatt a thyng, wit*h*oute þe whilk all oþ*er* þinges may nott p*ro*fett. And he askid hym what was þatt, & he said; "Contricion; ffor þuf all," he said, "I p*ro*mytt to lefe my syn, yit my co*n*sciens said vnto me: 'what & I mend, I sall fall vnto syn agayn'; ffor my harte more declynyd vnto þat þan not for to syn. & þ*er*for I had no faste purpos in gudnes, & so be þe consequent, I had no p*er*fite cont*r*icion, & þ*er*for I am dampned."

CCIX.

Contricio p*er*fecta ecia*m* in iudicio dei pecc*at*a remittit quo ad culpa*m*, et quo ad penam.

Jacobus de Vet*r*iaco tellis how þ*er* was a damysell þat synnyd wit*h* hur[1] fadur in syn of lichorie, & hur moder on a tyme purseyvid itt & blamyd hur & reprovid hur þ*er*for, vnto so mekle, sho slew hur moder. And when hur fadur wiste þis, he had hur in hatered; and when sho pursayvid þis, as hur fadur was slepand vndernethe a matres, sho smoryd hym odead, & þan sho become a com*m*on wom*m*an. And on a tyme a gude holie man p*re*chid, and hur happend to be at his s*er*mon; and he tolde mekull of þe m*er*cye of all-myghti God, vnto so mekull þat when his s*er*mon was done, sho come vnto hym wit*h* grete cont*r*icion, & shrafe hur

[1] MS. þ*er*.

of all hur synys, & asked hym if þe m*er*cie of God was so grete as he p*re*ched att it was. And he answerd & said þat it was mekull more; and þan sho bad hym enioyne hur penans, for sho trustid mekill in his m*er*cie. And he vmthoght hym þat he cuthe not so sodanlie enioyn hur helefull penance for hur syn þat was so grete. And he bad hir abide vnto after meate, & þan he wold p*re*che agayn; "& þan," he said, "I sall giff þe penans." And sho insswerd hym agayn & sayd; "Sur, I trow ye be in dispayr of my sawle heale." & he sayd; "Nay! bod in stede of penance, I enioyn þe to abyde here in þi prayers so lang." And so sho did. And in þe mene-while sho had so mekull sorow & contricion for hur syn, þat hur harte breste in two, & sho dyed. And þis was onone told þis p*re*chur how it was, & he com*m*awndid þe pepull h*er*tely to pray for hur; and as þai wer in þ*er* prayers, þar come a voyce vnto þai*m* fro hevyn, þat sayd; "Pray not for hur, for sho is in hevyn. Bod pray vnto hir þ*er*, for to pray for you."

Cont*r*icio aliqu*ando* excitatur in corde *pecca*t*or*is ex*empl*o bono. Sup*r*a de Abb*a*te. vij[1].

Cont*r*ic*io* p*er*fect*a* volu*n*tate*m* fac*it* pro *fact*o reputari. Inf*r*a de volu*n*tate.

Cont*r*ic*io* in fine ho*min*em saluat. Inf*r*a de milite *et sup*r*a* de ambicione. iij.

Cont*r*ic*io* ecia*m* imp*er*fect*a*[2] qu*ando*q*ue* iuuat. Inf*r*a de obstinacione. ij.

Cont*r*icio ecia*m* negantes d*eu*m ei reconsiliat. Inf*r*a de negacione dei, *et* sup*r*a de ambicione. iij.

Cont*r*icio p*er*fecta ecia*m* vsurarios saluat. Inf*r*a de test*amento*[3] *et* de vsurario.

Contricio p*er*fect*a* ecia*m* latrones *et* homicidas saluat. Supra de Abb*a*te vj. *et* de apostata. iij.

Contumelias pacient*er* sustinet humilis. Infra[4] de humilitate. ij.

[1] MS. vj. [2] MS. inperfecta. [3] MS. testið. [4] MS. Supra.

CCX.

Conu*er*cio. Conu*er*ti facit pecc*a*tore*m* aliqu*ando* consideracio p*er*petuitatis pene infernalis.

Fulco [1] telles how þat M*ar*ciliensis þat was bisshopp of Tholosan told of hym selfe; "when I was yong & giffen vnto vanyties of þis werld, I began ans sodanlie [*to think*] of þe evurlastyngnes of þe payn of hell, and I said in my harte; 'and it war putt vnto þe to lig alway in a softe bed & a delicatt, so þat in no man*er* of wise þ*ou* sulde pas oute þ*er*of, and þou might not suffer þatt, how may þou þ*er*for sustene in þe euerlastand & bitt*er* payn of hell, if it happen þe to be dampnyd thedur?' And be þis occasion I lefte all þingis and made me a monke."

CCXI.

Co*n*uerti ecia*m* fac*it* pecc*at*orem co*n*sideracio ac*er*bitatis pene inf*er*ni.

We rede in 'Libro de Dono Timoris,' how þat þ*er* was a yong man þat was riche and delicate, and he made hym a freer p*re*chur. And his frendis come vnto hym & wold hafe had hym oute of his ordur; and þai said vnto hym þ*at* he myght not suffer þe austeritie of his ordur. þan he vmthoght hym & said vnto hym selfe; "The bitt*er* payn of hell, þat is vntollerable vnto me, and þerfor I hafe chosyn me rather to suffyr þis payn þan þatt."

Co*n*ue*r*sus ad[*d*]iscens l*itt*eras efficitur p*e*ruersus. Inf*r*a [de demone. vii.

Conue*r*sus neq*u*am punitur. Inf*r*a de histrionib*us*. iij.

CCXII.

Conu*er*ti ecia*m* facit aliqu*ando* pecc*a*tore*m* consideracio mortis subite.

We rede in 'Lib*ro* de Dono Timoris,' how som tyme þ*er* was a noble clark þat was a grete baron son; and he went & made

[1] Arund. MS. Fulco Marsilens*is*: episcopus Tholosamus. Harl. MS. Fulco Marsilione: epi*scopus* Tholosa*nus*.

hym a freer pr*e*chur. And when his fadur hard tell of þis, he vmthoght hym þat he wold dryfe þase freers oute of þe land, & take his son fro emang þa*im*. And when þe freers hard tell of þis, þai all sam*en* went vnto þis baron *with* all þe mekenes att þai cuthe, and told hym þat þai tuke not his son & made hym freer in violent, bod he offerd hym þ*er*to on his awn gude will. And he said þai said wrang, & þ*at* he sulde prufe & evur he myght mete *with* his son. And so þai lete his fadur & hym speke sam*en*, & he trowed þat onone *with* a wurd he sulde averte his purpos. And he said vnto hym on þis man*er* of wise; "Son, þou hase husely trubled me becauce þou hase made þe a freer. Bod not forthi, & þou will lefe þine ordur & go home *with* me, I sall forgiff þe all." And þis yong freer answerd hym agayn & sayd; "Fadur, I wull nott go home *with* you bod if ye wull beheste me þ*at* ye sall fordo ane ill custom þat is *with*in your lord-schup." And his fadir said he suld do what att evur hym plesid to byd hym do, and bad hym tell hym what þis custom was. And þis yong freer said it was þis, thatt als sone dyes a yong man as ane olde man. And when his fadur hard þis, he tuke a grete *com*punccion in his harte & lete hym alone *with* þe freers, and went home agayn, and nevur desirid hym after. *et* c^{9}.

Conu*er*tu*n*tur ecia*m* aliqui ex conside*r*acione p*ro*p*r*ii corporis ne in inferno comburantur. Inf*r*a de obstinacione.

Conu*er*sus aliqua*n*do efficit*ur* [perversus [1]] *et* dampnatur. Inf*r*a de obstinacione.

Conu*er*tuntur aliqui solo corde religionis habitu*m* assumentes *et* no*n* corde vel p*r*oposito. Infra de Nouicio.

Conu*er*sio ad religione*m* ecia*m* infirmo corporalit*er* p*r*odest. Inf*r*a de voto.

[1] From Latin MSS.

Conu*er*tu*n*tur aliqui occ*asi*one confusionis alicui*us*. Sup*ra* de confusione. j.

Conu*er*tu*n*tur ecia*m* aliqui ex hijs que vident in defu*n*ctis sibi apparentib*us*. Infra de sciencia nigromantica.

Co*n*u*er*tuntur aliqui ex ben*e*ficio sibi p*r*estito. S*upra* de contricione.

Conu*er*tu*n*tur ecia*m* aliqui exemplo bono. S*upra* de Abb*a*te. vij.

Conu*er*tu*ntur* aliqui exhortacione bona. Sup*r*a de Abb*a*te. iij.

Conu*er*tu*n*tur aliqui or*ati*one *sanctorum*. Inf*r*a de be*a*to Dom*ini*co. iiij.

Cor. Cor ho*minis* no*n* potest saciare quicquid est in mu*n*do. Infra de Saciare. Et supra de ambicione.

Cor ho*min*is eleuatur ex honore exhibito. Sup*r*a de augurio. ij.

Corpori nocet aliqu*ando* gaudiu*m*, *et* p*r*odest dolor. Infra de gaudio.

Corporales delicias[1] secu*n*tur frequent*er* miserie *et* calamitates corporales. Inf*r*a de delicijs. j.

CCXIII.

Corporale Altaris sang*u*inem emisit.

We rede in 'Gestis Beati Gregorij,' how þ*er* was a wurthi mañ þat was knoweñ *with* Saynt Gregur; and he sent vnto hym̃ messangers and prayed hym̃ to send hym̃ som̃ relikk*is* owd*er* of appostels or martyrs. And he reseyvid þai*m* honestlie & helde

[1] MS. diuicias. Latin MSS. delicias.

þai*m* *with* hym a gude while, and went *with* þai*m* vnto dyvers placis of Saynttis þat þai askid relikk*is* of, & sang mes þ*er*. So att þe laste he tuke smale pecis of ilk corprax whar þat he sang, and putt þai*m* in small boystis, & selid þai*m* p*ri*valie & gaff þai*m*; and þai tuke þai*m*. And as þai went hamwerd þai said ilkone to oþ*er*; "we have had a fonde iorney and wate neu*er* what p*re*cious þing we hafe broght hame vnto our lord." And þai brak þe pope seale & oppynd þies boystis, & þai fande no þing bod smale pecis of lyn clothe. And *with* indignacion þai come agayn vnto Rome & told ane archedekyn how þai had done. And at þe laste þai wer broght afor Saynt Gregur; and he said his p*ra*yers & did mes. And þan he tuke one of þies little pecis of clothe, & cutt it in sonder in þe myddest *with* a knyfe; & onone blude come oute þerof, & made all þe clothe blodye. And when þies messangers saw þis, þai had grete wonder þ*er*off, & þai fell on þ*er* kneis and þankid almiȝtti God; and þan þe pope putt þai*m* in þe boystis agayn & selid þai*m* & gaff þai*m* þai*m* agayn, & bad þai*m* be stedfaste in belefe. & þus þai went home vnto þ*er* lorde *with* grete myrth & ioy, and delyverd þies relikk*is* vnto hym. *et c*.

CCXIV.

Corporale immu*n*diciam sp*irit*ualem non sustinet.

Cesarius tellis how som tyme þ*er* was a non att was sacristan. So on a day sho wasshid þe corprax & gaff it vnto a damysell to dry; and onone as sho tuchid it þ*er* apperid a dropp & a spott of blude. And when þe Sacristan saw it, onone sho wasshid it agayn; & als sone as þe damysell tuchid it, þer apperid a noder spott of blude. & þan sho lete þe p*ri*ores & all hur susters se it; and þai had grete m*er*vaile þ*er*off, & went vnto þ*er* prayers, & besoght God att þai myght hafe a knowlege what it ment. And þai serchid þis damysell, & fand þat a man had liggyn by hur & gettyn hur *with* childe.

CCXV.

Chorizare. Chorizantes aliqu*ando* visibilit*er* puniu*n*tur.

We rede how þat a preste þat hight Tullius on a tyme opon þe Yole-evyn said mes in a kurk of Saynt Magnus. And þ*er* was in þe kurk-garthe a grete meneya of men & women dawnssand in a cercle and syngand carals, & lettid dyvyne *serves* wit*h* þ*er* noyse & þ*er* cry. And þis preste com*ma*wndid þai*m* to lefe & þai wold not for hym. And when he saw þai wold not lefe, in his mes he prayed vnto God & Saynt Magnus þat it mot please þai*m* at þai sulde abide so still vnto þe yere end; and so þai did. And all þat yere nowder rayn nor snaw fell opon þai*m*, nor þai wer neu*er* hongrie nor thrustie, nor þ*er* clothes ware nott; bod eu*er* þai went aboute syngand carals as þai had be mad folk. And þer was a yong man þat had his sister emang þai*m*, & he tuke hur be þe arm & wold hafe drowen hur fro þai*m*, & he pullid of hur arm; & þ*er* come no blude furthe, bod sho dawnsid on still: & þus þai did all þe yere to it was passid. And þan Hub*er*tus at was bysshopp of Colayn [*com*] & assoylid þai*m* & lowsid þai*m* oute of þis band, and recowynceld þ*er* befor þe altar. And þ*er* dyed of þai*m* þ*er* a man & ij wom*me*n; and all þe toder slepid iij dayes & iij nyghtis to-geder; and som of þai*m* had a tremblyng of all þ*er* bodie evur aft*er* ewhils þai liffid. And þis happend in a town of Duche-land, in þe yere of owr Lord M.L.X.

CCXVI.

Correpcio. Corrigu*n*tur aliqui p*er* moniciones s*ib*i f*a*ct*as* a bonis.

We rede in 'Libro de Dono Timoris,' how þ*er* was a religious man þat was passand contemplatyfe; and on a tyme he was sodanlie ravisshid vnto his dome. And þ*er* he saw ij grete men, of þe whilk þe tane was ane Erle, and þe toder a grete p*re*latt; and þai wer hugelie accusid befor our Lord. Agayns þe whilk, þuf all hym̄ semyd passand grevid, neu*er*-þe-les, be prayers of som̄ of þai*m* att wer of þat cowrte, he putt our his sentans and said vnto þis religious man̄ at he suld make þai*m* hafe knowlege hereoff be his Abbott; & so he did. And þis Erle, for drede of þis vysion̄ at was told hym̄, forthoght his syn̄ & did penans þ*er*for, and dyed a gude man̄. And þis prelatt sett lightly be þis visyon̄ & þis warnyng, and wold nott amend his life. And afterward hym̄ happend to be fon̄ sodanlie dead in his bed on̄ a nyght. *et c*.

CCXVII.

Corrip*er*e debet pat*er* filiu*m*, *et* p*re*latus subditum.

We rede in þe same buke how þ*er* was a yong man̄, & he was tenderlie broght vp & noþing correcte nowd*er* of fadur nor moder when̄ he did wrong; so he become a thefe, & stale grete gudis. And on̄ a tyme he was taken̄ & demyd to be hanged: and as he was led vnto þe galos he desyrid at he mott se his fadur or he dyed; and he was broght. And he besoght hym̄ to forgiff hym̄ all offensis at he had made vnto hym̄, & so he did; & þan̄ he prayed hym̄ to kis hym̄. And as he kissid hym̄, he bate of his fadur nece; and þai þat wer abowte hym̄ had grete m*er*vayle þ*er*off, and said ffellie vnto hym̄ þ*er*for. And he answerd þai*m* agayn̄ & said; "I sulde hafe done hym̄ more skathe and I had myght, ffor he is cauce of my dead; for he chastid not me when̄ I was yong, bod let me fall to gou*er*nans & to mysreule at I am now dampned to my dead for, & mon be hanged."

Corripiendi su*n*t p*ar*uuli. Sup*r*a de blasfemia.

CCXVIII.

Corripiendi sunt rebelles ecia*m* si impacient*er* ferant.

Helynandus tellis of a philosophur þat hight Policartus[1] þat was a techur of þe Emp*er*our Troian̄, þat had ane vnthrifti servand & ane ill; & on̄ a tyme he had done a grete faute. And þis

[1] Harleian MS. Policarpus.

philosophur his maist*er* gart in his awn presens take off his clothis & bete hym wele nakid; and[1] as þai bett hym he cryed & sayd þat his maist*er* was no trew philosophur, þat had writtenn so fayr a buke of mekenes as he did, & for all þat was turnyd in-to wrath agayns hym. And be þis mene, he said, his techyng was contrari vnto his warkis. And his maist*er* answerd hym agayn & sayd; "Semys it to þe þat I am angri becauce þou erte bett? And þink*is* þ*o*u at it is yre, at I pay þe at I aw? þou seis I hafe no burnyng een, nor no spome at my mouthe, nor I cry not lowde, nor I wax not rede, nor trembles nott, nor hase no synge on me þat sulde be yrefull." And in þe mene-while he bad hym þat bett hym þat he suld contynue as he began ewhill þai ij disputid; "And *with*-outen any yre þou sall se me correcte þis ill servand, & teche hym rather to be meke & speke fayr, þan for to flite or strife *with* his maist*er*."

CCXIX.

Cosme & Damyani.

Ther was som tyme a man þat had a speciall deuocion vnto Saynt Cosme & Damyan, & þe canker happend into þe the of hym & had wastid it nerehand away. And on a tyme as he was slepand, hym thoght þies ij saynttis come vnto hym, & þai broght *with* þai*m* oyntementt*is* & playsters. And þe tone of þai*m* said vnto þe toder; "Whar sall we take vs flessh, þat we may fill þe hole *with* agayn when we hafe cut oute þe rotyn flessh?" And þe toder answerd agayn & sayd; "In þe kurk garth of Saynt Petur ad Vincula[2], ffor þis day was þ*er* a man of Ynde[3] new berid; and þ*er*for go feche vs of þat, at we may fill þe hole *with*." & þis man of Ynd hight Maurus; & þai went & fechid his bodi, and þai cut of þe þe of þe whik man & þan of þe dede man, & putt þe dead mans the vnto þe whik mans, & anoyntid þe wownd dili-gentlie; & þai tuke þe seke man the & put it *with* þe bodie of þis Maurus, and layd hym agayn þ*er* he was. And þan þis seke man wakkend, and felid at hym aylid no sore, & putt down his

[1] MS. as. [2] MS. Saynt Petur Aduincula. [3] Latin MSS. Ethiops.

hand vnto his hambe, & he felid no hurte; & he garte light a candyll, & lukid, and his the aylid nothyng. And þan he was fayn & rase oute of his bed; and he told vnto euer-ilk man what he had sene in his slepe, & how he was helid. And þai at he told it vnto, went vnto þis Maurus grafe, & lukid; & þai fand his legg away, & þe whik mans leg layd þer in-stede þeroff in þe grafe with þe dead mans bodie.

CCXX.

Credere. Credendum est non cito contra amicum.

Valerius tellis how on a tyme it was told vnto Plato þat Democrates[1] his disciple had said mekull ill agayns hym; & he wold giff no fayth þerto. So he att told itt, askid hym whi þat he wold not truste hym, & he said he was redie to profe it at he had told hym. [*Than*] this Plato answerd & said; "It is not trowable at he þat I hafe luffid so lang, att I sulde not be luffid of hym agayn." And so he wold gif no truste vnto þe complaynt vnto he spak with hym hym selfe.

CCXXI.

Credere cito periculosum est iudici.

We rede in Cronicles, how on a tyme þe Emperour[2] had a wyfe, þat wold at ane Erle of his on a tyme had liggen by hur. And when sho desirid hym þervnto, he excusid hym & said he wold not do such a truspas vnto his lord. And sho saw þat, & went & accusid hym vnto þe Emperour, and said he wold hafe defowlid hur. And þe Emperour tuke it vnto so grete wrath, þat he garte smyte of his head with-owten Iugement; and he was neuer[3] olife agayn. & þan þe emperour desyrid his wyfe at þis erle mot be knowen after he was dead be beryng of a hate yrn, at luke wheþer he war innocent or noght; & sho grawntid. And þe day of Iugement was assigned, and many wedos & maydens callid vnto þe

[1] Latin MSS. Zenocrates.

[2] Latin MSS. Otto *tertius* imperaor.

[3] Neuer *omitted, and added above the line.*

dome; and þis Erlis wife come *with* hur husband heade in hur arm. And sho asked of þe Emp*er*our what deade he war wurthi to hafe, þat slew a man wronguslie. And he said his head war wurthi to be smetyn off. And sho answerd hym agayn & sayd: "Thou ert þat man, þat at fals suggestion off þi wife slew my husband. And for to make prefe here-of, I oblissh me to bere þe hate yrn." And when þe Emp*er*our saw þis, he had grete m*er*vell, & com*m*ytt hym selfe to abide what punyssment at sho wolde deme hym vnto. So be p*r*ayer of bisshoppis & oþ*er* worthi men he tuke respecte *with* hur furst for x, ten dayes, & þan for viij, & þan for vij, & þan for vi. And in the mene while he garte examyn þe cauce. And when he knew þe trewth, he gaff hur for his rawson iiij castels þat er in þe bisshop[*ryk*] of Lunens. And be respecte at he had of þe dayes, þai er callid, Decimu*m*, Octauu*m*, Septimu*m*, & Sextu*m*, yitt vnto þis day.

CCXXII.

Credendum no*n* est de facili referentib*us* aliorum defectus.

We rede ex 'Dictis Pat*rum*,' þat a c*er*tan religious man on a tyme said vnto þe abbott Pastor, þat he was so trubbled att hym burd lefe his place, becauce at hé hard c*er*tan wurdis of a bruther of his þat hym thoght plesyd hym noght. And þis Abbott bad hym at he suld nott trow þies wurdis, for þai wer not trew. And þe toder said þai wer trew, for a trew broder of his tolde hym þai*m*; and þe abbott sayd he was not trew at told hym, ffor he sayd, & he had bene a trew bruther he sulde noght hafe said so. And þan he askid hym of þe balke & þe mote, what þai wer; and he told hym whatt þai war. And þan he bad hym vmthynk hym in his awn harte þat þis balk was his awn synys, and þis litle mote was þe synnys of þe toder man.

Credere cito cont*ra* vxore*m* no*n* debet vir. Inf*ra* de regina v*el* imp*er*at*r*ice.

Credendu*m* no*n* est om*ni* ve*r*bo. Sup*ra* de consilio *et* infra de paciencia, iij. Et supra de accusacione. iij.

CCXXIII.

Credend*um* no*n* est om*ni* spiritui an*te*q*u*am p*ro*bandi sint vtru*m* su*n*t ex deo vel non.

We rede in 'Vitis P*atrum*,' how þe devuƚƚ, made hym̄ in liknes of a gude angeƚƚ, come vnto a solitarie at his fadir vesett eu*er*-ilk day, and bad hym̄ be war of þe devuƚƚ, for he was besy eu*ere* day to begyle hym̄; "and tomorn̄," he said, "he wiƚƚ come to þe in liknes of þi fadur; and þ*er*foꝛ now venge þe on̄ hym̄, & luke at þou hase a sharpe ax redie, at when̄ he com*m*ys nere the, gif hym̄ so grete a strake on̄ þe hede att he p*re*sume no moꝛ to com̄ vnto the." And þis ankir trowid þ*at* he had bene ane angeƚƚ at had bene sent vnto hym̄ fro God Hym̄ selfe to giff hym̄ þis cownceƚƚ; & on̄ þe day after his awn̄ fadur come vnto hym̄ at vissit hym̄, and he wit*h* ane ax killid hym̄, and was takyn̄ þ*er*for & hanged evyn̄ furth-wit*h*.

Crimen falso imponitur. Infra de infamia.
Cristus. Cristianus, vbi agitur de *Cristo* inf*ra*.

CCXXIV.

Crudelitas. Crudele est malu*m* p*ro* bono[1] reddere.

We rede in þe storie of Nero, when̄ Senec at was his maister askid hym̄ his ffe for his labur, he answerd agayn̄ & said; "Maister[2], þou muste dye; for als lang as þou liffis I may hafe nō reste; ffor I hafe bene als ferd for þe as a barn̄ wold hafe bene, & yitt is." And þan̄ Seneca answerd agayn̄ & said; "Sur, sen̄ me bus nedis dy, I pray þe grawnt[2] me att I may dy what mane*r* of dead at me likis to chese my selfe." And Nero grawntid hym̄, & bad hym̄ chese it hastelie, ffor hym̄ burd nedis dye. And þan̄

[1] MS. malo. [2] MS. Maistes.

Senec garte make a grete batth of warm watir & garte putt hym selfe þ*er*in, and garte latt hym blude of bothe his armys. And so he bled odeade. And be þis mean he was callid Seneca, quasi se necans; and be þis mean he was dead.

CCXXV.

Crúdelitas cont*ra* natura*m* detestanda est.

We rede in 'Historia Neronis,' how at þis Nero garte sla his moder & cutt hur in sonder, at he might se how he lay in hur wombe, & whar-*with* he was nurrisshid. And þe philosophirs reprovid hym þ*er*for & said, "þe law denyes, & rightwusnes forbiddis[1], att þe son sulde sla his moder þat sufferd so grete payn for hym in hur burth as sho did, & broght hym vp *with* so grete labur." And þan Nero said vnto þai*m*; "Make ye me to be *with* childe, and afterward to be delyver þ*er*off, at I may hafe v*er*ray knawlege whatt sorow my mod*er* had *with* birth of me when I was born." And þai answerd agayn & said þat it was not possible, þat was contrarie vnto natur. And he said bod if þai did itt, þai sulde dye ilkone. And þan þai made hym drynk*is*, and p*r*ivalie þai made hym to drynk a froske; and be þ*er* crafte þai made it to grow in his body & to wax. And so his bely began agayns natur to bolne, to so mekull att he trowid he was *with* childe; and þai made hym daylie to be dyett *with* such meatt as þai knew wolde nurissh a frosk. So on a tyme his belie warkid hugelie, & he said vnto þies lechis; "Take hede on me, ffor þe tyme of my birth is nere; ffor my belie warkis so, þat I may vnnethis draw myne and." And þan þai gaff hym a purgacion, and he spewid oute a grete froske and ane vglie to luke on, bludie & infecte *with* humers. And when Nero lukid þ*er*vppon, hym vggid þ*er*w*ith*, & he askid; "Had my mod*er* als mekull sorow for beryng of me, as I had for beryng of þis?" And þai said, ya. And þan he com*m*andid þat þis vglie burth of his sulde be norisshid & kepyd, and at it sulde be closid in a stone, as a snyle is in hur shell.

[1] MS. forbiddid.

CCXXVI.

Crudelitas dampnu*m* inferens rei pub*li*ce no*n* est toleranda [1].

We rede in þe same storie, how on a tyme Nero had grete m*er*vall whatkyn a thyng burnyng was; and he garte sett fyre in ane end of Rome, & it burnyd vij dayes & vij nyghtis. And evur he lay in a hy towre & beheld it; & when he saw þe low rise vp into þe ayr, hym thoght it was a fayr syght. And þan þe Romans wex grevid & wold suffre it no langer, & rase & pursewid opon hym, & drafe hym oute of þe cetie, & wold hafe slane hym & þai myght hafe getten hym. And when he saw þat he mot not esskape, he gatt hym a stowre, & gnew vppon þe tone end & made it sharpe w*ith* his tethe, & þrustid hym selfe evyn thrugh þ*er*w*ith*. And þus he made his end. Neue*r*-þe-les we rede in a noder place þat he was devowrid w*ith* wulfis [2].

Crudelis no*n* debet esse iudex. Infra de iudice.
Crudelis no*n* debet esse p*re*latus. Inf*ra* de p*re*lato.

CCXXVII.

Crux Cr*ist*i v*e*l crucifixus. Crucifixi ymago a Iudeis in despectu vuln*er*atur.

We rede how þat in þe tyme of Constantyne þe iiij [3], þe Iewis fand in a cetie ane ymage of þe crucifix; & þai broght it into a Iewis hows, & [4] þ*er* þai spitt þeron & strake it w*ith* þ*er* handis, & naylid þe fete þ*er*of vnto þe cros w*ith* naylis, & þai put vnto þe mouthe þ*er*of aysell & gall. And at þe laste þai oppend þe syde þ*er*of, & þ*er* come blude & watir; and þai sett ane ampull vndernethe it & kepyd it in. And ilkone of þai*m* att was seke, þai wold sprencle of þis blude on þai*m*, & onone þai war hale. So at þe laste þies Iewis forthoght att þai had done, and tuke þis ymage

[1] MS. tolleranda.
[2] MS. wulfid.
[3] Lat. MSS. In Siria, Ciuitate Bericho, Iudei ymagine*m* crucifixi inue*n*ientes in domo cui*us*da*m* Iudei, relicta*m* ibi a quoda*m* Cri*sti*ano qui ibi manserat, ea*m* iniuriose doposuerunt. et cet.
[4] MS. *repeats*, &.

& þe blude, & had it vnto þe bisshopp of þe cetie; and so þai wer cristend & turnyd vnto þe fayth. And of þis blude was sent to many cetis & kyngdoms; & yit to þis day it duse many meracles.

CCXXVIII.

Crucis signum magnam habet virtutem, eciam infidelibus.

Saynt Gregor tellis how þat a bisshopp of þe cetie of Fundan[1] had som tyme in his howse soiornand a non; & be fals temptacion of þe devull, on a tyme he was so tempid at he thoght he wold hafe at do *with* hur. So it happend a Iew to go will on a nyght, & cuthe fynd no place to reste hym in. And he went into a temple of Appollo, & *þer* he layd hym down & slepid. And abowte mydnyght, *þer* come a company of fendis, & *þer* chiftan was sett in a chayr emang*is* þai*m*, & garte þai*m* com befor hym, & examynd þai*m* of *þer* craftis. And when ilk one of þai*m* had tald hym all, ane of þai*m* steppyd befor hym at satt, & said how he had tempyd þis bisshopp *with* þis wom*m*an, & in a burte to giff hur a knokk on þe bakk. And þan *þer* chiftan com*m*endid hym, & chargid hym to *per*form at he had begon. And he com*m*andid þai*m* to seke aboute in þe temple, & luke who was *þer*in mo þan þai. And þis Iew hard þat & made a cros on hym; and þai soght aboute & fand hym. And onone as þai saw hym, one of þai*m* saw, & said; "ve! ve! vas vacuu*m* sed bene signatu*m*; wo! wo! here is a voyde vessall, bod it is wele m*er*kid." And *with* þis voyce, all þe fendis vanysshid away; and þe Iew rase vpp & went vnto þe bisshop of þe cetie & told hym. And he made mekull sorow for his syn, & put away þis wom*m*an & cristend þis Iew. *et c*[9].

CCXXIX.

Cruce signari debent om*n*es p*ro*pt*er* indulgencias.

Jacobus de Vet*r*iaco tellis of hym selfe & says; "On a tyme as I was in a town *pre*chand, *þer* was a man þat durste not com vnto þe *ser*mon for his wyfe, not in-to þe kurk. And he come to a

[1] Latin MSS. Andreas, Fundare civitatis ep*iscopus*.

wyndow & harde þe sermon; and when he had hard of þe ind[*ulg*]ence at longis vnto þai*m* at er m*er*kid w*ith* þe cros, for als mekull as he durste not com in att þe dure for his wyse, he crope in att þe wyndow in myddeste the peple, & tuke þe cros as þai did."

CCXXX.

Cruce signatis datur filius be*a*te virginis.

Jacobus de Vet*ri*aco tellis of hym selfe and says: "ans in my childed, when I was in a howse of Ceustus ordur, þ*er* I hard a sermon of þe cros. And mekill pepull lefte all[1] þe gudis att þai had, and come and wurshuppyd þe cros. So emang þai*m* was a bruther þat hight Symond, and he besoght God att he mott hafe som knowlege whatt mede þai sulde hafe att wurshuppyd þe cros; and on þe nyght after he was ravisshid in his spiritt, and þer he saw our Ladie Saynt Marie holdand hur dere son. And aftre þat eu*er*ilk a man w*ith* a contrite harte had taken þe cros, sho gaff vnto hym hur son." *et c*[9].

CCXXXI.

Cruce signati dolose puniu*n*tur eciam corporaliter.

Cesarius tellis how þat in þe bisshoppryk of Traiectens, ane vsurer tuke þe cros & lete as he wald go vnto þe Holie Land. And when he sulde go furth, he fenyd hym selfe seke & wayke, & sayd he myght not go, and hyrid a-noder to go for hym, & gaff hym bod v marc*is*, þuf all he myght have giffen hym xl[ti] marc*is*. So afterward when þai at wer burnyd wer bown furth, he satt w*ith* þai*m* in þe tavern & sayde vnto þai*m*; "ye wrichis, now ye forsake your wyvis and your childer, & your frendis, and all your other gudis, & puttis your bodis in p*er*els be-yond þe see; and I sitt att home w*ith* my wyfe and my childer, & w*ith* all[2] my gudis, and for v marke hase als mekull p*er*don as ye hafe." Bod almyghti God, att is rightwus, shewyng how mekull þe labur & expens*is* of pylgramys plesis hym, & how mekull desayte &

[1] MS. *repeats,* all. [2] MS. *after* all, al, *erased.*

blasfeme of bakbyters displesis hym̄, sufferd' þatt on̄ þe night after þe devuƚƚ come vnto hym̄ in liknes of a *ser*vand' of his awn̄, and broght *with* hym̄ ij grete blak hors, and bad hym̄ faste caste of his vppermest clothe, & go *with* hym̄ & lope on̄ one of þies hors. And þe cross at he had takyn̄ was sewid' opon̄ his ou*er*meste clothe, and so he vmthoght hym̄ þat he mott not esskape, & keste away his ou*er*meste clothe & onone lepid' on̄ þe to hors, & þe devuƚƚ lepid' on̄ þe tother; & *with*-in a while þai war led þ*er* dyvers paynys wer. And þe·devuƚƚ shewid' hym̄ þe seatt þ*er* he sulde sytt in paynys, and þe devuƚƚ sayd' vnto hym̄; "Now þou saƚƚ turn̄ agayn̄ into þi howse, bod *with*-in iij days þou saƚƚ dy, & turn̄ agayn̄." And þan̄ he was broght agayn̄, and men̄ askid' hym̄ whar he had bene; and he tolde þai*m* aƚƚ as is afor sayd'. And þan̄ a preste was broght vnto hym̄, þat counceld' hym̄ to shryfe hym̄ & do penance for his syn̄. And he wold' nott, bod feƚƚ in despar & dyed *with*outen̄ owder shrift or howsiƚƚ or contricion̄, & was berid' in heƚƚ. *et c*9.

Cruce signatus relinque*n*s amicos carnales m*e*ret*ur*. Inf*ra* de milite. iiij.

Crucifixi amore culpa inimici rem*i*ttitur. Inf*ra* de mis*er*icordia.

Crucem p*re*dicantes a deo remun*er*antur. Inf*ra* de p*re*dicac*i*o*n*e. j.

Cruce signati in via transfretac*i*o*n*is morientes gl*o*riose remun*er*antur. Infra de peregrino[1], *et* in multis alijs locis.

Cruce signatos crucifixus honorat. Inf*ra* de M*a*ria.

CCXXXII.

Cruce signata*m* vestem int*er* flammas illesam deus custodit.

Cesarius tellis how att þe cetie of Susas þ*er* was a cetysyn̄ at was m*er*kid' *with* þe cros. And in þe mene-while, or he went

[1] MS. perigrino.

furth, happend his howse to be burnyd, & all his other gudis safeyng onelie als mekull of a garment of his as þe cros þat he had taken was sewid opon, & þat was fon vnbyrnyd emang þe hate colis. And all þat saw it had grete m*er*vayle þeroff, at þe cros had so mekull m*er*vayle & vertue þ*er*in. *et c*⁹.

Culpa. Culpe respondet pena. Sup*ra* de agro, p*ri*mo *et* ij.

Curatus male intrans eccl*es*iam punitur. Sup*ra* de blasfemia. ij.

Curato eccl*es*ie po*ssu*nt coadaptari multa que dicuntur infra de p*re*lato *et* sacerdote.

Custodia. Custodire debet homo sensus suos. Sup*ra* de aspectu.

Custodiri no*n* potest mulier. Inf*ra* de muliere.

Dampnacio. Dampnatur homo qui toto tempore vite sue s*anct*e vixit, quia finalit*er* peccauit. S*upra* de carnis temptac*i*o*ne*. 3.

Dampnati no*n* iuuantur or*ationi*b*us* viuor*um*. Inf*ra* de or*aci*one. iiij.

Dampnatis no*n* p*ro*su*n*t suffragia. Infra de suffragijs. 3.

Dampnatus ab inferis ex speciali gr*at*ia reuocatur. Infra de or*atione* ij. et viij.

Dampnatis aliqu*ando* be*a*ta d*e*i genit*r*ix vita*m* inpet*r*auit. Inf*ra* de Maria.

Dampnu*m*. Dampnificare p*r*oximu*m* nemo debet reb*us* suis. S*upra* de colu*m*bis.

Dampnu*m* debet restitui dampnificato. Inf*ra* de restituc*i*o*ne*.

Dari no*n* debet hostia no*n* consecrata loco euk*aristi*e. Inf*ra* de euk*aristi*a et infra de or*ation*e. ij.

Dacio siue donu*m*. Dare no*n* debet vxor sine licencia viri. Inf*r*a de muliere.

Dare debent p*r*incipes lib*er*alit*er*. Inf*r*a de liber[*ali*]-tate.

CCXXXIII.

Dant *sancti* res *et* corpus suu*m* p*ro* deo.

We rede in 'Gestis Serapionis Abb*atis*' how þ*at* þis Serapion apon a day gaff his amett vnto a pure man, and it was cald weddur; & he mett a noder pure man, & he gaff his cote. And þan he was nere-hand nakid; and he sett hym down and ane evangill in his hand. And þan one of his brether come vnto hym & sayd; "Abba, who hase robbed you?" And he shewid þe euaungyll & sayd; "this hase robbid me." And wit*h*-in a while after he sold þis euau*n*gill, & gaff þe p*r*ice þ*er*-of vnto pure men. So on a tyme his disciple askid hym whar it was, and he sayd; "I hafe sold it & giffen it vnto pure men, becauce it says: 'vende que h*abes et* da paup*er*ib*us*.'" So on a tyme afterward þ*er* come a wedow vnto hym & askid hym som almos, for sho said sho had nowd*er* meate nor drynk to hur nor hur childer. And becauce he had no thyng to giff hur, he gaff hur his awn selfe, & bad hur sell hym; & so sho did vnto a lorde of Grece land. And wit*h*-in a while fro he had bene þ*er*, he co*nuer*tid all þat contreth & made it cristend.

Dari semp*er* debet elemosina. Inf*r*a de Elemo*si*na.

Data paup*er*i elemosina dat*ur* deo. Inf*r*a de elemosina, et de G*regorio* ij, *et* sup*r*a de Abb*ate*. iiij.

Dona excecant oculos iudicu*m*. Sup*r*a de balliuo. iiij.

CCXXXIV.

Debitu*m* cito debet solui alioquin debitor dampnu*m* incurrit.

Petrus Alphonsus[1] tellis how þ*er* was a porter of a cetie, and he had be a gifte of þe kyng of þat land þat ilk man or wom*m*an

[1] MS. Alphensus.

þat come in att his yate, þat was owd*er* crukyd-bakkid, or skabbid, or þ*at* had bod one ey, or war in þe p*ar*lesie, or a crepyll, he sulde hafe of þai*m* a peny. So on̄ a day þ*er* come in at þe yate a man̄ *with* a crukid bak, & he was wele cled & warm̄. And þe porter arestid hym̄ and bad hym̄ pay hym̄ a peny; & he wold nott. & þe port*er* gatt hym̄ be þe cloke & lifte vp his hude, & he fand þat he had bod one eye, and þan̄ he said; "Now þou awis me ij d." & he wold hafe bene away, & þe porter gatt hald on̄ hys hude, & it went off, & þan̄ his hede was skallid. And þe porter said; "Now þou awis me iij d." And þis man̄ saw at he mott nott gett away, & began̄ to defend hym̄; & his armys happynd bare, & þai wer skabbid. And þan̄ þe porter sayd; "Now þou awis me iiij d." And þus þai wrasteld to-gedyr, & þis man̄ fell, & þan̄ þai mott se he had a croked fute. And þan̄ þe porter said; "Now þou awis me v d"; and garte hym̄ pay itt. And so it happend hym̄ þat wold not pay a peny *with* his gude will, to pay v d ageyns his will. *et c*ꝰ.

CCXXXV.

Debitu*m* debet solui a debitore no*n* petente v*e*l mortuo.

Seneca tellis of a philosophur þat hight Pictagoricus[1], þat boght a payr of shone on̄ a tyme of a sho-maker, bod he had not money enogh to pay for þai*m*; & so he frustid hym̄, & *with*-in a few dayes, he come agayn̄ & callid at þe shomaker dure. And one answerd hym̄ *with*-in & sayd; "Wharto losis þou þi labur? þis sho-maker is dede." þan̄ þis philosophur, fro he hard þis, went home *with* his sylu*er*. So on̄ a tyme, when̄ he was be hym̄ selfe & þoght of þis sylu*er*, hym̄ thoght his conciens sayd vnto hym̄; "þou aw yone man̄ sylu*er*. Ga pay hym̄ þat att þou aw hym̄." And he went agayn̄ þ*er*with, & in at a hole in þe dure he putt ma penys þan̄ he aght, and putt away fro hym̄ þe p*er*ell of his will, þatt gruchid to pay itt.

[1] Arund. MS. Pictagor*us*.

CCXXXVI.

Decepcio. Decepiu*n*tur aliqui sub simulacione boni.

We rede in þe 'Cronicles of Rome,' how þ*er* was som tyme in þe cowrte at Rome a famos clerk þat hight Machomett, and he desyrid to hafe bene made pope [1], & myght not com þ*er*to. And herefor he wex wroth, & went fer þens our þe se; and þ*er*, wit*h* a symulacion, he gadurd sam*en* a grete multitude of yong folk vnto hym, & told þai*m* þat þai*m* burd hafe emangi*s* þai*m* a man to govern þai*m*. And in þe mene-while he vsid to putt whete-cornys in his ere, & he lernyd a white dowffe to stand opon his shulder & take þai*m* oute. So on a day he callid his pepull to-geder, & sayd þai*m* þat it was Goddis will þ*at* he suld be made rewler of þai*m*, whame þat God shewid for be þe Holie Gaste. And p*ri*valie þis dowfe was lattyn go; & onone sho light on Machomett shulder þ*er* he was emang þe prese of peple; & putt hur byll in his ere, & tuke oute þe cornys. And all þe peple at was aboute went at it had bene þe Holie Gaste þat had comm*e*n fro heven and descended on hym, & told hym þe wurd of God in his ere, & what at God wolde hafe done; & þus he was made rewler of all þe Sarracens, & desayvid þai*m*; & he made þai*m* a law att þai kepe yit, whilk þat is callid Machomett law.

Decipit demon bonos sub specie boni. Inf*r*a de demone.

Decipitur iudex freque*nter* si iudicet *secundu*m apparencia*m* ext*er*iorem. Infra de Iudicio humano.

Decipit vicinus vicinu*m*. Supra de Adult*er*io.

Decipiu*n*tur tam boni q*u*am mali p*er* demones multiplicit*er*. Infra de demone [2], *et* alijs locis.

[1] Latin MSS. in Rom*ana* curia honorem que*m* cupiebat assequi no*n* potuisset.
[2] MSS. de decem.

CCXXXVII.

Decipiu*n*tur aliq*ui* pe*r* artem magicam.

Heraclides tellis how þat a man of Egipte was stryken in-to a luste *with* his neghbur wyfe; and he mot neu*er* gett hur will. And he sayd vnto a nygramansyer to make hur to loff hym, & to hate hur awn husband. And he *with* hys crafte made hur a mere, so þat hur husband, when he wakend in his bed, he fand hur a mere lygand by hym. And when he spak vnto hur sho wold giff hym none answer. And he fechid pr*e*stis & lete þai*m* se, & ledd hur vnto þe wud as sho had bene a beste. And he went vnto þe cell of Saynt Machari *with* hur; and þe monkis blamyd hym becauce he come vnto þ*er* monast*e*ri *with* a mere. And he told þai*m* at sho was his wife, & at sho was forshapyn in his bed vnto a mere, & how att þat iij dayes he had etyn no meat. And Saynt Macharie wiste þ*er*-of wele enogh be a reuelacion; & his bretheri*n* went & told hym. And he come vnto þai*m* & sayd; "Ye er bathe as hors, & hase hors een. And hur þis is a wom*m*an, & sho is not transfigurd into þe lyknes of a hors bod vnto þ*er* sightis þat may be begylid *with* vanyte syght." And he made his prayers & kest hali watir on hur & onone sho was a wom*m*an agayn. & þan he garte refressh hur *with* meatt & drynk, & bad hur go home *with* hur husband; and at sho sulde eu*er* whils sho liffid say hur prayers & daylie here mes. For he said sho sufferd all þis becauce þe space of v weki*s* sho nowder hard dyvyne s*er*ves nor mes.

Decipiens p*r*ius aliquem[1] postea qu*ando*q*ue* ab eo decipitur. Infra de vindicta *et* de muliere.

CCXXXVIII.

Deceptor aliqu*ando* in actu decepcionis decipitur *et* forte ab eo que*m* decipe*r*e volebat.

Petrus Alphonsus[2] tellis how on a tyme ij burges went on a fer pylgramege, and þ*er* went *with* þai*m* a husband-man;

[1] MS. aliqu*ando*, Harl. MS. aliqu*em*. [2] MS. Alphensus.

and þai made þaim felows in þer vitals. And when þer vitall was nerehand gane so at þaim was left bod a little flowr, þe burges sayd, tone of þaim vnto þe toder; "we hafe bod litle bread, & our felow etis mykill." And þai ij tuke in cowncell to-gedur at þai sulde take þis flowr & make it all in a lafe & sethe itt; and ewhils it wer in sethyng þai sulde lay þaim down & slepe. And whilk of þaim iij dremyd þe mervolest dreme suld hafe þis lafe & ete it all be his one. And þus þai fenyd to begyle þis husband-man. And þai made þer counand, & þis husband consentid; þan þai made þis lafe & put it to sethyng, & layd þaim to slepe. And þis husband purseyvid þer suteltie, & ewhils þai wer slepand he tuke þis lafe halfe-soden & eete it & laid hym down agayn. Than þies burges wakend, and one of þaim sayd at he had dremyd a mervalus dreme; for hym thoght at ij angels oppynd hevyn yatis, & tuke hym & ledd hym befor allmyghti God. And þe toder sayd at hym thoght þat ij angels cutt þe erthe evyn in sonder, & led hym down vnto hell. And þis husband all þis tyme lete as he slepid & hard þaim well enogh; and þan þai wakkend hym & he starte vp as he had bene flayed, & sayd; "Who is þat att callis me?" And þai sayd; "We, þi felows." And he ansswerd & sayd; "Er ye commen agayn now?" & þai sayd; "Whethyr went we at we sulde com agayn?" And þan þe husband told his dreme, & sayde; "Me thoght att ij angels led þe tane of you vnto hevyn & þe toder vnto hell. And I trowid at ye sulde neuer com agayn, & rase & tuke þe lafe & eet it." & þan þai lukid whar it was, & it was gone, *et c^9*. And þan þe tane of þaim was wroth & sayd þai wer begilde; & þe toder sayd nay, & sayd; "Fallere fallentem non est fraus." *et c^9*.

Decipit aliqu*ando* discip*ulus* magistru*m*. Infra de vindicta.
Decipit aliqu*ando* vxor viru*m*. Inf*ra* de muliere.
Decipit mulier mulierem. Inf*ra* de muliere.
Decipit Demon ho*minem* sub spec*ie* boni. Inf*ra* de solitudine [1].

[1] MS. solicitudine.

Decipiu*n*tur aliqui v*er*bis multor*um*. Infra de v*er*bo *et* de p*ro*misso.

CCXXXIX.

Decipiu*n*tur aliqui quia aliqu*ando* non inueniu*n*t quod queru*n*t.

We rede in 'Libro de Dono Timoris,' how þ*er* was a lord þat had a fule, & þis lorde had also a gay falcon & a swyfte, þ*er* was [*bod*] such one in all þat land. And ilk man at saw it fle com*m*endid it & praysid it. So þis fole hard at ilk man com*m*endid þis falcon so, and p*r*ivalie on a nyght he gat þis falcon of his lordis & slew itt, and sothe itt, & ete itt. And when þe lord myssid þis hawke, he made grete sorow þ*er*for, becauce he wiste nott how it was loste. And he com*m*endid it gretelie in p*re*sens of þis fule; and when þe fule hard hym com*m*end it so, he answerd & sayd; "Forsuthe lord, it dught nott; ffor I ete neu*er* bitterer flessh þan it was." And so þis fule fand a noder þing þan he trowid.

CCXL.

Decima. Decimas bene solu*e*re est vtile.

Cesarius tellis how þ*er* was a knyght þat had so grete deuocion about payment of his tendis, & þat he wold eu*er* of rightwusnes pay þai*m* wit*h*-owten any tarying or wit*h*-oute dissayte or vexacion. And he had a c*er*tan vyneyard of þe whilk he had yerelie x ton of wyne. So it happend on a yere when he had gaderd all his vynys & brayed þai*m*, he had bod a ton of wyne. And when þis knyght saw þat, he sayd vnto his s*er*vand; "That at was myne, God hase taken it fro me; and yitt I will not take His parte fro Hym. And þ*er*for go byd þe p*re*ste feche þis ton of wyne for his tend." And þe prest did so. And þe same yere on a tyme, a bruther of þe same knyght*is*, at was a preste, went down be þe garthyn abowte þe M*ar*tynmes; and he saw all þe vynys hang full of grapis. And he went in-to his bruther & flate wit*h* hym for his neclegens, & sayd; "Whi hafe ye noght yitt gaderd your vynys, & þe yere is so-fortherlie paste?" And þe knyght sayd þat þai war gaderd lang befor. And þe preste sayd nay it was not so; "ffor," he sayd, "I was þeratt þis day, & I saw it grow full of vynys." And þe knyght & his meneya went & lukid, & þai fand it was so. And þai gaderd þaim & made wyne þeroff; & þer grew neuer ryper nor mor plentefull vynys in þat garth þan þase wer. *et* c^9.

CCXLI.

Decanus ad inferni curiam inuitatur.

Cesarius tellis how þat in tyme of Hereticus[1] þe Emperour, in þe kurk of Palernens was þer a certan dean þat sent a servand of his to seke a palfray of his þat hym wantid; & þer mett ane ald man þis servand & askid hym whedir he went & whatt he soght. And he said he soght his maister hors. And þis ald man teld hym þat þis hors was att þe Mownte of Gybber; "and þer," he sayd, "hase my lord kyng Arthur hym. And þat mownte byrnys evur on a grete low as it war full of burned-stone." And þis servand had grete mervayle of his wurdis, and þe alde man said vnto hym; "Saw vnto þi maister & charge hym at þis day xiiij dayes he com thedur vnto Kyng Arthur solempne courte. And if þou forgett & tell hym nott, þou sall be grevuslie punysshid þerfor." And þis servand went home & told his maister all at he sayd vnto hym *with* grete ferdnes. And when þe dean hard att he was sommond vnto þe courte of Arthur, he logh þerat & made a skorn þerof. And onone he fell seke, & þe same day att he was somond he dyed. *et* c^9.

CCXLII.

Dedicacio. Dedicacione ecclesie expellitur ab ea demon.

Saynt Gregur tellis in his Dyaloggis, how on a tyme a kurk of þe Arryans was gyffen vnto Cristen men; and þai garte halow

[1] Latin MSS. Tempore Henrici imperatoris.

itt. And þe relikkis of Saynt Sebastian, & Saynt Agnes & Saynt Agas[1] war broght thedur, all þe peple at was gadderd thedur felid þe grond in the kurk-dure quake, & mofe heder-ward & þedurward. And when þai wer *with*-in þe kirk, þai felid nothyng þeroff. And þai had grete m*er*vell here-off, and all-myghti God lete þai*m* all hafe a knowlege þat it was þe fend þat garte þe erth stir when he went furthe of þat place & it was halowd. *et c9*.

Defectus p*ro*ximor*um* no*n* su*n*t reuelandi indifferen*ter*. S*upr*a de celac*ione*.

Defunctis valent indulgencie. Inf*r*a de indulgencijs.

Defunctis p*ro*su*n*t suffragia. Infra de suffragijs.

Defu*n*cti adiuuantur or*ationi*b*us* viuor*um*. Inf*r*a de or*ati*o*ne*.

Defu*n*ctis valent misse p*ro* eis dicte. Inf*r*a de mortuis.

Defunctis [*conueniunt*][2] que infra dicuntur de mortuis.

Delectacio. Delectant[3] al*iquando* aliq*u*i in modicis. S*upr*a de Basilio.

Delectabile no*n* est videre malos. Inf*r*a de videre.

Deleccio mala est fugienda. Inf*r*a de p*er*ic*u*lis.

CCXLIII.

Delicie. Delicias corporales secuntur frequent*er* miserie et calamitates. *et c9*.

Petrus Damyanus tellis how som tyme þ*er* was a duke at had a wyfe þat liffed so delicatlie & so tenderly þat sho wolde nott wassh hur *with* comm*on* watirs as we do, bod sho wolde gar hur maydyns gader þe dew on somm*er* mornyng*is* at sho mot wassh hur *with*. And sho wold not tuche hur meate *with* hur

[1] Latin MSS. reliquie . . . sancte Agathe.

[2] From the Latin MSS.

[3] *Or* delectant*ur*. MS. not clear.

handis hur selfe, bod after hur carvur had cutt itt in morcels sho wold take it vpp *with* poyntels & crukis of gold & putt itt in hur mowthe. And sho wolde make hur bed so redolent savurand *with* spice þ*at* it was a m*er*vayle to tell off. And as sho liffid þus, be þe rightwusnes of God, sho was so smytyn *with* canker and seknes þat sho rotid so, & sho on life, þat no creatur mot fele þe stynk of hur; to so mekull at all folke lefte hur & all hur s*er*vandis, bod onelie a damysell þat was left to kepe hur; & yitt sho mott not com att hur for stynk *with*-oute sho had at hur nece many wele-saue*r*yng spycis; & yitt sho mott not tarie *with* hur no tyme for horrible stynk. And when sho had ligen þus many day sho dyed, & no body *with* hur. *et c*9.

CCXLIV.

Delicate viuentes in hoc sec*u*lo cogitare debent de penis inferni.

We rede in 'Libro de Dono Timoris' how þ*er* was a delicatt scoler of Bolañ, and he fled þe state of penance and he wold nowder here sermon nor no wurd of God, þat he suld not be movid to be a religious man. So it happend at a freer-p*re*chur, þat was his contrey-man & kend *with* hym, come & visett hym & luked how he did. And when þe scolar saw hym he sayd unto hym; "Freer, & þou will speke *with* me of God I charge nott, and if þou speke *with* me of oþ*er* thyngi*s* þou erte welcom." And þe ffreer ansswerd hym & sayd; "I sall speke furste of oþ*er* erandis, and att þe end I sall speke of God bod a wurd." And when he had said all his erandi*s*, be lefe of þis scolar vnnethis g*r*auntyd, þe freer sayd; "Maist*er*, I pray you for Goddi*s* sake þat þis nyght when ye lye in your bed warm happed, þat ye wold vmthynk you of þe bed þat is ordand in hell to þai*m* þat mon be dampnyd, þat liffis here in all þe delicatis att þai*m* liste hafe." And þan he askid whatkyn a bed þat was; & þan þe freer said þe saying of þe p*ro*phett Ysai; "Subt*er* te sternentur, *et c*9." And when þe freer had þus said, he went his ways, and þis scoler on þe nyght after as he lay in his bedd, he vmthoght hym̄ on̄ þies wurdis, & he mott not slepe a dele for thoght of þis bed in hell, unto so mekull þis þoght *pre*vaylid so on̄ hym̄ þat *with*-in a litle while after he made hym̄ a freer of þe same ordur. *et c9*.

CCXLV.

Delicie corporales *et pre*sentes i*m*pediu*n*t spi*rit*uales *et* futuras.

We rede in 'Libro de Dono Timoris' how som̄ tyme a husbandman̄ was biddyn̄ vnto a kyngis brydall, and as he went thedurward he wex passand thrustie, & he fand drovy watyr & stynkand, & drank þ*er*off. And his felows cownceld hym̄ not to drynk þ*er*of, bod to byde to he come att þe brydall, & þ*er* he sulde hafe gude wyne enogh, & clarett; & he wold not, bod fillid his body of þis stynkand watir, into so mekull at he began̄ to bolk, & his brethe for to stynke. And when̄ he come vnto þe kyngis yate *with* his felows, þai went in & he was holden̄ oute for his bolkyng & his stynkand brethe.

Qui delicantur corpore frequencius infirmantur. S*upr*a de abb*at*issa.

Demon impedit or*at*iones q*uan*tu*m* potest. Infra de Or*ati*one.

Demon s*anct*os plus in desp*er*acionem p*re*cipitat p*er* mulieres q*uam* p*er* alios. Supra de carne.

Demon gaudet qu*ando* s*anctu*m viru*m* p*re*cipitat in pecc*atu*m. S*upr*a de carne.

Demon temptat ho*min*es ieiunantes. S*upr*a de abstinencia.

CCXLVI.

Demon non est incaute nominandus.

Saynt Gregorie tellis how a p*re*ste þat hight Stephan on̄ a tyme was wate-shodd, and necligentlie he com*man*ddid his servand &

sayd; "þou devull! Com, doff my shone!" And at þis biddyng onone þe thwang*is* of his shone lowsid passand tite. And when þe prest felid þis, he was passand ferd and cried w*ith* a grete voyce & sayd; "þou wriche! Go fro me! Go fro me! ffor I spakk not vnto þe, bod vnto my servand." And so þe shone lefte vndofte vnto his servand did þai*m* off.

CCXLVII.

Demones in nocte apparent in formis viror*um* *et* mulier*um*.

We rede in þe 'Life of Saynt German' how þat on a tyme he was lugid on a night in a howse vp of land; and when all had suppyd þai sett þe burde agayn. And he had m*er*vayle þ*er*of and askid for wham þai did so. & þai told hym þai[1] sett þe burd for þase gude wom*men* þatt gase on nyghtis. And he thoght þat he wold se whatt þai wer, & awakid all þat nyght. And aboute mydnyght he saw a multitude of fendis com to þis burd in form & liknes of men & wom*men*; and he chargid þai*m* remow þai*m*, & he callid vp all þe meneya in þe howse & shewid þai*m* þies men and þies wom*men*, & askid þai*m* if þai knew any of þai*m*. And þai said at þai knew þai*m* wele enogh, þai wer all þ*er* neghburghs, bothe men & wyvis. And he sent vnto þ*er* howsis at þai sayd war þ*er*, & þai þ*a*t went fand þai*m* in þ*er* beddis. And þan he co*n*iurid þies fendis, & þai told how þai war fendis & come to dissayfe þe peple.

Demon ecia*m* religiosos ret*ra*hit ab or*atione*. S*upra* de be*a*to Benedicto.

Demon eciam s*anct*os sensibilit*er* qu*andoque* in corpore verberat. Sup*ra* de Antonio. Et inf*ra* de p*er*seu*er*ancia.

Demonis diu*er*se su*nt* temptaciones. Inf*ra* de temptacione.

[1] MS. þat.

Demone*m* sola humilitas confundit. Inf*ra* de humilitate.

Demon aliqu*ando* amicos vita corporali p*ri*vat. Inf*ra* Nicholai.

Demon Ep*iscop*os p*er* mulieres temptat. S*upra* Andree.

CCXLVIII.

Demones insistu*nt* morientib*us*.

Jacobus de Vet*ri*aco tellis how on a tyme when a sister of þe frate*r*nitie of Oegniez[1] was seke & bown to dye, Saynt Marie of Oegniez[1], as sho was in hur cell, sho purseyvid & saw a multitude of fendis rumyand abowte hur[2] sister bed, & sho bown to dye. And as hur sisters war sayand þ*er* prayers for hur, & trowid þat sho suld dye, sho ran vnto þe bed of hur seke sister & werid away wi*th* hur shirte þir evull spyrittis as þai had bene fleis, & said hur prayers alsso. And þai wythstude hur & chalangid hur sister sawle as þ*er* awn. þan sho mot suffer þai*m* no langer, & cryed on Criste for His bittyr passyon & His blude to helpe hur. And þan þies evull spiritt*is* laburd gretelie to hafe getten þis saule, and sho saw þat & sayd; "Lord, I becom borgh for þis sawle; for þuff all sho hafe synnyd, yit sho is confessid þ*er*of. And if oght be ignorans or neclegens be left behynd wi*th* hur, Lord, latt hur lyff, & I vnd*er*take sho sall amend hur." & so sho did; & þe fend*is* vanysshid away.

Demoni se com*m*endare p*er*iculosu*m* est. Sup*ra* de Com*m*endacione.

CCXLIX.

Demones p*re*sciunt mortem malor*um* aliquando.

Jacobus de Vet*ri*aco[3] tellis of Elebrandus þat was archebisshopp of Beme[4], how on a tyme his bed-felow tolde on hym & sayd;

[1] MS. Oegimez.
[2] MS. his.
[3] The Latin MSS. attribute this tale to Helinandus.
[4] Latin MSS. Remen*sis*.

"My lord on a tyme sent me ane erand vnto Attrebatt[1]; and when I and my *ser*vand wer in a wud, we hard a grete noyse of armyd men, & as vs thoght, of harnessid hors, and fendis cryand, & sayd; 'Now we hafe our purpas[2] of Arta[3], and onone we sall hafe our purpos[2] of þe bisshopp of Beam'; bod we may nott gett furth our hors, nowder *with* staffis nor spurris. And þan I sayd vnto my servand; 'Latt vs make crossis in our forhedis, & þan sall we go sekurlie.' And so we did. And when we come home, we fand þe p*re*fecte[4] of Arta[3] dead, and þe archbisshop of Beam bown to dye."

CCL.

Demon ecia*m* viuos in equo portat in infernu*m*.

Helynandus tellis how on a tyme, opon a solempne day, as þe erle of Maciscon[5] satt in his awn palas & many knyghtis abowte hym, sodanlie ane vnknowen man sittand on a hors come in at[6] þe pales yate, and, att þai all saw, rade evyn vp to hym þ*er* he satt, & said he come to speke *with* hym, & bad hym ryse & go *with* hym. And he myght not agaynstand hym, & rase & went vnto þe dure; & þ*er* he fand a hors redie. And he bad hym lepe on, & so he did; and þe toder tuke his bridyll-rene at come for hym, & at þai all saw, þai rade vp in-to þe ayre. And þe erle cryed as he war wude; "Helpe me my cetysyns! Helpe me my cetisyns!" And eu*er*-ilk man in þe cetie hard þis voyce, & ran oute; & þai mot a grete while se hym rydand in þe ayre. And at þe laste he was *with*-drawen fro þ*er* syght, & had vnto hell. *et c*⁹.

Demon bonos bellare facit. Sup*r*a de bello.

Demon iuuene*m* anulo desponsau*i*t. Inf*r*a de sponsalib*us*.

[1] Latin MSS. Attrebate*r*, Atrebate*r*.

[2] Latin '*pre*positu*m*' *misread as* 'purpos' = 'propositum,' *and repeated before* 'bisshopp of Beam.' Latin: Iam h*abe*mus *pre*positu*m* de Isrea, in proximo h*abe*bimus archiep*isco*pum Remens*is*.

[3] Arund. MS. de Arta; Harl. MS. de Isrea.

[4] MS. p*re*feste; Latin MSS. prepositu*m*.

[5] Harl. MS. Comes Matistonens*is*; Arund. MS. comes Mastisconens*is*.

[6] At *omitted and added above the line*.

Demon pecc*ata* confessa tradidit obliuioni. S*upra* de confessione.

Demon. Morientes tempta*n*tes p*er* or*atio*nem expellu*n*tur. Inf*ra* de mori*enti*b*us*.

Demon immittit ymagines eor*um* que nu*n*q*u*am visa sunt vel facta. Infra de temptacione.

Demones in morte vsurarios in corpore *et* in a*nima* vexant. Inf*ra* de Vsuris.

Demones ecia*m* ad obitus beator*um* veniunt. Inf*ra* de morientib*us*.

Demon corpus pecc*at*oris loco a*nim*e aliqu*ando* vegitat. Inf*ra* de suffragijs.

Demon in corpore humano cantat. S*upra* de cantu.

Demon sec*un*d*um* modu*m* suu*m* servit fidelit*er*. Inf*ra* de milite.

Demon accusat morientes. Supra de accusacione.

Demon decipit ambiciosos. Sup*ra* de ambicione.

Demon sibi adherentes ditat temp*o*ral*ite*r. Inf*ra* de Milite.

CCLI.

Demon sub sp*ecie* boni aliq*u*os ad mortem temporale*m* *et* ete*r*na*m* ducit.

We rede how on̄ a tyme þ*er* was a Iew co*n*uertid in þe bisshopprik of Colan̄; and he was emang monk*is*, & þai lernyd hym̄ on̄ þe buke to he cuthe rede wele. And þan̄ he garte write bukis, & þe monkis lettid hym̄ & wold not lern̄ hym̄ no more; & onone as he saw þat, he stale away from emang þai*m* and went his ways, to þe entent at he wold lern̄. And þan̄ þe deviƚ appered vnto hym̄ in liknes of ane aungeƚ, and bad hym̄ lern̄ faste, ffor he sulde be a bisshop̄. And a little while afterward he apperid vnto hym̄ agayn on þe same wise, and said vnto hym; "To-morn mon þou be a bisshop, ffor þe bisshopp is dead; & þerfor haste þe to go vnto þe cetie, ffor God will at þou be made bisshopp þer-of." And onone þis wriche privalie went his way; & þat night he was hostid with a preste nerehand þe cetie; and becauce þat he wold com wurthelie vnto þe cetie, he rase vp þat same nyght befor day, & stale þe prestis hors & his cloke, & went his way. Men on þe morn missid þe hors, & sewid after hym & tuke hym, & broght hym vnto a seculer iugement, & þer he was dampnyd. And þus he ascendid, nott as a bisshopp vnto þe chayr, bod as a thefe vnto þe galows.

CCLII.

Demon obstinatus est in malo.

Cesarius tellis how on a tyme when a devull had turment horrebly a man þat he was in, it was sayd vnto hym of a certan man; "Tell me, þou fend, if þou may com agayn vnto þe blis at þou hase loste; and if þou might, what wold þou do þerfor?" And þe fend answerd agayn & said; "And it war in my chose, I had leuer go vnto hell with a sawle þat I had desayvid, þan for to turn agayn vnto hevyn." & þai þat hard hym say so, had grete mervayle þerof, & þan he sayd agayn vnto þaim; "wharto merveil ye here-of? My malice is so mekull and I am so obstinatt & so fraward, þat I may not will nor desire nothyng att is gude nor profetable vnto my selfe." *et c9.*

CCLIII.

Demonis Penitencia.

Cesarius tellis how þat in Colan þer was a womman vexid with a fend, & be grace of God, a holie man drafe hym oute of hur. And þan þis holie man hard a noder fend & hym to-gedur, & saw þaim bathe. And þe tane said vnto þe toder; "O! þou wriche! why consentid þou to Lucifer? For þerfor we fell fro euerlastand ioy." And þe toder answerd hym agayn & sayd; "Whi did þou so!" And þai bothe forthoght it, & said' þe tane vnto þe toder; "Halde þi tong! þis penans is our late; ffor & þ*er* was a pyler of yrn̄ byrnand', sett full of sharpe rasurs, sett evyn̄ vp fro erth to hevyn̄, me had levir, & I mot suffer it & I had flessh, be drawen̄ þ*er*on̄ vp & down̄ to þe day of dome, *with* cou*n*and' at I mot com̄ agayn̄ vnto þat ioy þat I was in." *et c*[9].

Demon in ornatu vestiu*m* delectatur[1]. Inf*ra* de ornatu.

CCLIV.

Demon psallentes in choro impedit.

Cesarius tellis how on̄ a grete solempne nyght at matyns, þe Covent of Hemmerode, as þai war sayand' þis psalm̄; '*Domine*, quid multiplicati, *et c*[9],' þ*er* was so many fendis in þ*er* quere, þat *with* sight of þai*m* goyng vp & down̄, þe ta side falid' in þe psalm̄. And when̄ þe tod*er* syde laburd' to gar þai*m* say right agayn̄, þai whettid' þ*er* tethe agayns þai*m* & flayed' þai*m* so at þai wiste neu*er* what þai suld' say; bod þe ta syde cried' agayn̄ þe tod*er*, þai wiste neu*er* whatt. And nowder þe abbott nor þe p*r*iour cuthe bryng þai*m* vnto þe psalmodie agayn̄, nor none acordans. And at laste, ilfarandlie, þai made ane end' of þis little psalme, *with* grete labur and' confusion̄; & þan̄ þe devull & all his felashup̄ went away, & þe prior saw þai*m* fle a-way in liknes of dragons.

Demon nigromancia co*m*pellitur apparere. Infra de Nigromancia.

Demon ludit ad taxillos. Inf*ra* de ludo taxillor*um*.

CCLV.

Demon confessione*m* in qua*n*tu*m* potest impedit.

Cesarius tellis how þat in þe town̄ of Bon̄, in þe dioces of Colayn̄, þ*er* was a p*r*estis lemman̄; & hur irkid' so *with* hur syn̄ at sho hangid' hur selfe. And as sho did it þe rape braste, & sho was still on̄ life; and when̄ sho saw sho was delyverd' of þat deade,

[1] MS. dilectatur.

sho went & made hur a non. And þan be temptacion of þe devull, hur luffer come agayn & laburd to hafe hur as he was wunte; and sho wold noȝt grawnt vnto hym be no mene. And þan he hyght hur þat, & sho wold consent vnto hym, he sulde make hur a ladie. And þus he laburd hur nyght & day, & sho cuthe not avoyd hym; so sho kest on hur hali watir, & made a cros on hur, & he vanysshid away for a while. And þan þe devull come in his lyknes vnto hur agayn, & laburd hyr. And þan be cowncell of a gude man sho sayd hur Ave Maria; and onone as sho had sayd it, he fled away as he had bene stryken *with* ane arow, and durste not com nere hur; not-*with*stondyng he lefte hur not all. And a man cownceld hur to go shryfe hur; and as sho went, he come vnto hur & askid hur whyder sho was bown, & sho said; "I am bown to distroy bothe þe & me." And he sayd; "Nay, nay, do not so! Turn agayn!" And sho answerd agayn & sayd; "þou hase oftsithis confowndid me, & þ*er*for I will now go shryfe me." And evur as sho went he flow abown hur in þe ayr, as it had bene a[1] glede. And als sone as sho oppynd hur mouthe to shryfe hur, he vanysshid away *with* grete crying & yowlyng; and he appered nevur vnto hur afterwerd, nor sho hard hym neu*er* efter.

CCLVI.

Demon ecia*m* virginem corrumpit.

Cesarius tellis how þat in þe same town of Bon, how þ*er* was a preste þat had a doghter at was wedd, & hur husband was dead; & sho was so fayr þat he was ferd for hur, to so mekull þat evur when he went furth he wold spar hur in a lofte. So on a tyme þe devull apperid vnto hur in lyknes of a man, & spak vnto hur wurdis of luff to gar hyr inclyne to hym, to so mekull at he lay by hur & had at do *with* hur. And sho purseyvid at sho was desseyvid be a fend, & told hur fadur. And he was passand hevye and made mekull sorow þ*er*for, & had hur thyne owr a grete watir in-to a noder contreth, at sho suld be ferrer fro þis fend, &[2] at sho

[1] *After* a, g & half l, *erased.* [2] & *omitted and added above the line.*

sulde be bettur be changyng of þe ayr. And þis Devull myssid hur, & was wroth þer*with*, & come vnto þe preste & sayd; "þou cursid preste! Whi hase þou taken my wife fro me?" And when he had sayd so, he strake hym opon þe breste, at he spytt blude *with* iij dayes; & on þe thrid day he dyed. And we rede also how þat a fend held a woman vj yere, & come vnto hur ilk nyght in lyknes of a knyght, & lay *with* hur in bedd as he had bene a man. And onone as sho made ane oppyn [*confession*] þerof vnto Saynt Barnard sho was delyverd; and he come neuer to hur after.

CCLVII.

Demon decipit viros.

We rede of a scoler þat was a lustie yong man, & so he agreid *with* a wom*man* at he sulde com vnto hur on a nyght; & sho agreid þerto. So on þe nyght he come noght to hur, bod a fend in lyknes of hur come vnto hym & lay *with* hym all nyght, & lete hym hafe his liste. And on þe morn þis fend askid þis scoler if he wuste whame he had ligen *with* all nyght, & he sayd, ya, *with* such a wom*man*. And he sayd; "Nay, þou hase ligen & had at do *with* þe devull;" & þat he sayd it in such fowle wurdis at it wer shame to tell. & *with* þat þe devull vanysshid away.

CCLVIII.

Demon ecia*m* iocalia offert vt ametur.

We rede how þe devull luffid a yong wom*man*, and apperid vnto hur oft-sithis on þe night *with* grete lightis aboute hym, so þat all þe chawmer myght be seen *with* þe light, & þe droppis of þe seargis myght be sene; & he gaff vnto hur rynges & oþer iewels of gold, and many other þing*is*. And sho come vnto hur confession, & shewid þai*m* vnto þe preste. *et c⁹*.

Demon or*ationibus* s*anctorum* a malo inchoato impeditur[1]. S*upr*a Barnardi.

Demon impedit audire sermonem. S*upr*a de audire se*r*monem.

[1] MS. inpeditur.

Demon conscribit pecc*a*ta ho*min*um. Sup*r*a Augustini.

Demon insidiatur cl*er*icis in choro. S*upr*a de.

CCLIX.

Demonis forma est t*er*ribilis.

We rede in 'Libro de Dono Timoris,' how þ*er* was a religious man þat lay in his dortur wit*h* his brethir, and sodanlie as [*he*] lay, he began to cry vgsomlie. And þe covent rase and come vnto hym; and þai fand hym glorand faste agayns þe wall, & he wolde speke no wurd, bod he was evyn as he had bene flayed. So in þe mornyng he come to hym selfe, and þe[1] p*r*iour askid hym what hym aylid. And he said at he saw þe devull; "and his shap," he sayd, "was so vglie, it mot not be discryvid; bod I say þis," sayd he, "þat & þ*er* war a hate oven on þe ta side me, & þe shapp of hym on þat other p*a*rtie, me had levur crepe in-to þat hate oven þan ans behold hym agayn as I did."

CCLX.

Depositu*m* vsurarij non est s*er*vandu*m*.

Cesarius tellis how some tyme þ*er* was ane vsurer þat lent a certayn of mony vnto a selerer of þe Ceustus ordur; and he selid it & layd it in a kyste besyde a c*er*tan money of þ*er* awn. So aft*er*ward þis vsurar askid it agayn; and þe monke went vnto þe kiste, and he fand nowder þ*er* awn money nor itt. And he lukid & saw at no bodie had tuchid þe lokk bod hym selfe, & þe selis of þe sakettis safe, at he mot know no suspecion of þifte. þan he conseyvid in his mynd þ*a*t þe mony of þe vsuraris had devowrid and distroyed þe money of þ*er* monasterie.

Depositu*m* debet reddi eo m*od*o q*u*o com*m*issu*m* est. S*upr*a de Cautela.

[1] MS. þi.

CCLXI.

Deposit*um* no*n* debet recipi servand*um* nisi p*r*ius videatur.

Joh*annes* Beleth̄ tellis how on̄ a tyme þ*er* was a womm*a*n̄ þ*a*t had iij pottis fuƚƚ of gold', & sho delyverd' þai*m* to kepe vnto Julian*us* Apostata [1], for sho trowid' þ*a*t he was a gude holie monke befor̄ other of his brether. And' sho told' hym̄ not þ*a*t þ*er* was gold' in þai*m*. Than̄ þis monke tuke þies pottis, & fand' þ*er* was so mekuƚƚ gold' in þai*m*, & he stale it & fillid' þe pottis agayn̄ fuƚƚ of assh̄. And when̄ þe womm*a*n̄ come & askid' þe pottis agayn̄, he delyverd' hur þai*m*, & þai war fuƚƚ of assh̄; & sho said' at sho had' delyverd' [2] þai*m* vnto hym̄ fuƚƚ of gold'. Bod sho cuthe neu*er* gett no mendis on̄ hym̄ becauce sho had no witnes, and his brethir þe monkis, at war by, saw no þing abown̄ þe pott*is* bod' assh̄. *et c*[9].

CCLXII.

Desideriu*m* celestis patrie lac*r*imas corp*or*ales excitat.

Jacobus de Vet*r*iac*e* tellis þ*a*t he had sene bothe men̄ & wom*m*en sett vnto Godward' *with* so m*er*valos & so spi*r*ituaƚƚ affeccion̄, þ*a*t for desyre þai wex seke, & som̄ so mekuƚƚ, þ*a*t many yeris þai lay in þ*er* beddis, and myght not ryse vp bod seldom̄ tymys. & þai had none other cauce of sekenes bod at þ*er* h*er*tis was so sett vnto Godward', & of þe ioy of hevyn̄. And als lang as þai war in þ*a*t thoght þai war evur seke & at male ease. *et c*[9].

Desideriu*m* carnale est rep*r*imendu*m*. Sup*r*a de abstinencia.

CCLXIII.

Desperacio. Desp*er*acione*m* induc*u*nt tristitia *et* accidia.

Cesarius tellis how on̄ a tyme þ*er* was a religious man̄ þ*a*t liffid lovable emang his brethir fro his youthe vnto his age, so þ*a*t

[1] The Latin MSS. *explain*, aurum illud ne app*a*reret in orificijs ollar*um*, cin*e*re op*er*uit.

[2] MS. *has another* hym *here*.

þ*er* was none þat was more religious þan̄ he was. So on̄ a tyme hym̄ happend' to fałł in-to suche a sadnes & a hevynes, þ*at* he dowtid' of his syn*n*ys, & fełł in-to a dispayr. And he mot not be broght oute þ*er*-of *with* none auctorite of scriptur, nor he mot not be broght into no hope of forgifnes, not-*with*-stondyng he had not done no grete syn̄. And when̄ his brethir askid' hym̄ what hym̄[1] aylid' at he was fallen̄ into suche a drede & a dispayr, he answerd' agayn̄ & sayd'; "I may not as I was wu*n*te to do say my p*ra*yers, & þ*er*for I am̄ ferd' to be dampnyd'." And þan̄ he was putt in a fermorie ałł a nyght, & on̄ þe morn̄ he come vnto his maist*er* & sayd'; "I may no longer feght agayns God'." & þan̄ he went furth vnto þe myln̄-dam̄ of þe abbay, & þ*er* he lowpid' in & drownyd' hym̄. *et c*9.

Desp*er*andu*m* non est de aliquo. Sup*r*a de Abb*at*e *et* apostata.

Desperans sacerdos dampnatur. Inf*r*a de sace*r*dote.

CCLXIV.

Desp*er*anti ante mortem aliqu*ando* pena infernalis ostenditur

Petrus Clunacens*is* tellis how som tyme[2] þ*er* was in Pycardi a preste þat was fułł of vices & syn̄; so on̄ a tyme he p*ro*mysid' be councełł for to make hym̄ a monke in Ceustus ordur; bod he put it in contynance, and in the mene-while[3] he fełł seke[4]. And him thoght at þ*er* come vnto hym̄ ij dragons and wold' hafe devowrid' hym̄, bod be þe p*r*ayer of þe p*r*iour of þat ordur he was delyverd', and becou*n*and' þat he sulde fulfyłł his p*ro*mys at he had made, as he behestyd'. & þan̄ he coverd', and yitt he fulfillid' not his p*ro*mys, bod putt it in co*n*tynnance. And þan̄ he fełł seke agayn̄, & cried & sayd'; "Lo! a fyre occupyes me for to burn̄ me!" & he helde vp̄ þe coverlad betwix hym̄ & it; and yitt

[1] MS. *repeats*, what hym.
[2] MS. *repeats*, how some time.
[3] While *is repealed and erased*.
[4] MS. *repeats*, & in þe mene while he fełł seke.

þe prayers of þe monk*is* he was delyverd, and þan he fulfillid at he beheste. And þan he was ravisshid vnto þe dome, and þer he hard a sentans, at he sulde be dampned, put furthe agayn hym. And when he come agayn vnto hym selfe, þan he told his brether & sayd; "Lo! two fendis brynges a grete arow to slo me *with*:" & þan þer fell fro þis arow a drop þat þrillid his hand vnto þe bare bone. And þan he cryed agayn & sayd; "Now takis þe fendis me, & castis me into a frying pan to bole me þerin." And *with* þat he swelte.

Desponsat v*ir*go Maria se amantes. Inf*ra* de Maria[1].

Despectus. Despiciu*nt* sup*er*bi alios. Infra de Gl*or*ia.

CCLXV.

Detraccio est fugienda.

We rede in 'Vitis *Patrum*' how þer was ij religious men þat on a tyme went furth of þer abbay, & þai waxed faynt for travellyng; & so þai warr hostid *with* ane hermett, and he sett befor þai*m* suche as he had in his cell. So on þe nyght as þai lay sam*en*, he hard þe tone of þai*m* say vnto þe toder; "This h*er*mett hase bett*er* meate, & is bett*er* fed þan þai er þat liffis in abbays." And when he hard þai*m* say so he held his tong. And on þe morn he had þai*m* vnto a noder h*er*mett, & bad[2] at þai sulde hayls hym, & tell hym how he had made þai*m* at fare. And þai bad hym þat, & he had any gude meate, þat he suld kepe it & giff þai*m* nothyng bod potage. And he vnd*er*stude þai*m* well enogh, & held þai*m* *with* hym & garte þai*m* wurk *with* hym eu*er*-ilk day, & make skuttels & lepis of wandis evyn vnto evyn; & þan þai went vnto þ*er* prayers. And þan he sayd he was nott wunte to supp, bod he sulde supp for þ*er* sake; and he sett befor þai*m* sture brede & salte. And þan he sayd he wold fare better for þ*er* sake, and

[1] MS. Inf*ra* de amantes. The Latin MSS. *havc*, de Maria.

[2] Latin MSS. "Salutate eum ex me, *et* dicite ei; 'obserua *et* noli illud irrigare *scilicet* olera'." Quod ille intelligens, tenuit eos.

he sett befor a little aysell & garlykk; & when þai had suppid þai went vnto þ*er* prayers agayn vnto it was myrk nyght. & þan he sayd þat he myght not for þai*m* saw all his prayers. And on þe morn þai wold hafe gane þ*er* way & tuke þ*er* lefe, & he wolde not latt þai*m*, bod he sayd þat he wold for charite hold þai*m* iij dayes. And on þe night after þai rase and stale away & wolde no langer abide wit*h* hym.

Detractorib*us* no*n* est credendu*m*. Sup*ra* de credere.

Detrahend*um* no*n* est ecia*m* mortuis. Inf*ra* de mortuis.

Detrahit*ur* bonis frequent*er* iniuste. Inf*ra* de *sancto* Lupo.

Deviacio. Deuiare no*n* debet a iusticia iudex. Inf*ra* de iudice.

Devocio. Devotos sibi Maria ab opprobrio lib*er*at. Sup*ra* de abb*at*issa.

Deuocio qu*andoque* excitatur ex p*re*sencia be*a*tor*um*. Inf*ra* de lacrima *et* de visitac*i*on*e*.

Deuocio contra natura*m* subuenit. Supra de ap*ost*olis.

[1] Deuotos sibi Maria desponsat. Inf*ra* de Maria.

Deuocio qu*ando*q*ue* p*ro*rum*pit in lac*r*imas. Infra de lac*r*ima.

Deuocio excitatur ex su*m*pcione cibi sp*iri*tualis. sup*ra* de cibo.

Deuotis conceditur consolacio diuina. Sup*ra* de consolac*i*on*e*.

CCLXVI.

Deuotos sibi eciam in celo *sancti* remun*er*ant.

Cesarius tellis how þ*er* was som tyme a chylde þat kepid shepe of a wedous, and he had a grete deuocion vnto Saynt Nicholas,

[1] MS. *repeats this heading.*

vnto so mekull at halfe þe meatt at he had eu*er*e day, he wold' dele it vnto pure men̄ in wurshup̄[1] of Saynt Nicholas; & eu*er* he made his p*r*ayers vnto hym̄. So on̄ a tyme Saynt Nycholas aperid' vnto hym̄ in habett & lyknes of a fayr olde man̄, and bad hym̄ dryfe hys shepe hame. And he said' his huswyff wold' be wrothe þan̄, for it was ou*er*[2] tymelie of þe day. And þis Say[*nt*][3] com*m*and' hym̄ to do as he bad hym̄, & sayd'; "Son̄, þis day sall þou dye, & þ*er*for make þe redie, & go home & take þi sac*r*ament*is*; ffor I am̄ Saynt Nicholas at þou hase bene devote to, & I will rewarde the." And he went home; & his dame was wrathe & blamyd' hym̄. And he sayd' he had myster to com̄ home, ffor he mond' dye þ*at* same day And his huswyffe trowed' þat he had bene fond' & at he had sene som̄ þing in þe feld', and p*r*ayed' þe prest to inquere hym̄ þ*er*off. And he tolde þe p*r*este of all his vision̄, and he tuke his sac*r*amentis of holy kurk and dyed'; and' his saule went vnto hevyn̄.

Deuotos deus in sacramento altaris confortat. Inf*r*a de sacr*amento*.

CCLXVII.

Deuocio ad Sa*nct*os non debet impediri.

We rede in þe 'Meracles of Saynt Nicholas' how on̄ a tyme in a kurk þat was of þe holie cros, þe monk*is* of ane abbay desyrid' þ*er* p*r*iour att he wold' suffre þai*m* go þeder on̄ Saynt Nicholas[4] day, at þai myght syng þe storie of Saynt Nicholas, for þan̄ it was new made; and he wolde not latt þai*m*. So on̄ a nyght after, as þe p*r*ior and all his brether was in þ*er* beddis, Saynt Nicholas visible apperid' vnto þe priour in a ferdfull wyse, and he drew hym̄ oute of his bed be þe hare, & keste hym̄ apon̄ þe dortur flure. And he began̄ to syng þis antem̄, 'O! pastor eterne'; and sang it softlie vnto þe end'; & at eu*er*e wurd'[5] he gaff a lassh, & sang it wit*h* a grete tarying, to so mekull þat wit*h* his holie crying he wakend' all þe monk*is*. And þan̄ þai tuke þ*er* p*r*iour &

[1] MS. *repeats*, in wurshup̄.
[2] Harl. MS. *quia* nimis mane est.
[3] MS. Say.
[4] MS. *repeats*, on̄ Saynt Nicholas.
[5] MS. eu*er* ewurd'.

bare hym vnto his bed; & euere yere, fro thens furth, he bad hys brether on Saynt Nicholas day go vnto þat kurk and syng þe storie off Saynt Nicholas.

CCLXVIII.

Deus om*n*ia videt.

Petrus Damianus tellis how on a tyme þ*er* was a man þat stale his neghbur sew; and þis man at stale þis sew was a man þat luffid wele to h*er*ber pure folk. So on a tyme our Lord apperid vnto hym in lyknes of a pure man; & he was lang-harid & he prayed hym þat he wold for charite cutt it shorter. And *with* gude will he welcomd hym & sayd he wold, all redie; & he garte hym sett hym down, & tuke a payr of sisurs and began to clypp hym before. And in þe hynderparte of his head he fand ij p*ri*vay een lurkand; and he had grete m*er*vall þ*er*of & askid hym whi þai war þ*er*. And he answerd & sayd; "I am Ie*sus*, þat seis our all þis werld, and þies er þe een whar-*with* I saw þi neghbur sew at þou stale, & slew it & hyd it in a cafe." And *with* þat he vanysshid away. And þis man amendid hym & made restitucion p*ri*valie for hur vnto hym att aght hur, be advice of his confessur.

Dileccio. Supra, sicut de amicicia *et* amore.

CCLXIX.

Dionisius. Dionisij martiriu*m* be*a*to Regulo nu*n*ciavit deus.

We rede how on a tyme when bysshopp Regulus sang mes, and in hys canon he namyd þe apostels o-raw, & þan þe martyrs, sodanly he sayd; "Et be*a*tis martiribu*s* tuis [1], Rustico *et* Eleu-therio." And when he had sayd so, sen als mekull as he kend þies s*er*vandis of God at þai war olyfe, he had grete m*er*vale how þ*er* namys happend so sodanly in his mouthe, & he wiste no þing of þai*m*. And as he was in þis m*er*vall, þ*er* apperid vnto hym

[1] Latin MSS. et be*a*tis Martiribu*s* tuis, Dyonisio, Rustico *et* Eletherio.

iij dowffes sittand opon þe cros of þe awter; and þai had þe namys of þies holie martyrs writtyn *with* blude on þ*er* brestis. And onone as he saw þat, he vnderstude at þies holie sayntis was martyrd & putt to dead.

Discrecio. Discretus debet esse p*re*latus. Sup*ra* de Abb*ate*.

Discretus est a cibo abstinend*um*. Sup*ra* de Maria.

Disciplina. Disciplinandi su*n*t iuuenes ne insolescant. Inf*ra* de iactantia.

Discordia int*er* bonos non facile oritur. Sup*ra* de concordia.

CCLXX.

Dileccio. Dilig*i*t canis d*omin*um suu*m*, *et* est ei fidelis.

Solinn*us* tellis how þat Apius, Funius[1] & Puplius, & dyvers other *with* þai*m*, wer dampned att Rome; & when þai war dead, one of þai*m* had a hond, & he satt at þe galos att þai hang on iij dayes murnand for his maister, & wolde neu*er* eate meate of no mans hand. & when his maister was taken down, þai put brede in his maister mouthe, & he tuke it & eate it; & þan þai keste his maist*er* in-to Tybur, & eu*er* as he flett in þe watir, þe dogg swam *with* hym, & at his power held vp his head.

CCLXXI.

Diligit canis vsq*ue* ad mortem.

Solinus tellis how þat when Iasalicius[2] was slayn, his hond lay by hym & wold neu*er* eate meate after. And þe kyng saw þat, & garte make a grete fyre, & caste þe dead bodie in; & onone þe hunde folowid into þe fyre, and gruchid not to be burnyd *with* his maist*er* bodie.

[1] Latin MSS. Iunio.
[2] MS. Harl. Infelic*io* int*er*fecto. MS. Arund. Iasolicio int*er*fecto.

CCLXXII.

Discere. Discendu*m* est in om*n*i etate.

Valerius tellis of ane of þe vij sagis, & he wold' all-way say þat he was redie to lern̄; so hym̄ happend' on̄ a tyme for to fall seke, & was bown̄ to dye, and all hys ffrendis come aboute hym̄ & com-furthid' hym̄. And evyn̄ sodanlie, als seke as he was, he sett hym̄ vp emang þai*m*, & tuke a buke & lukid' þ*er*on̄; and þai askid' hym̄ whi he did' so, and he answerd' agayn̄ & sayd at he wold' lern̄ somwhatt of a disputacion̄, & þan̄ lay hym̄ down̄ & dye.

CCLXXIII.

Discendi multiplex est causa.

Jacobus de Vet*r*iaco tellis þat on̄ a tyme he askid' a passand wyse man̄ and a wele-letterd', how he had lernyd' so mekull. And he answerd' agayn̄ & sayd'; "I had iij sp*iritu*all maisters, and þe furste was drede, & the secunde was shame, and þe iij was luff. And me þoght evur in my mynd' þat I saw þai*m*, & ilkone of þai*m* a wand' in his hand' to bete me with. And becauce I was eu*er* ferde to be bett, I sesid' neu*er* to lern̄. And also me þoght þat my felows þat was yonger þan̄ I passid' me, and eu*er* I vmthoght me at I wold' not be lawer þan̄ þai. And so doctryne ffell somwhatt vnto me, & keste me in a grete luff þ*er*to, so þat I lernyd' not alonelie for drede nor yitt for shame, bod rather for p*er*fite luff & curage þat I had vnto lernyng."

Discretus debet esse confessor. S*upr*a de confessione.

Discrecio m*u*ltiplex est necessaria. S*upr*a, inf*r*a, in m*u*ltis locis.

Discursus impediunt co*n*solac*io*nem di*uin*am. S*upr*a de consolacione.

Discursus iuuenis est p*er*ic*u*losus. Infra de iuuene.

Disputand*um* no*n* est de m*er*itis *sanctorum* prot*er*ue. Inf*r*a Ioh*ann*is ut*r*iusq*ue*.

Dis*cur*rere no*n* de*b*et religiosus causa visitandi cognatos. Sup*ra* de affeccione carnali *et* de affectu.

Dissimulacio. Dissimulande su*n*t aliqu*ando* iniurie. Infra de Iniurijs. *et* c⁹.

Dissimulat deus. pec*catu*m vt postea plus peniteat. Supra de Consuetudine peccandi.

CCLXXIV.

Diuicie sp*iri*tuales p*re*ponende su*n*t corporalib*us*.

Valerius tellis how þat when Anaxagoras þe philosophur had traveld far for þe studie of philosophie, & when he come agayn he fand all his gudis destroyed; "Ya," he said, "no fors of my gudis & I hafe connyng & my heall of my bodie; for þies two er wurth mekull riches." And so he cowntid more be riches of co*n*nyng & of hele þan he did be riches of gudis.

CCLXXV.

Diuicie sp*iri*tuales ho*mi*ne inuito p*er*di no*n* possunt.

Valerius tellis how ane of þe vij sagis, when his enmys come into his contrey & tuke all his gudis & his riches & fled away þ*er*wit*h*, he was askid whi he folowd not on þai*m* & tuke som of his gudis fro þai*m*. And he answerd agayn & sayd; "Forsuthe whar-somevur I go, I bere all my gudis wit*h* me." For he bare þai*m* in his breste and noght on his shulder, & not be syght of his ene, bod rather in his mynd & his witt; "ffor þat," he sayd, "þat is closid in a mans mynde & in his harte may not be takyn away wit*h* no mans hand, nor þai may not stele nor fle away þ*er*wit*h*."

CCLXXVI.

Diuicijs p*re*ponende sunt condiciones bone.

Jacobus de Vet*ri*aco tellis how þ*er* was a pure man þat wit*h* þe labur off his handis vnnethis cuthe gett his lifelod, ffor when he had suppid, þ*er* lefte right noght ou*er* night vnto in þe mornyng; & evur he was merie, to so mekull þat eu*er*ilk night, when he was in his bed *with* his wife, he wolde, & sho, syng a sang m*er*elie at all þ*er* neghburs mott here; & þan þai wold fall on slepe. So þ*er* neghburs had grete m*er*vall þ*er*off, and one of þai*m* said; "I sall make swilk a way at I sall gar hym lefe hys syngyng." & in p*re*sens of som of his neghburs, opon a night he tuke a sachell full of sylver, & lete fall afor þis pure mans dure. And when at he rase & sulde go furth to seke his lifelod, he fande þis bagg, & he tuke it vp & turnyd agayn þ*er*-*with* in-to his howse & hid it. So on þe night after, als tyte as he was in his bed, he vmthoght hym in his mynde what he wolde do þ*er*-*with*; & he was ferd þ*er*for þat he war not culpid *with* felony þ*er*for, & also at no thevis sulde stele it from hym, or if so be at he boght or solde þ*er*-*with*, or boght any lande, he mond be suspecte, vnto so mekull at he was so occupyed in his thoght þat at þ*at* nyght he sang not, nor was not merie; bod a grete while after he was passand hevy & thoght-full. & þan his neghburs askid hym whi he was so hevie, and whi he sang nott as he was wunte to do; and he wolde nott tell þai*m* þe treuth. And þan he at aght þis money said vnto hym; "I knaw þe treuth; for suche a day & in suche a place þou fande my money, & tuke it vp at I & myne neghburs saw, & had it in-to þi howse." And when he hard þis he wex ferd & shamefull, & sayd; "woo wurth þat money þat hase turment me thus; for sen þ*at* I fand it I had neu*er* ioy in my harte; & I hafe bene trubbled in my witt eu*er* syne, more þan eu*er* I was before when I *with* grete labur of my bodie & my hand*is* gat my meat. And þ*er*for take þi mony þi selfe agayn, at I may syng & be mery as I was wunte to done." And so he did; and fro it was gone, þis pure man made als merie as evur did he.

Diuicie temporales impediunt sp*iri*tuales. Inf*ra* de fideiussore.

CCLXXVII.

Diuicias h*ab*ere et no*n* amare virtus est.

Saynt Gregur tellis of ane h*er*mett þat was a man of grete v*er*tue & lefte all man*er* of gudis for Goddis sake, to so mekle at he had no gude lefte bod a catt. And he prayed vnto God at He wulde vuchsafe to latt hym̄ witt who sulde be his felow in þe blis of hevyn̄. And it was answerd' hym̄ from̄ ałł-myghtie God & sayd', þat Gregur sulde be his felow. And when̄ he hard' þis he made mekułł sorow, & þoght his wilfułł pou*er*tie p*ro*fettid' hym̄ bod little, sen̄ Gregur þat had so mekułł riches sulde be his felow in hevyn̄. So on̄ a nyght as he was in his prayers, hym̄ þoght þat he hard' almighti God say vnto hym̄; "Gregur, þat is so riche of gudis, is als pure in his spiritt as þou erte, for þou hase more lykyng in þi pou*er*tie þan̄ he hase in his riches."

CCLXXVIII.

Doct*r*ina. Doctor debet ostendere *facto* quod ve*r*bo docet.

We rede ex 'Dictis P*atrum*' þat þe abbott Iohn̄ was askid' whi he liffid' so straytelie emang his disciples, & gaff þai*m* so strayte chargis & commaundment*is*, and he & þai bothe mott hafe com*m*en̄ vnto hevyn̄ be other menys. And he made sorow & answerd' agayn̄ wit*h* grete wepyng, and' sayde; "In ałł my life I did neu*er* myne awn̄ wiłł, nor I taght nevur no man̄ to do noght bod at I did' my selfe befor̄."

Doctor debet habere discretu*m* modum *et* gestum compositu*m*. Inf*r*a de p*r*edicacione.

Dolor. Dolend*um* est non de re que recup*er*ari non potest. Supra de Consilio.

Dolor qu*andoque* p*ro*dest corpori. Infra de gaudio.

Dolendu*m* no*n* est de morte amici te*m*po*r*alis. Inf*r*a de morte.

Doluspun itur g*r*auit*er*. Sup*r*a de adulterio.

CCLXXIX.

Do*mi*nicus ordinem p*er* be*a*tam vi*r*ginem p*r*edicatoru*m* impet*r*auit.

We rede how on a tyme when Saynt Dominyk was in his p*r*ayers at Rome, and laburd beselie vnto þe pope for confirmacion of his ordur, on a tyme he saw in his spiritt almyghti God in þe ayre, shakand iij speris like as He wold hafe destroyed all þis werld. And our Ladie, His meke moder, come vnto Hym and askid Hym whatt He wuld do; & He sayd þat[1] He wolde destrow þis werld, *with* iij vicis þat was corrupte; þat was, *with* p*r*ide, co*n*cupiscens & avarice. And þan sho sayd; "Dere Son! Meng þi rightwusnes *with* m*er*cie! For I hafe a trew *ser*vand at sall call þis werld agayn vnto þe; & in eu*er*-ilk place shall destroy vicis." And þan hur Son was soberd & sayd; "I wold se hym at sulde be ordand vnto suche ane offes." & þan our Lady shewid Hym ffurst Saynt Do*mi*nyk, & þan Saynt Frauncys; & hur Son com*m*endid þai*m* gretelie. And aft*er* þis vision Saynt Dominyk mett Saynt Frawncis þat he neu*er* saw befor bod in þe vysion, & he kend hym wele enogh, & kissyd & sayd; "þou erte my felow; latt vs stond bothe sam*en*, & none adu*er*sarie sall p*re*vayle ayeyns vs."

CCLXXX.

Ad-huc de S*a*n*c*to Do*mi*nico.

We rede in his Legend how on a tyme, when he come home & fande his brether at þ*er* reste, & þe yate sparrid, he wald not waken þai*m*, bod *with* his holie p*r*ayers he oppynd þe yate, & he & his felow went in. And a noþ*er* tyme he had *with* hym a monk of Ceustus ordur, & on a tyme when þai wold hafe gone into a kurk to say þ*er* prayers, & fand þe dure lokkid, þurgh his prayers þe dure oppynd, & þai went in & sayd þar deuocions.

[1] Latin MSS. "Mundu*m*," inquit, "t*r*ibu*s* vicijs corruptu*m*, pun*i*re uolo."

CCLXXXI.

Domi*ni*ci preci*bus* ha*bi*tum ordinis virgo Maria attulit.

Also we rede in his Legend' ewhils Mayst*er* Raynald', at was dene of Aurilianens & a maist*er* of law, was essurid' vnto Saynt Dom*i*nyk to com̄ into his ordur, & hym̄ happend' for to faƚƚ seke, & was in despayr of lechecrafte, þis holie Saynt *pr*ayed feruentlie for his heaƚƚ. And our Ladie & ij virgyns w*ith* hur apperid' visible & enoyntid' þis seke man̄ w*ith* ane oyntement þ*at* ane of þies vi*r*gyns bare, & curid' hym̄ bothe sp*iri*tuallie & bodelie, to so mekuƚƚ þat fro thens furth̄ he felid' nevur movyng of his flessh̄ vnto syn̄; & sho schewid' hym̄ þe abbett of þe ordur at þe toder vi*r*gyn̄ broght.

CCLXXXII.

Domi*ni*ci or*at*io semp*er* auditur.

We rede also in his Legend' how þat Saynt Domynyk on̄ a tyme [*come*] vnto a *pr*iour of Ceustus ordur, þat was a devote man̄ & famyliari w*ith* hym̄, that askid' hym̄ in *pr*ivatie & *pr*ayed' hym̄ to teƚƚ hym̄ som̄ of þe gracis at God had giffen̄ hym̄; and he answerd' agayn̄ & sayd'; "I tolde neu*er* man̄ at I saƚƚ teƚƚ you, and I warn̄ you teƚƚ no man̄ whils I liff, ffor I latt you witt þat I askid' neu*er* of God no thyng bod I had my desyre." So þis *pr*iour thoght þat he wold' prufe þis, & said'; "Besoght[1] ye of God', & I *pr*ay you beseke it, at Maist*er* C[*lemet*] enter in-to your ordur, for your brether gretelie desyris hym̄, & he hase no wiƚƚ þ*er*-to; & he is a famos man̄ and a *gr*acious & a wele-letterd'." & þan̄ þis holie man̄ sayd'; "Ye hafe askid' of me a grete þing. Not-w*ith*-stondyng *pr*ay ye w*ith* me þ*er*for þis night, & to-morn̄ saƚƚ maist*er*

[1] Latin MSS. "Impetretis ergo a deo ut mag*ist*er C. Theutonic*us* intret ordinem ue*str*um."

Clemett com befor day & aske þe abett of our ordur." And so he did, & liffid in þe ordur many day in *per*seu*er*ans of gude holynes.

CCLXXXIII.

Dormiencium septem.

We rede in *þer* Legend, when Decius þe Emp*er*our *per*sewid Cristen men, *þer* was vij yong Cristen men, & þai fled all sam*en* for drede off þis Decius vnto þe mownt of Celion beside þe cetie of Ephesim, whar þai war born, & *þer* þai hid þ*aim* in a den. And þai warr accusid vnto Decius Ceſar at þai war *þer*, & he garte close vp þe den mouthe at þai sulde not com oute, bod at þai sulde dy *þer*. And as God wold, sodanlie þai fell on slepe; and *þer* was o*þer* *pr*ivay Cristen men þat wrate *þer* martirdom & put it betwix ij stonys. And þan when Decius & all his kynrid was dead CCCLXXIJ [*yeris*], after þe xxx^ti^ yere of Theodoce þe Emp*er*our, þat was a C*r*istenman & made grete sorow for ane heresye þat þan began at rise in þ*aim* þat trustid not in vprysyng of flessh, almighti God raysid þ*aim* in þis man*er* of wyse. Ther was in þe cetie of Ephesie a cetisyn þat went vnto þis mownt & þoght to make *þer* a stable for his catell. And he oppynd þis den, and when it was oppyn, thies Saynttis rase vp and trowed at þai had slepid bod a nyght; and one of þ*aim* þat hight Malchus, þat vsid to seriff þ*aim*, þai sent hym in-to þe cetie to by þ*aim* bread, & for to witt whatt Decius sayde. And he tuke wi*th* hym v *soldi* of *þer* money. And when he come att þe cetie yate, he saw a cros set vp *þer*-opon, & he had grete m*er*vayle; and þan he went vnto eu*er*-ilk yate, & he fand it so. And þan he went agayn vnto þe furste yate, & he trowid þat he had dremyd, and wi*th* grete ferdnes he went into þe cetie. And when he hard þat eu*er*-ilk man was a Cristen man, and [*purseyvid*] at þe cetie was o*þer*wice biggid, & at he cuthe know no man at he saw, he askid if þat was þe cetie of Ephesim; and ane answerd hym & sayd ya. & he tuke oute his sylu*er* to by bread wi*th*, & he was taken onone, & þai sayd at he had fon a tresur, & þai putt a rape aboute his nekk & harlid hym [1] þurgh þe cetie to þer bisshop; & he trowid at þai had drawen hym vnto Decius Cesar. And when þe bisshop askid hym if he had fon any tresurrie, he answerd & sayd þat he had þat syluer of his fadur & his moder. And þan he askid hym whyne he was, & who was his fadur & his moder; & he said; "þai dwell in þis Cetie, in suche a place, & here-in I was born & þis be Ephesim." And þer was no man þat kend nowder his fadur nor his moder; & he luked aboute hym if he saw any of his cussyns, and he was evyn emang þaim as he had bene fond. And þan þe bisshopp said vnto hym; "How may it be trew at þou had þis syluer of þi fadur, & þe scriptur of þaim is mor þan ccclxxij yere old, & þai hafe þe figur of Decius Cesar made opon þaim?" And þan he had grete mervell & sayd; "Liffis not Decius Cesar yit?" And þe bisshop sayd; "Nay, son, þer is none now in all þis land þat is callid Decius, bod here hase bene a noder emperour of long tyme." And þan þis Malchus; "In þis I hafe a grete mervayle, ffor yisterday I saw Decius com into þis cetie, & þis be Ephesim, bod no man trowis me; bod folow me & ye sall trow my felows." And þan þe bisshopp vmthoght hym, & sayd vnto þe iustice; "þis is som vision att God will shew vs." And þai rase vp & fand betwix ij stonys letters selid with gold; & þe bisshop garte semble þe peple, & red it befor þaim. And when þai come at þe den, þai lukid opon þies Sayntis [2], and þai fell evyn down in-to wele-sauerryng rosis. And when þe Emperour hard tell of þis, he come vnto þaim & he saw þer facis shyne, & fell down on kneis befor þaim & wepid, and halsid þaim & þankid God. And þan Maximian said vnto hym; "For þe almyghti God hase raysid vs, þat þou may trow vndowtable at þe rysyng of deade folk sall be trew. For now we hafe ryssyn & liffid, and we wer evyn as a childe is in his moder wambe, bod slepid & felid no hurte." And with þis þai lenyd þaim down, þat all folk saw, & yeldid vp þer sawlis vnto allmighti God. *et c⁹.*

[1] MS. þaim.

[2] Harl. MS. videntesque facies *sanctorum* in spelunca *quasi* rosas florentes, procidentes glorificauerunt *deum*.

CCLXXXIV.

Dormicio. Dormiend*um* no*n* est in or*atione* p*ri*vata.

Cesarius tellis how þ*er* was a young monk þat was a gude liffer, & he was so wayke & so feble þat hym̄ yrkid' to liff[1]. And on̄ a nyght when̄ matyns was done, he lenyd' hym̄ down̄ opon̄ a tre befor̄ ane altar vnto Laudes tyme, as was his ordur, & þ*er* he fell on̄ slepe. And our Ladie, Saynt Marie, come &[2] putt opon̄ hym̄ & sayd'; "No*n* est hic locus dormiendi; here is not þe place off slepyng, bod rather of praying." And wit*h* þat he wakend' & luke aboute hym̄ who spakk, & he saw þe bak of a wom*m*an̄, & p*er*seyvid' at itt was a wom*m*ans voyce at spak.

Dormire paru*m* debet suffic*er*e religioso. Infra de labore.

CCLXXXV.

Dormiend*um* no*n* est in choro.

Cesarius tellis of ane olde monk þat was a grete sleper; so on̄ a nyght as he stude at þe psalmodie at matyns & slepid', hym̄ thoght at he saw in his slepe, standand' befor̄ hym̄, a long man̄ & a difform̄, þat held' in his hand' a lang, grete, clayie wispe[3], as it had wypid' hors. & he lukid' angrelie of þis monk & said' vnto hym̄; "Wharto stondis þou her̄ al night & slepis?" And he hytt hym̄ in þe face wit*h* þis clayie wispe. And wit*h* þat he wakend', & was ferd' at he suld' hafe strekyn̄ hym̄. And he plukkid' his hede so hastelie bakk, at he brakk it behynd' hym̄ on̄ þe wall. *et c*[9].

Duplicitas semp*er* est vitanda. Inf*r*a de honore parentu*m*.

Dux. Ducis vxor siue ducissa delicate viuens eciam in p*re*senti punitur. Sup*r*a de delicijs.

[1] Latin MSS. sed uite sancte adeo debili*s* erat corp*ore*, vt eum viu*ere* ted*er*et.

[2] Latin MS. *et* ueste eum ferien*s*.

[3] MS. *repeats here*, in his hand.

Dux malus in infernu*m* portatur. Inf*ra* de Inuidia.
Dux bonus in fine conu*er*titur. Infra de morte.

CCLXXXVI.

Ebrietas. Ebrius grauit*er* punitur.

Cesarius tellis how þ*er* was a pylgram at, when he fand gude wyne on a tyme, he seld his slavyn & drank it þ*er*-att. And he drank so mekull at he was dronken, and fell evyn wude, to so mekull at men trowid at he was [1] v*er*elie dead. So his spiritt was takyn & led þ*er* paynys was, and þ*er* he saw þe devull sitt in a hy tre, as him thoght, couerd *with* burdis. And emang oþ*er* þ*er* was broght befor hym þe abbott of Corbeyꝰ; and þe devull rase vp & haylsid hym & servid *with* a drynk mengid *with* burnston on a burnyng chales. And when he had dronkyn, he was com*m*andid vnto þe depe pitt. And when þe pylgram saw þis he was passand ferd. And þan þe devull cryed *with* a hy voyce & said; "Bryng hedur þat lord of ours þat late seld hys pylgram clothyng & drank it att þe gude wyne, and was dronkyn." And when þis pylgram hard þis, he lukid vppon his gude aungell þat broght hym thedur, & said, & he wold delyver hym fro thens, he suld neu*er* after be dronken. And so he come agayn vnto hym selfe, and notid þe day & hour, & went & shrafe hym & did his pylgramege, & come home agayn vnto his awn land. And he fand att þe same Abbott dyed þe same tyme at he saw his saule com*m*ytt vnto p*er*petuall payn.

Ebrietatis causas sapientes fugiunt. Sup*ra* de abstinencia.

CCLXXXVII.

Eccle*s*ia de vsuris *et* rapinis construi no*n* debet.

We rede how on a tyme, when ane vsurar of his ravyn & his vsurye had byggid a kurk, he desirid a bisshopp to com & halow

[1] MS. *repeats*, was.

itt. And as þe bisshop and his clergie did þe offes of consecracion, he was war of þe devull syttand vppon þe hy altar in a chare, þat said vnto hym; "Why halows þou my kurk? Sese! for þe iuridiccion þeroff longis vnto me; ffor it is byggid all of ravyn & vsurie." And with þis, þe bisshopp & his clerkis wer ferd & went þer ways. And onone as þai wer getten oute þer-of, þer was a grete noyce þer-in, & þe devull sett fire þerin & burnyd it vp & destroyed itt euere dele, att all folke mott se. *et c*[9].

Ecclesie dedicacione expellitur demon. Supra de dedicacione.

Ecclesie sepultura parum prodest aliquando. Infra de sepultura.

CCLXXXVIII.

Ecclesiis non sunt bona temporalia subtraenda.

Petrus Damyanus tellis how som tyme þer was ane erle þat was of gude name and liffid well; and when he was dead, a man of religion was ravisshid in his spiritt, and[1] he saw [*þis erle*] in hell in a grete degre, syttand vppon a hy leddir in myddest of burnand paynys; and as hym thoght, þat stie stude evyn in myddeste of hell. And þan he askid whi þis erle þat was so gude a man and liffid so rightwuslie, was so turmente. It was tolde hym þat it was for a possession þat he had taken fro þe kurk off Metence, þat was giffen vnto God & Saynt Stephan; and for þis, fro hensfurth, all his sequele at holdis þis same possession & knowis þerof mon be punysshid vppon þis same stye.

Elacio cordis semper causatur ex adulacione et ex vestium apparatu. Supra de augurio.

Elacio cordis aufert graciam a deo concessam. Infra de locucione.

[1] Harl. MS. vidit . . . *dictum* cuiusdam scale erecte(s)* inter stri- Comitem in inferno, in supremo gradu dentes *et* crepitantes flammas.

* Arund. MS. erecte.

CCLXXXIX.

Eleccio. Eligi semp*er* debet melior ad offic*ium*.

Petrus Clariuall tellis how in a Cathedrall-kurk of Fraunce þ*er* fell a[1] dis-corde for chesyng of þ*er* bisshopp. So þai *com*promysid vnto a cardinall þat was þ*er*, þat he sulde chese þai*m* one of ij, whame þai namyd. And þis Cardinall tuke councell att þis holie man Petrus Clariuall, whethur hym was bettir to chese to be bisshopp; and he ansswerd agayn & sayde, þat of ij fals penys þe bettur may nott be chosyn.

Eligi no*n* debet puer in p*re*latu*m* vel iudice*m*. Inf*ra* de puero.

Eligi no*n* debet p*re*latus racione carnalitatis. Inf*ra* de p*re*lato. Et sup*ra* de abb*at*e.

Elemosina semp*er* est danda. Sup*ra* de dacione *et* dono.

Elemosina paup*er*i negari no*n* debet. Inf*ra* de paup*er*tate.

Elemosina eciam in p*re*senti deus reddit. Sup*ra* de auaricia.

Elemosina temp*er*ata auget, negata, temporalia toll*it* qu*ando*q*ue*. Sup*ra* de auaricia.

CCXC.

Elemosina temporalia auget.

Petrus Damian*us* tellis how som tyme þ*er* was a bisshopp þat thurstyd gretelie to drynk wyne, and com*m*andid it to be broght vnto hym; and þe butler powrid furth all þat was in þe flakett & broght it vnto hym. And sodanlie þ*er* come a pure man & prayed þai*m* to giff hym it, or els he monde dye for threste; and þe bysshop com*m*andid it to be giffen vnto hym. And when he

[1] MS. *repeats*, a.

had dronken it he cryed for more, & said his thriste was not slakid; and þe bisshop bad giff hym more. And þe butler said at þer was no more; and þan he bad þai*m* go vnto þe vyne-garth & luke if þer war lefte any vynys growyng, & feche hym. And when þai come þer, þe vyne-garth, at no frute was in befor, was growyng full of rype grapis.

CCXCI.

Elemosina reddit plus q*u*am datur.

Petrus Damianus tellis how som tyme þer was a pure husband-man, and he had no mor money lefte to by hym *with* soule vnto his bread bod a peny; and sodanlie þer come a pure man & askid hym a peny for Godd*is* sake, & he gaff hym þis peny *with* gude will. And so he went home & sett hym down to his meatt, and his wife sett bread befor hym & no soule. And sodanlie þer come in ane vncuth man hastelie *with* xx *soldi* bon in a clothe, & putt it in his hand, & said his lorde sent hym it. & he thankid hym & prayed hym bide & drynke. And ewhils þai went at feche hym a drynk, sodanlie he was away.

CCXCII.

Elemosina remun*er*atur in p*re*senti.

We rede in 'Gestis Ioh*ann*is Elemosinarij' how þer was a knyght at was robbid, and he come vnto þis Ioh*anne*s & told hym of his myschefe; and he com*m*andid a s*er*vand of his to gyff hym xv li*bra* of gold, and he gaff hym bod v li*bra*. And þer come a wedow vnto hym *with* a byll, & xv [1] markis of gold wretyn þ*er*in, & he tuke it & delyvird it vnto his men, & askid þai*m* what þai gaff þe pure man, & þai said xv li*bra*, as þai had in com*m*andment; & he had knowlege at þai did wrong & askid þai*m* þe byll agayn, and þer was wretten þ*er*in bod v [2]. And þan he askid þe wedow how

[1] Latin MSS. dedit ei . . . noticiam exennij v. centenarior*um* auri.

[2] The Latin MSS. further explain that Iohannes said, "Si dedissetis xv ut iusseram, que attulit v. centenaria xv attulisset."

mekull at sho had writtem, & sho said xv, bod x was away; and sho said sho trowed it was Goddis will att sho suld offer bod v. And þan his *ser*vand was ashamyd & grawntid treuth, & tellid hym all, & besoght hym of forgifnes.

CCXCIII.

Elemosina remun*er*atur in futuro.

Saynt Gregorie tellis how som tyme þ*er* was a shomaker þat wold wurk all þe weke day, & on þe Satturday[1] he wold evur go vnto þe kurk. So þ*er* was a gude halie man, & he saw be revelacion of þis man, þat a howce was byggid for hym in hevyn, and þai at bigid it wroght alway on þe Satturday; and he spyrrid of þat mans life, & he fand how þ*at* he wroght all þe weke day, & what at he mott safe ou*er* his meatt & his clothe, he wold go vnto þe kurk vpon þe Satturday & giff it vnto pure men.

CCXCIV.

Elemosina facta de rapinis *et* iniuste acquisitis no*n* valet.

Petrus Damianus tellis how som tyme þ*er* was a bisshopp, and in a visyon he saw a pope at hight Benett, att wold new be dede, & hym þoght he saw hym bodelie syttand on a blak hors. And þis bisshopp said; "Allas! erte þou nott pope Benett, at is newlie dead?" & he said; "Yis, I am þat same vnhappy man; and here," he sayd, "I am grevuslye turment, bod I despayr nott of þe m*er*cie of God, & I may gett any helpe. And þ*er*for I pray þe go vnto my successur, & bid hym do almos for me in suche a place, for þat almos at is giffen for me hedur-toward p*ro*fettis me noght, for it was all of robbery & of wrong-getten gudis."

Elemosina debet fieri de vestib*us*. Inf*ra* de histrionib*us*.

[1] Latin MSS. die Sabbato.

CCCXV.

Elemosina no*n* debet esse causa vane gl*or*ie.

Heraclides tellis how a halie wom*man* of Rome, þat hight S*ancta* Melama[1], broght on a tyme vnto abbott Pampus[2] iij c. li*bra*, & he thankid hur þ*er*for & bad God reward hur[3]; & he gaff it vnto his s*er*vand & bad hym go devide it emang his brethir. And sho stude still and þoght sho suld hafe had owd*er* grete lovyng, or grete blissyng, for þis gifte; & when sho hard he wold say no mor, sho said vnto hym: "Sur, I latt þe witt þ*er* is in þatt pokett iij c. li*bra*." & yit he lukid not vp; & þan he said: "Doght*er*, þou sulde say þis easyelie when þou hase gyffen þine almos[4]. And þ*er*for be still & luke aft*er* no lawde of man, bod of Hym þat þou giffes it for; ffor He þat made all þing of noght, He can reward þe when att Hym plesis; & þ*er*for luke aft*er* no noþ*er* thank nor reward bod of Hym."

Elemosina data amore alicui*us* s*an*cti ipsi datur, *et* in p*re*senti aliqu*ando* remun*er*atur. Inf*ra* de p*er*egrino.

CCCXVI.

Elemosina ecia*m* no*n* ex deuocione data valet.

Ioh*annes* Elemosinarius tellis how þ*er* was a riche tol-gadurer þat hyght Peirs, & he luffid no pure men nor wold giff þai*m* none almos; & when þai come to his howse he wold shute þai*m* oute, & giff þai*m* noght. So on a tyme þ*er* was a grete meneya of pure men samen, & þai made grete *com*playnt emang þai*m* how þai cuthe gett none almos of þis riche man, þis Peirs Toller. So emang þai*m* all ane starte vp & sayd; "I dar lay wit*h* you all a grete wageour att I sall þis day or evyn gett almos on hym." & þai laid a wageour agayns hym. So þis pure man went vnto

[1] Harl. MS. Melana.
[2] Harl. MS. Paulo. Arund. MS. Pambo.
[3] MS. hym.
[4] Latin MSS. "Si inde, o filia, hoc offerens, competenter hoc diceres."

his howse & stude at þe dure, & askid almos. So þis Peirs bad hym pakk, & said he sulde hafe none; and euer he cried for almos & wold not sease. So þis Peirs wex wrothe *with* hym, and soght a stone to caste at hym, & he cuthe fynd none. So þer happend a servand of his awn to com in at þe dure in the mene-while *with* a baskett full of ry lovis, and in a grete tene he tuke ane of þies rye lovis & slang it att þis pure man, and gaff hym a grete strake þer*with*; & þe pure man was fayn of þis lafe & tuke itt & went vnto his felous & told þai*m* how he had it at þe hand of þis Peirs Toller. And *with*[*in*] ij dayes aft*er* þis man fell seke, lyke to dye. And he was takyn in a vysyon & hym þoght at he was broght befor a iuge, & hym þoght þer was fowle blakk men þatt putt all his ill dedis in a wey-skale. And on þe tod*er* hand hym þoght þer was fayr men, bod þai wẹr passand hevy, & said þai had no gude dede of his to putt in þe tod*er* wey-skale agayns his ill dedis, bod alonelie a rye lofe þat he had giffyn God halfe agayn his wyll. And þai putt it in þe tod*er* wey-skale, & yitt it was þe lighter be a grete dele, & þan þies men bad hym eke more weght to putt in þat wey-skale agayns his evull dedis, or els þies blak men wulde take hym. And *with* þat he wakend & was delyverd, & sent after þe preste & tolde hym all þe cace, & said in þis man*er* of wyse; "Sen a rye lafe þat I keste in ane anger fro me *pro*fettid me so mekull, þan I wote well þat & I giff all my gudis for Godd*is* sake, att þat will gretelie profett me." And so he did afterward & become a gude man.

Elemosina occulte debet dari. Sup*ra* de amicicia.
Elemosinam impedit avaricia. S*upra* de auaricia.

CCXCVII.

Elemosina*m* deus aliqu*ando* sibi datam ostendit.

Ioh*annes* Elemosinarius tellis how on a day afterward, when þis same Peirs was arayed in þe beste clothyng at he had, a pure shipman at was nere-hand nakid come vnto hym & askid hym almos, & he gaff hym his vppermeste garment. And when he had it, onone he sold itt. And when Peirs had knowlege þ*er*of, he was somwhat trubblid in his mynd & said; "I was nott worthi at þis pure man sulde were my clothe, nor hafe me in remembrance." And on þe nyght after, when he was on slepe, he was war a man þat was bryght*er* þan þe son, & hym thoght he said vnto hym; "Peirs, whi wepis þou? Knowis þou þis clothyng?" & he said; "Ya, sur." And our Lord sayd agayn vnto hym; "þat clothyng at þou gaff þe pure man, þou gaff it me; and þis is it at I am cled in."

CCXCVIII.

Elemosina eciam viuis p*ro*dest quando p*ro* eis fit.

Ioh*ann*es Elemosinarius tellis how som tyme þ*er* was [1] a man þat was taken *with* [2] þe Persies & putt in-to p*ri*son. So other p*ri*soners of his awn contre þat was *with* hym esskapid & went home vnto his contrey, and told his wyfe þat he was dead & berid. And his wyfe & his frendis garte iij yere to-gedur þe p*re*ste eu*er*-ilk a day do a colett for hym in his mes. And in þe iiij yere hym happend esskape and com home. And þai war fayn on hym & told hym how þai had done for hym. And when þai had tolde hym, he said þat eu*er*-ilk a day at þat colett was said for hym, aboute mes-tyme, þ*er* come a fayr man & lowsid hym oute of his yrnys. And so he was lowse all day afterward to nyght come; and þan he wold lay hym down, & on þe morn he felid hym-selfe bon agayn in yrnys as he was befor.

CCXCIX.

Elemosina*m* recipiens *et* no*n* orans p*ro* dante punitur.

Cesarius tellis how som tyme þ*er* was a pylgram þat tuke sekenes, and dyed in his pylgramege. And he bewitt þe preste his slavyn, & þe preste tuke it, bod he had litle charge of þe saule. So it happend afterward at þis preste made hym a monke in Ceustus

[1] *After* was, þat, *erased.* [2] MS. *repeats,* with.

ordur; and as he lay on a nyght in his dortur, he was ravisshid in his spiritt, & had vnto þe place of paynys, þ*er* he saw many sawlis grevuslie punysshid. And he hid hym behynd þe dure. So he was war of þis slavyn, þ*er* hym þoght, at þe pylgram had giffen, and þe devull askid who aght it; & þai told hym at it was þe prestis at stude behynd þe dure, & at a pylgram had giffen hym itt to pray for hym, & he had owder litell prayed for hym or noght. And þe devull [*said*][1]; "Latt vs reward hym"; & he tuke þis slavyn & putt it in hate, bulyng, stynkand watir, & clappid þe preste in þe face þ*er*-*with*. And *with* þat he wakend & cryed; "Helpe me! helpe me! ffor I am so burnyd þat I dye." And þe monkis his bruther rase vp & come vnto hym, & þai fand all his face & his head burnyd all þe flessh nerehand of, & hym halfe dead; & þai tuke hym vp & had hym in-to þ*er* ffermorye, & þan he told þai*m* þ*er*-of. & ilk-one of þai*m* sayd mes þat day for þis pylgram; & onone after þis monke amendid & was als hole as he was befor.

CCC.

Elemosina p*ro*pt*er* vana*m* gl*or*iam f*act*a non p*ro*dest.

Cesarius tellis of a vision þat was sene in Balmarie[2], how þat a ryche lord, att was dead, vppon a nyght apperid vnto his wife, and sho askid hym whatt estate he stude in; & he ansswerd agayn & sayd þat he was dampnyd. And sho askid hym whi he said so, & said; "Whatt p*ro*fett*is* you your grete almos-ded, & þe h*er*berie at ye did?" And he said þai p*ro*fett hym no thyng vnto evurlastand life, for he sayd he did þai*m* nott be way of charite, bod rather for vayn glorie. And sho askid hym mekull mor, & he said þat he myght nott abyde & tarye *with* hur, for his maister þe devull bade hym *with*-oute þe dure. And he said, & þe levis of all treis in þis werld wer turnyd into tonges, þai might nott all tell his paynys. And þan his maist*er* callid hym; and when he wente all þe castell shuke *with*.

[1] Latin MSS. ad quod diabolus.
[2] Arund. MS. Balbaria. Harl. MS. Balwaria.

CCCI.

Elemosina que fit de re que, *et*-si in se non fuit rapta, tamen si de re[1] rapta ortu*m* h*abuer*it, no*n* valet.

Cesarius tellis how som tyme þ*er* was a riche man, and vnd*er*nethe þe colour of almos-dede, he made pure men a feste. So emang þai*m* þ*er* was one and he wold not ete, nor a nod*er* þat satt by hym þat wold hafe etyn, he wold not latt hym, bod eu*er* as he putt meatt vnto his mowth, he tuke it fro hym. And þai att wer aboute hym askid hym whi he wold nott suffre þe man to eatt; and he answerd & said; "I will nott att he syn; ffor þis almos is done of stoltherie." And þai said he leyid, ffor he þat did þe almos was a gude man. And he answerd agayn & said; "Nay, I lee nott; ffor þis calfe þat is devidid her in almos emang pure men, in þe v gen*er*acion fro hyne was of a cow þat he had stollen." And þai þat wer aboute had grete m*er*vall here-off.

Elemosine vsurario*rum* ecia*m* non su*n*t grate deo. Inf*ra* de vsuris.

CCCII.

Elemosina in centuplu*m* redditur deo.

Iacobus de Vet*ri*aco tellis how at þ*er* was a bisshopp þat made a *ser*mon, & in his sermon he said at þai þat delte þ*er* gudis to pure men suld hafe þ*er*for a hondrethfolde reward. And þ*er* was a riche man at hard hym, & all þe gudis att he had, he putt þai*m* vnto þe bisshopp, & he delte þai*m* vnto pure men for Goddis sake. So hym happend to dy, & his childre tuke a sute agayn þis bisshop & askid þ*er* fadur gudis agayn. And he was not in power to giff þai*m* agayn. Not-wit*h*-stondyng he was a holie man, & had a com*m*andment be revelacion, and he and þai to-gedur suld go vnto þ*er* fad*er* grafe; & so þai did, & tuke hym vpp. & þai fand in his hand a quytans, wreten & selid wit*h* his awn seale, þat he not alonelie had reseyvid agayn all þe gudis at he

[1] MS. se.

had delyverd þe bisshopp̄, bod also þatt he had reseyvid a hondreth tymys mor. And when̄ þis riche mans childer saw þis, þai lete hym̄ alone & sewid hym̄ no more.

Elemosina eciam in presenti redditur in centuplum. Infra de Hospitalit[*at*]e.

CCCIII.

Elemosinam recipientes ab vsurarijs puniuntur.

We rede in 'Legenda S*an*c*t*i Fursij,' when̄ þe sawle of hym̄ was passid oute of his bodye, ffendis accusid hym̄ befor almighti God, and þai cuthe not fynd nothyng to accuse hym̄ off, bod at he had on̄ a tyme taken̄ a cape of ane vusurar, & þis sentans þai fand agayn̄ hym̄. And gude angels stude on̄ þe toder syde & pleyid agayns þai*m*, and almighti [*God*] gaff eniugement þ*at* his sawle sulde go agayn̄ vnto his body & do penans þ*er*for. So wit*h* þis þ*er* was a fend wrothe, & in a tene he tuke þis vsurar saule & keste in his face. And so his saule come vnto his bodye; and eu*er* after þ*er* was in his saule[1] a spott as it war byrnyd *with* þis vsurar saule. Yit not-wit*h*-stondyng þis holie man̄ had nott þis cape of þis vsurar[2] bod as almos-dede.

Elemosinarius p*er* p*re*ces paup*erum* lib*er*atur a dampnacione. Ex mirac*u*lis B*ea*te Vi*r*ginis vt infra Laurencij.

Eleuatur cor ho*min*is quando honoratur. Sup*r*a de Augurio.

CCCIV.

Ep*iscop*us a demone citatur.

We rede in 'Libro de Dono Timoris,' how on̄ a tyme a bisshopp̄ happend to fall seke, and a fend come & somond hym̄ to com̄ afor

[1] Saule, *for* face, Lat. MSS. app*a*ruit in facie.

[2] MS. vsusar.

þe pope, & for to giff rekynyng of his adminystracion. So vppon þe day at was assigned hym, hym thoght þat he was drawen vnto iugement befor þe pope, and at þe devull suld article agayns hym for to giff a rekenyng. And he cuthe not giff a due rekynyng; so hym thoght hym was assignyd a day to take his full sentance on, and her-for he wex passyng hevy, and callid all his howshold aforn hym, & told þaim how it was. So a noder day hym thoght at a fend come & constreynyd hym to com to his rakenyng befor þe hye iuge of hevyn, and he vgged so with þe fend þat he cryed hugelie, & said he wold nott go with hym; & he clekid a pyler in his armys to hold hym by þat he suld nott take hym, and with þat his head was plukkid off & he dyed.

Episcopus de religione sumptus, cibaria delicata vitare debet. Infra de Gula.

Episcopus a demone temptatur. de Andrea supra.

Episcopus bonus deuote moritur. Supra de Communione.

CCCV.

Episcopus a sanctis accusatur.

We rede in 'Libro de Dono Timoris,' how þer was in þe cetie of Turan a gude man; and he vsid of costom to com on þe night to matyns vnto þe cathedrall-kurk þer. So on a tyme hym happend com tymelie, & he fand þe yatis opyn, & he saw a grete light in þe kurk, & a iuge syttand in a trone. And hym þoght þer come Saynt Martyn & many oþer Saynttis with hym, and accusid þe archbisshopp of þe same kurk, & he was cityd & come. And he was sett in a chayr in his pontificall aray, and he was grevuslie accusid and wold giff none ansswer, to so muche þe iuge wex wroth with hym, & smate þe chayre & hym bothe owr with his fute. & with þat þe vision vanysshid away, & þis gude man went vnto þe bisshoppis place, & spirrid how þe bisshop did; & his meneya went in-to his chawmer & lukid, and fand hym stark dead in his bed sodanly.

CCCVI.

Episcopalis status periculosus est.

Cesarius tellis how on a tyme þer was a monk of Clariuall þat was chosyn to be a bisshopp; and he forsoke to take it & wold not agre þerto, nowder be commandment of his abbott nor yitt of þe archbisshopp. So with-in a while after hym happend to dy, and on þe night after he apperid to a man þat he luffid, a bruther of his, and he askid hym of þis inobediens, whether it noyed hym or nay. And he answerd agayn & said nay, it noyed him not; "ffor," he said, "si episcopatum suscepissem, eternaliter dampnatus essem. And I had taken þe bisshopprike, I had bene dampnyd for evur." And he ekid to & sayd a full ferdfull wurd, & þat was þis, þat þe estate of þe kurk sulde happen so, at it suld not be wurthi to be gouernyd bod with reprevable bisshoppis.

Episcopus habens iusticiam secularem diligenter debet auertere quid balliuis suis precipiat. Infra de iudice.

CCCVII.

Episcopus debet esse sobrius.

Petrus Damyanus tellis how þer was som tyme a bisshopp, & he garte ordand for hym selfe a lawmpron; and when he had said mes, he garte giff þis lampron vnto a pure man for Goddis sake.

Evagacio cordis. Euagatur cor frequenter in oracione. Supra Barnardi.

CCCVIII.

Eukaristia sumpta ab infideli a combustione eum protexit.

We rede how on a tyme þer was a childe þatt was a Iew son; and he was fayr and gentyll, so þat cristen men childre luffid hym passandlie wele, vnto so muche þat vppon a tyme þai desyrid hym to go into a kurk of our Ladye wit*h* þai*m*, and þer for to take þe sacrament as þai did; and he did so. And onone as he come home he tolde his fadur, & he was hetand aue oven, and he was so wroth þer-with þat he tuke þis chylde, his awn son, & keste hym in þe hote ovyn. And þe childes moder saw how he had putt hym in þe ovyn, & how þe low come oute at þe mouth þer-of; & sho wex evyn wude and ran oute att þe dure and cryed as sho war wude. And cristen men had grete mervall & ran into þe Iewis howse, and wit*h*-drew þe fyre oute of þe oven mouthe, and fand þe child in þe ovyn, syttand opon þe hate colis, right as had syttyn opon fayr flowris; and hym aylid no rew sore. And þai tuke hym furth, & he told þai*m* all þe cace. And onone þai tuke þis Iew, his fadur, & threste hym in-to þe oven; and onone þe fire had made a nend on hym, so þat þai cuthe nowder fynd of hym bone nor lith. And þan þe childe told þai*m* how þat wom*m*an[1] þat was in þe kurk þer he had etyn bread wit*h* his felous, syttand in a chayr, þat had a little chylde syttand on hur kne wappid in a clothe, coverd hym wit*h* hur mantyll þat þe fyre shuld nott burn hym. And so þis childe and his moder, and many other Iewis, wer cristend enspeciall for þis fayr meracle of þe sacrament.

CCCIX.

Eukaristia propter fidei roboracionem versa est in carnem.

Saynt Gregur tellis how þer was a wom*m*an at Rome, and sho had grete devocion to make offrand vnto þe pope, and in esspeciall opon þe Sononday. So opon a day sho come wit*h* other to be howsyld of þe popis hand, and when þe pope sulde howsell hur, & said; "Corpus D*omi*ni n*ost*ri, Iesu Cri*sti*, et c^9," sho smylid; & he pursayvid itt, and wit*h*-drew þe sacrament fro hur, & laid it on þe altar fro þe toder. And when he had done, he callid þis wom*m*an on syde, and askid hur whatt þing was in hur harte þat

[1] MS. *repeats*, þat wom*m*an.

sho smylid whe[*n*] he sulde hafe howseld hur. And sho answerd agayn & sayd; "Sur, I vmthoght me þat þat porcion of bread was of þe same offrand þat I made *with* myne awn handis; and when I hard you call itt a body, þan I smylid." And evyn furth-*with* þis holie man hereof made a *ser*mon vnto þe peple, & he & þai fell in þ*er* prayers vnto almyghti God, & evyn opynlie, at þai all saw, þis porcion turnyd in-to a little fynger all bludy. And when þis wom*m*an & all þe peple saw þis, þai war passand fayn [1], & mekull more stirrid into deuocion & confermyng of þe faithe þan þai wer afor. *et c*[9].

Eukaristia lib*er*at a purgatorio. Inf*r*a de *pro*-p*r*ietario.

Eukaristia sustentatur aliquis sine aliquo cibo. S*upr*a de cibo.

Eukaristia vbiq*ue* est adoranda. Infra de Milite.

CCCX.

Eukaristie loco n*u*lla alia hostia administrari debet.

We rede how þat when Hugo de Sa*nc*to Victore, þat was ane excellent doctur and a devoute in religion, agayn he sulde dye laburd gretelie in sekenes & no meate mott hold, he prayed his brethir *with* a grete instans for to giff hym þe sac*r*ament. And his brethir þoght þai wuld somwhat slake his truble, and þai tuke a symple oste & broght hym in-stead of þe sac*r*ament. And he co*n*seyvid in his spiritt at þai did wrong, & sayd; "God hafe m*er*cie of you, brether, whi wuld ye hafe disseyvid me? For þis is not my Lord at ye hafe broght." And þai had grete m*er*vell here-of, and went and fechid þe sac*r*ament. And when he saw þat he myght not resayfe it, he held vpp his handis vnto hevyn and p*r*ayed on þis man*er* of wyse; "Ascendat filius ad patrem *et*

[1] MS. fayr.

spiritum sanctum qui me fecit[1]." And in þies wurdis saying he swelte; and þe sacramente evyn̄ þ*er* emang þai*m* vanysshid̄ away.

Eukaristie loco falsus den*ar*ius malo rustico administratur. Inf*r*a de oblacione.

Eukaristie su*m*pcio ecia*m* obstinatu*m* de obstinac*ion*e *et* dolentem reuocat ad penitenciam. Infra de obstinacione.

Eukaristia a religioso p*ro*p*r*ietario no*n* potest sumi. Inf*r*a de p*ro*p*r*ietate.

CCCXI.

Eustacij Placidi.

We rede in þe Legend̄ of Saynt Eustace þat befor̄ was callid̄ Placidus, how on̄ a tyme as he went on̄ huntyng att þe harte, emang alƚ oþ*er* he fand̄ a fayre harte, and hym̄ he pursewid̄ & folowd̄. So at þe laste þis harte turnyd̄ agayn̄ & lukid̄ on̄ hym̄, and he beheld̄ þis harte, and he saw betwix his hornys a cros and þe ymage of our Lord̄ Iesu, þat spakk vnto hym̄ be þe mouthe of þis harte, & tolde hym̄ & taght hym̄ þe faythe of þe kurk̄, & bad hym̄ teche þe same vnto his wyfe & his childer; and so he did, & þai trowid̄ þer-in. And þai war cri*st*end̄ at Rome; and Placidus was callid̄ Eustachius, and his wife was callid̄ Theospita, and his sons Agapitus and Theospitus. And opon̄ þe morn̄ our Lord̄ aperid̄ vnto hym̄ in þe same place & in þe same figur, and tolde hym̄ þat he sulde suffer mekuƚƚ þing bod he sulde giff hym̄ þe v*er*tue of paciens. So *with*-in a little while after, dead̄ come and tuke alƚ his hows-meneya, and thevis come and robbid̄ hym̄ of alƚ his gudis, so þat hym̄ was lefte right noght, bod was almoste nakid̄. So on̄ a nyght he fled̄ away *with* his wife & his childer, and went our att a ferie, and had nothyng to pay for his ferilay,

[1] Latin MSS. "Ascendat filius ad p*a*trem *et* spiritu*m* *sanctum*, ad deum qui fecit illu*m*."

[&] þe maist*er* of þe shipp tuke his wyfe from hym for his ferilay, mawgre his tethe, becauce sho was a fayr wom*m*an. And he made grete sorow & went on his wayis w*ith* his childer. So hym happend to com vnto a watur, and itt was so grete he myght nott bere þai*m* ou*er* bothe att onys. So he tuke þ*at* one on hys bak & bare it our, & lefte þ*at* other behynd; and when he come agayn for þe toder, & was in þe myddeste of þe watir, þ*er* come a lyon on þe tone syde & tuke þ*at* one of his barnys, and a wulfe on þe tod*er* syde & tuke þat oþ*er*. And he, when he was in þe myddeste of þe watir, saw þis, and mornyd & made mykill sorow, & luhid þe hare of his head, and turnyd agayn & went on his wayis mornand. Not-w*ith*-stondyng, at he wyste not, hurde-men & plew-men rescowid his childer fro þis lyon & þis wulfe, & þai war bothe nurisschid & broght vp in þe next town. So Eustace wiste nevur what he moght do, & he become a mans hird-man, & kepid his catell xv yere; and almighti God kepid his wyfe. Than þe Emp*er*our of Rome happend to be oppressid w*ith* enmys, and he vmthoght hym of þe nobylnes of þis Eustas, and he sent ij knyghtis to seke hym in eu*er*e place; so þai happend to com by hym þurgh þe feld þ*er* he walkid, and þai askid hym if he war oght wer of a pylgram at hight Placidus, & his ij sonys & his wife: and he said he saw þai*m* noght. Neu*er*-þe-les he knew þai*m*, and he had þai*m* home vnto his maist*er* howse; and as he *ser*vid þaim, be dyvers tokens þai kend hym wele, & þai tuke knowlege vnto hym and kissid hym, & spirrid hym of his wyfe & his childer; and he told þai*m* at his wife was taken from hym, & how his childer war dead. So þai broght hym vnto þe Emp*er*our, and he resayvid hym w*ith* mekull ioy and wurshup, & made hym maist*er* of þe knyghtis as he was befor. And he fand few knyght*is* þat war able vnto þe were, and he garte gadur to-gedur yong men þ*at* wer able vnto chyvalrie, emang þe whilk was his ij sons broght; and þai plesid hym gretelie. So þurgh þe grace of God þai*m* happend to hafe þe victorie of þ*er* enmys. And as God wold, þis ij yong men war att hoste in þ*er* moder howse, and be knowlege þat ather of þai*m* told other, how þai war takyn fro wylde bestis, athir of þai*m* knew other well enogh; and þ*er* mod*er* þoght of þis in hur harte, bott sho knew nothyng þeroff. So *with*-in a little while, when sho saw þis maist*er* of þe knyghtis, sho knew hym well enogh & he hur; and sho askid hym of þ*er* childer, & he told hur how þai war devowrid *with* wylde bestis. And þan sho told hym how þies ij yong men had told hur, and he was passand fayn & sent for þai*m* & knew þai*m* wele enogh. And þai wer all passand fayn to-gedur, and thankid God. And afterward þai wer all m*ar*tyrd same*n* for Goddis sake.

Exactor talliar*um* g*r*auit*er* punitur. Infra de gula.

CCCXII.

Exco*mmun*icacio. Exco*mm*unicatus [1] ab om*n*ib*us* debet evitari.

Jacobus de Vet*r*iaco tellis how som tyme in þe bisshopprik of Lincoln þ*er* was a smyth, and he dispysyd þe sentens of þe kurk; and þai cursid hym. So on a day he satt at meatt *with* oþ*er* folk, and þ*er* come in-to þe howse vnto þai*m* a swyne of Saynt Antons. And he tuke bread & keste vnto it, & said; "Now sall itt appere wheþ*er* þis Anton swyne will eatt of my bread þat am cursyd, or nay." And þe swyne smellid þe bread & wolde not eate it. And þan he bad one of his felous take þe same bread & giff it; and so he did, & yitt it wold not tuche it. And þe toder þat satt aboute gaff it of þ*er* bread, and onone þe swyne eate itt.

Exco*m*municatus [2] qua*n*tecu*m*q*ue* auc*tori*tatis eccle-*s*iam int*r*are no*n* debet. Sup*r*a de adult*er*io.

CCCXIII.

Exco*mmun*icacio lata in viuu*m* *eciam* post mortem durat.

We rede in þe 'Legend of Saynt Benedicte' how on a tyme þ*er* was ij wurthie nonnys in a monast*er*ie, and oft sithes, *with* þ*er* vnthrifti

[1] MS. Exco*m*minicatus.

[2] MS. Exco*m*minicatus.

language, hym̄ at had rewle of þai*m* þai *pro*voked & stirrid to be angrie and wrothe. And þis holie man̄ purseyvyd þis, & gaff þai*m* a charge & said; "Amend, & correcte your tongis, or els here I curse you." And þai wold not amend þai*m*; & wit*h*-in a little while after þai dyed, & was berid in þe kurk. And þ*er* was ane vsage, þat eu*er*e day afor mes, a deken̄ stude vp̄ & said; "He þat is curste, go his ways!" So þ*er* was a noryss of þairs þat eu*er*-ilk day offerd for þai*m*, & sho saw þai*m* rise oute of þ*er* gravis & go oute of þe kurk. And sho went & told Saynt Benett; he tuke ane offrand hym̄ selfe and gaff vnto þ*er* nuress; "Goo & offyr for þai*m* þis offrand, and fro hyne furth þai sall not be cursid." And so sho did; and when̄ þe dekyn̄ cryed as he was wunte to done, þai war neu*er* after sene go furth of þe kurk.

Exco*m*municacio non debet cito p*ro*ferri. Sup*ra* de absolucione.

CCCXIV.

Executoris necligencia *quandoque* testatorem retinet in purgatorio.

Turpin*us* the Archebisshopp̄ tellis how som̄ tyme in þe felowshipp̄ of greatt Charles, þ*er* was a knyght þat happend seke, & he made his testament and comm*a*wndid a cussyn̄ of his to take his hors, and he dyed, and sell itt, & giff the pryce þ*er*-off vnto pure men̄ & clerkis, to pray for hym̄. And when̄ he was dead he sellid a nod*er* hors & spendid þe price þ*er*-of for hym̄ in meate & drynk. And wit*h*-in xxx^ti^ dayes after, þis dead man̄ apperid vnto hym̄ and sayd; "Be-cauce I gaff my gudis for the to deale for my sawle, & þou did not as I bad þe, þou sall vnd*er*stand þat all my synnys er forgiffen̄ me; bod becauce þou hase wit*h*-holden̄ myne almos þis xxx^ti^ dayes, & lattyn̄ me be in purgatorie, þerfor I latt þe wett, þat to-morn̄ sall I be taken̄ into paradice, & þou sal be putt in hell." And þe same day as he rade wit*h* his felows, & told þai*m* all þis cace, sodanly þ*er* began̄ a cry in þe ayre, as it had bene of lyons, wulvis & beris; and sodanlie he was taken vpp *with* fendis, & putt þ*er* he was ordand to be. And his felows went & soght hym; and his body was fon dead oppon a hy hill & revyn in sonder, iiij day iorney from þe place þ*er* he was taken.

CCCXV.

Exemplu*m* bonu*m* plus monet q*u*am p*re*dicacio subtilis.

Saynt Bede tellis in 'Gestis Anglor*um*' how, when Englond was oute of þe belefe, þe pope sente in-to it to p*re*che a bisshop þat was a passyng sutell clerk, & a well-letterd; and he vsid so mekull soteltie & strange saying in his s*er*mons, þat his p*re*chyng owder litle p*ro*fettid or noght. And þan þ*er* was sent a nod*er* þat was les of co*n*nyng of l*it*eratur þan he was, & he vsid talis & gude exsample in his s*er*mon; and he *with*[1]-in a while[2] conu*er*tyd[3] nere-hand all Englond.

Exemplo vni*us* debet alius edoceri. Infra de Iudice.
Exemplu*m* bonu*m* aliqu*ando* conu*er*tit pecc*at*orem. Sup*ra* de Abb*at*e.
Exemplu*m* malu*m* multis nocet. Infra de monacho.

CCCXVI.

Exemplu*m* a meliori est sume*n*du*m*.

We rede in 'Vitis P*at*rum' how on a tyme þ*er* was two, þat was to say, a man, & a wom*m*an his wyfe. And þe man was a holie man, bod he was infortunatt in werdlie[4] thyngis, to so mekull þat on þe day at he was berid on, þ*er* fell suche a wete and a rayn, þat ij dayes aft*er* þai mott nott berie hym. And his wife was ane ill liffer, bod scho was fortunatt; and when þai war bothe dead, a doght*er* at þai had began to vmthynk hur whedur of þ*er* lyvis sho wolde folow. So aft*er*-ward hur happend to be in a trans,

[1] MS. *repeats, with.*
[2] MS. *has,* he, *again here.*
[3] MS. coneruertyd.
[4] MS. werlrdlie.

& hur thoght sho saw a fayr place & a merie; and *þer* hur þoght sho saw hur fadur, and sho hawsiđ hym̄ and kyssyd hym̄, & besoght hym̄ at sho mott abyde *þer* stiłł *with* hym̄. & he saiđ nay, sho mott nott; bott and sho led hur lyfe as he diđ, he saiđ sho suld com̄ thedur. And onone sho was removiđ fro thens, & had vnto a noder place. And *þer* sho lukyd behynđ hur, & sho saw hur moder in ane horrible turment. And sho made sorow, & cryed on̄ hur doght*er* & saiđ; "Dogh*ter*! Se what I suffer for myne vnclene lyfe!" And *with* þatt sho come agayn̄ vnto hur selfe, & thankid God of þat att sho had sene. And scho confermyđ to folow þe lyfe of hur fadur, and so sho diđ, and afterwarđ sho was a holie wom*man̄*.

CCCXVII.

Facundia necessaria est clerico.

Valerius tellis how þat when̄ Demostenes moght not easylie bryng furth *cer*tayn̄ *let*tres, he laburđ so agayn̄ a vice & ane impediment in his mouthe, þat no man̄ myght speke fayrer þat at he wolđ speke þan̄ he diđ[1]. So on̄ a tyme hym̄ happend go vnto þe se-side, & *þer* he harde grete noyse & dusshyng of þe wawis to-gedur; and he gaff grete hede *þer*-to. And evur when̄ his[2] mowthe was fułł of sentance & reson̄, he wolde speke mekułł, & be long in spekyng; and when̄ it was tome, þan̄ it was redie & as it had bene lowse.

Fallacia mulieris. Infra de muliere.
Falsitas testiu*m* nocet. Infra de testimonio.
Falsum iurans punitur. Inf*ra* de iuramento.

CCCXVIII.

Falsu*m* impositu*m* debet denudari.

We rede in 'Legenda *Sanctorum* Prothi *et* Iacincti,' how Eugenia, þat was Philip̄ dogh*ter* þat was governer of Alexandria,

[1] The latter part of this tale differs from the Lat. MSS., which give the well-known version.
[2] MS. he.

wold not be wed vnto a wurthi man þat wold hafe had hur when sho was xv yere olde. And sho fled away and gatt hur mans clothyng, & fenyd at sho sulde be a man, & went vnto ane abbay & made hyr [1] a man of religion; and sho callid hur selfe Eugenius. And when þer principall was dead, sho was made principall. So þer was in Alexandria a wurthi womman, a wedow, þat was passand riche, and sho trustid at he had bene a man, & fell in ane amorositie vnto hym, vnto so mekull at sho fenyd hur seke & sent for hym, and said sho wold speke *with* hym. And when he was befor hur bed, & none was þer bod þaim two, sho wold hafe halsyd & kyssyd þis Eugenius, & told hym þe matir, and desyrid hym to hafe at do *with* hur. And he vgged þer-*with*, and wold not consent vnto hur, bod reprovid hur & blamyd hur for hur desyre. And þan sho was ferd at he suld discure hur, and sho began to cry, and said at þis Eugenius wolde hafe ravisshid hur. And all hur howsemeneya come and hard, and went & tolde þis Philipp, & bare witnes þeroff. And þis womman accusid him als-so, als strongli as sho cuthe. And þan þis Eugenius was broght befor þis Philipp to giff ane answer, & he suffyrd mekull truble. And so at þe last, when he saw it wold no bettyr be, he began to speke & said; "Now it is tyme to speke, ffor it is not right at a lichur putt a fals cryme vnto þe servand of almiȝtty God; and þerfor, to declar þe treuth, I sall shew my selfe whatt I am." And *with* þat þis Eugenius *with* a knyfe cutt down all hur cote, & shewid at sho was a womman, & sayd vnto þis Philipp; "Forsuthe þou erte my fadur, and þi wyfe Elendia is my moder, and I am Eugenia your doghter." And when hur fadur & hur moder hard þis, þai tuke hur in armys & kissid hur. And þai & all þer howsold become crestend, þat war haythen befor and vncristend.

Falsitas punitur. Infra de honore.
Fama necligi no*n* debet. Sup*r*a de falso.
Fama aliqua*n*do pe*r*ditur sine culpa. Infra de Infamac*i*o*n*e.

[1] MS. hym.

CCCXIX.

Fames multa mala cogit fac*ere*.

We rede in þe 'Cronicles' þat when Titus had vmsegid Jer*usal*em ij yere, þ*er* was such a honger in þe cetie þat þe fathir fro þe son, & þe son fro þe fadir, and þe husband fro hys wife, and þe wife fro hur husband, not alonelie tuke meate oute of þ*er* handis, bod also þai wold refe it furth of þ*er* mowthis. And when þ*er* meate faylid þai*m*, þai dyed so thik for hungre þat þai mot not suffre þ*er* caryons lygg *with*-in þe cetie for stynke, bod þai keste þai*m* ou*er* þe wallis. And þan Titus saw how þe dykis was fyllid *with* carion, & at þe contre began to be corrupte *with* savur of þai*m*, þan he made his prayers & said; "Lord! þou seis I do nott þis, þai do itt þ*er* selfe." & þai had so mekull honger emang þai*m* att þai eete þ*er* shone & all þing þat was made of leddur. So þ*er* was emang þai*m* a riche huswiffe, and a wurthie, and all hur gudis was taken fro hur, & no thyng lefte hur þat sho might eate. And sho had no child bod one; & þat sho slew, & sethid þe tone halfe þ*er*of. And onone as þe lurdans in þe cetie felid savur of sodyn flessh, þai ran in-to þe howse & askid hur parte; & sho tuke þe toder p*ar*te & shewid þai*m* & told þai*m* how sho had done *with* hur awn barn. And þai vggid þ*er*-*with*, & went þ*er* ways. And so in þe secund yere Ier*usal*em was yolden vpp, and xxx Iewis war sold for one penye becauce þai solde Criste for xxx^{d}. And, as Iosephus tellis, lxxxxvij thowsand war solde, and xi C. Ml. was slayn & p*er*isshid for hu*n*gre.

Fames t*er*renor*um* est insaciabilis. Infra de sacietate. Fame temptantur ieiunantes. Sup*ra* de abstinencia.

CCCXX.

Familiaritas[1] ecia*m* m*at*ris ad p*ro*p*r*iu*m* filiu*m* nimis expressa est p*er*iculosa.

We rede in þe 'M*er*acles of Our Ladie, Saynt Marie' how som tyme in Rome þ*er* was a wurthie wom*man*, and scho had *with* hur

[1] MS. Familieritas.

husband a son, and þatt sho broght vpp passand tendurlie, & luffid it so wele þat, when he was a grete yong sprynhold, sho wold kys hym & halsse hym & lat hym lig *with* hur as he had bene a barn. So on a tyme when hur husband was gone of pil*gr*amege in-to a fer land, as hur son lay by hur he had at do *with* hur, and belife sho was *with* childe; & þan sho wex passand hevy, & had grete sorow in hur harte, and sho fell to hur *pr*ayers as sho was wunte to do, & besoght God & our dere Ladie to helpe hur. So at þe laste sho traveld; & when þe barn was vnnethis born, sho slew it & ekid syn vppon syn, & keste it in-to a sege. And þan þe fende had despite her-att, and þoght for to gar hur be destroyed, & made hym in habett like a clerk, and come afor þe iugges & þe men of law, and desyrid þa*im* to here hym, & he sulde tell þa*im* a huge m*er*vayle for any man to here, & a passand cruell dede: "ffor such a wom*man*, at ye trow is a passand halie wom*man*, is a passand wikkid wom*man*, & a crewell, & full of syn. For sho conseyvid a childe of hur awn son, & yit also when it was born, sho slew it & keste it into a sege." And þai had grete m*er*vell here-of, & said þai trowid it was not so. And he bad feche hur & examyn hur; "& in þe mene while make a fire, and if sho grawnt or be co*n*victe þ*er*-in, latt kaste hur whik in þe fire & burn hur." And if sho wer nott, he bad þa*im* take and burn hym. And sho was fechid and broght befor þe iuggies & þe men of law; and þan þe iuge sayd vnto hur; "Wom*man*, we hafe her a new *pro*phett in Rome, & he, þuff all vs for-thynk it gretelie, hase accusid þe in grete trispasis. And þerfor þou muste owder knowlege þi trispas, or els þou must excuse þe þeroff." And þan sho askid of þe law a respecte, & had it grawntid. & scho went home & made grete sorow for hur trispas, and went vnto a preste, & *with* hartlie cont*r*icion sho shrafe hur & told hym all how sho had done. And he saw þat scho wepid & made grete sorow, & *com*furthid hur, and enioynyd hur in penans to say bod one pat*er* nost*er*. And he bad hur at sho sulde *pr*ay ha*r*telie vnto our dere Ladie to helpe hur. And so sho did, *with* grete deuocion. And so vppon þ*er* courte-day, sho was sent aft*er* agayn; & sho come [1]

[1] *After* come, n, *erased.*

onone *with* all hur houshold, & hur frendis *with* hur. And sho was sett in myddeste þe courte, at all men might se hur; and þan þe Iustis chargid all to be pease, & said vnto þis clerk at accusid hur; "Loo! her is sho at þou hase accusid. Say now vnto hur & þou hase oght at say." And þis fend beheld þis wom*m*an, & had grete m*er*vayll off hur, what sho sulde be. & þan he said; "This is not þatt synner nor þ*at* man-queller þat I accusid; ffor þis is a holie wom*m*an, and Marie, þe moder of Criste, stondith by hur & kepis hur." And þan all þ*at* evur was aboute had grete m*er*vayle, & lifted vpp þ*er* handis & saynyd þai*m*. And þe fend myght not suffre þis & vanysshid away *with* a grete reke and a stynkkand; and þus þis wom*m*an was delyverd. *et c*[9].

CCCXXI.

Familiaritas mulieris eciam *sanctis* nocet.

We rede in 'Legenda *Sancti* Remigij' how þ*er* was one þat hight Geneland*us*, & he was a wurthi man, & wed Saynt Re[*mi*]gius [1] sister doght*er* vnto his wife. And so be concell of þis gude holie man þai dep*ar*tid [2]; and þis Genelandus was made bisshopp of Lúgdun, and he was a gude clerk & a wurthi p*re*chur. And his wife wold oft sithis com vnto hym becauce of instruccion, & to here hym p*re*che. And so att þe laste, be temptacion sho conseyvid, & was *with* child *with* hym; and when þis child was born, þis bisshopp, þe fadur þ*er*off, garte call it Latro, becauce it was getten be stoltherie. Not-*with*-stondyng, becauce of suspicion, he suffred his wife com to hym agayn as sho did befor; and belife scho was *with* childe agayn. And when þe childe was born, þe fadur garte call it Vulpiculus. So at þe laste hym repentid, and went vnto Remigius, and shrafe hym to hym & knowlegid his syn. And he closid hym vp in a cell vij yere, & in þe mene while he gou*er*ned his bisshopprik. And at þe vij yere end, ane angell aperid vnto þis Genelandus [3], & told hym at his syn was forgyffyn

[1] MS. Saynt Regius.
[2] Lat. MSS. Et se religionis causa mutuo absoluissent.
[3] MS. Gelelandus.

hym, and bad hym go furth, & opynd þe dure and savid þe seale hale at Saynt Remigius sett on itt. And þan þis Genelandus layd hym down in þe dure opon þe erth in liknes of a cros, & said vnto þe aungell; "And my Lord, almighti God Hym selfe, com vnto me I will not away bod if my maist*er* Remigius at sparrid me here com & take me furth." And þan, be com*m*andment of þe angell, þis Remigius come vnto hym & tuke hym oute, & had hym vnto Lugdon & restorid agayn vnto his bisschopprik. And he was a halie man all his life-dayes after; and when he dyed, þis Latro his elder son was made bisshopp aft*er* hym.

Familiaritas[1] ecia*m* mulieris sapientib*us* est p*er*iculosa. Inf*r*a de m*u*liere.

CCCXXII.

Fatuitas. Fatuitate*m* causa humilitatis s*an*c*t*i similant aliqu*an*d*o*.

Heraclides tellis how som tyme þ*er* was in a monast*er*ie of nonnys a maydyn, and for Godd*is* luff sho made hur selfe evyn as a fule, & meke & buxhom to eu*er*-ilk bodis com*m*andment; & sho made hur selfe so vile, & so grete ane vnd*er*lowte, þat ilkone vggid *with* hur, to so mykell þat þai wold not eate *with*[2] hur, bod ilkone strake hur & skornyd hur: & evur sho tuke it in plesans. So sho passid neu*er* þe kichyn, bod bade þ*er*, & wasshid dysshis & skowrid pottys, and did all man*er* of fowle labur. And sho satt neu*er* at meatt, bod held hur selfe content *with* crombys & crustis þat war lefte at þe burd; & þer-*with* sho liffid, and sho war nevur shone nor hose, & sho had nothyng on hur head bod revyn clothis, & raggid. And sho was s*er*uyciable to eu*er*ilk creatur, and wold do no bodye wrong, and what at evur was done vnto hur, þ*er* was none at hard hur gruche þ*er*-*with*. So emang all þies, be þe com*ma*wndment of ane aungell, Saynt Patryk, at was a holie man & liffid in wildrenes, come vnto þis same monast*er*ie, and callid befor hym all þe nonnys & all þe susters of þe place, at he might

[1] MS. Familieritas. [2] MS. *repeats*, *with*.

se þaim, and sho come not: & þan he said; "Ye er not all here." And þai said; "Yis, fadur, we er all here, outtakyn one þat is bod a fule." And he bad þaim call hur; and als sone as he saw hur he knew in his spiritt þat sho was mor halie þan he. And he fell down on his kneis befor hur & said; "Spirituall moder! giff me þi blissyng!" And sho fell down on kneis before hym & said; "Nay, fathur, rathur þou sulde blis me." And with þat þe susters of þe howse had grete wonder, & said vnto hym; "Fathir, suffer not þis eniorie, for sho is bod a fulle." And he said; "Nay, sho is wise, & ye er bod fules; ffor sho is bettyr þan owder ye or I." And þan all þe susters fell on þer kneis befor hur, & askyd hur forgifnes of wrangis & iniuries þat þai[1] had done vnto hir, ffor[2] scho forgiffes þaim ilkone with all hur harte.

Feruor fidei laudabilis est. Infra de Martirio.

CCCXXIII.

Festinacio, licet aliqu*ando* nimia, tame*n* est bona[3].

Jacobus de Vet*ri*aco tellis how som tyme þer was a man þat had a guse, & sho warpyd eu*er*-ilk day ane egg. And on a tyme he vmthoght þat he wold hafe all þies eggis at ons, & he slew his guse & oppend hur, and he fand bod one egg in hur. And so for grete haste þat he had of þat at was for to com, he loste all. *et c*9.

CCCXXIV.

Festinacio nimia ho*min*em retardat.

The same Jacobus tellis how, on a tyme in France, þer was a grete meneya of men rydand in a carte. And agayn evyn þai ou*er*tuke Saynt Martyn rydand vppon ane ass, & þai askyd hym if þai myght com *with* day vnto P*ar*iss. And he said; ya, & þai drafe bod playnlie & softelie. And þai gaff no hede vnto his

[1] MS. þai þa.

[2] The MS. *has a contraction sign above* ffor.

[3] Lat. MSS. Festinacio nimia non est bona.

wurde, & drafe faste, & garte þ*er* carte ryn̄ als faste as þe hors mot preke. So þai*m* happend' breke þ*er* whele; & Saynt Martyn̄ went bod softelie & he come to P*ari*ssh̄ at a gude howr̄, lang befor̄ evyn̄, whar þai lefte behynd' w*ith* þ*er* hastynes.

CCCXXV.

Fides trinitatis confirmatur p*er* mirac*u*lu*m*.

We rede how, on̄ a tyme, in þe Cetie of Nazarenc*is*[1], when̄ þe bisshopp̄ was at mes, he was war of iij clere droppis, all̄ elike mekill̄[2], dropp̄ opon̄ þe altar̄; & þai flewid' to-gedur & turnyd' into a p*re*cious stone. And he garte take þis stone & sett itt in myddeste of a cros of gold' emang many other p*re*cious stonys; and onone as it was sett in, all̄ þe other p*re*cious stonys fell̄ oute. *et* c9.

Fides corroborat*ur* p*er* eukaristia*m* p*ro*tegentem a co*m*bustione. Sup*ra* de Eukaristia.

Fides roboratur p*er* corporale sanguinolentu*m*. Sup*ra* de corporali.

Fides roboratur p*er* crucifixu*m* sang*u*inolentu*m*. Sup*ra* de c*ru*cifixo.

Fides roboratur p*er* eukaristia*m* in carne v*er*sam. S*upra* de Eukaristia.

Fides fracta displicet Deo. Infra Iacobi.

Fides contra natura*m* aliquando subuenit. S*upra* de Ap*os*tolis *et* August*ino*.

Fidelis est canis d*omi*no suo. Sup*ra* de dileccione.

CCCXXVI.

Fidelitatem racione inuidie multi deseru*n*t.

Justinus tellis in 'Gestis Alexandri' how at Alexander had a hy naturall̄ witt aboue all̄ other men̄, vnto so muche þat his

[1] Lat. MSS. in urbe N*asatense*.

[2] Latin MSS. vid*i*t tres guttas clarissimas, equales magnitud*in*is.

knyghtis had such a faith in hym, at als lang as he was present þai trustid þat, & þai had bene vnarmyd, yit þer enmys sulde nott hafe ouer-commen þaim, & at what peple at þai sulde feght *with*, þai trustid to our-com þaim, & what cetie at þai vmsegid, þai trustid to gett & wyn itt. For þer was neuer enmy þat he faght *with* bod he ouer-come hym, nor neuer cetie þat he segid bod he wan it, nor neuer peple nor nacion att he rase agayn bod he had þe ouer-hand of þaim. And neuer-þe-les, at þe laste end, he was ouer-commen, & not in batell be feghtyng *with* his enmys, bod[1] *with* gyle & dessayte of ane of his awn knyghtis þat poysond hym *with* a drynk.

CCCXXVII.

Fidelis seruus corpus suum pro domino suo exponit.

Valerius tellis how som tyme þer was a man þat hight Papulion[2], and be chance be þe peple he was condempnyd vnto dead. And þer was knyghtis sent be þe law to punyssh hym after þe decre. And he had in his howse a servand þat luffid hym hugelie wele, and when he wiste at þies knyghtys war commen to sla his maister, he did on his maister clothyng, & putt on his ryng on hys fynger, & put oute his maister at a postern, & went in-to his maister chawmer hym selfe. And onone þies knyghtis come & fand hym in þe chawmer, and þai went he had bene Papulion hym selfe, & slew hym in-stede of his maister. *et c9.*

Fidelis amicus omnia sua exponit pro Amico. Supra de Amicicia.

CCCXXVIII.

Fideiussor pro alio nullus fieri debet de facili.

We rede in '*Vitis Patrum*' how som tyme þer was ane holie hermet, & on a tyme hym happend to be herberd at a mason

[1] Lat. MSS. *sed* insidiis suorum et fraude civili.
[2] Lat. MSS. Papinion.

howse. And be þ*er* com*m*onyng sam*en* at evyn, þis hermet fande wele þat þis mason despendid his adlyng, one *parte* in suche thyng as hym nedyd, & a noder *parte* in almos-dede, and þe thrid *parte* in h*er*beryng of pure folk. And here-for þis h*er*mett, when he come at home at his cell, made his *pr*ayer vnto God, and besoght Hym at He wold multiplie þis mason gudis, becauce he spendid þai*m* so wele. And þan it was ansswerd hym in a vision, þat it wold not be expedient vnto hym þat he had mor gude þan he had. And þe h*er*mett said yis, & said at he wold becom his borgh. And vppon þat it was grawntid hym, vnto so mekull þat vpon þe morn, as þis mason was brekand ane old wall, he fand a grete som of golde stoppyd in a hole. And he tuke it, & gaff our his crafte, and went to cowrte in-to þe emp*er*our howshold. And belife he was so grete *with* þe Emp*er*our at he was made a baillay; & þan he was a grete oppresser of pure men. So it happend þis h*er*mett in a vision was taken & led vnto þe dome; and þ*er* he saw aungels compleyn of þis mason. And it was ansswerd þai*m* þat his borgh suld ansswer for hym; and þis h*er*mett was passand ferd, and besoght our Ladie, Saynt Marie, to helpe hym. And scho gat grant at þis h*er*met sulde be sent vnto hym to make hym to amend hym. And when he come at hym & told hym here-of, he sett lityll þ*er*-by, & wold not amend hym, nor speke a wurd vnto þis h*er*mett, bod *with* his staff he bett þis h*er*mett all to clowtis. And þis h*er*mett was sorowfull & went home agayn vnto his cell. And on þe night after, he was ravisshid agayn vnto þe dome, and accusid as he was befor, bod our Ladie, Saynt Marie, helpid hym wele. And *with*-in a little while after þis Emp*er*our dyed, & a noder was made in his steade, þat wold hafe tane þis mason & punysshid hym for his mys-gou*er*nans. And he fled, & all his gude was loste, vnto so mekle he was fayn to turn agayn vnto his crafte, & do as he was wunte to do; & þan he felid at he had displesid God, & amendid hym & devydid his adlyng in-to werkis of charitie as he did befor. *et c*[9].

Filij par*um* curant de a*ni*mab*us* parentu*m* post mortem. Infra de morte.

Filij no*n* su*n*t maledicendi a parentib*us*. Inf*ra* de honore.

Filij p*ro*pt*er* deu*m* derelinq[*u*]unt parentes. Infra de visitacione.

CCCXXIX.

Filia diligent*er* debet custodiri.

Seutonius Ph*ilosoph*us tellis how þat Augustus Cesar garte ordand' so for a doght*er* & a sister doght*er* þat he had, þat he mott wunte þai*m* & make þai*m* p*er*fite in wirkyng of wull; and he forbad þai*m* to speke any thyng bod opynlie, and dischargid' þai*m* þe co*m*pany & spekyng w*ith* of any strangiers. So it happend' a wurthi mañ Licrinius, for to com̃ to þe Emp*er*our doght*er* & halsid' hur, & sho wolde speke no wurd' agayñ. So aft*er*ward' it wald' tolde þe Emp*er*our, and he wrote vnto hym̃ & said' at he had done hym̃ a litle sober trispas, for als mikell as he come to haylse his doght*er* cont*r*ary vnto his com*m*andment.

Finem malu*m* qu*and*oq*ue* habent mali. Infra de sa*lut*a*re*.

Fletus malus v*e*l multiplex. Infra de lacrima.

Fornicacio. Fornicaria mulier infamat aliqu*ando* innocentes. Sup*ra* de accusacione. Et infra de infamia.

Fornicacionem com*m*ittu*n*t aliqui incaute se custodientes. Sup*ra* de Confidencia.

Fortitudo semp*er* est laudabil*is* in vtentib*us*[1] ea. Inf*ra* de milite.

Fortitudo animi. Infra de morte.

Forcior aliqu*ando* est vnus q*u*am plures. Sup*ra* de com*m*estione.

[1] Arund. MS. bene ute*n*tibus ea.

CCCXXX.

Fortes nimis sunt canes vt in alio lat*ere*.

Solinus tellis þat þ*er* er bred in Albanye hondis þat & þai be set at any maner of beste, þai will kill it & halde still what at evur *þaim* happynd to mete. So when kyng Alexander went into Ynde, þe kyng of Albany sent hym ij of þies hundes, and þe tane of þai*m* wolde nowder luke on swyne nor on bere, and he wald eate no meat, in his kenell þ*er* he lay. And kyng Alexand*er* garte lowse hym & lete hym go. And þe toder, evur when he was com*m*andid be þai*m* at folowid hym, he wold sla lyons or any other wylde beste. So þai lete hym se ane olyfante, and he chasid so þat he was werie; and at þe laste he pullid hym down & killid hym,

Fortuna est variabilis[1]. Infra de gl*o*riac*io*ne *et* ordinacione.

CCCXXXI.

Francisci. De S*anct*o Francisco.

We rede how som tyme þ*er* was a wom*m*an þat had a grete deuocion vnto Saynt Frawncis; so hur happend to dye, and þe *pre*stis come & sang hur a dirige. So sodanlie sho spak vnto one of þe prestis at stude abowte hur, & said; "Fadur, I wulde be shrevyn; I was dead & com*m*aundid vnto a grevus *pre*son for a syn þat I was neu*er* shrevyn of, þat I sall now confess me off to the. Bod Saynt Frawncis prayed for me, at my saule mott com agayn vnto my bodye & confes þat syn, & so hafe forgyfnes þ*er*of."

[1] So Harl. MS. The Engl. MS. *has*, inenarrabilis.

And þ*er* sho shrafe hur þ*er*off, & tuke hur absolucion̄, & onone aft*er* sho swelt agayn̄.

Fraus. Fraudem debent om*nes* vitare. Infra de negociacione.

Fuga. Fugienda est turba. Infra de turba.

CCCXXXII.

Fur. Furis audacia magna est frequent*er*.

We rede in 'Libro de Dono Timoris' how þat a thefe come p*r*ivalie on̄ a nyght vnto a philosophur bed' þ*er* he lay, & nemelie he drew at þe cou*er*lad' att lay on̄ hym̄, & wolde hafe stollen it away. And he felid' at one pullid' at itt, & put vp his hand' & drew it agayn̄. And wit*h*-in a while after, þis thief drew agayn̄, & he held'; and þus þai did' twice or thrice. And when̄ þai had long done so, þe philosophur spak vnto hym̄ & said'; "þou vnhappie man̄! Take þe cou*er*lad, & go þi wais þ*er*-wit*h*, & latt me lygg in reste."

Fur videtur aliqu*ando* qu*ando* credit no*n* videri. Sup*ra* de deo.

CCCXXXIII.

Fures qu*andoque* associant se in furtis suis.

In a town̄ in Normundie þar standis a kurk wit*h*-oute þe town̄, vppon̄ a hyll; and ij thevis mett þ*er* in ane evynyng, and þai made cou*nan*d' at þe tane of þai*m* þat night sulde go stele a lambe, and þe tother sulde go stele nuttis. And he þat had' furste sped' sulde furste com̄ vnto þe kurk, & þ*er* abide his felow in þe porch. And he þat stale þe nuttis was sped' belife, & come furste, & satt down̄ & abade his felow, & krakkid' nuttis in þe kurk-porche & ete þai*m*. So wit*h*-in nyght, late, þe clerk come to þe kurk to ryng curfur. And onone as he come in þe porche & harde at one was þ*er*, & he trowed it had bene þe Devull; and als faste as he cuthe he ran home vnto þe prestis howse & was passand ferd, & said þe Devull was in þe kurk-porche. So þ*er* was in þe howse a halte man, & he scornyd þe clerk, & said þat he dughte nott. So þ*er* was a noder yong strong felow, & þis halte man said vnto hym, and he wolde bere hym to þe kurk in his nekk, he sulde go luke whether þe Devull war in þe kurk-porche or nay. And he said yis. And þis halte crepyll was sett vpp in hys nek, & he bare hym vnto þe kurk. And þis thief at was in þe kurk-porche saw a man com & a thyng in his nekk, & he trowed it had bene his felow at had broght a lambe. And when he was nerehand at þe porche dure, he cryed vnto hym & sayd; "Est ne crassus? Is it not fatt?" And so þis yong felow at bere þis crippill hard what he said, & ansswerd agayn & said; "Whethur he be fatt or lene I sall lefe it *with* the." And *with* þat he keste hym fro hym, & ran hame als faste as he cuthe. And þis cripyll gadurd his strenth vnto hym, & began at ryn home alsso. And yit he was furste at þe howse þan þe yong man at bar hym. And evur aft*er* he went on his fete þat stude not on þai*m* vij yere before.

Furis societas p*er*ic*u*losa est. Sup*r*a de Angelo *et* h*er*emita.

CCCXXXIV.

Fures possu*n*t dici multi p*r*incipes *et* p*r*elati.

Saynt Austyn tellis how þ*er* was a maist*er* of a ship þat hight Dironides, & he was a grete robber be þe se; so on a tyme hym happend to be taken & broght befor kyng Alexander. And kyng Alexander askid hym whi he vsid suche robburi *with* his shupp; and he answerd agayn & said; "Whi laburs þou to hafe d*omina*cion of all þis werld, and I þat vsis bod a little schup, I am callid a thefe, and þou þat vsis to rob & refe *with* a grete navie of schuppis erte callid ane Emp*er*our? And forsuthe, þou sall v*er*elic know, þat, & rightwusnes be removid away, what er kyngisdoms?

Not els bod grete thyfte; & what er little kyngdoms? Not els bod little thifte. And þus, þou erte a grete thefe, & I am bod a little thefe."

Fures in presenti sepe puniuntur. Supra de agro.

CCCXXXV.

Furtum non potest celari.

We rede in 'Legenda Sancti Patricij' how som tyme þer was a man at stale his neghbur shepe, & ete it; and þis man at aght þis shepe come vnto Saynt Patryk, & told hym how a shepe was stollen from hym: & he chargid oft sithis þat who som-evur had it sulde bryng it agayn, and no man wolde grawnte it. So on a haly day, when all þe peple was in þe kurk, Saynt Patrik spirrid & commandid, in þe vertue of Iesu, at þis shepe sulde blete in his belie þat had etyn itt, at all men might here. And so it did; & þus þe thefe was knowen, & made amendis for his trispas. And all oþer þat hard euer after was ferd to stele.

CCCXXXVI.

Furtum committendo eciam bruta se peccasse cognoscunt.

Seuerius[1] tellis how som tyme þer was ane hermett þat dwelt in wyldernes, and euer-ilk day, at meate tyme, þer come vnto his yate a sho-wulfe; and sho wulde neuer away or he gaff hur somwhatt at eate. So on a day þis hermett was with a noder bruther of his in occupacion, & come not[2] home att meate-tyme of þe day. And þis wulfe come & fand hym not þer, & was war of a litle bread in a wyndow, & sho brak in & tuke it, & eete it & went away. And when þe hermett come home, he fand þe crombis of þe bread at þe wyndow, & he demyd who had takyn it. And þis wulfe knew hur defaute, & wolde not com at þis hermett a sennett afterwerd. And when þis hermet myssid þis wulfe, at vsid to com

[1] *For* Severus. [2] Not, *omitted and added above the line.*

daylie vnto hym, he made his prayer vnto God; & þis wulfe come agayn vppon þe sennet day, bod sho stude of ferrom, & durste not com nere hym. And sho layd hur down & held down hur head, as sho suld aske hym forgyfnes; and he tuke it for a confession, & bad hur com ner hym boldly, & he suld forgiff hur. & sho come to hym & fell down on kneis; & he forgaff hur, and gaff hur als mekyll to brede as he was wunte to giff hur. And fro thens furth evur aft*er*, scho come at tyme of þe day, and did hur offes as sho was wunt.

Furtu*m* restituere[1] ecia*m* bruta a*nim*alia compelluntur p*er* or*acion*em. Inf*ra* de orac*ion*e.

CCCXXXVII.

Furtu*m* ecia*m* nimiu*m*[2] in purgatorio punitur.

Cesarius tellis how som tyme þ*er* was a preste of þe Templer ordur, and when he was a childe hym happend for to fall seke, and he askid for to be enoyntyd, and he was not. So hym[3] happend to dy, & when his saule passid furth of his bodye, he askid helpe, and ane angell come, & said it was euyll done att he dyed w*ith*-oute enoyntment. So þis sawle was p*re*sent before þe iuge, so þat þe child saw hym & was passand angry agayn hym. And þan come þe devull, & accusid þis childe, & said; "Lord! þis childe stale ane halpeny from his bruther-german, & nowd*er* yit hedurtoward did penans þerfor, nor rewardid itt agayn." And þan owr Lord answerd hym agayn, & said; "Wold þou at I dampnyd þis childe for suche a lityll thyng? Bod þou sall vnderstand att my rightwusnes is mengid w*ith* m*er*cie." And þan p*ra*yed[4] for þis childe þe xxiiij seniores; and so þis childe was forgyffen his tryspas. Neu*er*-þe-les, be þe commandment of our Lord, he was casten in-to a byrnand pitt, whar-in he sufferd so mekle payn, þat he cuthe not aft*er*ward tell w*ith* his mouthe. And after þis he was drawen oute of þe pitt, & þan hym thoght þat þe iuge shewid hym frendlie

[1] MS. sustenere. Lat. MSS. *as above.*

[2] Lat. MSS. minimum.

[3] *After* hym, hyn, *erased.*

[4] MS. prayer.

chere; and þan he gaff a sentance þat his saule sulde be restorid agayn vnto þe bodie, and so it was. & when he come vnto hym selfe, he told all att was abowte hym how it had happend hym; and all þat hard hym had grete *mer*vell here-off. And be signes þat þai fand of burnyng opon his bodie, þai knew at all þat he said was trew. *et c*⁹.

Gallus mortuus revixit [1]. Sup*ra* de blasfemia.
Galline intestina in bufonem [2] su*n*t v*er*sa. Inf*ra* de gula.

CCCXXXVIII.

Gaudiu*m* quandoq*ue* nocet corp*or*i.

We rede in þe 'Storie of Ap*ro*cryfatt*is* [3]' of Titus and Vespacyan, how þat when Titus hard tell þat his fadur Vespacian was made Emp*er*our, he was strykyn *with* such a ioy and a comfurth, þat he was shronken all his synowes to-gedur in a lumpe, as it had bene *with* a crampe. And Iosephus hard tell how he was þus fallen seke, & serchid þe cauce of his sekenes, & þe tyme at it tuke hym in. And he conseyvid at he tuke it *with* a h*er*telie ioy and a comfurth þat he tuke when he hard tell of þe sublimacion of his fadur. And þan he vmthoght how þat a sekenes may be curid *with* þe contrarie, & he garte spur if þ*er* war any man þat Titus was wrothe *with*, or grevid agayn, or þat he wold not suffer com in his sight. And belyfe þai told hym of one [4]. And þan he come to Titus & sayd; "And þou desyre to be hale, þou bus p*ar*don & suffer all þai*m* þat com*m*ys in-to þi p*re*sens *with* me." And Titus grawntid at he suld so do. And Iosephus garte sett a burd in þe chawm*er* anence his bed, and he garte Titus be sett att meatt at þe burd-end, in a chayr, & he sett þis servand, at he was so wrothe *with*, on his right hand, & himselfe on his lefte hand. And Titus saw at it was þis man at he was wrothe *with*, & remembred hym how þat he mott say nothyng

[1] MS. reviuixit.

[2] MS. co*m*bustionem. Lat. MSS. in bufone*m*.

[3] Lat. MSS. Historia Apocriphi.

[4] Lat. MSS. *et* erat ibi s*er*uus adeo Tito molestus, ut sine uehem*en*ti turba*ci*one nulla tenus in ip*su*m respic*er*e posset.

vnto hym; & he was so angred & so trubbled in his mynde, vnto so mekull, þat he þat *with* a cald for ioy was shronken to-gedur, þan *with* a hete of angrynes hys synos rached & lowsid. & þus he gatt vp on his fete, and was curid, & tuke hys[1] servand vnto grace, & forgaff hym his truspas; & evur after, fro thens furth, he luffid þis Iosephus specialli befor all oþ*er*.

Gaudiu*m* est aliqu*ando* causa mortis corporalis. Infra de morte et gu*er*acione.

Gaudia celi sup*er*ant om*n*em melodia*m*. Inf*r*a de nouicio.

Gaudent mali de malis. Infra de p*re*dicacione.

CCCXXXIX.

Germani Antissiodorens*is*.

We rede in his Legend how þis Germanus was Duke of Normundye[2]; & aft*er*-ward his wyfe, be þ*er* bother consent, was made a non, and he was made bisshopp of Antissiodorens*is*; & þai delte all þ*er* gudis vnto pure folk. And he punysshid so his bodi xxx^ti^ yere to-gedur, þat he neu*er* eate bread of whete, nor potage, nor salte; nor dranke neu*er* wyne bot twyce in þe yere, att Yole & att Pach. And all oþ*er* tymys he drank watir & wyne to-gedur, and furste he wold eatt ass*is* & fyne barlie bread. And nowder wynter nor somm*er* he ware no clothe bod hare, & aboue it a cote & a cowle; & þase wolde he neu*er* doff vnto þai war clene worn away. And his bed was bod of sek-clothe & of hare, & he had no cod at his hede bod a stone, & he ware bod seldom shone nor gyrdell aboute hym. And so & he do nott m*er*acles it is a grete m*er*vayle.

CCCXL.

Gl*or*iari siue gl*or*ia. Gl*or*iandum no*n* est de delicijs naturalib*us*.

Saynt Austyn tellis how þat Alcibiades[3], þat was Socrates discipyll, was a passand fayr man & a riche, & ane eloquent

[1] MS. hym. [2] *For* Burgundye. [3] MS. Abibiades.

speker; and here-in he had grete pride. And when Socrates purseyvid þis, *with* his disputacions he provid hym bod a wriche & a naturall fule, so þat he garte hym wepe for tene. And þan Tullius said þat þ*er* sulde a myserie and a wrichidnes folow þe ioy att he had, & þat sulde be p*ar*tid in-to ij fortuns. And ane sulde be [1] þat he had riches, favour, and witt at his awn wyll. And a noder fortun sulde folow hym after-ward, and þat sulde be outelawrie, myserie & hatred of þe contre; & at þe laste he sulde hafe a vylans dead.

Gloriandu*m* no*n* est de virtutib*us*. Infra de iactantia.

CCCXLI.

Gloriandu*m* non est de dictis vel factis.

Valerius tellis þat when Sophocles wex ane alde man, he sent a man of his, at he luffid passand wele, vnto a iustyng; and þ*er* he wan þe victorie aboue all oþ*er*. And when he hard tell þ*er*off, he tuke so mekull comfurth & ioy vnto hym, þat evyn sodanlie he fell down & dyed.

Gl*or*ia vana semp*er* est fugienda. Inf*ra* de vanitate. Gl*or*ia vana oritur aliqu*ando* ex bonis op*er*ib*us*. S*upr*a Barnardi.

CCCXLII.

Gl*or*ia mu*n*di paru*m* durat.

Esopus in 'Fabulis' tellis how þ*er* was a hors þat was arayed *with* a brydyll of gold, & a gay saddyll, & he mett ane ass þat was ladyn; & þis ass made hym no reu*er*ens, bod held evyn furth his way. So þis prowde hors was wrothe þ*er*-*with*, & said; "Bod at I will not vex my selfe, els I sulde sla þe *with* my hynder fete, becauce þou wolde not voyde þe way, & giff me rowm to pass by þe." And when þis ass hard hym, sho made mekyll sorow.

[1] MS. *repeats*, & ane sulde be.

So *with*-in a little while after, þis hors, þat was so gaylie cled', was wayke & lene, & had a sare gallid' bakk; & þe ass mett hym vndernetħ a carte, ledand' muke vnto þe felde: & þe ass was fayr & fatt. & þan þe ass said' vnto hym; "Whar is now þi gay aray at þou was so prowde of? Now blissid' be God', þou erte put to þe same occupacion at I vse, & yit my bak is haler þan þyne. & þ*er*for now þi gay gere helpis þe nott." *et c*.

CCCXLIII.

Gracie agende su*n*t deo de om*n*ib*us* que videntur.

Helinandus[1] tellis how som tyme þ*er* was a freer, & he said he saw neu*er* þat þing bod he tuke a comfurtħ *with* þe sight þ*er*off. And a noder askid' hym what comfurtħ he had' when he saw a fowle tade? And' he said'; "yis, als oft sithes as I se a tade, I vmbethynk me, & thankis God' þat gaf me so fayr a form, & so fayr a liknes as I hafe, lyke His awn selfe, whar þat He myght, and He had wald', hafe made me als fowle & als vglie as a tode is."

CCCXLIV.

Gregorij S*an*c*t*i.

We rede how on a tyme, when Saynt Gregur was a chyld', our Lord' apperid' vnto hym, at his mod*er* yate, in liknes of a pure shipman, and askid' hym his almos. & he had' bod' xd' in his purs, & he gaff hym vjd' þ*er*off. And belife after, þe same day, he come agayn, & askid' hym mor; & þan he gaff hym þe toder iiijd'. And agayn evyn he come agayn, & askid' mor; & he had no thyng at giff hym, bod' a sylu*er* dissch þatt his moder had giffen hym potage in, & þat he gaff hym. And he was fayn þ*er*-of, & went his wayes þ*er*with. And efterward', our Lord' lete hym se be reuelacion, þat Hym selfe was þat shipman þat he gaff þat syluer dissħ vnto.

Gregorius antiphona*m* Regina celi p*r*imo cantari audiu*i*t ab a*n*gelis. Inf*r*a de Maria.

[1] MS. Heliandus.

Gregorius Deu*m* hospicio recepit. Inf*ra* de hospitalitate.

Gregorius Traianu*m* ab inferis reuocauit. Infra de or*atione*.

CCCXLV.

Gregorio celebranti angeli respondent.

On a tyme wheñ Saynt Gregur opoñ Pacħ day sang mes in Rome, in S*ancta* Maria Maiori, and sayd', "Pax D*omi*ni," *et* c⁹, Aungels of ouř Lorde answerd' hym̄ and sayd'; "Et cu*m* sp*iritu* tuo." And herefoř þe pope at þat kurk̄ ordand' þe stacioñ vppoñ Pacħ day. And iu witnes here-of, wheñ þe pope synges þ*er* oñ þat day and says, "Pax D*omi*ni," þ*er* answerd' no body hym̄.

CCCXLVI.

Gula aliqu*ando* in pecc*atu*m carnis innocentes inducit.

Petrus Damianus tellis how oñ a tyme as a monke bare fryed' fruturs in-to þe fratur, he was prikkid' wit*h* glotonny, and onone he wit*h*drew one of þai*m*, & keste it in his mouthe, & ete it p*ri*valie at none of his neghburs saw. And onone aft*er* he was strekyñ wit*h* a luste of his flesscħ, at he laburd' hym̄ selfe in sucħ form̄ as he did' neu*er* befoř, vnto so muche, at wit*h* his awñ hand fretyng he had a pollucioñ of his sede. And so-aft*er* þe morsełł at he stale, onone þe fende entird' in-to hym̄.

Gula*m* refrenare expedit. Sup*ra* de Ep*iscop*o et Abb*ate*.

Gulosi cibu*m* sumu*n*t sine ben*e*diccione *et* puniu*n*tur. S*upr*a de ben*e*diccione.

CCCXLVII.

Gulosi in cibarijs vetitis[1] contra deu*m* vtuntur.

Cesarius tellis how þ*er* was som tyme a wurthie man þat hight Otto de Normu[*n*]borg*is*[2], þ*at* made grevus accions ayeyns his neghburs; and sodanlie he was streken w*ith* a grete sekenes, and he had a passand payn þ*er*-w*ith*, ffor all lentren tyme he had such ane appetite to ete flessh, at he wold not alonelie hold hym contente in etyng þ*er*of hym selfe, bod also he compellid all at was aboute hym to do þe same. And when he had done so all þe lentren, and Gude Fryday come, his meneya spakk vnto hym & sayd; "Sur, þis day is Gude Friday, & þe day of þe passion of our Lord, and þis day chr*isten* men liffis in abstinence; & þ*er*for it is not lefull to eat flessh as þis day." And he answerd agayn & sayd; "This day I sall ete fflessh as I hafe done hedirtoward." And so he did. And on þe Pach day it happend m*er*valuslie w*ith* hym, for when other trew crysten peple ete flessh, evyn be þe dome of almighti God he tuke such ane vgsomnes w*ith* flessh, þat he mot not eate it, bod ete fyssh. & so he did eu*er* whils he liffid after.

CCCXLVIII.

Gule *peccatum* q*uam* detestabile sit visibilit*er* deus ostendit.

Cesarius tellis how þ*er* was som tyme monkes þ*at* war prestis, and opon þe fastynggang evyn þai satt etand & drynkand in a prest howse vnto mydnyght; and at mydnight þai satt still & ete on as þai had nevur etyn a morsell. And so when cokk*is* krew & þai war bown at ryse, þe gudeman of þe howse sayd; "Yit we will not parte or we ete somwhatt." & he bad his servand feche þai*m* a[3] hen, "þe beste at þou fyndis sittand next þe kokk, & sla hur & roste hur." And he went & fechid hur, & slew hur & skaldid hur & oppend hur. And when he putt in his hand

[1] MS. vetidis.
[2] Harl. MS. Normanburgis.
[3] *After* a, rostid, *erased.*

att draw hur, he went he had drawen furth all hur guttis, & he drew oute a gre[*te*] whik tade. And *with* þat he gaff a grete cry; and þai come all & luked whatt hym ayled. And he lete þai*m* se; and when þai saw att þe hen-bowels was turnyd in-to a whik tade, þai vnder-stude at þai had s*er*vid þe Devull & displesid God; & þai were all confusid & went þ*er* ways. *et c*⁹.

CCCXLIX.

Gula impedit ho*min*em ne penit*ent*iam sibi iniu*n*ctam p*ro*ficiat.

Cesarius tellis how þ*er* was on a tyme, in þe bisshoppryk of Colayn, a c*er*tan meneya of knyghtis þat was att grete were *with* a grete lord. & þai gaderd þai*m* same*n* in-to a strang place & h*ar*nessid þai*m*, & tuke þe keyis & gaff þai*m* vnto ane of þ*er* servand*is*, att þai went had bene a trew man. And þis servand went & agreid *with* his maist*er*s enmys, & made þai[*m*] com at mydday, when þe knyghtis was on slepe; and he oppynd þe yatis & lete þai*m* com in, and gaff þai*m* his maist*er*s swerdis[1]. And þai come on þai*m* & slew þai*m*. So afterward þis wrichid traytur was co*m*puncte, & forthoght his dede; & he wente vnto þe pope & shrafe hym, and tuke his penance. And ofte sithes he brakk his penance, and eu*er* he went vnto þe popis penytaw*n*ser agayn, & tolde hym. So on a tyme þe penitawncer wax wery on hym, and he askid hym if þ*er* war any thyng þat hym selfe wold grawnt to doo for penance. And he said, yis, he mott neu*er* ete garlykk. And his confessur bad hym go home, & enionyd hym for his penans þat he sulde neu*er* whils he liffid eatt garlykk; & he grawntid þ*er*to and went home. So on a tyme afterward, hym happend com in-to a garth þ*er* garlykk grew, & he began to hafe a liste to eatt þ*er*off, and he durste not negh itt. So on a noder tyme he come vnto þe same garth, & he had such a luste vnto þis garlykk, þat he brakk his penance & tuke þ*er*off, & ete it raw, þat befor he myght nowder ete raw nor soden. And belife

[1] MS. swerders.

after hym for[1]-thoght itt, & went vnto þe penytawnser & told hym; & he *with* grete indignacion putt hym from hym, & wold enioyn hym no mor penans, bod reprovid hym.

CCCL.

Gula religiosos aliqu*ando* decipit.

Cesarius tellis how som tyme þ*er* was a monk of Ceustus ordur, and hym happend be made a bisshopp, and afterward a cardinall. So on a tyme hym happend to ride, & emang all þe felaship þat was *with* hym he spak vnto a monk þat was bod lightlie letterd, & said; "Tell vs now som gude wurd or som gude tale as we ride." And he excusid hym faste, & said he cuthe nott; & be no mene cuthe he gytt excusid. So at þe laste he began att tell, & said vnto þis cardynall; "When we shall be dead & broght into paradice, þan sall Saynt Benett com & take vs in, þat er cullid *with* grete ioy & myrth. And þan he sall speke vnto þe, þat is a bisshop & a cardynall, & say, 'Whatt erte þou?' And þou sall answer agayn & say, 'ffathur, I am a monke of Ceustus ordur.' And he [sall say][2], 'Nay, þat erte þou nott; ffor a monke is nott so gaylie arayed as þou erte.' And þan þou sall alege many thyng*is* for þe. And þan sall Saynt Benett giff a sentance, & bid þe porters oppyn þi bodye & luke what at þai fynd þ*er*-in; 'and if ye fynd þar cale & peas & benys, & no noder meatt, latt hym com in *with* þe monkis: & if ye fynde þ*er*in grete ffissh, or delicatt meatis, lat hym stand þ*er*oute.' What may þou þan say, þat now faris so wele, and we far so ill?" So þis Cardinall smylid, & com*m*endid hym for his gude tale.

CCCLI.

Gulosi in morte a demone degluciuntur.

Saynt Gregor tellis of a monk þat hight Theodorus, þat eu*er* fenyd hym as he had liffid in grete abstinens, & in p*ri*uatie be hym selfe, he wold evur eate when hym liste. So hym happend to fall

[1] for, *omitted and added above the line.* [2] MS. said.

seke, & was bowñ at dye. And sodanlie he begañ to cry, & sayd þat þe devuł in liknes of a dragoñ swalod hym̃ hand & fute, & put his hede in his mouthe, and sweluđ his sawle. And evyñ in þis saying he deyid.

Habitus religionis aliqu*ando* a deo inuenitur. S*upra* Dom*ini*ci.

Habitus monachalis apostate cont*r*ito morienti *eciam* post mortem a deo redditur. Sup*ra* de apostatis *et* inf*ra* de volu*n*tate.

CCCLII.

Hereticus recipiscens a co*m*bustione lib*er*atur.

Cesarius tellis þat in þe cetie of Attrabicens oñ a tyme þ*er* was takyñ many h*er*etik*is*; and for drede of dead þai forsuke þ*er* fals title. And þai wiłł prufe þai*m* wi*th* a hate burnyng yrñ, & þai þat war fou*n* giltie war burnyd. And emangi*s* þai*m* þ*er* was a wurthi clerk, and þe bisshopp entretid hym̃ to lefe his h*er*esie, and do penans þ*er*for. And he ansswerd agayñ & sayd, he knew wele he had errid, bod it was to late to do penaunce. And þe bisshop ansswerd hym̃ agayñ & said, þat v*er*ray penans was neu*er* done ou*er* late. So þai callid a preste, & he confessid hym̃ of ałł hys synys; & þe hate yrñ was in his hand, and be þe v*er*tue of confessioñ, ałł þe hete of þe yrñ vanysshid away, & þ*er* it had burnyd hym̃, sodanlie it helid agayñ. And þañ þai broght hym̃ befor þe iuge, & tolde hym̃ þe matir, & lete hym̃ se how his hand was byrnyd & sodanlie in his confessioñ helid agayñ. And þus he was savid, and ałł þe toder war dampned.

CCCLIII.

Hereticus p*er* contricionem a pena lib*er*atur, et recidiuus ecia*m* in pena*m* relabitur.

Cesarius tellis þat in þe cetie of Argentyne þ*er* was ane h*er*etike, at was purseyvud be burnyng wi*th* a hate yrñ; bod he renayid

& shrafe hym̄, & tuke his penance. And when̄ he had done, his wyfe chiddid hym̄ & said; "O þou vnhappye man̄! Whatt hase þou done? For þou sulde titter hafe putt þi bodie in a hondreth fyris, þan̄ for to recede away fro so provid a faithe." And so þe fals cownceƚƚ of his wife, he turnyd agayn̄ vnto his fals error þat he was in befor. And onone he was taken̄, & þe hate yrn̄ layd in his hand, and it burnyd hym̄, & his wife was burnyd also hir hand*is*, evyn̄ vnto þe hard bonys. And þan̄ þai war lattyn̄ go, & þar handis war so sore at þai might not forbere crying; & þai durst not cry in þe cetie for purseyvyng, & þai went vnto þe wuddis. & þer þai war so turment *with* þer burnyng, at þai cryed and yowlid as þai had bene wulvis, vnto so mekuƚƚ, at þai of þe cetie fand þai*m* & broght þai*m* home, & keste þai*m* bothe in a grete fyre. And onone þai war burnyd vpp̄ vnto verray assh.

Hereticus p*re*te*r*mittens forma*m* no*n* baptizat. Sup*r*a de baptismo.
Herodis Agrippe. Supra de Augurrio.
Herodis nequicia. Infra de nequicia.

CCCLIV.

Hillarij. De vita eius.

We rede in his Legend, how þat a pope þat hight Leo was dampnid of h*e*resye, and he gadurd sam*en* to a cownceƚƚ aƚƚ þe bisshopp[*is*]. And þis Hillarius come to þis cownceƚƚ vncallid; and þe pope hard teƚƚ att he come, & warnyd at no man̄ sulde rise nor giff hym̄ rowme. And when̄ he come in, þe pope said vnto hym̄; "þou erte Hillarie & a Frawnche man̄!" And he answerd agayn̄ & said; "I am̄ no Franche man̄, bod I am̄ bisshop̄ of France." And þe pope answerd agayn̄ & said; "And I am̄ Leo, þe pope, and a iustis." And Hillarius answerd hym̄ agayn̄ & sayd; "Thuff aƚƚ þou be Leo, yitt þou erte noght of þe trybe of Iuda; & þuff aƚƚ þou be a iustis, yitt þou sittis noȝt in þe seate of magestie." Than̄ þe pope wex wrothe, & said; "Bide a while vnto I com̄ agayn̄, and I saƚƚ giff þe att þou adlis." And *with* þat he rase & went his ways. And Hillarius sayde; "And þou com̄ not agayn̄, who shaƚƚ answer for the?" And he answerd' agayn̄ & sayd'; "Dowte not I saƚƚ com̄ agayn̄ onone, and meke aƚƚ þi pride." And he went vnto a seage, & sett hym̄ down̄ þer-on̄ to ease hym̄. And þer he feƚƚ in-to suche a flux, þat aƚƚ his bowels ran̄ oute att his hynderhend'. And þer he deyed' in grete myserie. And in þe mean̄ while þis Hillarius saw att no man̄ rase vnto hym̄, and mekelie he sett hym̄ down̄ opon̄ þe erthe & sayde; "*Domini* est terra," *et c*[9]. And onone, þurgh þe ordinance of allmighti Godd', þe erthe att he satt oppon̄ rase vpp̄ als hy as þe toder bisshoppis satt att was aboute hym̄. And þan̄ come tythand*is* at þe pope was myserablie dead'. And þan̄ þis Hillarie rase, & confermyd' aƚƚ þies bisshoppis in þe trew fayth. & þan̄ he wente home agayn̄ in-to his awn̄ bisshoprykk.

CCCLV.

Hirundo singulis annis eadem loca repetit.

Cesarius tellis how[1] som̄ tyme þer was a husband'-man̄, þat had bygand' in his howse eu*er*-ilk yere many swalows. So at tyme of þe yere when̄ þai wer bown̄ att goo, he tuke ane of þe old' swalows, & he wrate a byƚƚ *with* þir wurdis þer-in; "O Irundo[2]! vbi habitas in yeme?" & he band' it vnto þe fute þer-of, & lete hur goo; for he knew be exp*er*iens þat sho wold' com̄ agayn̄ þe nexte yere. And so sho flow hur wais *with* other in-to þe lande of Asie; & þer sho biggid' in a howse aƚƚ wynter. And so þis gude man̄ of þe howse on̄ a tyme beheld' hur. And he tuke þis burd', & lowsid' þe biƚƚ, & lukid' whatt was þer-in; & he tuke it away, & wrate a noder of þies wurdis; "In Asia, in domo Petri." & he knytt it vnto hur fute, and lete hur go. And sho come agayn̄ att somm*er* vnto þis husband' howse, whar sho had bred befor; & he tuke hur & lowsid' þis biƚƚ, & redd it. & he told' þe storie þer-of vnto many men̄, evyn̄ as it had bene a m*er*acle.

[1] MS. hom̄.

[2] MS. Irunde.

CCCLVI.

Histrionib*us* nichil est dandu*m*.

We rede in 'Gestis Franco*rum*' how Philypp, at som tyme was kyng of France, on a tyme when he saw mynstrallis & iogullurs hafe gay clothyng & grete giftis giffen þai*m* oute of courte; and he p*ro*mysid *with* all his harte, þat als lang as he liffid, þ*er* sulde no mynstrall were no clothe at langed vnto his bakk. For, he said, hym had levur clethe Criste þ*er*-*with*, or pure men, þan for to giff þai*m* to mynstrallis. "For," he said, "it was no nod*er* to giff to mynstrals bod for to offyr to fendis."

CCCLVII.

Histriones aliquando maliciose se vindicant.

Iacobus de Vet*ri*aco tellis how som tyme þ*er* was ane abbott of Ceustus ordur; and when he was a monke, he was a passand hard man, & a sparand. So hym happynd be made hosteler, to kepe gestis in þ*er* ostrie, afor he was made abbott. So on a tyme þ*er* come vnto þis abbay on a day a mynstrall, & was sett in þe ostrie att dyner. And þis monke servid hym of passand gray bread, & thyn[1] potage, & a little salte; & he had no drynk bod watir. & at evyn he was layd in a uyll bedd, & a hard. And opon þe morn þis mynstrall was ill plesid, & vmthoght hym how þatt he mott venge hym on þis monke at had servid hym so evull. So as he went furth of his chamber þ*er* he lay, hym happend to mete *with* þe abbot, and þis mynstrall come vnto hym & haylsid hym, and said; "My lord, I thanke you & your wurthie covent of grete cher at I hafe had here, & of grete coste þat I hafe taken of you; ffor yone gude lib*er*all monke, your hostley, servid me yistrevyn at my supper wurthelie, *with* many dyvers costious mece of ffissh, & I drank passand gude wyne. And now, when at I went, he gaff me a payr of new butis, & a gude payr of new knyvis, and a poynt to hym þai*m* *with*."

[1] MS. thyng.

And when þe abbott had hard þis, onone he went vnto þe closter, & callid þis monke befor all[1] his covent, & betid hym grevuslie here-for, & putt hym furth of his offes for þis mynstrall saying, þus all he war not wurthi.

CCCLVIII.

Histriones non sunt accusandi.

Valerius tellis how on a tyme þe cetie of Massalience[2] wold suffer no mynstrall com *with*-in it, & if any happend at com, þai wold reprufe hym. So þ*er* was a philosophur, & he reprovid þai*m* of þe cetie þ*er*-of, & tolde þai*m* þat þai sulde *with*-in a while hafe war mynstralls þan þai war. And so it happend *with*-in a while aft*er*, þe cetie was evyn full of comm*on* wom*men*; and þan þai purseyvid at it was trew at he told þai*m*.

Homagiu*m* *factu*m est Diabolo. S*upr*a de ambicione, iij. *et* de amore. iij.

Honestas est morib*us* servanda. S*upr*a de amicicia. iiij^a. *et* c^9.

CCCLIX.

Honore*m* parentib*us* no*n* exhibentes puniuntur.

Cesarius tellis how som tyme þ*er* was a yong man þat hight Henrye, & his moder was a wedow & a riche wom*mon*. So þis yong man on a tyme keste hym to begile his moder, & sayd vnto hur; "Gyff me all þi gudis, at þurgh name of þai*m* I may richelie be marid & gett a gude wyfe; and þ*ou* sall hafe þai*m* agayn when I am marid. And in þe mene while I sall honestelie p*ro*vide for þe." And sho grantid to hym, & gaff hym it. So belyfe aft*er* he was wedd, and *with*-in a while aft*er* he was wed, hys wyfe garte hym putt hur oute; & so sho had nothyng bod att sho beggid hur meatt, & evur when sho come & co*m*pleynyd hur vnto hym, he

[1] MS. *repeats*, all.

[2] Lat. MSS. Civitas Massiliensis.

sparrid his eris & wold not here hur. So on a day he & his wife satt at meat to-gedur and his mod*er* come vnto his dure & knokkid, & askid meatt for Goddis sake. And he said; "Lo! yonder is þe devull at cryes at þe dure!" And his moder come in & besoght hym to hafe m*er*cie of hur & giff hur som meatt; & he flate w*ith* hur as he had bene wude. So at þe laste he bad a childe go feche þe reu*er*sion of a pulett þat was sett in a kiste, & giff hir it. & þe childe went & lifte vp þe kiste lid, & whar þe pullett was on þe platir he fand nothyng bod a wrethyn serpent; & he was ferd, & told his maist*er* what he saw. And þan he sente a mayden & bad hur go feche it, & sho come agayn & was ill flayed, & told hym at sho had sene þe same. And he rase vp in a wreth hym selfe, & sayd; "& þe devull lig on þe dubbler, I sall go feche hym." & he liftid vp þe kiste lid & stowpyd vp to take þe platir. & þe serpent clappid aboute his throte, & dubbled evyn aboute his nekk; & evur as he eatt, sho ete; and ay þe more at þai laburd to gett hur lowse, þe faster clave sho, vnto so mekull at his vesage was so bolnyd at his ene fell oute on his chek*is*. & so he liffid xiij yere & more, blynd, & alway þis s*er*pent aboute his nekk. And he was carid vnto dyvers placis of pylgramege, & cuthe gett no bute. And his moder at þe laste hadd co*m*paciens of his payn & forgaff hym, & þan he dyed.

Honoratur qui facit quod debet *sine* accepc*io*ne p*er*sone. Sup*ra* Amb*r*osij. ij°.

CCCLX.

Honorandi su*n*t parentes in secreto, sed non in pub*li*co.

Helinandus[1] tellis of ane þat hight Taurus, þat was rewler of þe cetie of Athenys. So on a tyme þe p*r*ince of Crete come vnto Athenys, & broght w*ith* hym his son & his ayre. And þis Taurus desyrid þai*m* to com dyne w*ith* hym, & so þai did. & he bad þe

[1] MS. Heliandus.

fadur sytt hym down, and þe fadur bad his son sit down furste, for cauce at he had a gou*er*nans & a maist*er*shup of þe pepull at Rome. And þan Taurus sayed vnto þe prince; "Sit þou furste down befor þi son vnto we examyn þe cauce, whethir is wurthi to sit aboue att the table, þe fathur or þe son." And when he was sett, þai sett a chayr þan for his son. And þan Taurus sayd to þai*m* at satt abowte; "In oppen placis, & þ*er* þe son hathe a reule, or a maist*er*shupp, or a gou*er*nans abown þe fadur, þ*er* it is semand þat þe fathur suffer þe son to hafe a prioritie. Bod att home, or in oþ*er* priva placis, or in gude felowshupp whar þai walk sam*en*, or etis sam*en* or sittis sam*en*, þ*er* suld all publicall honor and wurshup sese betwix þe fadur & þe son, & þ*er* suld naturall curtasy & honor be kepid: þat is to say, þar þe son suld wurshup þe fadur or þe mother, & lett for no thyng."

Honorande sunt reliquie *sanctorum*. Infra de reliquijs.

Honore exhibito cor h*omin*is eleuatur *et* sup*er*bit. Sup*r*a de augurrio.

Honorandi su*n*t *sancti* in cantu *secundum* me*r*ita sua. Infra Thome martiris.

CCCLXI.

[1] Honorant se mutuo [2] *sancti*.

We rede in þe 'Life of þe H*er*mett Saynt Paule' how on a tyme Saynt Anton come to luke how he did, & he resayvid hym wurshupfullie. So at tyme of day when þai suld go to meatt, a raven come & broght hym ij smale lavis. And Saynt Anton had m*er*vell here-of; and þan Saynt Paule sayd vnto hym; "Almighti God eu*er*-ilk day hase s*er*vid me þus, and þis day He dubbles itt for þi sake." And þan betwix þai*m* þ*er* was a meke

[1] This heading has been transposed from Tale CCCLXII, and the heading of Tale CCCLXI to CCCLXII; Saint Martin is the 'hospes' of Antisiodorens in the Lat. MSS., which, however, follow the same order of headings as that of the Eng. MS.

[2] MS. nutuo.

stryfe whethur of þa*im* suld blis þe brede; and Paule bad his oste do it, & he bad hym do itt. So at þe laste þai put bothe þ*er* handis þ*er*to & did it to-gedur; and þan þai partid þe brede evyn betwix þa*im*.

CCCLXII.

Honorandi su*n*t hospites. *et c*.

We rede how on a tyme when þe Normond*is* destroyid France, the bodie of Saynt M*ar*tyn was translatt vnto þe cetie of Antysiodorence; and þer, for grete m*er*vals & m*er*acles at it did, þ*er* was grete offrand made therto. So þ*er* fell a grete debate be-twix þe men off Turans[1] & of Antisiodorens, for skiftyyng of þis money betwix þa*im*. So þai made a cou*n*and, at þai suld take a lepre man & lay hym all nyght betwix þe bonys of Saynt Martyn & Saynt German, at luke be v*er*tue of wheþ*er* of þa*im* he was curyd; & þai to hafe þe money; and so þai did. & on þe morn, when þai come & lukid hym, þat side at was next Saynt Martyn was curid & hale, & þe tother syde was lepre; & þan þai turnyd & layd þe sare syde to Saynt M*ar*tynward, & þe hale syde vnto Saynt German ward. And on þe toþ*er* morn he was hale ou*er* all his bodie. And þus þe men of Turence had þe offrand.

Honorare se mutuo debe*n*t om*n*es eiusdem status. Infra de Reu*er*encia.

CCCLXIII.

Honorare. Horas canonicas necligent*er* dicentes puniu*n*tur.

Cesarius tellis how þat in ane abbay of Saynt Saluaturs, of Ceustus ordur, þ*er* dyed a damysell of þe age of x yere or mor. So opon a day when all þe covent of þe nonnys stude in þe where at

[1] St. Martin's body had been translated from Tours; St. German's remains were at Antisiodorens = Auxerre.

þ*er* serves, sho come vp̄ in-to þe where & lowtid̄ up̄ vnto þe altar; & þan̄ sho went vnto þe place þ*er* sho was wunte to sytt in, & bade þ*er* still̄ to sho had said̄ evynsang & com*m*endacion̄ of our̄ Ladie. And att þe colett sho bowed down̄ vnto þe erthe, & when̄ it was done sho went hur wayis. So þ*er* was a noder damysell̄ of þe same age, þat hight M*a*rgrett, þat satt next hur; & sho saw hur & teld̄ þ*er* abbatis all̄ at sho had sene, & [*t*]he Abbatis bad hur þat, & scho come agayn̄ on̄ þe nexte day, sho suld̄ aske hur how it stude w*ith* hur. And on̄ þe morn̄, at þe same howr̄, sho come agayn̄, and þan̄ þis M*a*rgrett sayd̄ vnto hur; "Gude suster Geretrude, fro whens come þou, & what duse þou now here at vs when̄ þou erte deade?" And sho answerd̄ agayn̄ & sayd̄; "Sust*er*, I come hedur to make satisfaccion̄, for I rownyd̄ oft sithis w*ith* þe in þe where in s*er*ves-tyme, & said̄ not oute þe wurdis full̄. And þ*er*for̄, in the same place þ*er* I truspasid̄, am̄ I com*m*anddid̄ to come & make a sethe. And þ*er*-for̄ be þou war of rownyng in þe where, at þou suffer not þe same payn̄ when̄ þou erte deade." And opon̄ þe iiij day sho said̄; "Suster, now I trow þat I hafe fulfillid̄ my penance, & fro hyne furthe þou sall̄ se me no mor̄." And þus sho was had vnto hevyn̄ w*ith* aungell̄-sang. *et c*⁹.

Hore non su*n*t p*re*te*r*mittende. Sup*ra* Augustini. ij.

CCCLXIV.

Horas be*a*te Marie Virginis deuote dicentib*us* apparebit in hora mortis. *et c*⁹.

Cesarius tellis how þat in Spayn̄, in ane abbay of þe ordur of Ceustus, was þ*er* a yong monk þat was passand̄ devowte in saying of our̄ Ladie s*er*ves & hur howres, vnto so mekull̄ þat not alonelie att eu*er*-ilk vers, bod at eu*er*-ilk wurd̄ at he said̄, he had mynde of hur; and þis he vsid̄ many day w*ith* grete labur. And when̄ he had̄ vsid̄ þis xvj yere, hym̄ happend̄ fall̄ seke and drew to deadward̄. And a bruther of his askid̄ hym̄ how he did̄, and he said', wele, and' told' hym̄ þat our Lady Saynt Marie had visett hym̄ & tolde hym̄ þat he sulde dye opon̄ þe vij day after þatt, and go vnto hevyn̄. And he told' hym̄ þat our Lady sayd' vnto hym̄, þat for gude *ser*ves & trew at he had done hur, sho sulde do vnto hym̄ þat sho did neu*er* vnto no noder. And *with* þat sho tuke hym̄ abowte þe nekk and kissid' hym̄. And on̄ þe vij day, as he told' þ*aim*, he deyid', & passid' vnto God' *with* a grete sang of angels. *et* c⁹.

CCCLXV.

Hospitalitas libent*er* exhib*er*i debet, quia qu*andoque* Chr*istus* in ea recipitur.

Saynt Gregur tellis how som̄ tyme þ*er* was a husband'-man̄ whilk þ*at* vsid', & all his howse-meneya, gretelie to h*er*bar pure folk; and he vsid' ilk day to hafe att his burde owder pylgrams or pure men̄. So on̄ a day þ*er* was a pylgram̄ emang þe pure men̄, and so as he was wunt to do he servid' þ*aim* of watir; & when̄ he suld' take þe lavur & powr̄ watir on̄ þis pylgram̄ handis, sodanlie he was away. And he lukid' abowte for hym̄, & cuthe not fynd' hym̄; and he had grete m*er*vell here-off. And þe same night when̄ he was in his bed', almighti God' apperid' vnto hym̄ & said'; "Other dayes þou hase reseyvid' me in my membrys, and yisterday þou receyvid' [*me*] to þine hoste in myne awn̄ p*er*son̄." *et* c⁹.

CCCLXVI.

Hospitalitatis gr*a*tia soluend*um* est int*er*dum ieiuniu*m*.

Cassianus tellis how on̄ a tyme when̄ he & other war sam*en* in þe land' of Egipte, þai fastid' not on̄ þe Fryday. And so þ*er* was c*er*tayn̄ p*er*sons þat askid' hym̄, whi he and' his felowshipp brak þ*er* faste so as þai did'. And' he answerd' agayn̄ & said'; "I faste always, for I hafe not halfe meate enogh; & þ*er*for, be way of charite, & for to gar my felows eate at þai be strong to do þ*er* pylg*ra*mege, I breke my faste to make þai*m* at eate when þai wold nott."

CCCLXVII.

Hospitalitas subtracta ecia*m* bona temporalia aliqu*ando* subtrahit.

Cesarius tellis how som tyme ther was ane Abbott of þe Blak Ordur, þat was passand m*er*cefull in hospitalitie, & anence pure men. And he helde servand*is* evyn therefor, & ay þe more att he gaff in hospitalitie or to pure men, ay þe mor God blissid his howse, and multiplied þe gudis þ*er*of. So hym happend to dye. And after his dead, his successur was covatus, & he putt oute þies offisurs at his p*re*decessur had ordand to do wark*is* of m*er*cy. And þe charitie at was giffen vnto pure men in þe toder abbott dayes, he wit*h*drew itt, and herefor almighti God wit*h*-drew His hand; & he put in offisurs at war hard & strayte, & wald vse none hospitalitie, for he sayd it was ane vndiscrete defawte. And wit*h*-in a while his cornys faylid, so þat he & his brethir had skantlie at þai myght eate. So vppon a day a man happend att com & askid hospitalitie, and þe porter tuke hym in p*ri*valie, & wit*h* grete ferdnes, of suche littill meat as he had wit*h*-in hym, he servid hym & said vnto hym; "Now it is so þat I may serve þe of na bettyr meatt, þuff all I hafe som tyme sene in þis place þat, & a greate bisshopp had comm*en* hedur, he sulde hafe bene reseyvid wit*h* greate habundans & plenteth." And þis pure[1] man answerd hym agayn & sayd; "Two brether er putt oute of þis place, and þe tone was callid Dare, and þe toder Dabitur; and vnto þies two com agayn sall neu*er* plentie nor welthe be in þis monasterie." And wit*h* þatt, sodanly he vanysshed oute of his sight. And þis porter went vnto þe abbott & þe covent, and told þai*m*. And þai tuke þai*m* to cowncell att þai wald resume hospitalite, & giff almos agayn as þai war wunte. And so þai

[1] *After* pure, þ, *erased.*

did; and onone almighti God blissid þaim, & þai had als gude plentie as evur þai had afor of corn & all oþer gudes.

Hospites su*n*t honorandi. Sup*r*a de honore. ij & iij.

CCCLXVIII.

Hospitalitas ecia*m* bona temporalia conservat.

Sigilbertus tellis how a town þat hight Anthiochia was sub-u*er*tyd be þe sande of God, and be þis man*er* of wyse. Ther was a cetysyne þ*er*of þat was so giffen vnto hospitalite and almos-dede, to so mekull þat he wolde neu*er* day eate wit*h*-oute a pure man or a geste. So on a day hym happend go þurgh þe cetie to it was nyght, to seke owder a pure man or a geste to eate wit*h* hym, and he cuthe fynd none. So att þe laste he fand a fayr olde man standyng, & two felos wit*h* hym, in þe myddeste of þe cetie. And he p*ra*yed þai*m* com & be his hostis & eate wit*h* hym; and[1] he answerd hym in þis man*er* of wyse & said; "O, þou man of God! þou may not wit*h* our Symond safe þis cetie at it be not subu*er*tid." And wit*h* þat he keste þe sudurye at he held in his hand opon þe tone halfe of þe cetie, & onone þ*at* halfe & all þe howsis þ*er*of & þai þat dwelte in þai*m* was destroyed. & he tuke agayn his sudarie and wolde hafe casten it on þe toder halfe, and vnnethis his felows myght restren hym to spare it; and wit*h* þat he vanysshid away. And þis was done, & þan þe man was passand ferd & went home vnto his howse, & fand safe & thankid God þ*er*-of. *et c*.

Hospitalitate aliqu*ando* Deus recipitur. Inf*r*a Iuliani.

CCCLXIX.

Hospitalitatis gr*ati*a ecia*m* pl*ur*ies in die concedendum [*est*].

Cassianus tellis in þis man*er* of wise & says; "Som tyme þ*er* was a halie man þ*at* tuke me to hoste & refresshid me, & spirrid

[1] Harl. MS. Hoc responsu*m* accepit ab eo; "Non pot*era*s, o homo Dei, cum vo*s*tro Simeone hanc urbem saluare ne subuerteretur?"

me & exhortid me what I wold eate. And I answerd agayn & sayd I myght not eatt. And þan he answerd & sayd; 'þis day I hafe sett þe burd to dyvers brether vij sythes, & desyrid þaim att ete[1], and yit I am hongrie. And þou, at yit ete no þing, says now at þou may nott eate.' And on þis[2] maner þai war wunt in commyng of þer brether for to solve þer faste, and in refeccion of þaim þai helde it a charitiable contynans." *et c*9.

CCCLXX.

Hospitalitas regnum temporale confert.

We rede in þe 'Legend of Saynt German of Antissiodorens,' how on a tyme when Saynt German prechid in Britannye, and þe kyng denyed hym a benyfice, þat was to say, meat & drynk & herber. So þe kyngis nowte-hard come home with his catell fro þer pastur, & tuke provand in þe kyngis pales to his catell, & had it home vnto his tofall at he dwelte in. And he was war of Saynt German & his felos sare laburyng, & war passand calde & hongrie; and he reseyvid þaim buxsomly into his place. And he had no calfe bod one, & þat he slew vnto þer supper. And when þai had suppid, þis holie man gadderd samen þe bonys of þis calfe in þe skyn þer-of, and onone, at his commandment, þis calfe rase agayn whik. And on þe day next after, he went vnto þe kyng, and askid hym whi he denyed meat & hospitalitie vnto Saynt German & his felows, and þis kyng was so astonyd þat he cuthe not answer hym. And with þat he bad hym go furthe, & lefe his kyngdom vnto a better man þan he was. And þan Saynt German, be þe commandment of almyghti God, made þis nowterd & his wife to com aforn hym; and, at all men had wonder of, he made hym kyng. And evur sethen, þe kynges þat come of þe nowtherd kynred hase reingned vppon þe pepull & þe land of Brytany. *et c*9.

Hospitalitas non propter Deum facta parum valet. Infra de intencione.

[1] Harl. MS. hortansque singulos, cum omnibus cibum sumpsi.
[2] MS. *repeats*, þis.

Hospitis curialitate *et* libertate multi abutuntur. Sup*ra* de det*raccione*.

Hospes male receptus aliqu*ando* vindicat se de recipiente. Sup*ra* de histrionib*us*.

Hospicio receptus debet circa se *et* sua *esse* cautus. Inf*ra* Iacobi. ij.

Hospicio recipitur Deus sub spe*cie* leprosi. Sup*ra* de compassione.

Humilitas est semp*er* in om*n*ib*us* obseruanda. S*upra* de fatuitate.

CCCLXXI.

Humilitas sola diabolu*m* confundit. ā.

We rede in 'Vitis[1] P*atrum*' how oñ a tyme wheñ Macharius went furth̄ of his celł, þe devułł come oñ hym̄ wit*h* a ley & walde hafe smetyñ hym̄, & he myght noght. And þañ he cried & said; "Thow Macharie! Thow fastis oþ*er*-while, & I am refresshid wit*h* no man*er* of meate; & þou wakis oft-sithis, and I slepe neu*er*. And yit þi mekenes alonelie ou*er*com*m*ys me." *ā*.

Hum*i*lis verus humilia de se sentit. Infra de timore.

Humiliandi su*n*t iuuenes p*er* disciplinas. Infra de iactancia.

Humiliari debet homo ex consid*eracione* sui. S*upra* de ambic*ione*. ij.

Humilitas *eciam* a corp*or*ali morte lib*er*at. Inf*ra* de mis*ericordia*. i.

Humilitas *eciam* in potentatib*us* hui*us* sec*u*li inueni-t*ur*. S*upra* Ambrosij.

[1] MS. Vitas.

Hum*i*litate*m* ostendere debent religiosi *eciam* in pe*r*secuc*i*o*ne* iuris[1] sui. Inf*ra* de Religiosis.

CCCLXXII.

Humilis pacient*er* co*n*uicia tol*er*at[2]. *et* c⁹.

Saynt Gregor tellis of a holie man þat hight Constantinus, & he was passand litle of person & of a feble makyng. So on a tyme a buxtus man come fer fro vp o land to se hym, and when he saw hym, at he was so febull & of so little a statur, he trowed not at it had bene he; notw*ith*standyng ilk man tolde hym at it was he. And he dispysid hym & skornyd hym, & said; "I trowed at þis man had bene a grete man, and he hase nothyng of a man." And onone as þis holie man hard, onone he hawsid þis buxtos man & said; "þou alonelie is he þat hase had in me þine een oppyn & sene me." Be þe whilk þing it is for to trow what meknes he had, þat so luffid þis buxtus man þat despysid hym & set hym at noght befor; ffor be þe language at was sayd of hym myght men se what mekenes he had.

CCCLXXIII.

Iacobi Maioris.

We rede in his '*Me*racles' how xxx men of Lothoringia come vnto Saynt Iamys, & þai all bod one made hym a p*r*ivey athe of *ser*ves. So one of þai*m* fell seke, & his felows bade [*with*] hym xv dayes; neu*er*-þe-les þai lefte hym behynd þai*m*, and þer wolde none at bade *with* hym bod he þat was not sworn to kepe felowshup: & he bade *with* hym & kepid hym still at þe fute of þe Mownt Saynt Michell, & þ*er* on a day he dyed. And onone Saynt Iamys [*com*] & co*m*furthid þe whik man. And he had a gude hors, & he bad þis whik man[3] lay þe dead man ou*er*thwarte befor hym, & lepe on hym selfe behynd hym; and so he did. And opon þat night þai went xv day iorney and come ad Monte*m* Gaudii, whilk þat is bod halfe a lewke fro Saynt Iamys, and þ*er* þai lightid; & he bad hym charge þe chanons of Saynt Iamys to bery þis pilgram. And

[1] MS. viris. [2] MS. tollerat. [3] MS. may.

he bad hym tell his felows þat, for þai had broken þer faithe, þer pylgramege was no wurth nor of no valew. And he did as he was biddyn & tolde his felows as Saynt Iamys had chargid hym, & þai had grete wonder þeroff.

CCCLXXIV.

Iterum Iacobi.

We rede in his '*Meracles*' how þat a Duche-man & his son, abowte þe yere of our Lord M l xx, went vnto Saynt Iamys. And in þe cetie of Thososti[1] a syluer pece was put in his skripp[2] privalie, at he wiste not off; and on þe morn þai went þer wayis. And þer oste folowed þaim & tuke þaim as thevis; & he oppynd þer skrip, & onone he fande þis syluer pece, and þan þai war broght befor þe iuge. & onone þe sentans was giffen þat all þat þai had sulde be giffen vnto þer oste. & þe tane of þaim was demyd to be hangid, & þe fadir wold hafe dyed for þe son, & þe son for the fadur; bod neuer-þe-les þe son was hanged. And þe fadur made grete sorow & went his ways on to Saynt Iamys. And xxxvj dayes he come agayn þer away, & come vnto þe galos þer his son hang, & wepid & made mekle sorow. And his son, þat hang, spak & began to comfurth hym, & said; "Swete fathir! Wepe noght! ffor it was neuer so wele to me; ffor Saynt Iamys beris me yit vp, & fedis me with hevynlie swetnes." And when þe fadur hard þis, he ran vnto þe cetie & tolde þe peputt how it was; and þai come & tuke down þis pylgrem son hale & sownd. & þan þai tuke his oste & hanged hym, when he had grauntid how he had done.

CCCLXXV.

Iterum Iacobi.

Hugo de Sancto Victore tellis how on a tyme þe devull apperid, in liknes of Saynt Iamys, vnto a pylgram þat was bown to Saynt

[1] Lat. MSS. in urbe Tolosa. [2] MS. skipp

Iamys, & said þat he sulde be passand happie & so wer he wolde, for honor of hym, sla hym selfe. And he onone, as he bad hym, tuke his swerd & slew hym selfe *þer* he was hostid. And when his oste fande hym, he was passand ferd to be suspecte for hym. And *with* þat, he þat was dead turnyd vnto life agayn, & said þat when þe devull wolde hafe drawen hym vnto payn, Saynt Iamys come and delyverd hym & broght hym befor a iuge. And be þe sentance of þat iuge he was restorid agayn vnto life, & his wownd helid, þat ilk man might se itt.

CCCLXXVI.

It*eru*m Iacobi.

Hugo Clunacens*is* tellis how on a tyme *þer* was a yong man þ*at* went in pylgramege vnto Saynt Iamys. And hym happend to do fornicacion be þe way. And þe devull apperid vnto hym in fygur of Saynt Iame, & reprovid hym for his fornicacion & said *þer*-for his pylgramege was na wurth. And he cownceld hym for Goddis sake and his, to cutt of his membris and so to kyll hym selfe; and he did so, & was dead onone. And onone his sawle was takyn *with* fendis; & þurgh þe merett*is* & prayers of Saynt Iamys, onone it was delyverd, & þe bodie restorid agayn vnto life and hale, safeyng onelie hym wantid his membrys eu*er* after.

CCCLXXVII.

Iactancia maxime iuuenu*m* co*m*pescenda est.

Seuerus. He tellis how on a tyme *þer* was ij brethir, & þ*at* one was of xv yere age, & þe tother of xij yere; and as þai went sam*en* in wyldernes, þai*m* happend mete *with* a passyng grete neddur. And þai war bathe men of religion in ane abbay. And þe les of þai*m* tuke vpp þis nedder in his hand, & wappid it in his skyrte, and come home *þer*-*with*. And befor all his brether he putt it oute of his skyrte, & lete þaim se how þat it had hurte hym nothyng. And þar[1] brether tellid it ilkone vnto other, & said it was be faith & vertue att Godd had giffen þaim at it hurte þaim nott. So þer Abbott was a passand wyse man, & þurgh grete cowncell he tuke a wand and skowrid þaim bathe, & blamyd þaim þat þai lete þe vertue at God had giffen vnto þaim be knawen; to þe entent þat þer yong elde sulde nott wax wanton nor prowde, bod at þai sulde rather seryff God in mekenes þan for to hafe a ioy or a cunnfurth of such vertue as God had giffen þaim.

Iactantia in verbis vitanda est. Infra de presumpcione. ij.

Iactant se aliqui de virtutibus. Infra de obediencia. ix *et* x.

Ieiunium *eciam* cum quadam violencia est implenda. Supra de abstinencia. vj.

Ieiunio possunt adaptari omnia que supra dicuntur de Abstinencia, *et* multa que dicuntur infra de oratione *et* supra de cibo.

Ieronimi. Infra de leone asini custode.

Ignacij[2] martiris Infra de nomine.

CCCLXXVIII.

Ignorancia multa mala facit.

As Helinandus tellis, when[3] þe poett Omerus & many other shypmen apon a tyme war purposid for to com in-to ane yle, þe shipmen putt vnto hym a light question. *et c*.

[1] *After* þar, p, *erased.*
[2] MS. Ignasij.
[3] Harl. MS. Cum Homerus poeta aliquando in quadam insula uenisset, proposuerunt ei naute quamdam questionem facilem.

vt supra de confusione. i.

Ignorans clericus aliquando audacior est quam sciens. Supra de ceco.

Impedimentum. Impedit Deus aliquando malos aliquos ne impleant quod facere poterant vel precogitabant. Infra de signis.

Impeditur raptor oratione et compellitur restituere. Infra de Raptore nocturna.

Impedit communionem [1] pollucio nocturna aliquando. Infra de pollucione.

Imperator iudicium sine causa inferre non debet. Infra de Iudice. iiij.

Imperator obedire debet prelatis ecclesie. Supra de Ambrosio.

Imperator honorare debet personas ecclesiasticas. Supra de celare. ij.

Imperator eciam proprio filio in iudicio non parcit. Infra de Iusticia.

Imperatrix per beatam virginem de infamia liberatur. Infra de Regina.

Impetracio. Impetrat beata Maria vitam eciam dampnatis. Infra de Maria.

Impetracioni possunt multa adaptari que dicuntur de oratione. iij.

Impetratur peccatoribus gratia oracionibus. Infra de oratione.

[1] MS. commusione.

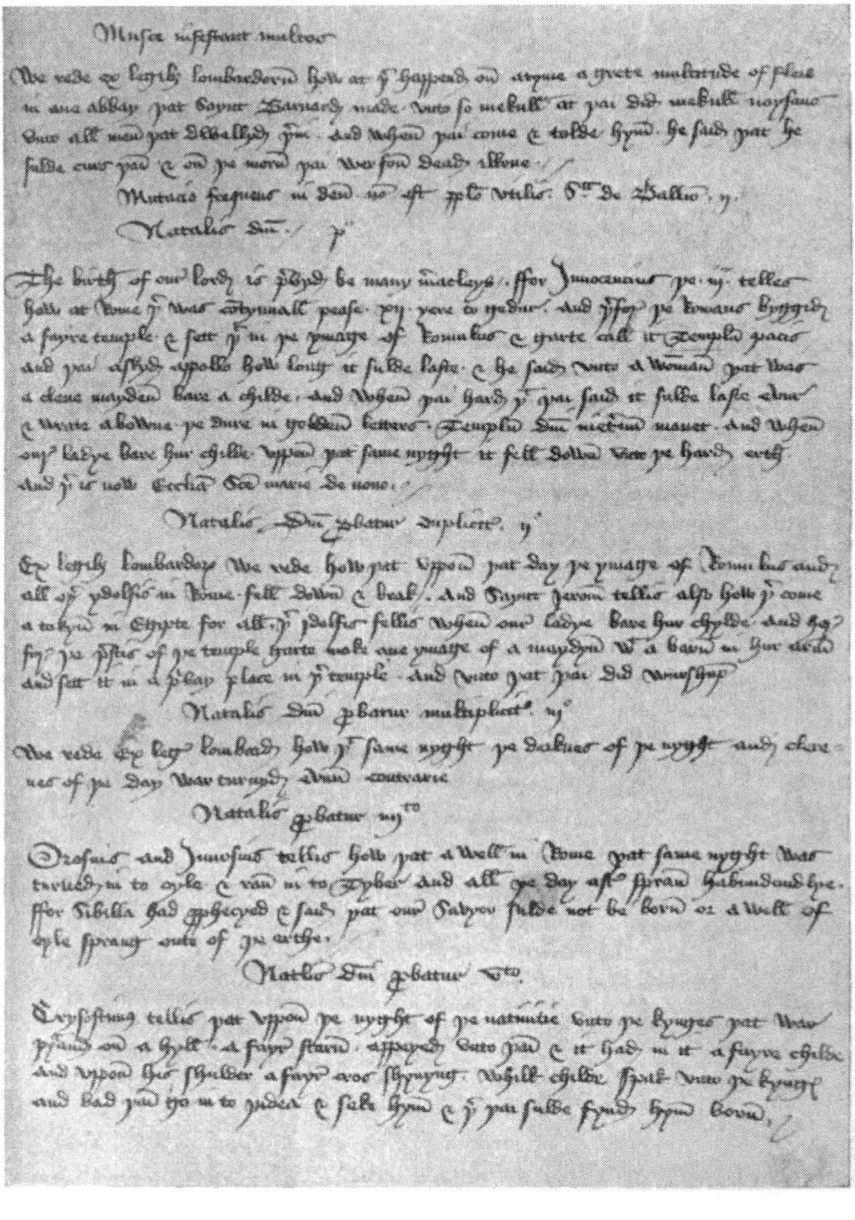

Musce infestant multos

We rede in legend of Lombardie how at it happend on a tyme a grete multitude of flies in ane abbay þat Saynt Barnard made, vnto so mekull at þai did mekull noysance vnto all men þat dwelled þer. And when þai come & tolde hym, he said þat he sulde curse þam, & on þe morn þai wer fon dead ilkone.

Mutacio saporis in dulcedinem est ipso [illegible]. [illegible] de Dulcio, ij.

Natalis domini. primo

The birth of our lord is proved be many merakyls. ffor Innocencius þe iij telles how at Rome þer was contynuall pease xij yere to gedur. And þerfor þe Romans byggid a fayre temple & sett þer in þe ymage of Romulus & garte call it Templum pacis. And þai asked Appollo how lang it sulde laste, & he said vnto a woman þat was a clene mayden bare a childe. And when þai hard þis þai said it sulde laste euer, & wrate abowne þe dure in golden letters: Templum pacis eternum manet. And when our lady bare hur childe vppon þat same nyght it fell downe vnto þe hard erth. And þer is now Ecclesia Sancte Marie de nova.

Natalis domini probatur dupliciter. ij°

In legend Lombardie we rede how þat vppon þat day þe ymage of Romulus and all oþer ydolsis in Rome fell downe & brak. And Saynt Jerom telles also how þer come a tokyn in Egypte for all þe ydolsis fellis when our ladye bare hur chylde. And þerfor þe prestes of þe temple garte make ane ymage of a mayden with a barn in hur armes and sett it in a preuay place in þe temple, and vnto þat þai did worschip.

Natalis domini probatur multipliciter. iij°

We rede in legend Lombardi how þis same nyght þe darknes of þe nyght and clerenes of þe day war turned euen contrarie.

Natalis probatur iiij^to

Orosius and Innocencius telles how þat a well in Rome þat same nyght was turned in to oyle & ran in to Tyber and all þe day after stran habundandlye. ffor Sibilla had prophecyed & said þat our Saveour sulde not be born or a well of oyle sprang oute of þe erthe.

Natalis domini probatur v^to.

Crysostimus telles þat vppon þe nyght of þe natiuite vnto þe kynges þat war prayand on a hyll a fayr starre appered vnto þam & it had in it a fayre childe and vppon his schulder a fayr croce schynyng, whilk childe spak vnto þe kynges and bad þam go in to Judea & seke hym, & þer þai sulde fynde hym born.

ADDIT. MS. 25,719, BR. MUS., leaf 131^a (REDUCED FACSIMILE)

Early English Text Society.
ORIGINAL SERIES. 127.

An Alphabet of Tales.

AN ENGLISH 15TH CENTURY TRANSLATION OF THE

ALPHABETUM NARRATIONUM

ONCE ATTRIBUTED TO

ETIENNE DE BESANÇON.

FROM ADDITIONAL MS. 25,719 OF THE BRITISH MUSEUM.

EDITED BY

MRS. MARY MACLEOD BANKS.

PART II. I–Z.

LONDON:
PUBLISHED FOR THE EARLY ENGLISH TEXT SOCIETY,
BY KEGAN PAUL, TRENCH, TRÜBNER & CO., LTD.
DRYDEN HOUSE, 43 GERRARD STREET, SOHO, W.

MDCCCCV

OXFORD

HORACE HART: PRINTER TO THE UNIVERSITY

NOTE.

Part II of the *Alphabetum Narrationum* brings the text to an end, and leaves introduction, glossary, index and general clearing-up for Part III.

The name of Étienne de Besançon still stands on the title-page; this is the last time it may be associated with this collection of Tales. The association is of so long and respectable a standing that it is worthy of an easy dissolution, though Étienne himself might possibly have felt no regret to see it brought about, as it assuredly has been by Mr. J. A. Herbert's article in the *Library* for January, 1905. Mr. Herbert sums up the case as stated by Mons. Hauréau, and adds evidence of his own weighty enough to dispose finally of the claims made for Étienne's authorship by Leandro Alberti, Quétif and Échard, and later writers.

There is a case for Arnold of Liège, but the verdict is a little in suspense. A definite attribution of authorship must wait for Part III, though it may be said forthwith that any testing of evidence hitherto undertaken serves only to strengthen Arnold's claims. For the present, however, readers must look for these in the article quoted above.

M. M. BANKS.

ERRATA

Page 4, line 9. *A note wanting from the* Latin MSS., *which begin,* Damianus. Abbas quidam.

P. 4, line 14, *for* mete *read* mece, *and delete* note 3. See p. 245, line 27.

P. 15, line 6. *A note wanting from the* Latin MSS., *which begin,* Humbertus. Quidam monachus.

P. 22, line 6, *for* Episcopus *read* Episcopus.

P. 29, line 8, *for* [þer] *read* [per].

P. 36, line 30, *delete the inverted commas after* hym̃.

P. 55, line 29, *add as note,* Latin MSS. Damianus. In monasterio quod Beatus Gregorius, etc.

P. 63, line 35, *for* ydolsis *read* ydolfis.

P. 71, line 5, *for* Clunacensis *read* Cluniacensis, *and passim.*

P. 72, line 15, *add as note,* Latin MSS. Iosephus. Cum quesitum fuisset a Tiberio Cesare.

P. 79, line 21. *A note wanting from the* Latin MSS., *which begin,* Gregorius. Quidam monachus.

P. 89, line 27, *for* ydolsis *read* ydolfis.

P. 104, lines 14, 26, *for* Jacobus *read* Iacobus, *and passim.*

P. 128, line 4, r *missing from* shrafe.

P. 147, line 22, *for* [de *read* [de].

P. 151, line 3. *A note wanting from the* Latin MSS., *which begin,* Tullius. Presbiter ecclesiae Sancti Magni.

P. 154, note 2, *for* imperaor *read* imperator.

P. 235, lines 12, 15, *for* Antissiodorens, *here and elsewhere,* Autissiodorens is a better reading.

P. 236, line 9, *for* vylans *read* vylaus.

P. 242, line 29, *for* at *read* þat.

P. 469, line 13, *add as note,* Latin MSS. Toletum.

CCCLXXIX.

Indulgencie valent defunctis. *et c⁹.*

We rede in 'Legenda Lomb*ardica*' how on a tyme a legatt of þe courte of Rome gatt a grete p*ar*don vnto his fadur, þat was dead, of þe pope. And he sent þ*er*-*with* a wurthi knyght in-to the contre of Albygen*sis* to a kurk þ*er* his fadur lay; & þis knyght taryd þ*er* þ*er*-*with* all a lentren. And þis done, vppon a nyght his fadur aperyd vnto þis legatt, clerar þan any light, and thonkid hym hartelie for his p*ar*don at he was delyverd by.

CCCLXXX.

Infamia. Infamatur aliquis sine culpa.

Heraclides tellis how som tyme þ*er* was a preste þat had a doghter, and sho happend to be corrupte & be *with* childe; and sho put þe cryme þ*er*-of apon a dekyn, & made a lye on hym. And þe bisshopp & þe preste hur fadur sent after hym, & inquyred hym þ*er*of; and he denyed itt. And þe bisshopp wax wrote þ*er*w*ith*, and said þat he was bod a lyer; and þe clerkансwerd agayn & said; "For suthe, sur, I hafe sayde as it is in my consciens, and ye wold here me now; for it was not I þat did þis dede." And when he had þus said, þai putt hym oute of his dekynshup, and garte hym wedd hur. And he com*m*endid hur vnto a monasteri & hym selfe was closid vp in a cell; & þ*er*, *with* grete prayers & wepyng*is* he besoght God at þe treuth mott be knawen. And when þe day of hur byrth drew nere, sho t*ra*ueld vij dayes to-gedur, & was hugelie vexid *with* grete paynys, so mekull þat sho mot nowder eate, nor drink, nor slepe, bod trowed hur selfe v*er*elie at sho sulde dye. And sho was passand ferd at sho sulde be dampnyd, and þan sho began to cry horrible & sayd; "Wo is me, wriche! for I am fallen into a dubble p*er*ill. Furst, for I hafe loste my maydenhed; and þe secund, I hafe putt a fals cryme vppon þe Deken." And þe susters of þe place hard hur, & went to þ*er* prayers for hur, at God wold vuchesafe at sho mot be delyver; bod it p*r*ofett nott, vnto so mekull þe bisshopp sent vnto þis Dekyn & bad hym pray for hur. Bod he wolde nott here þe messangers, nor giff þai*m* none ansswer. So at þe laste þe bisshop come vnto hym and bad hym lowse þat he had bun. And at þe bisshoppis com*m*andment he p*r*ayed for hur, & onone sho was delyver. And on þis man*er* of wyse þis dekyn was purgid of þis defame, & restorid agayn vnto his offes.

Infamat aliqu*ando* meretrix q*u*os ad pecc*atu*m trahere no*n* potest. Inf*ra* de m*er*et*r*ice.

CCCLXXXI.

Infamata fama aliqu*ando* restituitur.

Prudencius tellis in þe 'Life of Ioh*annes* Damascen*us*' how at þis Ioh*annes* was a passand holie man emang his brethir, & a mayden, and passand devowte vnto our Ladie; and bothe in Grew & in Latyn he was passandlie wele lernyd, in wrytyng & endytyng and syngyng. So on a tyme hym happend be taken wit*h* þe Sarrazens, and þat lord, þat happend to hafe hym in his parte, had a son. And þis Ioh*annes* Damascen*us* lernyd hym so in writyng & in endytyng & in syngyng, and in other þingys þat p*er*teynyd vnto þis sciens, so þat in writyng, in endytyng, & in voyce, his werk semyd no nod*er* bod at it had bene þis Ioh*annes* Damascen*us* his maist*er*. So the Emp*er*our Theodosius send for hym & payed his rawnson, & borowd hym; & his disciple wold hafe gone wit*h* hym, & he wold not latt hym. And ffor envy here-of this his[1] disciple, wit*h*-in a few yeris after, endityd a[2] lettyr & wrate þ*er*-in treson of þe Emp*er*our, & how he was in purpos to destroy hys roalm; and þis le*tt*re he garte hafe p*r*ivalie vnto Constantynople, & caste it in þe Emp*er*ours pales. And onone, as it was fon & redd, þe man*er* & þe form of þe lettir & of þe endytyng was knowen, at it was of þis Ioh*annes* Damascenus. And þe Emp*er*our when he saw it accusid hym, & þ*er*

[1] his, *omitted and added above the line.* [2] *After* a, luru, *erased.*

he was taken & fowle farn *with* & callid traytur. And when þe le*ttr*e was shewid hym, he answerd & said; "Forsuthe, surs, þis I knaw wele is þe form of my wrytyng & of myne endytyng, bod God I take to witnes þat I did it noght." And all men wondred & cryed on hym becauce he wolde not say þe treuth & graunt, & þai cryed & sayd he was wurthi to dy; & þ*er* he was broght befor þe iuges. And becauce he was þe Emp*er*our cussyn þai wold not deme hym to dy, bod þai demyd at his hand at he did þis trispas *with* sulde be cutt off. And when þis was done, in reprefe of þis felony at þai trowed þat he had done, his hand at was cut off, þai hang it in his awn kurk. So on þe night aft*er*, þis Ioh*annes* Damascenus *with* a hand come befor a speciall ymage of our Lady, & barid his wownd & shewid hur his arm. And mekelie he flate *with* hur & said in þis man*er* of wyse; "Behalde, swete lady! What rewardis is of vs þi servandis? Behold our reward! Lady, þow hase willid me, a synn*er*, þi servand, for my reward to suffre suche a turmentrie, at þou sufferd þe instrument of þine offes for to be þus cut off. For þis hand at is cutt off wrate oft sythis sangis of þi lovyng, & oft sithes sacred, & offerd þe flessh & þe blude of þi son." And when he had þus made his co*m*playnt & his prayers, he went vnto his bed; and as he was halfe slepand, halfe wakand, þe blissid mayden, our Lady Saynt Marie, apperid vnto hym *with* grete light & a gude chere, & said vnto hym; "My trew childe, what duse þou?" And he answerd agayn & sayd; "Allas! Lady, wharto askis þou me? For rather I sulde aske þe whar þou was when I sufferd þis. Behald, Ladie, how, bathe to þi shame & myne, þi hand of þi servand at was cutt of is hongen vp in þe kurk." And þan sho answerd agayn & sayd; "Son, be of gude comfurth in God!" And þis said, evyn att he myght see, sho went into þe kurk & broght his hand fro thens, & restorid it agayn vnto þe arm & made it hale. And he held vp his handis & thankid hur, & *with* þat sho vanysshid away. And on þe morn he rase & callid sam*en* his brethyr, & shewid þai*m* his hand; and onone, *with* a mery voyce & a lowde, he began our Ladie mes. And on þe morn, when þe Emp*er*our hard tell of þis m*er*acle, he come on his fete vnto hym & sett hym down on his kneis, and kyssid his hand, and askid hym if he knew any þat had his man*er* & form of writyng & endityng. And he told hym how þat he had lernyd one it; and þan þe treuth was serchid & it was fon who it was.

CCCLXXXII.

Infans in baptismo loquitur.

We rede ex 'Gestis B*e*ati Amandi' how þat when þe kyng of Fraunce had no chylde, he made a grete p*ra*yer vnto Allmiȝty God, & God sent hym one. And when it was born, he vmthoght hym whome he mot make to baptys itt. And so þis Amandus come in his mynde & he made hym to baptis it. And when it was namyd & crystend, þe childe answerd þat all myght here, and said, "Amen!"

CCCLXXXIII.

Infans vni*us* diei loquitur.

We rede in þe 'Legend of Symond & Iude' how on a tyme a dukis dog*h*t*er* happend to do fornycacion, & was *with* childe. And sho putt it vppon a dekyn, and hur fadur tuke þis dekyn & wolde hafe putt hym to dead. And þe Apostels Symond & Iude askyd when þe childe was born, and it was answerd þai*m* & said, þat same day in þe mornyng. And at com*m*andment of þe apostels, þis dekyn & þis childe was fechid afor þai*m*. And þe apostels sayd vnto þis yong child, "In þe Name, speke, þou yong childe, & tell if þis dekyn did þis trispas!" And þe yong childe answerd & said, at all men mot here; "þis dekyn fylid neu*er* his flessh *with* lichorye." And þan þis duke besoght þai*m* to spur who did þis trispas. And þe Apostels answerd agayn & sayd; "It is owr parte to excuse þai*m* þat er innocentis, and not for to discure þai*m* þat er mysdoers."

CCCLXXXIV.

Infernus. Infe*r*nal*is* pene consideracio induc*it* ho*m*i*n*em a[*d*] penitencia*m*.

Saynt Bede tellis in 'Gestis Anglor*um*' how þ*er* was a man þat was dead & restorid agayn vnto life, abowte þe yeris of our Lord cccc vj. And he was so ferd for paynys þat he had sene, þat he fled in-to wyldernes, & þ*er* biggid hym a cell beside a grete watir. And he wolde gang in-to þe watir *with* his clathis on vp to þe nek, and þan he wold com vp & latt þai*m* frese on hym vnto his flessh. And þan onone he wolde go into a hate bath, & þus evur whils he liffid, he sufferd ay þe tone aft*er* þe toder vnto he dyed. And when þai[1] att saw hym reprovid hym whi he did so, he answerd þai*m* agayn & sayd; "And ye had sene þat I saw, ye wold hafe done þe same *with* me þat I did." *et c*9.

Infernalis meditacio. Sup*r*a de Apostasia.

CCCLXXXV.

Infernalis pena est multu*m* acerba.

We rede in 'Libro de Dono Timoris' a grete me*r*acle & a solempne, how som [*tym*] at Parissh, a scolar þat was dead, in a garthyn apperid vnto his maister, and shewid hym þe payn of hell att he was dampnyd vnto in þis man*er* of wyse; he lete a drope of hys payn fall of his[2] fynger apon his maister hand, whilk þ*at* evyn furth-*with* a grete warke went þurgh his hand. So þat evur aft*er* vnto he dyed þ*er* was ay a hole þurgh his hand.

CCCLXXXVI.

Infernalis pena est magnitud*in*is inestimabil*is*[3].

We rede in 'Vitis P*at*rum' how on a tyme as Macharius went in wyldernes he fand a dead mans head, and he had grete m*er*vayll whose it was. And he com*man*did it to spek & tell hym, & so it

[1] MS. þat.
[2] *After* his, *maister, erased.*
[3] MS. inextinguibilis, Lat. MSS. *as above.*

did; and sayd it was a prestes head þat was a gentyle, þat was vncristend. And he askid it what þe saule þer-of was in payn. And it answerd agayn & sayd þat it was in hell, als depe as is fro hevyn vnto erthe, & he said þat it was als depe vnder-nethe hym. And þer he sayd wer fals cristen men. And a noder tale like þis tellis Saynt Gregur in his 'Dialoggis' of a grete man þat hyght Rep*er*atus; and on a tyme he was kepyd as dead & sodanly turnyd vnto life agayn. & he tellid how þat he had sene a grete kyngdom and it was all coverd ou*er*; and hym thoght þe heght þ*er*-of was als hy as is fro hevyn vnto erth.

CCCLXXXVII.

Infernalis pena est ete*r*na. Sup*r*a de Conue*r*sione.

A tale like vnto þe same tellis Saynt Gregur, how on a tyme þ*er* was a fond wom*m*an þat somwhatt vnderstude Latyn. And on a tyme as sho was in þe kurk at a Dirigie, sho harde þai*m* syng; "In inferno nulla est redempcio." And when sho had hard it, sho cryed *with* ane horrible voyce & sayde; "I will neu*er* com þ*er*, ffor þat is ane ill place for me to putt my truste in." *et* c[9].

Infernal*is* pena intolerabilis[1] est. S*upr*a de conue*r*sione.

Infernales pene horribiles su*n*t ad vidend*um*. Inf*r*a de sciencia nigromancie. *et* c[9].

Infernales pene viuis[2] aliqu*ando* ostendu*n*tur. Sup*r*a de cruce signatis, v., *et* infra de sciencia nigromanc*ie*.

Infernales pene su*n*t multiplices. Sup*r*a de elemosina, xj.

Infideles minus puniu*ntur* in inferno q*u*am mali Chr*ist*iani. Inf*r*a de Chr*ist*ianis.

[1] MS. intollerabilis. [2] MS. vicijs. Harl. MS. viuis.

Infideli defu*n*cto valuit oracio Sancti. Infra de or*a*-*cione*, iiij.

Infidelis a deo occiditur. Infra de vind*icta*, v.

Infidelis aliqu*ando* bonas leges condit. Inf*r*a de lege, j.

CCCLXXXVIII.

Infirmitas p*r*op*r*ia pacient*er* debet sustineri.

Saynt Gregoȝ tellis in his '*Dialoggis*' how som tyme þ*er* was a mañ þat hight Seruulus, and he was passand pure of gudis, bod he was riche of merettis. And alł his lyfe-tyme he lay alway in þe p*er*alysye, þ*at* he neu*er* rase oute of his bed, nor neu*er* put his hand vnto his mowthe, nor neu*er* myght turñ hym̃. And his moder and his bruther come vnto hym̃ to kepe hym̃ & seryff hym̃; and what at evur he gatt of almos ou*er* þat at þai expu*n*did, he made þai*m* to deale it vnto pure folke. And w*ith* any money þ*at* he gatt, eu*er* he boght hym̃ bukys of holie scriptur; and he garte religios meñ þat h*er*bard w*ith* hym̃ rede þai*m* vnto hym̃, to so mekle þat w*ith*-in a p*ro*ces he, þ*at* cuthe no wurd oñ þe buke, lernyd holie scriptur. And wheñ he knew hym̃ selfe þ*at* he drew nere his dead, he garte calł vnto hym̃ alł þais pylg*r*amys þ*at* he was wunte to herber, and com*m*awndid þai*m* þat þai sulde sitt abowte hym̃, & say þ*er* prayers & syng þe latynie vnto þat he dyed; and he sang w*ith* þai*m*. And evyñ as he was bowñ to dye, he spakk vnto þai*m* & sayd; "Be stiłł! be stiłł & holde your tongis! For ye hard neu*er* suche voyces as I here now songeñ in hevyñ." And as he was giffand hede vnto þai*m* his holie sawle passid furth of his bodye vnto blis.

CCCLXXXIX.

Infirmis est diligent*er* se*r*uiendu*m*.

Heraclides tellis how a mañ þat hight Eulogius forsuke þis warld so þ*at* he myght nothyng do be his one nor wirk[1]; and few of his gudis he kepid vnto hym̃ þat he myght liff vppoñ. And he

[1] Lat. MSS. *quia per se nichil poterat operari.*

mott nowder be in þe monaster*ie* *with* many, nor he myght nott liff be his one. On a tyme he fande a man þat had a sekenes þ*at* was callid Morbus Elefanticus, and he had it so fellie þat it had distroyed his fete & his handis, & all his membris bod his tonge. And þan þis Elogius, evyn as he had made a cou*n*ande *with* almyghti God, said on þis wise; "Lorde God! In þi name I sall take þis man, & take hym as þi *ser*vand, and kepe hym vnto þat he dye." And he sett hym on his ass, & led hym vnto þ*er* he was lugid, & kepid hym & *ser*vid hym his awn hand þe space of xv yere. And þan þis seke man be þe instinccion of þe devull desyrid to be away fro hym, & flate *with* hym & rep*re*vid hym, & said; "Thow come & stale me furthe of my howse becauce be me þou trowid to hafe welthe of gudis, and to requeuer helthe of þi bodie." And þan þis Eulogius spakk fayr *with* hym, & prayed hym to be in peace & said; "Gude sur! Say nott so, bod tell me & I hafe oght trispasid vnto the, & I sall amend itt." And he said; "Nay, go þi wayes, I will none of þi fagyngis! Lay me þ*er*oute opynlie; me misters none of þi refresshyng, ffor I desyre to eate flessh." And he garte ordan flessh soden & broght hym itt: and þan he wolde none þ*er*-off, & said; "I may nott dwell *with* þe, for I will go se þe peple." And þan Elogius tolde hym he sulde bryng in a grete meneya of brethir & latt hym se. And he ansswerd agayn & said; "I will se none suche distroyers as þ*ou* erte; hafe me agayn þ*er* þou tuke me fro!" þan þis Elogius layde hym in a bote & had hym vnto Saynt Anton þe Abbott, & tolde hym all his reule & how he wolde putt hym oute. And Saynt Anton said; "P*er*aventur, & þou forsake hym, a bettir man þan þou shall take hym in & fynde hym." And þan he said vnto þis seke man; "þ*ou* behaldis nowder wurthelie hevyn nor erthe; knowis þou not at þis is Criste att *ser*vis the? For all þe *ser*ves at hym þis duse the, he duse it for Cristis sake." And after þatt he comfurthid þai*m* bothe & said; "Childre, parte you nott in sonder, ffor ye mon be bothe savid. And þ*er*for þis temptacion happend you now, when ye er bothe nere at end of your life." And þis done, þai turnyd agayn vnto þ*er* cell, and *with*in xl^{ti} dayes after þai bothe dyed.

CCCXC.

Infirmitas corporalis aliquando prodest sp*irit*ui.

We rede in þe 'Legend' of Saynt Petronell,' þat was Saynt Petir doghter, how þat sho was a passand fayr w*om*man. And be þe will of hur fadur sho had þe axes. And on a tyme when þe disciples come & dynyd' *with* hym, þai said' vnto hym; "Sen all seke folk er helid' be þe, whi suffres þ*ou* þis Petronell[1] þi doghter to lye so sore seke?" And he answerd' þai*m* agayn & said' þat it was necessarie for hur. And becauce þai sulde nott trow þat it wer impossible þat sho sulde be hale be his wurdis, þ*er*for he said' vnto hur; "Thow Petronell! Rise swithe & seryff vs!" And onone at his wurde sho rase & servid' þai*m*. And when þai had etyn, he bad hur go vnto hur bed agayn, & so sho did & was als seke agayn in þe axis as evur was sho; and so sho lay many day vnto hym þoght att sho was p*ar*fite in þe luff of Godd'. And þan he made hur fissch-hale. And þan þ*er* come vnto hur ane erle þat hight Flaccus, & desirid' for hur fayrnes to hafe hur vnto his wife. And sho answerd' agayn & said'; "If þ*ou* desire to hafe me vnto þi wyfe, com*m*and' a c*er*tayn of maydens to com vnto me & bere me felachup vnto þi place." And so he did. And þan þis Pet*r*onell fastid' hugelie, & made devowte p*r*ayers vnto almyghti God', & tuke þe holie sacrament, and *with*[-*in*] iij dayes after sho passid' oute of þis warld'.

CCCXCI.

Infirmitas corporalis aliqu*ando* est appetenda[2].

We rede ex '*Dictis* P*atrum*' how som tyme þ*er* was ane olde man þat evur-ilk yere had a grete sekenes. So it happend a yere þat he was not seke, and þ*er*for he tuke a grete sorow & wepyd', and sayd vnto hym selfe; "Dereliquit me Deus, *et* c*etera*. Almighti God hase forsaken me, becauce He vissett*is* not me as He was wunt."

[1] MS. Peronell.

[2] MS. appitenda.

CCCXCII.

Infirmitas corp*or*alis aliqu*ando* de sup*er*bo facit humilem.

Jacobus de Vet*ri*aco tellis how som tyme in þe byesshoppryke of Parissħ þ*er* was a paress clerk̄, & he vsid' to com̄ vnto a knyghtis place w*ith* halie water evur-ilk wuke; & he cuthe neu*er* gett nott on̄ hym̄ bod flytyng & bannyng. And it happend on̄ a tyme þis knyght fell̄ seke, and when̄ þe clerke come w*ith* holi watyr & keste on̄ hym̄, he prayed' þis clerk to pray for hym̄. And he garte giff hym̄ a kirk̄. And þan̄ þis clerk̄ spakk vnto hym̄ & said'; "How is þis happend, sur, þ*a*t ye þ*a*t so ofte hase flittyn̄ w*ith* me, & bannyd me so oft, is now þus turnyd' at ye pray me now for to pray for you?" And þe knyght ansswerd' & said'; "Seis þou not how I am̄ seke, & how þe gowte is in my fute on̄ þe to syde?" And þan̄ þe clerk̄ said'; "Sur, I sall̄ pray God þ*a*t it may be also in þe toder fute." And þe knyght askyd' hym̄ what he said'. And þe clerk ansswerd' hym̄ agayn̄ & said'; "þou was als prowde as a lion̄ when̄ þou was hale, and now in þi sekenes þou erte made als meke as a lambe. And yit for þi gude I sall̄ pray for the."

Infirmus aliqu*ando* convalescit p*er* votu*m* religionis. Inf*r*a de voto.

Ingratus Deo de beneficio p*er*cepto ab eo me*r*ito pe*r*dit illud. S*upr*a de h*er*etico.

Ing*r*atitudinis viciu*m* incurrit vane glorians de beneficio p*er*cepto, *et* ideo me*r*ito illud p*er*dit. Sup*r*a de confessione.

Ingratus ho*min*i de beneficio ab eo recepto multu*m* est rep*r*ehensibil*is*. Supra de Infirmo.

CCCXCIII.

Iniuria p*r*opt*er* Deum debet dimitti.

We rede ex '*Dictis* Pat*rum*' how þat þe Abbot Hillarion̄, when̄ on̄ a tyme he visit a c*er*tayn̄ bisshopp̄, and when̄ þai war at meatt, þis bisshop sett befor hym a capon & bad hym eatt. And þe Abbott answerd hym agayn & said; "Sen I tuke þis abbett I ete neu*er* þing þat suffred dead." Than þe bisshop answerd hym agayn & said; "And I, sen I tuke þis abbett, suffred neu*er* man to slepe þat had oght agayn me. Nor I slepid nevur als lang as I had oght agayns hym vnto we war in charite." And þan þis Abbott said; "Fathir! fforgiff me; for þi conu*er*sacion is more þan myne."

Iniurie su*n*t aliqu*ando* dissimulande. S*upr*a de amicicia, viij *et* ix.

Inobediencia. Infra de obediencia *et* religione.

Insidie. Insidiantur supe*r*bi bonis op*er*ib*us*. Inf*r*a de sup*er*bia.

Insidiantur demones h*omin*ib*us* m*u*ltipliciter. Sup*r*a de demo*n*ib*us* pl*ur*ib*us* locis.

Insidiantur mali qu*andoque* bonis. Sup*r*a de carne, iiij.

CCCXCIV.

Intencio mala ecia*m* bonu*m* opus viciat.

Saynt Gregorie tellis how som tyme þ*er* was a holie man þat hight Fortunatus, & he was a bisshop. And on a day he drafe oute ane evull spiritt oute of a man þatt was vexid þ*er*-*with*, whilk spiritt agayn evyn fenyd hym selfe like a pylgrem, & went aboute in þe cetie þurgh þe stretis, & said & c*r*ied; "O! þou holie man, Fortunatt þe bisshopp, þat putt oute a pylgram oute of his hoste! And I seke now in his cetie þ*er* I mot be lugid, & I can gett no h*er*berie." And þ*er* was a man þat satt in his howse be þe fyre *with* his wife & his childre, and he come furth & askid hym what þe bisshop had done vnto hym; & he tolde hym. & he tuke hym in & herberd hym, and as þai satt talkand be þe fyre, þis same spiritt keste a barn of hys in þe fyre and burnyd it o dead. And *with* þat he flew away *with* a grete noyse. And þis sorie man purseyvid þat he þat he had resayvid was not putt oute be þe bisshopp, bod at it was ane ill spiritt þat come for to disclander hym[1].

Inuencio. Inuenta res debet restitui. Infra de promisso.

Inuidia inter religiosos inuenitur. Infra de obediencia.

CCCXCV.

Invidie stimulis agitati religiosi aliquando se excusant.

Cesarius tellis how som tyme þer was a monke þat was stirrid with envie, and he accusid a yong man vnto þe Abbott, & putt vppon hym grevus trispas. And þe Abbott belevid hym noȝt, & so oppynlie in þe chapiter he putt furth all þies trispas of þis yong man, when þer visitur was þer. And þe visitur belevid hym & putt þies trispas vnto þis yong man; and he said he was nott giltie, & þat he tuke God to witnes. Notwithstondyng he was commytt vnto prison; and onone after þis envious man fell seke and was ferde to dye. And þan he grauntid opynlie how he for envye had accusid þis yong man. And so þis yong man with grete ioy be his visitur was taken oute of prison agayn, & restorid vnto his olde estate as he was befor.

Inuident mali bonis. Supra de carne, iiij.

CCCXCVI.

Inuidia aliqualis eciam in puellis paruis reperitur.

Cesarius tellis how þat in Freseland in a nonrie þer was ij little maydens þat lernyd on þe buke, & euer þai strafe whethur of þaim shulde lern mor þan þe toder. So þe tane of þaim happend to fall seke, and sho garte call þe Priores vnto hur & sayd; "Gude ladie! suffre nott my felow to lern vnto I cover of my sekenes, and I sall

[1] Harl. MS. Qui miser orbatus . . . quia non hospitalitatis pietate delectabatur sed episcopi derogacione.

pray my moder to gif me vjd & þat I sall giff you & ye do so; ffor I drede þat whils I am seke, þat sho sall pas me in lernyng, & þat I wolde not at sho did; *et c*9." And at þis wurde þe priores smylid & hadd grete mervayle of þe damysell conseyte. *et c*9.

CCCXCVII.

Invidus in morte eciam non cessat.

Cesarius tellis þat when þe Duke of Siringie was deade, þer was harde a voyce besyde þe Mownt of Tybir[1], þat spat fyre, & it sayd; "Ordand fyre!" And a noder voyce ansswerd & sayd; "I wote neuer whatt, nor to whame I sall ordan." And þe toder said agayn; "Our gude & wele-beluffid frend, þe Duke of Siringie, commys hedur." And onone it was knawn þat in þe Empyre of Frederyke, vnto whome þies war wreten, þe same day & howr was Bertolfus[2], þat was Duke of Siringie, dead; þat was a grete tyrand and a robber bothe of riche men & pure men. And for als mekyll as he had no child, or he dyed he prayed þat all his tresurs, þat war of grete valow, mott be molten in-to a grete mace, & sayd vnto hym selfe; "I gnaw well at my cussyns will be fayn of my dead; and if þai fynd me tresurs, sone þai will devide þaim emang þaim. And if þai be all in a grete lompe þai er noght ethe to parte emang þaim." *et c*9.

CCCXCVIII.

Inuitis prestat Deus multa beneficia.

We rede in þe 'Legend of Saynt Martyn' how þat þer was two at war felowse to-geder, & þai war beggers; & þe tone was blynde & þe toder myght not goo. And he þat was blynde was a strong man & bare[3] the tother in his nekk, & he tellid hym alway how he sulde goo; and þus þai beggid many day & gatt mekle syluer. And when þai hard tell how þat att Saynt Martyn tombe many seke folke wer helid, opon þe day of his translacion it was vse to

[1] Arund. MS. *Montem* Geber. Harl. MS. Montem Ciber.

[2] Lat. MSS. Bertoldus.

[3] *After* bare, to, *erased*.

bere his bonys furth of þe kurk, and þai come thedir. And yit þai war aferd þat peraventur, and þai abade in þe strete þer his bonys war born thrugh, þat þai sulde be made hale; & þa[i] wold not be made hale for drede þer begyng sulde defayle þaim. And þai went furth of þat strete. And sodanlie þaim happend mete with his shryne in a noder gate, & þer þai war made hale agayn þer wyll.

CCCXCIX.

Iohannis[1] Euuangeliste.

Cassianus tellis how on a tyme a man come & broght Saynt Iohn Euuangeliste a pertrykk whikk, & gaff hym it; and he tuke it & held it in his hand & strakid it & made mekyll þer-off. And þer was a yong felow at saw & skornyd hym, said vnto his felows att stude abowte hym; "Will ye se yone olde felow how he laykis with yone byrd as it wer a yong barn?" And Saynt Iohn be þe Holie Gaste purseyvid þis, and callid þe yong man vnto hym & askyd hym what þat was at he held in his hand. And he ansswerd agayn & said þat it was a bow. And he askid hym what he did þerwith, and þe yong man sayd; "I shute burdis & bestis þerwith." And þe apostell askid hym whi it was vnbendid, and he said, for & he helde it allway bendyd, it wolde be þe wayker to shute away his shaftis with. Than þe apostell ansswerd hym agayn & sayde; "Son, on þe same wise mans freletie wolde be passand wayke & it wer allway bendyd in þoght of contemplacion; ffor as þe egle emang all burdis fleis hyest & seis nexte þe son, & yit hur muste nedelyng com down vnto þe law placis, right so mans witt, when it withdrawis it a little from contemplacion & hase a litle comfurth, afterward it is mor ardent vnto hevynlie matyrs." *et c*.

CCCC.

Iohannis Baptiste *et* Iohannis Euuangeliste.

We rede in '*Legenda Lombardica*' how som tyme þer was ij docturs of dyvynyte, and þe tone of þaim luffed in esspeciall afor

[1] MS. Iohannes.

aƚƚ oþ*er* Sayntt*is* Saynt Iohn̄ Baptiste[1], & þe tod*er* Saynt Iohn̄ Euua*n*geliste, into so mekuƚƚ þat betwix þai*m* þai made grete disputacions of þ*er* ioy & þ*er* excellence, vnto so mekuƚƚ at ather of þai*m* war passand' besy to fynd' resons & auctorities to p*re*fer þe Saynt Iohn̄ þat he luffid' *with*. And so þai poyntid' a day of disputacion̄. And in þe menewhile ather of þies Sayntis aperid' vnto his doctur at held' *with* hym̄, & sayd'; "We er wele acordid' in hevyn̄, and þ*er*for̃ dispute nott of vs in erthe." And when̄ þai mett same*n*, ather of þai*m* aforn̄ aƚƚ þe peple tellid' other þ*er* vision̄, and thankid' Almiȝti God & þase holie sayntis.

CCCCI.

Ioh*ann*is Baptiste.

We rede ex '*Legenda* Lomb*ardica*' how one þ*a*t hight Pawle, þat was historiog*ra*phus Longobar*dorum*, and a dekyn̄ of þe kurk of Rome, and afterward' a monk of Cassynence, on̄ a tyme when̄ he sulde hafe halowid' þe pascaƚƚ, hym̄ happend to wex dom̄, þat he cuthe not als mekuƚƚ as say A, þat is þe furst voweƚƚ. And he made hys prayer vnto Saynt Iohn̄ at he mott speke agayn̄, & in wurshup̄ of hym̄ he made þis ympne, "Vt queant laxis, *et* c9," & als tyte as he had made þat he mot speke.

CCCCII.

It*erum* Ioh*ann*is Baptiste.

We rede in þe same 'Legend'' how som̄ tyme þ*er* was a huswyff þat punysshid' hur selfe *with* fastyng & p*ra*yers. And eu*er* sho prayed Almyghti God' to send hur som̄ of þe relikkis of Saynt Iohn̄ Baptiste. And sodanly apon̄ ane altar̃ sho saw a thombe þat was passand white, and sho was glad þ*er*of & tuke itt. And' þ*er* come vnto hur iij bysshoppis, when̄ þai harde teƚƚ þat sho had such a relyk, & desyrid' to hafe p*ar*te þ*er*of; & sho lete iij droppis

[1] MS. Saynt Iohn of Baptiste.

of blude dropp opon a clothe, & þai cut it in sonder & tuke ilkone of þaim a drop, and went home þerwith & was passyng glad.

Iohannis Damasceni. Infra de infamia.

CCCCIII.

Ira aliquando est dissimulanda.

Valerius tellis how on a tyme ane arschedekyn[1] þat was callid Carentinus, on a tyme when a bondman of his had grevid hym, he said on þis maner vnto hym; "Had I not bene angred vnto þe I sulde hafe putt þe vnto grete punyssment." And so he had levur lefe þe blame vnpunysshid þan fulfyll þe movyng of his yre. We rede also of Plato, when on a tyme he was grevid agayns his servand for a tryspas, ffor drede þat he sulde be vengeable & pas mesur, he commytt þe chastiment of his seruand vnto þe fre liste of a noder man.

Ire signa. Supra de Correcione, iij.

Irasci non debet iudex corrigendo. Supra de correccione, iij.

CCCCIV.

Iracundus naturaliter eciam solus existens irascitur.

We rede in 'Vitis Patrum' how som tyme þer was a brother þat was passand angrie in hym selfe. So on a tyme he said vnto hym selfe; "Þou bodie! & þou war be þine ane, þou sulde not be so ofte movid vnto angrynes." So he went vnto wildernes & liffid be hym selfe. & on a tyme he tuke a little pott & fillid itt full of watyr, and he turnyd vp þe pott & powrid it oute. So þe secund tyme he fyllid it & wex angrie & powrid it oute agayn; and þan he wex so tene þat he tuke þe vessell & brakk it all to gobettis. And þan he come vnto hym selfe & knew þat he was stirrid to wrath be a fend. And þan he said; "Lo! þuff all

[1] Harl. MS. archidiaconus Canentinus.

I be be myne ane, neu*er*-þe-less I am ou*er*-comme*n* wit*h* angrynes." And þan he turnyd agayn vnto his felashup; for whar þer is labur & felashup commonlie þ*er* is paciens & Goddis helpe.

CCCCV.

Iracu*n*dus ecia*m* visibilit*er* punitur.

Cesarius tellis how som tyme þ*er* was a riche mans doghter, and sho was so angrie þ*at* whare at evur sho war sho made stryfe & debate; & yit sho lete hur selfe holye & sho mott nott restrene hur tong. So at þe laste hur happend to dye, & þai berid hur in þe kurk porche. And on þe morn when folk come vnto þe kurk, þai saw reke com oute of hur grafe, & þai had m*er*vell þ*er*-of, & was ferd & opynde it, & keste oute þe erthe. & þai fande þe vpper halfe of hur bodie to hur navill burnyd clene away wit*h* fyre, & þe lawer p*ar*tie lay hale, in betokynyng þat sho was a clene maydyn bod yit sho was passand angrie.

Irreu*er*encia facta s*an*ctis punitur. Sup*r*a de blasfemia, iij.

CCCCVI.

Iudei expectantes Messiam p*er* cl*er*icu*m* decipiuntur.

Cesarius tellis how som tyme in þe cetie of London[1] a clerk gatt a Iewis doghter wit*h* childe; & he was ferde for grevans of hur fadur & hur moder, & he gatt hym a long rede & come on þe night to þe wall þ*er* hur fadur & hur moder lay wit*h*in. & he put þe vpper end of þe rede in at a hole, & he spakk in att þe toder end & said; "O! ye rightwus folk, in God wele-beluffid!" & callid þai*m* be þ*er* names & bad þai*m* be merie, for þ*er* dought*er* had conseyvid Messias & yit sho was a mayden. And wit*h* þ*at* þe man was estonyd & askid his wife if sho hard þis voyce, and sho said nay; & þai made þ*er* prayers at þai myght here it agayn. And þe clerke stude still & harde þai*m*; and as he did befor, he spakk

[1] Harl. MS. Lomodonensi*s*. Arund. MS. Lomo*ni*densis.

agayn. And when þai hard hym þai war passand fayn, & trowid þat it had bene trew; & vnnethis þai abade a day vnto þai grapid þ*er* dogh*ter* bodie & fand at sho was wit*h* childe. & þai askid hur how sho conseyvid, and sho answerd as þe clerk had bedyn hur, & sayd; "I wote neu*er* wheþ*er* I be wit*h* childe or nay, bod I know wele I am a mayden & had neu*er* at do wit*h* man." And þ*er* was hur fadur & hur moder so ioyfull þat onone þe noyse ran þurgh þe cetie þat þ*er* dogh*ter* was wit*h* childe wit*h* Messias. So tyme come sho sulde be delyver, & þ*er* come vnto hur many Iewis wit*h* grete myrth & ioy, & abade to sho war delyver at þai mot se what sho had born. And in hur travellyng sho had grete payn, & at þe laste wit*h* grete sorow & crying sho bare a dogh*ter*, þat cryed & grete & made mekyll mornyng. And when þai saw þis þai all war confusid passynglie, to so mekill þat ane of þai*m* in a tene tuke þis childe be þe legg & threw it agayn þe wall & killid it. *et c*.

Iudei filius in fornace*m* missus p*er* be*at*am Maria*m* est lib*er*atus. S*upr*a de eukaristia.

Iudei canonicu*m* accusantes vsu*m* loque*n*di p*er*diderunt. Sup*r*a de cont*r*icione.

Iudei ymagi*n*em c*r*ucifixi v*er*be*r*antes sang*u*ine ex ea p*r*osiliente conue*r*si su*n*t ad Chr*istu*m. Sup*r*a de cruce.

CCCCVII.

Iudex iniuste iudicans puniendus est.

Helinandus tellis[1] of Cambises, þat was Cyrus[2] þe kyng of Perce son, when he had optenyd his kyngdom & fande a iustis þat had giffen a wronges eniugement, he com*m*andid at he sulde be flane, & his son to be made iustis after hym; & at þe sete at his son suld sitt in for iugement sulde be couerde wit*h* his fadir

[1] of Cambises *added above the line.* [2] MS. Ciri.

skyn̄, at he sulde hafe mynde of hys[1] faders iugement & of þe payn̄ att he had þerfor̄, and so at he sulde be ferde to giff a fals eniugement.

Iudex a u*er*itate no*n* debet deuiare p*ro*pt*er* amiciciam[2]. Sup*ra* de amicicia.

Iudex debet e*ss*e sobrius maxi*me* in potu. S*upra* de abstinencia, vij.

Iudex no*n* debet eligi puer. Inf*ra* de pu*er*o.

Iudex no*n* debet constitui paup*er* vel auarus, vt supra de balliuo.

Iudex cito credere no*n* debet. Sup*ra* de credere, ij.

Iudex v*er*itate*m* vendere *et* aliena rap*er*e no*n* debet. Inf*ra* Laur*encij*, ij.

Iudex debet astutus esse in causis obscuris inq*u*irendis. Inf*ra* de m*u*liere.

CCCCVIII.

Iudex sine causa reu*m* absoluere no*n* debet.

Cesarius tellis of a bisshop þat was a holie man̄ & a devowte, and on̄ a tyme in þe Lentren̄ he red owr̄ his psalter, and when̄ he come at þis place in his psalter, "*Quis loquetur potentias Domini, auditas* [*faciet*] *omnes laudes eius?*[3]" sodanly ane of his iustis come in vnto hym̄ and askid' hym̄ what he sulde do *with* a man̄ þat had done a grete cryme & a trispas. And þis bisshopp̄ was full̄ of mercie and bad hym̄ spare hym̄ for þe holie tyme. And *with* þat þe Iustis turnyd' agayn̄ purposyng to lat hym̄ go. And þe bisshop red on̄ on̄ þe psalter þ*er* he lefte, & onone he fande þis verce, "Beati qui custodiunt iudiciu*m et faciunt* iustici*am* in om*ni* tempore, *et* c*9*." And *with* þis he was flayed' as he had bene resond' be almighti God. And onone he garte call̄ þis iustis agayn̄ &

[1] MS. hym̄.
[2] MS. amicisiam.
[3] *This comes after*: Confitemini Domino, quoniam in saeculum misericordia eius.

said' vnto hym̄; "Serche diligentlie þe cauce & deme hym̄ rightwuslie." And so be þe voyce of þe prophett he þat was giltie loste his lyfe.

CCCCIX.

Iudex debet esse adeo iustus vt *eciam* propinquis delinque*n*tib*us* no*n* pa*r*cat.

Valerius tellis of one þat hight Zaleucius þat was a iustis. And on̄ a tyme hys son̄ for avowtrie was condempnyd' afor̄ hym̄ þat bothe his een̄ sulde be putt oute. And all̄ þe cetie wit*h*stude it for wurship̄ of his fadir a grete while, vnto so mykill̄ he was evyn̄ ou*er*com*m*en̄. And at þe laste, becauce he wolde þe law war kepid trewlie & not broken̄, he garte furst put furth̄ one of his awn een̄ for his son̄, & syne one of his son̄ een̄, at his son̄ sulde not hafe bothe putt oute. And so be temp*er*ans of a m*er*valos evynhed'[1], ather of þai*m* loste ane ee. And þus he shewid' hym̄ selfe bothe a rightwus man̄ of law & a m*er*cyfull̄ fadur. *et* c*9*.

Iudex debet esse co*m*positus in sensib*us* ext*er*ioribu*s*. S*upr*a de aspectu.

Iudici malo freque*n*t*er* succedit det*er*ior. Sup*r*a de balliuo[2].

Iudices[3] freque*n*t*er* mutare no*n* expedit. Sup*r*a de balliuo, ij.

CCCCX.

Iudex bonus no*n* debet differre iusticia*m*[4] sine causa r*ati*onabili.

Helynandus tellis of þe Emp*er*our Traiane, how on̄ a tyme when̄ he sulde go vnto batell̄ and lepid opon̄ his hors, a wedow come

[1] Arund. MS. sibiqu*e* mirabili equitatis temp*er*ame*n*to, se misericordi*e* p*a*trem *et* iustu*m* legislatore*m* ostendit.

[2] MS. balneo.

[3] MS. Iudeces.

[4] So Lat. MSS. Eng. MS. causam.

& tuke hym be þe fute; & wit*h* grete sorow & lamentacion sho *pr*ayed hym at sho mott hafe right of þai*m* at had slayn hur son wrongualie. And sho said; "Sur! þou reingnes as emp*er*our, & whi lattis þou me suffer þis fowle eniurie?" And he said he sulde make it to be amendid when he come agayn; and sho askid hym how sho sulde do & he neu*er* come agayn, and he said his successur sulde make hur to be asethid. And sho askid hym how scho sulde know þat; "and if he do," sho said, "whatt will þat *pr*ofett the? And if no man make me a sethe, yit þou erte dettur vnto me, & þou mon be rewardid aftir þi warkis. And þi successur is bon for the, bod a noder mans rightwusnes sall not delyvir þe for þat at þou sulde hafe done þine awn selfe." And wit*h* þies wurdis þis Emp*er*our Traiane was somwhat movid & lightid of his hors, and in his awn p*er*son he exsamynd þe wedous cauce, & he comfurthid hur & made hur to hafe a due satisfaccion for hur hurte.

CCCCXI.

Iudicia Dei frequent*er* sunt occulta.

Iacobus de Vet*r*iaco tellis how som tyme þ*er* was ane h*er*mett þat was tempid wit*h* þe spiritt of blasfemyng, vnto so mek[ill] [1] he thoght in his awn mynd þat þe domys of Almiȝtti God wer nott rightwus, þat sufferd synners & ill men to hafe *pro*sp*er*tie & welefar of þis warlde, & gude men & rightwus to hafe disease & tribulacion. And þ*er* apperid vnto hym ane angell on a tyme in a mans liknes, & said vnto hym; "Folow me & þou sall se þe *pr*ivay Iugementt*is* of almiȝtti God." So þai come vnto a gude mans hows þat h*er*berd þai*m* al nyght [2], & made þai*m* gude chere. & on þe morn when þai went, þe aungell stale þe sylu*er* copp at þai dranke of, & tuke it wit*h* hym; whilk cop þe gudeman luffid beste of any thyng þat he had. And þai wente þ*er* wayse, & on þe nexte nyg[*ht*] þai h*er*berd wit*h* ane ill man & a wykkid, whare þai wer reseyvid wit*h* ill will & fure ill. And þe copp at he tuke fro þe toder man, þe angell gaff hym itt. And þis hermett thoght

[1] MS. mekyng. [2] MS. *repeats*, *with* gude chere.

ill *þer*-*with*, bod he sayde noght. And on þe iij nyght þai wer hostid at a gudemans howse *þat* reseyvid þaim *with* gude will & made þaim wele at fare. And on þe morn he sent a *servand* of hys furth *with* þaim to teche þaim þe way, & when þai war all on a bryg þis aungell keste þis mans *servand* our þe bryg & drownyd hym. And þis h*er*mett saw & had grete m*er*vayle þer-of & yit he said noght; and on þe iiij nyght þai war herberd in a gude mans howse & had grete chere. And he had a yong childe þat wepid all nyght & wolde nott lat þaim slepe, and þis aungell rase vp & wrathe þe nekk in-sonder þ*er*off. And when þe h*er*mett saw all þis, he thoght þat he wolde sodanlie stele away & lefe hym, & trowid þat he had bene rather ane aungell of þe devull þan off God. And þan þe aungell bad hym abyde, & sayde vnto hym; "Almiȝtti God sent me vnto þe at I mot shew þe His privay domys. The furste man at reseyvid vs so wele, luffid *þat* copp abown all oþ*er* thyngis; þ*er*for I tuke it fro hym for his gude, & gaff it vnto hym at reseyvid vs *with* ill will, at he may resayfe his mede in þis werlde. And our thrid oste *servand* *þat* I drownyd, he was purposid als tite as he had comm*en* home, to hafe slayn his maister. And so I delyverd our gude oste fro dead, & þe toder fro manslaghter, at his punyssment myght be les in hell. And our iiij hoste, befor he had a childe, did grete almos dede, bod als sone as his childe was born, he *with*drew his hand, & þoght to be covatus & gadir gudes vnto his childe. And þ*er*for I hafe taken fro hym þe cauce of his covatice, at he may be as he was befor. And þe saule of þe in*n*ocent childe I hafe putt in Paradice." And when þe h*er*mett hard þis, he thankid God & tuke his lefe at þe aungell; & fro thens furth he was delyverd fro al man*er* of suche temptacion.

CCCCXII.

Iudiciu*m* humanu*m*. Iudicantes *secundum* apparenciam ex*teri*orem frequenter decipiuntur; vt patet.

Som tyme þ*er* was a kyng, & he garte make iiij kistis of tre. And ij of þaim he fillid full of stynkand banys of dead folk, & he garte cover þaim clene abown with platis of golde; & þe toder ij he fillid full of fyne precious stonys; & enoyntid þaim withoute with pykk & tarr. And þan he callid aforn hym all þe wyse men of his cowncell, and askid þaim whilk of þies war moste wurthie. And þai said þase at war coverd with golde, & þe toder þai reprovid & sett at noght. And þan þe kyng sayd; "I wiste wele ye walde say so." & þan he commawndid at oppyn þies kystis at war giltid; & so þai war, & þar come oute of þaim a fowle stynke & ane ill. And þan þe kyng said; "This is a figur of þaim þat er cled withoute with gay aray, and within er full of syn & ill dedys." And he garte oppyn þe toder, and þer come oute a swete smell at all men myght fele. And þan þe kyng sayde, "This is a figur of þaim þat er cled with feble clothis withoute, & within hase a grete fayrnes in þer sawle, & er full of gude warkis."

Iudicare non debent religiosi seculares. Infra de religiosis *et* supra de Basilio.

CCCCXIII.

Iudicandum non est de proximis eciam peccatoribus.

We rede in 'Legenda Iohannis Elemosinarij' of a yong man þat ravisshid a non. And when clerkis broght þis man befor Johannes Elemosinarius, þai reprovid hym & said he was wurthi to be cursid as he þat had slayn ij sawlis, þat was to say, bothe his & hurs. And þis holie man, Iohn, snybbid þaim, & said; "Not so brether, not so! ffor I sall shew you ye do ij synys; ffurst ye do agayns þe commandment of God þat sais; 'Nolite iudicare.' And þe secund, [*ye wote noght*[1]] whethir þai forthynk þer syn & hafe done penans þerfor or noght, nor whethir þai contynue in syn to þis day or noght."

Iudicium plurimorum aliquando comprobatur. Infra de suspicione.

Iudicando aggrauantes facta aliorum aliquando eciam visibiliter puniuntur. Supra de contricione, iij.

[1] Harl. MS. "secundo, quia nescitis pro certo si usque hodie peccent aut peniteant."

Iudici*um* medicor*um* de infirmis frequenter no*n* evenit. Supra de Basilio, ij.

CCCCXIV.

Iudicij vltimi aduentu*m* inc*er*tu*m* est ho*m*ini*bus* quantu*m* ad tempus.

We rede of a husbandman þat on a tyme went fro home, & he lefte behynd hym to kepe his place iij servandis, and he tolde none of þai*m* when he wolde com home. So emang þies iij servandis þ*er* movid a question of þe com*m*yng home of þ*er* maister, when it sulde be. And one said he wolde com home sone, & þe secund said nay, it wolde be lang or he come home. And þe iij said; "Forsuthe I wote neu*er* when he will com home." And so it is c*er*tayn at þe thrid said þe moste trew. And so it is of þe laste day, þe day of dome; we wote wele it mon com, bod we wote neu*er* when, nor what tyme.

CCCCXV.

Iudiciu*m* vltimu*m* debet timeri.

We rede of a kyng þat traveld be þe way wit*h* his baronage in a gay kyngis charyott. So hym happend to mete ij men cled in hevie clothyng, whilk þ*at* war ill hewid, & had pale facis, and þe kyng come down oute of his chariott & wurshuppid þai*m*. And his baronage tuke it to ill, & be þ*er* cowncell his bruther resond hym þ*er*for. And in þat realm þis was þe custom, þat vnto þe yate of hym þat sulde be iugied vnto dead, sulde þe kyngis messanger be sent befor, to make ane oyas. And when þai come home þe kyng garte þ*at* be done befor his bruther yate. And þat done, his bruther & his wife & his childer come in a mornyng clothyng vnto þe kyng, wepand & makand sorow. And þan þe kyng spak vnto his bruther & sayd; "O, þou fule! If þou hafe dred þe bedell of þi bruther, whome þou knowis þou trispasid no3t vnto, how durste þou take on hand to chalange me becauce I mekend me befor þe bedels & þe messangiers of allmighti God

whome þat I know þat I hafe grevid many tymys & ofte, and þat grevuslie?"

Iudicio vlti*mo* reddit*ur* racio de om*n*ib*us*. S*upra* de ep*iscopo*, *et* inf*ra* de risu *et* de me*r*catore. Iudicio vlti*mo* reddet*ur* cuil*ibe*t iux*ta* op*era* sua[1].

CCCCXVI.

Iuliani Confessoris.

We rede how þat when Saynt Iulian was a yong man & went on huntyng, he pursewid on a tyme after a harte. & þis harte turnyd agayn & spak vnto hym, & sayd; "Thow þ*at* mon sla bothe þi fadir and þi moder, whar-to pursewis þ*ou* me?" And he had grete wonder here-of, and becauce þis sulde not happyn hym, he went away oute of a fer contreth & servid a wurthi prince: & he made hy*m* a knyght and gaff hym a warde, a grete gentylwom*m*an, vnto his wife. And his fadur & his moder at home, hafyng grete sorow þat he was gone oute of þe contrey fro þai*m*, went & soght hym many mylis. So on a tyme when he was furthe, be a sodan cace þai*m* happynd to com vnto his castell. And be wurdis at þai said þ*er*, his wyfe vnderstude at þai war fadir & moder vnto hur husband, be all þe p*ro*ces at sho had hard hur husband say. And when scho had made þai*m* wele to fare, sho laid þai*m* sam*en* in hur awn bedd; and þis Iulian come home sodanlie in þe mornyng & wente vnto his chambr, & fand þai*m* ij sam*en* in þe bed. And he, trowyng þat it had bene one þat had done avowtry wit*h* his wyfe, he slew þai*m* bothe and went his ways. & he mett his wife fro þe kurkward, and sho tolde hym how his fadir & his moder was com*m*en, & how sho had layd þai*m* in hur awn bedd. And þan he began to wepe & make sorow, & said; "Lo! þ*at* at þe harte said vnto me, now I a sarie wriche hafe fulfillid itt." & þan he went oute of contre & did penans, & his wyfe wolde neu*er* forsake hym. & þ*er* þai come vnto a grete watir, þ*er* many war p*er*isschid, and þ*er* he byggid a grete hostre;

[1] A Tale of Silvanus in illustration omitted from the English MS.

& all þat eu*er* come he herbard þai*m*, & had þai*m* ou*er* þis watyr. And þis he vsyd a lang tyme. So on a nyght aboute mydnyght, as he lay in his bed and it was a grete froste, he hard a voyce cry petifullie, & sayd; "Iulian! com & feche me owt, I pray the!" And he rase onone & went out þe watir, & þ*er* he fand a man þat was nerehand frosyn to dead, and he had hym out, & broght hym into his howse & refresshid hym, & laid hym in his awn bed & happid hym. And wit*h*in a little while he þat was in þe bed, þat semyd seke & like a leppre, ascendid vnto hevyn & sayd on þis man*er* of wyse; "Iulyan! Almighti God hase reseyvid þi penans. And wit*h*-in a little while ye bothe shall com vnto Hym." And wit*h* þat he vanysshid away. *et c⁹.*

CCCCXVII.

Iuramento aliquos compellere no*n* est bonu*m*.

We rede how on a tyme a gude, trew, innocent man lent vnto one of his neghburs a c*er*tan þing, & when he wold hafe had it agayn he said he had borowid none swilk on hym, & wolde nott giff hym it agayn. And he was co*m*pellid to swer þ*er*for, & sware; & þus þe gude, trew man loste it. So vppon þe same nyght þis man was ravisshid vnto þe dome of Almighti God. And he was askid on þis man*er* of wyse; "Whi hase þou made yone man to swer ane athe whilk þou knew was a fals athe?" And he ansswerd agayn & said; "For he gaynsaid me þe þing þat I lent hym." And þan þe iustis said vnto hym; "It had bene bettir to þe to hafe loste þi þing þan for to lat hym lose his saule." And þ*er* þe iusti*s* com*m*awndid þat for his truspas he sulde be bett. And wit*h* þat he wakend & grapyd his bakk, & it was passand sare & full of yeddyrs & wowndis as he had bene betyn. And þus his trispas, aft*er* he was þus amendid, was forgiffen hym.

CCCCXVIII.

Iurare sup*ra* reliq*u*ias *sanctorum* falsu*m* est p*er*iculosu*m*.

We rede how som tyme ij men war at debate, & þat grete; and þe iustis cuthe nott witt whethir of þai*m* was gyltie. And he broght þaim bothe vnto ane altar & garte þaim purge þaim be þer athe. And he besoght þe aposteƚƚ at aght þe altar to send hym̄ son̄ takyn̄ þat he mot knaw þe treuthe. And when̄ he þatt was giltie sware [1], he began̄ to wax aƚƚ seke & iƚƚ at ease. And þe iustis purseyvid it, & he said; "Owder is þis gude aposteƚƚ Petur passand mercefuƚƚ, or els he differs þis martyr. And þerfor," he said, "we wiƚƚ go vnto Pancrace grafe." And when̄ he þat was gyltie sware on̄ Pancrace grafe, he wold hafe takyn̄ his hand away bod he myght nott, bod it held hym̄ stiƚƚ. & *with*-in a little while after, þer he swelte. *et c*°. And so yit vnto þis day in þat [2] contrey þai swer yit vppon̄ Saynt Pancras tombe, and any þing be in varyans emang þaim.

Iuliani Apostate. Infra de *sancto et* de signo de vindicta *et* de vsu.

Iusticia aliqu*ando* temp*er*anda est. Sup*ra* de Iudice, iij.

Iusticie execuc*io* no*n* debet differri sine causa. Sup*ra* de iudice, iiij.

CCCCXIX.

Iustitia ecia*m* in p*ro*p*r*io filio debet excerceri.

We rede how on̄ a tyme, when̄ a son̄ o Traiane rade prowdlie þurgh þe cetie, hym̄ happend of raklesnes *with* his hors to kyƚƚ a wedow son̄; and þe wedow *with* mekiƚƚ sorow [*com̄*] & tellid Traian̄ þe Emperour. And he gaff þe wedow in-stede of hur son̄ his son̄, þat had done hur þe trispas, and magnified hur *with* riche giftis.

CCCCXX.

Iusticia *eciam* exer*c*eri debet in p*ro*p*r*iis parentib*us*.

Herkenwaldus [3] tellis of ane þat hight Bormar, þat was a noble man̄ and a myghti, & in dome he sett by no man̄. So on̄ a tyme

[1] Arund. MS. *et nichil* mali pass*us* esset, iudex, ei*us* malicie consci*us*, exclamauit; "Senior iste Petr*us* aut nimis mis*e*ricors est, aut iunioribus defert."

[2] MS. þan.

[3] MS. Harl. Herkyndaldu*s* de Bornayr*e*, vir nobilis, etc.

he feƚƚ seke & lay in his bed in his chambre, and as he lay he hard' in þe nexte chambr̄ by hym̄ grete cryyng*is* as it had bene of wom*m*en̄. And he spurrid' what it was & þai wold' not teƚƚ hym̄. And þan̄ he sent one of his childer þedur and warnyd' hym̄, a payn̄ of puttyng oute of bothe his een̄, to teƚƚ hym̄ þe treuth̄. And þan̄ he went & saw it & com̄ agayn̄, & wit*h* grete drede tellid' hym̄ what it was & said'; "Sur! my felow, your sister son̄, wold' þ*er* hafe opp*re*sid' a wom*m*an̄ & defowlid' hur, and þis was þe cauce of þe cry." And at þis wurd' he was gretely grevid', and bad ij of his knyghtis go & hang hym̄. And þai said' þai sulde, and went furth̄ & tolde þe yong man̄ what his eam̄ had bydden̄ þai*m* doo. And þai bad hym̄ wit*h*draw hym̄ oute of his eam̄ sight at he saw hym̄ not, & þai sulde teƚƚ hym̄ at þai had done as he bad þai*m* do; for þai durst not sla þis yong man̄. And wit*h*-in a few howris þai come agayn̄ vnto þ*er* maister, & tolde hym̄ þai had done as he com*m*anddid' þai*m*. And vppon̄ þe fifte day aft*er* þis yong man̄, trowyng þat his eam̄ had forgetten̄ þis trispas, putt oppyn̄ þe chambr̄-dure & lukid' in. And onone as þis seke man̄ saw hym̄, he callid' hym̄ vnto hym̄ & gaff hym̄ fayr language, & made hym̄ to sitt down̄ by hym̄. And sodanlie wit*h* his one arm̄ he gatt hym̄ aboute þe nekk, & held' hym̄; & wit*h* þe toder arm̄ he drew his knyfe & shewid' it in his throte & kyllid' hym̄. And aƚƚ þat was aboute wondred' þ*er*of & vgged þ*er*wit*h*. So his sekenes swagid' a littyƚƚ, & þan̄ he sent for þe bisshoꝑ Herkenwaldus[1], and he come wit*h* þe sacrament & shrafe hym̄, & howseld' hym̄ not[2]. & he made grete sorow & had grete contricion̄ in his harte for his syn̄. And in his confession̄ he spak no wurd' of þe slayng of his cussyn̄. And þe bisshoꝑ had grete m*er*vaƚƚ þ*er*of, & said'; "Whi layn̄ ye þe mansslaght*er* of your cussyn̄ at ye slew?" And he answerd' agayn̄ & said'; "Sur, was þat a syn̄?" & þe bisshop said', ya, it was a crueƚƚ syn̄. And þe seke man̄ answerd' agayn̄ & said'; "I am̄ a Iustis & hafe þe law in gou*er*nans, & nowder I deme it a syn̄, nor I wiƚƚ neu*er* aske God forgifnes þ*er*of." Þan̄

[1] Harl. MS. Ep*iscopus* uocat*us* cu*m* sacri*s* aduenit. Herbinbald*us*, cum multis lacrimis *et* cordis contric*i*one, om*n*ia peccat*a* sua confessus e*st*, tacita iuuenis interfect*i*one.

[2] MS. not *added above the line.*

þe bisshopp answerd & said; "I will neu*er* gyff you þe sac*r*ament or ye shryfe you þeroff." þan þis Iustis answerd hym agayn & said; "Non ex rancore, sed ex zelo iusticie *et* Dei timore illu*m* int*er*feci; I slew hym not of rankor nor of il will, bod for luff of rightwusnes & drede of God; ffor þ*er* was neu*er* man luffid his sister son bettyr þan I did hym. And þ*er*-for & ye deny me þe holi sac*r*ament þat is Goddis bodie, I betake bothe my body & my saule vnto þat holie sac*r*ament, þat is God Hym selfe." And þus þe bisshop went away & wulde not howsyll hym. And onone after, þis seke man sent for hym agayn. And when he come att hym, þis seke man bad hym luke in his box if þe sac*r*ament war þ*er*. And so he did & fande rigt not þ*er*in. þan þis seke man said vnto hym; "Lo! þat at ye denyed me, Almigtti God Hym selfe hase giffen me & not denyed me." And *with* þat he oppynd his mouthe, & þai mot se þe sac*r*ament þ*er*in; and þan he dyed. And þan þe bisshopp was ferd & had grete sorow herefor, & prechid þis in eu*er*-ilk place for a grete m*er*acle.

CCCCXXI.

Iuuentus facit ho*m*in*es* diligent*er* mulieres considerare.

We rede of a p*ro*feste of þe ordur of P*re*monstracence, on a tyme as he rade with a yong man, a bruther of his howse, þai*m* happend to mete a fayr yong damysell; & þis p*ro*feste stoppid his hors & haylsid hur honestelie, & sho stude still & lowtid vnto hym & thankid hym. And when sho was passid þai*m* a littyll, þis p*ro*feste þoght he wold prufe þis yong man & said vnto hym; "Me þoght þis was a passand fayr maydyn." & þis yong man answerd & said, so þoght hym. And þan þe p*ro*fest said agayn; "A thyng difformys hur hugelie, þat is sho hase bod one ey." And þe yong man said; "Sur, forsuthe sho hase bothe hur ene, ffor I behelde hur graythelie." And þan þe p*ro*fest said vnto hym; "And I sall considur þi bakk, ffor þou sulde be of so mekyll symeplenes, & þou met a wom*m*an þou suld not luke wheþ*er* sho had bothe hur een or bod þe tane." And þan he turnyd agayn vnto his monasterie & said vnto his brethir; "Ye repruvid me for I take no yong men furth *with* me." And þan he tellid þai*m* þe cauce, & snybbid þis yong man & chastid hym for his truspas.

Iuuenes puelle pulc*ri*tudi*n*em corporalem abscondere debent. Infra de temptacione *et* sup*ra* de abscondere.

Iuuenis no*n* debet p*re*fici mulierib*us*. Sup*ra* de carne.

CCCCXXII.

Karolus. De statura *et* vita Karoli regis.

This kyng Charlis was of a fayr statur, for he was viij fute long & wele shapyn & awfull to sight; & he was passand large of renys, & he was clenlie bothe in bely & in armys & had grete theis; & he was a passand wyse knyght & a bitt*er* & strong of lym. & his face was in lenthe oderhalfe palme (and his berd a fute long), & his nese emyddiste þ*er*of & halfe þat lenth. & his fored was a fute long, and he had een like a lyon þat shane as a p*re*cious stane, and his browis was a palm brede. And if he had bene wrathe & lukid on a man he wolde hafe flayed hym. And his gyrdyll was viij fute lang *with*-oute þat at hang. And he ete bod littyl brede, bod at ans he wolde ete a q*uarter* of a weddur, or ij hennys, or a guse, or a swyne shulder, or a pacok, or a crane, or a hale hare. And he wolde drynk bod esy wyne, bod if it war medlid *with* watir. & he was of suche strenthe þat, at a strake *with* his swerd, he wald cut in sonder ane armyd knyght syttand on a hors fro þe crown of þe hede vnto þe sole of þe fute, & his hors als; and he wolde lightlie breke iiij hors shone at ans, and he wold lifte eselie to his hede ane armyd knyght stondyng on þe luff of his hand. And he bare tables *with* hym þat he bare all his actis in. And he drank bod seldom mor þan thrise at his meat. And he luffid wele to ride and bere armys, and he made his doghters to be clothe-makers, & for to lere at spyn on þe rokk, at þai sulde nott be ydill. And at Coleyn he garte byg ij briggis our þe watir of Reine. And when he come to Rome he wold light a myle *with*-oute þe town, & go vnto þe cetie apon his fute, & kys eu*er*-ilk kurk dure, & giff grete rewardis vnto eu*er*-ilk kurk. And he delyverd þe Holie Lande oute of Saracens hand*is*, and come fro thens-ward be Constantynople; and he broght thens many wurthi relikk*is*, þ*at* is to say, parte of þe crown of our Lord, whilk þat florisshid in his syght, and ane of þe naylis þat our Lord was naylid vnto þe cros *with*, and His sudarie, & our Ladie sarke, and Saynt Symeon arm. And all þies he putt in a kurk of our Ladye þat he byggid, and he fowndid & byggid als many abbays as þ*er* was l*ett*res in þe Abce. And in eu*er*-ilk one of þai*m* he lefte a letter of golde. And at þe laste, when his son Lowis was crownyd, he was full of gude werk*is* & decesid, and was berid at Aquis Gr*anum* in a kurk of our Ladye þat he byggid. And yit or he dyed he callid samen all his p*re*lattis, & gaff þai*m* all his tresurs to distribute þai*m* whar þai*m* þoght nede emang þ*er* kurkis.

CCCCXXIII.

Kat*er*ine Virginis.

Som tyme þ*er* come a monk of Rothomagence vnto þe monkes & þe abbay þat is on þe Mownte of Synay, and þ*er* he abade in s*er*ves of God & Saynt Katryn vij yere. And he was a passand devoute man; and he prayed evur vnto Saynt Katryn at he mott hafe som relykk of hur bonys. And sodanlie, as he satt at his prayers, þ*er* was putt in his hand, at he wiste nevur how come, hur little fynger; and he thankid God þ*er*of, & Saynt Katryn, & had it home vnto his monast*er*ie, and þ*er* it is wurshuppid vnto þis day.

CCCCXXIV.

It*erum* de S*ancta* Kat*er*ina.

We rede of a man þat was passand devoute vnto Saynt Katryn, & made his prayers speciallie vnto hur[1] a long while & besoght hur to helpe hym. So aft*er*werd he forgatt hur, & made nott his

[1] MS. hym.

prayers nor his offrand' vnto hur, nor did hur nott wurshup as he was wunte to doo, bod cesid' þeroff. So on a tyme as he was in his prayers he fell on slepe, and hym þoght þat he saw in a vision a grete multitude of virgyns goyng on a raw by hym. And emang þaim ane þat was passand' shynand' & fayr forby all þe toder, when sho come nere hym sho coverd' hur face þat he sulde not se hur, and so sho passid' away by hym & he mot se all þe toder facis bod hurs. And he had grete mervell what sho was at shynyd' so forbe all þe toder, & hid hur face þat he sulde not se hur. And one of þaim, when he spurryd what sho was, tolde hym at sho was Katryn, whilk þat he was wunte to know & to do wurshup to. "And becauce," sho said, "at þou hase now forgettyn hur & giffes none almos-dede in wurshup of hur, nor makis no prayer vnto hur nor wurshuppis her noȝt as þou was wunte to do, þerfor sho covers hur face when sho passis by the, att þou sulde nott know what sho was becauce þou had forgetten to know hur." *et c*ꝰ.

CCCCXXV.

Labor manuum est necessarius.

Arsenius all his life-tyme he vsid' at sitt & wurk a crafte *with* his handis, & he had evur so mekill þoght of þe Passion of our Lord, þat he had alway in his bosom a clothe to wype his ene *with*, he wepid' so when he thoght þeron. And all þe night he wolde be in his prayers & slepe nott, & in þe mornyng when he was wery for wakyng & liste slepe, þan he walde say þus; "Com, þou vnthrifti servand, slepe!" And so sittand' he wold' slepe a while, and þan onone he wolde rise & say; "Itt sufficis vnto a monk, & he had neuer so grete labur, to hafe a nyght slepe ans in a yere, or ilk nyght to hafe ane howr slepe."

CCCCXXVI.

Laborem in presenti Deus reddet in futuro, *et* quanto plus laborauerunt, tanto magis merentur. *et c*ꝰ.

We rede of ane hermet þat dwelte in wildernes, and þe watir was passand farr fro his cell. And on a tyme as he went for watir he wex irk, & sett hym down & said; "Whatt nedis me þus to labur when I may dwell harde be þe watir & I will?" And alssone he was war of a man þat folowed after hym & tellid his fute-steppis, and he askid hym & said; "What erte þou?" And he said agayn; "I am þe aungell off God sent for to nowm*er* þi fute-steppis, at þi mede may a nod*er* day be rewardid vnto þe aft*er* þat þi labur is." And þan þis h*er*mett *with* a strong wytt removid his cell v myle ferrer fro þe watir. *et c*[9].

CCCCXXVII.

Lac*r*imar*um* habu*n*dancia multu*m* valet ad co*m*passione*m*.

On a day when S*anct*a [*Maria*] de Oginiez[1] satt þinkand of þe benefice of Almighti God, how largelie he gaff þai*m* vnto mans kynd, sho tuke suche a co*m*punccion & fell opon such a wepyng, þat as sho went abowte in þe kurk men mot hafe folowd hur steppis be þe confluens of þe teris of hur een þat fell down on þe payment, vnto so mekull þat a long tyme sho mot nowder luke on þe crucifyx nor speke, nor yitt here no noder speke, of þe Passion of Criste, þatten evur sho fell in swone as sho had bene dead. & þ*er*for to restrene hur wepyng sho lefte thynkyng of þe manhede of Criste & toke hur to vmbethynkyng of His godded, at be þinkyng þ*er*of sho mott take a comfurth. Nevur-þe-les hur wepyng was evur mor & more when sho thoght of His godhed, als mekull as it was when sho thoght of His manhede. And þus hur sorow was renewid and hur sawle prikkid *with* a swete co*m*punccion. *et c*[9].

CCCCXXVIII.

Laborare debet monachus vt cogitaciones malas euadat.

Paulus H*er*emita, þat was a moste p*r*ovid man emang alde fadurs, on a tyme when he liffid in wildrenes, & had bod esi fude bod of þe frute of þe palm tre, and if he wroght oght *with* his handis no man wolde giff hym noght þ*er*for becauce he was so fer fro townys & no man come nere hym, becauce he wold somwyse be

[1] MS. S*ancta* Deoginiez.

occupyed ilka day, he wald gaddur sam*en* a grete meneya of palmelevis & bryn þai*m*, in exsample þat he did som bodele labur for his sustentacion; *pro*vand be þatt a monk myght not be in a place *with*-oute laboryng *with* his handis, or els he mot not esskape many ill thoghtis & vnthrifti. *et* c⁹.

CCCCXXIX.

Lacrimar*um* impetus retineri no*n* possu*n*t quia flante sp*irit*u vehementi fluu*n*t aque.

On a day befor þe Gude Fryday, [1] Maria de Oginiez, when þe passion of Allmyghti God neghid nere, sho þoght sho wold suffer a passion hur selfe in wurshup of His passyon; and sho fell vpon a grete wepyng & a sorow & a syghyng þ*er*for. And so as sho sat þus wepand in þe kurk, a preste come to hur & blamyd hur & bad hur lefe hur wepyng & say hur *pra*yers in sylens. And sho, knowyng wele enogh at sho mot not forbere wepyng, rase vpp & went furth of þe kurk and hid hur in a *pri*vay place far thens; & þ*er* sho wepid & besoght Almighti God in hur *pra*yers þat he wolde shew vnto þis preste þat a man may not restren hym fro wepyng when it flewis vppon be grace of þe Holie Gaste. And on a day as þis preste was att mes, be prompyng of þe Holie Gaste he fell on suche a wepyng þat he was nerehand strangled þ*er*-*with*. And ay þe mare at he laburd to restrene hym þe more he wepyd, vnto so mekull at nott alonelie hym selfe, bod also his buke & all þe altar clothis war all bod water *with* his wepyng. And aft*er*ward þis holie maydyn come vnto þis preste and teld hym all þis als playnlie as sho had sene it hur awn selfe, & said vnto hym; "Now ye hafe lernyd be exp*er*iens þat a man may not *with*-draw hym fro wepyng for þe passyon of Almighti God, when he thynkys þ*er*on & is movid þ*er*to be the Holie Gaste."

Lacrime contricionis impetrantur or*ationi*b*us* san*c*tor*um*. Infra de Or*ati*one.

Laicus no*n* debet stare in choro *et* audire diuina. Sup*r*a Ambrosij.

[1] MS. *has another* when *here.*

CCCCXXX.

Lantgrauius Lowicus.

We rede how þat þis Lantgrauius Lowicus was a passand grete tyrand and a mysdoer. And agayn þat he sulde dye he com*mawndid þaim* at was aboute hym þat als tyte as he was dead þai sulde clethe hym in a monk*is* cowle of þe Ceustus ordur, bod not or he war dead; & so þai did. And when he was so cled, one of his knyghtis lukid opon hym & said þus in skorn; "Lo! hym þis is not now like my lord in all his v*er*tues, ffor he was a wurthi knyght, & now he is a passand gude monke & kepis his sylence passand wele." So his sawle was broght vnto þe *prince* of Hell syttand opon þe pytt bra, & he held a copp in his hand & said vnto hym; "Welcom, our wele-belufid frend! Shew hym," he said, "your chawmers!" And belife was shewid hym all þe paynys. And þan he sayd vnto hym agayn; "Drynk, frend, of my copp!" And þuf all he war not [1] welewillid þ*er*to, yit he was co*m*pellid to drynk; and als sone as he had done þ*er* come oute stynkkand flawmys oute of his ene, his nease-thrillis, & his eris. And after þis he said vnto hym; "Now þ*ou* sall se my pitt þat is wit*h*outen bothom." And belife it was opynd & he casten þ*er*in.

Latroni possu*n*t adaptari que *supra* dicuntur de ffure, et infra de p*re*done *et* raptore.

Laudacio. Lauda*n*t multi alique*m* in co*m*par*ac*io*n*e alt*er*ius. S*upr*a de co*m*par*ac*ione.

CCCCXXXI.

Laudem appetu*n*t aliqui de bonis op*er*ib*us*.

We rede how on a tyme, when a man spirrid Macharius whi he sufferd so mekull honger in wyldernes, þat [2] mot wekelie hafe

[1] Not *omitted, and added above the line.*

[2] Harl. MS. qui in monasterio ebdom*adis* integris abstinens non sensisse esuriem.

byddyn̄ in his abbay & suffred no honger, he answerd agayn̄ & said; "For here is no wittnes of þi faste þat sulde nurissh þe *with* lovyng, nor at mot susteyn̄ þe. And þ*er* mans serves & refresshyng of a vayn̄ glorie makis þe fatt."

Laude*m* nolu*n*t aliqui acq*u*irer*e* p*er* facta enormia. Inf*r*a de memoria.

Laudes adulatoris contempnu*n*t sapientes. Sup*r*a de adulacione.

Laudem fugiu*n*t aliqui ne in ea dilectentur. Inf*r*a de vanitate.

CCCCXXXII.

Laurencij Martiris.

We rede in '*Legenda* Lomb*ardica*,' of Eusodia þat was doght*er* vnto Theodose þe Emp*erour*, how sho was vexid *with* a fend, and was had vnto Constantynople to þe body of Saynt Stephan to be curid. And þis fend spak *with*in hur & said; "I will not pas oute on̄ hur bod if Stephan com̄ to Rome, for so it is þe apostels will." And so, be þe consent of þe pope & þe Emp*erour*, þe bodie of Saynt Stephan was sent vnto Rome be þe Grekis, *with* cou*n*and at þai suld bryng vnto Constantynople þe bonys of Saynt Laurens. And when̄ þai come at Rome *with* hym̄ & sett down̄ his bodie in eccl*es*ia S*anct*i Petri ad Ui*ncu*la, þase at sulde bere hym̄ myght gett hym̄ no ferrer. And þan̄ þis fend cryed agayn̄ in þe maydyn̄ & sayd; "Ye labur in vayn̄, for he hase not chosyn̄ his seate here, bod att his bruther Laurens." And þai bare þe bodye thedur, & onone þe maydyn̄ was hale. And Saynt Laurens, as he had bene ioyfull of his bruther com*m*yng, remowid hym̄ vnto þe ta side of þe sepulcr, & left þe toder syde voyde vnto his bruther. And þan̄ þe Grekis putt þ*er* handis to take Saynt Laurence away, & þai fell down̄ vnto þe erth as þai had bene fonde. And *with*-in x dayes after þai war all dead. And þan̄ a voyce was harde in Rome þat sayde; "O, felix Roma! *et c*. O! þou happy Rome, þat sparris bothe in a grafe þe bodie of Saynt Laurens þe Hyspany, & þe bodie of Saynt Stephan of Ier*usa*lem."

CCCCXXXIII.

Laurencius accusat facientes sibi iniuriam.

We rede in þe 'Meracles of our Ladie,' how at Rome þer was a yong man þat hyght Stephan, þat vsid gladlie to take giftis & so for to forbar right of many folke in þe law. And he wronguslie tuke away & held in possession vnto hym selfe iij howsis of Saynt Laurens kurk, and a garthyn of Saynt Agnes kurk. So hym happend to be seke & sulde dye, and hym þoght he was broght befor þe iugement of Almighti God. And onone as Saynt Laurens saw hym, he come vnto hym *with* a grete indignacion & iij tymys he thrustid hym be þe arm, & þat sare, & crusid it att it warkid gretlie *with*. And Saynt Agnes nor none oþ*er* vyrgyn wold nott ans luke on hym, bod turnyd þ*er* facis fra hym-ward. And þan þe iustis gaff a sentans of hym & said; becauce he tuke oþ*er* mens gude fro þai*m* & selde þe treuth for takyng of giftis, he sulde be putt into þe place at Iudas þe traytur was in. And þan come Sanctus P*ro*iectus, whome þis Stephan had had grete deuocion to in his life, & p*ra*yed Saynt Laurens & Saynt Agnes to forgiff hym. And so our Ladye & þai p*ra*yed for hym vnto þis iustis, to so mekull he g*ra*untid þat his saul [*sul*]de[1] goo agayn vnto his body, & þ*er* he sulde do penans xxx^{ti} dayes. And our Ladie gaff hym in com*ma*ndment þat he sulde daylie say þis psalme, 'B*ea*ti immaculati,' whils he liffid. And when his saule come vnto his bodie agayn, his arm was als bla & als sare *with* þe thrustyng of Saynt Laurens as he had suffred it evyn on his body, whilk takyn was apon hym ewhils he liffid. And þat at he had wronguslie takyn away, he restorid itt and did penans þ*er*for. & opon þe xxx^{ti} day he passid vnto Almighti Godd.

CCCCXXXIV.

Laurencius se honorantes in necessitate adiuuat.

We rede in '*Legenda* Lomb*ardica*' when þe Emp*er*our Henrie and Ranegunde[2] his wyfe abade alway clene vi*r*gyns, þurgh

[1] MS. his saulde goo. [2] MS. Ranegude.

instigacion of þe fend, he suspecte his wyfe *with* a knyght, & made hur for to gang on hate coles, barefute, xv fute lang. And als sone as sho began to ga sho said in þis man*er* of wise; "Lord Criste! As þou knowis that I am vnfylid bothe of Henry my husband & all oþ*er*, so I beseke þe helpe me!" & *with* þat þis Emp*er*our was esshamyd & gaff hur on þe cheke *with* hys nefe. And þan a voyce sayde vnto hur; "Marie þat is a mayden hase delyverd þe becauce þou erte a mayden." And þan sho passid þurgh all þis grete fire vnhurte. And eft*er*ward, agayn þis Henry sulde dye, a grete multitude of fendis come be þe cell of ane h*er*mett, and he oppynd his wyndow & askid one of þai*m* what þai wer. And þai answerd agayn & said; "We er a legion of fendis þat bownys vs vnto þe dead of þe Emp*er*our Henrie, to luke if we can fynd any thyng of owrs in hym." And he chargid hym to com agayn by hym & tell hym how þai had done. And he come agayn & tolde hym þai had not sped, & said; "Ewhils þe fals suspecte þat he had in his wife & all his od*er* ill dedis war weyed in a weyscale *with* his gude dedis, þat swythyn Laurens broght a grete hevy pott of gold. And when his evull dedis was like to hafe bene þe heviar, he kest it in-to þe tother weyscale, & it was hevyar & weyed all down. & *with* þat," he said, "I was angrie, and starte vnto þe pott & brakk of þe tone ere þ*er*off; and þis pott was a chales at þis Henre had giffen vnto Ceustus ordur, in wurshup of Saynt Laurens. And becauce it was so grete, he garte make it ij eris, at it mot be liftid vp by." And þis Emp*er*our was dede þe same tyme as þe h*er*mett had knowlege. And he garte luke þe chales and [*þe*] ta ere wantyd, as þe fend sayd.

CCCCXXXV.

Leonis Pape.

We rede in his 'M*er*acles[1]' how Leo þe pape opon a Pace day said mes in a kurk of our Ladie, and as he was howsylland cristen men, ilkone in þ*er* ordur, a c*er*tan wom*m*an kissid his hand, þurgh

[1] Latin MSS. Ex Miraculis Beate Virginis.

þe whilk he had a huge temptacion in his flessh. And so þis holie man þoght he wolde venge þis temptacion in hym selfe, & þe same day þat hand at slanderd hym so, privalie he cut it off & keste it fro hym. And in þe mene while þer rase emang þe common peple a gret murmor whi þe pope said not mes as he was wunt to doo. Than þis Leo made his prayer vnto our Ladie, Saynt Marie, & commytt hym all vnto hur providens; and sho onone come vnto hym & with hur holie handis sho restorid his hand agayn vnto his arm, & commawndid hym for to go furth & do his mes, & offer þe sacrament vnto hur son as he was wunte to do. And than þis Leo prechid befor all þe pepyll, & tolde þaim what had happend hym, and shewid þaim his hand how it was cott off, & þorow our Ladie restorid agayn vnto his arm. *et c.*

CCCCXXXVI.

Leonardi Confessoris.

We rede in his Legend how þer was a knyght presond in Bretany, & he made his prayers speciallie vnto Saynt Leonard to helpe hym. And onone, at all men saw & might know hym, Saynt Leonard apperid in myddest of þe mute-hall, & went into þe preson & brak his fetters & put þaim in þe mans hand, & opynlie emang all men he broght hym furth þorow þaim. And all þat saw had so mekull wonder þerof þat þai war passynglie astonyd.

CCCCXXXVII.

Legatum male custoditum amittitur.

We rede how som tyme þer was a man þat when he dyed bewytt vnto iij sonnys þat he had ane ass, so þat one suld labur it a day, and a noder a noder day, and þe iij þe thrid day, & at þai sulde vpholde it & giff it meate emang þaim. And opon þe furste day þe eldeste bruther had þis ass, & laburd it sore and gaff it nothyng to eate, ffor he vmthoght hym þat his medyll bruther suld hafe it þe secund day & he wolde giff it meate enogh. And on þe secund day þis secund' brother had þis ass, & laburd' it sore, & gaff it no mor' meat no mor' þ*an* his furste bruther did'; ffor he vmthoght hym̄ þ*at* his thrid bruther, þat was richest of þai*m* ałł, sulde hafe it oñ þe thrid' day, & he said' he wold' giff it enogħ. And vppoñ þe thrid day þe iij bruther had it, & laburd' it & gaf it no meate, ffor he vmthoght hym̄ þat his ij brethir had bothe had' it, & þai had giffeñ it meat enogħ, for þai war richer meñ þañ he. And þus for grete labur & no sustentacioñ þis ass dyed'; & þus for þ*er* covatis none of þai*m* had gude oñ itt.

Legatarij debent p*ro* legatoribus[1] orare. Sup*ra* de elemosina, xi[2].

Leo virginem defendebat a corrupcione. Inf*ra* de vi*r*ginitate, iij.

CCCCXXXVIII.

Leo custodiebat asinu*m* ex p*re*cepto be*a*ti Ieronimi.

Oñ a day wheñ Saynt Ieroñ satt *with* his brethir, sodanlie þ*er* come a haltand lioñ & went into þe abbay. And onone as þe brethir saw hym̄ þai fled ałł, and Saynt Ieroñ rase & mett [*him*] as he had bene a geste. And þis lyoñ lifte vp̄ his sare fute & lete hym̄ se it, and he callid' his brethir & garte one of þai*m* wassh it, & layd' salvis & medcyns þ*er*to, made of h*er*bys, & onone þis lioñ was hale and was als meke as a hors. And Saynt Ieroñ chargid hym̄ þat he suld' evur[*e*]day take charge of & kepe ane ass þ*at* broght hym̄ & his brethir feweł fro þe wud, & he wolde eu*er*ilk day at dew tyme hafe þis ass of þe felde & bryng it hame, & kepid hur surelie. So oñ a day as þis ass was pasturand', þis lyoñ liste wele slepe, & layde hym̄ downe & feł apoñ a sad slepe; and þ*er* come m*er*chandes *with* camels be þis ass away, & saw at no bodie was stirrand', & þai tuke þisass *with* þai*m*. And wheñ þai war gone, þis lyoñ wakend' & myssyd' his felow, & soght here & þ*er* romyand' & couthe not fynde hit. And wheñ he saw he cuthe not fynd' it, he went home ałł hevylie vnto þe Abbay, & stude at

[1] MS. legatarijs. Lat. MSS. legatoribus. [2] MS. iij.

þe yate oferrom & durste com no ner becauce he broght not hame þe ass; & he durste not com in as he was wunte to do. And þe monk*is*, when þai say hym at he come home & broght not þe ass *with* hym as he was wunt to do, & þai trowed he had etyn hur, & here-for þai *with*drew his meate fro hym at þai war wunte to giff hym & wold not giff hym it, bod bad hym go & ete þe hynder-end of þe ass as he had etyn þe for-end. And þan Saynt Ierom chargid þis lyon to do þe ass offes, & to bryng home wod on his bak daylie to þe kychyn as it was wunt to do; & mekelie he did it as he was com*m*andid & gruchid nothyng þ*er*w*ith*. So on a day as þis lyon was walkand be his one, he was war of þies m*er*chandis com of ferrom *with* þ*er* camels ladyn, & þis lyon ass[9] at he kepid emang þai*m*. And *with* a grete romying he ran opon þai*m*, & all þe men fled & war passand ferd, and all þies camels & þis ass, bothe *with* m*er*chandis as þai war ladyn, he broght vnto þe Abbay. And when Saynt Ierom saw, he com*m*awndid his brethir to giff þies catell meate, and þan to abyde þe will of God. & þan þis lion come into þe abbay as he was wunte to do, & wente to Saynt Ierom & syne fro monk to monke, & fawnyd þai*m* & lowtid vnto þe erth, evyn as he had askid þai*m* forgyfnes. And þan þe m*er*chandis come & knew þ*er* fawte & askid Saynt Ierom forgyfnes; & he forgaff þai*m* when þai confessid how þai did, & lete þai*m* hafe all þ*er* gudis agayn. And þai gaff þe abbay to amendis a messur of oyle, and band þai*m* & þ*er* successurs for evur more yerelie to giff vnto þ*at* abbay þe same messur, and so þai do yerelie vnto þis day.

Lena impetrat quod petit. Infra de or*atio*ne.
Letania cantari[1] debet. Sup*r*a de cantu, vj.

CCCCXXXIX.

Leprosus. Leprosis seruire est deo se*r*uire.

Theobaldus, þat was þe noble Erle of Campanye, *with* grete deuocion wold visit layser howsis,' and befor his castell-yate þ*er* dwelte a layser. And þis lord had in condicion, þat als ofte as

[1] MS. cantaria.

he come be his howse away he wolde go in & wassh hys fete & giff hym̄ almos. So it happend afterward þis layzer dyed & was berid, & þe erle wiste [*not*]. So hym̄ happend afterward com̄ be þis howse & wiste not at þe layzer was dead, bod he went in as he was wunt to do, & þ*er* he fand, not þe layzer, bod Almyghti God in þe layser clothyng, and he did hym̄ *ser*ves as he was wunte to do; and in his harte he felid a grete swetnes. And when̄ he was gone furth, one of his men̄ tolde hym̄ þ*at* þis layzer was dead & berid in suche a place. And als tite as he harde þis, þis trew man̄ thankid Almiȝtty God, whome þ*at* he adlid to serve in His awn̄ pr*e*sens; and afterward he *ser*vid Hym̄ ofter in his membres. *et c*9.

CCCCXL.

Leprosis seruire credens deo servit.

In Frawnce þ*er* was a man̄ of grete mekenes & m*er*cie, & inspeciall vnto laysers, vnto so mekull þat wharesom-evur he mett þai*m* he wolde giff þai*m* almos. So on̄ a tyme hym̄ happynd to mete a man̄ þat was passand horrible lepre, & wolde hafe giffen̄ hym̄ almos. And he said; "Nay, I will no money. Bod I pray þe wype þe filthe fro my nease." And þis man̄, furste wit*h* his fynger & syne wit*h* his sarke skirte, wypid it als softlye as he cuthe. Þan̄ þe layser man̄ sayd; "I may not suffer so mekyll sharpnes, & þerfor I pray þe lykk it away wit*h* þi tong." And he neu*er*-þe-les, þuf all his natur vggid þ*er*-wit, yit he lykkid it away wit*h* his tong. And sodanlie oute of þe layzer nese in-to his mouthe þ*er* fell ij precious stonys [1], & furthwit*h*, evyn̄ at he say, þis layser stevend vp̄ vnto hevyn̄. *et c*9.

Leprosi sp*ecie* deus hospicio recipitur. S*upr*a de hospicio.

Leticia*m* aliqu*ando* gerit paup*er*tas, *et* diuicia tristiciam. S*upr*a de diuicijs.

Lex. De Lege, *et* c9 [2].

[1] Lat. MSS. Subito gemma preciosissima in os suum de naribus leprosi cecidit, et, ipso uidente, ad celum ascendit.

[2] A discourse on Law *omitted here.*

CCCCXLI.

Leges imp*er*ator*um* debent obseruari.

Commestor Mallius Torquetus[1], þat was a conselur of Rome, when he had betyn his son wit*h* a wand, he strake hym wit*h* ane ax, becauce he faght wit*h* his enmys agayns þe com*m*andment of þe concelurs; & neu*er*-þe-les ȝit he ouer-come þai*m*. *et c*9.

Leges quas imp*er*atores faciunt *eciam* ipsi observare debent. Inf*ra* de p*re*lato.

CCCCXLII.

Lib*er*alitas. De Lib*er*alitate.

Lantigonus[2], þat was kyng of Macydony, on a tyme when a pure man[3] askid hym a peny, he answerd agayn & said þat it was mare þan a pure man[4] sulde aske. And þan he askid hym a halpeny, & he answerd agayn & said; "It is les þan it semys a kyng for to giff." And Senec stude by & saw, & he said þis was a fowle cauillacion, when he mot nowder se þe kyng giff þe pure man a peny, nor þe pure man resayfe a halpeny of þe kyng; ffor þ*er* is no þing so mekull made of as is þat þyng þat a man giffis wit*h* his gude wyll. *et c*9.

CCCCXLIII.

It*er*um de Lib*er*alitate.

We rede of þe Emp*er*our Titus, how þat he was so lib*er*all of gifte þat on a day when no man come & askid hym noght, he sayd at evyn vnto hys men; "O, ye frendis! This day hafe I loste!"

Lib*er*acio. Lib*er*at Maria incarc*er*atos. Inf*ra* de Maria, ij.

[1] Harl. MS. Manli*us* Torquat*us*.
[2] Lat. MSS. Antigonus.
[3] Lat. MSS. amic*us*.
[4] Lat. MSS. plus *es*se q*u*am amic*us* deb*er*et petere.

Lib*er*ant diu*er*si *sancti* diu*er*sos. S*upra et* inf*r*a in locis suis.

Libido. Infra de muliere.

Lingua mala multu*m* est detestabilis. S*upr*a de exco*mmuni*caci*one*.

Lingua aduocati est venalis. S*upr*a de Aduocato, iiij.

Lingua mala turbat multos. S*upr*a de Iracu*n*dia, iij.

CCCCXLIV.

Locucio. Loqui no*n* debent religiosi de reb*us* p*er*tinentib*us* [1] ad uitam.

Whe͞n a meneya [2] of brether war at a calacio͞n & þai spak to-gedur of þingis þat p*er*teynyd' vnto þe bodie, þ*er* was one alde ma͞n emang þai*m* þat hyght Corpreys. & he rase & went away, & knokkid' o͞n his breste & said'; "Wo is þe, Corpres! For þou levis þase þingis þat God com*m*andid' þe, þat is to say, meknes & paciens & sike oþ*er* thingis lyke, and [3] spekis nothyng of swilk þingis as God askis of þe." *et* c⁹.

CCCCXLV.

Loquend*um* est de reb*us* p*er*tinentib*us* ad saluaci*on*em a*nim*e *et* edificaci*on*em p*r*ox*i*mi.

O͞n a tyme whe͞n Saynt Petur p*r*echid', þ*er* was so͞m þat wolde mofe vnto hy͞m vnp*ro*fitable questions, & þa͞n he wolde say vnto þai*m*; "Þe tyme is shorte, & þe dome of God drawis nere, & þ*er*foʳ befoʳ al thyngi*s* latt vs seke how & of what man*er* of wise we sulde doo to gett vs eu*er*-lastand life."

CCCCXLVI.

Loquentes multu*m* v*er*ba stulta puniu*n*tur.

Som tyme þ*er* was a no͞n þat was chaste of bodie, bod sho wold' nott restrene hur tong fro fowle langwage; so hur happend to dy

[1] MS. imp*er*tinentib*us*. Harl. MS. *as above*.

[2] MS. meneza.

[3] Harl. MS. et loqu*eri*s de hijs que de*us* no*n* requirit a te.

& be berid in þe kurk. And opon þe night after, he þat kepid þe kurk saw hur broght befor ane altar & cut in sonder evyn be þe myddeste. & þe [*tone*] parte was burnyd and þe toder parte putt in þe grafe agayn; and on þe morn þai mot se þe prynte apon þe m*er*byll stonys, like as a woman had bene bodelie burnyd þ*er*.

Loquendu*m* no*n* est indifferent*er* cora*m* om*n*ib*us*. Sup*ra* de augurio [1].

Loqui no*n* debemus de def*ectibus* alior*um*. Sup*ra* de iudicio, iij [2].

Loquendu*m* est semp*er* caute *et* no*n* est demon deno*min*andus. Su*p*ra de demone.

CCCCXLVII.

Loquendu*m* no*n* est nimis supe*r*be.

In þe iiij yere of Iustinyan was þ*er* ij bisshoppis, and þ*er* enmys come on þai*m* & pullid þ*er* tongis oute of þ*er* hedis. Afterward be revelacion þai wer restorid vnto þ*er* tongis & mot speke, & did many m*er*acles. So at þe laste þai began to wax prowde of speche, and onone, as God wold, þai wex bothe dom, & did neu*er* m*er*acles after. And Saynt Gregor tellis in his 'Dialoggis' þat þe tone of þai*m* fell vnto þe syn of lichorie, & her-for God deprivid hym of m*er*acles-doyng; and þe toder of þai*m* fell vnto pride, & loste all þe v*er*tue of his m*er*acles-doyng.

CCCCXLVIII.

Lucru*m* quod cito adquiritur cito expenditur.

Ther was som tyme in a cetie a passand curios barbur, and for eu*er*-ilk man þat he shufe he tuke a peny, and at þe weke-end he mot pay for his burd & putt in his purs ij or iij *shelyng*. So hym happend on a tyme to here tell of a nod*er* cete þat barburs tuke for ilk man shavyng in a shelyng, and he tuke his instrument*is*

[1] MS. augurrio. [2] MS. i.

wi*th* hym̄ & þoght he wolde go dwell þ*er*. Not-wi*th*stondyng, or he went, all þat evur he gatt of his wynnyng he spendid it & made hym̄ mery þ*er*wi*th*. So he come vnto þe toder cetie & sett vp his crafte, & on̄ þe furste day he gatt mekull money. And he was fayn̄ þ*er*of & wente vnto þe bowcherie & thoght to by hym̄ flessh vnto his supper, & it was spitefull dere, and so wi*th*-in a while he conseyvid þat, if all he tuke neu*er* so mekull for a mans shavyng, yit his meat & his drynke koste so mekill þat he mot not spare no sylu*er* bod spendid it eu*er* as he gatt it. And þan̄ he vmthoght hym̄ & said vnto hym̄ selfe; "I spend all my wynnyng of my meatt & my drynk & can̄ not safe a peny, þuf all I take a shelyng for a shavyng, and when̄ I tuke bod a peny for a shavyng, I couthe wele spar som̄ sylu*er* eu*er*-ilk day, & now I can̄ not so, for here I may not get my lyfelod." And he gatt his gere to-gedur & went agayn̄ vnto þe toder cetie & right not in his purs.

CCCCXLIX.

Ludus debet esse honestus.

When̄ Altibiades Socrasticus was wi*th* ane eame of his & lernyd þe vij scians liberall, his[1] eame gaff a tromper a trompe þat is callid Tibia, to thentent þat he sulde lern̄ his cossyn̄ to trompe þ*er*wi*th* & to syng þ*er*wi*th*, ffor in þat contre it was a commo*n̄* mynstralcy. And he sett þis trompe to his mouthe & began̄ to blaw, & it was foyste & ill-saverd & garte hym make grete chekis, & as hym̄ þoght, it deformyd his face when̄ he blew þ*er*in. And her-for he keste it fra hym̄ & brak it. And be exsample of hym̄, þat he luffid it nott, he chargid all þe contre þ*er* he dwelte afterward þat þai sulde neu*er* vse þat mynstralcie, and so þai vsid it neu*er* vnto þis day.

CCCCL.

Ludit miles ad taxillos cu*m* demone.

In þe Cetie of Susan̄, wi*th*-in þe dioces of Colan̄, þ*er* was a knyght, and he was so giffen̄ vnto playing at þe dice, at nyght

[1] MS. he.

& day he was evur redie to play *with* any þat wolde com̄; and he was passand fortunat in playing & temyd many mans purs. So on̄ a nyght þe devulƚ come in a mans liknes & desyrid' to play *with* hym̄, & he went in-to þe howse *with* hym̄, & a grete sakett fulƚ of mony in his hand', & þai played to-gedur to þis knyght had nere-hand' loste alƚ þe mony þat he had'. And þis knyght, when̄ he had loste, began̄ to wax angrie & said'; "Þou erte þe devulƚ, hope I." And þan̄ þe tod*er* said'; "Now we hafe played enoghe, and vs bus now go." And he tuke þe knyght be þe nekk & drew hym̄ oute þurgh̄ þe thakk of þe howse. And his body breste & his bowels cleuyd' on̄ þe sclathe stonys. And on̄ þe morn̄ his bowels was fon̄, bod what at wurthed of þe bodie cuthe neu*er* man̄ telƚ to þis day, & þai went & berid' his bowels.

Ludus aviu*m* in hoc sec*u*lo punitur. Sup*ra* de Aue.
Lupi confessoris. Supra de Amore.

CCCCLI.

Lupus puella*m* invasit.

We rede how on̄ a tyme a wulfe ou*er*come a damyselƚ & gatt hur be þe arm̄ in a town̄, & sho cryed' faste; & eu*er* when̄ sho cryed he wolde strene hur sore, & when̄ sho held' hur tong he sparid' hur. Notw*ith*stondyng he haylid' hur vnto þe wud' vnto a noder wulfe þat had a bane stykkand' in his throte, and he was gretely turment þer-*with* & he gapid' wyde. & þe[1] damyselƚ saw þe bane stik in his throte, & sho put in hur hand' in his mowthe & pullid' it oute. And he & his felow broght hur agayn̄ vnto þe town̄ safe & sownd', & lowtid vnto hir and went þ*er* wayes. *et c*⁹.

CCCCLII.

Lupa vindicauit quantu*m* potuit.

In companye scolers on̄ a tyme had remedy & went to play þai*m*, & þai fande in þe wud a wulfe den̄; & þ*er* was wulfe-whelpis

[1] *After* þe, j, *erased.*

þerin, bod þ*er* dam̄ was away. So one of þies scolers cut of all þe fete of þe wulfe-whelpis, and when̄ þe scolers was gone þe wulfe come vnto hur den̄ and fand hur whelpe fete cut of. & sho gat oute & folowid opon̄ þies scolers, and sho sewid alonelie on̄ hym̄ þat did þe dede. And he was passand ferd & clambe vp in-to a tre, and when̄ sho saw sho mot not gett hym̄, sho began̄ to skrape & grafe abowte þe rowte *with* hur naylis. & when̄ sho saw sho mot not so com̄ to hym̄, sho cryed & gaderd sam*en* a grete meneya of wulvis to helpe hur. And in þe mene-while þe scolers tolde men̄ in þe town̄, and þai come oute *with* clubbis and staffis & flayed þies wulvis[1] away, & broght þis scolar hame emyddeste of þai*m* all. Þe wulfis folowid þai*m* oferrom̄, bod sho alonelie come evur on̄ þai*m* & wolde not lett for þai*m* all, bod come rynand in emang þai*m* & gatt þis scolar be þe nekk, & onone sho werid hym̄. And þai fell vpon̄ hur & slew hur. *et c*.

CCCCLIII.

Lupor*um* more currit *et* vlulat aliquis.

Petrus de Lombardia tellis & says; "I saw ans a yong man̄ þat was born̄ in Fraunce & broght vnto he was at mans age[2], and he cuthe gang on̄ his fete & his handis as a beste and crye like a wulfe."

Lupanari expositam vi*r*ginem custodiui*t* deus. Inf*r*a de vi*r*gine.

CCCCLIV.

Luxuria multa mala facit.

In þe Cetie of Susace was þ*er* a wom*m*an̄ þat keste hur harte hugelie on̄ a clerk þat had fayr een̄, to hafe at do *with* hym̄, vnto so mekull at sho said vnto hym̄; "And þou will hafe at do *with* me all my gude sal be thyne." And he excusid hym̄ & wolde nott. And sho saw þat & went vnto þe iustis & accusid hym̄, & said he

[1] MS. wufvis.
[2] Harl. MS. educatus vt more lupor*um* semp*er* ad manus *et* pedes sciuit curr*er*e atq*ue* ululare.

wold' hafe oppressid' hur. And þe iustis sente for hym̄ & dampnu*m*[1] for lichori vnto p*ri*son̄. And sho co*n*tynod stiƚƚ in hur fals syn̄ & luste, & gatt a stye & clam̄ vp at a hy waƚƚ to a wyndow of þe p*ri*son̄, & clambe our & lepyd down̄ vnto hym̄ & laburd' hym̄ to hafe att do wi*th* hym̄, and he wolde not grawnt vnto hur. And als tyte as sho was fon̄ wi*th* hym̄ þai went & tellid' þe iudgies, and þai trowid' he had bene a wyche & vsid' sorcerye, & demyd' hym̄ to be burnyd', and so he was. & when̄ his ribbys was burnyd' þat men̄ myght se his longis, he began̄ to syng "Ave Maria," at aƚƚ folke hard'. And onone one of þe wom*m*ans cussyns putt a grete colle in his mouthe & said'; "I saƚƚ putt away þi p*r*ayers." & wi*th* þat he worod' hym̄; & his bonys war berid' in þe felde & did many grete m*er*acles. And now vpon̄ his grafe is þ*er* made a wurthi kurk.

Luxuriosa mulier. Infra de muliere, iiij.

CCCCLV.

Luxuriosa mulier co*n*ceptu*m* infante*m* necat.

We rede of a non̄ of þe dioces of Colan̄, and sho conseyvid' & bare a child' & when̄ it was born̄ she slew it. So aft*er*ward' hur happend faƚƚ seke & was bown̄ to dye, and sho shrafe hur of aƚƚ hur synys outtakyn̄ þis syn̄ of þe slayng of hur childe; and þan̄ sho dyed'. So afterward' sho apperid' vnto a cussyn̄ of hurs at p*r*ayed for hur, and sho bare in hur armys a burnande childe, & said'; "þis childe I conseyvid', & when̄ it was born̄ I slew it. & þ*er*for euer I mon̄ bere it abowte & it is a passand' byrnand' fyre vnto me. And if I had bene shrevyn̄ þ*er*of I had had grace, & now I mon̄ hafe none for I am̄ dampnyd'."

Luxurie pecc*atum* com*m*ittu*n*t *eciam* religiosi, vt hic *et* sup*r*a *et* inf*r*a diu*ersis* locis.

Luxuria religiosos religione*m* relinquere facit. Inf*r*a de Maria, vij.

[1] *For* dampnatus est?

CCCCLVI.

Luxuriosam mulierem diabolus ad infernum portauit.

We rede of a prestis concubyne, þat when sho was bown to dye sho cried opon þaim at was aboute hur with grete instans, & bad þaim gar make hur a payr of hy bottois & putt þaim on hur leggis for þai war passand necessarie vnto[1] hur, and so þai did. And opon þe night after þe mone shane bryght, and a knyght & his servand was rydand in þe feldis to-gedur, and þer come a womman rynand fast vnto þaim, cryand, & prayed þaim helpe hur. & onone þis knyght light & betaght his man his hors, & he kennyd þe womman wele enogh, & he made a cerkle abowte hym with his swerd, & tuke hur in vnto hym; & sho had nothyng on bod hur sarke & þies buttois. And belife he harde a blaste of ane vgsom horn at a hunter blew horrible, & huge barkyng of hundis, and als sone as þai hard, þis womman was passand ferde. And þis knyght spirrid hur whi sho was so ferd, & scho tellid hym all; and he light & tuke þe tressis of hur hare & wappid it strayte abowte his arm, & in his right arm he helde his swerd drawen. And belife þis hunter of hell come at hand, & þan þis womman said; "Lat me go, ffor he commys." And þis knyght held hur still, & þis womman pullid faste & wolde hafe bene away. So at þe laste sho pullid so faste at all hur hare braste of hur heade, & sho ran away & þis fend folowd after & tuke hur, & keste hur ouerthwarte behynd hym on his hors at hur hede & hur armys hang down on þe ta syde, & hur legis on þe toder syde. & þus, when he had his pray, he rade his ways, and be þan it was nere day. & þis knyg[*ht*] went in þe mornyng vnto þe town, & he fand þis womman new dead, & he teld all as he had sene, & shewid þe hare at was wappid abowte his arm. And þai lukyd hur head þer sho lay, and þai fande how all þe hare was plukkid of be þe rutis. And þis happend in þe bisshopprik of Magentyne.

[1] *After* vnto, h, *erased*.

CCCCLVII.

Luxuriosam mulierem canes dentib*us* com*m*inuerunt.

In þe dioces of Coleyn þ*er* was a yong damysell þat was rakles & lichoros. So at þe laste, aft*er* grete sekenes, hur happend to dye, and as sho lay nakid on þe flure, cou*er*de *with* a shete, all þe doggis of þe town come sam*en* into þe howse, & drew of þe shete and pullid hur all to gobettis so þat vnnethis þe husband*is* [1] myght dyng þai*m* away. And þan þai gaderd sam*en* þe pecis of hur body & berid it. And þe dogis come agayn vnto hur grafe & skrapid vp þe pecis agayn, & bate þai*m* as þai did befor in sonder, & faght ilk one *with* oþ*er* als faste as þai myght, to þai had all etyn hur for oght at any man cuthe lett þai*m*.

Luxuria int*er* alia pecc*ata* impedit confessionem. Sup*ra* de cont*r*icione.

Luxuria *eciam* a sene difficile vincitur. *Supra* de Andrea.

Luxurie possu*n*t adaptari ea que sup*ra* dicu*n*tur de adult*er*io, Andrea, carnis temptacione *et* fornicacione [2].

Macharij Abbatis. Macharij humilitas demone*m* confu*n*dit. *Supra* de h*um*ilitate.

Macharius [3] de occisione culicis [4] se mordentis penitenciam egit. Inf*r*a de vindicta.

Macula nocet ho*mini* multipliciter [5]. Sup*ra* de debito.

Machometi. Sup*ra* de decepcione, j.

[1] *After* husbandis, þe h, *erased.*
[2] MS. *et* infra de fornicacione.
[3] MS. Macharij.
[4] MS. Harl. pulicis. MS. Arund. culicis.
[5] MS. multiplex.

CCCCLVIII.

Magdalene p*re*cib*us* filius p*ro*creatur *et* nutritur p*er* ipsam, *et* mater a morte eius meritis suscitatur.

We rede ex '*Legenda Lombardica*' how þe Duke of Marsilie & his wife þurgh techyng and p*re*chyng of Marie Magdalen war turnyd vnto þe faith; and þai had no child, & þai p*ra*yed vnto hur at þai myght hafe a childe. So his wife happend to be grete *with* childe, and Mary Magdalen markid þai*m* bothe *with* þe cros, for þai desyrid to see Saynt Petur þe appostell, & to be enformyd of hym; and þe wife was grete & wolde nott lefe hur husband. So as þai wer vppon þe se it fell a grete storme of wedur, so mekull at þai all, & in speciall þis wom*ma*n *with* childe, war passynglie trubbled & dissesid, vnto so mekull þis wom*ma*n was delyver of a childe & dyed. & when þis childe was born it laytid aft*er* þe moder papp, & wepid and made grete murnyng. And þe fad*er* þ*er*of wepid & said vnto hym selfe; "Allas, wriche! þou desyrid a childe & now þou hase loste bathe þe moder þ*er*of and þe childe." And þe shipmen wolde hafe casten hur bodie into þe see, and hur husband gatt grawnte of þai*m* at sho sulde be had to land, & so sho was; & hur husband laid hur þ*er* wappid in a mantyll dead, & hur childe whik in hur arm. And þan he said *with* grete wepyng; "O þou Magdalene! Wold God þou had neu*er* commen vnto Marsilie, and wold God my childe had bene born þ*er*. Bod þat I purchasid be the, I beteche it to God & þe to kepe." And so he went vnto þe shupp agayn & come vnto Rome vnto Saynt Petur, and told hym all þe case. And Saynt Petur comforthid hym & said vnto hym þ*at* God was of power to turn his sorow into ioy. And he informyd [*hym*] in þe faith, and shewid hym all þe conu*er*sacion of Criste, & þe placis of His passion; & he went agayn vnto shipp. And after þe space of ij yere afterward he landid at þe same place þ*er* he lefte his wyfe, and he was war of a little childe þ*er* on þe see-bank, playing hym *with* little stonys, and he had grete m*er*vall what it was & went þ*er*to. & onone as þe childe saw hym & had neu*er* sene man befor, he ran vnto his moder breste, &

crepid vnder-nethe þe mantyll & hid hym. And when his fadur come at hym & lifte vpp þe mantyll & fand it was a fayr, whikk childe, "O þou, Marie Magdalen!" he said, "how happy war I if my wyfe war now on life & myght go home *with* me into myne awn contreth, ffor I knaw wele enogh at þou, whilk hase nurisshid my childe, is of power to rayse my wife fro dead to life, & þou will." And at þis wurd þe womman was olife & rase vp, and said; "O, þou Magdalen! þou erte of grete merett, whilk þat in my childyng was medwife vnto me, & evur syne hase helpid me in all my nedis!" And when hur husband hard hur speke, he was fayn & sayd; "Wom*man*, liffis þou?" And sho answerd; "Ya, & I hafe [*bene*] *with* þe in eu*er*ilk place þ*er* þou hase bene." And sho tellid hym all & faylid neu*er* a wurd. And þan þai all sam*en* wente hame vnto Marsulie, þ*er* awn contrey. And when þai come at home þai fell on kneis befor Marie Magdalen & thankid hur h*er*telie, & tolde hur all how it had happend þai*m*.

CCCCLIX.

Magdalena*m* angeli ad celu*m* eleuant.

We rede in '*Legenda Lombardica*' how, on a day, Marie Magdaleyn in þe vij canon howris was liftid vp in-to þe ayre *with* angels, and *with* hur bodelie eris sho hard glorios sangis of hevynlie companys, þu[*r*]gh þe whilk eu*er*ilk day sho was fed, & wyth þe same aungels had in-to þe ayr & broght down agayn, so þ*at* sho mysterd nor desyrid no bodelie meat. So opon a day þ*er* was a solitarie preste at dwelte bod a little þine, and *with* his bodelie een he saw how sho was daylie liftid vp into þe ayr *with* angels, & þ*er* holden ane howr space, & how angels *with* mery sang sett hur down agayn þ*er* sho was.

CCCCLX.

Magdalena deuotos sibi ad pentitenciam adducit.

We rede in '*Legenda Lombardica*' how þ*er* was in Flandres a clerk þat hight Stephan, & he fell vnto so grete syn & folie so þat he vsid to do all man*er* of folie, bod he wold nowd*er* do nor here nothyng þat was gude. Neu*er*-þe-les he had grete deuocion vnto Marie Magdaleyn, & wurshuppid hur day & fastid hur evyn, and wold go in pylg*ra*mege vnto hur grafe. So on a tyme sho aperid vnto hym in lyknes of a fayr wom*m*an, bod sho had wepyng een, and sho said vnto hym; "Stephan, whi duse þou ill dedis agayn my gude merettis? Whi ert þou not movid wit*h* no com-punccion for þi syn? And I hafe prayed so hartlie for þe sen þou had deuocion vnto me, and þ*er*for rise & forthynke þe, for I will not forsake þe to þou be recownceld." And fro thens furth he felid so mekull grace yett in hym þat he forsuke þis werld, & tuke hym vnto religion & shrafe hym & did penance, & lifid a gude life & died a holie man. And when he dyed Mari Magdaleyn was sene at his dying, & had his sawle vnto hevyn in ane angell lyknes.

Magistro est exhibenda reu*er*encia. Infra de peticione.

Mag*ist*ro possu*n*t adaptari que dicu*n*tur de doctore *et* predicatore.

Magus multa signa facit. Inf*ra* de Simone Mago.

Magus arte sua multos decipit. S*upra* de decepcione.

CCCCLXI.

Mansuetus homo ab om*n*ib*us* diligitur.

We rede in þe Cronicles how Titus þe Emp*er*our was full of all vertues, to so mekull he was callid þe delitis of all mans kynd; and þai þatt war co*n*victe of coniuracion, he tuke þai*m*[1] to familiarite & forgaff þai*m*, & he wolde deny nothyng to no man þat askid hym, becauce he wolde at no man went hevylie fro hym, & þat day hym thoght was loste at he gaff no thyng on.

Mansuetus iniurias remittit. Inf*ra* de paciencia, ij.

Malicia sac*er*dotis no*n* polluit sacramentu*m*. Inf*ra* de sac*er*dote, ij.

[1] *After* þaim, toke, *erased*.

Malicia societatis nocet ecia*m* bonis. Inf*ra* de societate, i *et* iij.

Malicia mulieris multa mala facit. Infra de muliere, ix *et* x.

Malicia mulieris qu*andoque* in caput suu*m* reu*er*titur. Inf*ra* de muliere.

CCCCLXII.

Maria deuotis sibi ecia*m* honore*m* mu*n*di p*ro*curat.

We rede in 'Our Ladie M*er*acles' how som tyme þ*er* was a noble knyght of Kurkby þat was deuowte vnto our Ladie, and on a tyme as he went vnto þe were, he went in-to ane abbay þat was fowndid of our Ladie & was in his way, & þ*er* he hard mes. And when ilk mes was done after oþ*er*, & he for wurshup of our Ladie wold not go or he had hard þai*m* all, at þe laste he wente furth of þis abbay & hastid hym vnto þis turnament. He mett meneya com*m*and fro þe turnament, & all was done; þai said at he had foghten manlelie in þe batell & born hym passand wele. And þai stude still vnto all come aboute, & ilk man *with* a hale voyce com*m*endid & said he had foghten wurthelie. And þ*er* come som & offerd þai*m* vnto hym & said þat he had taken þai*m* p*ri*soners in þe batell. So þe man was discrete and purseyvid how our Ladie had rewardid hym, & he gaff vp all werldlie þingis & s*er*vid hur Son & hur eu*er* after whils he liffid.

CCCCLXIII.

Maria incarc*er*atos lib*er*at.

We rede in hur 'M*er*acles' how þ*er* was a wedow þat had no childe bod a son, whilk þat sho luffid passandlie. So on a tyme hym happynd to be taken *with* his enmys and putt in p*ri*son, and his moder was passand devowte vnto our Ladie & made hur prayers hertlie vnto hur for hur son. And so sho saw at it p*ro*fettid nott, & sho wente vnto þe kurk þ*er* our Ladie was berid, and þ*er* was a fayr ymage of our Ladie *with* hur Son opon hur kne, and be hur one sho sett hur down on hur kneis & said vnto our Ladie on þis *maner* of wyse; "Thow blissid Ladie! I hafe ofte prayed vnto þe for my son, & þou hase not hard me, & þerfor as my son is takyn fro me, so sall I take þi Son fro the, & kepe hym in wed for my son." & sho tuke away þe ymage of our Ladie Son þat satt on hur kne & had it home, & wappid it in a clene shete, and putt it in hur arke & lokkid it, & was ioyfull & trowid sho had a gude wed for hur son. And on þe night after, our Ladie apperid vnto þe yong man and lowsid his fetters, & oppend hym þe prison dure & lete hym furth & sent hym vnto his moder, and bad hym say vnto his moder þat sho suld bryng hur hur Son[1] agayn for sho had sent hur hurs. And þis yong man come vnto his moder & tellid hur all how our Ladie had delyuerd hym. And sho was passand fayn, & bar agayn þe ymage-childe vnto þe kurk and said, "Blissid Ladie, I thank þe at þou hase giffen me my son agayn, & behold, lo, I bryng þe thyne agayn."

CCCCLXIV.

Maria deuotos sibi a morte liberat.

We rede in hur 'Meracles' how som tyme þer was a thefe, & he had a grete deuocion vnto our Ladie, & said hur salutacion oft vnto hur. So at þe laste he was takyn *with* thift & hanged, and our Ladie come & held hym vp iij dayes, hur awn handis, so þat he felid no sare. So þai þat hanged hym happend be cace to com by hym away, & fand hym mery and liffand; and þai trowed he had not bene wele hanged. & þai wer avysid to hafe stykkid hym *with* a swerd as he hang, and as þai wold hafe stryken hym, our Lady putt it away *with* hur hand, so at þai noyed hym noght. And he told þaim how our Ladie helpid hym, & þai tuke hym down & lete hym. & he went vnto ane abbay & þer servid our Ladie ewhils he liffid.

[1] MS. Sons.

CCCCLXV.

Marie virginis horas deuote dicentes per ipsam a miserijs seculi liberantur.

We rede in hur 'Meracles' how þer was a devowte clerk, and euer-ilk day he wolde say deuotelie þe howris of our Ladye. So his fadur & his moder dyed, and he was þer heir & had a grete heritage. So he was compellid & cownceld be his frendis to take hym a wyfe, and so he did. & on þe day at he was wed, as he went hamward fro þe kurk, þer was ane abbay of our Ladie in his way, & he had forgetten to say his howris & went into þe abbay to say þaim, & sett hym down on his kneis befor owr Ladie & said þaim. And sodanlie our Ladie spak to hym & said; "O, þou fule, & vnwise clerk! Whi forsakis þou me, þi best frend [1], & takis a noder spowse?" And with þis wurdis he was gretlie compuncte & went hame & made a nend of his weddyng. & att evyn he lefte his wife & all his lifelod, & went vnto þe abbay & made hym a monke, & servid God & our Ladie all his life. *et c⁹.*

Marie placet missa de eadem [2] dicta. Infra Thome martiris, v.

CCCCLXVI.

Marie se commendans ab incendio liberatur.

We rede in hur 'Meracles' of a man & a womman þat wunte nere þe cetie of Lugdun, abowte þe yere of our Lord M. C., & þai had no childe bod a doghter. & þai marid hur with a yong man, & þai helde hym in þer howse, & þe moder luffid hym als wele as sho did hur awn doghter. And kurste tongis said þat sho luffid hym not alonelie for hur doghter sake, bod rather becauce sho lete hym lig by hur in-stede of hur doghter, & sho hard tell þeroff & was ferd þat sklanderd sulde rise of hur betwix hym & hur, and

[1] MS. frendis. [2] MS. eo.

p*r*ivalie scho slew hym when hur husband & hur dogh*ter* war away, & layd hym in hur dogh*ter* bed. So in þe mornyng, as þai satt at den*er* sho bad hur [1] dogh*ter* go wakyn hur husband, & byd hym rise. And sho went & fand hym dead, & cryed, and sho & þe moder made bathe mekull sorow; neu*er*-þe-les sho forthoght hur þ*er*of, & wente vnto þe preste & shrafe hur, & tolde hym all how sho had done. So afterward þis womman & þis preste fell at debate, and he disclanderd hur & tolde hur cowncell, & vpbrayed hur þ*er*with. And when it come to knowlege of þe yong man fathir & his moder, thai garte take hur & bryng hur befor a iustis, & þ*er* sho was demyd to be byrnyd. And scho wepyd & betuke hur vnto our Ladie. And when þe fyre was kyndled abowte hur, sho stude still vnhurte, and hur enmys kyndled þe fire ner hur & it p*r*ofetid þai*m* noght. So þai tuke fork*is* & stowris & thruste hur down *with*, & it stedid þai*m* of noght. And þan þe iustis had grete m*er*vell & beheld hur graythlie, & he cuthe se no takyn of burnyng on hur, bod alonelie wowndis þat sho had *with* þe fork*is* & þe stowris. So sho was takyn furth & led hame, & balmyd & refresshid; and *with*-in iij dayis after sho, p*er*seu*er*and in grete lovyng*is* of our Ladie, gaff vp hur gaste, and passid vnto Almighti God.

CCCCLXVII.

Maria ad se co*n*fugientes deo reconsiliat.

We rede in hur 'Meracles,' þ*at* aboute þe yere of our Lord CCC vij [2], in þe land of Cecilie, [*was*] one þat hight Theophil, at was chauncelur vnto a bisshopp, & was wise & gracious. So on a tyme he was putt oute of his offes, and her-for he fell in a grete sorow & a dispayr. And so hym happend speke *with* þe devull, and be com*m*and of hym he forsuke Criste & His moder, & he renownced his faithe, and herefor he made hym a cyrographatt wretten, & selid it with his awn ryng. And when it was selid he delyverd it vnto þe devull, and band hym to do hym s*er*ves whils he liffid. So *with*-in a while after, be p*ro*curyng of þe fend, he was

[1] MS. our. [2] Lat. MSS. xxxvij.

restorid agayn vnto his offes. So *after* hym forthoght, and callid opon our Ladie, & made his *pr*ayer vnto hur; & sho apperid vnto hym and blamyd hym for þat at he had done. And be hur com*m*andmend [*he*] forsuke þe devull and tuke hym vnto God & our Ladie, and he was broght befor a iustis. And þe devull shewid þis cirographatt, and our Ladie tuke it fro hym & laid it on Theophill breste, þ*er* he was slepand. And when he wakid he fand it, & was passand fayn þ*er*-of, and evyn opynlie, befor þe bisshopp & all þe peple, he stude vpp & co*n*fessid hym. And all men had grete m*er*vayle þ*er*-off, & he did his penans þat was ioyned hym þ*er*for, & wit*h*-in a while aft*er* he decesid & made a gude endyng.

Marie salutacio causa est mirac*u*li post[1] mortem. S*upr*a de an*n*unc*iacione* dom*in*ica.

Maria p*ro*tegit a combustione. Sup*r*a de eukaristia.

Maria lib*er*at de infamia. S*upr*a de infamia, ij, *et* de abb*a*tissa, j.

Maria ordine*m* p*r*edicatoru*m* attulit. S*upr*a Dom*i*-*n*ici, iij.

Maria deuotis sibi in necessitate adiuvat. S*upr*a de familiaritate.

Maria horas de se dicentib*us* apparet in morte. Sup*r*a de horis, ij.

Maria consolatur suos. Supra de consolacione.

CCCCLXVIII.

Maria offic*iu*m se*r*uitor*um* suor*um* eis absentib*us* implet.

Som tyme þ*er* was a non þat hight Betres, a passand fayr wom*m*an, & sho was sacristan of þe kurk and sho had grete deuocion vnto our Ladie; and oft sithis men desirid hur to syn.

[1] *After* post, p, *erased.*

So at þe laste sho consentid vnto a clerk at go away *with* hym when complyn was done, and or sho yode sho went vnto ane altar of our Ladie & said vnto hur; "Lady, as I hafe bene deuoute vnto þe, now I resigne vnto þe þies keyis, for I may no langer susteyn þe temptacion of my flessh." & sho laid þe keyis on þe altar & went hur wayes vnto þe clerk. And when he had defowlid hur, *with*-in a few dayes he lefte hur & went away; & sho had nothyng at liff on & thoght shame to gang home agayn vnto hur clostre, and sho fell to be a common woman. And when sho had liffid in þ*at* vice xv yere, on a day sho come vnto þe nonrie yate, & askid þe porter if he knew evur a non in þ*at* place þ*at* hight Betres, þ*at* was sacristan & keper of þe kurk. And he said he knew hur on þe beste wyse, and said sho was a wurthi womman & a halie of barn little, "& eu*er* hase kepud hur clene & in gude name." And sho vnderstode not þe wurdis of þis man, & went hur wayis. And our Lady apperid vnto hur & said; "Behold! I hafe fulfillid þine offes þis xv yere, and þ*er*for turn agayn now into þi place & be agayn in þine offes as þou was, & shryfe þe & do þi penance, for þ*er* is no creatur her at knowis þi truspas, for I hafe eu*er* bene for the in þi clothyng & in þine abbett." And onone sho was in hur abbett & went in & shrafe hur & did her penance, and told all þ*at* was happend vnto hur.

CCCCLXIX.

Marie salutacio fantasma disp*ar*ere facit *et* demone*m* fugat.

We rede how þ*at* þe fend oft sithis in liknes of a gude angell apperid vnto ane ancres. So at þe laste he told hur þ*at* he come to comfurth hur, and sho had a grete comfurth þ*er*of, & told hur confessur of his apperans. & he was a gude man & bad hur, when he come agayn, þ*at* sho sulde [*bid him*] [1] shew vnto hur our Ladie, Saynt Marie; and if he did so þ*at* onone as sho saw hur sho sulde say, "Ave Maria." And þe next tyme he come agayn sho desirid hym þ*at* sho mot se our Ladie, and he said it nedid not, ffor it suffisid vnto hur his p*re*sens. And eu*er* sho desyrid hym more

[1] Harl. MS. 'Dic ei vt ostendat *tibi* beatam Maria*m*.'

& mor̄ at sho mot se our̄ Ladie. So on̄ a tyme þis fend formyd̄ hym̄ selfe in lyknes of a fayr wom*man*̄, and apperid̄ vnto hur. And onone as sho saw hur, sho fell̄ on̄ kneis befor̄ hur and said̄; "Ave Maria." And onone sho dispayrid̄ away as a fantasie. Hec valet ad decepc*ionem* demonis.

So fure it on̄ a tyme þe Devull̄ aperid̄ oft sithis vnto ane h*er*mett in lyknes of a man̄ of law, so a nod*er* wise man̄ cownceld̄ hym̄ þ*at* when̄ at he come, he suld̄ say his Ave Maria; and so he did̄. & þe fend̄ flow away in liknes of a whorle-wynd̄ & gnaystid̄ his tethe, & warid̄ hym̄ þat taght hym̄ to say it.

CCCCLXX.

Marie salutacio imm*i*ttit timor*em et* malu*m* cogitatu*m* emittit.

Som̄ tyme a non̄, tempid̄ for luff of a yong man̄, wold̄ hafe gane into þe werld̄, and sho mot not gett oute bod if sho had went þurgh þe kurk. And so as sho went þurgh̄ þe kurk sho[1] set hur down̄ befor̄ our Ladie, as sho was wunt to doo, & lowtid̄ down̄ & said̄ hur Ave Mar*ia*. And sodanlie þ*er* come on̄ hur so grete a drede þ*at* sho mot no ferrer go furth̄; and so it happend̄ oft sithes w*ith* hur. And at þe laste sho was tempid̄ w*ith* so grete temptacion̄, to so mekull̄ at sho thoght at sho suld̄ pas furthe by our Ladie & nothyng lowte vnto hur, nor at sho wold̄ not say hur Ave Maria. And þis done þe devull̄ tuke a power in hur, and gaff hur a hardynes to go oute of hur ordur w*ith*, & þus on̄ a tyme sho went hur wayes & fulfillid̄ þe luste of hur flessh.

CCCCLXXI.

Marie ymago infeccionem aeris fugat.

Saynt Gregor̄, when̄ þat he was pope, agayn̄ þe infeccion̄ of þe ayre þat was cauce in Rome of grete dead̄ & mortalitie[2], he garte make solempne p*ro*cessions: and ane ymage of our̄ Ladie þat Saynt

[1] MS. & set. [2] MS. *inserts* and *here*.

Luke had payntid, evyn after þe lyknes of our Ladie, he garte bere befor þe procession. And onone þis infeccion of þe ayr vanysshid away and fled fra þe ymage, and a grete reste & a quietnes come. And abown, þe aungell in þe ayr enence þe ymage sang; "Regina celi letare, All*eluia* ! Quia que*m* m*er*uisti portare, All*eluia* ! Resurrexit sicut dixit, All*eluia* !" And onone Saynt Gregur & his felashupp addid þ*er*to & sang; "Ora p*ro* nobis Deu*m*, All*eluia* !"

Marini qui ecia*m* Marine d*icitur*. S*upra* de accusa*cione*, iij.

CCCCLXXII.

Marthe corpus p*er* d*ominu*m sepelitur.

We rede in 'Leg*enda* Lomb*ardica*' þat [*when*] Saynt Martha was dead at Clarascon[1], apon þe day afterward at Pictagoras[2] our Lord apperid vnto Saynt Francon[3], þe bisshopp, as he was at mes and aft*er* þe epistull was fallen on slepe in his chayr, and said vnto hym; "My welebeluffid Franco[4] ! Ryse tite & folow me !" And so he did; and sodanlie þai come vnto Therascon bothe to-gedur, and þai sang aboute þe bodie of Saynt Martha, & all þ*at* was abowte answerd þai*m*. And þus þai did all þe offes, & layd hur in hur grafe. And at Pictagoras, when all þe sang aft*er* þe epistull was done, & þe dekyn suld go rede þe gospell & take þe blissyng of þe bisshopp, he was on slepe. And þe dekyn went to hym & wakend hym, and þan he said; "Brethir, whi wakkend ye me ? For our Lord Iesu Criste had led me vnto þe bodie of Martha his hoste, & he & I hase berid hur. And þ*er*for send faste thedur for to feche vs our gold ryng & our glovis, þ*at* we hafe lefte þ*er*, whilk þat I betuke vnto þe sacristan when we putt hur in hur grafe. And becauce ye callid me so tyte or þe mes was done, þ*er*for I hafe lefte þai*m* behynd me." And þai sent a messanger onon & fand all as þe bissl opp said, bothe þe ryng & þe gluvis, & broght þai*m* home. And in tokyn here-of þe sacristan kepid þe ta glufe, & so þai hafe it yitt for a relikk.

[1] Harl. MS. Tharasconem.
[2] Latin MSS. Petragoricas.
[3] Harl. MS. *beato* Frontoni Epi*scopo*.
[4] Harl. MS. "Dulce mi Fronto !"

CCCCLXXIII.

Martini, Episcopi *et* Confessoris.

Seu*er*us [1] in his 'Dialoggi*s*' tellis how on a ffestiuall day a pure nakid man folowid Saynt M*ar*tyn vnto þe kurk-ward, and he com*m*andyd his archedekyn to garr hym be cledd, and he lachid þ*er*in. And Saynt Martyn saw þat, & went in-to his secretorie & doffid his cote & gaff it vnto þis pure man, and bad hym go faste his wayis þ*er*wit*h*. And þan þe archdekyn desyrid at he wold go to mes, & he, spekand of hym selfe, said þat he mot not go to mes vnto þis pure man was cled. And so in a tene þis archdekyn went in-to þe m*ar*kett & boght a sary old cote for vd, & broght it vnto Saynt M*ar*tyn & said he cuthe not fynd þis old pure man. And Saynt M*ar*tyn bad hym giff hym þe clothe, & þe pure man suld nott want itt. And in a tene he threw it vnto hym, and he tuke it & went p*r*ivalie & gatt it on hym, & þe slevis þ*er*of come bod vnto his elbow, & þe lenthe þ*er*of was bod vnto his kne; and so he went vnto mes. And as he was att mes, a byrnyn*g* globe aperid abown his head, whilk þ*a*t many folk saw, and for þat he was callid Par Apo*st*olis, Evyn vnto þe Apostels. And vnto þis m*er*acle addid maist*er* Iohn Beleth, and says þat when he was at mes and sulde lifte, as þe vse is, his lyn slevis slafe bakk, & his armys was bod small, and þe slevis of þe olde cote come bod vnto his elbow, and so when he liftid, his armys war bare. And þan a m*er*valos wrethe of golde & p*r*ecious stonys was sene aboute his armys, þat coverd his armys vnto his elbow.

Martinus eciam inuitis beneficia p*r*estitit. Sup*r*a de invitis [2].

CCCCLXXIV.

Martini sepulture int*er*fuit Ambrosius.

Opon þe same day at Saynt M*ar*tyn decesid, Saynt Ambros þe bisshopp was att mes at þe cetie of Mediolan, and as he lenyd on

[1] MS. Severius. [2] MS. inimicis.

þe altar, betwix þe *pro*phesie & þe epistull, he fell on slepe; and þ*er* was none at durste wakyn hym. And þe subdekyn sulde go rede þe pistell, & he durst not go or þe bisshop assigned hym. And so þai stude þe space of ij or iij howris abydand hym. So at þe laste one of þai*m* wakend hym & said þe peple recedid away, and desyrid hym to com*m*and[1] þe dekyn to rede þe epistill. And þan he said; "Brether, be not trubled, ffor my bruther Martyn is passid vnto God and I did þe obseruance at his beryall. & becauce ye wakend me so sone I hafe lefte þe laste colett vnsaid." And þan þai notid þe day & þe howr, and þai fand at Saynt M*ar*tyn was decesid þe same tyme, & passid vnto Godd.

CCCCLXXV.

Martirium sustinent aliqui ex magno fervore.

Saynt Ambrose tellis how on a tyme when a grete multitude of cristenmen war drawen vnto m*ar*tirdom, þ*er* come a mayden of hur fre liste with a h*er*telie desyre vnto þai*m* for to be slayn wit*h* þai*m*. And þan a ryche man þ*at* was a paynom spak vnto hur & said; "Wom*m*an, whedur rynys þou so faste?" And sho answerd agayn & sayd; "I go vnto my frend þ*at* hase biddin me wit*h* oþ*er* vnto þe weddyng þ*er* grete daynttys er." And so he vmthoght hym at sho callid Criste hur frend, and at she ran to be m*ar*tyrd, & trowid sho had bene a fule & skornyd hur, & said; "Say vnto þi frend at send me ane of his rosis." And so sho was m*ar*tird emang oþ*er*. & als sone as sho was dede and fallyn down, a fayr chyld come vnto hym wit*h* a white copp full of rosis þat saverd passand wele, & told hym at þe wom*m*an frend þat was passid sent hym som of his rosis as he had askid. & he sett þai*m* down & onone he was vanysshid away. And þis man was passand ferd & co*m*puncte, for als mekull as it was not rose tyme; and he vmthoght hym at God of cristen men had callid hym vnto m*ar*tyrdom. And evyn furth-wit*h* he went vnto þe place of þe m*ar*tyrdom and said he was a cristen man. & onone

[1] MS. com*m*andid.

he was hedid & cristend in his awn blude, & broght vnto þe rosary of paradyce.

Mater tenere diligit filium suum. Infra de morte, ij[1], *et* de visitacione, ij[2].

CCCCLXXVI.

Matrimonium contrahi debet magis inter personas bonarum condicionum quam diuitum.

Iustinus tellis how on a tyme a man askid cowncell at Theristides[3] of Athenys wheþer[4] hym was bettir giff his doghter vnto a pure man, or to a riche man. And he ansswerd agayn & said; "I hafe levur þe money of þe man þan money be boght vnto þe man."

Matrimonio debet accipi vxor prudens magis quam diues. Infra de vxore.

CCCCLXXVII.

Matrimonio plus queritur substancia frequenter quam persona.

Agellius tellis how þat Caton som tyme had a doghter, and when hur furst husband was dead sho come & askid hur fader whi he wold not make hur to hafe a noder husband. And he ansswerd hur agayn & said; "For I can not fynde a man bod he wolde titter hafe þi gudis þan þi selfe."

CCCCLXXVIII.

Matrimonialis coniunccio periculosa est.

Valerius tellis how on a tyme a yong man come vnto Socrates & askid hym cowncell, whether hym was bettir wed hym a wife or nay. And he ansswerd hym agayn & sayd; "Ather of þaim

[1] MS. iij.
[2] MS. j.
[3] Harl. MS. Thimistidem.
[4] Vtrum filiam suam pauperi *sed* ornato, uel locupleti *sed* parum probato collocaret.

is a grete penance to do, for & þou be not wed, þou may happely syn in fornicacion, or in avowtrie, or els be ill defamyd & sklandred & neuer be at no certantie *with* þi selfe. And if þou be wed þou may happen wed a shrew at will be þi maister, and þou bus be ferd for hur frendis, & euer be besy & labur, & ofte in stryfe and debate, & suffer many grete wurd & say nothyng agayn, & hafe a snowryng cowntenance, & happelie bryng vp oþer mens childer. & if þou do nott wele to þi wyfe þou sall be bostid *with* hur frendis, & þus þou sall euer liff in trubble & in dissese."

CCCCLXXIX.

Mat*r*imonialis coniu*n*ccio tediosa est.

Theofrastus þe philosophur sayd, a womman is owder fayr or fowle, and if sho be fayr onone sho sall be luffid & desyrid to be had, and if sho be fowle sho will desyre to be had. And þerfor it is hard to kepe þat at many men desyris, and it is hevie to hafe þat in welde þat no man dedengnys to hafe.

Mediatrix mulier. Infra de muliere.

Medicor*um* iudicia de infirmis no*n* semp*er* eveniu*n*t. S*upr*a de Basilio.

Medicus p*ro*p*r*ietarius monachus in s*ter*quilinio sepelitur. Inf*r*a de p*ro*p*r*ietate, ij.

Medicus debet infirmis ea que sunt salutis sue p*ro*pon*er*e. Infra de p*r*edestinac*io*n*e*.

Meditac*io* inferni penitentem corp*or*alit*er* extenuat, *et* meditacio paradisi exhilarat[1]. S*upr*a de apostasia.

CCCCLXXX.

Memoria*m* sui acq*ui*ru*n*t aliqui p*er* aliq*ua* f*a*cta int*er*du*m* *eciam* mala[2].

Valerius tellis & says how þat, som tyme[3], certayn folk, for to assecute euerlastand memorie, dowtis not for to do grete

[1] MS. exhillarat.
[2] So Harl. MS. The translator's heading is incomplete.
[3] MS. *adds* som while *here*.

trispas, whase namys he said þat he kennyd nott. So þ*er* was a man þat spirrid Ermodeus how clere he might be had[1]; he answerd agayn & said, þat & he slew any wurthi man, it suld turn hym vnto grete[2] glorie. And so he slew one þat hight Philipp, and he was taken & putt to dead þerfor. And aft*er*-ward it was fon þat he did it be com*m*andment of þe Dyan of Ephesie[3], for sho wolde hafe burnyd þe temple. *et c*9.

CCCCLXXXI.

Memoria mulieris in corde viri remanere no*n* debet.

We rede in 'Vitis P*atrum*' how þat a noble wom*ma*n, ane olde wyfe[4], come vnto ane abbot þat hight Arsenius, to se hym, & he prayed þe bisshop at sho suld not se hym, & he wold not graunt þ*er*to. So sho come vnto his cell dure, & fand hym þ*er*-att, & fell down on hir kneis aforn hym. & he wit*h* grete dedeyng tuke hur vpp and said vnto hur; "And þou will se my face, se itt now." And sho for shame durst not luke vpon hym, bod sho went away & prayed hym to pray for hur vnto God, & hafe hur in his mynde always. And he said, nay, he wold nott, he sulde pray God to do away þe mynd of hur oute of his harte. And when sho hard þis, sho was gretelie trubbled, and went in-to þe cetie & fell into þe axis. And when þe bisshop come to vyssit hur, sho said vnto hym; "I am so hevie þat I mon dy." & þe bisshopp answer[*d*] hur agayn & said; "Knowis þou not at þou ert a wom*ma*n? And þe devull tempis men wit*h* wom*me*n, & speciall haly men. And þerfor yone man said vnto the as he did. Bod þuf all he said so, yit he prayis for þi saule." And so he comfurthid hur and sho wente home vnto hur awn place. *et c*9.

Memoria mortis est m*ul*tum vtilis. Sup*ra* de conu*er*sione, iiij, et de confessore, v, *et* infra de morte.

Memorie labiles[5] su*n*t aliqui. Inf*ra* de muliere, iiij.

[1] Lat. MSS. *quo modo* subito clarus poss*et* h*a*beri.

[2] MS. *repeats* grete.

[3] Harl. MS. Sic eciam inuentum est, quod Diane Ephesei sic templum incend*ere* uellet, ut op*ere* pulch*er*rimo consu*m*pto nome*n* suu*m* p*er* totu*m* orbe*m* innotesceret.

[4] Lat. MSS. Matrona qued*am* nobil*is et* senex.

[5] MS. labilis.

CCCCLXXXII.

Mendacium eciam corporaliter nocet.

We read in '*Legenda Lombardica*' how Iulius & Iulianus wer brether, and þai bygid a kurk, and be commandment of þe Emperour Theodoce, all þat evur come by þaim þai wold gar þaim abyde, & helpe þaim. So þer happend a meneya com þer-away [*with*] a carte, & þai laid ane of þer felows in þe carte, & coverd hym with a clothe as he had bene dead. And when þai come be þis werke, þies ij saynttis bad þaim abide with þer carte & helpe þaim, and þai said þai had in þer carte a dead man & þerfor þai had nede at haste þaim away. And þe sayntis answerd þaim & said; "Whi lie ye? Go your wais, & as ye say so be it vnto you." And when þai war passid, þai callid vppon þer felow and þai fand hym starke dead. And fro þens furth þer was nane at come þer-away at durst ans make a le vnto þies sayntis. *et c*[9].

CCCCLXXXIII.

Mendacium aliquibus temporaliter nocet.

Ex '*Legenda Lombardica*' we rede how þat a grete aduocatt of þe Ceustus ordur was made a monk, & he went oft sithis for to defend cawsis of þe abbott, & euer he was casten & had þe war. And þe abbott & þe monkis wax wrathe with hym & said vnto hym; "How is it at þou fallis alway in our cawsis, and whils þou was in þe werld þou prevaylid alway in oþer mens cawsis?" And he answerd þaim agayn & said; "While I was secular I was not ferd to lie, ffor oft sythes be my fraudis & be my lesyngis I ouercome myne aduersaries. And now becauce I dar say no þing bod treuth, it happens me þe contrarie." And so he was commawndid vnto his cloystur.

Mentiri non debet religiosus. Infra de religione.

Mendacium eciam punitur in presenti. Infra de periurio *et* de paupertate.

CCCCLXXXIV.

Mercator*um*[1] vita amota[2] co*m*putacione, a multis approbatur.

We rede in 'Libro de Dono Timoris,' how ane Erle of Pictauence cled hym dyu*ers* tymys in pure mans clothyng whils he had sene all man*er* of craftis & offes. And when he had serchid all þies, he said at þe m*er*chand crafte war þe beste crafte þat he fand, & þe beste offes, war not a thyng war, þat is[3] to say, cowntyng & rekynyng in þe end. For, he said, at evyn when þai come home þai made rekkenyng of þe leste peny at þai reseyvid, and at þai expu*n*did, and he þat made not a gude rekynyng was casten in *pris*on & holden þ*er*.

CCCCLXXXV.

Mercatores in empcione *et* vendicione freque*nter* me*n*ciu*n*tur vt lucrentur.

Cesarius tellis of ij cetisens of Colayn confessid þai*m* of ij man*ers* of syns, & þe tane was leyng & þe toder manesweryng. And þai tolde þe preste þat *with*-outen þies ij þai myght nowder by nor sell. And þe p*re*ste told þai*m* at þies was grete synnys, bod he bad þai*m* vse þai*m* on þis man*er* of wyse; "Furste lofe yo*ur* gude as ye will giff it, and it sall be wele *with* you, I warand." And þai p*ro*mysid hym þai sulde so doo þ*at* yere. Bod be lettyng of þe devull þat yere þai wan no thyng, and at þe yere end þai come vnto þe preste & tolde hym. And þe p*re*ste told þai*m* at it was bod a temptacion of þe fende, & bad þai*m* trow hym; bod he said, "Feste it faste in your mynde, and þink at ye will kepe hit fro hens forwhard, and it sall be wele enogh *with* you." And so þai did, and *with* a few yeris þai war passand riche men.

Mercator de bonis suis *et* no*n* de alienis debet m*er*-cari. S*upra* de abb*ate*.

[1] MS. Marcatorum. [2] MS. ammota. [3] MS. it.

Mercator[1] vicium rei non debet celare. Infra de negociacione.

CCCCLXXXVI.

Mensura semp*er* debet esse iusta.

Cesarius tellis how in þe bisshopprik in Colan som tyme þ*er* was a wedow at was a brewster, & vsid to sell ale, & fyre happend in þe town & byrnyd a grete dele þ*er*off. And when sho saw it come nere hur howse, sho wold nothyng remow furth of hur howse, bod tuke hur mettis & hur messurs at sho fillid ale wit*h*, and sett þai*m* at hur dure wit*h*-oute, & said; "O, þou rightwus & m*er*cifull God! If I hafe rightwuslie & trewlie mesurd wit*h* thies mesurs to þai*m* at I selde ale to, I beseke ye at þis tyme to behalde my myster, and at þou wolde vuchesafe to spare me and my hows & my howsold þat is þ*er*-in. And if I hafe wit*h* þies messurs messurd wrang, or disseyvid any creatur, þan, Lord, I will at my howse be burnyd & all þe gudis at I hafe." Lo! þis was a m*er*valos faythe of þis womman! And yit was þe m*er*cie of God mor m*er*valos, ffor when þe fire come at hur howse, at all folk saw & had grete wonder þ*er*off, as God[2] wold, þe ffawme at had burnyd all þe town-end to thedir sesid, & wold burn no man*er* of þing of [*hur*] howse, nowder thak nor tymmer. & yit not-wit*h*-standyng, all þe howse semyd clene our wit*h* fire as it had burnyd, & yit was it nothyng hurte wit*h* þe fyre, nor no gude of hurris þat was þ*er*in. And þe fire sesid & burnyd no ferrer, þat a hondreth men cuthe not sease befor. And here-by hur neghburs vnderstude þat hur messurs warr gude & trew. *et* c*9*.

CCCCLXXXVII.

Meretrix. Mulier accusat quos ad pecc*atu*m *tr*ahere non potest.

Cesarius tellis how som tyme þ*er* was a common womman þat was fayr, and sho folowid a grete lord fro town to town, for þe lordis men synnyd wit*h* hur eu*er* when þai*m* liste, and þe lord

[1] MS. marcator. [2] MS. gold.

wiste not. & at þe laste þe lord preste accusid hur vnto þe lord, & þe lord garte call hur befor hym, & sho denyed itt and accusid þis *preste*, & said he co*m*plenyd on hur becauce sho wold not consent vnto hym, and þis sho oblisshid hur to prufe. So at þe laste sho fenyd hur contrite, & come vnto þis same *pre*ste & shrafe hur. And in þe end of hur confession sho said þat sho was so tempid *with* his luff þat bod if sho had itt sho sulde sla hur selfe. And þis *pre*ste was aferd on hur & had no faste purpos to syn *with* hyr, yit he assigned hur a place & a tyme þ*er* he suld com vnto hur; and sho was fayn þ*er*of & went & tellid þe lord how þe prest had *pro*missid vnto hur. And þis p*re*ste come to þe place befor þe howr, & he made in þe same place a bed of dry wud, & put stra þ*er*in & put fyre vnd*er*-nethe in tow, & coverd it clenlie *with* a shete. And belife sho come & þe fyre began to kyndell in þe bed, & þe prest went þ*er*to, & laid hym down þ*er*on, evyn in þe fire, & bad hur com vnto hym. & þe fire rase all abowte hym & sho callid on hym & wold hafe had hym þine, & he lay still & was nothyng burnyd, nor his clothes nowther. And þan þis wrichid wom*m*an was conpu*n*cte & reknowlegid hur selfe þat sho accusid þis holye man of v*er*ray rancor & ill will. And þis done þis holie preste went & made hym a monk.

Meretrix multa mala facit. Infra de muliere pl*ur*ib*us* locis.

Meriti causa est aliqu*ando* temptacio. Infra de temptacione.

Meretur homo relinquens om*n*ia p*ro*pt*er* de*um*. Inf*ra* de milite, iiij.

CCCCLXXXVIII.

Miles malus p*er* sera*m* pen*itent*iam saluatur.

Cesarius tellis of a knyght þat[1] on a tyme was taken *with* his enmys & slayn. And when he saw þat hym burde nedelyngis dy, he said þies iij wurdis, "D*omin*e, miserere mei. Lord, hafe

[1] MS. þan.

m*er*cie on me." And when he dyed, a man þat was vexid *with* a fend was delyverd. So aft*er*ward þe fend come agayn vnto þis man and vexid hym hugelie, more þan he did afor. And a gude holie man come vnto hym & askid hym whi þat he did so. And he ansswerd agayn & said; "We war many fendis gadurd sam*en* at þe dead of swylk a knyght, and becauce we gatt nothyng þ*er*, þ*er*for all þat I can sall I venge me in hym þis." And þis holie man spirrid hym þe cauce how þai had no power of þat knyght, and he ansswerd agayn & sayd þat þe knyght sayd alonelie iij wurdis or he dyed, "be þe whilk all þe power þat we had in hym was loste."

CCCCLXXXIX.

Miles punitur et saluatur.

Cesarius tellis how on a tyme þ*er* was a knyght of Saxon, þat was cled in new skarlett clothes, and on a day as he was rydand, he mett a husband-man dryvand his carte. And *with* þe sprenclyng & dasshyng of þe whelis, þis knyght*is* clothis war al todasshid *with* myre. And þis knyght, as a prowde man & a tyrand, drew hys swerd & smate of þe ta legg of þis husband be his kne. So afterward þurgh þe grace of God he wex sorowfull for his syn, & made hym a monk of þe Seustus ordur. And *with*-in a few yeris aft*er* he was made monke, þ*er* began to brede a sur like a sylk threde in his legg, on þe same syde & in þe same place whar he cutt of þe husbandman legg. And be little & little it began to rote, so þat att þe laste mawkis bred þ*er*in. And þan he wex fayn & sayd; "Now I trow for to hafe forgyfnes, ffor I se on my body þe syngne of Iob." And so he liffid many day in grete co*n*tricion, and at þe laste, þurgh þis maledie, he dyed & yeldyd God a gude sawle.

CCCCXC.

Miles demone[1] vt famulo vtitur.

Cesarius tellis of a knyght þat dwelte in Saxon, and he was famos & noble in armys, and his name was Albert Stobberd. So

[1] MS. deuocione.

on a day hym happend to com vnto a place *þer* a damysell was vexid *with* a fend, and onone as he come sho began to cry and sayd, "Ecce! amicus meus venit. Lo! my frend is com*men*." And evur as he come inward sho bad gyff hym rowm, and lat hur frend com ner hur. And þuf all he war wrothe *þerwith*, yitt he smylid & said; "þou fende, þou ert bod a fole! Wharto vexis þou þis wom*man* on þis man*er*, *þat* is so innocent? Lefe hur & go *with* me vnto turnamentis & batels." And þis fend said he wold gladlie go *with* hym and he wold latt hym entre into his bodie, "or els to lat me in þi sadle or in þi brydill, or in som other *par*te at long*is* vnto the." And þis knyght had grete *com*passion of þis noble maydyn and said; "And þou will pas from hyne I will grawnt þe a plyte of my gown vnder-nethe a condicion, at þou sall not hurte me, bod when at I will, onone þou sall pas fro me." And he beheste hym *þat* he shuld. And *with* *þat* he went oute of þe maydyn & come in-to a plite of þe gown and made *þer* a grete movyng. And from *þat* howr þis knyght had so gret a strenth & a *com*furth, at whoso-eu*er* he wold he mot ou*er*thraw þai*m*, & whom so eu*er* hym liste take, and þai war ne so swyfte, yit he mott take þai*m*. And when þe knyght satt in þe kurk at his *pr*ayers, þis fend made a grete gruchyng and said hym thoght *þat* he taryd long *þer*. And he kaste holie watir on him [1], þis fend wolde byd hym war at he tuchyd not hym. So on a tyme þis knyght happend to com in-to a kurk whar *þer* was made a *ser*mon of þe cros. And þan þe fend said vnto hym; "What duse þou her?" And þis knyght anss werd agayn & said; "Now I wull forsake þe & seryff Almightie God." And þe fend answerd agayn & said; "What displesans haste þou fon in me? I neu*er* yit hurte þe, bod I hafe broght þe vnto mekull wurshup and riches, and þurgh me þou erte made passyng glorious." þis knyght answerd hym agayn & said; "Loo! now I behold þe cros, and I com*man*d þe now, in vertue of Hym *þat* was done on þe cros, *þat* from hens furth þou nevur turn vnto me agayn." And *with* *þat* þis fend lefte hym. And þis knyght burnyd hym *with* þe cros, and went to beyond se, & *þer* he *ser*vid Almightie God ij yere.

[1] MS. he.

And aft*er* þat he come home agayn̄, and byggid' ane hospitall. And þ*er*in he abade all his life aft*er*, & serryffed seke folk of swilk as þai*m* nedud'. And so in peas þ*er* he endid' his life.

Miles executor n*e*cligens punitur. S*upra* de execuc*io*ne.

Miles ludo avium deditus punitur. S*upra* de avib*us*, j.

Miles obstinat*us* in pecc*at*is dampnatur. S*upra* de accusacione.

Miles spoliat modica occasione habita. Inf*ra* de mo*na*cho, iiij.

Militi p*er* be*a*tam vi*r*ginem *gratia* dei ecia*m* temporalia p*er*dita restituu*n*tur. Inf*ra* de negacione, j.

CCCCXCI.

Miles c*r*uce signatus vx*or*em *et* libe*r*os relinque*n*s multu*m* meretur.

Iacobus de Vet*r*iaco tellis how on̄ a tyme a knyght þat was m*ar*kid' *with* þe cros went from̄ his awn̄ place to beyond' þe se. Or he wente, afor a grete parte of his frendis, he callid' all his childer aforn̄ hym̄, & he hawsid' & kyssid' þai*m* frendlye, & kyssyd' þai*m* tenderly, & wepyd swetelie. So one come in & callid on̄ hym̄ & said'; "Sur, your felows abydis you, lefe þies childer & com̄ your wayes!" And þis knyght answerd' agayn̄ & sayd'; "I do þis to make me mor hevie & sad when̄ I parte *with* þai*m*, at my mede may be þe mor for þe levyng of þai*m*."

Militis vxori aliqu*ando* sac*er*dos copulatur. S*upra* de confessione, vij.

Miles amore c*r*ucifixi culpa*m* inimico remittit. Supra[1] de M*a*r*i*a.

Miles obstinatus p*er* imp*er*f*ec*tam cont*r*içionem a pecc*at*o retrahit*ur*. Inf*ra* de obstina*cio*ne, ij.

[1] MS. Infra.

Miles corpore Chr*isti* p*er*cepto *eciam* corporal*iter* efficitur forcior. S*upra* de com*m*unione, iiij [1].

Miles p*re*do p*er* aliquas or*ati*ones dictas saluatur. Inf*ra* de remun*er*acione.

CCCCXCII.

Miles devotus reu*er*encia*m* fac*it* deo et sacramentis.

Cesarius tellis how som tyme þ*er* was a knyght of France. And he was of suche devocion, þ*er* whare-somevur he saw Goddis bodye he wolde fall down and wurshup it, and it had bene evyn in þe myre. So it happend on a tyme þat he was cled in gude clothes, & he went into a cetie, and þe strete þat he rade in was passand myrye. And sodanlye hym happend mete þe p*re*ste *with* Godd*is* body, and onone as he saw itt, he avysid hym a while & said vnto hym selfe; "What wyll þou do now? And þou knele down here þou losis all þi gay clothyng. And if þou do it nott, þou erte breker of a helefull condicion at þou was wunt to vse." And *with* þat, *with*-outen more, he lightid of his hors and sett hym down in þe myre on bothe his knethis, and held vp his hand*is* and wurshuppid þe sacrament. And our Lord, þat wurshuppid þai*m* at wurshuppis Hym, shewid þis m*er*acle þurgh his power, at þ*er* was not on all his clothis a drope of [2] myre nor a spott of clay. And when he saw þis, he had grete m*er*vell & lepid vp vppon his hors agayn. And evur fro thens furth, he was mor comforthed in þe faith þan he was afor, and thankyd Almighti God.

Militu*m* magistri quales d*e*bent e*ss*e. S*upra* de bello, ij.

Miles demones e*ss*e non credidit. Inf*ra* de nigromancia.

Miles videt vision*em* de p*ar*adiso. Inf*ra* de p*ar*adiso.

[1] MS. iij. [2] MS. *repeats*, of.

Miles malus post mortem apparens t*er*ret suos. Inf*ra* de mortuis xvi & xvij.

CCCCXCIII.

Miles d*eb*et esse constans in p*r*elio *et* corpus expon*er*e p*er*iculo[1].

Iustinus tellis of a knyght of Athenes þat hight Cinigrus how on a tyme when he saw hys enmys had done grete slaghter, and þai gaderd mekull gude to-gedur & had it vnto a ship, and when þai wer all þ*er*in, he gatt hold on þe ship & held it w*ith* his right hand & wold not lat þai*m* go. And þai saw þ*at*, and smate it of. And when it was of, he gatt hold þ*er*on agayn w*ith* his lefte hand, and held it, & þai smate it of. And when he saw bothe his handis was of, he gatt held it w*ith* his tethe. And þus nowder for los of bothe his handis, nor for no oder hurte at he had, he wolde not lefe, bod faght as he had bene a wude beste, tyll att þe laste þai smate hym down & kyllid hym.

Miles magn*us* *et* senator vrbis h*er*emita efficit*ur*. Inf*ra* de solitudi*ne*, ij.

Miles crudel*is* per infirmitatem mansuetus efficit*ur*. S*up*ra de infirmitate, ij & v.

Miles devotus be*at*e vi*r*gini *eciam* temp*or*al*iter* honorat*ur*. S*upr*a de Maria vi*r*gine, j.

Mimo p*oss*u*n*t adaptari que dicu*n*tur s*upr*a de histrionib*us*.

CCCCXCIV.

Minucio. Minuc*i*one al*iquando* p*er*dit*ur* scie*n*cia prius h*ab*ita[2].

Cesarius tellis how som tyme þ*er* was a clerk þat was wele and sufficientlie letterd. And on a tyme he garte latt hym blode, and

[1] MS. *paradiso*; Harl. MS. *as above*. [2] *Heading supplied from* Harl. MS.

when he had bled he loste all his letterall connyng, right evyn as he [1] had loste *þaim* be blode-lattyng [2], so þat he knew not a *lettre* nor cuthe not vnderstand a lattyn wurd; not-*with*stondyng he was refte no thyng els. And þis he tolde vnto many men. So *þer* was a man on a tyme cownceld hym & sayde, "þe same day twelmo[*n*]th at þou was lattyn blude on, and þe same howre," he sulde lat hym blude agayn, and so *per*aventur he sulde gytt agayn his con*n*yng. And so he did, & he requoverd hys con*n*yng agayn als wele as evur he had it.

CCCCXCV.

Misericordia impendit*ur* inimico crucifixi amore.

Cesarius tellis how in Ducheland *þer* [3] was a knyght þat happend sla þe fadur of a noder knyght. So be chawnce his son att was slayn happend to take hym at slew his fadur. And he drew his swerde and wold hafe taken hym and slayn hym. And he fell on kneis befor hym & said; "Sur, I beseke you, ffor His luff þat dyed on þe cross & had m*er*cy of all þis werld, þat ye wold hafe m*er*cie on me now." And *with* þies wurdis he was co*m*puncte, & tuke hym vpp & sayde vnto hym; "Loo, in wyrshup of þe holie cros, & for His sake þat dyed þeron, at He may forgyf me my synnys I forgyff þe, not alonelie þe truspas at þou hase done vnto me, bod from hens furth I shall be þi frend." And *with* þat he tuke hym abowte þe nekk & kyssyd hym. And *with*-in a little while after, þis same knyght burnyd hym *with* þe cros & went vnto þe holie land. And when he come at þe kurk of þe sepulcre of our Lord, he went in-to it as other did. And, at all folk saw, þe ymage of þe *cr*ucifix bowed evyn down & lowtid vnto hym. And when þai at saw vnderstude not vnto whome he did it, þai all went aforn þe rude ilkone aft*er* oþer. And itt inclynyd vnto none of *þaim* bod vnto hym. And þai axked hym what was þe cauce, and he tolde *þaim* all as is aforn sayd.

[1] MS. *repeats*, he. [2] MS. blode lastyng. [3] MS. þat.

CCCCXCVI.

Misericordia dei om*n*ib*us* est ape*r*ta.

Maist*er* Alexander, þe bisshop of Mylan, tellis how som tyme þ*er* was a scoler off Bolayn. And on a nyght as he lay in his bed, hym þoght he was be his one in a grete felde, & þ*er* he was war, as hym þoght, of a grete tempeste, & a huge, of storm & evull weddur com oute of þe north. And he hym selfe was gretelie giffen to syn and wrichidnes. So hym þoght he was feid for þis storm & was nere evyn, & he ran als faste as he myght & gatt hym to þe town, and come vnto a howse & knokkid at þe dure & prayed þai*m* latt hym com in. And a wom*m*an wit*h*in answered hym & said; "I am Rightwusnes att dwellis here, and þou þat erte nott riȝtwus may nott com in here." And þan he went vnto a noder dure & knokkid, & prayed þai*m* latt hym com in. And one wit*h*in answerd hym & said; "I am Trewth at dwellis[1] here, & þou þat luffis not trewth sall not com in here." And þan he went vnto þe iij dure, & knokkid & prayed at he mott com in, & one answerd hym wit*h*in & said; "I am Pease þatt dwelles here, & becauce þat peas is not to wykkyd men, þerfor þou sall not com in here, ffor all my thothtes er of peas, & not of affliccion nor of dissese. Bod I cowncell þe att þou go vnto my suster þat dwellis by me att þe next howse, þat helpys all þat er in dissese." And he went vnto þe iiij dure & knokkid, and a wom*m*an answerd hym wit*h*-in & said; "I am M*er*cye þat dwellis here, and if þou will hafe me & be savid fro yone grete tempeste, þou muste go vnto þe howse of þe freer p*r*echurs in Bolayn & make þe a freer, & þ*er* þou sall be savid." And þis scoler wit*h* þis wakynd, & on þe morn he rase & went vnto þe freers & told þai*m* all his vysion & askyd þai*m* þe abbett & reseyvid it, & liffid þ*er* many a day & was a gude man & a holie.

CCCCXCVII.

Misericordia dei parata est *eciam* eu*m* negantib*us*.

Wee rede in '*Vitis* P*atrum*' how on a tyme þ*er* was a monke þat gretelie was tempid, & he went into a strete of Egipp; & þ*er*

[1] MS. dwellid.

hym̄ happend se þe doghter of a paynoms preste, & he axked to hafe hur vnto his wyfe. And þis preste wente vnto his[1] goddis in his temple, & axkid þaim cowncell & said þe monk wold algatis hafe his doghter to wyfe, "whethur sall I giff hur vnto hym̄ or nay?" And þe fend ansswerd hym̄ agayn̄ & said; "Gyff hur not vnto hym̄ bod if he furste forsake his God & his baptym̄." And he went & told þe monk, & he did all as he bad hym̄. And onone þer come oute of his mouthe a white duffe, whilk þat flow vnto hevyn̄. And þan̄ þis preste went agayn̄ and axkid cowncell att his god, and he answerd hym̄ agayn̄ & said; "Gyff nott yitt þi doghter vnto hym̄, for yitt his God helpis hym̄, þuf all he hafe forsaken̄ Hym̄." And þis preste come agayn̄ & tolde þe monke, and þis monke made grete sorow & said; "A, so wo is me! Loo! God duse me gude agayn̄ itt." And be þe cowncell of a gude holie olde man̄ he was shrevyn̄ and did penance, and adled afterward for to see þe duffe þat he had loste commyng agayn̄ vnto hym̄, and entred in att his mouthe.

Misericordie dei possunt adaptari multa que dicuntur supra de contricione et confessione, et alibi.

CCCCXCVIII.

Missa prodest viuis.

Saynt Gregur tellis how on̄ a tyme þer was a ship̄-man̄, & hym̄ happend be perisshid be þe see. And he had a gude frend, a preste, þat said a mes for hym̄ & offred þe sacrament for hym̄. And as þis preste was at þe sacryng of his mes, þis man̄ come al hole furthe of þe see, and come vnto þis preste and tolde hym̄ þat when̄ he was in þe se and alsmoste defaylid, sodanlie þer come one vnto hym̄ & broght hym̄ a lafe. & when̄ he had eten̄ itt, onone he was comforthed & had strenthe, & was takyn̄ vp into a ship̄, & so he was savid. And be his tellyng, þis preste knew þat þe same howr at þe lafe was broght vnto hym̄ he was att mess, & offred þe sacrament for hym̄.

[1] MS. our; Harl. MS. deos suos.

CCCCXCIX.

Missa it*er*um *et* alio mod*o* valet viuis.

Petrus Clunacen*sis*[1] tellis þat in þe dioces of Politañ, in Grece[2], þ*er* was a mañ[3] þatt wroght in a banke for syluer vre. And sodanlie þe banke fell and kyllid all þat was vnder-nethe. So þ*er* was one of þai*m* rañ in-to a corn*er* of þe banke and was savid; neu*er*-þe-les he mott nott gett oute. And his wyfe, trowyng þat he was dead, eu*er*ilk day garte do a mes for hym̃, and daylie at þat mes sho offerd a candell and a lofe of bread and a litle pott full of wyne. And oñ a tyme þe devull had envy at hur dede, & daylie iij dayes to-gedur, in a mans liknes, he mett hur and axkid hur whedur sho went, and evur sho tolde hym̃ þe cauce of hur gate. And he answerd hur agayñ & said; "Labur not to þe kurk in vayñ, for þe preste hathe done mess." And so þies iij dayes to-gedur sho owr-hippid & offird nott. So afterward þ*er* happend a mañ grafe in þe same banke. And sodanlie as he wroght, he hard one speke & say; "Smyte softelie, for þ*er* is a grete stone bowñ to fall oñ me." And þis mañ was ferd with þis voyce, & callid dyvers folke to here it. And he grofe oñ, and belife he harde þe same voyce. And wi*th* þat he wroght oñ & fond þis mañ & tuke hym̃ oute quykk, & axkid hym̃ how he liffid þ*er* so long. And he told þai*m* þat eu*er*ilk day, outtakeñ iij dayes to-gedur, señ þe banke fell oñ hym̃ was broght vnto hym̃ a lofe of bread and a pygg wi*th* wyne & a light candyll. And wheñ his wyfe hard þis sho was passyng glad, & knew v*er*elie þat he was sustenyd wi*th* hur offrand, and at þe devull begylid hur þies iij dayes þat sho sulde nott gar mes be done, to thentent þat he wold nott þe m*er*acle of þe mes had bene p*ro*vid nor of þe sac*ra*ment nowther.

Missa p*ro*dest defu*n*ctis. Inf*ra* de Oculis.
Missa*m* p*ro* defu*n*cti*s* celeb*ra*re est vtile. Inf*ra* de sacerdote, j.

[1] MS. Climacens*is*. [2] Harl. MS. in diocesi Greciopolitana. [3] *For* men, Latin viri.

Missa it*er*u*m* valet defu*n*ct*is*. Inf*r*a de purgatorio, iij, *et* de pecc*at*o, iij, *et* de suffragio i *et* iij.

Missa debet celeb*r*ari cu*m* om*n*i diligencia. Inf*r*a de sace*r*dote, v.

Missa celebrari no*n* debet ab indigno. Inf*r*a de sace*r*dote, x *et* vj.

Missa*m* om*n*i die audire bonu*m* est. S*upr*a de Maria, i[1], *et* de decepc*i*o*n*e, ij.

D.

Monachus debet se humil*it*er habere *et* neminem iudicare.

We rede in 'Vitis P*atru*m' how one þat hight Ioseph axked abbott Pastor how he sulde make hym selfe a monke. And he ansswerd hym agayn & said; "And þou will fynd riste bothe in þis werld & in þe toder werld, in eu*er*-ilk cauce say vnto þi selfe, 'whatt am I?' And þan shall þou nevur deam no man."

DI.

Monachus in h*ab*itu suo debet mori.

Cesarius tellis how in an abbay of Ceustus ordur þ*er* was a monk þat was gretelie vexid with sekenes, & he doffid his cowle & did on his skaplorie, and so he dyed. And he was born in-to þ*er* oratorie, & þe monk*is* began att say þ*er* psalters for hym. And sodanlie he rase vp & callid þe abbot vnto hym. And his brethur war ferd & ran away, & þe abbott come vnto hym. And he said vnto þe abbott; "Sur, I shryfe me vnto you þat I dyed wit*h*owten my cowle vppon me. And when I trowed frelie to hafe entred into paradice, Saynt Bennett come vnto me & said; 'Whar is þine abbett? Here may þou nott enter wit*h*outen itt.'" & *one*, he said, axked hym whatt he was, and he tolde hym þat he was a monke of Ceustus ordur. And he said, "'& þou be a monke,

[1] MS. v.

whar is þine abbett?' and *with* þat oþ*er* þat was aboute prayed for me, and þus I was suffred com̄ agayn̄ vnto my bodye at I mott resayfe myne abbett of þe, and at I mott so be wurthie to entre into paradice."

DII.

Monachus passiones debet rep*r*imere.

We rede ex 'Dict*is* P*atrum*' how þat abbott Pastor said in his life; "He þat is evur *com*pleynand sulde nott be a monke, and he þat duse ill for ill is no monke, and he that is angrie is nott wurthie be callid a monke." *et c⁹.*

Monachus apostata penitens, *et* sic moriens, ecia*m* post mortem h*abitum* recup*er*auit. Inf*r*a de volu*n*tate, ij.

Monachus cibaria exq*u*isita comedere non debet. Sup*r*a de gula, v.

DIII.

Mo*n*achus in gestis ext*er*ioribu*s* debet om*n*es edificare.

Iacob*us* de Vet*r*iaco tellis how som̄ tyme þ*er* was a knyght þat happend in were to take a pure man̄. And þis pure man̄ prayed hym̄ to latt hym̄ gone, and gett his rawson̄. And þis knyg[*ht*] had petie off hym̄ & said; "Whatkyn̄ suertie shall þou lefe me for þi commyng agayn̄?" And he answerd agayn̄ & sayd; "I shall fynde you God to borgh & a cawson̄ be myne othe, for other þing I may not fynd you." And þus he went his ways and selde all his lyfelod, and yit he mott nott com̄ agayn̄ at þe day att he had poyntid; and here-for þis knyght wex passyng wroth. So on̄ a day, as he rode, he was wer of a monke þat was passand fatt & read, syttand prowdelie vppon̄ a fayr palfray, and rydyng passand secularelie. And þis knyght answerd to his sweyers

& sayd; "Wult ye se þis monke, þat be his ordur sulde ride on ane ass, hase a bett*er* hors þan I hafe." And wit*h* þat he rade vnto hym & tuke hym be the brydyll, and askid hym whose man he was. & he said he had no lord bod Almiȝti God. And þan þe knyght sayd vnto hym; "Thi lorde is a suertie bon vnto me, & I will att þou for him make a sethe vnto me." And wit*h* þat he garte hym light, and tuke þe hors from hym. And wit*h*-in a while after come þis pure man and broght þe knyght his rawnson, & prayed hym to forgiff hym att he kepid not his day. And þe knyght wolde nott take his money, bod bad hym take it agayn; for, he said, his borgh had payed hym for hym & delyverd hym. And when þe pure man harde þis he was passand fayn & tuke his money vp agayn, and went home als merie as he mott be & thonkid God.

Monachus ecia*m* post mortem ab abb*at*e suo est a pecc*at*is suis absolutus. Sup*ra* de absoluc*ione*.

DIV.

Monachus in se debet esse magne penitencie, *et* leues *et* dissolutos rep*r*ehendere.

In 'Lib*ro* Purgatorio B*e*ati Pat*ri*cij,' we rede how som tyme þ*er* was a monk þat entred into þe purgatorie of Saynt Patrykk, and evur aft*er* whils he liffid he had wowndis all ffressh & new, whilk he tuke þ*er*. And he was also evur in grete penaunce, and evur when he saw any yong monk lagh vnmesurable or otherwyse be lewidlie governyd, he wold cry & say; "O! wold God þou wist whatkyn byttyr payn is giffen for mysgov*er*nans, for þan þou wold nowd*er* do nor say as þou dose." *et c*[9].

Monachus recup*er*au*i*t de vacca quod potuit. Inf*r*a de simplicitate.

Monachus p*r*op*r*ietarius in sterquilinio sepelitur. Inf*r*a de p*r*op*r*ietate, ij.

DV.

Monialis in om*n*ib*us* debet esse paciens.

Saynt Ambros tellis how þ*er* was som tyme a gude huswyfe, & sho besoght ane abbatice at sho wulde g*ra*unte hur a non for to dwell *with* hur awhile for recreac*i*on, & sho g*ra*untid hur one whilk þat was a gude buxsom, and was as a s*er*vand in þe howse, bothe vnto hur and all hur meneya. & sho servid hur all a yere & grevid no creatur in þe howse. So at þe yere end þis abbatis come & visitt þis huswyff & þis non. And þis huswyff p*ra*yed þis abbatis to take home hur non agayn, for, sho said, sho mot wyn no þing by hur, sho was so pacient and so buxsom & so s*er*visable in all þingis, & will nowder truble hur selfe nor oder folk. And sho p*ra*yed hur to send hur one at sho myght wyn somwhatt bye. And þan sho sent hur one þat was a maydyn and vncorrupte, bod sho was debatus & passyng angrie & eu*er* chidand; & alway gruchand agayns hur huswyffe, & wolde flite *with* hur and *with* all þe howse-meneya. And when þe yere end was done, þis abbatice come agayn & visitt þis huswyffe, & þan þis huswyfe spak vnto hur & said; "Ye hafe now giffen me a gude non, whilk I wold þat neu*er* sulde parte *with* me; ffor I hafe won als mekull mede be suffryng of hur inpaciens þis yere as I loste be þe mekenes of þe toder þe laste yere." And so þis non was *with* hur all hur lyfe. *et c*[9].

Monialis debet esse casta *et* constans. S*upra* de castitate, iij.

Monial*is* bona m*i*ttit occasiones videndi viros *et* p*ro*pinquos carne. Sup*r*a de affectu carnali.

Monial*is* cu*m* puritate cordis *et* corporis debet sacras vestes contractare. Sup*r*a de corporali.

Monial*is* absentis off*iciu*m su[*p*]plet be*a*ta Maria. S*upr*a de Maria, vij.

Monial*is* amore carnali capta mo*n*aste*r*iu*m* vvlt relinquere. S*upr*a de Maria, ix.

Monial*is* debet ad om*n*es *et* in *omnibus*[1] esse humil*is*. S*upr*a de fatuitate.

Monialis luxuriosa. S*upr*a de luxuria.

Monial*is* temptata fu*it* carnalit*er* *et* postea sp*ir*itualit*er*[2]. Inf*r*a de temptacione, vij.

Moniali p*ossu*nt adaptari multa que dicu*n*tur inf*r*a de muliere.

DVI.

Mors aliqu*ando* ex gaudio causat*ur*.

Valerius tellis how som tyme at Tracie þar was a grete fray w*ith*-oute þe town, and þ*er* was a wedow had hur son þ*er*, and all was nerehand slayn þat þ*er* was. & when wurde come in-to þe town, þis wedow went hur son had bene slayn, & sodanlie hur happend to mete hur son in þe yate, þat sho went had bene dead. And sho was passand fayn & hawsid hym aboute þe nekk, & kyssyd hym, & evyn furthw*ith* for ioy sho swelte & was dead.

DVII.

Mors citius p*r*ouen*it* ex gaudio q*u*am ex t*r*isticia.

Valerius tellis how after þe same fray þ*er* was a wom*m*an in þe cetie, and message come vnto hur at hur son was dead; and scho went home vnto hur howse & was passand hevye. So at þe laste sho sett hur down to mete, and sodanlie hur son come in, and als tyte as sho saw hym, for ioy sho wex evyn oute of hur mynde. And so it was mor suffrable vnto hur, þe sorow of dead, þan was þe mirthe of life.

Mors aliqu*ando* causatur ex confusione. S*upr*a de confus*ione*[3] *et* inf*r*a de silencio, ij.

[1] MS. hom*inibus*.

[2] MS. Monial*is* carnalit*er* fuit *et* postea.

[3] MS. confuc*ione*.

Mortis cogitacio mitigat temptacionem carnis. Supra de cogitacione, iij.

Mors aliquando differtur orationibus sanctorum. Supra de Basilio, ij[1].

DVIII.

Morte subita moriuntur aliquando peccatores, eciam in actu peccandi.

Petrus Damyanus tellis how som̄ tyme þer was a prynce þat hight Salamitanus[2]. So on̄ a day hym̄ happend' to luke vp vnto a hyłł, and he saw bruste oute at þe top of þe hiłł grete low & smoke. And when̄ he saw it he said' vnto þaim at stude abowte hym̄; "Withouten̄ dowte þer is som̄ curste ryche man̄ dead' & gane vnto hełł, ffor þer is swilk a custom̄ in þat contreth̄, þat when̄ þe dead' of a curste riche man̄ drawis nere, þat hyłł wiłł caste oute low & stynk of pykk and burnte stane." And when̄ þis was said', apon̄ þe nexte nyght after, as þis prince thoght he was sekur enoghe & lay in his bed with a strompett, sodanlie he dyed'. Whame, as sho teld' afterward', sho suffred' lyg long vppon̄ hur body, and at þe laste sho felid' he was no man̄ bod a stynkyng caryon̄, & keste hym̄ of hur.

DIX.

Mors eciam omnes ditissimos spoliat.

We rede in 'Cronicles' of ane þat hight Saladinus, when̄ on̄ a tyme he knew þat he sulde dye att Damaske, he callid' his hansman̄ vnto hym̄ & said'; "þou at was wunt to bere my banor vnto batełł, bere now þe banor of my dead', þat is to say a fowle clothe, þurgh̄ ałł Damaske, & cry & say þus, 'Behold'! þe kyng of þe Orient is bown̄ to dye, and he mon̄ nothyng bere with hym̄ bod þis fowle clothe.'" And onone after he dyed', & was won̄ in þe same clothe.

Morientes in hora mortis temptati per orationes sanctorum adiuuantur. Supra de demone, iij[3].

[1] MS. iij. [2] Lat. MSS. Princeps Salamitanus, Salanitanus. [3] MS. iiij.

Mors est timenda. Inf*r*a de timore.
Morte imp*r*ovisa[1] moriu*ntur* aliqu*ando* aliqui. S*upr*a de Arc*h*idiacono.

DX.

Mors *omn*ia facit relinquere.

We rede in 'Libro de Dono Timoris' how þat þe kyng of Lothoringe, þat was bod a yong man, on a tyme when he was in a trans of dead, he beheld his palas & his grete howsis and sayd; "O! þou Lord God! How mekull þis werld aght to be dispysyd! For I, þat hase had so many grete palas and so many howsis to lygg in, þis nyght I wate nott whythir I mon goo, nor who þat mon take me to he*r*berye."

DXI.

Mors q*u*ant*um*cu*n*q*ue* magnos humiliat.

Petrus Alphonsis[2] tellis how þat when kyng Alexand*er* was dead & his tombe was gaylie made of sylver & of golde, in his palas þ*er* gader in many philosophers. And ane of þai*m* said; "Alexand*er* yisterday made tresur of golde and now it is evyn contrarie, for golde makis tresur of hym." And þan a noder said; "Yisterday wolde not all þis werld suffis vnto hym, and þis day for yerdis of grond alonelie sufficis hym." And þan þe thrid said; "Yisterday he had rewle of all þe peple, and þis day þe peple hase rewle of hym." Than þe iiij said; "Yisterday he myght hafe delyverd many peple fro dead, and þis day, for all his power, he mot [*not*] esshew dead." Than þe v said; "Yist*er*day he led a grete hoste, and today he is led of þai*m* & putt vnto beryall." Than þe sext sayd; "Yisterday he thristid down þe erth, and þis day þe erth þrustis hym down." And þan a noder said; "Yisterday þe peple dred hym gretelie, and þis day þai sett right not by hym." And þan a noder said; "Yisterday

[1] MS. inprovisa.

[2] MS. Alphensis.

he had bothe many frendis and enmys, and þis day all er in lyke vnto hym."

DXII.

Mortis eciam consideracio multu*m* valet ho*mini* in dignitate co*n*sti*tu*to.

Ysidorus tellis how som [*tyme*] þ*er* was a custom, þat on þe furste day of þe crownyng of þe Emp*er*our of Constantynople, when he was in his moste ioy, a mason sulde com & bryng hym iiij or v man*er* of stonys of marble and say vnto hym on þis man*er* of wyse, and byd hym chese of þies of whilk he wolde hafe his grave made. And so it was wunt to be done in þe cowrte of Rome, for when þe Pope was chosen þ*er* was broght aforn hym a pece of lyne-tow, & when fyre was sett in it, þan was sayd vnto hym; "Thus gose þe ioy of þis werld away, as þis fyre bryng*is* þis tow in-to a spark, and afterward in-to right noght."

DXIII.

Mortis ce*r*titudo q*ua*ntu*m*cu*n*q*ue* differetur m*u*ltos induc*it* ad bonu*m*.

We rede in 'Libro de Dono Ti*m*oris' how þ*er* was a man þat had mekyll co*n*nyng in li*ter*atur of phisyk*is*, and he was giffen vnto vanyties of þis werld. So on a tyme hym happend to be at matyns on a Sonday, & þ*er* he harde in þe legend of lang life of olde fadurs, and how alway in þe end of ilkone it was sayd, 'Mortuus est, he is dead.' He vmbethoght hym þat it wold happen so on hym, and he liffid neu*er* so lang, and when he conseyvid þis, he dispysid þe werlde & entred into þe ordur of freer p*re*churs. And þ*er* he was made a freer p*re*chur at vniu*er*sitie of Paryssh, and he was a man of grete auctoritie and holynes.

DXIV.

Mortis ce*r*titudo multu*m* te*r*ret aliquos immortalitate*m* appetentes.

We rede in 'Historia Dragmanor*um*,' how þat þies Dragmans, like philosophurs, beand in wyldernes, dispysyd all werldly thyngis.

And kyng Alexander sent message vnto þa*im* & said, aske what þai wold & þai sulde hafe it. And þai wrote vnto hym agayn & said; "Grant vs þat we shall nevur dy, for þat we desyre moste of all." And he wrote vnto þa*im* agayn & sayd; "When I am mortall & mon dy my selfe, how mot I graunt you þat ye sall nevur dye?" And þai wrote vnto hym agayn & sayd; "Sen þou knowis at þou mon dye, whi duse þou so mekull ill & puttis þi selfe in so many p*er*els?"

Mortis certitudo inducit ho*min*em ad p*ro*visione*m* necessario*rum* p*ost* mort*em*. Inf*r*a de p*ro*-videncia, ij.

Mortis ce*r*titudo confirmat ho*minem* in bono i*n*-choato. Inf*r*a de sortilegio.

Mortui corpus aliqu*ando* vegetur[1] a demone. Inf*r*a de suffragijs.

DXV.

Morit*ur* homo aliqu*ando* du*m* est in ma*io*re festo.

We rede in 'Libro[2] de Dono Timoris' how at þe cetie of Dyvyon þ*er* was ane vsurar þat wed a wyfe, and þ*er* was made abown þe porche-dure many ymagis of stone. And emang other þ*er* was made ane ymage of ane vsurar wi*th* a grete purs in his hand of stone, and sodanly as þis vsurar stude at þe porche-dure to be wed, þis ymage of þe vsurar abon lete fall þe purs of stone apon þe vsurar head þat shulde be wed, & kyllid hym.

DXVI.

Mors ho*min*em qua*n*tu*m*cu*n*que adnichilat.

We rede in þe 'Gestis of Alexander' how at þ*er* was sent on a tyme vnto Alexander þe kyng a stone, and when it was put in þe balance to be weyed in þe to skale, it weyed more þan[3] all þat evur þai cuthe put in þe toder skale. And when þai put

[1] MS. vegetatur. [2] MS. *repeats*, in Libro. [3] MS. þat.

a little powder þ*er*on, it weyid les þan [1] any thyng did at þai cuthe put in þe toder skale. And when þai say þis, many wise men had grete merveH þ*er*of. And emang*is* þai*m* ane said vnto kyng Alexand*er*; "þis stone shewis vnto you what ye er; ffor now ye wey mor þan duse all þe werld, for it may skantlie bere you. Bod fro ye be deade and a little powder of erth casten on you, þan shall ye be les þan any thyng þat is in þis werld."

DXVII.

Mortis horror aliquos ad bonu*m* inducit.

We rede in '*Libro* de Dono Ti*mo*ris,' when þe kurk of Crepsie [2] shulde be halowed, & for þat þai wolde take oute þe bodie of ane erle þat was berid þ*er*, þai fand a tade sittand on his face knawand, & many wormys and serpentis, to so mekull at all þat þ*er* was fled, all bod a son of his awn. And he come to it & saw it, & tuke hym so mekull þoght þ*er*for þat he lefte all his gude & tuke hym to pou*er*tie, & was so pure at efterward he beggid his meat. And so he p*er*severd many day. So hym happend on a tyme to com vnto Rome, & þ*er* he become a collear to gett hym meat wit*h*, & he had no noder place to lig in bod vnder-nethe a grece in þe howse of a cardinall. And þ*er* he lay vnto he dyed, and made a gude end. And on þe nyght when he dyed, all þe bellis of þe kurk rang be þ*er* one.

Mortis ti*mo*r reddit ho*min*em tristem *et* cogitatiuu*m*.
Infra de timore, iij & iiij.

Mortuis valent suffragia *et* or*ati*ones *et* obla*cio*nes.
Sup*ra* de missa, iij, *et* inf*ra* de suffragio, iij.

DXVIII.

Mortis memoria indu*ci*t ho*min*es ad pen*itenti*am.

We rede in '*Libro* de Dono Timoris' how on a tyme þ*er* was a cursid knyght, and he wolde do no penance þat was enionyd

[1] MS. þat.

[2] Harl. MS. Cresby.

hym̄ for his syn̄ be Pope Alexander. & so þe Pope gaff hym̄ his ryng, & enionyd hym̄ to penans for to bere itt, vnd*er*nethe þis condicion̄, þat evur when̄ he lukid þ*er*-vppon̄, he sulde vmthynk hym̄ of his dead. And when̄ he had worn̄ it many day, and done as he bad hym̄, he turnyd agayn̄ vnto þe Pope, & said þat he was redie to fulfyll whatt penans at he wolde enioyn̄ hym̄. & so he did & was a gude man̄.

DXIX.

Mortuis p*ro*dest penitencia a viuis fac*ta* loco defu*n*ctor*um*.

Maist*er* Nicholas, þe Archebisshop, tellis how som̄ tyme þ*er* was ij felowis at war passand trew to-gedur, and ane of þai*m* happend to do a grete syn̄. So be councell of þat oþ*er* he went vnto Rome & shrafe hym̄ þ*er*of, & hym̄ was enionyd þ*er*for iij yere penance, & þis taken̄, hym̄ happend fall into a grete sekenes. And he made grete sorow at he might not fulfyll his penance, and his felow beheste hym̄ þat, & he dyed, he shuld do itt for hym̄. And when̄ he was dead & his felaw had done þis penance for hym̄, in þe end of þe furste yere he þat was dead apperid vnto hym̄, and þe thrid p*ar*te of his bodie was passand white and þe toder ij p*ar*tis blak as pykk. And in þe end of þe secund yere he apperid vnto hym̄, & ij p*ar*ties of his body white & þe iij blakk. And in þe end of þe iij yere he apperid vnto hym̄ all white, and thankid hym̄ gretelie for his delyv*er*ans.

DXX.

Mortuis valet restitucio ablator*um* fac*ta* p*ro* eis.

We rede in '*Libro* de *Dono* Timoris' how a duches son̄ was bown̄ to dye, & he was shrevyn̄ & yit he was bod ix yere olde. And when̄ he was dead he aperid vnto his moder & told hur he was in grevus payn̄, becauce[1] he had not payed dettis þat he had borowid of his fadur meneya to play hym̄ wi*th*, becaus

[1] MS. *repeats*, becauce.

he had no thoght þ*er*on̄ when̄ þat he dyed'. And his moder garte spyr att whome he borowid' it, & garte pay it vnto þai*m*. And afterward' þe child' apperid' vnto hur agayn̄, & lete hur hafe knowlege that he was delyverd oute of payn̄, & put in grete ioy and felicitie.

DXXI.

Mors pulcritudi*n*em *et* om*n*es gr*ati*as corporales destruit.

We rede of ane, Isabell, þat was hy Whene of Navern̄, and when̄ sho drew nere hur dead' sho garte light many lightis aboute hur bed', and garte feche in many knyghtis & grete men of þe cetie. Sho sayde vnto þai*m* on̄ þis man*er* of wyse; "Vmthynk you & se þat I, þe Whene of Navern̄, þe Cowntas of Ca*m*panye, and þe doght*er* of þe Kyng of Fraunce, whilk þat was clere & fayr & discrete, and gracious in eu*er*-ilk mans sight, now, as ye see, dead wyll com̄ to me & destroy all þies."

Mori debet religiosus in h*ab*itu suo. Sup*ra* de mo*n*acho, ij.

Morientes aliqu*ando* demones asser*u*nt. Inf*ra* de vsurario, ij.

Mortui ecia*m* in odio morie*n*tes p*ost* mortem illud retine*n*t. Inf*ra* de odio.

Mortuor*um* pecc*atoru*m corp*or*a *eciam* post morte*m* visib*i*lit*er* puniu*n*t*ur*. S*up*ra de luxuria.

DXXII.

Mortui aliqu*ando* monent viuos p*ro* eis vt ablata restituant.

Cesarius tellis how þ*er* was a knyght, þat hight Fredericus of Kelle, when̄ he was dead apperid' vnto a man̄ sittand' vppon̄ a blak stede, & oute of his nese-thrilles come a grete reke & flawm̄

& he was coverd all with skynnys & bare a grete lumpe of erth betwix his shulders. And þe man þat he apperid vnto askid hym if he war Fredericus, and he answerd agayn & said he was. & he axkid hym fro whyne he come, and what all þat bement att he saw. And he answerd hym agayn & said; "I am in grete paynys, and þies skynnys I tuke fro a wedow & now I fele þai*m* burnand vppon me. Also þ*er* was solde vnto me wronguslie a c*er*tayn porcion of land, & now it burnys on my bakk & thrustis me down. Bod & my childer wulde restore it agayn, my payn mon be lestend." And þus he vanysshid away. And when his childer hard tell of þ*er* fadur wurdis be þis man þat spak *with* hym, þai wolde not yelde þis lande agayn, bod had levur at þ*er* fadur sawle war evur in payn þan at þai p*ar*tid *with* þis lande.

DXXIII.

Mortui aliqu*ando* apparentes infestant viuos.

Cesarius tellis how þat in þe bisshoppryk of Tryuarens þ*er* was som tyme a knyght þat hight Henrie, & he vsid robborie, avowtrie, inceste, & to be mane-sworn. And when he was dead he apperid vnto many folk. So at þe laste he apperid vnto a doght*er* þat he gatt in avowtrie, & afterward lay by hur hym selfe, and he wolde nowder lett for crossyng nor strykyng *with* swerd. And when he was stryken, he mott not be wowndid, and þ*er* come fro hym swilk a sownd like as þe bed had bene dongen on *with* mellis. So at þe laste, when he wold no wyse away, thurgh cowncell of þe arche-bisshopp þai tuke holy watyr on a Sonondày, & keste on hur & ouer all þe chawmer. And when þis was done þai saw hym nevur after.

DXXIV.

Mors amicor*um* debet pacient*er* tolerari [1].

Valerius tellis of ane þat hight Anaxagor, a whilosophur, when one tolde hym þat his son was dead he answerd agayn & sayd;

[1] MS. tollerari.

"Tell me not þat I wate, ffor I knew when he was born þat he sulde dye." Also Oracius tellis of a bisshop þat hight Iovis [1], how on a tyme as he was halowand a howse, as he was enoynttand þe poste *with* his hand, ane come & teld hym þat his son was dead; and he nowder removid his hand fro þe poste, nor left his obser-vance for no sorow, þat he sulde not be sene of þe peple to do mor þat longed vnto a fadur þan vnto a bisshopp. Also we rede of Socratic*us*, when þat he did his offrand, one lete hym witt þat þe more [2] of his sons was dead, he wold not lefe his offrand, neu*er*-þe-les he doffed his crown. Neu*er*-þe-les he spurrid how he dyed, & it was told his son dyed & faght manlelie in þe felde; & when he harde teld of þat he tuke þe crown agayn & dond it on his head, and said he made mor gladnes þat his son dyed manlely þan sorow for his dead.

DXXV.

Morientes lib*er*antur a temptacionib*us* demonu*m* pe*r* deuotas or*ati*ones.

Saynt Gregur tellis þat in his monast*er*ie þ*er* was a childe þat hight Theodor*us*, whame he was passand fell & grevus *with*, & þis childe wolde be passand wrothe *with* any þat tolde hym oght for his gude, and gladlie he wold not here þai*m*. So be proces of tyme hym happend to be seke & lay in trans of dead, and when all þe monk*is* stude aboute hym he began to cry, & sayd; "Go your ways! Go your ways! For I am gyffen vnto þe dragon to devowr. Now he hase swolod in-to his mouthe my head, bod for you he may not swolow me all. Gyff hym rome þat he no langer turment me, bod þat he may do att he come for to do." And one of þai*m* bad hym sayn hym, & he said he wold fayn bod he myght nott. So þai fell vnto þ*er* prayers devoutelie, & þan þis seke childe began to cry, & sayd; "I thank all-myghti [*God*], for þurgh your prayers þe dragon is fled & I am delyverd."

[1] Harl. MS. Oraci*us*, quoq*ue* Iouis pontifex.

[2] Harl. MS. maiore*m* e duob*us* filijs.

DXXVI.

Mortuis no*n* est detrahend*um*.

We rede ex 'Legenda Lombar*dica*,' how þat in þe monast*er*ie of Saynt Gregor þ*er* was a monk þat was so vexid *with* þe axis at he was like to dye. & his brethir said þ*er* psalters aboute hym, trowyng þat he sulde dye. And when þai had done þai began to bakbyte hym. So yitt hym happend to turn agayn vnto lyfe, & he lifte vp his ene & smylid & said; "God forgyf you, brethir! Whi wolde ye bakbyte me? Ye hafe done vnto me a grete impediment, ffor I was bothe at onys accusid bothe of you & of þe devull and I wiste neu*er* to whethur dissease I might answer. And þerfor when ye se any man bown to dy, bakbite hym not, bod hafe co*m*passion on hym, at ye make hym no lettyng when he co*m*mys afor þe strayte iugement of almyghtie God."

DXXVII.

Mulierem tangere no*n* est bonu*m*.

Thar was a man of religion þat on a tyme went o-gateward[1] *with* his moder. And when þai come vnto a watyr, & he sulde bere our his moder, he[2] tuke his handis & wappid þai*m* in his skirte, at he sulde not tuche þe handis of his moder. And when he had born hur our, sho askid hym whi he did so. And he answerd agayn & said, "þe body of a wom*m*an is fyre, & becauce I thoght what wom*m*en er, þ*er*for I wold not tuche þe for perell þat mot happen þ*er* vppon."

Mulier debet cauere ne[3] ornatu, v*e*l pulc*r*itudi*n*e, v*e*l alloq*u*io p*ro*vocet viru*m*. S*upr*a de abscondere.

Mulier casta est amanda. Sup*r*a de castitate, ij.

Mulierib*us* naturalit*er* inest compassio. S*upr*a de co*m*passione, ij.

Mulier diligent*er* debet custodiri. Sup*r*a de ffilia.

[1] Latin, cum matre sua *iter faceret*.

[2] MS. & he.

[3] MS. ne donis ornatu.

Mulier vltro se ingerit viro. Sup*ra* de casti*tat*e, v, et de luxu*r*ia, i.

Mulier amore castitatis *eciam* pro*pr*ia memb*r*a corporis debet conte*m*pnere. S*upra* de casti*tat*e, iij.

Mulier amore casti*tatis* *eciam* pro*pr*ia*m* pat*r*iam debet relinquere. S*upra* de Clemente.

Mulier amore casti*tat*is *eciam* corpus pro*p*r*ium* exponit pe*r*iculo. Vt *supra*.

Mulieris coh*ab*itacio no*n* est secura viro. S*upra* de c*r*uce, ij, *et* de carne, i.

DXXVIII.

Mulier *eciam* amicu*m* nititur decip*er*e.

Valerius tellis of one þat hight Zenoc*r*ates Platonicus, whilk þat was a man of such v*er*tue, þat he wolde lat no man swere for no man*er* of cauce, bod att eu*er*e man sulde be trowid be his playn wurd; & he was ffamilier vnto a wom*m*an of Athenis. So on a day as sho spak *with* oþ*er* wommen, sho trustyng gretelie in þe familiaritie of þis philosophur, sho laid a grete wageor at sho sulde bryng hym oute of þe purpos of chastite. So þis philosophur on a tyme come vnto hur, & sho made hym mery of wyne so þat he liste slepe. & sho lenyd his head down in hur kne, & of his awn wyll þ*er* he lay a grete while. And evur sho talkid vnto hym wurdis to p*ro*voce hym to luste of his bodie, and yit be no wyse myght sho induce hym þ*er*to, & so he went his wais & sho loste hur wageor. And when þe toder wom*m*en axked hur þat at sho had loste, sho ansswerd agayn & said, þ*a*t sho layd hur wageor of a man & not of a stokk, for he was a stokk, sho sayd, & no man.

DXXIX.

Mulier virtuosa.

Valerius tellis how þ*er* was a man þat hight Ninus, þat had a wyfe. & when he was dead, on a day as scho was byndand vpp hur head, it was lattyn̄ hur wit þat Babylon̄ defaylid in batall. And *with* þe ta syde of hur heade vnbun vpp̄ sho ran̄ to feght agayn̄ þaim of Babilon̄, & neu*er* wold sitt at bynd vp hur head vnto all was won̄ & þai ffled. & þ*er*for is ane ymage made of hur & sett vp̄ in þis man*er* of wyse.

DXXX.

Mulier luxuriosa.

Orosius tellis of one þat hight Se*m*iramis, þat was burnand in lichorie & thristie in blude, made ane ordinans and a constitucion̄ þat for no man*er* of reu*er*ens nor inceste þ*er* sulde no lettyng be, bod at betwix þe fadur & þe moder & þ*er* childer, als ofte as þai*m* lykid, it sulde be lefull to hafe at do same*n* or for to hafe to wyfe or husband. So on̄ a tyme sho desyryd hur awn̄ son̄ to hafe at do *with* hur, and þ*er* in despite he slew hur.

DXXXI.

Adhuc de muliere luxuriosa.

We rede in 'Cronicles' of þe wyfe of Claudius, how þat sho was so gyffen̄ vnto luste & lykyng, þat furste p*r*ivalie and syne opynlie sho wold expownd hur selfe, & cowncell þ*er*to other noble wom*m*en̄, so þat sho þoght þat sho had neu*er* enogh þ*er*of. And at þe laste þe Emp*er*owr & hur husband to-gedur slew hur; and sho was so forgettell of mynd þat when̄ þai slew hur sho askid þai*m* whi þai wolde not com̄ & hafe att do *with* hur.

Mulier sup*er*ba *et* despiciens viru*m* q*uandoque* postea viro capitur. S*upr*a de Assenech.

Mulieres no*n* expedit videre. Infra[1] de videre.

Mulier rixosa pacient*er* a viro est toleranda[2]. Inf*r*a de paciencia.

Mulier loquax g*r*auit*er* punitur. S*upr*a de locucione.

[1] MS. supra. [2] MS. tolleranda.

Mulieris nequicia co*m*p*a*rat*ur* se*r*penti. Inf*r*a de serpente.

Mulier adultera viru*m* suu*m* co*n*te*m*pn*i*t. Sup*r*a de adult*er*io, j.

Mulier bona debet esse que ducit*ur* in vxore*m*. Inf*r*a de vxore.

Mulier debet esse quieta *et* no*n* vaga. Inf*r*a de vxo*r*e.

Mulier ad peccandu*m* est parata si requiratur. Inf*r*a de silencio, ij.

Mulier naturalit*er* ad se att*r*ahit affec*tu*m viri. S*upr*a de co*n*cupiscencia, j.

Mulier temptat viru*m*. Inf*r*a de temptacione, v.

Mulier aliqu*ando* feruens est ad [1] bonu*m*. S*upr*a de martirio.

DXXXII.

Mulier i*n*fidelis est marito suo morienti.

We rede how a wom*m*an, when hur husband lay in dead thrawis, callid hur mayden & bad hur go by hur iij yerdes of h*ar*dyn, 'to wynde my husband in." And sho answerd agayn & sayd; "Dame, ye hafe enoghe of fayr lyn clothe. Take þ*er*of iiij yerdis and wynd hym in." And sho was wroth [2] & said; "May not iij yerdis of h*ar*den s*er*riff hym well enogh?" So þis man at lay seke happend for to here hur, and when he come to hym selfe, als ill as he myght, yitt he said; "Ya, make it shorte enogh þat it be not fylid w*ith* clay [3]."

DXXXIII.

Mulieres qu*ando*q*ue* p*ro* parua re litigant.

We rede in 'Libro de Dono Timoris' how þ*er* was ij women pleyd befor a iuge for a clew of threde. And þe iuge axkid ather

[1] *After* ad, h, *erased.* [2] *After* wroth, s, *erased.*
[3] *A hand with* Nota *above it points to this tale.*

of þai*m* whar-of þe bothom at þe clew was won on was. And þe tane said it was on a cole & þe toder said it was on a lyn clowte. And þan he rewardid at þe clew sulde be won of, & sho at said sothe of þe bothom sulde hafe it.

DXXXIV.

Mulieres[1] attente respice*re* no*n* de*b*ent religiosi.

We rede in 'Vitis P*atrum*' how on a tyme a monk ran for to se maydens as þai come sam*en* goyng be þe way. And when he had sene þai*m* he turnyd oute of þe way. And þan ane olde wyfe at was wi*th* þur maydyns sayd vnto þis monk; "And þou wer a p*ar*fite monke þou sulde not behalde vs, nor know þ*at* we wer wommen."

Mulier papa creatur. Inf*r*a de papa.

Muliere*m* demon incu*m*bens infestat. S*upr*a de demo*ne*, xj *et* xij.

Mulier nobil*is* ecia*m* viro aliqu*ando* se ingerit. Inf*r*a de temptac*io*ne, vj.

Mulier molestia carnis est temptata. Inf*r*a de temptac*io*ne, vij.

Mulier*um* ornatui congaudet demon. Inf*r*a de ornatu, ij.

Mulier viru*m* suu*m* in remotis p*ar*tib*us* pe*r*gentem debet exp*e*cta*re* diu an*te* qu*a*m nubat. Inf*r*a de pe*r*eg*r*ino *et* sup*r*a de celacione, j.

Mulier secretum e*st* male celans. Sup*r*a de celacione.

DXXXV.

Mulier mala decipit viru*m* suu*m*.

Petrus Alphons*is*[2]; how som tyme a man went to wede hys vynys, and his wyfe trowid þat he wold hafe tarid long and callid

[1] MS. Muliere. [2] MS. Alphensis.

hur luff into þe hows. So þis man happend to be smyten in þe ee *with* a twyste, so þat he mot not se, & he mott hafe no ruste þerof & went home. And when he knokkid at þe dure þe wyfe was ferde, & hid hur luff in a chawm*er* & aft*er*ward oppynd þe dure. And hur husband went in & wolde hafe gane vnto þe bed; and sho axkid hym what he wolde do at þe bed, and he tellid hur all as it had happend hym. And sho bad hym sitt down & latt hur charm þe hale ee, þat it happend nott þe same. And sho putt hur mowthe vnto þe hale ee to likk it, vnto hur luff was gone his way, at hur husband wiste nott. And þan sho bad hur husband ryse, & sayd vnto hym; "Now I am sekur of þis ee. And now if you like ye may go vnto your bed and riste you." And so he did.

DXXXVI.

Mulier vna alia*m* in maleficijs iuuat.

Petrus Alphons*is*[1] tellis how som tyme þ*er* was a man þat went on pylgramege, and he betuke his wyfe to kepe vnto hur moder vnto he come home. And when he was gone sho sent for hur doghtur lemman to sup *with* þai*m*, & þai ete & drank sam*en* & made merie. And sodanlie þe gudeman come vnto þe dure & callid, and sho was gretelie trublid þ*er*-*with*, & hid hur lemman in þe chawmer and þan lete hur gudeman com in. And he was wery & wete, & bad þai*m* go make his bed. And þis olde wyfe bad hur dogh*ter* bryng a shete & latt hym se it þat he sulde lig in, or sho made þe bed. And sho broght a fayr shete, and þe olde wyfe toke þat one end þ*er*of, & þe yong wyfe þe toder, and held it vp on ege als hy as þai might aforn þe chawm*er* dure, & þus þai hid þe gude man at he might not se to he was gone, at þai had hyd, oute att þe chaw*m*ber dure. And þe gude man bade styll & had a mokk[2]. And þa*n* þis olde wyfe said vnto hur doghter; "Ga now & make þi husband bedd *with* þis shete at I made myne awn handis sen he went." And he said; "Dame, can ye wefe such clothe?" "Ya, son," sho said, "forsuth I hafe wroght mekull suche sen I was born."

[1] MS. Alphen*sis*

[2] Latin, et marit*us* delusus remansit.

DXXXVII.

Mulier mediatrix aliam ad peccatum inducit.

Petrus Alphonsis[1] tellis how som tyme þer was a wurshupfull man þat went on pylgramege, and he had a gude wyfe and a chaste. So þer was a yong man þat luffid hur passandly, & wolde hafe giffen hur grete giftis to hafe had his luste on hur, and sho wolde not on no wyse. So at þe laste he fell seke for sorow at he mot not spede, & lay in his bed. So þer come in ane olde wyfe & vysitt hym & askid hym what was þe cauce at he was seke for. And he oppynd his herte vnto hur & tolde hur all þat hym aylid. And sho said hym þurte not be seke her-for, sho euthe help hym well enogh. And he promysid hur a gude rewarde to helpe hym. So sho had a little bykk whelpe, & sho held it fastand ij dayes. So on þe iij day sho made a cake of mustard & mele & gaff it, & it ete it. And for bytuernes of þe musterd it began hugelie to grete, & þe een þerof to ryn. So sho went vnto þis gude wyfe hows, and þis whelpe folowid hur. And sho, becauce sho was ane olde wyfe, welcomyd hur fayre, & gaff hur meat & drynk. So at þe laste sho askid hur what þis whelpe aylid to wepe þus. And sho ansswerd & said; "Dere Dame! it is no mervell if I make sorow & wepe, for þis whelpe was my doghter, & was a full leall maydyn, & a gude & a fayr. And becauce sho wolde not consentus vnto a yong man þat luffid hur, to be his luff, þus sho was shapen to be a biche whelpe." And *with* þat sho lete as sho swownyd & wepid sore. So þis gude wyfe made mekull sorow, & said; "What mon I do? Allas! for I am in þe same cace; ffor a yong man luffis me & I hafe dispysid hym, and I am aferd þat I sall oght be mysshapend." And þan þe olde wyfe ansswerd & cownceld hur to consent vnto hym, & latt hym hafe his liste at sho wer not forshapyn & made a byche whelpe. & sho prayed hur to go for hym, and so sho did & fechid hym vnto þis womman, & þer he had his luste & his desyre; & þis false alde when had a gude reward of ather partie.

[1] MS. Alphensis.

DXXXVIII.

Mulier difficile custoditur.

Petrus Alphons*is*[1] tellis how som̄ tyme þ*er* was a yong wed man̄, and þurgh consell of ane olde wyse man̄ he closid his wyfe in a hye chawm*er* þat had no dure butt one, and a wyndow, & evur as he come owder in or oute, he sparrid þe dure faste. And on̄ þe night he wolde hyde þe keyis at his bed head. And þus he did a long tyme. So on̄ a tyme when̄ hur husband was away, sho lukid furth at þe wyndow, and sho was war of a fressh yong man̄, & onone sho wex iolious on̄ hym̄. And to þe entent at sho mott gett oute vnto hym̄, iij nyghtis or iiij, by & by sho made hur husband dronken̄. And on̄ a nyght p*ri*valie when̄ he was on̄ slepe, sho stale þe keyis fro his head & oppynd þe durys. And p*ri*valie sho went vnto þis yong man̄. So hur husband wakynd & myssid hur, & compasid þat *with*-owten̄ a cauce sho wolde not hafe desyrid [*hym*] to drynk so faste on̄ evyns as sho did, & said no þing bod lay still & slepte. So when̄ sho had had hur luste, sho come in agayn̄, and he lete as he myssid hur noght. So on̄ a night afterward, he fenyd hym̄ selfe dronken̄, and þe same night sho rase vp as sho did afor, and went vnto hur luff. And onone as sho was gone, he rase p*ri*valie & folowid hur & come vnto þe dure & sparrid it faste, & went vp agayn̄ & stude in þe wyndow wachand. And at þe laste he was war of hur com*m*and in hur sark. And sho knokkid, & he axkid who was þ*er*? And sho besoght hym̄ forgyff hur at sho went furth, & to latt hur com̄ in. And he said sho suld not com̄ in, bod sho sulde stand still þ*er* & he suld shew hur vnto hur fadur & hur moder in þe aray at sho was in. And þe vse was þat þai þat wer fon̄ þ*er*-oute at mydnyght, wachemen̄ sulde take þai*m* & on̄ þe morn̄ sett þai*m* on̄ þe pyllorie, þat all men̄ myght wonder on̄ þai*m*. And when̄ sho saw þat on̄ na wyse he wolde lat hur in, sho said sho sulde lepe into a draw-well at was bod a litle frō þe dure, & drown̄ hur selfe, rather or sho war takyn̄ & shamyd. And when̄ sho saw for all þis at he wold not lat hur in, sho tuke

[1] MS. Alphens*is*.

vp̄ a grete stone & keste in-to þe draw weƚƚ, and bad fare-wele for evurmoꝛ. And when̄ he herd it faƚƚ in-to þe weƚƚ, he went it had bene sho had loppyn̄ in-to þe weƚƚ, and he was somwhat asstonyd, and he oppyn̄ þe dure faste, & ran̄ vnto þe weƚƚ at luke if he mott gett hur oute. And sho had hid hur be þe waƚƚ & saw þe dure was oppyn̄, & whippid in & lokkid þe dure faste, & gatt hur vp in-to þe wyndow. And when̄ he hard sho was getten̄ in, he said; "O, þou fals womman̄, and fuƚƚ of þe devuls crafte! Lat me com̄ in!" And sho said, nay, he sulde nott. And þ*er* sho held hym̄ oute vnto wache-men̄ come & tuke hym̄, & had hym̄ vnto *prison̄*. And on̄ þe morn̄ sho went vnto hur fadur & hur modir, and told þai*m* how þat he went oute on̄ þe nyght to his strompett*is* & for-suke hur, & þ*er* þai come vnto þe *prison̄* aƚƚ sam*en* & made playnt on̄ hym̄. And þ*er* in his sarke & his breke he was sett on̄ þe pelloryе, at aƚƚ folk wonderd on̄ hym̄, & þus maliciouslie sho put hur blame opon̄ hym̄.

DXXXIX.

Mulie*r*is malicia qu*andoq*ue in caput suu*m* redundat.

We rede in 'Cronicles,' when̄ kyng Albyon̄ was at Veron̄ at a grete feste, he commanddid his butler to feche hym̄ a copp þat he had made of þe heade of þe furst husband of Rosamond, at was his wyfe, whame he had slayn̄ in bateƚƚ; & he garte fyƚƚ it fuƚƚ of wyne & dranke þ*er*of, & gaff Rosamond his wyfe & made hur to drynk þ*er*of. And he bad hur drynk *with* hur furst husband, and sho *con*seyvid what he ment & was passand wrothe *with* hym̄. So þ*er* was in þe cowrte a duke þat held[1] a chawmerer of þe whene, & sho had knowlege þ*er*of. And on̄ a tyme when̄ þe kyng was fro home, opon̄ a nyght sho went into þis chawmerer bed, & sent *pri*valie vnto þis duke a message as it had comm*en̄* from̄ hur chawmerer, & bad hym̄ com̄ & lye *with* hur; and þ*er* þis duke lay bye hur. And when̄ he had done sho said vnto

[1] MS. *repeats*, þat held.

hym̄; "Knowis þou what I am̄?" and he said; "Ya, þou erte þe chawmerer, my lemman̄." And sho said, "Nay, I am Rosamond, att þou has done þis dede *with*; & chese þe oon̄ of ij. For owther þou sall sla kyng Albyon̄ at slew my furst husband & garte me drynk of his head, or els I sall tell hym̄ what þou hase done, & make hym̄ to sla þe. And þerfor venge me of hym̄ þat made my husband head in a copp, or els þou sall dye þerfor." And he said, nay, he wold not do it hym̄ selfe, bod he promysid hur att he sulde gett a noder þat sulde do it. And sho gart hide þe kyng*is* armor & his batell-ax at stude at his bed-head, & his swerd at hang sho gart bynd it, so at it mott not com̄ oute of þe shethe. And when̄ þe kyng was in his bed & of slepe, þis manwheller come in, & þe kyng gat his swerd & wold hafe drawen̄ oute, & it wold not; & so he was slayn̄. And þan̄ he tuke Rosamond, & all þe knygis tresur & ffled vnto þe Cetie of Raven̄[1]; & þ*er* he wedd hur. And hur happend þ*er* on̄ a tyme to se a fayr yong man̄, & sho wex amoros of hym̄, and þoght þat sho wolde hafe hym̄ to hur husband. And sho gaff hym̄ þat had wed hur poysen̄ to drynk, and kyllid hym̄. And when̄ he felid þat it was venom̄, he garte hur drynke of þe reu*er*cion̄. And sho wolde nott, & he tuke oute hys swerd & bad hur drynk it, or he sulde kyll hur. And so sho drank it, & þ*er* þai wer both dead.

DXL.

Mulier vbiq*ue* ab om*n*ib*us* est fugienda.

We rede in 'Vitis P*atrum*' how þe abbot Semestras had c*er*tan̄ disciples þat on̄ a tyme said vnto hym̄; "Sur, [*go*] we into þe werld a while, & latt vs dwell þ*er*." And he answerd agayn̄ & sayd; "Go we þan̄ whare no wom*m*an̄ is." And þai answerd hym̄ agayn̄ & said; "Whar is þat place þat a wom*m*an̄ is not in, bod if þat it be in wyldernes?" And þan̄ þe abbott answerd agayn̄ & said; "Therfor I pray þe, lat vs abide in wyldernes."

Mulieris memoria in corde viri esse non debet. Sup*ra* de me*mori*a, ij.

[1] Lat. MSS. Ravenna.

Mulier luxuriosa in *p*ro*p*riu*m* filiu*m* impet*it*. S*up*ra Andree, ij.

Mulieris spec*ie* diabolus s*anct*os temptat. Sup*r*a Andree, iij.

DXLI.

Mulieris nobil*is* vi*r*tus qu*andoque* apparet in morte.

Iustinus tellis of ane þat hight Olimpias, and when she saw armyd men come and wold hafe slayn hur, sho went & cled hur in gay clothyng, & tuke ij maydens *with* hur and went to mete þai*m*. And when þai saw hur in þat aray, þai wer astonyd at sho did so & þai went agayn vnto þ*er* maisters [*& teld*] how þai fand hur not ferd nor fleand fro dead, nor at sho was not ferd for swerd nor wownd, nor wepid wom*m*anlyke, bod resayvid armyd men mekelie *with* ioy & murth, and obeyid hur to vndergo dead. And þus sho was delyverd.

DXLII.

Mulier *et* viuens *et* moriens honestatem debet se*r*vare.

Iustin*us* tellis of þis same wom*m*an, how on a tyme[1] sho was stryken *with* a swerd & fell down & dyed, & yit *with* hur clothis & hur hare sho coverd hur theis, so þat none vnwurshup of hur bodie sulde be sene. Also we rede of the whene of Narvan[2], þat hight Isabell, & was doght*er* vnto Saynt Lowyce þat was kyng of Fraunce, þat if all sho was yong and passand fayr, neu*er*-þe-les sho wolde neu*er* lyg *with* Kyng Theobald, at was a fayr yong man at had wed hur, bod in hur sark, nor lat hym lig *with* hur bod in his sark & his breke. Nor þ*er* was neu*er* none of hur maydens, nowder *p*rivalie nor apert, þat nowder in bath nor in wasshyng saw als mekull as hur ancle bare. And when sho dyed, sho com*m*andid hur maydens þat þai sulde wapp all hur bodye & hur

[1] MS. tyme when.   [2] Harleian MS. de regina Navarre.

membres in a long webb & sew it, at when becauce of sethyng hur membrus burde be cutt, þe clothe sulde be cutt, at þai þatt cutt hur sulde not se none partie of hur body bare.

Mulier sine assensu viri non debet dare magna. Infra de vxore.

Mundi debent esse qui contractant sancta vasa et vestes. Supra de corporali.

Mundi pericula sunt evitanda. Infra de risu et de periculis.

Mundo possunt adaptari que supra dicuntur de contemptu mundi, de diuicijs et morte.

DXLIII.

Munera parua ab amicis data sunt non spernenda.

Senec tellis how þat when þe disciples of Socrates come and broght hym many giftis, he had a pure scolar þat hight Escharmes, þat come & offerd hym selfe vnto hym and said; "Sur, I giff you þe beste þing þat I hafe, þat is myne awn bodye." & he said þat oþer þat gaff hym small giftis helde þer beste giftis behynde, & so wolde not he doo, bod he prayed his mayster to take þat pure gifte, & so labur it with all his diligens, att it mott be better & fayrer for his sake. And his maister ansswerd hym agayn & sayd; "I have tane a grete gyfte of þe bod if þou þinke þi selfe little, and giff þi selfe besylie for þine awn profett to do all thyng at I command the."

Munera magna non debet dare vxor sine licencia viri. Infra de vxore.

DXLIV.

Munera accipere non debet princeps vel prelatus.

Valerius tellis of one Marchus Thurius, þat was þe nobyllest cowncelor within Rome. & on a tyme a grete man come vnto hym & faud hym syttand at his supper be þi fyre, & all his meat on a tre-dubler. And he offerd vnto hym & wold hafe gyffen a grete porcion of syluer vessell, & bad hym were þaim for his sake. & he forsuke þaim & wolde not take þaim. And he was wrothe þerwith & said; "Ye sall nevur tell þat Marchus Thurius had lere be lorde of riches þan for to be maid riche of wisdom. For vmthynk you þat ye neuer saw me ourcommen in batell, nor yit be corrupte with money."

Murmurare non debet pauper cui datur elemosina. Infra de paupertate.

DXLV.

Mures *eciam* homines aliquando inuadunt.

We rede in 'Cronicles' þat in þe tyme of þe iij Henrie þe Emperour, how þer was a riche man on a day satt at his meate. And sodanlie he was vmlappid with a grete flok of myce, and sodanly þai lefte all [1] at was in þe howse, & pursewid vppon hym. & men tuke hym and had hym vnto a ship on þe watir at he mot so esskape þe myce, & voyde þaim fro hym. And þai lepid after hym in-to þe watyr, & come to þe shupp & gnew it þurgh. & so he mott on no wyse kepe hym fro þaim, vnto so muche att he was had to land agayn; & þer þe myce fell on hym & kyllid hym, & ete hym vp euere morsell vnto þe bare bonys.

DXLVI.

Musce infestant multos.

We rede ex 'Legenda Lombardica [2]' how at þer happend on a tyme a grete multitude of fleis in ane abbay þat Saynt Barnard made, vnto so mekull at þai did mekull noysans vnto all men þat dwellyd þerin. And when þai come & tolde hym, he said þat he sulde curs þaim, & on þe morn þai wer fon dead, ilk one.

Mutacio frequens iudicum [3] non est populo vtilis. Supra de ballivo, ij.

[1] MS. *repeats*, all. [2] MS. ex legibus Lombardorum.
[3] MS. iu den. Harl. MS. iudicum.

DXLVII.

Natalis D*omi*ni, p*ri*mo.

The birth of our Lord is p*re*vyd be many m*er*acleys, ffor Innocencius þe iij telles how at Rome þ*er* was co*n*tynuall pease xij yere to-gedur, and þ*er*for þe Romans byggid a fayre temple, & sett þ*er*in þe ymage of Romulus, & garte call it Templu*m* Pacis. And þai askyd Appollo how long it sulde laste, & he said vnto a wom*ma*n þat was a clene mayden bare a childe. And when þai hard þat, þai said it sulde laste evur, & wrate abowne þe dure in golden letters; 'Templum D*omi*ni [1] in et*er*nu*m* manet.' And when our Ladye bare hur childe, vppon þat same nyght it fell down vnto þe hard erth, and þ*er* is now Eccle*si*a Sa*nc*te Marie Noue [2].

DXLVIII.

Natalis D*omi*ni p*ro*batur dupliciter, ijo.

Ex 'Legenda Lombardica [3]' we rede how þat vppon þat day þe ymage of Romulus and all oþ*er* ydolfis in Rome fell down & brak. And Saynt Ierom tellis also how þ*er* come a tokyn in Egipte for all þ*er* idolfis fellis when our Ladye bare hur chylde. And her-for þe p*re*stis of þe temple garte make ane ymage of a maydyn wi*th* a barn in hur arm, and sett it in a privay place in þ*er* temple, & vnto þat þai did wurshup.

DXLIX.

Natalis D*omi*ni p*ro*batur multipliciter, iijo.

We rede ex 'Le*gen*da Lombard*ica*' how þat same nyght þe derknes of þe nyght and clerenes of þe day war turnyd evun contrarie.

[1] Lat. MSS. Templum Pacis. [2] MS. Sa*nc*te Marie de nouo.
[3] MS. Legibu*s* Lombardor*um*.

DL.

Natalis *pro*batur, iiij^{to}.

Orosius and Innosins[1] tellis how þat a well in Rome þat same nyght was turned in-to oyle & ran in-to Tyber, and all þe day af*ter* spran habundandlye; ffor Sibilla had *pro*phecyed & said þat our Savyor sulde not be born or a well of oyle sprang oute of þe erthe.

DLI.

Nat*a*lis D*omi*ni *pro*batur, v^{to}.

Crysostim*us* tellis þat vppon þe nyght of þe natiuitie, vnto þe kynges þat war prayand on a hyll, a fayr starn appered[2] vnto þai*m*. & it had in it a fayre childe, and vppon his shulder a fayr cros shynyng, whilk childe spak vnto þe kyng*is* and bad þai*m* go in-to Iudea & seke hym, & þ*er* þai sulde fynd hym born.

DLII.

Natalis D*omi*ni *pro*batur, vj^{to}.

We rede in '*Legenda* Lomb*ardica*' how þat vppon þat day þ*er* apperid in þe este iij sonnys[3], and somwhat befor þat tyme af*ter* þe dead of Iulius Cesar.

DLIII.

Natalis D*omi*ni *pro*bat*ur*, vij^{mo}.

Innocencius þe iij, pope, tellis how þat Ottouianus þe Emp*er*our, þat all þe werld was subgett vnto, and be his reson he plesid so vnto þe senaturs of Rome, þat þai wolde hafe wurshuppid hym as Godd. And he callid Sybilla þe *pro*phetice vnto hym, & axkyd hur if evur þ*er* sulde be any born þat sulde be gretter þan he was.

[1] Harl. MS. Innoce*ns* iij.

[2] MS. appeyed.

[3] Harl. MS. qui paulati*m* in vnum corp*us* solare redacti s*unt*. Eusebi*us* in Cronici*s*, *et* Mag*iste*r in Histori*a* Scolastica dicunt q*uo*d no*n* ipso die appar*uer*i*nt* tres soles, *sed* au*tem* *per* aliquod temp*us*, *scilicet* post mortem Julij Cesaris.

So it happend on þe yole-day, and þis Sybyll was in þe Emp*er*our chawm*er*. And evyn aboute mydday þ*er* apperid aboute þe son a golden cercle, and in myddeste of þe cercle was þ*er* standand a fayr maydyn and a chylde in hur armys. And sho shewid þis vnto þe Emp*er*our, and þe Emp*er*our had grete m*er*vail here-of, & said þat he hard a voyce þat spak, saying, "Hec est ara celi." And Sybyll said þat childe sulde be mare þan he was, and þ*er*for sho bad hym wurshup hym. And þat chawm*er* is consecrate a kurk in honor of our Ladie, & is callid to þis day S*an*c*t*a Maria de Ara Celi[1]. And fro thens furth þe Emp*er*our wurshuppid þis childe & wolde wurshup none oþ*er* goddi*s*. And vnto þis sentans accordis Timotheus, historiagraphus, and Orosius for þe moste p*ar*tie.

DLIV.

Nat*a*lis p*ro*batur, viij^uo^.

We rede ex '*Legenda* Lombardi*ca*' how þat þe oxe & þe ass, knowyng m*er*volosly Almighty God layd in a cryb befor þai*m*, þai fell down on þ*er* kneis and wurshuppid Hym. And Saynt Ierom tellis þat vppon þat nyght all þat eu*er* labured in vicio sodomitico was slayn, so þat not in þe kynd þ*a*t Almiȝty God had taken fro thens furth þ*er* sulde be fon so mekull vnclennes. For als Saynt Austyn sayd; "videns Deus viciu*m* cont*ra* natura*m* in natura humana fieri, fere desijt incarnari."

DLV.

Negacione*m* dei inducit freque*nter* malu*m* consiliu*m* *et* inopia siue paup*er*tas.

Cesarius tellis how þat in þe dioces of Leodenens*is*[2], besyde Florens, þ*er* was som tym a yong knyght & noble in tornament*is*, & giffen vnto vanytis of þis werld, vnto so mekull þ*a*t þ*er* aboute he consumyd all his gudis, so þat he fell evyn in despayr. Vnto so mekull þat on a nyght he garte a man of his lede hym in-to a wude, & þ*er* þai raysid the devull as þai was wunt to do, & made

[1] MS. Cela.

[2] Harl. MS. Leodiens*is*.

hym to speke with þaim. And þer he bad þe knyght make no charge of his povertie, & he askid hym if he wold hafe riches agayn, & ioy, as he was wunt to hafe. And þe knyght said, ya, he wolde, and it mot be done be God Almyghtie. And þan hys man sayd vnto þe fende; "Here hafe I broght you a noble man, my maister, at ye may restore hym vnto þe degre at he was in afore tyme." And þe fende saide, hym burde furst forsake Almyghti God & make homage vnto hym. And þis knyght, þuf all it war tremland & makand sorow, neuer-þe-les, in hope of requoveryng agayn of þat at he had loste, þurgh cowncell of þis man he did itt. And þan þe fend said hym burd nede forsake Goddis moder. And þe knyght answerd agayn & said, þat wolde he neuer doo. And þus he partid away fro þaim, and went agayn vnto þe town. And þer was a kurk in his way, and he went in and sett hym down on his kneis befor ane ymage of owr Ladye, & wepid & made grete sorow, at all þe kurk rang *with*. So evyn þe same howr, a knyght þat had boght all his lifelod befor, happend com by þe kurk away, & hard grete noyse & went in, & when he fand þe knyght, þat he kend well enogh, cryand & makand his prayer so devowtly, he had grete mervell, & drew hym be-hynd a pyler & stude still, & þogght he wolde wit what all þis bement. And, at bathe þies knyghtis hard, our Ladie spak vnto hur Son & said; "O, þou swete Son! Hafe mercie of þis man!" And þe childe at satt on hur kne wolde not speke agayn vnto his moder, bod turnyd his head awayward fro hur. And sho prayed hym agayn, & sayd þat þe man was dessayvid, and *with* þat he turnyd his bak opon hur and said; "This man hase denyed me, what shulde I do vnto hym?" And þan þe ymage of owr Lade rase vp & sett hur Son apon þe altar, and fell down on hur kneis at His fete and said; "I pray þe, swete Son, þat for my sake þou forgyff hym his syn." And onone þe child liftyd vp His moder and said vnto hur; "Moder, yit I neuer denyed þe thyng att þou axkid me. And now, beholde, for þi sake I forgyff hym." And þan þis knyght was fayn, & rase & went his ways furth of þe kurk, and was passyng sadd & hevy for hys syn, & glad þat it was forgyffen hym. And þe toder knyght folowid hym privalie, &

ou*er*tuke hym̄ & axkid hym̄ whi his een̄ war so wate & so bownyd'. And he answerd' agayn̄ & said' þe wynd garte itt. And he said' agayn̄; "Sur, I knaw þe cauce of your truspas weH enogħ. And Sur," he said', "I hafe a doght*er* & no mo childer, and if ye wuH wed hur I saH giff you aH your lyfelod' agayn̄, & you ij I saH make heyris of aH my riches." And he thankid' hym̄ & wed hur, & was afterwerd' a gude man̄ & a ricħe.

Negant *eciam* deu*m* religiosi. Sup*ra* de mi*seri-cordia*.

Nega*cio*nem dei induc*it* amor carnal*is*. S*upra* de amore.

Nega*cio*nem dei inducit ambicio digni*tatis*. Sup*ra* de Maria, vj[1].

Neganda no*n* est paup*er*i elemosina. Inf*ra* de paup*er*e, ij[2].

Necligencia ho*min*is impedit ne ei ab aliquo sub-ueniatur. S*upra* de cogitacione.

Negligencia executor*um* nocet testatori. S*upra* de executore, j.

Negligencia vtenciu*m* aliqua re p*er*dit*ur* aliqu*ando* ip*s*a res. S*upra* de legato.

Necligencia dicendi horas. S*upra* de Augustino, ij.

DLVI.

Negociatores sine fraude debent em*er*e *et* vendere.

Tullius tellis how on̄ a tyme it was disputid' betwix Diogenes & Stocius[3], þat was his disciple. And Diogenes sayd'; "AH þe vices of a thyng þat is selde aw not to be expowndid' to hym̄ þat byes it, bod ewhils it is constitutt be þe law; ewhils neu*er*-þe-les oþ*er*

[1] So Lat. MSS., Eng. MS. *has*, de iniuria, iij.
[2] MS. iij.
[3] Arund. MS. int*er* Diogenem, Babilon*i*u*m* stoicu*m*, et discipulum ei*us*, Antipa*trem*. Harl. MS. int*er* Diogenem, Babiloniu*m* storcum, etc.

thynges er done wit*h*outen̄ gyle." And his scoler ansswerd hym̄ agayn̄ & sayd, þat when̄ þe byer trowes att þe thyng be gude, & puttis truste in hym̄ þat sellis it, þe sellar aw to tell þe byer & þ*er* be any fawte þ*er*in. Than̄ Diogenes sayd; "It is one to be styll & anoder to layn̄, and þe tane is not *pro*fitable to þe to here, nor it is not nedefull to me to say." And þan̄ his scoler sayd; "And it be dampned at Athenys at a man̄ sall not tell þe way vnto hym̄ þat travels, mekull mor̄ dampnable it is wittandlie to suffer a man̄ fall in-to error." Than̄ Diogenes sayd; "He hase not garte þe bye þat stirris þe not to bye; and þou byes þat þing at plesis þe, and he praysis þat þing þat is his awn̄. And whar þe dome is in þe byer, þ*er* is no begyle in þe seller. And þ*er*for [1] a [2] seller aght to layn̄ nothyng vnto þe byer [3], neu*er*-þe-les hym̄ thar not tell hym̄ bod if he wyll, for what-som̄-evur langis to hym̄ þat byes it, longes to hym̄ þat sellis, to witt how þat he sall sell."

Nequicia mulieris comp*ara*tur s*er*penti. Inf*ra* de s*er*pente.

DLVII.

Nequicia Herodis.

We rede in 'Cronicles' how þat Herode, when̄ he hard tell þat þe Iewis abade *with* grete myrth agayn̄ he sulde dye, he garte gadur sam*en* all þe noble yong men̄ of Iudee, & garte spar þai*m* in a *pri*son̄, & com*m*andid vnto Salome his wyfe þat als tyte as he war deade, þat sho sulde sla þai*m* ilkone, at on̄ þat man*er* of wyse all Iudee sulde make sorow when he was dead as wele as þai dyd in his lyfe. And so was done.

Nero. S*upra* de crudeli*tate*, *et* inf*ra* de p*ro*digali*tate* *et* Simone.

DLVIII.

Nicholai confessoris.

We rede in his '*Mer*acles,' how som̄ tyme þ*er* was a Iew þat hard tell of þe m*er*acles of Saynt Nicholas, and he garte make ane

[1] MS. *repeats*, and þerfor. [2] MS. & [3] MS. seller.

ymage of hym, & sett hym to kepe all his gudis. And when þe Iew on a tyme was fro hame, thevus come & stale away his gudis, & when he come and fand þai wer away, he began to reprufe þis ymage, and bett itt sore. And Saynt Nicholas apperid vnto þies thevis, & shewid þai*m* how his body was betyn for þat gude att þai had stollen, and thretid þai*m* at þai sulde be hanged bod if þai had þis gude agayn & restorid it, & teld þai*m* at he was Saynt Nicholas, in whose kepyng þis Iew had putt all his gudis. And þies thevis wer fferd, and broght all þies gudis agayn, and tolde þe Iew þis m*er*acle. And he was turnyd & þai, bothe, and become gude men; & þe Iew was cristend.

DLIX.

Nicholaus scolarem suscitauit.

We rede in his 'M*er*acles' how þ*er* was a gude man þat vsid yerelie, becauce of a son þat he had þat was a scolar, apon Saynt Nicholas day for to make a grete feste, & dele grete almos in wurshup of Saynt Nicholas. So þe devull had a dispite þ*er*att, & come to þe dure in a pure mans liknes, & axkid almos vppon þe Saynt Nicholas day. And þe gude man sent hym almos *with* þis scoler, and þ*er* þe devull strangeld þe childe & kyllid hym. And when þe fader come vnto þe dure and fande his son dead, he made mekull sorow & had vp þe dead childe in-to a chambr, and sett hym down on his kneis & made his co*m*playnt vnto Saynt Nicholas, & said; "Loo! Saynt Nicholas! behold, is þis your reward of þe wurshup þat I hafe þis many day done vnto you?" And as he was þus complenand þe childe oppynd his ene & rase vp & was olyfe agayn.

DLX.

Nicholaus iuuene*m* de captiuitate p*at*ri restituit.

We rede in his 'M*er*acles' how þat a man þurgh þe merett*is* of Saynt Nicholas had a childe, whilk þat when he was a yong man was taken in þe were *with* þe Aragans[1], & depute into *ser*ves *with* þ*er* kyng. So it happend vppon Saynt Nicholas day þis yong man broght þe kyng wyne in a copp of golde, and as he held it befor þe kyng he remembred hym þat it was Saynt Nicholas day, & how his fadur as þat day was wunte to make a grete feste. And sodanly he gaff a grete sigh, and þe kyng wold algatt*is* wete þe cauce at he sighed for, and he told hym evure dele. And þis vncrestend kyng thrett hym & said; "What at evur þi Nicholas duse, þou shall dwell here *with* vs." And *with* þat sodanlie þ*er* come a grete wynd, & smate down þe howse and liftid vp þe childe *with* þe copp in his hand & þe wyne in it, & sett hym evyn at his fadur dure. And he went in & fand his fadur & all his frendis at dyner, & þ*er* he teld þai*m* all how it happend. And þai war passand fayn & thankid God & Saynt Nicholas.

Nicholaus indeuotos sibi ve*r*berat. Sup*ra* de deuocione, ij.
Nicholaus deuotos sibi remune*r*at. Sup*ra* de deuocione, j.

DLXI.

Nig*r*omancie[2] ars est valde pe*r*iculosa.

Cesarius tellis how som tyme þ*er* was a knyght at wold not trow at þ*er* was any fendis. So on a tyme he come vnto one þat was callid Philip, þ*at* was practyse in nyg*r*omancye, and p*r*ayed hym to latt hym se som fendis. And he re[*cu*]sid & said he durst nott; & yit he laburd hym beselie. So on a day, aboute none, þis Philip garte þis knyght put his swerd abowte hym, and at a gateshatyll, *with* a[3] swerd he made a cercle aboute þis knyght, and bad hym kepe hym wele *with*in þis cercle, ffor and any membre of hym come *with*oute itt, he mond lose itt vnto tyme þat he come agayn vnto hym. And he bad hym, & he saw any bodie, nowd*er*

[1] Lat. MSS. ab Agarenis. [2] MS. Nigromancia.
[3] *After* a, w, *erased.*

giff þai*m* right not, nor take right not of þai*m*, and he tolde hym þat þai wolde bothe tempe hym & flay hym; bod & he wolde do so he bad hym, he sayd, þ*er* shuld nothyng noy hym. And when he was gone & þe knyght was be his one in þe cercle, belyfe þ*er* come as it had bene grete fludis, & a nowd*er* tyme as it had bene gru*n*tyng of swyne, and now blastis of wynd. And now hym þoght he saw a man als hye as treis, and when he come nere þe cercle he axkid þis knyght what he wold, & bad hym aske & he suld tell hym. So he lukid opon hym & hym thoght he was a grete man & a blakk, & of grete difformytie, so þat he durste not verelie behald hym. So att þe laste þis knyght spak & said vnto hym; "I hafe desyrid gretelie to se þe." And he axkid hym, whareto. And þe knyght said, for he had hard tell mekull ill of hym. And þe fend answerd hym agayn & said; "Men demys me oftsithis wit*h*owten cauce, and I do no man skathe bod if he gar me. And Philip þi maist*er* is my frend, & I do all þat plesis hym, for I grevid hym nevur yitt, vnto so mekull when he callid me & bad me now com vnto þe, I come." And þe knyght askid hym whar he was when he callid hym. And he said he was als far beyonde þe se as þe se was fro thens; "& þ*er*for," he said, "it is right at þou reward me for my labur." And þe knyght axkyd hym what he wold hafe, and he said owder his gown or his gyrdyll, or a shepe of his flokk; & þan he askid a hen, & att þe laste a cokk. And þe knyght said hym evur nay, and wold giff hym none of þies. So þe knyght axkid hym whare he had so muche con*n*yng as he had, and he answerd agayn & said at þ*er* was none ill done in all þis werld bod he knew itt. "And to so mekull," he said, "þou in such a town & in suche a howse loste þi maydenhede, and swylk synnys & swilk hase þou done." And þis knyght cuthe not agayn-say itt. And þan þe devull put furth his hand as he wold hafe taken hym, and þe knyght was ferd & fell bakward in þe cercle, & cryed as he had bene wude. And als sone as þis Philip harde hym, he come and made all þis fantasies to vanyssh away. And evur aft*er*, fro þat howr forward, he was pale & ill hewid, & trowid alway at þ*er* war fendis. And afterward he amendid his life & become a gude man.

DLXII.

Nigromantici discipulus a demone rapit*ur et* deportatur.

Cesarius tellis how at þe cetie of Tholett þ*er* was ane þat held' a skule of nygromancy, and his scolers on̄ a tyme desyrid' þ*er* maist*er* þat he wolde prufe þat befoȓ þai*m* þat he taght þai*m*. And þ*er* maist*er*, þuf aƚƚ he wer il-wyllid' þ*er*to, on̄ a tyme led' þai*m* into þe feld', and w*ith* a swerd' he made a cercle aboute þai*m*, & he bad þai*m* if þai saw any thyng nowd*er* gif it nor take þ*er*-off, bod at þai sulde holde þai*m* iustelie w*ith*in þe cercle. And þan̄ he went a littyƚƚ fro þai*m*, & began̄ to say his enchawntmentis. & belyfe fendis þat war callid' come, som̄ in liknes of a man̄, som̄ of a wom*m*an̄, & som̄ makand mynstralcy, & som̄ dawnsand'. And emang þai*m* þ*er* was ane like a fayȓ womman̄, fayrer þan̄ aƚƚ þe toder was, and sho p*ro*furd' a golde ryng vnto ane of þe scolers ofte sythes, & lang he forsuke it, & at þe laste he tuke it, and onone sho clekid' hym̄ oute of þe cercle & þe ryng, bothe, & onone sho was away w*ith* hym̄. And his felos began̄ to cry, & þ*er* maist*er* come onone, & þai told' hym̄. And onone he callid' vp þe maist*er*-fend', and tolde hym̄ of þe wrong at was done vnto his scolar, and desyryd to haffe hym̄ agayn̄. And þis fend' callid' aƚƚ þe toder fendis vnto a cownceƚƚ, and reprovid' hym̄ þat did þe dede. And he excusid' hym̄ & sayd' he dyd no wrong, becauce þe scoler was inobedyent vnto his maist*er*. Neu*er*-þe-les a sentans was gyffen̄ at he sulde be delyverd' agayn̄ vnto his maist*er*, for he was a behufable scolar vnto his maist*er*, and þus he was restoryd' agayn̄ vnto his maist*er*. And fro þat day forward' his felows þoght att his face was lene & pale, evyn̄ as he had bene taken̄ oute of his grafe. & he told' his felows what he saw at heƚƚ yatis, & told' þai*m* it was a cursid' scule at þai wer at, & desyrid' þai*m* to lefe itt. And he went and made hym̄ a monk of Ceustus ordur, and afterward' was a hali liffer.

Nigromantica*m* scienciam adipiscens dampnatur.

Inf*r*a de sciencia, iij.

DLXIII.

Nomen Chr*ist*i semp*er* est in corde h*ab*end*um*.

We rede in 'Legenda B*e*ati Ignacij,' þat when he was in dyvers grete turment*is*, he wold neu*er* sease of calling of þe name of Cryste, & þe turmenturs axkid hym whi he rehersyd þat name so ofte. And heansswerd agayn & sayd; "I hafe þ*at* name wretten in my h*er*te, & þ*er*for I may not sese fro calling þ*er*-vppon." And when he was dead, þai tuke his harte oute of his body, & cut it sonder be þe myddeste. And þai fand all his h*er*te written w*it*hin w*it*h þies namys, Ies*us* Chr*istus*, & all of letters of golde. And herefor many oon trusted in hym & was cristend.

Nomen acq*ui*run*t* aliqui *eciam* p*er* aliq*ua* mala op*er*a. S*upr*a de memoria, i.

DLXIV.

Nouicius d*eb*et semp*er* in deuoc*io*ne p*ro*fiscer*e* *et* no*n* tepescere.

We rede in 'Vitis P*atrum*' how þ*er* was one þat wolde entir into religion, and he lete his moder hafe knowlege of his purpos. And sho cowncelд hym nay; & he wold not lefe his purpos for hur, bod sayd þat he wolde go safe his sawle. And when he was entred into þe religion & governyd hym wele, & was fervent in þe begynnyng, fro he had co*n*tynued awhile he began to wax slaw, & yrked w*it*h þe strate[*nes*] of his religion. So on a tyme hym happend to fall seke & lay in a trans. So hym þoght þat he was broght vnto his dome, & þ*er* hym thoght he fand his moder þat was dead. And when sho saw hym sho sayd vnto hym; "Son, how is it w*it*h the? Come þou hedur to be demyd w*it*h vs? Whar is it now at þou said vnto me, 'I will go safe my sawle?'" And at þis wurde he was confusid, & wuste nevur what he suld say vnto hur agayn. And w*it*h þat he wakend of his t*r*ans, & amendid of his sekenes, and vmthoght hym þ*at* for he wex somwhatt yrke in his religion he was in way of dampnacion, & he turnyd hym̄ vnto þe fervor & þe luff þat he had' vnto his religion̄ at his furste entre, and' said' vnto hym̄ selfe; "I þat myght not abyde & suffer þe blame & chalange of my moder, how may I abyde þe blame of Aƚƚmiȝttie God & aƚƚ his aungels & aƚƚ þe saynttis off hevyn̄!"

Nouicius confirmatur in religione ex co*n*side*r*acio*n*e penar*um* inferni. S*upr*a de co*n*ue*r*sio*n*e [1].

Nouici*us* confirmatur in religione ex ce*r*titu*d*ine mortis. S*upr*a de co*n*ue*r*sione.

Nouicij dissoluti debe*n*t corripi. Supra de correccio*n*e, iij.

Nouicij or*ationi*b*us* iuuantur ad pe*r*seue*r*and*um*. Inf*r*a de or*aci*one.

Nouicio p*ossun*t adaptari multa que dicuntur s*upr*a de co*n*temptu mu*nd*i, conue*r*s*i*one [1], monacho, et inf*r*a de religione *et* obediencia.

DLXV.

Nupcie sec*un*de no*n* su*n*t appetende.

Ieronim*us* tellis how on̄ a tyme þ*er* was a yong wedow þat hight Ann, and' when̄ hur husband was dead' sho thoght sho wolde not [2] be wed' wit*h* a noder man̄. Hur frendis come & cownceld' hur yis, & said vnto hur; "Thow erte yit bod of a myddiƚƚ age, & a fayr̄ womman̄ & a listie, take þe a noder husband'." And sho said'; "Nay, þat wiƚƚ I not doo; ffor & I hafe als gude a husband' as I had befor̄, I wiƚƚ evur be ferd' þat I saƚƚ lose hym̄, & if he be yƚƚ, me wyƚƚ gretelie repent þat I had' ane iƚƚ after a gude."

DLXVI.

Obediencia debet esse parata.

We rede in 'Vitis P*atrum*' of a monk þat was a writer, þat hight Marchus, & as he was writand' & in makyng of ane O,

[1] MS. co*n*ue*r*sacio*n*e.   [2] *Added above the line.*

his abbott callid, & he lefte it half vnmade & went at his call, becauce he wolde not breke his obedyans.

DLXVII.

Obediendum est eciam in impossibilibus[1] a viris perfectis.

Senek[2] tellis how þat vnto a man þat shulde entre in-to religion þe abbott declarid þe grevus laburs þerof, & how þat hym burd doo all suche þing as was commanddid hym; & he was nothyng ferd þerfor & recusid nott to com into religion, bod promysid to be always pacient & obedient. So afterward his maister þoght at he wold prufe hym, so be cace it happend at þe oven of þer abbay was hate, redie to sett bread in; and his maister commawndid of obedyans to go into þis ovyn. And he left not to do his maister commandment, bod went in boldlie with a gude belefe; & when he was in þe oven, þe hete þerof turnyd in-to cold, so þat he felid nothyng bod as it had bene sprencled ouer with dew.

DLXVIII.

Obediunt perfecti eciam contra spem optinendi quod precipitur.

Seruius[3] tellis how on a tyme þe same abbott þoght þat he wold prufe a novace, & he tuke a dry stowre þat he vsid to bere in his hand & smate it into þe erth, & bad a novice þat he sulde watir it evurilk day vnto þat it waxid grene & bare liffis agayn kynde. And he did as he commandid hym, and evur-ilk day bare a grete pott full fro a watur ij myle thens, & watyrd þis stowr unto he had done it a yere; and yitt he wex nott werie bod did on as he did afor. And þuf all hym thoght þer come no frute on his warke, yit hym thoght he wolde not breke his obediens, bod endurid in his labur all þe secund yere. And in þe iij yere when

[1] *So* Arund. MS., Eng. MS. in possibilibus.
[2] Arund. MS. Seuerus. Harl. MS. Seuarius.
[3] Lat. MSS. Severus.

þis watir-ber sesid not of his labur, þis stowr at was dry florisshid, & bare levis & frute. And he went vnto his abbott & told hym, & he tuke all his monk*is* *with* hym & come & saw it & sayd; "Loo! brethur, þurgh v*er*tue of fulfyllyng of obediens, þis dry stowr agayn kynde is now fayr florisshid & beris levis."

DLXIX.

Obediens verus no*n* attendit quid p*re*cipitur.

Cassianus tellis how on a tyme þ*er* was ane abbott þat com*m*awndid his dissiple & said vnto hym; "Go, ryn," he said, "als faste as þou may, and als tyte as þou may turn me yone grete stone." And onone his dissiple a grete stone, þat many men myght not hafe turnyd, now *with* lifte at his head & now at his breste, *with* grete strenth he turnyd it ou*er*; & he swett so þat all his clothis warr wett thrugh, for he supposid þat nothyng was com*m*andid vnto hym þat was impossible to doo.

DLXX.

Obediencia pe*r*fecta amore*m* naturalem postponit.

Cassianus tellis how som tyme þ*er* was oon taken in-to ane abbay, & he broght *with* hym his son of viij yere olde; and he was disseverd fro hym & put in a-noder cell. So þis abbot þoght þat he wolde [*prufe*] his obedians & his affeccion, & he com*m*aundid hym to caste his son in-to a grete watir. And onone as he had com*m*andid hym, he gatt his son in his armys and come vnto þe watur-syde, and wold hafe castyn in his awn barn bod at þ*er* was monk*is* þat wachid what he wolde doo & lettid hym. And yitt for all at þai cuth do he keste it in, & onone þai gatt it oute and savyd itt olyfe.

DLXXI.

Obediunt qu*andoque* creature *eciam* insensibiles[1].

Saynt Gregorie tellis how þat in þe cetie of Placens þe watur þat was[2] cald Padus rase vp opon a grete spate and owryode all þe

[1] MS. ininsensibiles.

[2] MS. wald.

feldis þat langid vnto ane abbay. & þ*er* was a gude, holie man þat hight Sabinus, a bisshopp, and when he saw þis he garte a notorie of his write a byll & caste in þe flude, and þis was þe wrytyng; "Sabinus, þe *ser*vand of owr Lord Iesu Criste com*mandis* vnto þe, Pado, þat our þi bank*is* þou pas no mor fro hens furth, nor at þou hurte nott landis þat longis vnto þe kurk." And his notarie did as he bad hym. And onone þe watir fell of þe kurk-land and come vnto þe bownd*is* at it was wunte to ryn in; and nevur aft*er* vnto þis day rase it ou*er* þe bank*is* nor passid þe bowndis.

DLXXII.

Obediu*nt* sa*nct*is *eciam* bruta a*nim*alia.

Saynt Gregorie tellis how þat Florencius, þe servand of Almighti God, dwelt alone be hym selfe in a cell, & he had v or vj shepe. And he made his prayer vnto Allmyghti God & besoght Hym at He wold send hym somwhatt to dwell *with* hym to co*m*furth hym. And onone as he had made his prayer, he fand at his cell-yate, standand, a bere, whilk þat lowtid vnto hym and fawnyd hym, & was nothyng wylde. And he co*n*seyvid at it was sent hym be Almyghti Godd, & bad it go hafe his shepe furth & kepe þai*m*, & at it sulde bryng þai*m* home at sex of þe clok at evyn; and it did trewlie as he bad it. And in þe mornyng he com*m*andid it not to com home or ix of þe clok, and he fastid evur to it come home. And evur þis bere did as he bad itt, and so he tarid long fastand o days[1]. And he had iiij disciples þat war wrothe *with* þis bere becauce it held þai*m* long fastand o days, & þai dwelt *with* anod*er* man in þe wyldernes þat hyght Euticius. Becauce þ*er* maist*er* did no swilk takens, and privalie, þai slew þis bere. And þis holie man bade of his dener to evyn, & evur lukid aftur þis bere, & she come nevur home. So opon þe morn he went vnto þe felde and fand þis bere slayn, and als sone as he saw hur[2] he knew wele

[1] Harl. MS. cepit ex hoc fama eiu*s* longe lateq*ue* crebresce*re*; cui inuidentes, quatuor discip*u*li Euthici, eo quod magist*er* eor*um*, Euthiciu*s*, signa no*n* faceret, latent*er* vrsum occidunt.

[2] MS. hym.

enogh who did itt, and he fell opon a wepyng, more for þe malice of his bredur þan for þe dead of þe bere. And þus he said vnto hym selfe; "I trow þat in þis life at vengeange sall be taken on þai*m* for þe*r* males." And belyfe aft*er* it happend as he said, ffor þies iiij brethur war onone streken wit*h* a sodan sekenes, & rotid abown erde at þai stynkyd wit*h*. And her-vppon þis holie man had conciens & tolde his brethur þat hym forthoght at he had sayd. And all þe dayis of his lyfe he had sorow þerfor, & wepud & made muche murnyng, and held hym selfe as a crowell man & a vengeable homycide.

DLXXIII.

Obediencia p*re*fertur alijs[1] virtutib*us*.

We rede in 'Vitis P*atrum*' how som tyme iiij brethir þat was cled all in pylchis come vnto ane abbott þat hyght Pambo, & ilkone of þai*m* tolde hym þe v*er*tue of oþ*er*, when þai war away at þai spak off. So one of þai*m* was a grete faster, and anoder was passand pure, and þe iij had passand mekull charitie, and þe iiij had xij yere dwelte in obediens emang olde men & brak neu*er* his obedyens. And þan þis abbot Pambo sayde; "I saw þ*at* þe v*er*tue of hym þis is mor þan of all þe toder, ffor ilkone of you þe v*er*tue þat he hase holdys it þurgh his awn wyll, and he this makis his wyll his s*er*vand. And such men er acordable in religion, and speciallie þai þat p*er*seu*er*s þerin vnto þ*er* lyfis end."

DLXXIV.

Obediencia d*e*b*e*t aliqu*ando* a su*per*iori p*ro*bari.

Cesarius tellis how som tyme þ*er* was a husband þat had a s*er*vand þat was p*ro*fetable & trew vnto hym. And when he hard tell of þe inobediens of Adam, owr form*er* fadur, he had grete dedeyn þ*er*att. And on a tyme he said vnto his mast*er* þat hym þoght þat Adam was a grete fole, þat wolde not kepe his maist*er*s com*m*andme*n*t. "For," he sayd, "& ye com*m*andid me a

[1] MS. alij.

thyng I sulde not breke itt." So *with*-in a few dayes afterward his maist*er* delyverd hym a box at was sparrid, bod nott bod at he myght oppyn itt, and said vnto hym; "þis boyste I delyver þe; bod I charge þe att þou oppyn it natt, for & þou do, þou sall lose my *gr*ace, & I wull giff þe no hyre." And when he had takyn þis box and was be his one, he turnyd it abowte & sayd vnto hym selfe; "I am now be myne one, whatt & I oppyn þis boyste? Na man may se me & I doo." So þus he was ou*er*com*m*en with temptacion and oppynd þis boyste. And þ*er* was þ*er*in a little burde, & it flow away; and þan he was passand hevy & fell on kneis befor his maist*er* & askid hym forgyfnes, bod he had it no3t.

DLXXV.

Obediencia ecia*m* aliqu*ando* in minimis[1] no*n* se*r*uatur.

Cesarius tellis how som tyme þ*er*for þ*er* was a knyght þ*at* had a wurthi gentyll-womman vnto his wyfe, and a gude, whilk þ*at* had a grete skorn & a hethyng agayns [*Eve*], þat sho sulde be so vnobedient vnto Adam hur husband. And þis knyght blamyd his wyfe herefor and said þat sho was inobediente vnto hym in les þing þan evur was Eve vnto Adam. And sho sayd nay, & he yis. So he chargid hur in payn of xl[ti] mark þat opon þat day at sho shulde be wasshid or bathid, at sho sulde not entre in-to þe cowrte nor into þe dyke barefute. And lo! so m*er*valoslie it happend; ffor fro thens furth sho was so turment *with* temptacion þat on a tyme when sho was bathid, sodanlie sho sterte oute of hur bathe & went barefute in-to þe cowrte & in-to þe dyke vp to þe kneis. And one at saw hur come & tellid his lord, & he come vnto þe ladie & teld hur þat sho had broken hur obediens in les þing þan Eve did, & þ*er* he blamyd hur gretelie & made hur pay hur money at he had putt hur in payn of evurilk dele.

Obed*ienc*iam tollit aliqu*ando* temptacio gule. Sup*ra* de gula.

[1] MS. nimis. Harl. MS. *as above.*

Obedire nolens qu*andoque* visibilit*er*[1] punitur. Inf*ra* de religione.

Obediunt p*er*fec*t*i suscip*er*e penitencia*m* qua*m* no*n* me*r*uerun*t*. S*upr*a de accusaci*on*e.

DLXXVI.

Obediencia debet impl*er*i usq*ue* ad reuocaci*on*em p*re*cepti.

We rede in 'Vitis P*atrum*' how a gude, symple man, þat hight Paule, left all his gudis & went vnto Saynt Anton þe abbott. And þe furste nyght þis abbott com*ma*wndid hym at he sulde sitt hym down in his prayers vnto he come vnto hym. And he sett hym down befor þe olde man cell dure & made his p*ra*yers, and nowder for þe dew of þe nyght, nor yit for hete of þe day, he wold not move hym nor go away or his maist*er* come. So it happend on a tyme when he was emang his brether, he askid þai*m* whethur was furste, Criste or His p*ro*fetti*s*; and so Saynt Anton was ashamyd wi*th* his question & com*ma*undid hym to go his wais & holde his tong. And onone he did so; and fro thens furth he kepyd sylens so ferventlie, at he wold neu*er* speke bod when his fadur com*ma*wndid hym.

DLXXVII.

Oblacio no*n* debet fieri nisi de bono.

Iacobus de Vet*r*iaco tellis how som tyme þ*er* was a husband-man þat was ane yll payer of his tenndis, and he wold seldom offer bod if it wer on solempne dayis, and þan he wold offer a fals peny or ane yll. So on a passch-day hym happend emang oþ*er* to com vnto þe howselburde, and þe preste, þ*at* knew þat he vsid evur to offer a fals peny, when he had gyffen oþ*er* men þ*er* howsell, he gaf þis husband, in-stead of his howsell, þe same yll peny þat he offerd.

[1] MS. invisibiliter. Harl. MS. *as above.*

And he chewid & feld at it was hard, & grapid in his mouthe what it was, & he fand it was þe same fals peny þat he had offerd; & when he saw it he had grete mervell þerof, and made mekull sorow. So when mes was done, he come vnto þe preste wepand & sayd; "A! sur, my syn is so grete þat it happend me þis day at þe sacrament att ye gaff me is turnyd in-to a fals peny." And þe preste ansswerd hym agayn & said; "This thyng happynd not vnto þe *with*-oute som cawce, and þerfor þou haste done som horrible syn. Tell me what it is!" And *with* grete shame he tolde hym in confession, & said; "I shryfe me þat I was so attemptid *with*[1] covatice, þat evur when oþer folk offerd gude syluer I offerd alway ane ill penye." And þan þe preste said vnto hym; "This was þe iugement at þou tolde me off; and herefor in-stede of þe sacrament þou fand in þi mouthe ane ill peny. And þerfor þou moste make restitucion." And so he did, & promysid þat evur after fro thens furth he sulde trewlie pay his tend & offer gude syluer. And so þe preste asoylid hym & gaff hym his howsell, and evur after he was a gude man.

Oblacio sacramenti in missa valet ad viuos *et* defunctos. S*upra* de missa.

DLXXVIII.

Obligatus p*ro* aliquo, vel hic vel in futuro, p*er*soluet illud ad quod se obligauit.

Petrus Damianus tellis how þer was a monke þat was a grete synner, & grete penance at was enionyd hym he besoght one þat was familiarie vnto hym to helpe hym to do. And he vndertuke to do þat one halfe of his penance, & bad hym be not ferd þerfor. So hym þis at band hym selfe þus, *with*-in a while after deyid, and he was a gude man emangis his brethir; and *with*-in a little while he apperid vnto þis oþer monk. And he axkid hym how it stude *with* hym, and he said; "Ill & hardlie, not for my selfe bod

[1] *After* with, ov, *erased.*

for the; ffor when̄ I was fre of myne awn̄ selfe I bande me for þe. And þ*er*for̄," he saiđ, "go, & pray þe covent at þai fullfyłł ałł þat at I p*ro*mysiđ to do for the." And when̄ þat was done he apperiđ vnto hym̄ agayn̄, and lete hym̄ witt þat onone he was delyverđ þurgħ his brethir p*r*ayer.

Obligare se[1] p*ro* aliquo no*n* semp*er* est securu*m*. S*upr*a de fideiussore.

Obliuio scitoru*m* prius causatur aliqu*ando* ex minucione. S*upr*a de minucione.

Obliuissi debet confessor ea que in confessione audiu*i*t. S*upr*a de co*nfessione*, iiij.

Obloque*n*du*m* no*n* est sa*nc*t*is*. S*upr*a de blasfemia, iij.

DLXXIX.

Obstinacio. Obstinatus[2] in peccatis suis dampnatur sepius.

Saynt Bede tellis in 'Gestis Anglor*um*' of one þat was turnyđ in name bod he was shrewiđ in condicions, and when̄ he was correcte he wolde not amenđ hym̄ bod was ay longer war; bod becauce he cuthe gude skyłł of ane offes, þ*er*for̄ he was suffred more. So at þe laste hym̄ happend to fałł seke, and he garte całł ałł his brethir aforn̄ hym̄, and was ałł comen̄, he telliđ þai*m* his sete was ordanđ in hełł, noght ferr fro Pylatt & Cayphas. And when̄ his brethir cryed on̄ hym̄ & bad hym̄ aske m*er*cye & do penans for his syn̄, he saiđ he might not forthynk his syn̄, for iugement was passiđ agayns hym̄. And þus he dyeđ in wrichidnes.

Obstinacio impedit restitucio*n*em forisf*ac*toru*m*. Inf*ra* de vsurario, vj *et* x.

Obstinac*i*o impedit contricione*m*. Supra de cont*r*i-

[1] MS. Obligare se semper *pro* aliquo.

[2] MS. Obstinatutus.

cione, v, *et* de heretico, ij ; de accusacione, *et* de aduocato, iiij.

Occasionem querit potens *et* princeps contra impotentem. Infra de potente.

Ocium est semper fugiendum. Supra de labore, ij.

DLXXX.

Ocium detestantur sancti.

We rede in 'Vitis Patrum' how som̄ tyme þer was ane hermett in wyldernes, neuer-þe-les, þuf aƚƚ he mott nott seƚƚ þaim, yit he wolde make baskettis and swyllis of palme levis, þat he sulde not be ydiƚƚ, and for to kepe his harte fro yduƚƚ thoghtys & vanyties þat wiƚƚ com̄ in a mans mynd' and he be not occupied'.

Ociosa verba non sunt dicenda. Infra de verbo, j, & ij.

DLXXXI.

Ociosa verba precipue in ecclesia non sunt dicenda.

Iacobus de Vetriaco tellis at þe devuƚƚ wrate in a kurk aƚƚ maner ydul wurdis þat was wretten̄ þer[1], and when̄ he had not parchement enogħ to write on̄ he drew it oute with his tethe & his handis, & he drew so faste at he rappid' his head' agayn̄ þe waƚƚ. And þer was a holie man̄ at saw hym̄, and he askid' hym̄ what he did', and he tolde hym̄ aƚƚ þat is befor' said'.

DLXXXII.

Oculi sunt reprimendi.

We rede in 'Vitis Patrum' of one þat hight Gladius[2], when̄ he had bene lang in his ceƚƚ, xx yere or more, yit he lukid' neuer vp, nor neuer saw þe rufe þerof within.

[1] Lat. MSS. verba ociosa que ibi dicebantur. [2] Harl. MS. Claudius.

DLXXXIII.

Oculus est inimicus cordis.

We rede in 'Gestis Petri Clareuall*is*' how on a tyme, when he had þurgh raklesnes loste ane of his een and was made monoc*ulus*, afterwarde in his sporte he wolde say he had loste ane of his enmys, & at he was mor dredefull for þat ee þat was lefte hym þan for þe los [1] of þe toder ee.

DLXXXIV.

Odore contingit peccare.

We rede in 'Vitis P*atrum*' off ane þat hight Arseni*us*, þat was a passand grete laburer w*ith* his handis, when he was in wyldernes he wolde nevur skyfte his clothis bod ons in a yere, to so mekull þat when he doffid þai*m* þai stynkid. And þan he wolde say vnto hym selfe; "For þe vntement and gude savurs þat I hafe felid in þe werld, þ*er*for it is necessarie to me to fele þis stynke."

Odore nimis delicati *eciam* corpo*r*al*iter* puniu*n*tur [2]. S*upr*a de delicijs.

Offertorio p*ossu*n*t* adaptari que s*upr*a dicu*n*tur de oblacione.

Officialis malus est ammonendus [3].

DLXXXV.

Oracio debet esse co*n*tinua *et* cu*m* reue*r*encia.

Saynt Ierom tellis how som tyme þer was a man þat hight Iohn, & in a banke vnd*er*nethe a grete stone he co*n*tynued iij yere in his prayers, and all-way standdand. And he neu*er* satt nor lay, nor neu*er* slepid bod standand, and he had neu*er* meate bod on þe Sonday when a preste come vnto hym and said a mes aforn hym; and þat was his fude. So at þe laste he was our-com*m*en & myght

[1] MS. *repeats*, of þe los. [2] MS. peruniuntur.
[3] *Reference missing in the* MSS.

stand no langer, for his legg*is* & his fete warr rotyn vnderneth hym & ware come oute of þa*im*. And when þies iij yere was done, aungels come vnto hym & helid hym.

Or*atione* impeditur raptor *et* restituere co*m*pellitur. Inf*r*a de raptore, ij.

DLXXXVI.

Oracioni devote obediunt bruta.

Saynt Gregur tellis how on a tyme when þe holie man Boniface stude vppon a grece lenand our, þ*er* come a fox & tuke a hen evyn befor hym. And when he saw þat, he went in-to þe kurk & fell down in his p*r*ayers & said; "Lorde! Plesis it þe at I may not eatt of þat at my moder bryngis vp? Lorde, behald, sho bredis hennys, & þe fox com*m*ys & eatis þa*im*." And when he had done his p*r*ayer he rase & went furth of þe kurk; and onone þe fox come agayn, & þe hen att he had takyn lete hur fall owte of his mouthe. And *with* þat he fell dead befor þis holie man.

DLXXXVII.

Oracio *eciam* dampnatos ad vita*m* *et* pene*tent*iam revocat.

Petrus Damascen*us*[1] tellis how on a tyme þ*er* was a monk at was dead, & was born in-to þe kurk whils a mes sulde be songen for hym. And when þe Agnus Dei was said, þis dead monke rase evyn vp sodanlie & spakk & blasfemyd God & bannyd Hym, & spitt vppon þe c*r*ucifix, and wolde hafe revyn down þe ymage of owr Ladie. & he said vnto þe monk*is*; "Wharefor syng ye or prayes for me? I am dampnyd and in þe paynys of hell." And þan þe monk*is* *with* all þ*er* hertis prayed for hym, & did of þ*er* clothis & bete þ*er* selfe for hym, & made tunsions on þ*er* breste. So at þe laste, þurgh þ*er* prayer, he come agayn vnto

[1] Lat. MSS. Petrus Damianus.

hym selfe, and began to dispice þe fend & lofe God & our Ladie, & wurshuppid þe cros & askid confession & penance. And þ*er* he confessid hym þat after he had forsaken all þe werld he had fallen in-to fornicacion & laynyd it, & was neu*er* shrevyn þeroff. And þus he liffid to on þe toder day in p*ra*yer & in penance. And þan he passid vnto God.

DLXXXVIII.

Oraciones no*n* iuuant finalit*er* dampnatos.

Iacobus de Vet*ri*aco tellis þat when Saynt Marie of Oigniez[1] apon a day had made hur p*ra*yer vnto God for a c*er*tayn dead man, hur was bydden at sho sulde no mor pray for hym; "ffor he is reprovid of Almiȝtty God." And when þat he vnhappelie was slayn in turnament, he was dampnyd vnto evurlastyng payn.

DLXXXIX.

Or*ati*onib*us* iuuantur a*n*im*e* in purgatorio.

Iacobus de Vet*ri*aco tellis how on a tyme þis Saynt Marie of Oigniez[2] was in hur cell, and sho saw afor hur a grete multitude of handis haldyng vp as it had bene to p*ra*y vnto hur. And sho besoght God to latt hur hafe knowlege what it bement. And it was ansswerd hur at þai war sawlis of þai*m* þat war in purgatorie, þat besoght hur to p*ra*y for þai*m*. And sho was fayn þerof & p*ra*yed speciallie for þai*m*.

Oracio avis audita est. Sup*ra* de aue, ij.

Oracione Deus aliqu*ando* mortem tardat. S*upra* de Basilio.

Orantes impedit demon. Sup*ra* de or*acione*, iij.

Or*aci*ones aliquas dic*er*e om*n*i die vtile est. Inf*ra* de remun*er*a*cione*.

Or*acioni* cordis plus attendit deus q*uam* vocis. Sup*ra* de A*nnunciacione*.

[1] MS. Ogimet. [2] MS. Oxninez.

DXC.

Or*acioni* corde est attenden*dum*.

Saynt Ierom tellis how þat when Hillarion had lefte all man*er* of oþ*er* þing*is* and was giffen alonelie vnto his prayers, he sufferd many snybbis of þe fend; & when he was in his prayers þe fend apperid vnto hym in many lyknessis. So it happend on a tyme when he was in his prayers, becauce he wolde be lett *with* no man*er* of sight, he sett hym down on his kneis & on his elbowys, & layd his face down vnto þe erth. And onone þe devull come & sett hym stridlyng*is* on his bakk, & dang hym in þe sydes *with* sharpe spurris, & laid on his head *with* a swip & said; "Wharto syttys þou þus scornand & nappis?" And he was als hevy on his bakk as it had bene a grete sekk full of barlie.

DXCI.

Orantes illuduntur a demonib*us*.

We rede in 'Vitis P*atrum*' how on a tyme þe devull said vnto þe Abbott Macharie; "Go we vnto gaderyng sam*en* of our brethir." And he askid hym what he had at do *with* þe gaderyng sam*en* of þai*m*, and þe fendansswerd hym agayn & said; "Knowis þou not at *with*outen vs þ*er* is no gaderyng? Com and þou sall se our besynes." And he went *with* hym & saw, & þ*er* was all þe kurk our as it had bene littyll men of Ynde, & let þe monkis to make þ*er* prayers, & turnyd þai*m* in wom*m*en liknes & made þai*m* thynke on þai*m*, & sam*en* þai garte slepe & be wery of þ*er* prayers. And when þis holie man saw þat, he made his prayers vnto God, & sodanlie þai vanyshid away.

Oracionib*us* iuuantur morientes. S*upr*a de morte, xix.

Oracio p*r*edonis ei vitam p*r*olongat. Inf*r*a de remuner*acione*, viij.

DXCII.

Oracione reuocatur ab inferis dampnatus.

We rede in 'Gestis Beati Gregorij' how on̄ a tyme as Saynt Gregor̄ walkid befor̄ þe palace of Traian̄ and vmthoght hym̄ of his mekenes, he began̄ to fall opon̄ a sore wepyng. And he prayed hym̄ so long for hym̄ at Saynt Petur altar̄, wepyng & makyng sorow, vnto a voyce spak vnto hym̄ & sayd, þat Traiayn̄ þurgh his p*r*ayers was delyverd oute of þe payn̄ of hell; bod it bad hym̄ at fro thens furth he sulde bewar, & not p*r*esume hym̄ to p*r*ay for none vnc*r*istend man̄ þat was dampned.

DXCIII.

Ordinacio dei *non* potest impediri.

We rede in 'Cronicles' þat in þe yere of our̄ Lorde M l xv, the erle þat was callid Corandus[1], beyng ferd on̄ a tyme for þe emp*er*owr̄ wreth, ffled *with* his wife in-to a wudd, & *þer* he hid hym̄ in a tufall. So þe Emp*er*our happend on̄ a tyme to com̄ to þis wud on̄ huntyng, & folowid a dere so lang at it was nyght, & he cuthe fynd none of his meneya; so hym̄ happend com̄ to þis tofall. Bod þe Erle was gone & þe ladie was *þer* be hur one, grete *with* childe; so hym̄ burde nedis be h*er*berd *þer* *þa*t nyght & sho, als ill as sho myght, made hym̄ a bed. & þat nyght sho traveld & was delyverd of a son̄, and when̄ þe childe was born̄ þe emp*er*our hard a voyce say vnto þe childe; "Childe! þis emp*er*our sall be þi fadyr-in-lay." And vpon̄ þe morn̄ þe Emp*er*our rase & went his wais, & com*m*andid ij of his squeyers to feche þis childe in þe wud, & for to sla itt & bryng hym̄ þe harte *þer*off. And when̄ þai saw þis childe þai had co*m*passion̄ *þer*on̄, and þai gat a hare & tuke þe harte *þer*of, & broght it vnto þe emp*er*our, and lefte þe childe lygand in þe wudd. & onone aft*er* *þer* come a duke & fand þis childe, and he sent it home vnto his wyfe becauce he had no childe hym̄ selfe, and bad þai*m* tell hur

[1] Lat. MSS. Conrad*us*.

at he had getten it, & bad name it Henrie. So when þis chylde was waxen he was fayr & semely & wele-spoken, and passand gracious. And when þe emp*er*our saw at þis childe was fayr & wyse, he tuke hym into his cowrte. So on a tyme he keste in his mynde a dowte wheþ*er* þis was þe childe at he com*m*aundid to sla or nay. And he thoght he wolde be sekur, and he garte make a l*ett*re vnto his wyfe in þis man*er* of wyse; "As þou luffis þi lyfe, onone as þou hase red þis l*ett*re sla þis childe"; & he sent þis childe *with* þe same lett*er*. So as he went vnto þe whene-ward hym happend com into a kurk, & he was werie forgone & lenyd hym down & fell on slepe; & his purs at þe lettyr was in hang oute of his bosom. So þ*er* come a preste & fande hym & opynd his purs & lukid þe lett*er*, and hym vgged *with* þe wykkydnes at was þ*er*-in, & he skrapid oute, "pueru*m* hu*n*c necab*is*," & sett in þies wurdis; "puero filia*m* mea*m* dabis." And so he went furth *with* þis l*ett*re & he was wele welcomd; and onone he wed þe Emp*er*ours doghter. So when þe Emp*er*our come home & saw how it was, ffro he wiste þat he was ane erle son his sorow began to slake. And he made mekull off hym, & aft*er* when þe Emp*er*our was dead he was made Emp*er*our. And in þe place þ*er* he was born he byggid a wurthie abbay.

DXCIV.

Ornatus im*m*oderatus corp*or*is dampnacio*n*is est causa.

We rede in 'Libro de Dono Timoris' how som tyme þ*er* was a holie ladie in Fraunce. So on a tyme sho was ravysshid in hur spirutt and sho saw a cowntas dead þat sho was passand familiarie *with*, and sho saw hur drawen *with* fendis vnto hell. And sho made grete sorow, & cried & said; "Allas! Allas! I sary wrich, I was chastie enogh & a grete almos-deler, & I am now dampnyd & for none oþ*er* þing bod for varios & prowde arayment þat I luffid passand wele; & when I was snybbed þ*er*for yitt I wolde not lefe it[1]."

[1] *This and the following tale are marked* Nota.

DXCV.

Ornatus immoderatus causa est exultacionis demonum.

Cesarius tellis how som tyme þer was a preste at hight Catus, & on a tyme he saw a womman com fro þe kurk, & he met hur at þe kurk-dure. & sho was gaylie atyrid in cowrchevis, and sho had a passand lang tayle folowand hur, and þer was þer-vppon dawnsand a huge multitude of fendis, as it had bene blak men of Ynde, skornand with þer mowthes and clappand with þer handis. And þai war als thykk as it had bene fyssh in a nett. So he commaundyd all þe peple to stand styll, and he coniurid þies fendis at þai sulde nott go away, & he made his prayer & besoght God att þe peple myght se þaim; & so þai did. And when þis womman saw at þe fendis had so mekull power on hur for þe pryde of hur clothyng, & at þe peple yrkid for to luke on hur, sho went home and skyftid hur clothyng & wold neuer were tayle after. And bathe vnto hur and all oþer at say þis vision it was ane occasion of mekenes, & at þai sulde neuer after vse prowde clothyng.

Ornare se potest mulier interdum per virum. Infra de vxore, iij.

DXCVI.

Ornatus vestium non debet esse nimis sumptuosus.

Helynandus tellis how som tyme þer was a kyng in Yngland þat hight Gillelmus, and he wolde were no clothyng bod of a huge price; and if it war light of price, & it war neuer so gude, he wold hafe grete dedeyn þer-att. So on a tyme hys chamberlayn did on hym a payr of new hose, and he axkid hym what þai coste, & he sayd iij s.; and he grynnyd & had grete dedyn þeratt & said vnto hym; "þou hureson! What saw þou evur kyng were hose off so vile a price? Go," he sayd, "faste, & bryng me a payr of a marke price." And he went furth & broght hym a payr þat was mekull better þan þe toder, bod he made a lee of þe price of þaim. And when þe kyng saw þ*aim* he said; "Ya, thies acordis vnto a kyng to were." And fro þ*at* tyme evur afterward his chawmberlayn tellid hym þe p*r*ice of his clothyng as hym lyste, and as it plesid hym. And bod if he said it coste mekull he wold not were it.

Ornatus vestiu*m* qu*andoque* eleuat cor ho*min*is in sup*er*bia*m*. Sup*ra* de aug*u*rio, ij [1].

DXCVII.

Paciencia. Paciens *eciam* ab inferiorib*us* suis iniurias tollit.

Saynt Ierom tellis how Socrates had ij wyfis, & oft sithes ather of þ*aim* wold flite w*ith* other, & evur he wolde do bod scorn þ*aim*. And att þe laste þai wex bothe wrothe w*ith* hym & callid hym bellud chule, & said his nease droppid & his een ran, and þe harys on his browis war lyke swyne-brustyls. And þus þai made hym fayn fle fro þ*aim* & leve þaim be þ*er* one. And a man axkid hym whi he wold not bete þaim, and he ansswerd agayn & sayd þat womman, ay þe mor sho was bett, þe wars was sho.

Paciens iniurias illatas de naturalib*us* defec*ti*b*us* pacient*er* tol*er*at [2]. Sup*ra* de castitate.

Paciens ab indignis iniurias tollit. Inf*ra* de paup*er*tate, iiij.

Paciens e*qu*animit*er* tol*er*at [2]. Sup*ra* de Anthonio.

Pacient*er* co*n*uicia ferre signu*m* est humilitat*is*. S*upr*a de humilitate, ij.

Paciens *eciam* infamia de c*r*imine falso sibi imposito [3] pacient*er* tol*er*at [2]. Sup*ra* de infamia.

Pacient*er* debet sustineri infirmitas corp*or*ales. S*upr*a de infirmitate.

Pacientes debent esse religiosi in amissione te*m*poraliu*m*. Infra de religioso [4].

[1] MS. iij.
[2] MS. tollerat.
[3] MS. inposito.
[4] *Reference from* Arund. MS.

Paciens obiurgac*iones et* contumelias pacient*er* portat. S*upr*a de moniali, xiij.

DXCVIII.

Paciens bonu*m pro* malo reddit.

We rede in 'Gestis Ioh*annis* Elemosinarij' how on a tyme when a cussyn of his had a grete wrang of a tavurner, & when he made playnt vnto þe pat*r*iarke, he mott gett no comfurth, and þe patryarke said vnto hym; "Who is he att dar gaynsay þe or oppyn his mouthe agayns þe? Truste, son, vnto me, þat I shall do to-day vnto hym suche a thyng þat all Alexandria sall hafe m*er*vell þeroff." And when he hard þis he tuke a grete comfurth, & trowid þat he wold gar hym be grevuslie betyn. And þan when Iohn saw he tuke a grete comfurth, he kyssid his breste & said; "Son, & þou will be cussyn vnto my mekenes, þou bus make þe to be betyn & suff*ir* stryfe & debate of ilka man, for a trew thoght is nowder of flessh nor blude, bod it is knowyn of trewth of þe mynd." & onone þai sent for þis man, and he made hym fre of al man*er* of t*r*ibutt & pension. And all þat evur hard þis had grete m*er*vayle and vnderstude what he ment when he sayd; "I sall do vnto hym suche a thyng þat all Alexand*ria* shall hafe m*er*vell þ*er*off."

DXCIX.

Pacientes iniuste deus in fine *eciam* in hac vita honorat.

We rede in 'Legend Longab*ardica*' of ane þat hight Theodora, a noble wom*man* & a fayr, þat had a husband at Alexander in tyme of Zenonis þe Emp*er*our; and hur husband was a gud man & a riche, and dowtid God. So þ*er* was a yong man þat wex passand ameros of hur and begylid hur be þe mene of ane alde wyfe, þat tolde hur at Godd knew not þat at was done on þe nyght, bod alonelie þat at was done on þe day. And þus sho made hur to latt þe man lygg by hur. So afterward, when sho come to hur selfe, & felid at sho had done wrong and at God knew all maner of þing þat was done, sho wepid & made much sorow & garte cut hur head, & gatt hur mans clothyng of hur husbandis & did it on hur & went vnto ane abbay far thens & made hur a monk, & sayd hur name was Theodorus. & þer sho liffid a gude haly lyfe and did meracles. So on a tyme hur[1] happend to be hostid with his camels at sho drafe vnto þe cetie be þe commandment of þe abbott, at a mans howse þat had a fayr doghter; and on þe night sho come vnto þis Theodora & wold have lyggyn with hur, & sho wold not latt hur. So with-in a while after þis wenche was with barn, and sho said at þis Theodora had gettyn itt; and hur abbott gretelie blamyd hur þerfor, and when þe childe was born it was broght & layd in hur skurte. And sho & it was putt furth of þe abbay for vij yere, and with mylke & swilk as sho cuthe gett [*sho nurisshid it*]. And in þis menewhile sho was gretlie tempyd with þe devull to syn, bod he prevaylid not on hur. And when vij yere was gone þe abbott consydurd hur paciens & tuke bothe hur & þe childe in agayn. And þer sho & it to-gedur was sparyd samen in a cell. And þer with-in ij yere to-gedur sho passid vnto God; and yit sho had enformyd þis child or sho dyed in lernyng & in holie liffyng to persevur. And þat night at sho dyed, þe Abbott þoght at he saw all þe ordurs of Aungels & Patriarkis & Prophettis & all Saynttis com & feche hur sawle vnto hevyn; & hym thoght þai made grete ioy. And þer was a voyce at sayd vnto hym; "þis Theodorus was falsly accusid of þis childe-gettyng." And with þat þe Abbott wakend and callid vp his brether, and went vnto hur cell & fand hur dead; and when þai nakend hur þai fand sho was a womman. And he garte call þe wenche fadur & said vnto hym; "Lo! now, whethur he this corrupte þi doghter or nay." And all men had wonder her-of. So þer come a voyce vnto þe Abbot & bad hym go in-to þe cetie. And so he did, & þer mett hym a man, and he axkid hym whyter he was bown. And he said; "My wyfe is dead & I go to se hur." And þe Abbott & he went samen

[1] MS. hym.

wepand, and *with* grete devocion þai beryd hur. And þan hur husband made hym monke & dwelte in hur cell, & was a gude man evur whils þat he liffid. And þis childe *per*sevurd in gude wark*is* & was made a monk in þat same place. And afterward, when þe Abbott was dead, he was chosyn vnto Abbott.

DC.

Paciens vilia a vilib*us* pe*r*sonis tol*er*at [1].

We rede in 'Gestis Alexij' þat þis Alexius was þe son of Eufemian at was a wurthi offesur in þe Emp*er*our hall, and he was made rewler of iij M I childir at wer all cled in sylk & had gurdils of gold. And þis Eufemyan & Aglaes [2] his wyfe war passand m*er*cyfull & full of gude werk*is*; and þai had no childe bod þis Alexius, and hym þai maryed vnto a wurthie wom*m*an of þe emp*er*our howsold. So vppon þe nyght aft*er* þai war wed, he desyrid his wyfe to kepe hur in clene virginytie. And when sho had g*r*auntid hym, he lefte hur a gold ryng and a bygyrdyll full of gold, and went p*r*ivalie away from hyr & fled far thens into Syrie, vnto þe cetie of Egissam, whar þ*er* is ane ymage of oure Lord þat nevur was made be mans hand. & þ*er* he come in-to ane almos howse at was callid Syndo, & þ*er* he satt in ane entry emang pure men, & liffid of almos þat was giffen þai*m*. And his ffadur sent men þurgh all þis werld to seke hym. So one of þai*m* at soght hym come þurgh þis entry & gaff hym almos, and he knew hym wele enogh, bod he knew not hym. And þan he said vnto hym selfe; "Lord, I thanke The at Þou hase made me to reseyfe almos of myne awn servand." So all þies messangers come agayn & tolde his fadur þai cuthe not fynde hym, and he & his wyfe & his doghter made mekull sorow for hym. And when he had bene in þis hospitall xviij yere in pou*er*tie & in Goddis s*er*ves, þe ymage of our Ladie spak vnto hym þat kepid þe kurk, & said; "Make þe man of Almyghti God to com in, for he is wurthie þe kyngdom of hevyn." And þis kep*er* wiste not whome sho

[1] MS. toll*er*at.

[2] MS. Alglaes, *with the first* l *erased.*

ment off, and sho said; "He þat is *with*oute þe dure, þat is he." And when he was broght in & þis was knowen vnto all his felows, þai began to wurshupp, and he saw þat & fled away fro þai*m* & gatt our þe see. And as God wold, hym happynd to land at Rome, and when he conseyvid þat he said vnto hym selfe; "I sall ga dwell vnknowen in my fadurs hows, and I sall bere no grete coste of hym." So he come vnto his fadur place & sayd vnto his ffadur when he mett hym; "Thow *ser*vand of Almyghti God, take me into þi howse at I may liff of þe crombis com*m*ys fro þi burd, for þi son sawle þat was a pylgram." And he tuke hym in for his son sake, & com*m*andid hym into a place in his howse, & gaff hym meate euerilk day from his awn burd, & made hym his awn *ser*vand. And he did all þing þat evur any bodye bad hym, & none knew hym, ffor *with* fastyng & *with* wakyng he made hym selfe lene and oute of knowlege, and her-for þe *ser*vandes of þe howse wolde skorn hym, & stryke hym, & powr watyr at þai had wasshid vessell in vppon his head; and all þis he suffred xvij yere & nevur was knowen. So at þe laste he knew be reuelacion at his dead drew nere, and he wrate all þe cowrs of his lyfe in a grete roll. And vppon þe Sononday at evyn þ*er* was a voyce hard in þe kurk at Rome, þat said; "Venite ad me om*n*es *qui laboratis et onerati estis, et ego* [*refficiam uos*]." And all þat hard it fell down on þ*er* kneis & had grete m*er*vell þ*er*off. And þan it said agayn; "Go, seke þe s*er*uand of God, at he may pray for Rome." And þai soght hym & cuthe not fynde hym. So þai hard it say agayn þat he was in þe howse of Eufemyan; and þan þe pope and þe imp*er*our, a bisshop & ane archdekyn come vnto þis mans howse and desyrid to se þis pure man & bad hym luke graythelie whethir it war his son or nay, for he was a man of gude life & of grete pacyens. And Eufemianus ran in-to þe howse vnto hym and fand hym dead, and his face shane as it had bene ane angell. And he had a roll in his hand, & Eufemyan wolde hafe takyn it & sene it, & he wold not latt it goo; bod when þe pope come he lete it go alredy. And when it was red befor his fadur, at all þe peple hard, his fadur wex nere-hand mad & drew of þe hare of his head & of his berd, & fell down vppon þe body of his son & sayd; "A! son, full wo is me þ*at* I se þe þus lygg in a bedd & may not speke vnto me." And þan his moder come, & when sho saw hym sho swonyd & made grete wepyng & said; "Allas! son, whi did þou so vnto vs, þat when þou saw þi fadur & me wepe for owr son þou wolde neu*er* shew þe vnto vs? þine awn *ser*vand*is* hath done þe grete wrong, & þou hase evur suffyrd it." & evur sho swonyd & cryed & made mekull sorow, & sayd; "All þat bene here, I p*r*ay you wepe *with* me, ffor xvij yere I hafe had myne awn son in my howse daylie, & knew hym noght." And þan his wyfe come & made þe maste sorow of all. And þan þe pope, þe Emp*er*our, þe bisshop & þe archedekyn tuke vp his body on a bere, & bare it on þ*er* awn shuldres vnto þe beryall; & þai myght nott pass away þ*er*-*with*, ffor nerehand all Rome was gadurd þedur, & þe peple was passand thrang. And þai garte caste golde & syluer by þe way at peple sulde be besy þ*er* aboute & so lat þai*m* pas, bod þe peple lukid nowder aft*er* þe gold nor yit þe sylver, bod evur was besy abowteward for to tuche his bodye. So at þe laste *with* grete labur þai broght hym vnto his grafe. And þ*er* þe peple abade vij dayes & made grete lovyng vnto Almyghti God. & þ*er* [*he*] was berid & his grafe coverd *with* golde and p*r*ecious stonys; and fro his body þ*er* come a passyng gude odur. And he dyed xvij Kal*ends* of Auguste, in þe yere of our Lord CCC xviij.

Paciens in amissione membror*um* pacient*er* tole*r*at[1]. Inf*r*a de oc*u*lo, ij.

Paciens *eciam* mort*em* *pro* deo tole*r*at[1]. S*upr*a de martirio.

Paganus aliqu*ando* bonas leges condit. Sup*r*a de lege, j.

DCI.

Papa. Papa mulier creatur.

We rede in 'Cronicles' how som tyme þ*er* was a yong damysell, and a luff of hurs went away *with* hur & broght hur in maus

[1] MS. toll*er*at.

clothyng vnto Rome; and þer sho went vnto þe scule and wex so parfyte in connyng þat sho had no make in all Rome. So att þe laste, be ane hole consent, sho was chosyn to be pope and was made pope. And when sho was pope hur luff lay with hur & gatt hur with chylde, so he wiste not at sho was with childe to sho was evyn at travellyng[1]. So hur happend on a day to com in procession fro Saynt Peturs vnto Saynt Iohn Latarenens, and þer sho began at travell, and bare hur chylde betwix Colliseum & Saynt Clemett kurk; & þer sho dyed, & þer þai berid hur. And becauce of þat detestable dead, þe pope vsid neuer syne to com þer-away with procession, and here-for hur name is not putt emang other popes namys in the Martiloge.

Papa per diaboli procuracionem creatur. Supra de ambicione.

DCII.

Papa multipliciter dehonestatur.

We rede in 'Cronicles' of one þat hight Formosus, at was furste a cardynall & syne pope. And pope Iohn cursyd hym & degradid hym agayn vnto the lay astate, and made hym swere þat he sulde nevur com in Rome, nor desyre nor take þe papeshup on hand. Neuer-þe-les after-ward, of þis pope John successour he was asoylid, & restorid to com agayn vnto Rome; and he tuke þe popeshup agayn on hand. And when he was dede, Stephanus VI garte take his bodye, & doff all þe his pope clothyng & clethe hym in lay wede, & garte cutt of[2] ij of hy[s] fyngers of ather hand & cutt of bothe his handis & keste hym into Tybur. So vnto þis Stephan succedid John, and he reprovid all þe warkis off Stephan, & provid þe warkis of þis Formosius. Than after hym come Sergius III, & he garte take Formosius oute off his grafe & vnordurd all þat he had gyffen ordurs to, & garte caste hym in Tybur. And ffysshers happend at ffynd hym in þer nettis, & þai broght hym

[1] Harl. MS. *verum autem partum ignorans*, cum de *Sancto* Petro, &c.

[2] Harl. MS. *et* duobus digitis dextere abscisis, manu priuauit, *et* eam in Tiberim iactari precepit.

into Saynt Peturs; and wheñ þai broght hym̄ in, aƚƚ þe ymagis in þe kurk, att aƚƚ meñ myght se, as he come by þai*m* lowtid' vnto hym̄ & wurshuppid' hym̄. And here-by þai wyste he was a gude mañ.

Papa bonus. S*upr*a de Gregorio.

Pape p*ossu*nt adaptari multa que inf*r*a dicu*n*tur[1] de p*r*elato, *et* sup*r*a de morte.

DCIII.

Paradisus. Paradisi disposicio.

Saynt Gregur tellis how som tym̄ at Rome þ*er* was a knyght þat feƚƚ seke, & was evyñ bowñ to dye & lay in a trans. And wheñ he come agayñ vnto hym̄ selfe, he said' þat he saw a bryg, and vndernetħ it rañ a grete blak watur at keste owte intollerable savurs & stynkis. And wheñ he was passid' þis brygg, oñ þe toder syde of þis watyr was fayr medows & grene, & fuƚƚ of gude flowris wele savurand'. And þ*er* he saw a grete co*m*pany of white meñ in albys; and þ*er* was suche a gude savur emang þai*m* at þai war saciatt & fulfyllid' þ*er*-wit*h* as it had bene wit*h* meate or drynk. & þ*er* he saw dyvers mansions for evure mañ, at war fuƚƚ of grete light. And þ*er* was byggid' a howse, and aƚƚ þe sydis þ*er*off wer off fyne gold', for he cuthe not wytt whose it was. And þ*er* was many habitacles apoñ þe banke of the same watir; and he said' he saw many oñ þis brygg þat, þurgħ felyng of þe iƚƚ savur oñ þe watur, þai feƚƚ in-to itt.

Parentes frequent*er* visitare no*n* expedit religiosis. S*upr*a de affec*t*u carnali.

Parentes debent filij honorare. Sup*r*a de honore, j.

Parentes no*n* de*b*ent filijs maledic*er*e. Inf*r*a de Steph*ano*.

Parentes su*n*t relinquendi pe*r*fec*t*is. Inf*r*a de relinquere.

[1] MS. *repeats*, infra *after* dicuntur.

Paruulus male disciplinatus *eciam* deu*m* blasfemans dampnat*ur*. S*upr*a de blasfemia.

P*at*ris necligencia circa correccione*m* filior*um* frequent*er* est ips*is* filijs in det*r*imentu*m*. Supra de blasfemia.

Pater filios[1] instruere debet. S*upr*a de ffilia, j.

Patriarchia. Infra de veste.

DCIV.

Pauli Apostoli.

We rede in his legend how on a tyme when Pawle was hostid att þe Ile of Mustelan, þ*er* come ane erdur in-to his skurte and hurte hym noght, & he keste it in þe fyre. & þe gude man was wrothe, ffor all þat evur was born of the kynred of þat p*er*son at he was at hoste *with* was neu*er* hurte *with* þase venomos bestis. And when þ*er* childer war born, þai wolde put þies serpent*is* in þe creduls *with* þai*m*, at þai mot prufe whethur þai wer þ*er* trew fadurs or nay.

DCV.

Paulus velu*m* restituit Plautille.

We rede of Saynt Pawle þat when he went vnto his passion, Plautilla, at was his disciple, delyverd hym hur curchyff to wype þe swete of his face, & to covur his een in þe howr of his passion. And when þe turmaturs smate of his head, evyn in þe strake he tuke þis curchyff and[2] gadurd þ*er*in all his awn blude. And he wappid [*it*] sam*en* [*& gaff it*] vnto þis Plautille[3]. When þe turmatur was gone, þis Ploattyll mett hym & axkid hym whare he had done hur maist*er* Pawle, and he teld hur þat he lay

[1] So Latin version. English MS. *has* liberos.
[2] MS. *repeats*, and.
[3] Harl. MS. Paulus in ipso ictu uelu*m* explicuit, *et* in eo sanguine*m* propriu*m* collegit, obuoluit, *et* tradidit Plautille.

with his felow dead *with*-oute þe cetie. And sho said agayn vnto hym; "Petur & Pawle is gone in-to þe cetie, & fayr crownys vppon þ*er* hedis, & þai er cled in gay clothyng." & sho tuke furth hur curchiff full [1] of blude & shewid hym & many oþ*er*. And herefor many folke become crystend.

DCVI.

Pauli caput p*ro*p*ri*o corp*or*i post mortem p*er* se coniu*n*gitur.

Dionisius tellis how þat many yeris after þe passion of Saynt Pawle, his [2] head was fon in þe felde *with* a hurd-man, & he sett it vp on a rodd. & oppon þe nyght a grete light shane þ*er*-oppon fro hevyn; and when þe pope hard tell of þis, he tuke þe hede & laid it at Saynt Paule fete. And, at mekull pepull saw, þe body of Saynt Pawle rase & turnyd it, & ionyd it vnto þe hede; & mekull pepull had grete m*er*vayle þ*er*off.

Pauli p*ri*mi [3] h*er*emite. Paulus honorat hospitem [4] suu*m*. Sup*ra* de honore, iij [5].

DCVII.

Paup*er* humil*is* ditabitur *et* paup*er* sup*er*bus pau-p*er*abit*ur*.

Iacobus de Vet*ri*aco tellis how som tyme þ*er* was ij pure men, ane meke and a noder prowde; bod þe meke man, whare-so-evur þai berid corn, he wold com *with* his glofe & ask þai*m* itt full, & no man grucid bot gaff hym. And *with*-in a while he was a [6] r[*i*]che man. And þe prowde pure man wolde com *with* a sekk and ax corn. And þe gretnes of þe sakk flayed ilk man so and þai wolde giff hym noght; and so he was neu*er* bod a pure man.

[1] MS. *repeats*, full.
[2] MS. he.
[3] MS. prime.
[4] *So* Latin MSS. The English MS. *has* hostem.
[5] MS. j.
[6] MS. *repeats*, a.

DCVIII.

Paup*er*i no*n* est neganda elemosina.

Sigilb*er*tus tellis how þ*er* was a pure man axkid almos of a shipman, and he wolde giff hym none. And the shipman bad hym lefe his almos-axking for þai had nothyng þ*er* bod stonys. And þe pure man answerd agayn & said; "Stonys be þai þan." & all þat evur was in þe ship was turnyd in-to stonys, & þe color & þe facion abade styll.

Paup*er*is m*er*itis bona te*m*poralia augentur. S*upr*a de ele*mosina*, iij.

Paup*er*i data elemosina datur deo. S*upr*a de abb*at*e, iiij [1].

Paup*er* plus dilectatur in mi*ni*mis q*u*am diues in magnis. S*upr*a de Basilio.

Paup*er*i est gratis consulend*um*. S*upr*a de Aug*ustino*, iij.

Paup*er*i datu*m* dat*ur* deo. S*upr*a de abb*at*e, iiij, *et* de G*r*egorio, i [2].

DCIX.

Paup*er* murmurans tol*er*andus [3] est.

We rede in 'Gestis Ioh*annis* Elemosinarij' when Ioh*annes* Elemosinarius, þat was pat*r*iark of Alexander, vnto a pure man þat axkid hym almos com*m*andid to be gyffen v d he had grete dedeyng at he wold gyff hym no more. And onone he fell at debate wit*h* hym, & began to flite. And when þe pat*r*iark s*er*vandi*s* saw þis, þai wold hafe betyn hym. And þis holy man Iohn sayd nay, and said; "Suffre hym, brethur, to ban me; ffor I am lx yere old and I have oftsithis blasfemyd almyghti God; & þ*er*for I may suffer a flytyng of þis man." And wit*h* þat he garte

[1] MS. iij. [2] MS. iij. [3] MS. toll*er*andus.

bryng a sacheƚƚ fuƚƚ of sylu*er* and lay befor hym̄, & bad hym̄ take enogħ þ*er*off.

Paup*er* no*n* debet fieri villicus aut balliu*us*. S*upra* de balli*uo*, j^o^.

Paup*er*[es honorare debent [1]] p*r*incipes *et* p*r*elati. S*upra* de iudicio.

Paup*er*es no*n* su*n*t deridendi. S*upra* de apostasia, j.

Pax. Pacem̄ semp*er* cu*m* om*n*ib*us* qua*n*tu*m* possib*i*le est debet h*ab*ere bonus chr*ist*ianus. S*upra* de odio *et* inuidia.

DCX.

Pecc*atu*m multiplex nocet ho*mi*ni.

We rede in 'Vitis P*atrum*' how som tyme þ*er* was a voyce at said vnto þe abbot Arseni*us*; "Com̄, and I saƚƚ shew þe werk*is* of men̄." And he went furtħ & he saw a man̄ of Ynde cuttant treis and makand a burdyn̄ þat he mot not bere. And þe voyce sayd; "Thies er þai þat ekys syn̄ vppon̄ syn̄." And þan̄ he saw a temple & ij men̄ syttand on̄ hors, holdand vp̄ a brade tre for þe whilk þai myght not entre in. And þan̄ þe voyce sayd; "Þies er þai þat beris rightwusnes wi*th* pride." And þan̄ he saw a man̄ standand vppon̄ a dyke, & filland a veseƚƚ with watir þ*er*off & puttant it in-to ane iƚƚ cistern̄. And þan̄ þe voyce said; "Thies er þai þat hase som gude dedis, and blendis þai*m* wi*th* evuƚƚ warkis."

DCXI.

Peccatores aliqui benigne *eciam* recip*er*e deb*ent* [2] s*ancti*.

Heraclides tellis & sais þat on̄ a tyme when̄ he visitt ane olde man̄ þ*at* had þe grace of p*ro*phecying & spak wi*th* hym̄, þ*er* come þe mayr of þe cetie, and he forsuke Heraclides & talkyd wi*th* hym̄.

[1] *Supplied from the* Latin MSS. The English MS. *leaves a blank.*

[2] *So* Latin MSS. The English *has* sunt sancti.

& aft*er*ward when þai com*m*oned to-ged*er*, þai com*m*ond of þis, at he sulde forsake hym & talk *with* þe mayr, & þan he said; "Wherefor hase þou reprovid me in þi saule? þou & I luffid wele athur of vs to com vnto oþ*er*, at ather of vs myght hafe solas & comfurth of other *with* owr talkyng; and he is gyffen all vnto þe devuls power, and vnnethis he may brethe in ane howr. And now he as a *ser*vand come hedur from his lorde to seke refute, it wer ane vnsondabyll thyng to do, if it sulde be he lefte & [*I*] taryd *with* þe [1] þat hase bene wunte beselye to call me vnto þi hele."

Peccatu*m* incurrit aliqu*ando* nimis de se p*re*sume*re*. S*upra* de carne, iij.

Peccata rem*i*ttu*n*tur or*ati*onib*us* s*anc*tor*um*. S*upra* de Basilio, iij.

DCXII.

Peccata venialia impossibile est vitare.

Iacobus de Vet*ri*aco tellis how þ*er* was a monk þat luffid passand wele clennes and innocentrie fro þe state of childyd vnto þe state of man. And he wold eatt, bod he wold not hafe delectacion þ*er*in, and he studyd for to put away syn, and for to luff [2] *with*-owten any syn. And becauce for ane impossible thyng [3] he fell into a dispayre, vnto so mekull þat he myght not liff *with*-owten venyall syn, [*he*] demyd hym selfe þat it was impossible þat he sulde be savyd.

DCXIII.

Peccantes simul in morte si*mu*l in vita puniu*n*tur.

Helynandus tellis how som tyme þ*er* was a colyer [4] & he was *ser*vand vnto religious men and vnto þe com*m*ontie of M*er*uernens.

[1] MS. if it sulde be taryd *with* þe & he left þat hase, *&c.*

[2] *Should be* liff; Harl. MS. ducere uitam sine om*n*i pecc*ato*.

[3] Harl. MS. et q*uia* laborabat ad impo*ssib*ile, decidit in desp*er*acione*m*, ad eo [ut] q*uia* sine veniali no*n* pote*ra*t uiuere, iudicabat se saluari impossibile.

[4] Lat. MSS. uir carbonarius, paup*er* *sed* religiosus, *et* comiti Munensi pl*ur*imu*m* familiar*is*.

So on a nyght as he was kepand his cole-pitt, & *þer* was a light fyre by hym, he was warr of a nakyd womman rynand, and ane on a blak hors *with* a swerd in his hand drawen, folowand aft*er* hur for to take hur. And as sho come, sho ran vnto þe cole-pytt, & *þer* he tuke hur & strake hur þurgh *with* his swerd; & when sho was nere dead he keste hur into þe fyre. And when sho was all to-swythyn, he drew hur oute, & layd hur befor hym on þe hors & rade away. And þis he saw dyvers nyghtt*is*; and all þis he tolde vnto þe said commontie[1]. So on a nyght *þer* come a felow[2] *with* þis colleyer vnto þe same place, and he saw all as þe colyer told. And he tuke þis hors-man be þe brydill when all was done, and askyd hym what he was. And he ansswerd agayn & said; "I was swilk a knyght, and þis was þe wyfe of swylk a knyght whome sho slow for my luff, att sho & I mot mor frelie hawnte our syn; and in þat syn we er bothe dead. And vnnethis when we dyed we forthoght our syn; and þus ilk a nyght I sla hur & burnys hur, and sho suffers mor payn *with* þe strake of my swerd þat I stryke hur *with*, þan evur sho did with dead; and *with* þe burnyng sho felis mekull mor." And þan he askid hym what hors þat was at he satt on, and he said; "It is a fend þat turment*is* vs." Than he askyd hym if any þing mot helpe þa*im*, & he sayd; "Ya, and ye wold gar syng so many messis & gar say so many psalters for vs, onone we sulde be helpyd & our payn relesid." And þus þai *par*tid, and þis man garte do þies messis & say þies psalters for þa*im*, & þai wer neu*er* sene aft*er*.

P*eccatu*m punit Deus qu*ando*q*ue* in hac vita. Sup*ra*, ambulac*io*, ij.

P*ecca*tor p*er* que peccat p*er* hec *et* punit*ur*. S*upra* de agro, i & ij.

P*ecca*ta esse remissa o*ste*ndit aliqu*ando* deus aliq*ui*b*us* signis. Inf*ra* de remissione.

[1] Lat. MSS. *Quod* ille *comi*ti *pre*dicto *per* ordine*m* narrauit.

[2] Ac comes vna cu*m* carbonario ad *pre*fatu*m* locum . . . venie*n*s.

Pecc*atum* qu*andoque* dissimulat[1] Deus ut plus puniat. S*upra* de dissimulac*ione*.

Pecc*ata* sua *eciam* bruta aliqu*ando* cognoscunt. Sup*ra* de furto, ij[2].

Pecc*ata* delet confessio qu*andoque* de memoria confessoris. S*upra* de confessione, iiij.

Pecc*ata* delet confessio de consciencia penitentis. S*upra* de confessione, iij.

Pecc*ata* celat confessio multiplex. S*upra* de confessione in pl*uribus* locis.

Pecc*atum* unu*m* qu*andoque* inducit in aliud. S*upra* de cont*ri*cione, vj.

DCXIV.

Pecc*ata* su*n*t causa adu*er*sitatu*m* que nob*is* eveniunt.

We rede in 'Vitis P*atrum*' how þ*er* was som tyme a gude mañ þat suffred wrong of a noder, and he co*m*pleynyd hym̃ vnto ane olde mañ. And þe old mañ answerd' hym̃ agayñ & said'; "He did' not þis, bod þi synnys did itt. And þ*er*for' blame not þis mañ in nothyng at he duse vnto þe, nor at is happend vnto þe, bod say at þi synnys hath adlid' þai*m*."

Pecc*atum* fetet cora*m* deo *et* angelis. S*upra* de Angelo, iij.

Pecc*at*u*m* on*er*at ho*min*em *et* an*im*am. Inf*ra* de simia.

DCXV.

Pecc*atum* trahit ho*min*em ad infernu*m*.

We rede in 'Vitis P*atrum*' how þat oñ a tyme wheñ ane ypocryte was dead', meñ þat wer p*re*sent aboute hym̃ hard' a voice say vnto fendes oñ þis man*er* of wyse; "Draw hym̃ oute wheder

[1] MS. dissimilat. [2] MS. iij.

he wiłł or nay. And as he gaf me no reste in þe synnys þat he did̛ beselie befor̛ me, on þe same man*er* of wyse giff ye hym̄ no reste."

P*ecca*tores portat demon ad infernu*m*. Sup*ra* de demone in pl*ur*ib*us* locis.

P*ecca*tor in inferno punitur. S*upra* de Lang*r*auio.

Pena infernal*is* est multiplex. S*upra* de inferno p*er* to*tu*m.

Pena*m* debita*m* minuunt suffragia. Inf*r*a de suffragijs.

Pena respondet culpe. Supra de agro.

DCXVI.

Penitencia pocius est hic facienda q*u*am in futuro.

Iacobus de Vet*r*iaco tellis & says; "Som̄ tyme I saw a holye wom*m*an̄ whilk þat when̄ sho was long dead̛, or hur body was beryd & layd in erth̄, hur sawle turnyd̛ agayn̄ vnto hur bodye. & sho had grawntid̛ at sho suld̛ liff styłł in þis werld̛, and sho sulde suffre in purgatorie penans for hur syn̄ & sho wold̛, & if sho wold̛ not, sho suld̛ suffre penance in þis werld̛: & sho tuke hur to suffre penance in þis werld̛. So a long tyme, as God wold̛[1], sho was gretelye turment, to so muche at sho wold̛ som tyme weltyr in þe fyre, and som̄ tyme in wynter sho wolde lay hur down̄ in frosyn̄ watyr & lay hur þ*er* a long while; and̛ som̄ tyme sho was constreynyd̛ to entyr dead mens gravis. So at þe laste sho had grace g*r*auntid̛ of almyghtie God̛ at sho was oft sythes ravysshid̛ in hur spyritt at sho led̛ dyvers tymys þe sawlis of þai*m* at wer dead̛ into purgatorie, & thrugh̄ purgatorie, & sho had no hurte, vnto þe kyngdom̄ of hevyn̄."

Penitere potest int*er*du*m* unus p*ro* alio. Infra de satisfaccione.

[1] MS. *repeats*, a long tyme, *here*.

DCXVII.

Penitencia p*erfecta* delet pec*cata* et nichil formidat.

Cesarius tellis how som tyme þ*er* was a blak monk þat fell in apostasye, & syne he was a P*re*monstracence & went oute; and at þe laste he was a monk of Ceustus. And evur he gaff hym vnto luste & lykyng of his bodie, & vnto oþ*er* in*n*um*er*able vices. So at þe laste, as God wold, he tuke þe ordur & habett of Ceustus ordur, and onone he shrafe hym and tuke his penance. And he did his penance trewlie, in wepyngi*s*, prayer, & fastyng, & in all oþ*er* thyngys. So at þe laste he fell seke and was bown to dye, & evur he *con*tynewid in syngyng, prayers-saying, and wurshippyng our Lady vnto þe stounde of dead. And in p*re*sens of his abbot & his brethyr he said on þis man*er* of wyse; "Wurshupfull brethur, I, a synner & a penytent, ye beryng me wytnes, covetti*s* of almyghtie God to hafe a space to make a clere *con*fession, & to do v*er*ray penans for my synnys. And if God wyll graunt me lyfe, I am redie to make a sethe, and for to vnder-go all man*er* of turment, and all man*er* of hard thyng & labur; ffor nothyng is hard nor inpossible vnto hym þat is v*er*ray penytent." And þus, emang þies wurdi*s*, wit*h* a grete compu*n*ccion & a grete forthynkyng, he gaff vp vnto God a gude sawle; and þ*er* was sene com vnto hym aungels, whilk þat bare his sawle into hevyn wit*h* a grete myrth & a ioy.

Penitencia magis unu*m* q*u*am aliu*m* attenuat. S*upra* de apostata, ij.

Penitere facit ho*min*em cogitac*io* penar*um*. Supra de delicijs *et* de inferno, i.

DCXVIII.

Penitencia modica[1] ex corde f*acta* placet Deo.

We rede in 'Vitis P*atrum*' how som tyme þ*er* was a monk þat askid abbott Pastor, & said on þis man*er* of wyse; "I hafe done a

[1] MS. inordita. Lat. MSS. *as above*.

grete syn̄, & I wilł[1] þis iij yere be penytent þerof." And þan̄ þis abbot Pastor ansswerd' hym̄ agayn̄, & sayd'; "þat is mekułł!" & þis monk bad hym̄ commawnd hym̄ a yere, & yitt þe abbott said' þat was mekułł. And þai at was aboute desyrid' at he sulde be enionyd' þerfor xl^ti dayes, and yitt þis abbott said' it was mekułł, & said' on̄ þis maner of wyse; "I trow þat & a man̄ forthynk his syn̄ *with* ałł his harte, & turn̄ not þerto agayn̄, at God wilł for iij dayes penans-doyng forgyff hym̄ hys syn̄."

Penitenciam impedit gula. Supra de gula, iiij *et* v^to.
Penitenciam facit peccator inductus. *Supra* de abbate, iij.
Penitencia debet esse firma *et* perseverans. *Supra* de familiaritate *et* infra de perseuerancia.
Penitencia in fine vite valet. *Supra* de peccato, iij.

DCXIX.

Penitencia nimis tarda nichil prodest.

Iacobus de Vetriaco tellis how on̄ a tyme Charlis þe Emperour garte całł befor hym̄ his iij sonnys, Gobardus, Lotharius, and Lodouicus; and he helde ane appyłł in his hand' & bad þaim ałł oppyn̄ þer mouthes. & þe ij yonger oppynd' þer mouthis, & þis Gobardus wold' nott. And he gaff vnto þe ij yonger, þe tone a kyngdom̄, and þe toder a dukedom̄. And when̄ þis Gobardus saw, he said' vnto his fader at he wolde oppyn̄ his mouthe & hafe parte of þis appyłł. And his ffadur ansswerd' hym̄ agayn̄ & sayd'; "Þou oppynd' þi mouthe to late, & þerfor I wyłł nowder gyff þe appyłł nor land'." And hereof come a proverb þat is said' in Franche, "A tart bea[2] Gobard, qe eu la tere nout parte."

Penitent simul qui simul peccant. *Supra* de peccato, iiij[3].

[1] *After* will, not, *erased*. [2] MS. 'Acarbea Gobard,' &c. [3] MS. iij.

Penitencia viuor*um* fac*t*a p*ro* mortuis valet eis. S*up*ra de morte, xiij.

Penitencia debet a confessore acceptari qua*m* a con-fitente p*otes*t extorquere. S*up*ra de *con*fessore.

DCXX.

P*er*egrinu*m* demon subito reportauit [1].

Cesarius tellis how som tyme in þe town of Halybach, þ*er* was a knyght þat hight Gerard, and he had grete deuocion vnto Saynt Thomas þe apostell. So on a tyme þe devull in lyknes of a pure man come vnto hym, & askyd hym gestynnyng for Saynt Thomas luff; & he grauntid hym it. And when he was gone vnto his bed, þis knyght sent vnto hym his beste furryd gown to happ hym *with* for colde, and he vppon þe nyght had þis cape away, & wolde not be fon in þe mornyng. And þe knyght*is* wyfe was wrothe here-*with*, & blamyd hugelie [2] hur husband for h*er*beryng of pure beggers, & said; "Þou sulde nevur do hym mor gude." And þis knyght answerd hur agayn mekelie & said; "Saynt Thomas is in power to do me als gude a turn as my gown was wurth." So on a tyme aft*er* þis knyght wold go in pylgramege vnto þ*er* Saynt Thomas lay, and he brak a golde ryng in ij befor hys wyfe, & he guf þe tone halfe vnto his wyfe and sayd; "Trust vnto þis tokyn, & I send þe itt, and abyde my com*m*yng home vnto v yere be passyd." And sho said yis & tuke þis ryng, & he went his ways. So after dyvers yeris he come vnto þe cetie of Saynt Thomas, and when he was in þe kurk & made his prayer vnto Saynt Thomas, & com*m*endid in his prayers his wyfe and his childer & his meneya, he was war of þe fend walkand vp & down in his furryd gown. And þe fend come vnto hym & sayd; "Gerard! knowis þou oght me?" And he said; "Nay, I know þe not, bod I know þat gown well enogh." And þan þe fend said; "I am þe devull þat in lyknes of a pure man was h*er*bard *with* þe, and I stale þi gown; & herefor I hafe bene gretely

[1] MS. temptauit. Lat. MSS. *as above.* [2] MS. *repeats,* hugelie.

punysshid. And I am chargid at I shall onone hafe þe home agayn vnto þi place safe & sownd, for als mekull as þis day þi wyfe is wed *with* a noder man; for now it is xv yere sen þou come fro hur." And *with* þat, when he had offerd, he tuke hym vpp in Ynde, and onone he broght hym home to his awn yate in Ducheland. And his wyfe & hur husband, att war wed þat same day, wer at meatt, & he come in & keste in hur copp þ*er* sho satt þe halfe of þe golde ryng. And when sho saw it sho tuke þe tud*er* parte þ*er*-of & putt þ*er*to, & þai acordid; & here-by sho wyste he was hur husband, and þ*er* sho forsuke hur new husband & tuke hur to hur olde.

DCXXI.

P*er*egrinos d*eu*s in morte consolatur.

We rede in 'Vitis P*atrum*' how som tyme þ*er* was ij brethir, & þe tone was a pylgrem, and þe toder gaff hym vnto quiete & ryste. So it happid at þis pylgram dyed, and angels tuke his saule & flow up vnto hevyn þ*er*-*with*, & wolde hafe broght it in. And þan our Lord said; "He was a little necligent, bod becauce he was a pylgram, þ*er*for take hym in." So onone after his other bruther dyed, and a gude olde man, þat saw aungels com to þe furst & not to þe latter, he axked our Lord why þis was. And our Lord answerd hym agayn & sayd; "Þis pylgram in all his life had no comfurth of none of his frendis, and þ*er*for me behuvis comfurthe[1] hym *with* myne angels; bod his bruther in his life had co*m*furth of his gude frend*is*, & þ*er*-for I comfurthid hym not *with* myne aungels."

DCXXII.

P*er*egrin*us* a deo remun*er*atur.

Cesarius tellis how som tyme þ*er* was a cetysyn of Tulpytt þat hight Cono, & he went *with* other pylgramys vnto þe see; and þ*er* he fell passand seke and dyed. And when he was dead-

[1] MS. comfuthe.

lyke, he began to wax passand mery, and his felows axkid hym whatt was cauce att he was so merye. He answerd agayn & sayd; "Whi sulde I nott be mery? Our Ladie was here & sayd vnto me, 'Cono! becauce þou left þi wife, þi childer, & all þi gudis for þe luff of my son, I shall wele reward þe.'" And *with* þat he cryed & said; "Behold! I se hevyn oppyn & a seatt ordand for me." And *with* þat he passid away, & his sawle went vpp vnto hye hevyn.

P*er*egrino inclinat ymago crucifixi. S*upr*a de mis*er*icordia.

P*er*eg*r*inacio mentalis valet. Infra [1], Petri martiris.

DCXXIII.

P*er*icula mu*n*di su*n*t p*er*timenda [2].

We rede in '*Dictis* Barlaam' how som tyme þ*er* was a man þat fled from ane vnycorn, and hym happend fall in-to a grete pytt. And as he fell, hym happend *with* his handis to gett holde be a buske at grew in þe syde of þe pytt, and his fete wer strayte in a vessell [3]. So he lukid aboute hym & he saw ij myce, ane white & a noder blakk, & daylie þai gnew vppon þe rute of þis buske, to it was nerehand in sondre. And he consydurd þe depenes of þis pytt, & he saw þ*er*-in ane vglie dragon spowtand fyre. So he lukid vnto þe grownd þ*er*off, & þ*er* he saw iiij neddyr-hedis knytt to-gedur. So he lukyd wpward, & he saw a dropp of hony drope in þe bewis of þis buske, & he, negligent of þe said p*er*els, he thoght he wold not lefe, bod he wold hafe þis drope of honye. *et c*9. Moralit*er* sic. Frendis! Be þis vnycorn is vnderstond deade, & be þis pytt þe werld, and be þis buske þe lenthe of our lyfe, whilk þat be howris of þe day & of þe nyght, as a white mowce and a blak, cuttis it down; & be þe iiij neddyrs is vnderstand þe iiij elementis þat mans body is made of, & be þe dragon

[1] MS. Supra.
[2] *So* Lat. MSS. The English MS. *has* percanenda.
[3] Harl. MS. pedib*us* uase quodam impressus, *for* pedibus base quadam lubrica impressis.

is vnd*er*stand hell, and be þis drope of hony, þe swettnes of þis life, whilk who-so covatt*is* er casten in þe said p*er*els.

Peri*cu*lis possu*n*t adaptari multa que dicuntur su*pr*a de morte *et* de mu*n*do.

DCXXIV.

Peri*ur*iu*m* ecia*m* in hac vita punitur.

Cesarius tellis how þat þe dean of Bononye [1], beyng in þe dioces of Colayn, lent vnto a bruther þat he had xx marc*is* of cone of mony of his kurk. And when þis dean was dead, his [2] bruther, a knyght, denyed þis said dett. And þe chanons, þat had no prefe þ*er*-in, made þis knyght for to swere þ*er*for, and so he did, and forswore hym. Bod when he went fro Bononye, whar he sware, vnto his awn howse-ward, hym happend to stand in myddest of þe way styll, & mott go no ferrer nor yitt turn bakk. And his tong was taken from hym, vnto he p*ro*mysid in his harte þat he sulde turn agayn vnto Bonon & knowlege his manesworn athe & restor þe said money vnto þe chanons agayn. And so he did & was hale.

Periurio possu*n*t adaptari que sup*r*a dicuntur de iuramento.

DCXXV.

Perseu*er*ancia. Perseu*er*andu*m* semp*er* est in bono

We rede of one þat hight Iohn, þat was ane ankyr, þat was a man þat had lede ane ill lyfe. And when he was co*m*pu[*n*]cte, he garte spar hym selfe in a grafe, and þ*er* he wasshid away his synnys wit*h* salte teris, and he lay on his kneis & his elbows, and wolde not lifte vp his een nor name þe name of almyghtie God, bod þar he enduryd a long tyme in his prayer. So þ*er* come fendis into þis grafe vnto hy*m*, and cryed vppon hym & sayde;

[1] Harl. MS. decanus Bonnens*is*.

[2] MS. *repeats*, his.

"Þou cursid caytuff! Whatt duse þou here? For when þou was fulfyllid *with* al *maner* of syn & vnclennes, & now þi strenth sufficies not to do no syn, now þou will liff in chastite and seme a gude man. Turn agayn vnto vs, ffor þou erte one of vs." And þan a noder spak vnto hym & sayd; "What hopis þou att þis place shall do þe gude? Do as þou hase done befor, & lyff in luste & lykyng of þi flessh; ffor what payn mott þou suffer mor in hell þan þou suffres now?" And eu*er* he lay styll & nothyng wold say. And when þe fendis saw þatt, þai bett hym & gaff hym many a sore wownde, and þat anys, twyse, thryce, to so mekull þat att þe laste þai lefte hym halfe deade. And þai cryed *with* a hedus noyce & sayd: "Vicisti! Vicisti!" And *with* þat þai vanyshid away, and nevur aft*er* apperid vnto hym.

P*er*seue*r*ans in bono eciam mortem contempnit. Inf*r*a de silencio, ij.

P*er*seue*r*are debent novicij in deuocione. Supra de Novicio.

DCXXVI.

Peticio. Petitur aliqu*ando* cont*r*ariu*m* uolito.

Valerius tellis how on a tyme Grete Alexander was streken in a grete yre, & thoght to kaste down þe cetie of Lapsatu*m*. So hym happend mete sodanlie one þat was callid Anaximetes, þat was his p*re*ceptur & his maister, and he was ashamyd to mete his maist*er* becauce he was in suche ane angre, and he grawntid his maist*er* þat what þing som-evur at he wulde axke hym, he wolde grawnt hym itt. And when þis Anaximetes hard þis he said; "Sur Kyng, I aske at þou dof þine envie ayeynste þe cetie of Lapsatt." And he grawntid hym it. And þus þurgh his ben*e*fice was þe cetie savid.

Petri Ap*ost*oli. Petrus cu*m* voluit Petronillam sanauit *et* cu*m* placuit eid*em* infirmitatem reddidit. Sup*r*a de infirmitate, iiij.

DCXXVII.

Petri Martiris.

We rede in his Legend how on a tyme when he was at þe cetie of Melayn[1] & *pre*chid þ*er*, he disputid with a maist*er* þat hight Hesiarcha[2] in *pre*sens of all þe *pre*lattis of þe cetie. And þis Hesyarcha said vnto hym; "O! þou fraward Petur! And þou be als holie as þies fond peple trowis, whi *pra*yes þou noght þi God to putt a clowde betwix þai*m* & þe son, at þai dye nott for so grete hete as þai d[oo]?" And þis Petur answerd hym agayn & said; "And þou will *pro*mytte me at þou shall renownce þine heresie, I shall do as þou hase axkid." And þe heretykis, trowyng at þat myght not be done, cryed oppon þis maist*er*, and bad hym make a *pro*mys. And yitt he wolde nott. Neu*er*-þe-les þis Petur, to shew þe power of almightie God, and at He was former of al thyngis visible and invisible, made his *pra*yer & made a cros agayn þe son; and þ*er* apperid betwix þe son & þe peple a little clowde like a tent þat coverd þe peple fro þe son. And befor þar was no clowde in all þe ayre.

DCXXVIII.

Petrus mortuum suscitauit.

We rede also in his Legend how þ*er* was som tyme a wom*man* in Flawndres, and when sho had born iij childer sho *pra*yed Saynt Petur for to helpe hur. And sho bare þe iiij childe and it was dead, and sho tuke þis childe & broght it vnto Saynt Petur & besoght hym h*er*telie þ*er*for. And onone þis dead childe become whik. And when it was ordand þat at his baptym he sulde be callid John, þe preste, not wittand what he suld say, namyd hym Petur; and þat name remaynyd with hym ewhils he liffid.

[1] Lat. MSS. Ap*u*d Mediolan*em*.

[2] Harl. MS. et quemd*am* magi-str*u*m h*er*esiarcham examinante.

DCXXIX.

Petrus monialem absentem sanau*i*t [1].

We rede also in his Legend how þ*er* was a non in Lombardye þat had þe gutt grevuslie in hur kne, and sho cuthe not be helid with no medcyn. And when sho hard tell at it was bod xiiij day iorney fro hur place vnto Mylayn, þat at sho mot not do with hur bodye sho thoght to go in hur mynde. And ilka day sho sayd a hondreth patyr *noster*, and þus sho thoght ilk day to make a iorney. And onone as sho began þus for to go in hur [2] mynde, sho wex evur bettur and bettyr. And when sho did hur laste day iorney, & in hur mynde went vnto his tombe, kneland on hur kneis as sho had bene at hys tombe in hur prayer, sho said our hur psalter with a grete devocion. And be sho had done it, sho felid bod a litle of hur sekenes. And so sho turnyd agayn with hur prayers as sho began, and be sho had done all hur day iorneys, sho was al hole & sownd as evur sho was.

Pietas. Pietati co*n*ueniunt multa [que d*icunt*ur sup*ra* de el*emosina*, hospitalitate, leprosis et paup*er*ib*us* [3]].

DCXXX.

Pigricia. Pigricia semp*er* est uitanda [4].

Saynt Ierom tellis how som tyme þ*er* was ane olde monke, & he thoght to comfurth a slaw bruther of his, and sayd vnto hym in þis man*er* of wyse; "Som tyme þ*er* was a man þat had lande to be sawen, bod becauce of his negligens it grew full off thornys & breers. So he bad his son go & clence itt of þai*m*. And when he come þ*er*to, & saw þ*er* was so grete multitude of thornys & breers, he began to fayle in his h*er*te & sayd vnto hym selfe; "When shall I hafe clensid all þies?" And with þatt he layed

[1] MS. absentem nominauit *et* sanauit.
[2] MS. his.
[3] *From the* Harl. MS.
[4] *Heading from the* Arun. MS.

hym down & slepyd. And when his fadur knew how he did, he sayd vnto hym; "Son! wurke & clence evurilk day als mekull grownd as þou occupyes when þou lyes on þe erthe & slepis." And he obeyed his fadurs commawndment and did so. And þus be little & little he clensid all þis grownd.

Piscator. Infra purgatorij, iij.

Pollucio nocturna aliqu*ando* no*n* imped*it* com*mu*nione*m* *et* aliqu*ando* impedit. Sup*ra* de com*m*unione, v.

DCXXXI.

Potencia. Potentes frequent*er* queru*nt* occasiones *con*tra paupe*r*es.

Esopus tellis in his fables how þe lambe & þe wulfe war bothe thrustie, and þai come bothe vnto þe watir to drynk; & þe wulfe dranke abown, & þe lambe benethe. Than þe wulfe sayd vnto þe lambe; "Whi haste þou trubled þe watyr vnto me?" And þe lambe answerd hym agayn & sayd; "How sulde I make þe watir drovy when itt come fro the vnto me?" And þan þe wulfe said; "Whi[1] bannys þou me?" And þe lambe sayd; "Nay, I ban þe nott." And þan þe wulfe said; "Thi fadur did vnto me mekull ill, and now I sall venge me of the." And wit*h* þat he ran on þe selie lambe and worod itt. And þis had þe lambe þat did no tryspas

Potus supe*r*fluus est vitandus. S*upra* de abstinencia, ebrie*tate* *et* gula.

DCXXXII.

Preceptu*m*. P*r*eceptu*m* *eciam* indiscretu*m* nocet subdito inobedienti.

Cesarius tellis how þ*er* was a monk som tyme of Ceustus ordur þat dyed, and he apperid vnto a bruther of his and requirid hym

[1] MS. whan. Lat. MSS. *cur*.

of his estate. And þe dead monk answerd agayn & sayd; "I trowed neu*er* God had bene so strayte, ffor He thynk*is* of þe leste thyng. Bod God," he said, "for-giff our prelattis, for þai make vs oftsithis to vnder-go great paynys, & many. And He byndys hugelie þe p*re*ceptis of þai*m* when þai com*m*awnd anythyng vndiscretelie, & þ*er* subgett*is* giffis little hede þ*er*to, or els sett it at noght; & so it is reservid vnto þe laste iugementt."

Precepto co*n*veniu*n*t que dicu*n*tur sup*ra* de obediencia.

DCXXXIII.

Predestinacio. P*re*destinac*io*ni innitentes multi decipiu*n*tur.

Cesarius tellis of one þat hight Lodowicus, Lattg*ra*vi*us* Thurungie, þat was a letterd man, & he was deseyvid wit*h* suche ane errour at he said hym burd nedis be savyd & he wer destanyed þ*er*to, or els he sulde be dampned and he war destanyd þ*er*to. And also he said he mott not fle þe howr of his dead, nor nowd*er* lenthe it nor shorten itt; and for þis, wit*h*-owtyn any drede, he gaff hym vnto all man*er* of vices. So att þe laste he fell in a huge sekenes, & he garte gett hym a leche, and p*ra*yed hym to take hym in cure and amend hym of his sekenes. And þis leche was wele lernyd, not alonelie in lechecrafte, bod also in dyvynyte, and knew wele enogh his errour, and said vnto hym in þis man*er* of wyse; "Sur, and þe day of your dead be com*m*en, þan it wer in vayn þat I sulde do any cure vppon you." And þe seke man axkid hym why he sayd so, & said; "I know well enogh bod if I hafe sone helpe I mon dy befor þe tyme." Than þe leche sayd vnto hym; "And ye trow at your lyfe may be lenthend be þe v*er*tue of medcyns, wharto denye ye to do penance, þat is medcyn of þe sawle?" And þan þis Lattg*ra*vi*us*, consydurand þe v*er*tue of his wurdis, sayd vnto hym in þis man*er* of wise; "Fro hens furth be þou þe leche of my sawle; ffor be þi medycynable tong I trow at God shall delyver me from my moste errour."

DCXXXIV.

P*r*edicacio. P*r*edicandu*m* sincere [1] est p*r*op*ter* deum.

Cesarius tellis how þ*er* was ane of þe P*r*emonstraceneis ordur þat, when he had prechid of þe cros, he dyed and apperid vnto his felow. And he axkid hym how at it stude *with* hym, and he ansswerd agayn & sayd; "When I dyed devuls vmbelappid me [2], and ane of þai*m* sayd, 'þou kepyd neu*er* trewlye þine ordur.' And a noder said, 'þou p*r*echid neu*er* trewlie for Godd*is* cauce.' And I vnderstude at þai said bothe trewlie, and I was nerehand in despayr becauce þ*er* was none att ansswer for me. And þan almyghti God held me *with* His hand & sayd; 'ffolow Me, ffor þou p*r*echid for Me.' And onone þe fendes fledd, and I folowid Cryste vnto evurlastand ioy; and I had none other payn bod alonelie þis drede."

DCXXXV.

P*r*edicatori infundit deus aliqu*ando* scienciam.

Cesarius tellis how some tyme þ*er* was a symeple monke, & he was bod ane ydiott, bod he was devowte. And on a tyme hym thoght in his slepe þ*at* he was ravisshid in-to hevyn, & was cled in aray like a dekyn befor God, as he sulde hafe red þe gospell. And when he sulde hafe axked þe blissing [3], hym þoght at þis was sayd vnto hym; "Fro þis day forward þou shall hafe con*n*yng & v*er*tue in p*r*echyng þe wurd of God." And he was gretelie m*er*vaylid of þis vision at hym þoght he saw so oppynlie, and þoght he wold rede þe gospell þat day, if so wer at þe sacrestan ordand hym suche a stole and a vestement as he saw in hevyn; ffor þan he wold trow at his vision wer trew. And so when he come in-to þe revestiarie, & saw þe stole and þe vestiment at was layd furth for þe dekyn, he knew it wele enogh; & þan he was c*er*tayn of his vision and went vnto his abbott & tolde hym all þat he had

[1] MS. scincere.

[2] MS. þai*m*. Lat. MSS. circumde*derunt* me demones.

[3] MS. blissid. Harl. MS. a quo cum benedict*ionem* acciperet.

sene. And he com*m*andid hym go rede þe gospell & for to preche. And so he did, and he fell vnto p*r*echyng and p*r*echid so clerklie at vnto þis day his saying is taken for auctorite. And all men þat hard hym had grete m*er*vayle how þat he, þat had no con*n*yng befor, had so con*n*ynglie p*r*echud, & had so grett p*er*feccion in co*n*yng.

P*re*dicantes demon nititu*r* impedire. Sup*ra* de auditu.

DCXXXVI.

P*re*dicator ea que p*re*dicat debet facere.

Ioh*annes* Anachorita was a monk in wyldernes, and was enowrned w*ith* þe flour of all mane*r* of v*er*tues; and he was in bodye lyke vnto ane aungell. And he was sent ilk day his fude from almyghti God, ffor evure day he wold go into his cafe, & þ*er* he fand a burd, & bread sett þ*er* vppon þat was passand white & of a m*er*valus swetnes. & when he had etyn þ*er*-of, he wold þonk God & go vnto his prayers and his ympnes. And when he began to hafe a ioy of his merettis, onone þ*er* entred into hym c*er*tan desyris of his witt be little & litle, at he mot vnnethis p*ur*seyve þai*m*, and aft*er*ward gretter, vnto so much at he wexid necligent, & mor slow in his prayers þan he was wunte to be. And so þ*er* folowid in his h*er*t fowle thoght*is* & wykkid, & he made no charge to correcte hym for þies little thyngis. So on a tyme when he was strekyn w*ith* a grete luste of his flessh, he went into his cafe to take hym bread, and he fand bread, bod it was browne*r* somwhatt þan[1] þe toder was; & he had grete m*er*vell þ*er*off & was passand hevye. Notw*ith*stondyng he ete þ*er*of and refresshid hym. And vppon þe toder day his thoght*is* grew apon hym, & on þe nyght hym thoght he lay be a wom*m*an; neu*er*-þe-les in þe mornyng he went vnto his prayers, & stude w*ith* a waveryng ee and a waveryng mynde. So he went into his

[1] MS. þat.

cave to take hym meate, and he fand a lafe, bod it was passand brown, & hard þerwith, and as it had bene gnawen all aboute with myce. And þan he began to make sorow & weppyd, bod his sorow was not so great to distroy þe flawmys of his ill thoghtis. So at þe laste he was ouercommen with thoghtis, to so much þat at mydnyght he rase & went vnto þe cetie; and when it was day he was war of a lityll cell of freers & he was werye, & þer he restid hym. And þe brethur began to axke of hym, as of a wyse fadur, who may esshew þe temptacions of þe devull & evull thoghtis. And þan he sufficientlie techand þaim turnyd agayn vnto hym selfe & sayd; "How may I command other men & is deseyvid my selfe?" And þan he said vnto hym selfe þus; "O þou wriche! Do furste þi selfe at þou techis oþer men to do." And he tuke his lefe at his brethur & ran als faste as he myght into wyldernes vnto his cafe agayn, & þer he sparrid hym selfe þerin, & cled his bodie in hare & putt askis on his head. & þer he lay a long tyme in prayers & wepyngis, vnto ane angell come vnto hym & sayd; "Almighti God hase reseyvid þi prayers and þi penance, bod fro hens furth bewar at þou wex no mor prowde, and so be deseyvid when þou leste wenys."

DCXXXVII.

Predicator devotus vbique feruenter predicat.

We rede in þe 'Gestis of Bede' when for grete age his sight faylid hym, he had a leder to lede hym to townes & castels, & in evur-ilk place þer he come he wolde preche þe wurde of God. So on a tyme as þai went þurgh a valie full of stonys, his leder in a skorn tolde hym at þer was a huge peple, þat bade vppon hym in sylence to here hym preche, and þan he began ferventlie to preche. And when he had done, & concludid his sermon with '*per omnia secula seculorum*,' onone, as men sais, þe stonys with a hye voyce cried & sayd; "Amen! *Venerabilis pater*!" Som says þat aungels answerd & sayd; "Amen! *Bene, venerabilis pater, dixisti*!"

DCXXXVIII.

P*r*edicator discrete debet p*r*edicare *secundum* condiciones audientiu*m*.

Valerius tellis how som tyme þ*er* was at Athens a yong man þat hight Polloni*us*, & he was gyffen to suche luste of his bodie þat he had grete ioy in his infame. So on a tyme he was at a feste, & he satt þ*er* not alonelie vnto þe son sett, bod also vnto þe morn at þe son rase. & he was full of wyne and of gude meatis, & had enoyntid hym *with* p*r*ecious oyntement*is*, he cled hym in gay clothyng, & made hym a gay head & went home. So hym happend se þe scolehowse dure oppyn of one þat hight Zenoc*r*ates þat was techand; he went in at he mot here what he said. And when all þe scolers loghe at hym & had grete disdeyn at he come in, þis Zeno*cr*ates *with* a merie chere began to p*r*eche hym of sobernes and temperans, not-*with*-stondyng all þ*a*t he sayd befor. And þurgh sadnes of his wurdis þis Polloni*us* was gretelie movid, so þ*a*t he keste of þe hatt þat was on his head, & aft*er*ward he keste of his gay clothyng & was passand glad of his p*r*echyng. And at þe laste he lefte all his luste & lykyng þ*a*t he had in lychorie, and become a gude man. And þus *with* medcyn of ane howr he was helid of all hys infame. *et c*.

DCXXXIX.

P*r*edicacio cu*m* bono modo *et* gestu multu*m* valet.

Valerius tellis of one þat hight Eschines com*m*endid gretelie Demostenis eloque*ns*[1]; and he said he consydurd þ*er*in a bytt*er* strenth of een and a ferdfull chere, and a hevye burdyn, & in evure wurd a sownd of voyce, & at he knew þ*er*-in þe spedefull movyngi*s* of þe bodie, vnto so mekill þat nothyng mot be putt vnto þe nede þ*er*off. Neu*er*-þe-les a grete p*a*rte of Demostenes wantys when it is red, mor þan when it is hard.

P*r*edo. P*r*edonem deus in hac vita remun*er*at si aliqua bona ab eo sint facta. Infra de remun*er*ac*io*ne.

[1] MS. Eschines Demostenis commendid gretelie eloque*ns*. Harl. MS. Eschines Demostenis eloquentia*m* commendabat.

DCXL.

Prelatus racione carnalitatis no*n* debet eligi.

Valerius tellis of one Fabius, þat was a grete cowncelur of Rome; & he govern[*id*] nobyllie aft*er* his grawncer & his fadur þe offes of cowncell þat he bare. So on a tyme þe peple desyrid gretelie þat his son sulde be made a cowncelur of Rome, and he alone, als muche as he myght, laburde to lett it. Notwi*th*stondyng he was not dowtand of þe v*er*tues of hys son, for he was passand con*n*yng, bod for cauce he wold not hafe many maisters in one howshold.

P*re*latus no*n* debet eligi puer. Inf*ra* de pue*ro*, iij.
P*re*latus no*n* debet eligi paup*er* v*e*l auarus. *Supra* de balli*uo*.

DCXLI.

P*re*latus debet condescendere morib*us* subdito*rum*.

Valerius tellis how on a tyme þe consullis of Rome desyrid gretelie one þat hyght Manliciosus [1] to be of cowncell *with* þai*m*, and evur he excusid hym & sayd nay, & said his syght faylid hym; bod nevur-þe-les þai all laburd hym hugelie therto [2]. And evur he bad þai*m* take a noder in-to þat wurschup, ffor he said; "And ye make me to bere itt, I may not suffer your maners, nor ye may not suffer me to hafe rewle abown you, nor ye wull not fulfyll my com*m*andmentt*is*."

DCXLII.

P*re*latus no*n* debet se ingerere.

Hugo Florianens*is* tellis when þe knyght*is* of Rome saw Vaspasyan, at he was a nobyl man and a redy to cowncell, and comfurthable to yong men in batell, þai beroght hym at he wold take gov*er*nance of þe empyre of Rome. And when he denyed

[1] Harl. MS. Cu*m* co*n*sulatu*s* Manlio, *seni*, . . . offer*r*eretur.

[2] MS. *repeats*, hugelie, *here*.

þai*m* & sayd he was not wurthie þ*er*to, & þai laburd hym þ*er*to daylie, at þe laste he grauntyd vnto þai*m*, þuf all it wer agayns his will, at he wulde furste tytter take þe charge of þe empyre rather þan þe wurschup þ*er*off. And when he had reseyvid þe empyre he sayd þat in his begynyng onone he wold clens þai*m* at wer fowle, & putt vnwurthi men oute of þ*er* placis and fulfyll þair rowm *with* honeste men. And he was neu*er* prowde nor statelye, bod all-way consydurd of what kynryd at he come; & he wold neu*er* do grete punysshment for offens.

DCXLIII.

P*re*latus non debet sup*er*bire.

Helinandus tellis how som tyme in þe kyngdom of Iurie þ*er* was a hurd-man þ*at* hight Gygens, þat on a tyme aft*er* a grete rayn he went down in-to a law crak in þe erde, and þ*er* he fande a man dead, syttand vppon a hors of bras. And vppon his fynger he fande a ryng, be þe whilk he made hym selfe invisible, & lay be þe whene; & als sone as sho knew þis sho garte sla þe kyng [1], & he vsurpid þe kyngdom. And Valerius tellis þat when he had getten þe kyngdom be þis chawnce, he wexid so prowde þat he axkid cowncell of Apollo his god, if þ*er* war any in þis werld þat was happyer þan he was. And Apollo ansswerd hym agayn & sayd; "þou sulde be bettur *pro*vid *with* sekurtie of a shep*er*de tofall þan for to hafe a grete hall & lathis, & giff þi selfe to grete charge and besynes; for it is bettur vnto a man [*hafe*] bod att hym ned*is* vnto his lyfe, and so for to hald hym plesid, þan for to gett hym sam*en* grete tresurs & evur lyff in drede and covatyce."

DCXLIV.

P*re*latus no*n* debet esse crudel*is* nec fac*er*e vnde odio habeatur.

Valerius tellis how on a tyme when Dionisius Situlus shewid hym selfe vnto his [*suggettis*] [2] mor to be a tyraunt þan a prince,

[1] MS. kyngdom, -dom *erased*.
[2] Lat. MSS. subditis suis; Engl. MS. tyrandis.

he was so hatefull vnto all men at all folk desyrid at he had had a myschefe. Neuer-þe-les one old wyfe evurilk day in matyn-tyme prayed vnto þer goddis to kepe hym hale & sownd. And when he axked hur þe cauce at sho did so for, and sho answerd hym agayn & sayd; "Me had levur hafe þe a grevus tyrand as þou erte, þan þou sulde dye & a war succede after þe; and þerfor I bow down my head & prayes for the." & when he herd hur say þus[1] he wexid confusid & ashamyd, and began to forthynk and amend hym.

Prelatus aliquando morte subitanea moritur. Supra de archidiacono.

Prelatus a demone aliquando deportatur. Supra de demone, v.

Prelatus eciam malus[2] debet subditos in disciplina tenere. Supra de abbatissa[3], i.

DCXLV.

Prelatus debet esse communis et affabilis [omnibus][4].

Seutonius tellis how þat when Titus was made emperour, he vsid to make mony ryall festis, & he wold dispyse no cetysyn, bod gladlie wold speke with þaim & here what þai sayd; & he wold neuer gyff o man bettyr gyfte þan a noder. And he was so beneuolus at he wold latt none go away from hym with-owtyn a gude hope. So on a tyme his howshold-men cownceld hym at he sulde not do so, and he answerd þaim agayn & sayd þer sulde no man go hevylie away þurgh þe wurdis of a prince. So on a day when he went to supper, he vmthoght hym how þat he had þat day nothyng nowder gyffen nor lent, and he said unto hym selfe; "Diem perdidisti." Also Eutropius tellis of Troiayn, þat when his frendis blamyd hym for he was so hamelie with evure man, he answerd agayn & said; "Ane emperour sulde be such a

[1] MS. *repeats*, þus.
[2] MS. malos.
[3] *Reference from* Lat. MSS.
[4] *From* Lat. MSS.

man outeward anence his commons as he wold þai war inward vnto hym agayn."

Prelatus pauperes debet habere in reuerencia. Supra de iudicio vltimo.

Prelatus non debet cito credere contra subditos. Supra de accusacione, iij.

Prelati aliqui nolunt audire nisi placencia. Supra de adulacione.

Prelati debent beneficia dare dignis. Supra de beneficio, ij.

Prelati non debent munera suscipere. Supra de munere, ij.

Prelatus debet esse liberalis. Supra de liberalitate.

Prelatus debet fugere rapinam. Infra de rapina, j.

DCXLVI.

Prelatus statuta sua servare debet.

Valerius tellis how one þat was callid Licinius ordand a law, þat no man suld by our 1 acre of land; and he boght many ma. And vnder grace of a fenyng he excusyd hym þerof & gaff parte þeroff vnto his son. And for þis he was accusyd, furst þat he made a law & chargid it to be kepyd, & syne þat he was furste at brak it hym selfe.

Prelatus non debet esse nimis rigidus vel durus. Supra de abbate, ij.

Prelato possunt adaptari fere omnia que dicuntur supra de abbate.

Prelatus debet esse constans in execucione officij sui. Supra de Ambrosio, j.

Prelatus infirmis debet condescendere. Supra de leproso, i, & ij.

P*re*latus debet co*m*pati pecc*ato*ribus. Su*pra* de abb*a*te, ij.

P*re*positus dampnatur. Sup*ra* de demone, v.

P*re*sciencia. P*re*scitus potest saluari. Su*pra* de p*re*destinacione.

P*re*sciunt demones aliqua futura. Sup*ra* de demo*ne*, iv [1].

DCXLVII.

P*re*su*m*pcio. P*re*sumu*nt* aliqui plus q*u*am deberent de statu suo.

We rede in 'Vitis P*atrum*' of ane abbott þat hight Iohn, þat þoght he wold seryff allmyghtie God in man*er* as aungels duse, and he doffid all his clothis and he stude all a weke so in wyldernes. And when he was like to perissh for hunger & was shrewidlie wowndid *with* waspis & fleis, he turnyd agayn vnto his bruther dure, & knokkid þ*er*-att. And he axkid who was þ*er*, and he sayd; "I, Iohn." And his bruther answerd agayn & sayd; "Nay, it is not Iohn, for Iohn is made ane aungell & wyll be no mor emang men." And he said agayn; "Forsuthe I am he." And he wold not oppyn þe dure, bod lete hym alone stondyng þ*er* vnto in þe mornyng on þe toder day. And þan he oppynd þe dure & said vnto hym; "And þou be a man, þou hase myster to hafe þe dure opynd, and to hafe meatt and warm þe; and if þou be ane angell, wharto desyris þou to come in-to my cell?" And þan þis Iohn sayd agayn vnto hym; "Bruther, I pray þe forgyff me, ffor I know my selfe þat I hafe synnyd."

P*re*su*m*ptuosus aliqu*ando* cadit in pecc*atu*m. Sup*ra* de carne, iij.

P*re*su*m*pcio nimia de se ipso aufert dei ben*e*ficia. S*upra* de p*re*dicare, iij.

P*re*su*m*pcio est aliqu*ando* occasio desp*er*acionis. Sup*ra* de pecc*ato*, ij.

[1] MS. v.

P*resumunt* aliqu*ando* religiosi nimis de statu suo in co*mparacione* se*cu*larium. S*upra* de Basilio, j.

P*resumptuosus* debet humiliari ex consideraci*one* sui. S*upra* de consid*eracione*, ij.

DCXLVIII.

P*resumptuosum* est ve*rb*[*a*] subtilia *et* alta loqui.

We rede in 'Dictis Pa*trum*'[1] of ane ankyr, when he come vnto þe cetie of Pemenen, þ*er* was a gude man reseyvid *with* gladnes hym. And as þai satt, þis ankyr began to talke of holie writt, and of privaties of hevyn. And þan þis olde man turnyd his face vnto a noder of his brethir, and wold nothyng ansswer þis ankyr; and so he went furth and was passand hevye. So a disciple come vnto þis olde abbott & sayd; "For þe come þis man hedur, þat had grete myrth at home in his awn place, and þou dedeynys not now to speke vnto hym." This olde abbott answerd hym ayeyn & sayd; "He is a man of hie placys, & spek*is* all of hevynlie thyngis; and I am a man of law place, and vnnethis I may vnderstond erdlie thyngis." And þis dissiple went furth & tolde þis ankir what he said. And he was gretelie co*m*puncte here-*with*, & went in-to þis olde abbott agayn & said vnto hym; "What shall[2] I do, ffadur abbott? For þe passions of my sawle hase lordschup on me." And þan þis old abbott had ioy of hym & sayd; "Now þou erte welcom, fadur. Oppyn þ*er*for my mowthe and I sall fulfyll it *with* þi gudis." And *with* þis wurd þis ankir was gretlie comfurthid & sayde; "Forsuthe it is a gude way at þou holdes, & a trew." And þan he thankid þis olde abbott & went agayn vnto his awn region.

P*resumptuosus* freque*nter* credit habere gra*tias* quas no*n* h*abet*. S*upra* de cantu[3] et de obedi*encia*.

P*rinceps* debet e*sse* co*mpositus* in aspe*ctu*. S*upra* de aspectu.

[1] MS. *repeats*, we rede.
[2] MS. shat.
[3] *So the Latin versions.* The English MS. *has* cantiri.

P*r*inceps no*n* de*b*et es*s*e odiosus subditis. S*upr*a de p*r*elato.

P*r*incipi p*oss*u*n*t adaptari multa que dicu*n*tur *supr*a de abb*a*te, iudice *et* p*r*elato.

P*r*inceps subito moritur. Sup*r*a de morte, iij.

P*r*inceps debet humilit*er* suscip*er*e correcc*io*n*em*. Sup*r*a de Ambrosio [1].

P*ro*bacio. P*ro*bat deus aliquos. Inf*r*a de temptac*io*n*e*, vij.

DCXLIX.

P*ro*digalitas multa mala facit.

Seutoni*us* tellis how þ*a*t Nero þe emp*er*our was so statelie þat he trowed þe frute of [2] riches and of money was no nodur þing bod ordynance made for a mans exp*e*ns, vnto so mekull at he wuld nevur were a garment twyce, and he wold fyssh *with* a nett made of gold wyre, and all þe duris of his pales was made of evurye & enowntid *with* p*re*cious oyntement*is*. And he had rownd chawmers þ*er*in, þat day & nyght turnyd abowte as þe firmament duse. And yit at þe laste hym þoght he had not tresur enogh, bod he gart punyssh and sla dyvers ryche men at he myght hafe þ*er* gudis.

DCL.

P*ro*missio. P*ro*missu*m* debet solui.

Petrus Alphonsis [3] tellis how som tyme þer was a knygh[*t*], and hym happend on a tyme to lose a sakett and a thowsand talent*is* þ*er*in and a s*er*pent of gold; and a pure man happend to fynd itt. And he garte cry it in þe m*ar*kett, & p*ro*mysid in his cry þat he þatt had fon itt sulde hafe for þe fyndyng þ*er*of a hondreth of þe talent*is* *with* gude will. So þis pure man at fand it þoght hym had levur hafe les *with*-owten syn þan more

[1] MS. anbrosio.
[2] MS. *repeats*, of.
[3] MS. Alphensis, *as elsewhere, for* Alphonsus.

wit*h* syn̄, þuf all his wyfe agayn̄-said it, [&] gaff agayn̄ þis sakett vnto þe knyght & askid þ*er*of a hondreth talentis as he p*ro*mysid in his cry. Bod þe riche man̄, when̄ he had þe sakett agayn̄, wolde not pay þe salfay, and he said þ*er* was ij serpentis of gold in þe sakett, & at þe pure man̄ had wit*h*-drawen̄ þe tone of þaim̄. And þe pure man̄ said nay; so he co*m*pleuyd of þis pure man̄ & þai war bothe broght afor þe knyg. And evur-ilk man̄ held wit*h* þe riche man̄, & none wit*h* þe pure man̄. So þ*er* was a philosophyr & he had grete petie of þis pure man̄, and sayd vnto þe kyng in þis man*er* of wyse; "Sur kyng! It is mekull to trow vnto þis riche man̄, for he wold not say at he loste ij s*er*pentis of gold bod if he did so. And on̄ þe toder p*ar*tie, þis pure man̄ at fand þis gude, and he had not bene a gude man̄ and a trew, he mot hafe holden̄ all þis gude p*r*ivalie, & nevur giffen̄ it agayn̄. And þ*er*for. call þe riche man̄ & say vnto hym̄ in þis man*er* of wyse; 'This sakett and þis gold is not þine, for þou says þou lost ij s*er*pentynys & here-in is bod one,' & kepe þis styll in your hand*is* & gar cry agayn̄ in þe m*ar*kett a sakett wit*h* ij s*er*pentynys þ*er*in." And when̄ þis riche man̄ hard þis, at he sulde be þus betyn̄ wit*h* his awn̄ staff, he grawntyd vnto þe kyng at he said þ*er* was ij s*er*pentynys in þe sackett when̄ þ*er* was bod one, becauce he wold nott hafe gyffen̄ þe pure man̄ a hondreth talent*is* to safye, as he p*ro*mysid he sulde do. And when̄ þe kyng hard þis, he made þe riche man̄ to pay vnto þis pure man̄ þis hundreth talentt*is*, as he p*ro*mysid he sulde doo.

P*r*omittu*n*t multi multa que no*n* soluu*n*t. S*upr*a de amicicia [1].

Promocio [2]. P*r*omocione*m* in temp*or*alib*us* impedit aliqu*ando* auaricia. S*upr*a de auaric*i*a, iij [3].

DCLI.

P*r*op*r*ietas. Prop*r*iu*m* no*n* debet habere religiosus.

Cesarius tellis how som tyme in Pycardye, þ*er* was ane abbay of Ceustus ordur, þ*er* was a lewid monk, and hym̄ happend fall seke

[1] MS. amicisia. [2] MS. promosio. [3] MS. ij.

and lyke to dye. And he was shrevyn, and þan þe sacrament was broght to hym and he was howseld; and when it was in his mouth he myght nowder chew it nor swelow it. Neu*er*-þe-les þe same day, a little befor, he had etyn a hen be his ane. So hym happend sone for to dye, and when he was dead þ*er* was fon with hym v *soldi*, not of clene syluer bod of coppur; and her-for it was demyd þat he myght not ressayfe his sac*ra*ment.

Propriu*m* aliqu*ando* est causa confusionis religioso. Inf*r*a de simonia, i.

DCLII.

P*ro*p*r*ietarius in sterquilinio sepeliri debet.

Saynt Gregor tellis how som tyme þ*er* was a monk in ane abbay, and he was a leche, & he had a noder bruther, monke in þe same place. So hym happynd fall seke, bown to dye, & þ*er* was fon emang his medcyns iij nobles of gold. And when Saynt Gregur saw þai*m* he made mekull sorow what he sulde do here-in, in clensyng of hym þat was bown to dye, and in exsample also of þai*m* at warr olyfe. And herefor he com*m*awndid at none of his brethyr bod his full bruther sulde speke with hym, nor gyff hym no wurd of comfurth, bod at his bruther sulde tell hym þat his brethir vggid with hym becauce he kepyd golde p*r*ivalie vnto hym selfe. And when he wiste þis he made mykyll sorow, and in þis sorow and wepyng he decesid. And when he was dead, Saynt Gregor com*m*andid he sulde be beryd in a myddyng, and at þe money sulde be casten on hym, and at þai sulde say when þai keste it; "pecunia tua tecu*m* sit in p*er*dic*io*nem." þurgh þe whilk þing it sulde be bothe punyssment to hym þat dyed, & ferdfulnes to þai*m* þat liffid, at þe bitt*er*nes of dead mott do away his syn, and at þis penance done vnto hym mot flay þai*m* att war on lyfe. And þus it was done. So afterward þe monk*is* durste nevur p*r*ive to þ*er* selfe kepe no man*er* of þing, and it war nevur so feble. And when xxx dayes war passyd he had co*m*passion of þis monk, and garte say mes for hym xxx dayes. And when þies war passid he apperid vnto his bruther german, & sayd vnto hym; "Vnto now it was bod ill wit*h* me, bod now I thank God it is wele, ffor þis day I reseyvid my howsyll."

P*ro*p*r*ietarius monachus est excommunicandus [1]. Sup*ra* de absoluc*io*n*e*, ij.

Prop*r*ietarius *eciam* post mortem absoluitur. Sup*ra* de absoluc*io*n*e*, ij.

Propria volu*n*tas est deserenda. Infra de volu*n*tate, j.

Propositu*m* bonu*m* debet impleri. Inf*r*a de voto *et* volu*n*tate.

DCLIII.

Prosp*er*itas est aliqu*ando* signu*m* adu*er*sitatis future.

We rede in þe 'Legent of Saynt Ambr*os*' how on a tyme as Saynt Ambros went to Rome-ward and was h*er*berd at a riche man howse in a town in Tussie, he emang od*er* carpyng*is* askid hym of his astate. And he answerd agayn & sayd; "Sur, my state was evur happie & glorious, ffor I hafe at will grete riches, many *ser*vandis, many childer, & many cussyns, and all þies I hafe evur had at my liste. And I had nevur none adu*er*sitie." And when Saynt Ambros hard þis, he had mekull m*er*vell & sayd vnto his felows; "Ryse, go we hyne, for God is not in þis place; and þ*er*for haste us hyne at þe vengeange of God tak vs not here." So in þe mornyng þai [2] gatt þai*m* faste vp & wente þ*er* wayes; and when þai war passid a little, þai lukid behynd þai*m*, and sodanly þe erth oppynd and swolud þis man & all þat longid vnto hym, at þ*er* was nothyng left aboue erde. And when Saynt Ambros saw þis, he sayd vnto his felaschup; "Lo! brethur, how m*er*cyfull at God is! For He sparis þai*m* at He sendis adu*er*sitie & truble in þis werld, & how felly He is grevud vnto þai*m* at He sendis p*ro*sp*er*ite and no dissese." And in witnes here-of yit vnto þis day in þat [3] place þ*er* is a passand depe dyke [4], callid þe riche man pitt of Tuscan [5].

[1] MS. excominicandus.
[2] MS. þat.
[3] MS. þan.
[4] MS. *repeats*, dyke.
[5] *This Legend has two hands pointing to it, nota, written above them.*

DCLIV.

Providencia dei infallibilis est.

We rede of þe kyng of Crete he was a semelie man, & he had a nygromancier in his courte at hight Estus. And þis kyng had a doghter, and þis Estus happend to gett hur *with* childe. And when it was born, for tene þis kyng hur fadur garte caste it oute in þe wud emang wylde bestis. So *with*-in a while aft*er* hunters fand it in a cafe emang wyle bestis, & þ*er* it was nurisshid *with* hur mylk. And when it was broght home in a strayte gate whar catell vsyd to com by, and when he saw þai wolde do it no skathe bod rather norysshid it, he com*m*aundid at it sulde be casten vnto hundis þat long had bene kepyd fastyng, at þai mott destroy itt, & þai wold do it no skathe. & þan he garte caste it emang swyne at þai mott devowr it; and þ*er* it was nurisshid on a sew papp. And when he saw þ*a*t, he garte caste it in-to þe occian; and when it was casten þ*er*, þis Estus, þe fadur þ*er*of, be his craft broght it vnto þe land agayn whikk; & þ*er* it was nurisshid *with* a hynde. And fro thens furth it wexid so swyfte of fute at whare at evur þe h*ar*tys went it wold go *with* þa*im*. So at þe laste it was taken in a snare, & broght to þe kyng & gyffen hym to a *pre*sent. And onone he knew it & had co*m*passion þ*er*off, & garte name it & nurtur it; & þe name þ*er*-of was Avidus. And aft*er*ward he made it his successur. And þis kyng Avidus, as we rede, was furste þat evur garte tame oxen & lern þa*im* to draw; and he was furst þ*a*t evur fand pleugh, & he taght men to plew & to saw whete & oþ*er* cornys[1].

Providet Deus suis in necessarijs. Sup*ra* Bene*d*icti et de hospite, iij, *et* iiij.

DCLV.

Providencia in futuru*m* est laudabilis.

Barlaam tellis how þat in a cetie beyond se þe cetysyns had suche a custom þat euerilk yere þai wolde chalange a strange

[1] *A sidenote here has a small hand pointing to the words* [*Su*]pra de [*in*]vencione aratri.

man, & chese hym vnto þ*er* kyng þat knew nothyng of þe lawis of þe cetie. And alway fro he war chosyn he suld hafe his com-*mandmentis* fulfyllid vnto þe yere end, & what at evur he bad be sude be done. And when þat yere was gone, when hym thoght he was in his moste sekurtie & his moste mirthe, sodanlie þe cetyzens wolde rise vppon hym and wolde take from hym þe kyngis crown & nakyn hym & harle hym þurgh þe cetie, & send hym in-to ane yle in þe se þ*er* he sulde nowder hafe mete nor clothe, bod at he sulde þ*er* dye for honger & sorow. So on a tyme þ*er* was a man made kyng þat vnderstude þis custom & þis law at þai hadd, and when he was made kyng he garte opyn þe kyngis tresurie, and sent a grete copye þ*er*off into þis yle. And when his yere was done & he was sent into þis ile, he had habundance enogh of riches at he had ordaud for be hys wisdom ewhyls he liffid as a kyng in þe cete.

Prudencia necessaria est multis. Sup*ra* de cautela *et* p*ro*visione.

DCLVI.

Puer despo*n*sauit ymaginem beate Marie V*ir*ginis.

We rede in þe '*Mer*eclas of Our Ladye' how som tyme þ*er* was a felaship of childer þ*a*t vsid to play at hand-ball befor a kurk; and þ*er* was one of þai*m* þat had on his hand a ryng whilk þat a maydyn þat luffid hym be flesshly luff had gyffen hym. And he was ferde at he *with* his faste rynyng at þe ball sulde breke it, and he went in-to þe kurk to gyff som bodie it to kepe to he had laykid hym. And when he come befor þe ymage of our Lady, he stude m*er*vellland and beheld hur fayrnes, & he set hym down on his kne and deuotelie sayd afor hur his Ave Maria. And when he had done he said vnto hur; "Forsuth, Ladie, þ*o*u erte fayrer þan any oþ*er* & mor fayr þan sho þat gaff me þis ryng, and þ*er*for I forsake hur. I, fro hens furth, I will luff the, so at þ*o*u wyll luff me agayn." And he p*ro*furd þe ryng vnto þe ymage fynger, and þe ymage put furth hur fynger streght & he putt it on. And þan þe fynger closyd agayn vnto þe ymage as it was are. And when he saw þis he had grete *mer*vell þ*er*off & callid his felous & tolde þai*m* & lete þai*m* se itt. So afterward hym happend breke þis p*ro*mys and was wed, and on þe furste nyght at he was wed our Ladie come & lay betwix hym & his wyfe, & putt furth hur hand & lete hym se þe ryng on hur fynger, & reprovid hym þat he had broken his beheste. So wit*h* þat he wakynd & grapyd aft*er* þe ymage[1] & fand hur not þ*er*, & lay styll & trowed þat it had bene bod a fantasye. So afterward sho apperid vnto hym & thretid hym att he was ferd for hur. And when he wakend on þe morn, at evyn p*ri*valie he forsuke his wyfe & all his gudis & went to wyldernes, and þ*er* devotelie he servid our Ladie vnto his lyfis ende.

DCLVII.

Puer ex actib*us* suis qu*and*oq*ue* declarat qualis sit futurus.

We rede in 'Cronicles' how on a tyme kyng Agibu*n*dus, kyng of Lombardie, soiornyd in Germanye, he fasted & walkid abowte, & he fand casten in piscina*m* vij childer be a common womman for to sla þai*m*; and all þies þis same com*m*on wom*m*an had born. And when þis knyght saw þai*m* he had grete *mer*vayle and put down a spere-shafte vnto þai*m*. And ane of þai*m* gat þe shafte wit*h* his hand be þe end & helde it styll. And þe kyng had *mer*vell here-of & pullid hym vp, & garte nuryssh hym and namyd hym Lawncelott[2], þat is als much to say as he þat sal be a grete man in tyme to com. So afterward hym happend to be of so grete nobylnes þat when þe kyng was dead þe Lombardis made hym þ*er* kyng.

Puer in purgatorio punitur. Sup*ra* de blasfemia.

DCLVIII.

Puer no*n* debet eligi in p*re*latum vel p*re*sulem.

[3] Helinandus tellis how þat Adrianus þe emp*er*our on a tyme wolde algatis make his son emp*er*our in his life. And his p*ri*nces

[1] MS. ymange.
[2] Harl. MS. Lamissionem. Arund. MS. Lancissionem.
[3] *This Exemplum is corrupt and part has been omitted from the Latin versions.*

ansswerd hym̄ agayn̄ & sayd' þat it longid' not alonelie vnto þe blude to hafe rewle; bod rather vnto þe adlyng*is* & vnto the governance. And so his desyre contynued', and efterward he conseyvid' in his mynd' þat childer sulde furste be broght vpp̄ and exc*er*cysed in vertues, at þai mot be p*ro*vid what gou*er*nance þai wolde be off or þai war putt vnto any wurshup̄.

Puer a demone temptatur. Sup*ra* de blasfemia.

Puella debet abscondere sua*m* pulcritudinem. Sup*ra* de abscondere.

Puella debet solicite custodiri. S*up*ra de ffilia.

DCLIX.

Pulc*r*itudo corp*or*is debet abscondi ne alijs sit dampnosa.

Valerius tellis how þ*er* was a fayr yong man̄ þat hight Spurann*us*, and he was so pratie & so defte at yong wom*m*en̄ wex evyn̄ fond' on̄ hym̄, and he was ferd at þai or þ*er* fadurs shulde desyre hym̄ to be maryd or to fall vnto syn̄. And he wowndid' hym̄ selfe his visage and his mouth to make hym̄ disfygurd' at þai sulde not desyre hym̄, and þoght hym̄ had lyffer be deformyd' & liff in halynes, þan̄ daylie be a p*re*paratyfe to oþ*er* folk luste & syn̄ & wykkydnes.

Punicio. Puniu*n*tur corizantes. Sup*ra* de corizare.

Puniu*n*tur gulosi. Sup*ra* de gula, vj, *et* de benediccione.

Punitur quis p*er* hec que peccauit. Inf*ra* de religiosis, iij.

Puniu*n*tur pecc*at*ores diue*r*si diue*r*simode. Sup*ra* *et* inf*ra* in locis suis.

DCLX.

Purgatorius. Purgatorij pene su*n*t diue*r*se.

Iacobus de Vet*ria*co tellis þat when Saynt Marie of Oginiez p*r*ayed for a c*er*tayn sawle vppon Saynt Petur day þe apostell, Saynt Petur aperid vnto hur and tolde hur þe paynys at it was in & þe cawsis þ*er*off, and how at it was turment *with* huge hete becauce it luffid passynglie þis werlde & þe lustis þ*er*of. And som tyme it was gretelie turment *with* a huge caldnes, becauce it was slaw to do gudenes, & neclegentlie governyd þe chylder & þe howsholde[1]. And [som]tyme it was punysshid *with* hungre and threste, becauce it had grete dilectacion in meat & drynk. And sum tyme it was gretelie punysshid *with* nakidnes, becauce it had in þe life grete delectation in costious clothyng, & to be passynglie warm happed.

Purgatorij pena mitigatur or*atione*. S*upr*a de or*atione*.

Purgatorij pena soluitur missa. S*upr*a de p*ro*p*r*ietario.

DCLXI.

Purgatorij pena modico temp*or*e diu videtur durasse.

Iacobus de Vet*ria*co tellis how som tyme [*þer was*] a synner þat was correcte *with* a grete infirmytie, to so mykyll he prayed God to feche hym oute of þis werlde. And when he had lang prayed so, ane aungell come vnto hym and bad hym chese whethur he wolde stonde ij dayes in purgatorie or he wolde suffre his sekenes ij yere. And he chose þe furste, and decesid, and his saule went vnto purgatorie. So *with*-in ane houre after it was þ*er*, þe angell apperid vnto hym, and he axkyd; "What ert þou?" þe angell answerd hym agayn & sayd; "I am þe aungell þat apperid vnto the when þou was olyfe." And he said; "Nay, þou erte none aungell, ffor aungells wyll not lye; and þou erte bod a lyer, for þou tolde me þat I sulde be bod ij dayes in purgatorie,

[1] *A sidenote says,* [n]ota bene, *here.*

and I hafe stand þ*er*in many yeris." The aungell answerd hym agayn & sayd; "þ*ou* sall vnderstand at þ*ou* haste not bene here nott fullie ane howr." And þan he prayed þe aungell to bryng hym agayn vnto þis werld; for hym had leu*er* þ*er* suffer any sekenes at God wold send hym, þan for to be þ*er* a noder howr agayn in payn." And so his sawle was broght agayn vnto þe bodie, & mekelie he suffred sekenes ij yere, and þan he decesid.

Purgatoriu*m* suu*m* faciunt aliqui aliqu*ando* int*er* eos int*er* quos peccau*er*unt. S*upr*a de abb*a*te, viij.

Purgatorius plus timetur a bonis q*u*am a malis. Inf*r*a de ti*m*ore, iiij.

DCLXII.

Purgantur aliqui int*er* viuos.

We rede in '*Legend Lombardica*' how þ*er* was [1] c*er*tayn ffysshers in a town of Saynt Thebott*is* [2], and in h*ar*veste when þai went on fysshyng, and in-stede of fyssh þai drew in þ*er* nett a grete panell of yse. And þai war mor fayn þ*er*of þan þai wuld hafe bene of fyssh, ffor þ*er* bysshop had a grete surans in his fete, and þai laid þis yse vnder-nethe his fete & he had a grete remedie of his sekenes þ*er*bye. So vppon a day he harde oute of þis yse þe voyce of a man speke & say dyvurs wurd*is*, and þe bisshop coniured it & askid it what it was, & it answerd agayn & sayd; "I am a c*er*tan saule þat is punysshid for my synnys in þis panell of yse, and I myght be delyverd and þ*ou* wolde say for me xxx [*messis xl^ti*] [3] dayes to-geddur." And he granttyd at he sulde do so, & did. And when he had sayd halfe þe messis & was bown for to say þe toder halfe, sodanlie be þe suggestion of þe devull, all his household fell at were emang*is* þ*er* selfe, & ilkone of þai*m* was in poynt to kyll oþ*er*. And so þe bisshopp was trublid here-wit*h*, & lefte his mes-saying. And yit he fell vnto þai*m* agayn &

[1] MS. was a c*er*tayn ffysshers.
[2] Latin MSS. Theobaldus.
[3] Latin MSS. si quadraginta dieb*us* continuis .xxx. missas dic*er*es.

sayd þaim. And when he had sayd ij partis of þaim and was bown to say mes, one of his meneya come vnto hym & tolde hym at þer was a grete sege of men of armys layde abowte þe cetie; and herefor he put of his mess-saying þat day. And at þe iij tyme, when he had sayd all his messis bod[1] ane, þer come a man vnto hym when he was bown vnto þe laste mes, & tolde hym at þer was a grete fyre in þe cetie. And þe bisshop answerd agayn & sayd; "And all þe cetie burn vp stowte & rowte, I sall not ouerhypp nor lefe þis mes vndone." And onone as þe mes was done, þis yse resoluyd into watir, and þis fyre vanysshid away and was nevur sene after.

Pena purgatorij est acerba eciam si diuturna.

DCLXIII.

Pusillanimitas quando[2] retrahit a bono.

Cesarius tellis how þer was som tyme a knyght þat made hym monk of Ceustus ordur, to the intent at make a noder knyght at was his felaugh to do þe same. And þe toder knyght answerd & sayde he wold gladely[3] entyr in-to þe ordur bod he was ferd for lyce. And þe toder answerd hym agayn & sayd; "He is nowder wurthi nor noble knyght þat in þe batell of þe devull dredis nowder swerd nor spere, & is in þe batell of Cryste ferde for a few smale wormys. And þerfor bewar at þies lies take not fro the the kyngdom of hevyn." And *with* þis wurd þis knyght was confusid, & holilie and stronglie he tuke þe ordur and vttirly forsuke all þis werld.

DCLXIV.

Quies mentis in omnibus est querenda.

Saynt Ierom tellis of iij men þat luffid passand wele to-gedur, & þai all iij went and made þaim monkis. And one of þaim chose

[1] *After* bod, iij, *erased.* [2] Latin MSS. *quandoque.* [3] MS. goldely.

to condycion to make þai*m* att ane at was at debate, and þe secund chose hym to seryff þai*m* at wer seke, and þe iij luffyd alway to be solitarie and be hym selfe. And þe furste, when he had done mykyll & mott not agre þai*m* all þ*at* wer at discorde, he began to wax irke, & come vnto þe toder & tolde hym, & fande at he was irk also becauce he mott not seryff seke folk to plesans. And þies ij war acordyd sam*en* & come vnto þe thrid and tolde hym of all þ*er* trubbles, and p*ra*yed hym at he wold tell þai*m* what at p*ro*fettyd þai*m*. And he went from þai*m* a litell and put wat*ir* in a copp and sayd vnto þai*m*[1]; "Behold in-to þe watir!" And it was drovy, & so þai did & þai saw þ*er* awn facis as þai had lukid in a myrrour. And þan he said; "þus þai þ*at* er emang many men may not se þ*er* awn synnys no mor þan ye mot se your awn shadus in þis watir when it was drovye; and when þai hafe bene awhile in solatare place be þ*er* ane, þan þai may se þai*m*."

DCLXV.

Quies corpo*r*is a demone aliqu*ando* impedit*ur*.

We rede how on a tyme Abbott Isaac told in a collacion; 'Som tyme þ*er* was a moste holy fadur, and on a tyme as he went be a cell of ane of his brethur,[2] he was war of his bruther dyngand on a grete stone w*ith* a huge hamm*er*, and ane standand by hym lyke a man of Ynde, as he had prompyd hym vnto his wark. And þis gude olde fadur had m*er*vell of such ane illusion and trowid it was bod a dissayte. And he come vnto þe cell and haylsyd his bruther, & sayd; "What wark is þis at þou wyrkis?" And he ansswerd agayn & sayd; "Fadur, we hafe laburd agayn a harde stone, an vnnethis we may any thyng breke it." And þis olde man ansswerd hym agayn & sayd; "þou says wele, we hafe laburd, for þou was not be þine one; anod*er* was w*ith* the at þou saw nott, þat stude evur and prompyd the to wurk besylie."'

[1] Latin MSS. "Intendite in aqua*m*," *et* turbule*n*ta erat. Post modicu*m* it*er*um dix*it*; "Attendite q*ua*m limpida facta est aqua." Cumque intend*er*ent in aqua*m* vid*er*unt uultos suos.

[2] MS. *inserts*, and, *before* he.

DCLXVI.

Quies corp*or*is appetenda est a *sanc*tis.

Heraclides tellis & says of hym selfe; When variable thoghtis hase trublid me & bydden me go furth of my cell, and I had nothyng to do, I *com*pleynd vnto Anton of Antiocen oppon þis hevynes. And he answerd me & sayde; "When þies thoghtys com*m*ys vppon þe, answer þai*m* agayn & say, 'ffor *C*ristis sake I kepe þies wallis and will do, þuf I doo no noder thyng els.'"

DCLXVII.

Quietem corp*or*is *et* mentis nitit*ur* demon *eciam* visibil*iter* impedire.

Saynt Gregor tellis; "som tyme þ*er* was a man þat hight Martyn, and he led a solitarie lyfe. And þe devull had dispite here-att, & in lyknes of a s*er*pent he laburd & keste for to lett hym. And þis serpent on a tyme be hym selfe come into þe cafe whar þis Martyn led his lyfe in wyldernes, and when he was alone in his prayers, sho stude vp ryght befor hym, and when he wold lay hym down, sho wolde lay hur down. And on a tyme þis holy man putt furst his hand & syne his fute nakid vnto hur, & sayd; 'And þou hase lefe for to smyte me, I sall not lett the.' And when þai had vsid þis iij yere same*n*, at þe laste þis fals enmy, þe devull, was ou*er*com*m*en wit*h* his mekenes & vanysshid away from hym."

Rana. Rana*m* pep*er*it Nero imp*er*ator arte medicor*um*. *Su*p*r*a de c*r*udelitate, ij.

DCLXVIII.

Rapina om*n*is fugienda est *et* maxi*m*e a p*r*incipe vel p*r*elato.

Seutoni*us* tellis how on a tyme, when he had exhortid Tyberius Cesar þat he sulde eke þe tributis of his regions, the emp*er*our answerd agayn & sayd; "Nay, ffor it longis vnto a gude hurd to clypp his shepe, & not all at ons for to worow itt."

DCLXIX.

Raptor oratione restituere compellitur.

Saynt Gregor tellis how on a tyme a company of Gothomys[1] mett Libertinus, a gude holy man, rydand on his hors, and þai threw hym of his hors & tuke it from hym. And when þai had taken it from hym, he profurd þaim his whipp, & sayde; "Take þis with you at ye may gar þe hors ga with." And þai tuke it and went þer wayse. And als sone as þai war gone he fell vnto his prayers, and it happend at þai mott go no ferrer, nor with þer spurris gar þer hors go furth. So þai vmthoght þaim at þai had done wrang vnto þis holy man, and þai turnyd agayn & restorid hym of his hors. And þan þai went þer wayes, and nothyng lettyd þaim[2].

Rapine antecessorum debent restitui. Supra de ecclesia.

Rapine possunt adaptari ea que dicuntur supra de fure.

DCLXX.

Raptus spiritualis. Rapitur aliquando anima extra se.

Iacobus de Vetriaco says; "I saw som tyme devote wommen, þat was so hugelie ravissid with thoght of holy liffyng, þat of all þe day þer was no witt in þaim vnto none oute-ward thyng bod was evyn as þai had bene on slepe. And þai myght not be wakynd with no maner of criyng, nor þai myght fele nothyng sore and þai had bene nevur so prykkid." And he says he saw a noder womman nerehand of xxx[ti] yere old, and sho was kepyd with so grete luff be hur spowse in þe clostre, at sho mot be no ways go furth þeroff. And neuer so many men had drawen hur be þe hand, ffor oft tymys sho was enforcid to be drawen oute, bod it was in vayn bod if þai wuld hafe rugid hur in sonder. Also he says þat he had sene a noder womman þat som tyme xx[ti] sythes on þe day was besyde hur selfe, whilk þat in his presence opon a day was

[1] Arund. MS. *exercitus* Gothorum.
[2] Tales DCLXVIII and DCLXIX *marked*, Nota, *in the margin*.

vij sithes ravysshid. And in what state som evur sho was ravissid sho abade in þat astate vnto sho was turnyd owte of hur ravisshyng. And hur hand*is* hang vp in þe ayre vnmouable aft*er* þe disposicion at sho was ravisshid in, at sho was garte shew a bodely ioying. *et* c⁹.

Rebellio. Rebellis punitur. Inf*ra* de religione, ij.
Recidiuu*m*. Recidiuu*m* nocet. Sup*ra* de heretico, ij.
Recognic*io*. Recognoscere debem*us* ben*e*ficia nob*is* impensa. Sup*ra* de beneficio, i.
Recreacio int*er*du*m* vtilis est religiosis. Sup*ra* Joh*ann*is Euang*e*liste.

DCLXXI.

Recreacio *eciam* moderata om*n*ib*us* est necessaria.

Valerius tellis þat when Socrates þe wyse clerke wexid alde and taght his scolers, he wold not alway bynd þai*m* in at lernyng, bod som tyme to avanyssh away þ*er* labur he wolde suffer þai*m* to have recreacion, to cauce þai*m* to be more dyligent & craftie in þ*er* lernyng afterward, at þai sulde not be yrke of þ*er* labur. And herefor þis wise philosophur, Socrates, [*usyd*] for to lope on a rede betwix his leggis, as barnys rydys, and ryde wit*h* þai*m* as þai do to make þai*m* sporte.

Redempcio nulla est in inferno. Sup*ra* de inferno, iiij.
Reddicio. Reddit deus centuplu*m*. Su*pra* de elemos*in*a xiiij, et de dec*im*is.
Reddu*n*t aliqui malu*m* p*ro* bono. Infra de serpente.

DCLXXII.

Reg*in*a qu*an*to dignior tanto mag*is* casti*tat*e*m* sua*m* se*r*vare debet.

We rede in þe 'M*er*acles of our Ladie,' how som tyme in Rome þ*er* was ane emp*er*our þat had a fayr wyfe & a chaste. So[1] on a

[1] MS. som.

tyme þis emp*er*our sulde travell furth oute of contre fro his empyre vnto other grete regions, and he putt a bruther þat he had, & also all his empyre, vnto gou*er*nans of his whene. And when he was gone, his bruther wexid' fond' of þe whene, & at þe laste he oppynd' his harte vnto hur, & sho forsuke hym vttirlie and wolde not graunte vnto hym; notw*ith*standyng he wolde not lefe, bod laburd' hur daylie þ*er*in. So at þe laste when sho saw he wolde not lefe, sho sparrid' hym in a towr horn faste, and gou*er*nyd' þe empyre peasfullie. And when v yere was passid' þis emp*er*our come home, & be lefe of þe empryce his bruther was lattyn furthe of þe towr & come vnto þe emp*er*our and accusyd' þe emprice hugelie vnto hym, & sayd' þat sho was ane oppyn fornycatur nerehand' w*ith* evur-ilk man. And becauce he wolde not consent vnto hur to ly by hur, þ*er*for sho sparrid' hym faste in a towr, & herefor he said' he was lene and ill hewid'. And þis emp*er*our gaff our redelie truste vnto hym, & tuke a grete sorow in his harte, to so mykell at he fell down in swownyng & lay a grete while. So when he come vnto his spyritt*is* agayn he went furth, and þe whene mett hym & wolde hafe kissid' hym, & he wolde not bod gaff hur a grete strake, & felde hur vnto þe erth. And he comm*a*undid' ij of his men to take hur & hafe hur vnto þe wudd & smyte of hur heade. And þai tuke hur & had hur furth as he bad. & when þai come þ*er* þai sulde hafe smyten of hur head', þai wolde bothe hafe ligen by hur. And sho putt þai*m* by and cryed & made a grete noyse. And þ*er* happeud com by a wurthi man, & many men w*ith* hym, and harde hur cry & rade to hur & slew þies ij h*ar*lott*is* at was w*ith* hur, & tuke hur[1] home w*ith* hym & betaght hur vnto his wyfe. And sho made hur nuress of a little yong son at sho hadd'. So þis wurthi man had a bruder was a knyght, & he wexid so fond' on hur at he wiste neu*er* what he might doo, & oft wolde hafe had at do w*ith* hur; and evur sho putt hym bye. So on a nyght, as sho was on slepe in hur bed & þis yong bab by hur, he come privalie w*ith* a knyfe & cutt þe barn throte in sonder, & put nemelie þe knyfe in hur hand and sho of slepe; & so he lefte hur and went his wayes. So sho felde warm blude

[1] MS. hym.

ryn̄ aboute hyr in þe bed, & wakend þer-*with*. And when̄ sho saw how it was sho cryed', at þe lorde & þe ladie and all þe howshold' hard'. So þai come vnto hur at luke what hur aylid', and fande þe barn̄ dead'. And þe howshold' meneya wold' hafe slayn̄ hur, bod þe lorde and þe ladie wolde not latt þai*m*. So þe lord' com*m*andid' at sho sulde be delyverd' vnto shipmen̄, & at þai sulde hafe hur in-to a far contrey. And so sho was delyverd' vnto shipmen̄ & broght vnto þe ship̄. And onone þai wolde hafe ligen̄ by hur, and in no wyse sho wolde consent vnto þai*m*, and herefore þai wolde hafe drownyd' hur. Bod þugh grace of God þ*er* cowncell changid', and þai sett hur vpp̄ apon̄ a hy skar in þe see. And þ*er* our Ladie Saynt Marie apperid vnto hur & comfurthid hur, and' bad hur take ane erbe þat was vnder hur head' þ*er* sho lay & kepe it, & *with* þat sho sulde heale all þai*m* þat war lepre whar-som̄-evur sho come. And sho was þ*er* many day & had' no meat bod h*er*bys & gress. So on̄ a tyme þ*er* come shipp̄-men̄ by þe land', and sho cryed' vnto þai*m* and þai had petie on̄ hur, and tuke hur in-to þ*er* ship̄ & had hur vnto a haven-town̄; and onone þ*er* befor þai*m* all sho helid' a lepre man̄. And in þe mene while þis vnhappie man̄ þat had slayn̄ his bruther barn̄ þat sho kepid', was sodanlie fallen̄ lepre, and sho was broght vnto hym̄ & no bodie knew hur of all þe howshold'. So þe lord prayed hur to hele his bruther, and sho answerd' agayn̄ & sayd' sho myght nott bod if he in p*re*sence of þe lorde & þe ladie & oþ*er* viij p*er*sons shrafe hym̄ clene of all his synnys. And so he did', bod þat syn̄ at he did' anence hur, he wolde not shryfe hym̄ þ*er*of, and evur sho sayd' he was not full shrevyn̄. So he gatt assurans of his bruthir, & knowleged all his syn̄ how he had done. And sho answerd' agayn̄ & sayd'; "I am̄ þat same wom*m*an̄." And þ*er* sho helid' hym̄. And þe lorde wolde hafe garte hur wed hym̄ and sho wolde not, bod went hur way; & evur whar any was lepre sho helid' þai*m*. So at þe laste hur happend to com̄ to Rome, and þ*er* sho fand þe emp*er*our hur husband' bruther, at had done so vnto hur, lepre. And sho was fechid' to hele hym̄, & sho wolde not bod if he *con*-fessid' hym̄ oppynlie of all þe synnys at evur he had done befor all men̄; and so he did' & telde opynlie how he had done vnto hur, &

how þe emp*er*our had garte sla hur. And all þe peple þat was þ*er* & harde made sorow for los of so gude a ladie. So at þe laste sho lete þai*m* witt at it was sho, & helid in þe cetie all þat evur was lepur. And be þat tyme þe emp*er*our was dead, and þe pope sent vnto hur; & becauce þat in hur *tri*bulacion sho had made a vow of chastite, he made hur to take one abbet of religion. And þus sho endid hur lyfe in clene liffiyng. *et c*9.

Regina semp*er* honestate*m* sua*m* debet tenere. Sup*ra* de muliere, xvi.

DCLXXIII.

Religiosus no*n* debet se de secularib*us* intromittere.

Iacobus de Vet*ri*aco tellis how som tyme þ*er* was a knyght þat lefte all his possessions & his wurshuppis and his welefaris, and made hym a monk. And þe abbot saw at he was a wyse man and sent hym vnto þ*e* m*ar*kett to sell assis of þe abbay at was olde, & at he sulde by yong; þuff all he war displesid þ*er*-wit*h*, neu*er*-þeles he went, and wolde not breke his obediens. And when men axkid hym if þe assis wer gude & yong, he answerd eu*er* agayn & sayd; "Trow ye at our abbay is fallen vnto suche pou*er*tie at we sulde sell our gude assis & our p*ro*fetable?" So one come & axkid hym whi þ*er* taylis wer so pylde, and no hare lefte on þai*m*. He answerd agayn & sayd; "Becauce þai fall oft sythis vnder þ*er* lade & we lifte þai*m* eu*er* vp be þe tayllis, and þat is cauce þ*er* tayllis er bare." And þus he wolde nott layn þe treuth. So hym happend sell none of þai*m*, and come home vnto his cloystur. A noder lewid monke at was wit*h* hym at þe m*ar*kett accusyd hym evyn opynlie in þ*er* chapit*er* hows; and þe abbott dysplyd hym as it had bene for a grete truspas. And he answerd vnto þe abbott agayn & sayd; "I lefte many assis & mekull oþ*er* gude thyng in þe werlde, and I come hedur to seryff God & becauce I sulde nott lye, bod at I sulde safe my saule." And þus fro thens furth he was nevur sent oute forwarde.

Religiosus mentiri non debet. Supra de mendacio, ij.

Religiosus aduocatus esse non debet. Sup*ra* de mendacio, ij.

DCLXXIV.

Religiosus non debet excedere in potu.

Petrus Clunacens*is*[1] tellis how som tyme þ*er* was ane holie man. and as he lay in his p*ra*yers on Gude Fryday, he was ravisshid his spyrid fro his body vnto Pasch day. And when he come vnto hym selfe, he tolde how þat he saw a religious man of grete penance swolud of þe devull in drynk þat he was wunte to vse excesly. And þan he was drawen vnto his dome, and had noght Saynt Nicholas bene, he had bene dampned; bod Saynt Nicholas at he vsid to seryff deuotelie helpid hym. & so he was nott dampnyd, bod demyd vnto þe payns of purgatorie.

Religionis ingressus causat aliqu*ando* consideracio penar*um* inferni, p*er*icu*lor*u*m* mundi, penar*um* purgatorij, p*ro*p*r*ie complexionis. S*upr*a de co*n*ue*r*sione.

Religionis status securior est seculari. Inf*r*a de relinquere.

Religiosus in h*ab*itu suo debet mori. S*upr*a de monacho, ij.

Religiosus no*n* debet pompose incedere. Sup*r*a de mo*n*acho, iiij.

Religiosus p*ro*p*r*ietarius no*n* potest com*m*unicare[2]. S*upr*a de p*ro*p*r*ietate, i.

Religiosus p*ro*p*r*ietarius in sterquilinio sepelit*ur*. S*upr*a de p*ro*p*r*ietate, ij.

Religionis ingressus *eciam* infirmitate*m* corporalem sanat. Inf*r*a de voto, ij.

Religiosus humilem habitu*m* debet habere. Sup*r*a de abb*a*te, x.

[1] MS. Clymacensi*s*. [2] MS. com*m*i*u*icare.

DCLXXV.

Religiosus inobediens aliqu*ando eciam* a deo uisibilit*er*[1] punitur.

Cesarius tellis how som tyme þ*er* was ane abbot & he had a seke monke. And he saw þ*at* it was necessarie to hym to eate flessh, & he comm*a*undid hym þat he sulde eate flessh; and he was passand swaymos & wold nott. And for als mekull as God wolde shew þat obediens war bett*er* þan meat or drynk, þis inobedient monke onone turnyd into a wudenes, and ran wude into þe felde. And þ*er* he fande a dead dogg & all þe flessh on hym stynkid, and he fell to and ete of hym gredelie. And þus becauce he truspasid in flessh & wolde not eatt flessh when his abbott bad hym, þ*er*for he was punyssid in flessh-etyng, *et* c^{9}, for his inobedyance.

Religiosus no*n* debet carnalit*er* affici ad amicos. S*upr*a de affectu[2], ij.

Religiosos temptat demon. S*upr*a de demone in pl*u*rib*us* locis.

DCLXXVI.

Religiosus potest bellare sine armis in spe diuini auxilii defendendo ius suu*m* quod alit*er* h*ab*ere no*n* posset, q*u*od magis est no*n* bellare q*u*am bellare.

Petrus Damianus tellis how þat in þe p*ar*ties of Frawnce þ*er* was in a place a[3] grete debate betwix ane abbott & a myghtie seculer man for a possession of a lyfelod, so þat when þai had lang strevyn, ffavorers on bothe p*ar*ties arayid þai*m* evyn vnto batell. And þis myghti man come in-to þe felde *with* a grete company of armyd men *with* hym, & bownd hym to feght. And þis abbott, all þat come *with* hym to feght, he comm*a*ndid þai*m*

[1] MS. inuisibili*ter*. [2] MS. aspec*tu*. [3] MS. *repeats*, a.

stand oparte & latt hym & his monkis alone, and he sett all his monkis on hors, & made þai*m* cover þ*er* hedis wit*h* þaire cowlis. And in þis man*er* of armur he come vnto þe place þ*er* þai sulde feght; and onone his enmys, when þai saw hym, wer strekyn wit*h* suche ane vgsomnes at onone þai lightid of þ*er* horsis, & keste away fro þai*m* þ*er* armor & þ*er* wapyns and fell down mekelie vnto þe erde, & axkid hym forgyfnes and nevur after made chalange vnto þis possession agayn.

DCLXXVII.

Religiosi no*n* debent statu*m* seculariu*m* contempnere.

Saynt Ierom tellis of one þat hight Paphencius, whilk þat when he had long tyme vsyd aungell lyfe, he made his *pr*ayer vnto almightie God at he wold shew hym to whilk saynt of hevyn he sulde be like in blis. And it was shewid hym at he sulde be lyke vnto one Simphoniacus þat dwelte in þe next strete. And he went onone vnto hym and axkid hym of his reule & his gou*er*nans. And he tolde hym at he had vsid to be emang thevis & knew no gude dede, nor neu*er* did none, safeyng onelie at he gatt a damysell fro his felows, at þai had taken & defowlid, & savid hir honesti at þai lay not by hur. And he tolde hym also how he gaff vnto ane honeste wom*m*an in wyldrenes, goand wyll, iij c penys to rawnson hur husband & hur childer þat lay in sore *pr*ison. And þan þis Paphencius tolde hym hys vision and had hym wit*h* hym vnto wyldrenes, and wit*h*-in a little while after he dyed, and he saw his saule had vnto hevyn. A nodir tyme þe same was shewid hym of þe *pr*imat of þe cetie, þat was wed xxx^{ti} yere & evur kepud hym in chastitie from his wyfe, and he saw his sawle also had vnto hevyn. And the thrid tyme it was shewid hym þe same of a m*er*chand. And þan when he sulde dye and prestis come vnto hym, he said vnto þai*m*; "No man, nowd*er* thefe nor m*er*chand, sulde be despysid, for emang peple of evur-ilk degre is God plesud wit*h* som sawlis." And he tolde þai*m* in ordur all þat is aforn saide, and þan he passid vnto God.

Religiosus non debet discurrere. Sup*r*a de affec*tu*.

Religiosi [1] attente mulieres aspic*e*re n*on* debent. Su*pr*a de muliere, viij.

DCLXXVIII.

Relinquere. Relinque*n*di su*n*t parentes a viris p*er*fec*t*is.

Abbot Abraham on a tyme tolde in his 'Collasion,' how som tyme þ*er* come a yong man vnto Saynt Anton þe abbott, and rep*ro*vid þe life of ancharis and said at þai war of more p*er*feccion þat bade at hame *with* þ*er* fadurs & þ*er* moders, & ordand for þai*m* all þing att þai*m* mysterd and wroght beselie daylie, þan þai war at went into wyldernes and [2] abstenyd þai*m* fro daylie laburyng, and gaff þai*m* vnto nothyng bod vnto redyng and prayer. And Saynt Anton ansswerd hym & said; "Son, þou at duse þus, whethur was þou not hevie when þi fadur and þi moder happend any cace of adu*er*sitie? And also was þou not ioyfull when þai war in p*ro*sp*er*ite?" And he ansswerd agayn & said yis. And þan þis abbott sayd vnto hym; "þou sall vnd*er*stond þat in þe werld þat is for to com þou sal be demyd for to be in þ*er* co*m*panye, in whase co*m*pany in þis lyfe þou was conu*er*sand, owder in wynnyng or in los, in ioy or in sorow. And þ*er*for þuf all we hafe bothe ffadurs & moders, yitt vs hase levur lefe þai*m* & liff in wyldrenes & þ*er* take syke fude as God sendis vs, þan for to be in þe warlde & be sekur of fyndyng of our fadurs & moders."

Relinquentes om*n*ia p*ro*pt*er* deu*m* deus remun*er*at. Su*pr*a de p*er*eg*r*ino, iij.

DCLXXIX.

Reliquie s*anc*t*oru*m su*n*t honorande.

Cesarius tellis how þ*a*t som tyme in ane abbay of þe Ceustus ordur þ*er* was ij bodis of þe xj ml virginys, and in a were tyme þai [3] war sett aboue a vowte in þe kurk, & þ*er* þai stude long

[1] MS. religiose. [2] MS. *repeats*, and. [3] MS. þ*er*.

& was forgetten̄. So on̄ a tyme at mydnyght þai made sike a dusshyng in þe cace at þai lay in, att alƚ hard' in þe quere, and þus þai did' on̄ þe nyght ij or iij [*sythis*], vnto so mekuƚƚ at þe sacristanes said' at þai durste not lygg in þe kurk. And for alƚ þis *þer* was no wurshuꝑ done vnto þai*m*, bod alƚ way þai war nothyng lukid after. So on̄ a nyght in matyn̄ tyme, when̄ alƚ þe covent was in̄ þe where, þai alƚ saw befoꝛ þe altar ij fayr vi*r*gyns in maydyn̄ clothyng, inclynand þai*m*, & when̄ þai had done, went furth of þe kurk at a dure at evur befoꝛ was wunte to be sparrid'. So onone [1] þe monkis went vnto þe cace at þies ij vi*r*gynys lay in̄, & oppynd it, & *þer* was nothyng *þer*in. And þai had grete m*er*veƚƚ hereof, & sent vnto Colayn̄, and *þer* þe same bodis was fon̄ in þe same placis *þer* þai lay when̄ þai war furste giffen̄ vnto þe sayd abbay. *et c*ᵒ.

Remigij Remens*is*. Su*pra* de familiaritate, ij.

DCLXXX.

Remissio. Remissionis pecc*atorum* ostendit deus aliqu*ando* signu*m* aliquod.

Petrus Damianus tellis of one þat hight Arnulphus, þat was fadur of kyng Pypyn̄, and' grawnsur vnto great Charlis þat was duke of Lothoringia. So on̄ a tyme sodonlie he lefte his wyfe and his childre, and went into wyldernes. And on̄ a tyme as he went ou*er* a grete bryg þat was owꝛ a depe watir, when̄ he was at þe myddest of þe brygg *þer* þe watyr was depeste, *þer* he keste in his ryng *with* þis condicion̄, & sayd'; "When̄ I hafe þis ryng agayn̄, þan̄ *with*-outen̄ doute I saƚƚ truste at my synys is forgyffen̄ me, and' at I am̄ fullie asoylid' of þai*m*." And *þer* he abade in wyldernes many day in gude life. And in þe mene while dyed' þe bisshoꝑ of Methens*is*, and he was chosyn̄ vnto bisshoꝑ. And he abstenyd' hym̄ fro etyng of flessh. So on̄ a tyme *þer* was a ffyssch broght hym̄ to a p*re*sent, and he garte oppyn̄ itt befoꝛ hym̄ and fand' hys ryng in þe cudpoke *þer*off, & onone as he saw it he kend it. And it was ij day iorney fro þat bryg at he keste it dow[*n*]

[1] MS. on̄ one.

att, vnto þat place þ*er* þe fissh was taken at it was fon in þe bely off.

Remuner*a*cio. Remuner*a*t deus dantes aliquid p*er* se. S*upra* de elemos*ina*, i, ij, *et* iij.

DCLXXXI.

Remuner*a*t deus aliqua bona a pecc*at*orib*us* facta.

Cesarius tellis how som tyme þ*er* was a knyght þat was a grete robber and a thefe, and be com*m*andmend of Emp*er*our Frederyke he was taken & honged. And vpon þe iij day after he was hanged, a noder knyght come rydand be þe galows, and when he saw hym hyng þ*er* he sayd vnto his man; "O God! it was mekull petie at þis fayr man was hanged!" And his man ansswerd hym agayn & sayd; "Sur, þis was a noble knyght & your nere cussyn." So þis knyght & his man come ner, and thoght to take hym down & beryy hym; and as he hang he spakk vnto þai*m* & sayd; "Take me down, ffor I lyff yitt." And when þai had tane hym down he sayd vnto þai*m*; "Thuff all I was a synn*er*, yit I did a litle s*er*ves vnto almyghtie God, for þe whilk He had m*er*cie on me; ffor I vsid eu*er*e day to say iij pat*er* nost*er*, & iij ave maria, in wurshup of þe holie trynytie, & v *pater noster* & v ave maria in wurshup of þe v wowndis of our Lorde, and a p*ater* nost*er* in wurshup of þe aungell at I am betaght too, and also one vnto þe sac*ra*ment þat is daylie sacred þurgh all þis werlde, besekyng daylie almighti God, at I myght be wurthi to reseyfe þe sac*ra*ment er I dyed. And þat God hase grawntid me of His m*er*cie, and þ*er*for I pray you call vnto me a preste." And when þe preste come he shrafe hym, and þan he was howsled. And onone as þis was done he yelde vp his gaste, and þai tuke and berid hym[1].

Remuner*a*t Deus p*er*egrinos. Sup*ra* de p*er*eg*ri*no, iij.

Restitucio. Restituere nolens ablata punitur. S*upra* de apostatis.

[1] *This tale is marked* Nota [be]ne.

Restitui debent forisf*acta* antecessor*um*. S*upra* de ecc*les*ia, ij.

Restituere nol*u*nt mali filij p*ro* parentib*us eciam* post mortem eos monentib*us*. S*upra* de morte, xvij [1].

Restitucio valet vsurarijs. Infra de testamento, I°.

Restituere nolentib*us* negatur sepultura. Inf*ra* de sepultura [2], iij, *et* iv [3].

Restituere tenentur [4] executores p*ro* testatorib*us*. Sup*ra* in pl*u*rib*us* locis, *et* infra de reuiuiscere, de sac*er*dote et de sacramento.

DCLXXXII.

Reue*r*encia. Reue*r*eri *et* honorari debent [*se mutuo*][5] ho*m*in*es* eiusd*em* status.

Valerius tellis how þat in þe tyme þat þe vij sagis florisshid at Athenis, it happend in þe region of Niclase [6] at a man boght of þe ffysshers a draght *with* þ*er* nett, & at þat draght þai þai*m* happend draw a grete burde all of golde of a grete weght. And so þai fell at varyans for þis burde, þe fisshers & þai þat boght þe draght, for þai sayd þai solde hym noght bod ffissh, & he said he boght what at fortun wolde send hym. So þai had it vnto þe cetie, and broght it befor Appollo, & made þ*er* prayers vnto hym to send þai*m* som taken to whame þis burde sulde be demyd. And he answerd þai*m* & bad þai*m* giff it vnto hym þat was þe wyseste in all þe cetie. And so þai gaff it vnto one þat hight Talentus Millesius, þat emang þe vij sagis was moste noble, and he sent it vnto Byantes Priemo. And he wolde none þ*er*off bod gaff it vnto a noder, and so it went þurgh þai*m* all vnto it come at þe laste. And he gaff a iudgement at it sulde be halowid in wurshup of Appollo & gyffen vnto hym, and so it was.

[1] MS. xvj.
[2] MS. spepultura.
[3] MS. v.
[4] MS. tenend.
[5] *From the* Latin MS.
[6] MS. *repeats*, it happened, *here*.

DCLXXXIII.

Reuiuiscere v*e*l resurgere. Reuiuiscit aliqu*ando* homo ex gr*atia* sp*iritu*ali.

Saynt Gregur tellis how þ*er* was som tyme in Rome a noble cetysyn þat hight Romanus[1], and hym happend for to dye at Constantynople. & on þe morn when þai wold hafe opynd hym & sesond hym *with* spycis at he myght hafe bene curid[2], he rase vpp & was whikk. And he tolde þai*m* mekull þing at he had sene in hell, and at he neu*er* trowid befor, & he tolde also þat þe juge at he was broght befor, þat he callid hym noght Ro*manus*[3], bod Romanus Ferarius þat was nere-hand hym. And þus he þat ans was dead was on lyfe agayn & liffid many yeris.

Rex aliqu*ando* gl*or*iatur in vestibus. Sup*ra* de augurio *et* de ornatu.

Rex humilit*er* se habet ad subditos. Sup*ra* de iudicio vlti*mo*.

Rex malus a deo deponitur. Sup*ra* de hospit*a*litate, vi[4].

Rex sapiens. Sup*ra* de prudencia *et* p*ro*videncia.

DCLXXXIV.

Risus. Ridere no*n* debent h*ab*entes oc*ul*u*m* ad iudiciu*m* vltimu*m*.

We rede in 'Vitis Pat*ru*m,' how on a tyme ane olde man saw a yong man lagh, & he said vnto hym; "Son, how may þou fynd in þi herte to lagh? Mon not þou & I & we all befor bothe hevyn and erth gyf a rekynyng of all our lyfe? And þ*er*for me m*er*vels," he said, "at þow may fynde in þi harte to lagh."

[1] Latin, civis romanus, Stephanus nomine.
[2] MS. carid.
[3] Harl. MS. non petierat, 'huncSteph*anu*m,' *sed*, 'Stephanu*m* Ferariu*m*,' mortuus est. Arund. MS. *sed* 'Steph*anu*m Ferrariu*m*,' q*ui* erat iux*ta* eu*m*, q*uo* d*icto*, ille Steph*anus* mortuus e*st*.'
[4] MS. iiij.

DCLXXXV.

Ridere no*n* debent adu*er*tentes p*er*icula mundi.

We rede in 'Libro de Dono Timoris' how som̄ tyme þ*er* was a kyng, and if he made nevur so great a feste, he wolde neu*er* lagħ. So a frend' of his reprovid' hym̄ þ*er*for, & askid' hym̄ whi he did so, and he answerd' fenandlie. So after-ward' he ordand a chayre *with* rotyn̄ fete, and he garte sett it abown̄ a hate burnyng oven̄, and abown̄ it he gart hyng a swerd' *with* a wayke threde. And þis done, he garte se t hym̄ þ*er*in þat reprovid' hym̄ for he wolde not lagħ, & he garte sett aboute hym̄ iiij men̄ *with* iiij drawen̄ swerdis. And he garte bryng befor̃ hym̄ alƚ man*er* of delicious metis & drynkis, & alƚ oþ*er* thyng*is* þat sulde make hym̄ merie. So þan̄ þe kyng come in and stirrid' hym̄ to lagħ, and he answerd' agayn̄ & said'; "I may not lagħ when̄ I se þies p*er*els þat er aboute me." Than̄ þe kyng answerd' hym̄ agayn̄ & said'; "Than̄ vmthynk þe how mot I lagħ when̄ þ*er* er grete festis made afore me, þat seis behynd' me þe bitt*er*nes of my syn̄? And befor̃ me I se ane vnc*er*tantie of þat at is for to com̄, and on̄ my lefte hand' I see vexacions of p*re*sent adu*er*sities, and on̄ my right hand I se noyes þat com*m*ys after p*ros*p*er*ities. And alƚ þies I se as sharp̄ swerdis of þe sentans of alƚmyghti God'. And I se dead' hyng abown̄, whame I wate nevur what howr̃ wilƚ stryke me, and vndernethe me I se þe pitt of helƚ at I am̄ ferd' at falƚ into, & *with*-in me I se myne awn̄ freletie. And emang alƚ þies I am̄ sett in a frele seatt, oute of þe whilk I am̄ ferde daylie to falƚ. And þ*er*for̃ hafe þou no m*er*velƚ if I may not fynd in my harte to lagħ."

Rosa. Rose h*a*bentur tempore hyemali. Sup*ra* de martirio.

Rusticus delicijs nescit vti. S*upra* de delicijs, ij *et* iij.

Rustico falsu*m* den*ariu*m offerenti, idem ei *pro* com*m*unione exhibetur. S*upra* de oblac*io*ne.

DCLXXXVI.

Sacerdos debet frequenter pro mortuis celebrare.

Petrus Clunacensis[1] tellis how þ*er* was som tyme a bisshopp þat suspent a c*er*tan pr*e*ste in his dioces becauce he sang eu*er*ilk day for all crysten sawlis. So on a tyme aft*er*ward, as þis bisshopp walkid be his one in a kurk-garth, hym þoght at all þe dead folk at lay in þat kurk-garthe rase agayns hym, ilkone *with* a spade in þ*er* hand. And þai thrett hym & said; "Beholde! þis is þe bisshopp þat tuke fro vs our preste & suspend hym, at he may not say mes for vs. And þ*er*for c*er*tanlie, bod if he amend it vnto vs, he sall dye." And *with* þat he was so flayed he was like hafe dyed, & fell in a swownd[2]. And when he come vnto hym selfe agayn, he garte send aft*er* þe pr*e*ste and asoylid hym, & bad hym syng on for al crysten sawlis as he did befor.

DCLXXXVII.

Sacerdotis malicia non polluit sacramentum.

Iacobus de Vet*ri*aco tellis how þ*er* was som tyme a man, whilk þ*at* of ane vnwurthie prest þat he knew wolde nowder here mes nor resayfe his sac*ra*mentis. So on a tyme hym thoght in his slepe þat hym was passand thrustie, and þat he stude be a pitt *with* watir þ*er* a leprus man drew vp watir in a passand fayr vessell *with* a corde all of golde. And þ*er* come many one & axkid hym a drynk of þat fayr watir, & he gaff þai*m* & þai drank faste. And at þe laste þis man drew ner & wolde hafe had a drynk, & þe layser man drew bak his hand & wolde not lat hym drynk, & sayd; "How will þou take a drynke of a lepros man hand, þat will not here mes nor take þe sac*ra*mentis of a preste at þou knowis is in syn? Do no mor so, bod þink of þis vers; 'vim sac*ra*menti non mutat vita ministri.'" And *with* þat he wakynd.

[1] MS. Climacensis.   [2] MS. swownyd.

And fro thens furth he neuer gruchid after to here þat prestis mes, nor for to take his sacramentis of holie kurk of his hande.

Sacerdos indiscretus terret confitentes. Supra de apostasia, iij.

Sacerdos tenens vxorem militis *et* de hoc laico confessus, a confusione liberatur. *Supra* de confessione, vij.

DCLXXXVIII.

Sacerdos curatus infirmis debet esse paratus *et* petentibus omni tempore sacramenta ministrare.

Cesarius tellis of a preste at was a curatt, þat on a tyme satt playand at þe dice *with* a cussyn of his. And þer come vnto hym a man hastelie and tolde hym at his moder was seke and bown to dye, & bad hym in payn of þe perell þat wolde fall þeron þat he sulde com in all haste vnto hur & shryfe hur & giff hur hur sacramentis. And þe preste answerd agayn & said þat he wolde not vnto hys layke war done. And euer þe man stude still & laburd hym to ryse. So at þe laste þis preste said vnto his cussyn at he played *with*; "Cussyn, I compleyn me, & at þe I take wittnes, at þis felow will not lat me alone at my gamen, bod trubbles me and lettis me." So þis man saw þat his taryng profettid hym nott, & went his ways. And his moder dyed *with*outen howsell or shrufte. So it happend on þe iij day after, þe cussyn of þis same preste mett þis yong man at þe moder was dead of, and vmthoght hym of þe playnt at þe preste made of hym, & pullid oute his dagger & stykked hym. And after þis and many oþer synnys, þis preste happend fall seke & bown to dye. So a cussyn of his, at was his servand, cownceld hym to be shrevyn & forthynk hym of his truspas. He wolde nott bod fell into a despayr, & answerd hur & sayd; "Seis þou yone grete lathe euence vs? Forsuthe þer is not þerin so many strais as þer is fendis gadurd here aboute me, to take my sawle when I pas."

DCLXXXIX.

Sac*er*dos indigne celebrans *eciam* visibilit*er* sacr*amento* p*r*iuatur.

Cesarius tellis of a preste of Saynt Petur kurk in Colayn, how on a day when he had sacred his mes & layd down þe sacrament on þe altar, when he sulde take it agayn he cuthe not fynd it, nor all þe oþ*er* peple þat helpid hym to seke itt. Whar-for witty men þat knew hym supposid þat aungels had taken it from hym, & translat it into hevyn, þat he þat was a lichuros preste sulde not resayfe it vnto hym dampnacion; for it was not vnknowen at he had a lemman in þe town & held hur opynlie.

DCXC.

Sac*er*dos diligent*er* debet adu*er*tere q*uo*d hostia consec*r*anda nullu*m* h*ab*eat def*ectu*m.

Cesarius tellis how som tyme þ*er* was a p*r*este besyd Colayn, and when he was att mes & had sayd þe gospell & layde down þe sac*r*ament vppon þe corprax, sodanlie it was away. And he trowid at þat had happend þurgh som fallyng down, & he layd þ*er* a noder; and onone þat was removid ferrer þan þe toder was. And þan he tuke þe thrid, and onone it was casten of þe altar. And when he saw þat he was ferde for þat hoste behynd hym, and he consecratt a noder. And when mes was done, he tuke þis hoste & broght it vnto Colayn, & shewid it vnto p*ar*fite men & rehersid vnto þai*m* all þe mater. And þai brak it aforn hym and fand þ*er*in a lowse baken. And all þat was þ*er* thankid almighti God þat will algatt*is* at þe sac*r*ament be made of clene thyng.

DCXCI.

Sacerdotem indigne celebrantem p*r*iuat deus su*m*pcione sacramenti.

Cesarius tellis how þ*er* was a p*r*este in Fraunce, so hym happend on yole nyght to go fro þe ta town to þe tod*er*, whar he sulde say mes in bathe placis; so he was be his one, & hym happend to mete *with* a womman be hur ane. And so in þat same howr hym happynd to syn *with* hur, and so he mor dredyng þe shame of man þan Goddis vengeans, when he had said his matyns, he began solemplie þe furste mes. And when he had consecratt bothe þe bread & þe whyne, a white duffe light down on þe aw*ter* at þe preste saw, and sho suppid of all þat was in þe chales *with* hur neb, & tuke þe sac*ra*ment *with* hur and flow away. And þis preste was ferd, bod not as hym aght to be, and wyste neu*er* what he sulde do. Neu*er*-þe-les he said oute þe wurdis & fulfyllid þe sygnes of þe sacrament, and endid his mes. And þe same happend hym at þe secund mes, and also at þe iij mes þe same day. So at þe laste he repentid hym, and *with* a grete contricion he went unto ane abbott of Ceustos ordur & confessid hym, whilk þat, when he saw his contricion, enionyd hym for to ga to mes. And when *with* grete drede & sorow he had said mes, befor his su[*m*]pcions[1], þe same duffe come agayn. And þe same iij hostis at sho had had away syngnlelie, ilkone be þ*er* one, sho broght þa*im* agayn in hur byll, & layd þa*im* on þe corprax. And þe liquore of iij messis sho put oute of hur throte into þe chales, and went hur ways. And when þe preste saw þis, he was passand fayn and told his confessur all þis be ordur, and besoght hym at he mot be resayvid into þe ordur to be one of his brethur. And he grawntid hym so at he wulde furste go & be iij yere beyond se & þ*er* seryff seke folke of þ*er* religion, and so he did. And þis done, he come home; and þe abbot reseyvid hym & made hym a monke of his couent.

DCXCII.

Sacerdoti curato imputantur defectus subditor*um*.

Cesarius tellis how som tyme þ*er* was a preste, a curatt, at gaff hym all vnto etyng & drynkyng and lichorye. And he was necligent anent his parishyng, and gaff no hede vnto þ*er* sawlis. So hym happend to dye, & when he was dead his p*ar*isshyns at war dead vndernethe his cure, ilkone of þa*im* gat a grete stane,

[1] Latin, *ante sumpcionem*.

and accusid hym vnto hell, and said vnto hym; "We wer commytt vnto þe and þou haste forgettyn vs; ffor when we synd, þou nowder reuokid *with* nowder gude wurde nor exsample, and þerfor þou ert cauce of owr dampnacion." And *with* þat þai keste all þe stanys on hym, and he fell into þe pitt of hell and neu*er* efter apperyd.

Sacerdos malus tempestate perit. Inf*r*a de tempestate.

Sacerdotis[1] co*n*cubina punitur. Sup*r*a de luxuria, iij.

DCXCIII.

Sacietas. Saciari no*n* potest cor humanu*m*.

Say*n*t[2] Barnard sayd & tellis; "Som tyme," he sayd, "I saw v men whilk I cuthe not say bod at þai wer fond, for þe furste wald eate no meate bod gravell of þe se, and þe secund of þai*m* had a curage to fele all man*er* of yll savyr, and þe thrid wald stand be a byrnyng ovyn & evur gape to take in his mouthe þe byrnyng sparkis. And þe iiij wold sytt vppon þe pynacle of þe temple, and eu*er* gape agayn þe weddur. And þe v of þai*m* wolde luke behynd hym & scorn his felas, and yit he was more to be skornyd þan þai, for *with* all his myght he laburd to sowke his awn flessh & he wolde neu*er* nowder putt his arm nor his hand[3] vnto his mouthe. And in þai*m* all I cowde fynd no reson, bod at he be my consayte had suffred a passand hu[*n*]ggre, mor þan any of þe toder."

DCXCIV.

Sacramentu*m* altaris devote celebranti qu*andoque* apparet in sp*e*c*ie* pueri.

Cesarius tellis how som tyme þ*er* was a monke of Ceustus ordur, and vppon þe yole day he sayd mes at a privay altar *with* grete

[1] MS. Sacerdos. [2] MS. Saynd. [3] hand *written over* mouthe, *erased*.

deuocion and wepyng of teris. And when he had made his consecracion, he cuthe not se þe sac*r*ament in kynd of bread, bod in lyknes of a yong childe þat was passand fayr. & he keste suche a luff þ*er*-vnto & was so gretele delytid *with* þe fayrnes þ*er*-of, at he halsid it and kissid it *with* a grete dilectation. So at þe laste he was ferd at þai at stude aboute hym sulde thynke lang, and he layd it down on þe corprax, & he p*ro*cedid in þe wurd*is* of þe sac*r*ament aft*er* þe form. And it turned agayn into þe substance of þe sac*r*ament, and þan *with* grete ioy he p*er*formyd & fulfyllid furth his mes.

DCXCV.

Sacramentu*m* honorauerun*t* apes.

Cesarius tellis how som tyme þ*er* was a wom*m*an þat had many beis, & oft sithes þai dyed opon hur. So þ*er* was ane þat cownceld hur at sho sulde gett þe sacrament and lay in þe hyfe emang*is* þai*m*. So on a day sho went vnto þe kurk and shrafe hur, & fenyd at sho wolde be howseld, and so sho was. And onone as sho was howseld of þe prestis hand, whils he turnyd hym vnto þe altar, sho *with*drew þe sac*r*ament oute of hir mouthe & had it hame & laid it emang hur[1] beis. And onone þai knew þ*er* Maker, & *with* þ*er* wark in þe hyfe þai made a little chapell & þ*er*-in þai made ane altare, and abon þis altar þai layde þe sac*r*ament, and afterward fro thens furth þai encresid gretelie. So on a tyme þis wom*m*an oppynd þe hyfe, and fande þe wallis, þe wyndows, þe rufe & þe steple, þe duris & þe altar of þis chapell, all made be beis as þai wurke. And sho went and shewid it vnto þe preste & vnto hyr neghburs, and þe preste sersyd what was þ*er*in, & fand þe sac*r*ament. And he & all his p*ar*isshyn *with* greate ioy & mirthe[2] had it vnto þe kurk. And þe wom*m*an grawntid hur syn & was shrevyn agayn, and reseyvid þe same sacrament.

Sacramento p*ossu*nt adaptari multa que dicu*n*tur *supra* de sac*er*dote, eukaristia, com*m*unione, et cibo sp*iri*tuali.

[1] MS. his.

[2] MS. *repeats*, & ioy.

Sacra scriptura. Infra de sciencia *et* supra de Andrea, i.

Sacrista ecclesiam *et* res ecclesiasticas legitime debet custodire. Infra de silencio, iiij.

Sacriste absentis officium supplet beata virgo deuote. Supra de beata Maria, vij.

Salutacio Marie multipliciter valet. Supra de ave Maria, annunciacione dominica, et Maria, ac alijs locis diuersis.

Sancti aliquando accusant malos. Supra de episcopo, ij, *et* de archidiacono, *et* de elemosina, xv.

Sanctis non est obloquendum. Supra de blasfemia, iij.

Sanctis *eciam* bruta reuerenciam exhibent. Supra de obediencia.

Sancti se vindicare nolunt. Infra de vindicta, iij[1].

DCXCVI.

Sancta vasa *et* vestes semper munde debent tractari.

We rede in 'Legend Lombardica,' how Julianus Apostata on a tyme, at Antioche, gadurd samen halud vessell & halud clothis, and keste þaim samen & sett hym down vppon þaim and dispisid þaim *with* grete reprofe. And onone in þase placis he was so strekyn als fer as þai tuchid hym, þat als lang as he liffid after, wormes & mawkis bred in his flessh & eate it away. And of þat passion, ewhils he liffid, he mot neuer be delyverd. So afterward þer was ane þat hight Julianus also, þat was his stewerd, and be commandment of þe emperour he tuke þies halod vessell & pyssid in þaim & sayd; "Lo! þies vessell in þe whilk þe Son of Marie was sacrificed, now I pis in þaim[2]." And *with* þat sodanlie his mouthe was turnyd into his ars, & efter euer whils

[1] MS. iiij. [2] MS. *þeraim*.

he liffid, all þe filthe and þe degestion of his bodie come out at his mouthe, & noght at his nache.

Sanitas. Sanitate*m* recupe*r*ant aliqui miraculose. S*upr*a Dom*ini*ci, iij, *et* inf*r*a de voto, ij.

Sapiens tempore op[*p*]ortuno de n*e*cce*ssar*ijs sibi p*ro*videt. Su*pr*a de p*ro*videncia.

Sapientis est loco *et* tempore timere. Inf*r*a de timore, i.

Sapiencie possu*n*t adaptari multa que dicuntur su*pr*a de cautela, de consilio, *et* de pl*u*rib*us* alijs in diue*r*sis locis, *et* infra de studio.

DCXCVII.

Satisfaccio. Satisfacit viuus p*ro* mortuo.

We rede in 'Legenda Lomb*ardica*,' how som tyme þ*er* was a wom*m*an þat was a grete synner, to so mekull at sho had done homage vnto þe devull. And when tyme drew nere at sho sulde dye, hur son cownceld hur to be shrevyn. And sho answerd hym & sayd þat shrufte mot not p*ro*fett hur; not-w*ith*-stondyng he laburd hur so att sho g*r*antid, & bad hym feche þe preste. Bod or þe p*re*ste come, þ*er* apperid vnto hur many fendis, þurgh vgsomnes & drede of þe whilke sho dyed. And when hur son come agayn & fande sho was dead, he made mekull sorow, for he knew hur syn eu*ere* dele. And he went & shrafe hym of þat syn at sho had done, & did þ*er*-for vij wynter penance. And þat done, his moder apperid vnto hym & thankid hym, & tolde hym how þat þurgh his penance-doyng sho was delyverd out of payn.

Satisfaciend*um* est leso. Sup*ra* de agro, ij.

Satisfacit *eciam* vnus p*ro* alio. S*upr*a de obligacione.

Scandalu*m* est vitand*um*. Sup*r*a de abscondere.

DCXCVIII.

Sciencia sacre scripture op*er*e debet impleri.

We rede in 'Vitis P*atrum*' how when þe abbott Pambo was vnletterd, he went vnto a man þat was letterd and prayed hym to lern hym a salme. And when he had lernyd hym þe furste vers of þis salme, 'Dixi custodiam vias meas,' he wolde not lern þe secund vers nor no mor þ*er*of, bod sayd; 'Satis est,' it was enogh. "For," he said, "and I may fulfyll þis, it sufficies me." So afterwarde he was axkid of his maister whi he come not at hym ans in sex monethis, and he ansswerd agayn & said; "I hafe not yit fulfyllid þat wurde in dede." So long aft*er* he was axkid if he had fulfillid it, and he ansswerd agayn & sayd; "I hafe liffid þis xliiij yeris, and yit vnnethis I can fulfyll itt."

DCXCIX.

Sciencia *eciam* aliqu*ando* p*ro*curacione demonis [1] acquiritur.

Cesarius tellis how som tyme þ*er* was a scoler of Paryssh, & he had a dull witt and a forgettyll mynde, so þat he cuthe nothyng nowder lern nor holde. And evur-ilk man skornyd hym & callid hym idiott, and herfor he was passynglie confusid, so þat þe devull apperid vnto hym and axkid hym if he wulde do hym homage, and he sulde hight hym all man*er* of con*n*yng. And þis scolar wolde not, bod forsuke hym. And þan þe devull put a stane in his hand & sayde vnto hym; "Als lang as þou holdis þis stane in þi hand, þou sall know all man*er* of thyng." And *with* þat he rase & went into þe scule. And onone he put oute questions, & concludid all þat evur was in þe scule. And evur-ilk man had m*er*vell how þis idiott shulde hafe suche con*n*yng, and he wolde tell þe cauce vnto no man. So not lang after, hym happend fall seke, and of all þis he shrafe hym, & he keste away þe stane and þis dessayvable connyng to-gedur. And when he was dead

[1] So Latin MSS. The English MS. *has*, mentis.

and prestis and clerkis sang salmys aboute hym̄, devuls tuke his saule, an[*d on*] þe to syde of a vayle alƚ of burntstone þai playd' þ*er*wit*h* as wha played at þe fandyng of þe hand-balƚ our þis dale, and on̄ þe toder syde of þe valley oder fendis clekid' it wit*h* þer sharpe naylis; & þis passid' alƚ man*er* of oþ*er* paynys. Neu*er*-þe-les at þe laste, our Lorde had bene m*er*cyfulƚ of[1] hym̄ becauce he was deseyvid', and his saule was put vnto þe bodie. & sodanlie he rase, & alƚ þat was aboute hym̄ fled. And he come done of þe bere and went & made hym̄ a monk in Ceustus ordur, and þ*er* he turment hym̄ selfe wit*h* harde penance als lang as he liffid'.

DCC.

Sciencia nigromancie[2] est mors an*im*e.

Cesarius tellis of ij yong men̄ þat was at Tholence, & þ*er* þai studid' in nygramancye. So þe tane of þai*m* happend' to falƚ seke, bown̄ to dye, and þe toder prayed' hym̄ þat wit*h*-in xx dayes aft*er* his dissese he wold' apere vnto hym̄, & latt hym̄ witt how it stude wit*h* hym̄. And he grawntid', & he mot be suffred þ*er*to, wit*h* gude wilƚ, and þan̄ he dyed'. And wit*h*-in þe tearm̄ he apperid' vnto his felow, and he axkid' hym̄ of his estate. And he answerd' hym̄ agayn̄ & sayd'; "Wo is me, for I am̄ [*dampnyd*][3] for þe con*n*yng of dialetykk þat I lernyd'. And þ*er*for," he said', "I councelƚ þe att þou lefe itt." And he agreid' & did' aftur his cowncelƚ, and lefte hitt & made hym̄ a monk in Ceustus ordur, & þ*er* he liffid' alƚ his lyffe.

DCCI.

Sciencia nigromantica penas inferni videre facit.

Cesarius tellis of one Lodowicus at was þe son̄ of Lowis, Lant-grauius Thuringie[4], and he covett greteli to know how it stude wit*h* þe saule of his fadur. And he promytt a grete reward' vnto

[1] *After* of, our, *erased.*
[2] MS. nigramancie.
[3] Latin, 'Ve mi*hi*, dampn*atus* sum.'
[4] MS. latograuii Thiringie.

hym þat cuthe tell hym any thyng how it stude *with* his fadur at was decesid; & tell hym gude tythand*is* of hym. So þ*er* was a knyght at hard tell here-off, and he had a brud*er* þat was a nygromansyer, and he tolde hym here-of and bad hym do his labur herein. So he went vnto his crafte & callid vp a devull, and garte hym bere hym vnto hell. & þ*er* he saw many vgsom turment and many dyvers kyndes of paynys. And þ*er* he saw a fend sytt apon þe cou*er*yng of þe pitt, and when þe cou*er*yng was takyn of þe pytt, onone a trumpe all of fyre come oute of þe pytt, and made such a noyce at þe clerk went at all þis werld had bene at an end[1]. And þan he saw ascende oute of þe pytt flawmes of fyre all like burnston. And emang þai*m* he saw com vp þis Lowis Latog*ra*uius, & he put furth his hand vnto þe clerk & sayd; "I am her, þis wriched Lowys, som tyme lorde of þe cete. And now þou seis wele myne astate. Bod & my childer wolde restore agayn suche possessions, whilk when I liffid I tuke fro suche kurkis, þai myght do me grete remedie, and þat þou sall tell þai*m* be suche takens." And þis done, he went into þe pitt agayn. And þe clerk was broght agayn whik, neu*er*-þe-les he was pale & passand seke, and he teld þe fadurs sayingi*s* & þe tokyns vn-to his childer. And þai tuke it to no fors, nor wolde nott restore þe possessions agayn. & so it is to suppose þ*er* fadur saule abydis þurgh þ*er* necligens in p*er*petuall dampnacion.

Seculi ph*ilosoph*i. Infra de silencio.

Secretu*m* debet celari. Sup*ra* de celac*ione*.

Senex assuetus malis vix illa dim*i*ttit. Sup*ra* de Andrea.

DCCII.

Sepulture no*n* debent indifferent*er* in eccl*es*ia fieri.

Saynt Gregur tellis how som tyme þ*er* was a bisshop þat grawntid a place of beriall in þe kurk vnto a riche man þat hight Valerius Pat*ri*cius, þat was a synn*er* of his bodie. And vppon þe same nyght Saynt Faustyn, in whase kurk þis was done,

[1] MS. a nend.

apperid vnto þe keper of þe [1] kurk & said vnto hym; "Go & say vnto þe bisshop þat he caste oute yone stynkand flessh oute of my kurk, or els he sall dye *with*-in xxx[ti] dayes." And he had grete drede þ*er*off for to do itt, & wolde not do it. Vppon þe xxx[ti] day he went to bed in wharte & heall, & on þe morn he was fon dead in his bed sodanlie. Also Valentin*us* þat wont in Melayn, when he was berid in þe kurk of Saynt Sixtus, aboute mydnyght in þe same kurk was hard voyces and cryes, as þ*er* had bene men [2] at had bene drawn oute þ*er* agayn þ*er* wyll; vnto þe whilk voycis þe kepers of þe kurk ran, and saw ij vglie [3] þat band þis Valentyne fete, and *with* a grete noyce þai drew hym oute. And on þe morn þai soght for hym & þai fand his bodie *with*-oute þe kurk, casten in a fowle dyke, and his fete bathe bon sam*en* as þai saw hym drawen oute of his grafe.

Sepeliu*n*tur aliqui a Chr*isto*. Sup*ra* de Martha *et* Martino.

Sepultura in eccl*es*iam non impedit q*u*in ib*ide*m sepulti puni*a*ntur. Supra de locutione [4], iij.

Sepeliri debet in sterquilinio religiosus p*ro*p*r*ietarius. Su*pra* de p*ro*p*r*ietario, ij.

DCCIII.

Sepultura in eccl*es*ia*m* qu*ando*q*ue* paru*m* p*ro*dest.

Saynt Gregur tellis how som tyme þ*er* was ane yll man berid in Saynt Laurence kurk at Rome. And þ*er* was hard voyces com*man*d oute of his grafe, sayand; "Ardeo! ardeo! I burn! I burn!" And his wyfe, when sho hard tell of þis, garte oppyn his grafe & lukid what was þ*er*in; & þai fand þe clothis at he was wappid in, bod his body was clene away.

[1] *After* þe, keper, *erased.*
[2] MS. a men.
[3] Latin, duos det*er*rimos *specie*.
[4] *Reference from* Latin MSS.

DCCIV.

Sepeliri non debent vsurarij in claustris religiosor*um*.

We rede of ane archbysshop[1] þat hight Bysmytinus, at was a maist*er* of dyvynitie, and he tellis how on a tyme when þ*er* was ane vsurar berid in þe cloystur of ane abbay, he went oute of his grafe on þe nyght & cryed & mayd grete noyce, & threw of þe thakk of þ*er* dortur, & fure fule *with* þe monk*is* & flayed þai*m* & did mekull skathe. & on þe morn his bodie was fon *with*-oute þe cetie, and it was broght agayn & putt into þe grafe. Neu*er*-þe-les he did oft sithis as he did befor. So at þe laste, a holie man coniurid hym, & bad hym tell hym why[2] þat he wulde not suffre hym nor þe monk*is* to hafe no reste. And he answerd agayn & sayd; "It is of me in despayr, ffor as *with* myne vsuris I grevud God bothe day & nyght, right so I may hafe no reste nowder day nor nyght. Bod ye may be in gude reste and ye wold bere my bodie oute of your closter." And so þai did, and þai war nevur aft*er* grevid nor hard mar of hym.

DCCV.

Sepeliri non debet vsurarius nisi sub patibulo.

Iacobus de Vet*ri*aco tellis how som tyme þ*er* was ane vsurar þat wolde neu*er* restore his vsurie agayn, þuff all he war oft movid þ*er*to. So hym happend to fall seke & bown to dye, and callid þe preste & askid his sacramentis; and þe preste said he wulde gyff hym no sacrament bod if he restorid agayn his vsurie, and he wulde nott So þe preste went away from hym and his sekenes incresid on hym, and he was bown to dy. & þe preste come, and þai at warr aboute prayed hym to commend his sawle vnto almyghtie God, and he a[*n*]sswe[*r*]d agayn & sayd, evyn when he was in

[1] Arund. MS. arch*i*episcop*us* Bisuntinus.

[2] why, *omitted and added above the line.*

passyng; "I com*m*end his saule vnto all þe devuls in hell." And when he was dead, his frendis p*r*ayed þe preste at he mot be berid in som noke or som entre of þe kurk-garth, becauce of þ*er* honestie; and þe preste denyed þai*m* & wolde nott. And þis preste had ane ass þat did nothyng on dayes bod caryd bukis & vestementi*s* fro þe prestis howse into the kurk, and fro thens home agayn. And sho cuthe go no noder way bod vnto þe kurk & fro þe kurk. So þis mans frendis prayed þe preste at his bodie mot be layd vppon þe ass, and to what place som-evur at þe ass bare hym, at þ*er* he sulde be berid; and þe preste grawntid. & þai made a full bargan, trowyng at þe ass wold owder bere hym vnto þe kurk or els vnto þe prestis chawm*er*, becauce sho cuthe none oder way. And when his bodye was layd vppon þis ass, sho nowder declynyd vnto þe right hande nor þe lefte hand, bod bare hym evyn st[*r*]eght vnto þe galows, & evyn vndernethe þe galows sho shuke hym down. And þ*er* he was berid in sepultura p*atrum* suor*um*.

Sequela. Sequi plures no*n* semp*er* expedit. Sup*ra* de societate, iij.

Sermo. Sermone*m* audire impedit demon. Su*pra* de auditu.

Sermoni possu*n*t adaptari multa que dicuntur su*pra* de doctore, locucione, predicatore, et infra de v*er*bo.

DCCVI.

Serpens. Serpenti comp*ar*atur nequicia aliquor*um*.

Petrus Alphonsi*s*[1] on a tyme as he went be a wud-syde tellis how þat he fand a s*er*pent slayn wi*th* hurdmen, & bon vnto a stokk; and he lowsid hur becauce sho was som-what on lyfe, & layd hur þ*er* sho mot fele warmenes of þe son. And so when sho was a lytyll warmyd, sho crope aboute hym, and at þe laste sho tanged hym hugelie. And þan he said vnto hur; "What dois

[1] MS. Petrus Alphensi*s*.

þou? þou dose me ill for gude, and whi duse þou so?" And þe *ser*pent answerd hym agayn & said; "I do not bod my kynd." And *with* þat sho clappid hur faste aboute his legg. And he wold hafe had hur of & sho wold nott. And so, be þ*er* bother assent, þai callid vnto þai*m* a fox to gyff a iugemend wheder sho sulde lowse of his legg or nay. And þey told hym all þe matir how it happend. Than þe fox sayd; "In þis cauce I can gyff no dome be heryng, bod if I se at myne ee how it was *with* you bothe at your furste metyng." So þis serpend lowsid, & onone sho was bon vnto þe stokk agayn as he fand hur. And þan þe fox gaff his iugement & sayd; "O þou *ser*pent! & þou may now esskape, go þi wayes! And þou man!" he sayd, "I owncell þe not labur no mor to lowse hur."

DCCVII.

Seruiciu*m*. Seruire Deo est vtile.

We rede in 'Libro de Dono Timoris' how som tyme þ*er* was a kyng þat had a baillay, & he servid hym alway trewlie. So on a tyme hym happend fall seke, and þe kyng come & visit hym & offerd hym þat what þing at he wold aske, he sulde hafe it. And he answerd agayn & sayd; "I wulde beseke you at ye wulde delyver me of þis sekenes, for I am gretlie turment þ*er*-*with*." And þe kyng answerd hym agayn & sayd þat he wold do it *with* gude will and he myght, bod he sayd þat he myght nott. Than þe seke man answerd agayn & sayd; "Sen ye may not delyver me of my sekenes, here I promytt to Hym þat may delyver me, þat & He will delyver me þ*er*of, ffrom hens furth I shall seryff Hym alone, & nevur no man." And onone he coverd & tuke hym to þe *ser*ves of almyghti God, & wold nevur seruff man aft*er*.

Seruilis timor iniciu*m* est boni. Inf*ra* de timore *et* voto.

Seu*er*itas. Seuerus iudex. Sup*ra* de iudice, iij.

DCCVIII.

Signu*m*. Signis evidentib*us* aliqu*ando* impedit Deus malos vt non compleant quod ceperu*n*t.

We rede how Iulianus Apostata in dispite of *cris*ten men garte þe Iewis repayre and belde agayn ane olde temple, & gaff þai*m* grete gudis to þe bigyng þ*er*-of. And when þai had bygyd vp a grete dele þ*er*off wi*th* lyme and stone, sodanly þ*er* come a grete wynd & blew all down, and eft*er* þat þ*er* come ane erde-quake & shuke down þe reuersyon; & þan þ*er* come a fyre evyn oute of þe grond, & not alonelie burnyd itt, bod also all þai*m* þat come nere it. And þan, wi*th*-in a day or ij aft*er*, þ*er* apperid in þe ayre a syngne of þe cros. And sodanlie all þe Iewis clothis wer fyllid wi*th* blak crossis.

Signa plura *et* diue*r*soru*m* signoru*m* narraci*o*nes inuenies in libello de mirabilib*us* reb*us et* eventib*us*, que*m* deo auxiliante intendo co*m*pilare.

Signu*m* crucis. Supra de cruce.

DCCIX.

Silenciu*m* tenere est assu[*esc*]endu*m*.

We rede in '*Vitis Patrum*' how abbot Agothen bare in his mouthe iij yere a stone vn[to] he was lernyd to be styll and sylent. Also þ*er* was a noder bruder þat when he entred into religion sayd vnto hym selfe; "Thow & ane ass be bothe as one; ffor as ane as is betin & wyll not speke, and suffers wrang and answers not, right so sall þou bee; ffor & þou war putt fro þe burde, þou sulde not answer."

DCCX.

Silenciu*m* aliqu*ando* aliquis impon*i*t sibi in penam.

We rede in þe '*Life of Secundus Philosophus*,' how þat on a tyme when he was a child and went vnto þe skule, and hard tell þat evur-ilk womman was incontynent, when he was p*er*fite in philosophye he went home in-to his awn contre like as he had bene a pylgrem, wi*th* a skrypp & a staff. And his hare of his head & his berd war growen long. So he was hostid in his moder hows, and nowd*er* sho nor none of þe howshold kend hym. And he thoght he wolde prufe if it wer trew þat was sayd of wom*m*en, and he hight one of þe maydens x nobles to make hym to lye be his moder. And sho grawntyd vnto hym & his moder bothe. So at evyn he was broght in, and þai went to bed sam*en*. And sho trowid he sulde [hafe][1] had at do wi*th* hur, and when þai war in bed he halsid hur in his armys as a chylde sulde do þe moder, & lay styll & his breste vnto hurs all þe nyght & slepid. And when it was morn he rase, and his moder sayd vnto hym; "Wharto haste þou þus attempid me?" And he answerd agayn & sayde; "Nay, moder! It is not wurthi to me to fyle þat vessell at I come oute off, ffor I am Secundus, þi son." And when sho hard þis, sho was so confusid at sho mot not suffre it, bod fell in a deade swownyng & spak neu*er* wurd after. So þis Sec*un*dus, when he saw sho was dead, he vnderstude þat his wurdi*s* was cauce þ*er*off, and he kepid sylens & wolde not speke. So on a tyme aft*er*-ward, hym happend sodanlie to mete þe emp*er*our and he hailsid hym, & he wold not speke agayn. So þe emp*er*our com*m*awndid becauce he wold not speke, at his hede sulde be smyten of, and delyu*er*d hym vnto a man-wheller, and com*m*andid hym to labur hym be þe way to luke if he cuthe gar hym speke. And if he spak, he bad hym smyte of his head, & if he wolde not speke, he bad hym latt hym goo. And þis man-wheller said vnto hym as he went; "O, þou Sec*un*dus! Whi will þou dye? Speke, and þou mon liff." So he sett noght be his lyfe, bod bade vppon his dead and layd hym down & putt furth his nekk, redie to be hedid. And þis done, þe manwheller broght hym agayn vnto þe emp*er*our, and tolde hym how þat, vnto dye þ*er*for, he wold nevur speke wurd.

Silenciu*m* qu*and*oq*ue* venditur. Sup*r*a de aduocatis.

[1] MS. he.

DCCXI.

Silencium tenere debent religiosi.

Saynt Ierom tellis & says; "I saw Saynt Theon sparrid in a cell, solitarie, as it was sayd, xxx[ti] yere, and evur he kepid sylens." And of hym writis Socrates & says; "Theonas, þe fadur of iij ml monkys, at was moste connyng in *lettres* of grew & latyn, xxx[ti] yeris spak nevur wurde, savyng in his prayers."

DCCXII.

Silencium strictissimum tenere debent religiosi.

We rede of Zenocrates þe philosophur, how on a tyme as he satt talkand *with* oder folk, sodanlie he held his tong & wold not answer þai*m*. And when þai axkid hym whi he wolde not speke [1], he answerd agayn & sayd; "Som tyme me hase forthoght þat I spak, bod neu*er* þat I held my tong."

Also we rede in 'Vitis P*atrum*' how þat one alde monk kepid a passand strayte sylence. And on a tyme when þ*er* come vnto hym a man of grete auctoritie, þe brethir prayed hym at he sulde putt vnto hym som gude thyng for edificacion of his sawle. [*& he answerd again & said*] [2], "And he be not amendid be my silence, he may not be amendid be my wurd."

Also Guill*el*m*us* tellis how som tyme þ*er* was ane erle in Normondie þat was passand deuote vnto almiȝtty God. And he vsid oft sithis to vissit a kurk of monkis. So on a tyme he come tymelie on a nyght in a meke habett, and I can not say be whatt crafte, bod he gatt into þe kurk. And þe sacristan, trowyng at he had bene a thefe, bett hym & putt hym oute of þe kurk. And in þe mornyng, þe erle come into þe chapitur howse emang þe monkis, & com*m*endid þis sacristan becauce he was so diligent in his offes, & at he sparid hym not when he come at inordinatt tyme. And fro thens furth þis erle was so diligent in his offes & his prayers, at þ*er* myght none grevans lett his silens.

[1] MS. spele. [2] *The Latin version has the usual preface:* qui ait.

DCCXIII.

Siluestri confessoris.

We rede in his Legent how Constantyne þe emperour was made lepre, and þurgh cowncell of a bisshop [1] þer was iij Ml childer broght vnto Rome to be slayn, at he mot be bathed in þer warm blude & so be made hale. And when he saw þe moders of þies childer, shewand hym þer brestis & pulland of þer hare, & wepand befor hym, he made sorow & sayd; "How sulde I vse þis wykkid bath? It is bettur to me to dye for þe heale of þies innocentis, þan for to requovir my life for þer deade." And *with* þat he com*mandid* þe childer agayn to be delyverd vnto þer moders, and giff þai*m* grete giftis also. And vppon þat same nyght, Saynt Petur apperid vnto hym and Saynt Paule, & sayd vnto hym; "Becauce þou vggid to sla so mych innocent blude, our Lord Iesu Cryste sent vs to giff þe cowncell how þou sal be helid. Thow sall call Siluester þe bisshop [2] vnto the, & here hym, and þou sall be curid." And he garte call hym, & tolde hym all hys vision. And so Siluester told hym at þase goddis at he wurshuppid was no goddis, bod þe *servandis* of goddis, as þe son & þe mone, *et cetera*. And he shewid hym þer ymagis, at he mott verelie know what þai wer. And þus he was enformyd in þe fayth and cristend. And when he come oute of þe watir of baptym, he was clene of his lepre. And a grete shynyng was our hym, to so mekull as he said he saw almighti God; & þan he gaff mekull privalege vnto þe kurk.

DCCXIV.

Simia. Simie pecc*ato*r assimilatur.

We rede in 'Libro de Dono Timoris,' how þe pro*purtie* of þe ape is to hafe ij whelpis; & when þe hunter com*mys* & pursewis hur, sho takis þat at sho luffis bettur in hur armys, & þe toder lepis vp on hur bakk. And when þe hunter sewis hur sore, sho levis þat at is in hur armys & lattis it fall, & þe toder clevis still by hur.

[1] Latin, de consilio pontificis. [2] Latin, episcopus.

DCCXV.

Simon Magus.

Saynt Leo þe pope tellis how on̄ a tyme as Symon̄ stude befor̄ Nero, his shap̄ turnyd sodanlie, & now he semyd̄ one olde man̄ & now a yong man̄. And herefor Nero trowid̄ þat he had bene þe son̄ of God̄. So on̄ a tyme þis Symon̄ sayd̄ vnto Nero; "Becauce at þou shall verelie know at I am̄ Goddis son, command̄ my head̄ to be smytyn̄ of, & on̄ þe iij day I sall rice fro deade vnto life." And so it was. & when̄ þe turmetur trowid̄ þat he had smytyn̄ of his head̄, he strake of the head of a weddur, & hid̄ it & held̄ hym̄ away iij dayes at he was not sene. And þe weddur blude lay styll in a cake. And on̄ þe iij day he *pre*sent hym̄ vnto Nero, & bad hym̄ gar gedur vp his blude, for he þat was hedid̄ was ressyn̄ fro dead̄ vnto lyfe agayn̄ as he made his *pro*mys. And when̄ Nero saw hym̄ he had grete m*er*vayle, and trowid̄ at he had bene þe verray son̄ of God̄. So afterward̄ on̄ a tyme when̄ he was wit*h* Nero in a chawm*er*, a fend̄ in his lyknes spakk wit*h*-oute vnto þe peple. Bod when̄ Saynt Petur come, he vndid̄ all his crafte; and when̄ he was fleand̄ in þe ayr, þurgh his *pra*yer he made hym̄ to fall, & brak evure bone[1] of hym̄.

DCCXVI.

Simonia. Simoniace nullus debet elegi.

Cesarius tellis how on̄ a tyme when̄ þai sulde chese a new abbott at þe abbay of Saynt Denys in Fraunce, þe *pri*our of þe same monasterie come vnto þe kyng of France, & gaff hym̄ l li*bras*, & *pra*yed hym̄ to vuchesafe favur his *par*tie. And þe kyng wold̄ beheste hym̄ no thyng, bod tuke þe money & made hym̄ in a hope, & betuke þis money vnto his chamberlayn̄. So þe selerer of þe place wyste not of þis, nor þe thresurar nowder, and ather of þai*m*

[1] MS. evur ebone.

come vnto þe kyng & broght hym a grete som of gold & prayed hym favur þai*m*. & he tuke þe mony evure dele [1]. And when þe day come at þe abbott sulde be choseyn on, and þe kyng satt in þe chapytur-hows, and þies iij abade of þe kynges reward, þe kyng was war of a gude innocent monke, syttand in þe hyrn of þe chapitre. And he callid hym vnto hym and made hym abbott. And he excusid hym faste & wolde nott hafe bene, and alegid many thyng*is*. And emang oþ*er* þing*is* he alegid at þe abbay was gretelie endettid, & he was bod a pure man. And wit*h* þat þe kyng smylid, and answerd hym & sayd; "I sall giff þe onone M ɫ pond, and if þou myster I sall len þe als muche, and helpe þe & forther þe in þat I can. And þ*er*for take it on hand boldlie." And so he did, and þe kyng gaff hym þis gude at þai had broght hym. And þus þies symonyers war confusid, & belife þe abbay was wele rewlid and clere oute of dett.

DCCXVII.

Simonia com*m*ittitur sine pecunia.

Cesarius tellis how on a tyme a holie ancres sayd vnto ane abbott of Ceustus ordur, when he spirrid hur whedur it was expedient vnto hym to be abbott or nay, and sho said nay, it was not expedient unto hym to abyde abbott, ffor he entrid þerinto be symonye. And he answerd hur agayn & sayd; "What says þou? Says þou at I have done symonye?" And sho answerd hym agayn & sayd; "When þe day of your eleccion come, þou, desyrand þe abbotshup, went not symeplie as þou was wunte to do, bod þou said vnto þe symeple monk*is* on þis man*er* of wyse; 'It is not our wurshup to chese our abbott wit*h*-oute our abbay,' becauce þou knew þ*er* was none in þe abbay abyll to be abbot bod þou. And þus þou begylid þai*m* & was made abbott." And when he hard þis, he grawntid it & cuthe nott agayn-say it. & þan he gaff vp his abbotshup & become a closter monke.

[1] MS. evur edele.

DCCXVIII.

Simplicitas aliquando p*ro*dest.

Cesarius tellis how som tyme þ*er* was a noble castellan, and he vsid oft sithes to take catell & shepe of a c*er*tayn abbay of Ceustus ordur þ*at* was nere-hand hym. And when þe abbott & dyvers of þe monk*is* prayed hym to lefe, he wolde nott. So on a day he drafe away a grete drafe of þ*er* catell, and þe abbott sent vnto hym a monke þat was bod a symple man, and com*m*aundid hym þat what at evur he mot gett agayn of þis catell, he sulde wi*th*-owten delay resayfe it. So aboute mete-tyme, þis monke come vnto þe castell, and did his message. & þe knyght answerd hym & sayd; "Sur, ye sall furste dyne, & þan I sall gyff you ane answer." And as þe monke sat at meate emang oþ*er* men, he was servid wi*th* flessh as oþ*er* was, and þat largelie. So he vmthoght hym of þe catell of þ*er* abbay, and he ete of þis flessh a grete repaste; and þe knyght & his wyfe behelde hym grathelie. And when þai had dynyd, þis knyght callid þe monke osyde, & axkid hym whi he ete flessh when it was rewle of his ordur þat monk*is* sulde [*not*] ete flessh? And þe monke full mekelie answerd hym agayn & said; "Sur, myne obedyence cawsid me to eat flessh, ffor myne abbot com*m*aundid me þat of our catell at was tane away fro vs, I sulde resayfe agayn what at I mot gett. And I knew wele at þe flessh at was sett befor me was of our catell, and I trow þat I mon nevur requover mare. And þ*er*for in etyng, I resayvid als mekull as I myght." And when þe knyght hard þis, he was somwhat co*m*puncte wi*th* þe monk*is* meke answer, and he callid his men & com*m*aundid at þe monke sulde be restorid of als many catell agayn as evur he had tane fro þai*m*. And also he beheste at fro thens furth he sulde not noy þai*m*, bott rather restore þai*m*. And þe catell was delyverd vnto þe monk, and he went home wi*th* þaim & wi*th* his mesage to-gedur, and tellid þe abbott & þe covent all how he had done. And þai had grete m*er*vell here-off, & thankid God & was full fayn.

DCCXIX.

Simplex aliquando deridetur.

Cesarius tellis how þat som tyme in Colan þer was a chanon at was so symple & so vnconnyng þat he cuthe nott tell no maner of nowmer, nor tell whilk was od whilk was evyn[1], bod at he wald all way cownt ij thynges to-gedur. So on a tyme hym happend be made chanon of þe kechyng, and he had þer many bakon-flikkis in þe balkis. So on a tyme hym happend to tell þaim, and he cuthe no noderways tell, & he cuthe say none oder bod þus; "Lo, þer a baken-flykk & his felagh, and þer a noder bakon-flikk & his felow[2]." And so of all þe toder. So on a tyme one of hys meneya *with*-drew one of þies bakon-flykkis. So on [*a*] tyme afterward, þis chanon come into þe kechyn agayn, and tellid þies bakon-flykkis & fand at þai war od, & ane wantid. And he sayd vnto his menya þer-of, and þai prayed hym be in pease & go vnto his chawmer and þai sulde fynd it wele agayn or þat he come; and so he did. And whils he was away, his meneya *with*drew a noder bakon-flykk, and so þer was evyn behynd as þer was befor. And þan þai callid þer maister & bad hym go luke if he had all his bakon-flikkis, and he come & teld þaim agayn as he was wunte to dco, & fand þai wer evyn. And so he trowed at he had getten his flykkis agayn, & in a grete myrthe he sayde vnto his meneya; "O, ye felows! I mot hafe haldyn my tong & loste my bakyn-flyk." And when his servandis wolde eatt any gude meate, þai wolde threpe vppon hym at he was seke; and he wulde aske þaim whareby þai wyste, & þai wold say, "Yis, Sur, for your haris er passand bolnyd." & þan he wold trow he was seke, & lay hym down on his bedd. And þan þai wold ordand gude metis and gyff hym owder little or noght þeroff, & eate vp þe toder þer selfe.

Simplicitatem deus remunerat. Supra de contricione.

[1] **Harl. MS. vt nichil numerare sciret nisi in quantum res essent pares.**
[2] **MS. flelow.**

Simplicitas aliqu*ando* ad virtutem p*er*tinet. S*upra* de obediencia, xj.

Simulacio. Simulare stultu*m* tempore *et* loco aliqu*ando* expedit. S*upra* de fatuitate.

Singularitas in obseruancijs est aliqu*ando* occasio vane gl*or*ie. Sup*ra* de abstinencia, ij[a].

DCCXX.

Sitire non h*ab*ent aliqui ex co*m*plexione.

Solinus tellis how þ*er* er so*m* þat er so grete of bonys þat þai neu*er* nowder er thrusti nor swetis; and he sais he ca*n* consayve þat be many resons.

Sobrietas. Sobrius debet esse iudex. Sup*ra* de abstinencia, vij.

DCCXXI.

Societas malor*um* fugienda est.

Petrus Alpho*nsus*[1] tellis how o*n* a tyme ij clerk*is* went sam*en* befor a place þ*er* þar was many drynkers, and þai callid þai*m* in. And þe tone of þai*m* went into þai*m*, & þe toder wold nott bod went o*n* hys wais; and it was fer wit*h*-in nyght. So þe wachis of þe tow*n* fande all þies drynkers syttand sam*en*, & þe clerk wit*h* þai*m*, & becauce a ma*n* of þe tow*n* was robbid þat nyght, þai tuke þai*m* all & þe clerk wit*h* þai*m*, & hanged þai*m*. And þe clerke at bade wit*h* þai*m*, or he was hanged, sayd o*n* þis man*er* of wyse; "Quisq*uis* inique gentis consorcio fruitur, p*ro*cul dubio mortis immerite penas luc*ra*tur. What so*m* evur he be at vsis ill company, na dowte of he sall hafe ane ill dead."

DCCXXII.

Socio fatuo vel malo non est adquiescendu*m*.

We rede in 'Libro de D*ono* Ti*moris*' how o*n* a tyme ij brethur went sam*en* be þe way, and þe ton[e] was wyse & þe toder bod

[1] MS. Alphu*nsus*.

a fule. So þai come vnto a gate-shatyll þer þer was ij wa[yis], þat one a fayr way, & þat oþer a fowle way, and þe fule wolde not go be þe fayre way [1]. And þe wise sayd vnto hym; "þis way is bothe fayr & gude, & wuld lede vs to a gude herbarie." And þe toder sayd; "Nay, þis way, þuff all it be fowle & sharpe, yit it w[ill] lede vs vnto a gude herberie; and þerfor I cowncell þe latt vs go here-bye." So þis fule wolde not trow bod þat at he saw, & wold algatis go þe fayr way, and þe wise wold not lefe hym bod felud hym, þuf all it wer agayns his will. So as þai w[ent] samen, thevis mett *with* þaim, and þai garte put þaim in prison. And afterward þe kyng garte bryng befor hym all þat wer in prison. So þies ij war broght befor þe kyng and fell at stryfe befor hym, ffor þe wyse made playnt of þe fule, how þat he wolde not truste on hym of þe way, and þe fule complenyd of þe wyse becauce he folowid hym & wiste he was bod a fule. And þan þe kyng gaf a sentence & bat at þai bothe sulde be hanged, þe fule becauce he wold not trow þe wyse, & þe wise becauce he folowd þe fule.

Socij aliqu*ando* mutuo se decipiunt. S*upra* de decepcione, iiij.

Socius sociu*m* aliqu*ando* ad negandu*m* deu*m* inducit. S*upra* de negacione.

DCCXXIII.

Societatem pluriu*m* non expedit sequi.

We rede in 'Legenda Longabord*ica*' of one Richard, þat was kyng of Freseland, when he sulde be crystend in þe yere of our Lorde CCC, & he had putt þe tone fute in to þe funte [2], he helde þe toder oute, & sayd; "Whar er all þe noble men of my kyn? In hell or in Paradice?" And one tellid hym at þai wer in hell. And when he hard þat, he drew oute his fute of þe funt agayn &

[1] Harl. MS. Voluit fatuus p*er* viam delectabile*m* ire, sapiens aute*m* dixit, "Et si illa via sit delectabil*is*, tame*n* ducit ad malu*m*, alia, vero, lic*et* sit aspera, tame*n* ad bonu*m* hospitiu*m* ducit."

[2] MS. *has another* and *here*.

sayd; "Sanctius est plures quam pauciores sequi. It is more halie to folow many þan few." And þus he was deseyvid be a fend þat promysid hym to gyff hym þat day thrid day ane vnnumerable porcion of gude. And on þe thrid day he dyed sodanlie, & was perpetuallie dampnyd for evur.

DCCXXIV.

Solitudo. Solitudinem multi *propter* deum appetunt.

We rede in 'Vitis *Patrum*' how on a tyme a solitarie went into wyldernes, & he was cled all in a lyn sakk alone. And when he had walkid þerin iij dayes, he stude vp apon a grete stone, and he was war vndernethe it of a man fedand hym of grene *her*bis as it had bene a beste. And he went down privalie & gatt hym & held hym, and þis olde man was nakid & myght not suffre þe odur of a man, and gatt fro hym & ran away als faste as he myght. And þe toder ran af*ter* hym & cryed; "Abyde, & lat me speke *with* þe!" So he abade & spak *with* hym[1], and when þai come nere sam*en*, þe olde man bade & askid hym whatt he wolde. And he sayd; "Fadur, I pray þe, tell me a wurd at I may be savid bye!" And he answerd hym agayn & sayd; "Fle mans felowschupp & be still, & þou sall be safe."

Solitudo quietem a*nime et con*sciencie facit. Sup*ra* de quiete, i.

DCCXXV.

Solitudi*n*em elig*er*e inspiratur a deo.

We rede in 'Vitis *Patrum*' of one Arsenius, þat was of moste valow in þe emp*er*ours palas, and he besoght God in his prayers to drys hym into þe way of hele. And a voyce come to hym & sayd; "Fle mans felowshup & þou sall be safe." And so he did. *et c*[9].

[1] MS. *repeats*, and he abayde.

DCCXXVI.

Solitudinem relinquere suggerit [*diabolus*].

We rede in 'Vitis Pat*rum*' how þ*er* was one þat went into wyldernes, and he besoght God to send hym a place þ*er* he wold at he ristid and abade. And so þ*er* come ane agle, & he folud hur, as sho had bene ane aungell, whar þ*er* was a palm, & a well at þe rute þ*er*off. And when he had þ*er* many yeris liffid in penance, & had none od*er* mete bod of þe frute of þe palm & drynk of þe well, þe devull had envy at hym, & he come vnto hym in lyknes of a messanger. And when he had beholden hym grathelie, he sayd vnto hym; "Is not þis he þat I hafe soght? Yis, forsuthe it is he." And so he come to hym & sayd; "I hafe soght þe many day, & I cuthe not fynd þe. Go we home, for þi fadur is dead & þe heritage is happyd vnto þe; and þ*er* wyll many folke feght þ*er*for bod if þou com tytter home, and if þou com þai wull sease. And when þou hase it, þou may, and þou will, deale it for Goddis sake." And he grawntid vnto hym & come home vnto his fadur howse, and fand hym on lyfe. And when he saw þat he was confusid in hym selfe, and abade þ*er* in grete trubble and besynes. And at þe laste he dyed & made a wrechid end.

Solitarius aliquando in pecc*atum* labitur. S*upra* de p*re*su*m*pcione, j.

Solucio. Solui debet debitu*m* *et* p*ro*missu*m*. S*upra* de p*ro*misso.

DCCXXVII.

Sortilegijs no*n* est fides adhibenda.

We rede in 'Libro de Dono Timoris' how þat a wom*ma*n þat vsyd sorcerie happend on a tyme to fall seke and was bown to dye. And hur dogh*ter* cownceld hur to be schrevyn & take hur sac*ra*mentis, and sho wolde not. So hur neghburs come in & cownceld hur þe same, and sho answerd þai*m* agayn & said;

"I mon̄ not dye þus sone." And þai sayd; "Yis, ye er lyke to dye." And sho sayd'; "Nay! I am̄ *certan̄* at I mon̄ liff yit þis v yere." And þai axkid' hur how sho knew þat, and sho ansswerd' agayn̄ & said' þat on̄ þe furste day of Maij þe goke ansswerd' hur & sayd' v tymys, "Cukkow!" And be þat sho sayd sho wiste wele þat sho sulde liff v yere. And þus onone after in þis belefe, *with*-owten̄ any sacrament, sho dyed'. *et* c⁹.

Sortilegium quandoque fit de sacramentis. Supra de sacramento, ij[1].

DCCXXVIII.

Sortilegi puniuntur.

Cesarius tellis how som tyme *þer* was in Englond a wom*m*an[2] þat vsid' sorcerie. And on̄ a day as sho was bown̄ to eatt, sho hard' a craw cry beside hur, and sodanlie þe knyfe þat was in hur hande feƚƚ. & hereby sho demyd' at hur dead' drew nere, & so sho feƚƚ seke, bown̄ to dye. And sho sent af*ter* a monk̄ & a non̄ þat was hur childer, and chargid þai*m* in hur blissyng þat onone as sho war dead' þai sulde sew hur in a harte-skyn̄, & þan̄ at þai sulde close hur in a tombe of stone, and at þai sulde feste þe coveryng *þer*on̄ stronglie bothe *with* lead & strong yrn̄, & at þai sulde close þis stane & bynde it aboute *with* iij strang chynys, and þan̄ at þai sulde do mes & pray for hur aboute hur bodye. And if sho lay so sekurlie iij dayes, þan̄ sho chargid' þai*m* to bery hur vpp[on] þe iiij day in þe erth̄. And so aƚƚ þis was done, and ij furste nyght*is*, as clerkis was sayand' *þer* prayers aboute hur, ffendys brak þe yatis of þe kurk̄, & come in vnto hur & brak ij of þe chynys at was at ather end'; and þe myddyƚƚ chyne abade styƚƚ hale. And vppon̄ þe iij nyght aboute cokkraw, *þer* come in suche a throng of fendis, at þai at saw it semyd' at þe temple turnyd' vpsadown̄. So *þer* come a fend' at was maste vgsom̄ of aƚƚ, & hyer þan̄ any of þe toder was, and he come vnto þis tombe and callid' hur be hur

[1] MS. j.

[2] MS. wom*m*and'.

name & bad hur ryse. And sho answerd agayn & sayde sho mot not for þe bondis at was bon aboute þe tombe. And he bad lowse þai*m*, and onone at his com*m*andment þe chyne braste as it had bene hardis, & þe cou*er*yng of þe tombe flow off. And þ*er* he tuke hur oppynlie befor all men & bare hur oute of þe kurk. And þ*er* befor þe yatis þ*er* was ordand a blak hors, & þ*at* ane vglie, & here-vppon was sho sett. & þan onone sho & all þis felowshup vanysshid away.

DCCXXIX.

Spectacula vana vitanda su*n*t.

Fulgencius tellis how þat Dyogenes, when he wex olde, he was fellie vexid *with* þe fevurs. So on a tyme he sett hym down at a tre-rute in þe son to co*m*furth hym, and when he was gretelie turment *with* þe sekenes, & saw other men go vnto disportis & laykys, he sayd vnto hym selfe; "O! how fonde at men ar now on dayes! Lo! how þai faste ryn to se wonders & men feght, and lukis not aft*er* me þ*at* stryvis *with* so fell a sekenes as I do."

DCCXXX.

Sponsalia contrahuntur p*er* anuli tradicio*n*em.

Guille*lmus* tellis how som tyme at Rome þ*er* was a yong man þ*at* was new wed. So on a tyme as he was playand *with* his felows, he put furth his hand vnto þe ymage of Venus, þat[1] was made of bras, and delyverd hur his weddyng-ryng to kepe to þe play war done. And when þe play was done he come & axkid his ryng agayn, & he fand it on þe ymage fynger & þe fynger cruked into þe luff of hur hand. And he wraystid at hur fynger and he cuthe nott gett of þe ryng nor yit breke hur fynger, so he lete it alone. And on þe nyght aft*er* he come thedur *with* his servand, & he fand hur fynger streght & þe ryng takyn away. And he turnyd agayn & fenyd as hym aylid nott, & went to bed *with* his wife; and as he lay in his bed *with* his wyfe, he feld a blak myrk thyng welter betwix hym & his wyfe, and he mot fele it wele bod he myght noght se itt. And be þis obstacle he was lett fro halsyng

[1] MS. þas.

of his wyfe. And he harde a voyce say vnto hym; "Mecu*m* cc*n*cube: hafe at do *with* me, for þis day þou wed me; ffor I am Venus at þou put þe ryng on þe fynger of, and þ*at* sall þou neu*er* hafe agayn." And so it was a long tyme, and evur when he wold hafe liggen with his wyfe, he bothe felid þis in his bed & hard þe voyce þ*er*off. So on a tyme he tuke his lefe at his wife & his howshold, & wold walk fer oute of contrey. So hym happynd mete *with* a nygromansyer þat hight Palumbus, and he tuke councell at hym. & he wrote hym a *lett*re and delyverd hym it, and bad hym bere it befor hym in his hand vnto he com att þe nexte gateshatyll; and so he did. And agayn evyn he come to a place þ*er* iiij wayes met *samen*, & þer he saw com rydand & on fute a grete pepyll bothe men and wommen, som merie and som hevye. And emang oþ*er* he saw a womman gaylie arayed like a com*mon* wom*man*, and hur clothis war so thyn at he mot se all þat evur sho had; & at þe laste come þe lord of þis co*m*pany & lukid angrelie of þis yong man & axkid hym whatt he did þ*er*. And he, as it was taght hym, wolde gyff no wurde to answer, bod put furth his hand *with* þe letter þ*er*in. And þis fend knew þe seale of þe lettyr & durst not [*scorn it*][1], bod tuke it & red it, & onone he sent a meneya vnto Venus & tuke þis ryng fro hur ayayns hur will. And fro thens forward þis yong man come home & þis ryng *with* hym, & neu*er* after he was lettid to lyg *with* his wyfe nor nevur hard uoyce after.

Sompnus. Infra de vigilia.

Status religionis quo ad personas se h*ab*ent, sicut eximia et excelsa. S*upr*a de religione[2].

Status religi*on*is p*re*fertur statui sec*u*lari. Sup*r*a de co*n*temptu mundi.

Statutu*m*. Statuta supe*r*ior*um* debent ten*er*i. Supra de lege, ij[3].

[1] Harl. MS. Demon, notu*m* sigillu*m* non aude*ns* contempn*ere*, legit script*um*.

[2] Arund. MS. sic*ut* existenc*ia* et excelsa et al*ibi*. Harl. MS. S*upra* existencia et excessa et alibi.

[3] *Exemplum* Lex i *is omitted by the English translator, so the reference should be to* Lex, i.

DCCXXXI.

Stephani P*ro*thomartiris. Steph*an*us infirmos sanat.

Saynt Austyn tellis how on a tyme at Cesaria Capadocie þer was a wurthi womman þat had x sonnys. So on a day sho was gretelie vexid ayayns þai*m*, and gaff þai*m* all hur malyson. And onone þe vengeange of God folowid after, for sodanlie þai all were streken *with* a palcie, & þai waxed so pure at þai wavurd aboute here & þ*er*. And evur whar þai went, ilk man beheld þai*m* and wondred on þai*m*. And of þies x, ij come vnto Yponeus[1], and þ*er* befor ane altar of Saynt Stephan þai war curid.

Steph*an*i corpus co*n*iunctu*m* est corpori Sancti Laurencij. S*upr*a de Laur*encio*, j.

DCCXXXII.

Studiu*m*. Studere debent libent*er* cl*er*ici.

Agellius. Democritus, ph*ilosoph*us, when he was of a moste happy & riche fortun, he went vnto Athenys & lefte all to his frendis, for to by wysdom. And becauce in his mynd he sulde desire none thyng at he saw, he garte putt oute his een at he mott hafe his inward witt*is* mor whik. þuff all Tertullian*us*[2] tell at he garte putte oute his ene becauce he mot not se no womman *with*-outen perell of his chastitie, whilk þat is not contrarie to our entent.

Studiu*m* circa celestia rapit ho*min*em ext*ra* se. S*upr*a Augustini, iij.

DCCXXXIII.

Studendu*m* est amore celestium.

Saynt Gregorie tellis & says; "Anthonye þat dwelte *with* me in a monastarie many yeris, and euerilk day made his prayer

[1] Latin MS. Yponam venientes. [2] MS. Tritullian*us*.

to God *with* gretand teris. So on̄ a tyme when̄ he bethoght hym̄ of halie write, *with* a grete fervent desyre he soght not in þai*m* wurdis of con*n*yng, bod of co*m*punccion̄ & of wepyng, þ*at* his mynde be that mot be stirrid' to co*n*templacion̄ & religion̄ of holie lyfe, and not for to thynk of warldlie thy*n*gys."

Stulticia. Stulto socio no*n* est adquiescendu*m*. S*upr*a de societate, ij.

Stulticie co*n*ueniu*n*t que *supr*a dicu*n*tur de infirmitate.

DCCXXXIV.

Suffragiu*m*. Suffragia *fac*ta a bonis multu*m* vale*n*t.

We rede in 'Legend' Lombard*ica*,' som tyme a knyght þat was dead' apperid' vnto a nodir knyght þat was olife, and sayd vnto hym̄; "Frend', deme none ill of no man̄, and forgyff me if I hafe synnyd' oght agayns þe." And when̄ he axked' hym̄ of his asstate, he ansswerd' agayn̄ & said'; "I am̄ turment *with* dyvers paynys, bod I pray þe gar pray for me." So he axkid' hym̄ if he wold' at suche a preste & suche a preste[1] sulde pray for hym̄. He wold' not ansswer agayn̄, in man*er* as he had refusid' þai*m*, and he shuke his head'. So he axkid' hym̄ if he wolde at suche ane hermett prayed' for hym̄, and he said'; "Ya, walde God at he wolde pray for me." And he promysid' hym̄ at he sulde make hym̄ so to do. And he tolde hym̄ agayn̄ þat he sulde liff to þat day ij yere & þan̄ he sulde dye; & þus he dispayred away. And þe knyght amendid' his lyfe and at þe laste made a gude ende.

DCCXXXV.

Suffragia facta p*ro* defunctis grata su*n*t eis.

Cantor P*a*risienc*is* tellis how on̄ a tyme as a man̄ went aboute þe kurk-garth̄ sayand alway his De Profundis for all cristen̄ sawlis, so on̄ a tyme þis mans enmys sewid' after hym̄ into þe same kurk-

[1] Harl. MS. an a tali *et* tali sac*er*dote, &c.

garth, & he fled thedir. And onone all þe dead men rase, and ilkone of þai*m* a spade in his hand, and manlelie þai defendid hym and made his enmys so ferde at þai fled ichone.

Suffragiu*m* misse sp*iritu*alit*er* mortuis valet. S*upr*a de sace*r*dote.

Suffragiu*m* or*ati*onis *eciam* dampnato p*ro*fuit. S*upr*a de or*ati*one.

DCCXXXVI.

Suffragia non p*ro*su*n*t dampnatis sec*und*u*m* legacionem.

Cesarius tellis how som tyme þ*er* was a p*re*ste þat prayed speciallie *with* grete devocion in his mes & his other p*ra*yers for a prince of Almany þat was dead. And þ*er* apperid vnto hym a c*er*tayn saynt & sayd; "Whi laburs þou so for a man þat is dampned? It p*ro*fett*is* hym no thyng, for his saule is in þe depe pitt of hell." And þe p*re*ste answerd agayn & sayd; "Sur, he hase done me mykyll gude." And þe saynt bad hym sease & pray no mor for hym, for he was deade a yere or he was berid, and a wykkid spirit instead of a sawle nurisshid his body.

Suffragia cu*m* elemosina valent. S*upr*a de elemos*ina*, x.

Suffragia obligatos p*ro* alijs redemu*n*t. S*upr*a de obligac*io*ne.

Suffragia pena*m* debita*m* minuu*n*t. S*upr*a de apostatis.

DCCXXXVII.

Sup*er*bia. Sup*er*bus nec in vita nec in morte pare*m* vult h*ab*ere.

Com*m*estor tellis how when Alexander turnyd agayn into Babylon & his suster had poysond hym, he mot not speke, & herefor he wrate his testament his awn hand. And he wold not bewitt hys kyngdom hale vnto no a man, þat none of þai*m* at come *after* hym sulde be lyke hym in power, bod he made successurs of his kyngdom xij yong men þat had bene in his felowshup fro barn little.

DCCXXXVIII.

Sup*er*bus *eciam per* humilitatem gl*or*iam appetit.

Valerius Publeus [1] tellis how som tyme þ*er* was a cowncelour of Rome, and he luffid the peple so speciallie, vnto so mekull at he was callid to surname Plebicola. And he dwelte in þe m*er*ket-stede, & becauce his howse was hyer þan neghburs, he garte take þai*m* downe & make þaim evyn wit*h* his neghburs [2].

DCCXXXIX.

Sup*er*bia aliqu*ando* oritur ex bonis op*er*ib*us*.

Seuer*us* tellis how som tyme þ*er* was a saynt þat had a grete v*er*tue in castyng oute of ffendis, not alonelie when he was p*re*sent, nor in his awn wurd alone, bod somtyme when he was absent, and somtyme þurgh þe hem of his hare, and somtyme be his l*ett*res-sendyng. & he wulde heale many folk þat war seke, and herefor þurgh all þe wurld þ*er* come vnto hym mekull peple. And as it was sayd, he abstenyd hym bothe fro meat & drynk. Neu*er*-þe-les at þe laste he cachid a pride here-of in his harte, to so mekill þat his v*er*tue faylid in hym, and when he saw þat, he repentid hym & besoght God at he mott be made lyke þai*m* at he had curyd, & at þe fend myght hafe power on hym v monethis. And so it happend, & he was bon, & he did many wondres at all þe contrey spak of hym, how he was correcte wit*h* a fend and bon in bandys. And in þe v moneth he was delyvurd, not alonelie of þe fend, bod of all oþ*er* vanyties þat had behapped hym.

Sup*er*bia op*er*a de gen*er*e bonor*um* destruit. S*upra* de pecc*at*o.

[1] Arund. MS. Val*eriu*s Publi[c]*us*, consul roman*us*, plebe*m* adeo dilexit, &c.

[2] Arundel MS. Ide*m* edes suas in medio foro dirui fecit *quia* nimis excelse *super* cet*er*as app*ar*ebat, *quan*tumcu*m*q*ue* domi inferior tu*m* gloria *superior* euasit.

Superbia quandoque insidiatur bonis operibus ut pereant, sed propter hoc non sunt omittenda. Supra Barnardi, j.

Superbia non debet esse in corde religiosi. Supra de religione.

Superbia in paupere est ei nociua. Supra de paupertate.

Superbus fetet coram deo *et* angelis. Supra de angelo.

Superbiam frequenter sequitur humilitas. Supra de gloria, iij.

DCCXL.

Superbia virtutes adnichilat.

Cesarius tellis how som tyme þer was a man̄ þat was vexid' with a spyritt, and his frendis bad hym̄ vnto a mansyon̄ of Ceustus ordur. And when̄ þe priour[1] come he spak vnto þe fend' at was in hym̄, & sayd'; "Þis monk commandis þe to pas oute of þis man̄, and how dar þou dwell in hym̄ in þis place?" And þe fende answerd & sayd'; "I am̄ not ferde for hym̄ ffor he is prowde, & þat makis me to hafe power on̄ hym̄."

Superbia eciam[2] secularibus displicet. Supra de abbate, x.

Superbia frequenter manifestatur in ornamentis exterioribus. Supra de angelo *et* de ornatu per totum *et* de prodigalitate.

DCCXLI.

Suspicio diligenter examinata est falsa.

Saynt Ierom tellis þat it is wreten̄ in þe bukis of Ypocratis how þer was a man̄ þat þoght his wyfe sulde be punysshid', & suspecte

[1] Latin MSS. egressus prior cum quodam monacho iuuene quem nouerat uirginem corpore, ait demoni; "Si precepit tibi monachus iste ut exeas, quomodo audibis manere?"

[2] MS. in.

hur becauce sho bare a fayr barn at was not like nowder þe fadur nor þe modir. So þai bathe agreid at a leche sulde essone þe question. And a leche come, & he sayd[1] it was like þe clothe at was on the bed when it was getten, & þus þe wom*m*an was delyverd from hur suspecion.

Suspicione mouentur defacili viri ad vxores. S*upra* de p*ul*c*r*itudine.

Suspicio tollit*ur* v*e*l confirmatur p*er* p*ro*bacionem. Supra de Paulo[2].

DCCXLII.

Tactus. Tangi debet mulier nec a sanis nec ab infirmis.

Saynt Gregur tellis how som tyme þ*er* was a p*re*ste, & þ*er* was giffen hym a kurk and he governyd it *with* mekull drede, whilk[3] þat fro he had furste tane ordurs he luffid passynglie p*re*sbit*er*am sua*m*, for in that contre evur-ilk a preste hath a wyfe, bod he fled hur as he wold hafe done pestelens, and wulde not suffre hur com nere hym. And when he had bene xl^ti yere preste, a grete ffevurs tuke hym so þat he was bown to dye & tuke a passion of dead. And when his wyfe saw that, sho made grete sorow & went he had dyed. And sho lenyd down hur mowthe vnto his at luke if any brethe war in hym, and when he felid hur he spak vnto hur & sayd; "Go away fro me, wom*m*an, ffor yit þer is a sparke of lyfe in me, & þ*er*for remefe away þe caff at it burn not!"

Tactus mulieris movet carnem viri. Sup*ra* Leonis pape.

Taxillus. Taxillor*um* ludus displicet deo. Sup*ra* de ludo.

[1] Latin MSS. Ne forte talis pictura esset in cubiculo. Qua inuenta, mulier a suspicione liberata.

[2] *Reference supplied from the* Latin MSS.

[3] Latin MSS. qui ex tempore ordinis suscepti presbiteram suam ut sororem diligens, sed ut pestem fugiens, &c.

Taxillor*um* ludus est aliqu*ando* causa blasfemandi deum. S*upr*a de blasfemia.

DCCXLIII.

Te Deum devote cantantib*us* deuot*us* ympn*us* est.

Cesarius [*tellis*] how þat in Essex [1], in a monasterye of nonnys, þ*er* was a litle damysell, and on a grete solempne nyght hur maistres lete hur com with hur to matyns. So þe damysell was bod a wayke thyng, and hur maistres was ferd at sho sulde take colde, and sho com*m*aundid hur befor Te Deu*m* to go vnto þe dortur to hur bed agayn. And at hur com*m*andment sho went furth of þe where, þuff all it war *with* ill wyll, and abade *with*oute þe where & thoght to here þe residue of matyns. And when þis song, Te Deu*m*, was begon, sho saw hevyn oppyn & all þe quere of þe nonnys lifte vp into hevyn. And when þai come at þis place, "Tibi om*n*es angeli," *et* c9, sho saw all þe ordurs of angels, and evur-ilk angell bow down his head & knele down on his kne & hold vp þ*er* handys and wurshup God & syng *with* þai*m* att sang, "*Sanctus, Sanctus, Sanctus*," *et* c9. And þe same did þe apostels at "Te gl*or*iosus," and þe prophett*is* at "Te prophetar*um*," and þe martyrs at "Te martiru*m*." And afterwerd confessurs and virgyns & all oþ*er* did þe same. And when þai sang þe laste vers, "In te, Dom*in*e, speraui," þe quere of þe susters descendid agayn down vnto þe erth, and hevyn sparryd agayn after þai*m* [2].

DCCXLIV.

Tempestas. Te*m*pestati aliqu*ando* admiscentur demones.

Cesarius tellis how, in þe bisshoppryke of Treuen, on a tyme as a preste þat hyght Henry satt in þe tavern, þ*er* happend a storm & a tempeste in þe ayre, & þat a grete. And he & his clerk ran faste into þe kurk at [3] rang þe [4] bellis, and when þai come at

[1] Latin MSS. In Saxonia.

[2] *A marginal note has*, nota, de Te Deum.

[3] *& erased, and* at *added above.*

[4] MS. *repeats*, þe.

þe kurk-dure, a dynt of þe thondre smate þaim bathe down, so at þe clerk lay vnder-nethe þe preste, & he was nothyng hurte, and all þe preste membrys war all to-swythyn, and all þe tuder partie of his bodie vntuchid; and he was a ffornycatur. And his clothis war so revyn at neuer a pece of thayme was hale with a noder, outtake þat parte on his lefte arme þat his manyple was wunte to hyng on. And he had on a payr of new buttows, and þai wer al to-revyn as þai had bene revyn with fless-crokis, and þe solis war lyke as þai had bene sodden in hate watir. And þe clerk was passand ferd & had grete wonder hereof, and he saw fendis feghtand in þe kurk and ij shrynys þat war behynd þe hie altar fell down on the altar & brak. & þan come þe saynttis at þe relykkis of lay þerin, & withstude stronglie þe fendis, and þer was betwix þe saynttis & þaim a grete batell. So at þe laste þe fendis war ouercommen, & becauce þai mot not bere away with þaim þe prestis bodie, þai tuke a parte with þaim of þe kurk-rufe. Also þe clerk saw þe preste bodie oft sithis born vp to þe steple topp with strenth of fendis; bod thurgh helpe of þe saynttis it was ay broght down agayn.

DCCXLV.

Temptacio. Temptaciones demonum sunt diuerse.

We rede in 'Vitis Patrum' how Macharius þe abbott saw on a tyme þe devyll go in a mans lyknes. And he had on a lyn garment all to-revyn & full off holis, & it hang full of lytyll pottis. And þis abbot axked hym whither he went, and he said he went to giff his brethir a drynk. So he axkid hym wharto he bare so many pottis, and he said; "I bere taste vnto our brether, so þat if a pott please not to any of þaim I sall offer hym a noder, or a thrid, & so in ordur to som please hym." And when he come agayn, þis abbot axkid hym how he had done, and he ansswerd & said; "Þer was none at wulde consente vnto me bod one." So þis abbot rase & went vnto his brethir, & he fande onone þis bruther at was tempid, and with his exhortacion onone he converte hym agayn vnto gude lyfe. So onone afterward þis abbott mett þe devuƚƚ agayn̄ & axkid hym̄ whither he went, and he said he went vnto his brethir. And when̄ he come agayn̄ þis abbot axkid hym̄ how his brethur did. And he sayd, iƚƚ; "for," he sayd, "þai er aƚƚ halie men̄, & ane þat I had emang þai*m*, I hafe loste hym̄, for he is halier þan̄ þai aƚƚ, and þat duse me mekuƚƚ iƚƚ." And when̄ þis alde abbott harde þis he held vp his handis and thankid almightie God.

Temptat demon aliquos visibilit*er*. S*upr*a de Antonio et de q*u*iete, iv[1].

DCCXLVI.

Temptacio est magistra meriti.

We rede in 'Vitis P*atrum*' how on̄ a tyme þe disciple of ane alde monke was gretelie tempid w*ith* þe spirit of fornicacion̄, bod þurgh þe g*r*ace of God, manlelie he w*ith*stude it. And þis monke, when he saw hym̄ so grete labur þ*er*on̄, he sayd vnto hym̄; "Son̄, and þou wiƚƚ, I saƚƚ p*r*ay God to do þis temptacion̄ away fro the." And he answerd agayn̄ & sayd; "Thuf aƚƚ I hafe a grete labur in w*ith*stondyng þ*er*of, yitt I fele frute þ*er*in, ffor it cawsis me to faste & for to wake and giff hede vnto my p*r*ayers. And þ*er*for I p*r*ay þe p*r*ay Almyghtie God to gif me v*er*tue to sustene itt, and for to withstonde it manfullie."

DCCXLVII.

Temptat demon religiosos p*er* formas mulier*um* ymaginatas[2].

We rede in 'Vitis P*atrum*' how som̄ [*tyme*] þ*er* was in a monasterie a monk þat had a son̄. And he was so long nurisshid þ*er* & come not oute, att he knew not whatkyn̄ thyng wom*men̄* was. So when̄ he was wexen̄ vnto mans state, þe devuƚƚ apperid vnto hym̄ in lyknes and clothyng of a wom*man̄*, and he tolde his

[1] MS. iij.

[2] MS. ymaginatinas.

fadur whatt he had sene and axkid hym whatt it was, & he welde not tell hym. So on a tyme he went *with* his fadur into Egypte, and þ*er* he saw womm*en*. And þan he tolde his fadur at þai war swilk at he saw in his abbay in wyldernes, and his fadur had merve*ll* here-of & trowid at it was a disseyte of þe devull and said vnto hym; "Son, thies er seculer monkes þat vsis a noder man*er* of habett þan monkis or h*er*mett*is* duse." And onone þai went home sam*en* agayn, and he wolde nevur aft*er* latt hym com furth agayn oute of his abbay.

Temptatus h*er*emita a demone int*er*fecit p*at*rem suu*m*. S*upr*a de credere.

Temptatos adiuvat Marie salutacio. S*upr*a de Maria, ix.

Temptat demon ieiunantes. Sup*r*a de abstinencia, vj.

DCCXLVIII.

Temptans caro debet domari.

We rede in 'Vitis P*atrum*' how som tyme þ*er* was a yong man in ane abbay, and be no contenence nor none other gude werk he mot not distroy þe flawm of his flessh. So on a tyme when þis temptacion was knowen emangis his brethur, his abbott garte kepe hym strayte, and com*m*andid a sharp angry monke at he sulde flite *with* hym & bete hym, and lat hym compleyn hym to whome he wolde. So on a tyme þe monkis co*m*pleynyd vnto þe abbott & said þis yong monk had grete wrong. He began to wepe and was destitute of all helpe; and þus he was done to all a yere. And when þe yere was done, he was axkid if his ill thoghtis wer gone, or if he felid oght of þai*m*. And he answerd agayn vnto his abbott & sayd; "Fadur, how may I thynk of fornycacion when I may skantlie liff for sorow þat I suffer?"

Temptacione carnis *eciam sancti* int*er*du*m* vexant*ur*. Sup*r*a de carne, j.

Temptatur caro p*er* tactu*m* mulieris. S*upra* de Leone p*a*pa.

Temptacio carnal*is* a *sanct*is ben*e*ficia dei tollit. S*upr*a de p*r*edicatore, iij.

Temptacio carnalis accepta a *sanct*is demones letificat. S*upr*a de cruce, ij.

Temptacio carnal*is eciam* sanc*t*os in pecc*atu*m precipitat. Su*pr*a de carne, ij.

Temptacio carnalis ho*min*em inducit ad ne*g*and*um* d*eu*m. S*upr*a de amor*e*, ij.

Temptacio carnal*is eciam* sanc*t*os desp*er*are facit. S*upr*a de carne, iij.

Temptantur carne *eciam* senes. Sup*r*a de confidencia.

Temptacio carnis rep*r*imitur p*er* fetorem mulieris. S*upr*a de carne, vi[1].

Temptacio carnis *eciam* or*ati*onib*us* extinguitur. S*upr*a de abb*a*tissa, ij, et de Agnete *et* aliqu*ando* no*n* iuuatur. S*upr*a de M*a*ria, iij.

Temptantur aliqu*ando* aliqui re vili. S*upr*a de or*ati*on*e*, ix *et* x.

DCCXLIX.

Temptat viru*m* mulier ultro se ingerens.

We rede in 'Historiis Barlaam' how þ*er* was a kyng þat hight Abennyr, and he had a son̄ þat hight Icsaphatt, þat was chri*st*end. And he, purposand to wit*h*draw hym̄ fro þe purpos of cristendom̄ & chastite, he garte spar hym̄ in a chamber be his one, and he garte bryng in to hym̄ fayr yong wom*m*en̄ and clenlie arayed; and þai sat by hym̄ & halsid hym̄ & shewhid hym̄ fayr cowntenance

[1] MS. iij.

& laburd hym to luste & lykyng of his flessh. Nor he had no man þat he mott compleyn hym to nor aske councell þ*er*-of att, nor eate with bod þai, and þai war all commo*n* vnto hym. And þe devull had grete power in temppyng of hym, so þat he fell vnto luste and lykyng of his bodye. Not-wi*th*stondyng he vmthoght hym of God & began to wepe, & knokkid on his breste and besoght God to helpe hym. And þus he chasid away all his ill thoght*is*, and for all at þies wom*m*en cuthe do, his temptacion sesid so þat he fell not to syn.

DCCL.

Temptacio carnis sensu*m* aliqua*n*do alienat.

Cesarius tellis how som tyme þ*er* was a wurthi wom*m*en. So on a tyme as sho was be hur one in a castell þat sho dwelt in, sodanlie scho was inflammyd *with* þe fyre of luff at sho mot not suffre it. So sho met *with* þe portar & sho prayed hym to com vp *with* hur & ly by hur. And he as a gude man answerd hur & said; "Madame, what is þat at ye say? What is your witt? Behald Almyghti God & thynk of your awn wurshup." And sho tuke no hede to his saying, bod when he had refusid hur, as God wold, sho wente furth of þe castell vnto a grete watir þat ran vnder þe castell, and þ*er* sho sett hur vp to þe shulders in þe calde wat*er*, & þ*er* sho satt vnto all þis luste þat was in hur was slakid. And þan sho come vp agayn & thankid þe porter of his cowncell, and at he putt hur away from hym, & sayd; "And þou had giffen me ml marke of gold it culde nott hafe done me so mekull gude as þi cowncell did." And *with* þat sho went in agayn vnwemmyd.

DCCLI.

Temptacione carnis amota pe*r*mittit deus aliquo*s* cadere in dete*r*iorem[1].

Cesarius tellis how þat in Fraunce þ*er* was a religious mayden þat was made an anncras. And be þe temptacion of þe devull sho was gretelie tempyd *with* luste of hur flessh, and sho prayed h*er*telie

[1] MS. Temptacione carnis ammota p*er*mittit deus aliqua*n*do studere in det*er*iorem.

vnto almighti God at sho mot be delyverd of þis temptacion. So in hur *pr*ayers on a tyme ane angell apperid vnto hur and axkid hur if sho wolde be delyverd fro þis temptacion, & sho said ya, full fayn. And he bad hur say *with* gude will þis vers; "Confige timore *tuo* car*nes* meas, et c^9," & sho sulde be delyverd. And so sho did, and onone þe temptacion left hur. Bod onone after sho fell into a more *per*lious temptacion of God & of þe chr*ist*en fayth. And sho *pr*ayed God mor specialli þan sho did befor at sho mot be delyverd of þat temptacion. So on a tyme þe aungell apperid vnto hur agayn & said; "Suster, how is it *with* the?" And sho answerd agayn & said; "Nevur wars." Than þe angell askid hur if sho trowid at sho mott lyff *with*oute temptacion. "It is necessarie," he said, "vnto þe to hafe þe tone of þies temptacions, and þ*er*for chese þe whethur þou will hafe." And þan sho said; "I chese me vnto þe furste, ffor þuf all it be vnclene, yit it is kyndelie, and þe toder com*m*ys all of the devull." And þus þe spirut of blasfeme lefte hur, and þe temptacion of hur flessh turnyd agayn vnto hur.

Temptacioni carnis co*n*ueniunt*ur* multa que dicu*n*tur *supr*a de luxuria.

DCCLII.

Tempus necligere est valde periculosum.

We rede in 'Libro de Dono Timoris' how on a tyme a holie man, as he was in his *pr*ayers, he hard a voyce crying duelfullie in spiritt, & makyng mekull sorow. And when he axkid what it was, it answerd agayn & sayd it was dampned and it made mykull sorow for losyng of tyme, ffor in þat mene while, it said, it mot hafe done suche penance for þe truspas at it had done at it mot hafe bene delyverd fro payn.

Temp*er*ancia bona auget elemosinam. *Supr*a de elemosi*n*a.

Theodori, qui *et* Theodore. *Supr*a de paciencia, iij.

Theodosij imp*er*atoris. Infra de vanitate, j.

DCCLIII.

Testamentum vsurarij in morte factum valet.

Cesarius tellis how som tyme þer was ane vsurar, & he was a passanď riche mañ. So hym̃ happenď to faƚƚ seke, bowñ to dye. So he sent after ane holie abbott, & confessiď hym̃ & forthoght his syñ, & made his testament in þis maner of wyse & sayď; "Sur, and ye wiƚƚ answer for my saule, I wiƚƚ giff vnto you aƚƚ þat evur I hafe at do *with*, what at you plesis." And he grauntiď þerto & garte hafe aƚƚ his gudis vnto his abbay, and also þe mañ þat was seke. And evyñ as þai broght hym̃ into þe abbay he dyeď and þis abbott restoriď aƚƚ his vsuries and gaff grete almos for hym̃, and þe residue of his gudis he turnyď into þe vse of his abbay & his brether. So as þe monkis war in þer prayers abowte þe bodie of þis mañ, þai war war stondanď oñ his lefte syde iiij vglie spyrittis, and wheñ þai saw þaim þai wer so ferď at þai fled, aƚƚ bod one olde holie monke. And onone he was war oñ þe[1] right side of þis mañ, standanď, iiij white aungels enence þe fendis. And onone one of þe fendis sayď; "Dixit iniustus ut delinquat in semetipso, *non est timor* Dei ante *oculos eius*. And þis is fulfilliď in þis mañ." Thañ a noder sayd; "*Quoniam* dolose egit vt *inveniatur* iniquitas *eius* ad odium." And thañ þe iij sayď; "Verba [*oris*] eius iniquitas *et* dolus, *noluit intelligere* vt *bene* ageret." And þañ þe iiij said; "Iniquitatem *meditatus est* in *cubili suo*, *astitit* [*omni*] *uie non* bone, maliciam autem *non* odiuit." And þañ þai sayď aƚƚ to-gedur; "And God be rightwus & His wurdis trew þis mañ is owrs, for in aƚƚ þies is he giltie." And þañ þe aungels answerď agayñ & sayď; "Now we saƚƚ say þe residue of þe psalmys at ye hafe begoñ." And þerfor þe furste angeƚƚ sayď; "*Domine*, in celo *misericordia* tua, *et veritas tua usque* ad nubes." Thañ þe secund sayď; "Iustitia tua *sicut montes* Dei, [*iudicia tua*] abyssus multa." And þañ þe iij saiď; "*Homines et* iumenta saluabis, *Domine*, *quemadmodum multiplicasti misericordiam tuam*, *Deus*." And þañ þe iiij spak & sayď; "Filij autem *hominum* in *tegmine* alarum

[1] *After* þe, left, *erased*.

tuarum superabunt." And þan þai all cryed samen & sayd; "þis man is owrs, for he fled vnto allmyghti God and þedur sall he go; ffor he trustid to be vndernethe þe coveryng of His wengis." And þus þe fendis was confusid, and þus þe aungels had þis contryte saule away *with* þaim.

DCCLIV.

Testamentu*m* facientes freque*n*te*r* paru*m* legant p*ro* a*n*i*m*a sua.

We rede in 'Libro de Dono Timoris' of ane vsurar, when he sulde make his testament befor þe *pre*ste & many oþ*er* þat was bye, and he bewytt mekull vnto his frendis and nothyng ordand for his saule, þe *pre*ste spak vnto hym & sayd; "Sur, thynk of your sawle." And he answerd agayn & sayd; "Sur, ye say wele, ffor trewlie I had nerehand forgettyn itt bod now at ye thoght me on."

Testatoris a*n*i*m*a in purgatorio retinetur executoris necligencia. Sup*r*a de executore et in diue*r*sis alijs locis.

DCCLV.

Testi*m*o*n*iu*m*. Testes diligente*r* su*n*t examinandi.

Cesarius telles how a kyng of Fraunce, þat hight Philipp[1], had a baillay at Paryssh, & he covett gretelie his neghbur vyneyard to by, & he wolde not sell hym it. So his neghbur dyed, and þis baillay vmthoght hym of a fals wyle, and he hyrid ij felows on a nyght to go to þis mans grafe & take hym vp. And he & þai went on a nyght vnto his grafe & tuke hym oute of þe erth, and putt in his hand a bagg full of money, als muche as he had *pro*fyrd hym þ*er*for whills he liffed, & made hym to take of a seke *with* his awn hand in *pre*sens of þies ij men, notwit*h*stondyng he was dead, and he *pra*yed þai*m* bere witnes hereof, and gaff þai*m* a gude reward. So þai layde hym in agayn & fyllid þe grafe als wele as

[1] MS. *inserts*, þat, *here*.

it was before, and tuke þe money *with* þaim & went þ*er* ways. And on þe morn þis baillay entred into þis vyne-yarde & said it was his, and þe wydow had mekull m*er*vell here-of [&] said nay, it was not soo. And he said yis, he had boght it of hur husband in his lyfe & payed hym in his hand þ*er*for, and þat he offred hym for to prufe. So þis wedow saw sho cuthe not p*re*vale ayeyns hym, and went vnto þe kyng & made playnt on hym. And þe kyng com*m*aundid þe cauce to be examynd be men of law, bod þai examynd it not sufficientlie, to so muche þe sentans went *with* þe baillay ayayns þe wedow. And þan þis wedow made more sorow þan she[1] did afor, and sho come agayn vnto þe kyng and made a grete crying & a besekyng vnto hym to helpe hur. So þe kyng had compassion on hur & callid þe wittnes befor hym selfe, & sayd þat he wold examyn þa*im*. So he callid þat one oside into a p*ri*vay place and bad hym say his pat*er* nost*er*, þat he mott here it; and so he did. And þan he garte spar hym in a chambre and callid þe toder, & said vnto hym sadlie in þis man*er* of wyse; "Thi felow hase telled me all þe trewth of þe vynegarth als trew as þe pater noster. And trewlie, & þou discord fro hym, þou sall be punysshid þ*er*for, þ*a*t all Fraunce sall witt." So þis man was ferd & trowed at þis felow had tellid hym all as it was, and he fell down on his kneis befor þe kyng & sayd; "Lorde, hafe m*er*cie on me, for we wer hyrid for a c*er*tayn money be þe baillay, & þus we did & þus," and telde hym evurilk-dele as þai had done. And þe kyng was gretelie grevid at þis baillay & putt hym oute of his offes, and restorid þe wedow of hur vyneyard agayn. And he garte berie þe baillay all whik for disclanderyng of þis deade man.

DCCLVI.

Timere loco *et* tempore sapientis est.

Agellius[2] tellis how, on a tyme, when a wurthi philosophur was sayland our a grete watyr *with* many other, & þe wawys wex grete aboute þe shup, þis philosophur wex pale-hewid for ferde. So onone as all men wex still, þ*er* was a lichurus riche man in þe

[1] MS. he. [2] MS. Agellus.

shup, & he scornyd þis philosophur and blamyd hym for he was ferd, notw*ith*stondyng he was ferde hym selfe. And þis philosophur ansswerd hym agayn, & said he was not ferd for his lichorus bodie nor for his saule, bod for hym selfe, & þerfor no m*er*vell if he wexid pale.

DCCLVII.

Timeri semp*er* debet iudiciu*m* vltimu*m*.

We rede in 'Vitis P*atru*m' how, on a tyme, þ*er* was a monke þ*at* axkid his abbott & prayed hym tell hym a wurde at he mot thynke on. And he bad hym go & vmthynk hym alway, "as a thefe duse in preson þ*at* evur spirris whar þe iustis is and when þe session sall be, and evur is in sorow & mornyng for ferd of hangyng; so sulde þou & evur-ilk man thynk how þou mon com befor þe grete iugement of Almyghtie God, and þ*er* giff rekynyng of all þi dedis. And if þou thynk all-way on þis man*er* of wyse, no dowte of þou mon be savid."

DCCLVIII.

Timent ecia*m* p*er*fecti iudiciu*m*.

We rede in 'Vitis P*atru*m' when abbot Agathon was bown to dye, he lay iij dayes, & his een oppyn, & stirrid nott and his brethur callid nevur so faste on hym. So at þe laste he movid, & þai spakk vnto hym & said; "Abbay! whar erte þou?" And he answerd agayn & sayd; "In þe covent of all men, and I mon to my iugem*ent*." And þai comfurthid hym & axkid hym wharfor he was ferd, and he answerd ageyn & sayd; "W*ith* all þe strenth at I had I laburd to kepe þe com*m*aundment*is* of God, and I am bod a man and yit I wate nevur þuff my werkis hafe plesid God or nay, ffor þe iugement of Almiȝty God is oderwas þan is þe iugement of man. And þerfor I hafe none oþ*er* truste bod at I mon come to my iugement before þe hye seatt of Allmyghtie God."

Timere debet peccator v*bi*q*ue* q*uia* deus vbiq*ue* videt. S*up*ra de deo *et* abb*at*e.

DCCLIX.

Timere debent viri boni purgatoriu*m*.

We rede in 'Libro de Dono Ti*m*oris' how on a tyme as a *certayn* meneya of religious men spak sam*en* of purgatorie & was passand ferd þ*er*for, þ*er* was emang*is* þai*m* a lay man, & he sayd; "It is a grete m*er*vell of you, sen ye er so gude men & of so grete penans, þat ye hafe so grete drede. Sekurlie and secular men þ*a*t duse so mekull ill & duse so little penans þ*er*for knew it, þai wulde fall in a dispayr." And þan ane of þai*m* tolde hym ane exsample of a blynd man, as is tellid befor of þe blynd man. Also we rede of a preste þat was holden a holie man, þ*a*t in his lyfe did grete penance. And vnto one þat axkid hym whi he did so, he answerd & said þus; "And all þis town were full of fyre, me had levur be þ*er*in vnto þe day of dome þan for to be in purgatorie or in hell a day."

DCCLX.

Timere casum in pecc*atu*m om*n*es debent.

We rede in 'Lib*ro* de Dono Timoris' how som tyme þ*er* was a gude man þat fell to syn, and a noder gude man when he harde tell þ*er*off had grete sorow þ*er*for & sayd vnto hym; "Ille heri *et* ego hodie." Et supra de carne temptac*i*o*ne* *et* in pluribu*s* alijs locis diu*er*sis.

Timore mu*n*dano debent aliqui amittere res temporales. *Sup*ra de co*n*te*m*ptu mu*n*di *et* de diuicijs *et* infra de vsurario [1].

Timore humano timetur mors u*e*l pena corporalis. Supra de martirio, de morte, de penitencia *et* hic de timore.

Timore servili faciu*n*t aliqui aliqua de gen*er*e bonor*um*. *Sup*ra de cont*r*icione.

[1] MS. vsura.

Timore speciali timent s*ancti* ne op*er*a sua deo placeant. S*upr*a eod*e*m, iij.

Titus. Sup*r*a de p*r*elato, vj, et de fame.

DCCLXI.

Thome Martiris Cantuariens*is*.

We rede in his 'Legent' how þ*er* was in his dioces a p*r*este þat daylie sang mes of our Ladie, and he was accusid vnto þe archbisshop̄, Saynt Thomas, and he suspend hym̄ as ane ydiott & a man þat cuthe no gude. So oñ a tyme wheñ Saynt Thomas sulde sew his hayre, & hid it vndernethe his bed to wache ane howr þat he mot sew it in, our Ladie apperid vnto þis p*r*este and bad hym̄ go vnto þe archbisshop̄, "þat sho, for whase luff þou[1] was wunte say þi mes, hase sewid his hayre þat lyes in suche a place," & teld hym̄ þ*er* sho lefte itt, "and say þat sho byddis hym̄ relese þe suspensioñ þat he hase putt ayenys the." And he went & tolde hym̄, and wheñ he harde it & fand it was as he sayd, he[2] relesid his suspensioñ & bad hym̄ say mes styll of our Ladie, & bad him[3] kepe it p*r*ivay ewhils he liffid & discure hym̄ noght.

DCCLXII.

Thoma*m* Martirem honorant angeli.

We rede in his 'Legend' þat wheñ he was slayñ, & þe covent of Cantyrberie begañ for hym̄ þe mes of Requiem, sodanlie a co*m*pany of aungels was þ*er*, & wit*h* a hy voyce abowñ all þe quere þai begañ to syng mes, & said; "Letabitur iustus in D*omi*no." And onone as þe mouk*is* hard þai*m*, þai felowid and sang as þai did þe mes furth, as þai did, of a martyr.

Thoma*m* orans avis exaudita est. Sup*r*a de ave, ij.

Tonitruu*m*. Supra de tempestate.

[1] MS. þus. [2] *After* he, had, *erased.* [3] MS. his.

Torneamentum vicit miles absens. *Supra* de Maria.
Tribulacio. Tribulatos de*us* m*u*ltipliciter consolatur. Sup*r*a de infirmitate, de co*n*solac*io*ne *et* in alijs pl*u*rib*us* locis.
Tristicia nocet ho*mini*. *Supra* de desp*er*ac*io*ne, j. *et* de accidia, j.
Turba est fugienda. Supra de solitudi*ne*, j, ij *et* iij.

DCCLXIII.

Vanitas semp*er* est fugienda.

We rede ex 'Dictis P*atrum*' how som tyme þ*er* was a monk at Constantynople, & dwelte þ*er* in þe tyme of Theodoce þe emp*er*our in a litill cell *with*-oute þe cetie. And þe emp*er*our harde tell on hym & went vnto hym be his one at speke *with* hym; & when he come vnto hym he knew not at it was þe emp*er*our, & þis monke hastid hym & put wat*er* in a vessell, & tuke salte & a morcell of brede & servid hym þ*er*-off & þai ete to-gedur. And þan he sayd; "I am Theodos þe emp*er*our, & of devocion I come hydur. Ye er blissid þat er so sekur & so fre of your necessities in þis werld, & ye hafe a ristfull & a quiett lyffe forby þat I hafe; ffor suthelie I was blissidlie born in my realm, and now I liff þ*er*in & I neu*er* eatt nor drynk *with*-outen besynes." And *with* þat he tuke his lefe att hym and went his ways. So when he was gone, the same nyght þis monke co*m*pasid in his mynd & said vnto hym selfe; "Not alonlie many of þe peple, bod also many of þe emp*er*our pales, folowyng þe exsample of þe emp*er*our, will now com for to se me & do me wurshup as þe servand of God. And herof I suppoce þai wull not sease. And I am ferd leste þe fend vndergo me & make me gladlie to ressayfe þai*m*, & at my harte take a comfu[*r*]th be þ*er* lovyng & be þ*er* wurshup, and be þat at I sulde begyn to lose þe v*er*tue of my mekenes." And when he had þus consydurd in hym selfe, þe same night he went into wyldernes in Egypte, and dwelte þ*er* all his lyfe-tyme after *with* holie fadurs, oute of syght.

DCCLXIV.

Vanitatem *sancti per* humilitatem fugiu*nt*.

We rede also in 'Gestis P*atrum*' how oñ a tyme a iustice of a lande come for to se ane abbott, and wheñ he hard' teƚƚ at he come [1], he garte clothe hym̄ in sak-clothe and tuke in his hand bread' & chese, & sett hym̄ in his ceƚƚ-dure. And wheñ þe iustis saw hym̄ he dispysid' hym̄ and sayd'; "Is not þis þe mañ at we hafe hard' so mekuƚƚ teƚƚ off!" & *with* þat he went his way & wolde byde no longer.

Vana gl*or*ia appetit*ur* aliqu*ando* ex bonis op*er*ib*us*. S*upra* de elemo*sina et* de abstinencia.

Vanitas punitur in purgatorio. Sup*ra* de ave, i.

Vaspasianus. Supra de p*re*lato.

Vanitati possu*nt* adaptari m*u*lta que d*icuntur* sup*ra* de laude, gl*or*ia, *et* memoria.

DCCLXV.

Verbu*m*. Verbo no*n* est semp*er* adherend*um*.

We rede how som tyme a mañ had ane ass, & he rade hur, & a little soñ that he had folowid' hym̄ on fute. And þ*er* was meñ at mett þai*m*, emang þe whilk som̄ said'; "O, how fond' þis alde carle is, þat rydis hym̄ selfe & lattis hys soñ ryñ in þe myre," & wheñ þai war passid' þai lepid' oñ bothe. Thañ þai mett a noder meneyay, & þai sayd', "Forsuth, þies er bod' fulis, for þai wiƚƚ sla þis ass." And wheñ þai war passid', he and his son light & lete þe ass go tome. So þai met a noder meneya, & þai sayd; "þies meneya er fonde, for þai go bothe oñ þ*er* fete, and þat one of þai*m* mot ryde." þañ he sett his soñ oñ & went oñ his fete hym̄ [*self*]. And þañ þai mett a noder meneya þat sayd'; "Loo! Yone fonde alde carle, he gois oñ his fete hym̄ selfe & lattys his soñ ryde, þat mott bettyr go þañ he may." And þañ

[1] MS. *adds*, and, *here*.

he & his soñ tuke vp þis ass & bare hur. & þañ þer mett þaim a noder meneya and þai said: "Lo, þies fulies! How þai bere þis ass þat sulde bere þaim!" Thañ he sett downñ þe ass & sayd vnto his soñ; "Loo! soñ, here may þou se how þat evur we doo, alway meñ wiłł fawte vs & speke of vs. And þerfor it is not gretelie to charge of wurdis-spekyng and a mañ do wele."

DCCLXVI.

Verba aliqua*n*do inducunt ad credendu*m* quod no*n* est.

Iacobus de Vet*ri*aco tellis how som̄ tyme þ*er* was a pure mañ þat bare vnto þe m*ar*kett att sełł a lambe. So þ*er* was in þe m*ar*kett a iaper þat saw he was bod ane innocent, & he said vnto his felows; "Doo as I sałł tełł you, & we sałł hafe þis lambe from̄ yone felow." And he made þai*m* stand in dyvers placis in sonder in þe same way, ilkone aft*er* oþ*er*. And as þis mañ went by þai*m* þe furst sayd vnto þis mañ; "Mañ, wiłł þou sełł þat hunde?" And he answerd agayñ & sayd; "Skorñ me nott, for it is no hunde, it is a lambe." So he come vnto þe secund, & he axkid hym̄ hif he wold sełł hym̄ þat hund for a peny. And he was wrothe þ*er*-wit*h*, & said; "Ye doo bod skorñ me." So he come vnto the thrid, and he said in þe same wise. So þis mañ had grete m*er*vełł hereoff & waxed shamefułł. And þañ he come to þe iiij & þe v, & þai spirrid hym̄ in þe same wyse. So þis felow begañ to vmbethynk hym̄ what þis sulde mene, at so many meñ sulde spyr hym̄ of þis lambe if it war a dogg, & ałł acordid in one þat it sulde be a dogg & no lambe. So at þe laste he agreid vnto þ*er* oppynyons & sayd vnto hym̄ selfe; "God knowis þat I trowid it had bene a lambe, bod becauce it is a dogg I wiłł bere it no ferther." And wit*h* þat he keste it from̄ hym̄ & said he wulde bere it no langer. And wheñ he had casteñ it from̄ hym̄ he went his way, and þis iaper & his felows tuke vp̄ þis lambe & ete itt.

Verba ociosa no*n* su*n*t credenda. Sup*r*a de ocio, ij.

Verum semper dicere non semper expedit. Supra de adulacione, j.

Veritas non est celanda in necessitate. Supra de testimonio.

Veritati possunt adaptari multa que dicuntur supra de falsitate et mendacio.

DCCLXVII.

Vestes preciose contempnende sunt a sanctis.

We rede in 'Vita Iohannis Elemosinarij' how on a tyme þer was a riche man þat saw hym, & he was bothe a bisshopp & a patriarke, at he was bod in a pure clothyng & a vile, of xxxvj d' price he boght a garment and gaff it vnto þis patriarke. And þis Iohn, seyng þe devocion of þis man, tuke it. Bod all þat nyght he lay wakand & said vnto hym selfe; "Who sall say þat meke Iohn is cled with a garment of xxxvj d' price, and þe brethur of Cryst er slayn for calde? þou meke Iohn!" he said, "It sall not cover þe a noder nyght, ffor it is rightwus at þe brethur of our Lord be cled þerwith mor þan þou, vnhappy creatur!" And on þe morn he sent it into þe town for to sell, and he þat gaff hym it boght it, and offerd it vnto hym agayn & prayed hym were itt. And he tuke it & evur sellid it, & þe price ay þat he tuke þerfor he gaff it wnto pure folk. And evur þis man boght it agayn & gaff hym itt. So at þe laste þis holie man thankyd hym & sayde; "We sall se who sall defayle, I or þou." And þis man was evur ryche enogh als lang as he barkand with þis holie man, & evur þis holie man gaf þe price þat he sent hym þerfor vnto pure men.

Vestes preciose eleuant hominem in superbiam. Supra de augurio.

Via melior est tenenda. Supra de socio, ij.

Victoriam semper debent appetere pugnantes. Supra de bello, ij.

DCCLXVIII.

Vigilare debent in *orationibus* religiosi.

We rede in þe 'Lyfe of Saynt Arsenius[1],' þat when he saw þe son ryse he wolde turn his bak *þeron*, & lifte vp handis & his harte vnto hevyn to Almyghty God, & say his prayers. & so he wolde sytt all day to þe son shane on his face agayn, and þan he wulde turn hym & sitt in his prayers all nyght. And agayns morn, when he wexid werie & his natur wolde ruste, he wolde say vnto slepe; "Com, *servand*, & serif me." And evyn sittand he walde spar his een & slepe a while, and onone he wulde wake agayn & go vnto his prayers.

Vigiliam qu*andoque* inducit temptacio demo*nis per* so*m*pni s*ub*t*racc*io*n*em. S*upr*a de abstinencia. Vindicta. Vindicant se aliqui crudeliter[2].

DCCLXIX.

Vindica*ns* se an*te* morte*m* celeriter moritur[3].

We rede in þe 'Storie of Alexander,' how þat when Pausanias had wowndid Philip, þat was Alexand*er* fadur, þat hym burde nedis dye, Alexander gatt þis Pawsanias & broght hym vnto Philip; and he put a swerd in his fadur right hand and helpyd hym *with* his hand & slew hym. And when he dyed þis Philipp sayd; "Now þe end of my lyfe, nor my dead, nor none o*þer* thyng may hevy me ewhuls I hafe slayn hym þat hase slayn me. And, Alexand*er*, I hafe mynd of own god, how he said vnto þi moder at sho sulde bere þe son of vengeange." And *with* þat he lenyd hym down and swelte.

[1] MS. Arseme.

[2] *The tale from Valerius to follow this heading is missing in the* English MS.

[3] *Heading supplied from* Harl. MS. *with* celeriter *for* celerabili*us*.

DCCLXX.

Vindicant se aliqui subtiliter.

Petrus Alphonsis[1] tellis how som tyme þer was a kyng þat had a wardrop[er] þat was maister-shaper of his clothyng; and he had many servandis vnder-nethe hym of þe whilk ane was callid Nediu. And þai sewid & war at burd in a mans howse[2] þat hight Eunuchus. So on a day þai went to dyner, & þis Nediu was not þer, & þai ete hony & drank wyne, & had many oþer gude metis sent vnto þaim fro þe kyng. And when þai war att dyner & ete, þis Eunuchus axkid þaim whi þai abade not Nediu, and þer maister ansswerd & said at he wulde ete no hony and he war þer. So at þe laste þis Nediu come & fand þaim at dyner, & sayd; "Whi bade ye noght for me?" And Eunuchus tolde hym how þat his maister sayd he wolde eate no hony, & he held his tong & sayd noght. Notwithstondyng he began to vmthynk hym how he mot be vengid. So on a tyme he sayde vnto þis Eunuchus, "Bewar, ye & your howshold, of my maister at he do you no harm, for som tyme he will wax fond & is evyn brayn-wude." And þis Eunuchus ansswerd hym & said; "And I knew þe how when it happend hym I sulde bynd hym." And þis Nediu sayd; "When þou seis hym luke hedurward & þedurward & opon þe erde, & rap abowte hym with his handis and ryse oute of his seate & remow his stule, þan þou sall vnderstand þat he is wude." So within a while after þis Nediu on a tyme hid his maister sheris, and he myssyd þaim & began to caste þe stra hedurward & þedurward & luke aboute hym & rap on þe burd with his nefe, & ryse & remofe þe stule at he satt on. And when Eunuchus saw þis, he callid faste on his servandis & onone þai tuke hym & band hym faste. And evur he cryed; "Whi do ye so? What hafe I done?" And evur þai band hym strayter, and bete hym to he was nerehand dead. So at þe laste he come vnto hym selfe &[3] þai lowsid hym, and he axkid þaim whi þai did so. And Eunuchus tolde hym how þat Nediu sayd at he was wude. And þan his maister sayd vnto hym;

[1] MS. Alphensis, *for* Alphonsus.

[2] Arund. MS. in domo eunuchi regis.

[3] & *omitted and added above the line.*

"When saw þou me be wude?" And Nediu answerd hym agayn & sayd; "þou was wude, maister, when þou said at þou saw me nevur eat honye." And when þai þat was abowte hym harde þis, þai demyd at he had rightwuslie vengid hym, & so he satt *with* his awn skathe.

Vindicant se aliqu*ando* creature [1] irracionales. Su*pra* de bufone.

DCCLXXI.

Vindicare se nolunt s*an*cti.

We rede in þe 'Legend of Saynt Macharie,' how on a tyme as he cut hys hand *with* his knyfe, & it bled a grete dele becauce he brak þe knyfe, & when he had done he reprovid hym selfe becauce he did wrong [2], & went nakid into wyldernes & was þ*er* vj monethis. And þan he come home all tobittyn and skrattyd *with* thornys and breers.

DCCLXXII.

Vindicat se deus aliqu*ando* p*er* mortuos.

We rede in þe 'Historie of Saynt Basyll,' on a tyme when Iulianus Apostata wente to procede agayn þe P*er*sas, he bostid Basill þat [3] as he come agaynward to Capado[*ce*] he sulde destroy all Cesarie. And on þe nyght folowyng, þis Basill saw in þe kurk of our Ladie a multitude of angels, and in myddest of þai*m* a womman standand, and said vnto þai*m* abowte hur; "Call vnto me M*er*curius þat sall sla Iulian*us* Apostata, þ*at* blasfemys bothe me and my Son." And þis M*er*curi*us* was a c*er*tayn knyght þ*at* þis same Iulianus had slayn for þe fayth of Cryste, and was berid in þe same kurk. And onone þis M*er*curius was redie in his armur, and sho sent hym into þe batell. And onone þis Basyll

[1] ir- *omitted and added above the line.*

[2] Harl. MS. Du*m* *sanctus* Macharius pulice*m* se pungente*m* manu occidisset *et* m*u*ltum sanguin*is* ex illo emanasset, rep*re*hendens se ips*um* q*uo*d prop*ri*am vindicasset iniuri*am*, &c. Arund. MS. Du*m* *sanctus* Machari*us* calice*m*, &c.

[3] Latin MSS. quod in reditu Cesariam Capadocie destru*e*ret.

went to þ*er* he was gravyn̄ & opynd his grafe, & he fand nowder his bodie nor his armur þat was berid wi*th* hym̄, & þan̄ he axkid þe keper of þe kurk who bare away þis armur, and he sware grete athis at it was þ*er* þat same nyght. So þis Basilius went thens tyll on̄ þe morn̄, and þan̄ he come agayn̄ & fand bothe his bodie and his armur, and his spere bludye to þe myddyste. And þan̄ þ*er* come ane & sayd; "When̄ Iulian*us* Apostata was arayed in þe batell, þ*er* come ane vnknowyn̄ knyght armyd & a spere in his hand, apon̄ a hors, and he smate þe hors wi*th* þe spurris and wi*th* a bolde spyritt he rade at þis Iulyan̄, & manlelie wi*th* his spere he smate hym̄ thrugh; and when̄ he had done, sodanlie he vanyssid away." And as we rede in 'Hist*oria* Trip*ar*tita,' þis Iulian̄, when̄ he was hurte, he fyllid his hand wi*th* his awn̄ blude, and keste it into þe ayre & sayd; "Vicisti, Galilee, vicisti!" And in þis wrichid voyce he swelte, and all his childur lefte hym̄ þ*er* vnberid; & þe P*er*sis come & flew hym̄ and of his skyn̄ þai made a fute-skyn̄ [1] to þe kyng of Persis [2].

Vindicat *eciam* deus bonos in hac vita. S*upra de* obedie*n*cia, vij.

Vir. Viro ultro [3] s*e* ing*er*it mulier. S*upr*a de temptacione, v [4].

Viru*m* suu*m* decipit vxor. Sup*r*a de muliere, ix.

DCCLXXIII.

Virginitas *eciam* cu*m* det*r*imento corpo*r*is al*iquando* se*r*uatur.

Saynt Ierom̄ tellis how at a ffeste xxx[ti] archars come & slew a man̄ þat hight Phidones, & when̄ þai had done, þai garte bryng his doghters þat war maydens aforn̄ þai*m* at þai mot nakyn̄ þai*m*, & defowle þai*m* þ*er* on̄ þe payment whar þ*er* fadur was slone.

[1] Harl. MS. subte*r*ci*n*torium?

[2] MS. Kyng of Pars. Lat. MSS. regi Persarum.

[3] *So* Lat. MSS. English MS. *has*, multus.

[4] *The* MS. *gives a wrong reference, here corrected by the* Lat. MSS.

And þai fenyd þaim sorowfull, & band þaim samen & fell all samen into a pytt & drownyd þaim, becauce with þer dead at þai mot kepe þer virginite.

DCCLXXIV.

Virginitatem in filia amissam pater aliquando crudeliter punit.

Valerius tellis how Virgillius slew his awn doghter in þe markett, to þe entent þat hym had lere be callid þe slaer of a virgyn þan þe fadur of a strompett.

DCCLXXV.

Virgines iuuat deus virginitatem suam custodire.

Saynt Ierom tellis how on a tyme when a virgyn wolde not sacryfice þe ydolfis as þe paynom commauns did hur, þai led hur vnto þe bordell-howse, and þer come thedur a yong man to hafe defowlid hur. And sodanlie þer come a lyon rynnand þurgh þe cetie vnto þe bordell, & tuke þis yong man & held hym and lukid on þe virgyn & did hym no skathe, bod lukid what sho wolde command hym to do. And he prayed þe virgyn to command þe lion to lat hym goo, and sho did gude for ill and commawndid þe lyon to lat hym go. And þus he was delyverd, and þai þat saw had grete mervayle þeroff. And þe lyon went[9] his ways & þai lete hur go.

Virtus animi *eciam* in mulieribus inuenitur. Supra de muliere, iij *et* xv.

Virtus viri. Supra de muliere [1], ij.

Virtuti possunt adaptari multa superposita in diuersis locis.

Visio sive visus. Videt deus omnia *et* ubique. Supra de deo *et* abbate, iij [2].

[1] So Harl. MS. Eng. MS. de viro.

[2] MS. ij.

DCCLXXVI.

Videre mulieres vel malos viros no*n* multu*m* expedit.

Valerius tellis how Democritus put oute his awn̄ een̄ at he sulde not se gude to be iƚƚ, and Te*r*tulianus[1] tellis þat he made hym̄ selfe blynd', for he mot not se womme*n̄* wit*h*owten̄ co*n*cupiscens.

Visus est cohibendus. S*upra* de oculo, j, *et* de aspect*u*.

DCCLXXVII.

Videre malos no*n* est dilectabile.

We rede in 'Cronicles' how on̄ a tyme as Iulianus Apostata made his sacrafice at Co[*n*]stantynople vnto þe ymage of Fortun̄, his modir, the bisshop̄ of Calcidony, þat was blynd' for age, come vnto hym̄ & callid' hym̄ wrichid' Apostata. And he answerd' hym̄ agayn̄, & sayd'; "Thi Galile may not luff þe." And he answe[*r*]d' agayn̄ & said'; "Therefor God tuke from̄ me my syght at I sulde not se the at is wit*h*owten̄ petie." And Iulian*us* answerd' hym̄ nothyng agayn̄, bod went his ways home als faste as he myght.

Visiones multas ostendit de*us* diu*er*sis *per*sonis. S*upra* in pl*u*rib*us* locis.

DCCLXXVIII.

Visitacio *per*sonar*um* religiosar*um* aliqu*ando* *pro*fuit.

Iacobus de Vet*r*iaco tellis how on̄ a tyme þe chawntur of Camatens*is*[2] as he was in traveƚƚ, went oute of his way to visett dame Marie of Ogniez[3]. And ane of his felows said' vnto hym̄; "For God, what seke ye þ*er*? Wiƚƚ ye go kepp butterfleis as barnys duse?" And he feynyd' & went on̄. And as þai walkid' to-gedur

[1] MS. Terculianus. [2] Arund. MS. *Cameracensis* = *Cambray*. [3] MS. Ognnez.

his felow waxid werie in tarying for hym, and went vnto hym & com*ma*wndid hym to haste hym. And when he beheld þis holie maydyn, sodanlie he was changid in his witt, and fell vnto suche a wepyng þat a grete while he mot not abstene hym nor go furth of hur p*re*sens. And þan þe chawntur p*ur*seyvid þis & was meri, & sayd; "Go we! Whar-to sulde we stand here at kepp buttyr-fleis?" And he after grete sobbyng & teris vnnethis mot be had away, and sayd; "I p*ra*y þe forgyff me, for I wate nevur what I sayde. Bod now in þis holie wom*ma*n I hafe purseyvid be exp*er*yens þe vertue of God Almyghtie."

DCCLXXIX.

Visitacionem corp*or*alem amicor*um* no*n* m*u*ltu*m* sa*n*cti approbant.

We rede of þe abbott Pastor, þat many yere dwelte in wyldernes *with* his brether, & he wolde neu*er* se his moder. So on a tyme sho come into þe kurk, & wolde hafe sene hym & spokyn *with* hym; and he was war on hur he gatt hym into his cell & clappyd to þe dure faste. And sho come & stude att þe dure & wepud, & cryed vppon hym & p*ra*yed hym comfurth & speke *with* hur, & sayd sho wald fayn se hym. And he went vnto þe dure & sayd vnto hur; "Whar-to standis þou cryand þ*er*, þou olde wyfe?" And when sho harde hym speke, sho cryed faster þan sho did befor, & sayd; "Son, I wold se you, whi will ye not lat me se you? Am I not your moder þat gaff you at suke of my breste? And now I am olde & white-harid." And he answerd agayn & sayd; "In þis werld þou may not se vs, bod þou sall se vs in a noder werld." And sho said agayn; "Son, & I se you here, I sall also se you þ*er*." And þan he sayd; "Bod if þou lyff in gude lyfe as we do here, þou may happen not see vs þ*er*." And when he had so sayd sho went hur way, & was merie and sayd; "And I may se you þ*er*, I rak neu*er* if I se you nevur here."

Visitat deus p*er* tribulacio*n*es. S*upr*a de infirmitate, iij, *et* in pl*ur*ib*us* locis.

Visitat deus *per* consolaciones. *Supra* de consolacione *et* in pl*uribus* locis.

Visitatores conuentuu*m* aliqu*ando* false informantur. *Supra* de inuidia.

Vnccio extrema no*n* debet *preter*mitti ante mortem. Su*pra* de furto.

DCCLXXX.

Volu*n*tas *pro*p*r*ia deserenda est a religiosis.

We rede in 'Dictis P*atrum*' how on a tyme ane olde monke sayd; "Than I do my selfe mekull tribulacion, when I doo myne awn wyll."

DCCLXXXI.

Volu*n*tas *pro* facto reputatur qu*ando* no*n* adest facultas.

Cesarius tellis how som tyme þ*er* was a monke of Saynt Barnard*is*, and he lefte his habett & went into þe werld, and þ*er* he become a preste of a kurk; & he had a lemman dwelland *with* hym, & he gatt hur childer bothe sonnys & doghters. So lang tyme after Saynt Barnard happid to be hostid in þis apostata howse, and he knew Saynt Barnard, bod he knew not hym. And in þe mornyng when Saynt B*ar*nard was bown to ga, he mot not speke *with* hym for he was gane vnto þe kurk, and he sayd vnto ane of his sonnys; "Go & bere my message vnto þi fadur, & say I thank hym his gude h*er*berie." And þis childe was dombe born & spak neu*er* wurde. And he ran vnto his fadur & tolde hym all how þe abbott sent hym wurd. And when he hard his childe speke, for ioy he wepud, and he garte hym say his message ou*er* onys or twyce. And he axkid hym what þe abbot did vnto hym, & he said he dyd no thyng vnto hym, bod at he spak vnto hym and bod hym go say þies wurdies vnto his fadur. So þis preste was compuncte *with* so evydent a meracle, and hastelie he come vnto þis holie man. And *with* grete wepyng he fell to hys ffete & sayd; "A! holie fadur! Som tyme I was suche a monk of yours, and

I beseke your fadurhede to licent me to com̄ hame agayn̄ vnto myne abbay *with* you." And he answerd' hym̄ agayn̄ & sayd'; "Byde me here, and' I saƚƚ com̄ agayn̄ by þe & take þe home *with* me." And he answerd' agayn̄ & said'; "Sur, I am̄ aferd' in þe menewhile þat I saƚƚ dye." And he answerd' hym̄ agayn̄ & sayd'; "And þou dye in suche a contricion̄ & a purpas, doute not þou saƚƚ be a monke befor' Aƚƚmyghti God'." And *with* þat he went his ways. & when̄ he come agayn̄ he fand' hym̄ new dead' & berid', and when̄ he hard' teƚƚ þ*er*of he garte oppyn̄ his grafe. And þai þat wer aboute axkid' hym̄ what he wold' doo, & he said' he wuld' se how he lay in his grafe, a clerk or a monk; & þai said' at þai berid' hym̄ in clerk*is* clothis. And when̄ þe erd' was takyn̄ of hym̄, þai fand' hym̄ not cled' as a clerk, bod rather a monke, & in a monk*is* abbett. And þus he was magnyfied' of aƚƚ men̄, becauce his gude wiƚƚ tornyd' hym̄ as to your gude dede[1].

DCCLXXXII.

Votu*m* vouent aliqui raci*o*ne alicuiu*s* p*er*iculi, *et* lib*er*ati a p*er*iculo solu*er*e no*n* curant.

We rede in '*Libro* de Do*no* Ti*m*oris' how som tyme þ*er* was a man̄ þat had bothe a cow and a calfe vnto þe mownte of Saynte Michaeƚƚ, betwix þe bowndis of Bretayn̄ and Normondie, at he mot esskape þe flowyng of þe see þat vmwhile occupied' þat way. And þe flude come on̄ hym̄ and he c*r*ied' of Saynt Michaƚƚ & sayd'; "O þou blissid' Michaeƚƚ, delyver me & I saƚƚ gyff þe þis calve." And when̄ he was delyverid' he sayd'; "Saynt Micheƚƚ was bod a fule þat trowed' at I wolde hafe gyffyn̄ hym̄ my calfe." So afterward' hym̄ happend' to be taken̄ *with* þe same flude. And þan̄ he cryed' of Saynt Michaeƚƚ & p*r*ayed' hym̄ delyver hym̄ & he sulde gyff hym̄ bothe þe cow & þe calfe. So he was delyverd' & sayd' as he did befor'. So þe iij tyme he went thedur at feche home þis cow & þis calfe, & sodanlie as he come hamwerd', þe se-flude vmlappid' bothe hym̄ & þe cow & þe calfe, & drownyd' þai*m* aƚƚ thre, and þat onone.

[1] Arund. MS. et magnificatu*s* e*st* ab om*n*ibu*s* deu*s*, qui volu*n*tate*m* pro *facto* reputat.

DCCLXXXIII.

Votu*m* de ingressu religionis *eciam* ab infirmitate corp*or*ali sanat.

Cesarius tellis how som tyme þ*er* was a knyght þat hight Lodowyc*us*, & he ffell seke bown to dye, & wit*h* lefe of his wyfe he made a vow þat he sulde be a monk of Ceustus ordur & he mott covir of his seknes. And þat done, onone wit*h*outen swete or blude or hostyng, or any oþ*er* þing, at all men m*ar*veld off, agayns þe kynd of his infirmyte he becam to covir & was hale furthwit*h*.

DCCLXXXIV.

Vouere *et* no*n* reddere dampnabile est.

Petrus Damianus tellis how som tyme þ*er* was a riche hard man, and on a tyme he made a vow þat and he liffid x yere lang*er* he sulde make hym a religious man in þe monast*er*ie of Saynt Vincent. So when þe tearm was fulfillid þe abbott axkid hym, & he began to feyn & wolde nott. And in þe menewhile he fell in sekenes and he delte mekull to pure folk & was shrevyn, and semyd as he wer wele disposid, so he dyed. So on þe nexte night aft*er* þe abbott þog[ht] þat he saw[1] in a grete playn medow ane emp*er*our wit*h* all his co*m*panye, and hym thoght he saw c*er*tayn kep*er*s com lede þis man a grete pace. And þis abbo[t] cryed on hym & bad; "Abyde, bruther, & speke wit*h* me! Bruther," he sayd, "What aylis þe? Wheþ*er* erte þou in payn or in ioy?" And he wit*h* a hevie chere answer[d] hym & said; "Whar-to axkis þou me of ioy, þat is turment wit*h* so many paynes?" Aud þan he axkid hym what Saynt Vincent did vnto hym, and he answerd agayn & sayd; "He made me long to trayste in hym, bod now I am werie and hase loste my hope, and as I p*ro*mytt hym & kepid it not, now I am servid on þe same wyse."

[1] MS. *either*, say, *corrected to* saw, *or vice versa.*

DCCLXXXV.

Vsurarij pena aliquando visibiliter demonstratur.

Cesarius tellis how som tyme in þe cete of Metence þer was ane vsurer þat died, & he was passand covatus. And when he drew nere his dead, he prayed his wife to lay a bag full of syluer by hym when he was dead in his grafe; and so sho did. So afterward þaim happend oppen[1] þat same grafe agayn, & þai fand þerin ij tadis, ane in þe bag mouthe and a noder on his brest; & þat one of þaim drew oute penys of þe bag with his mouthe & þe toder tuke þaim at hym & putt þaim into his harte, right as he had sayd; "With mony we sall fyll þine vnsaciable harte." And when þai saw þis, þai wer so ferd at þai fled away & fillid þe grafe agayn.

DCCLXXXVI.

Vsurarijs aliquando apparent demones in morte.

Cesarius tellis how som tyme þer was ane vsurar at was bown to [dye][2], and hym thoght at he saw all þe felde full of crawis & crakis. And he began for to cry faste & sayd; "Allas! alas! Se, now þai com vnto me, ffor now þai er at þe dure. And now þai er in þe howse, and now þai [*er*] on my breste, and now þai draw my saule oute of my bodie." And in þis crying he dyed. And þe same nyght, at many folke bothe hard & saw, þai[3] lifte his bodie vp into þe howse-rufe, & lete it fall oftsithis & breke all to gobettis; and all þe lyght in þe howse was putt oute, and men & wommen fled. & on þe morn þai fand his bodie þer all to-reven & rente, and þai tuke it & beryd itt in þe felde emang bestis.

Vsurarij depositum non est seruandum. *Supra* de deposito, j.

[1] MS. oppend.

[2] Latin MSS. vsuraria moritura.

[3] Latin MSS. demones . . . cor tollentes usque ad tectum, &c.

DCCLXXXVII.

Vsurarius debet prius restituere *et* postea elemosinas facere.

Cesarius tellis how som tyme at Parissh þ*er* was a grete vsurar, so he fell vnto compunccion and he come & askid councell at ane þat hight Maurice, þat was bisshop þ*er*, how he mot be savyd. And þis bisshop had a kurk of our Ladie in byggyng, and he cownceld hym to giff his money holie þ*er*vnto. And he suspecte hym somwhat in his cowncell-gyffyng, and went vnto Maister Petur at was chawntur þ*er*, and he bad hym go gar cry oppynlie þat he was redie to restore vnto all men þ*at* at he had had wronguslie of þai*m*; and so it was done. And þis done he come agayn vnto þe chawntur, and tuke witnes at his consciens & said þat he had restorid agayn all þ*at* he had wronguslie gettyn vnto all þat come vnto hym, & þis he had somwhat lefte. And þan he said hym burde do almos-dede, & after þat go in his sarke & his breke þurgh þe cetie nakid, and so he did. And ane folowyd hym wit*h* a wande, cryand, "Behold, þis is þat man þat princes wurshuppid for his money!" And þurgh þis penance-doyng he his sawle was savid.

DCCLXXXVIII.

Vsurarior*um* elemosine no*n* placent deo.

Cesarius tellis how som tyme in Colayn þ*er* was ane vsurarie, and he fell vnto co*m*punccion & shrafe hym vnto a preste. And he sayd he wolde gyff all his gudis for Goddis sake, and þan þe preste bad hym cut shyvis of bread & fyll a kyste þ*er*wit*h* and lokk it. And so he did. And on þe toder day, when he sulde com & se it & opynd þe kyste, he fand þ*er* als many tadis as he put in shyvis of bread. And when he tolde þe preste þ*er*of, he sayd; "Loo, now, how þine almos at þou makis of þine vsurie plesis vnto God!" And he was ferd & axkid what he sulde do. And he said, "And þou will be savid, lyg all þis nyght nakyd emang yone v*er*myn̄." Lo! how grete con*tr*icion̄ he had! For þuff aƚƚ he did' it *with* a grete vgsomnes, he layd' hym̄ nakid emang þis vermyn̄. And þe p*re*ste lokkid' þe kyste and went his ways, and on̄ þe toder day when̄ he oppynd itt, he fand nothyng þ*er* bod þis mans banys. And he tuke þai*m* & berid' þai*m* in a porche of Saynt Geryon̄. And as it is sayd', þai er of so grete vertue þat vnto þis day no tade may abyde whykk wit*h*in þe bowndis of þat kurk.

Vsurarij condentis testamentu*m* om*n*ia debent reportari in manus executor*um*, et inde debent fieri restituciones. Sup*ra* de testamento.

DCCLXXXIX.

Vsurarius *et* si a pecc*ato* no*n* abstinet, saltem debet habere[1] intencionem restituendi.

Iacobus de Vet*ri*aco tellis how som̄ tyme þ*er* was a riche man̄, and þuf aƚƚ he had mekuƚƚ gude, nevur-þe-les to gett more gude he lete his money to hyre. Bod þe increce þ*er*of he durste nott turn̄ into his awn̄ vse, bod layd' it oparte at he mott restore it agayn̄ at his dead'-day, and so he did'.

DCCXC.

Vsurarij ecia*m* post mortem ab vsuris no*n* cessant.

Iacobus de Vet*ri*aco tellis how som tyme þ*er* was ane vsurar & he wolde nothyng restore when̄ he dyed', bod, for honor of þe werld', he garte deale large almos, and he bewytt in his testament a grete sowm̄ of money and þat he chargid' his sons & his frendis at it sulde be lent in vsurie iij yere after his decese, and at þai sulde gyff for his sawle aƚƚ þat multiplied' þ*er*of.

DCCXCI.

Vsurarius inuite moritur.

Iacobus de Vet*ri*aco tellis how som̄ tyme þ*er* was ane vsurar þat lay in passions of dead', and he began̄ to be passyng [*hevie*] & sorow-

[1] MS. habet.

full, & prayed his sawle t[o] abyde in þe body & he sulde purvay þerfor, and he promytt it gold & sylu*er* & all þe delytis of þis werld, & els he wold not gyff þer-for þe valour of a sh[red] clowte[1]. So at þe laste he saw his sawle wolde not abyde in his bodie bod at hym burde nedelyngi*s* dye, he wex passand wroth & sayd vnto his saule; "Þ*ou* sawle! I sulde hafe ordand þe a gude h*er*barie, bod sen þou erte so fond at þou will not abyde, I beteche þe vnto all þe devuls in hell." And þus he dyed and was berid in hell.

DCCXCII.

Vsurarij nomen est confusibile.

Iacobus de Vet*r*iaco tellis how som tyme þ*er* was [*a*] prechur þat in his *ser*mond told of þe myschevus crafte of vsurie, and when he had done his sermond, he bad at all men suld rise to his absoluci*on* in ordur as he callid þai*m* be þ*er* offes. And furste he bad smythis ryse, and so þai did & he asoyled [þaim], and þai went þ*er* ways. Than he bad ryse baxsters, and so dyd þai, and þus he callid vp ilk crafte after other. & at þe laste he bad ryse vsuraris, and þuff all þ*er* was ma in þe kurk þan þ*er* was of any oþ*er* crafte, yit þ*er* wolde none ryse, bod for shame þai hid þai*m*. And oþ*er* folke lughe & skornyd þai*m*, & all þies vsuraries rase and went oute confusid.

DCCXCIII.

Vsurarij a bonis no*n* debent sepeliri.

Iacobus de Vet*r*iaco tellis, when neghburs wolde hafe liftid vp þe bodie of ane vsurar þat was dead, & born hym vnto his grafe, þai mot not mufe it be no maner of wyse. And þai had grete m*er*vell þeroff. So emang þai*m* þ*er* was one olde wyse man, & he sayd; "Surs, ye know wele at þe custom in þis cetie is þis, þat when any man*er* of man dyes, þase men þat er of þe same crafte er wunte to bere hym vnto his grafe, as p*re*stis duse p*re*stis, & so of oþ*er*." So p*r*ivalie þai callid iiij at þai knew wele was vsurars, and onone þai liftid hym vp & had hym away, for þe devull

[1] Harl. MS. *non vnam pictam.*

wolde not lett his servand*is* to bere away his s*er*vant whar he lett gude me[*n*] to do itt.

Vsurarij sepultura est sub patibulo. S*upra* de sepultura.

Vsurarij aliquando moriu*n*tur du*m* su*n*t in maiori festo *et* securitate. Supra de demone, x[1], *et* alijs locis diu*er*sis.

Vsurarius restituens saluat*ur*. Su*pra* de testamento.

DCCXCIV.

Vsurarij restituere amittu*n*t aliqu*ando* timore paup*er*tatis.

We rede in '*Libro* de *Dono* Ti*m*oris' how som tyme a *pr*este movid ane vsurar when he was seke to dispose hym for þe heale of his sawle, and he tolde hym at iij þinges was necessarie vnto hym, þat is to say, fullie to be shrevyn, & to sorow for his synnys, and to make restitucion at his power. And he *gr*antid wit*h* gude wyll to do þe ij furste, bod he sayd; "How sulde I do þe thrid, for þan sulde I lefe nothyng to me nor my chylder." And þe *pr*este sayde bod if he did þus, he mot not be savid. And he axkid if wise men & scriptur sayde so, and he said ya, for suthe. And he answerd agayn & sayd; "I will nevur prufe whethur þai said suthe or nay, for I will make no restitucion." And þus he dyed, more dredand pou*er*tie in þis warlde þan evurlastand payn in þe toder werld.

Vulpes oracioni obedit. S*upra* de oracione, ij.

DCCXCV.

Vxor sine licencia viri sui exennia dare non debet.

We rede in þe 'Legend of Saynt Edmund, Bisshop of Canturberie,' how þ*er* was a wyfe þat luffid hym wele and wolde he had

[1] *A wrong reference apparently.*

had at do *with* hur, & oft sythis sho broght hym *presentis* to make hym lightlier to enclyne to hur entent. So he knew wele enogh hur entent, and axkid hur if sho broght hym þies *presentis* be consent of hur husband or nay. And sho sayd, nay, hur husband sulde nott wit what sho did vnto hym, nor yit what he did vnto hur. And he answerd agayn & sayd; "I will not take þi giftis *with*-oute consent of þi husband." And þus þe wom*man* *with* grete shame bare hur *presentis* agayn, and he was clere and fullie rid on hur.

Vxor de facili no*n* debet haberi suspecta a viro suo. S*upr*a de suspicione.

DCCXCVI.

Vxor modica occasione est zelotipa.

Saynt Ierom tellis of ane þat hight Gorgias, & þuf all at he war chastie, neu*er*-þe-les he had a fayr maydyn, and here-for his wyfe was passand hevy & sad. So his neghburs in þe contrey, ij of þai*m*, fell wrath, and þis Gorgias sent þai*m* a fayr buke þat he had co*m*pylid of concorde, & sayd; "He com*m*aundis you to concordans þat kepis [*not*] iij at concord in a howse, þat is to say, him selfe, his wyfe, and his maydyn [1]." So his wyfe had a grete envye at his mayden fayrenes, & here-for sho wold not sease, þuf all hur husband war not wurthie, daylie for to chyde hym, becauce sho mystryste hym, for þe mayden was fayrer þan sho.

Vxor rixosa pacient*er* debet tolerari [2]. S*upr*a de paciencia.

DCCXCVII.

Vxor a viro debet corripi si ornet se racione alt*er*ius viri.

Valerius tellis how a noble man of Rome þat was suspecte [3] of his wyfe, and here-for he sayd he wolde lefe hur, ffor þe law,

[1] Harl. MS. "Iste uob*is* precepit de concordia, qui se, uxore*m*, ancillam, tres in vna domo, concordare non potuit."

[2] MS. tollerari.

[3] Harl. MS. Roman*us* suspici*us* uxore*m* suam dimisit.

he sayd, was so þat a wom*man* sulde not make hur fressh & gay *with* hur husband gude, to gyff hym þat seis hur occasion to make hur husband cukwolde. & here-for he wolde not lat hur be gayl[ie] cled, to þe entent at sho sulde not be suspecte nor broght in blame.

Vxor casta multu*m* est amabilis. Su*pra* de castitate.

DCCXCVIII.

Vxorem non expedit ducere.

Ieronim*us*[1] tellis in 'Libro de Nupcijs' of ane Aureolus Theophrasti, & in þis buke he axkis if a wise man sulde wed a wyfe, and he says þuf sho war nevur so fayre, nor so wele taght, nor had nevur so honest fadur nor moder, yit nevur-þe-les, he says, a wyse man sulde not wed hur, for þis Aurelious sais it is not possible to a man to please bothe his wife & his childer; ffor wom*men*, he says, burd hafe gold & syluer & gay clothyng, & a servand and mayny o*þer* thyng*is*, & yit all þe nyght sho will lyg chat*er*rand & say[2] þat *þer*[3] is oder þat hase bettur curchus & er fressher arayed þan sho is, and if sho be wele arayed hur lykis . . . . to com emang no pepull and sho will say, "Lo! I am þe baddeste in all þis town!" Also sho will say vnto hur husbond; "Whi beheld þou þi neghbur wyfe, & whi spak þou *with* þi neghbur mayden?" And when he com*m*ys fro þe m*ar*kett sho will say; "What hase þou boght? I may not hafe a frend nor a felow for þe, nor luf of a noder man bod if I be suspecte." And *þer*for *þer* sulde no man make chesyng of his wyfe long befor, bod take such one as hym happend, whedur sho be fayre or fowle, or prowde or angry, & *þer*for þai sulde not be *pro*vid or þai war wed. A hors or ane ass, ane ox or a cow or a servand, all þies sulde be *pro*vid or þai wer boght or hyrid, bod a wom*man* sulde not a man se or he wed hur, þat he war not displesid aft*er* þai war wed. And if þou giff hur

[1] Harl. MS. *Ieronimus*. Fert*ur* Auriolus Theofrasti 'Libro de Nupcijs.'

[2] Arund. MS. "*Illa* ornat*ior* procedit *in* publicum *et* honorat*ur* ab om*n*ibu*s*, ego *autem in conuentu* femin*arum* despicior." Ait*que*; "Cur aspiciebas vicina*m*?" &c.

[3] þer *omitted and added above the line.*

all þi gude to kepe, yit sho wyll trow at þou kepis som þi selfe, and þus sho will suspecte þe & hafe þe in haterede, & happelie afterward poyson the. And if þou bryng men of craft in-to þi hows, as tailliours or oþ*er*, it is perell for hur vnclennes. So [if] þou forbyd hur it will cauce hur do truspas. Therefor what *pro*fett*is* a diligente kepyng of a wyfe when ane vnchaste wyfe may not be kepyd, ffor þe kep*er* of chastite is nede[1], and þ*at* sho þat is not lustie to syn, sho may be callid chastie. And if sho be fayr, oþ*er* men will luf hur, and if sho be fowle sho will be prowde, at cauce men make mekull on hur, and it is full hard to kepe þat wele þ*at* many men luffis, and it is full hevy to hafe þat no man wyll cheris nor hafe in welde. Nevur-þe-les a fowle wyfe may bettir be kepyd þan a fayr wyfe may, for þ*er* is no thyng bod som peple will giff þ*er* vew and þ*er* fantasye þ*er*-vnto.

Vxoris malicia qua*m* in viru*m* cogitat qu*andoque* in
caput suum redu*n*dat[2]. S*upr*a de muliere,
xiij[3].

Vxor infidelis est viro morienti. S*upr*a de muliere,
vj.

Vxor qu*andoque* est occasio dampnac*ion*is viro.
S*upr*a de h*er*etico.

Vxor fidelis est viro morienti. S*upr*a de missa, ij.

Vxor bona p*ro*dest viro. Su*pr*a de abb*a*te.

Vxor adult*er*a. Sup*r*a de adulterio.

DCCXCIX.

Chr*ist*ianus. Chr*ist*iani mali magis puniu*n*tur in inferno q*u*am infideles.

We rede in þe 'Life of Saynt Macharie' how on a day he fand a dead man head, & he spak þ*er*to & askid whose hede it was, & it ansswerd agayn & sayd it was þe head of a paynom. And he

[1] Infida *enim* custos castitatis *est* nec*ess*itas.

[2] MS. qu*andoq*u*e* vi capit.

[3] MS. xi.

askid whar þe saule þ*er*-of was, & it sayd in hell; & he axkid how depe, and it said, als depe as fro hevyn to erde. And he axkid if þ*er* was any dipper þan it, and it sayd ya, all fals crysten men, þai er depeste in hell.

Chr*istus*. Chr*ist*i ymago. S*upr*a de ymagi*ne*.

DCCC.

Ymago Chr*ist*i miracula facit.

Eusebius tellis of þe wom*m*an þat was callid Emorissa, þat was cle*n*syd of hur sekenes be þe tuching of owr Lordis hem, sho garte make ane ymage after Cryste wit*h* clothyng & His hem as sho saw Hym, & oft sithis sho wurshippid it, & sho sett it in hur garte, & all þe h*er*bys grew þ*er*[1] vnder-nethe þat befor was of no v*er*tue, when þai grew vp & tuchyd þe hem þ*er*off þai war of suche v*er*tue at þai heli[d] many folke þat war seke. And as Ierom tellis, Iulian*us* had it away & sett þ*er*[in] hys awn ymage, and belyfe a blaste of levenyng come & smate it down & burn[yd it].

Ymago c*r*ucifixi sang*u*inem emisit. S*upr*a de crucifixo.

Ymago b*ea*te vi*r*ginis infectionem[2] mitigauit. S*upr*a de Maria, x.

Ymago b*ea*te vi*r*ginis anulu*m* a puero suscepit. S*upr*a de puero.

DCCCI.

Ypocrisis. Ypoc*r*ita a demone deuoratur.

Saynt Gregorie tellis how som tyme þ*er* was a monke of grete estimacion in his gude thewis, & passand wele nurturd in all his oder gude werkis; as it p*ro*vid at end, he was not so

[1] MS. vppon, *erased*.   [2] MS. temptac*io*nem.

inward; for he was oþ*er*was þan he apperid. So hym happynd a hevynes of his bodie & fell seke, and he garte gadder to-gedur all his bredur vnto hym, and þai trowyng þat, & he dyed, at þai sulde hafe som grete thyng of hym, or els som thyng þat was delectable for to here it of hym. And when þai come aforn hym, þuf all he war gretelie turment & whakand, [yit] he was co*m*pellid to vttyr. And þan he sayd vnto þai*m*; "Brethir, when ye trow[yd] at I fastid wit*h* you I had meate privalie & eete, and þerfor I am now giffen vnt[o a] dragon to devowr, ffor wit*h* his tayle he hase vmlappid my kneis, & he hase [put] his head in my mouthe & suppyd vp my sawle. & wit*h* þat he stude vpp on his fete and onone he was dead.

Zelus. Zelotipus est vir freque*n*t*er* de vx*or*e. S*upr*a de suspicione.

Zelotipa est mulier de marito h*ab*ita modica oc-*casion*e. Su*pr*a de vx*or*e, ij.

Explicit.

Finis adest mete, nu*n*c explicit, ergo valete.
Pro merce tali, nu*n*qua*m* tantu*m* calamavi,
Sed retributum, fore largu*m*, iam puto tutum.
Preco Dei narrat, q*uo*d quarcus[1] ego vocor errat.

[1] *For* quartus?

CPSIA information can be obtained
at www.ICGtesting.com
Printed in the USA
LVHW081914011222
734419LV00010B/578

9 781377 012346